MW01421633

# ACCOUNTING AND CONTROL FOR GOVERNMENTAL AND OTHER NONBUSINESS ORGANIZATIONS

# ACCOUNTING AND CONTROL FOR GOVERNMENTAL AND OTHER NONBUSINESS ORGANIZATIONS

**Leo Herbert,** Ph.D., C.P.A.
**Larry N. Killough,** Ph.D., C.P.A.
**Alan Walter Steiss,** Ph.D.
Virginia Polytechnic Institute and State University

**McGRAW-HILL BOOK COMPANY**

New York   St. Louis   San Francisco   Auckland   Bogotá
Hamburg   London   Madrid   Mexico   Milan   Montreal   New Delhi
Panama   Paris   São Paulo   Singapore   Sydney   Tokyo   Toronto

This book was set in Times Roman by Publication Services.
The editor was Jim DeVoe; the cover was designed by Marian Recio;
the production supervisors were Joe Campanella and Friederich Schulte.
Project supervision was done by Publication Services.
R. R. Donnelley & Sons Company was printer and binder.

**Library of Congress Cataloging-in-Publication Data**

Herbert, Leo
   Accounting and control for governmental and other nonbusiness organizations.

   Includes bibliographies and index.
   1. Finance, Public—Accounting.   2. Corporations,
Nonprofit—Accounting.   I. Killough, Larry N.
II. Steiss, Alan Walter.   III. Title.
HJ9768.H47   1987   657'.835   86-15172
ISBN 0-07-028316-8

Material from Uniform CPA Examination Questions and Unofficial Answers, Copyright © 1966, 1970, 1971, 1972, 1973, 1974, 1975, 1976, 1977, 1978, 1979, 1980, 1981, 1982, 1983, 1984 by the American Institute of Certified Public Accountants, Inc., is reprinted or adapted with permission.

Material from the Industry Audit Guide, Audits of Voluntary Health and Welfare Organizations; Audit and Accounting Guide, Audits of Certain Nonprofit Organizations; Industry Audit Guide, Hospital Audit Guide, 4th Edition; AICPA Professional Standards, Volume A, U. S. Audit Standards, copyright © 1978, 1981, 1982, 1984, 1985 by the American Institute of Certified Public Accountants is reprinted with permission.

**ACCOUNTING AND CONTROL FOR GOVERNMENTAL
AND OTHER NONBUSINESS ORGANIZATIONS**

Copyright © 1987 by McGraw-Hill, Inc. All rights reserved. Printed in the United States of America. Except as permitted under the United States Copyright Act of 1976, no part of this publication may be reproduced or distributed in any form or by any means, or stored in a data base or retrieval system, without the prior written permission of the publisher.

2 3 4 5 6 7 8 9   DOCDOC   8 9 4 3 2 1 0 9 8 7

ISBN 0-07-028316-8

# ABOUT THE AUTHORS

LEO HERBERT is professor emeritus of accounting at Virginia Polytechnic Institute and State University. He received his B.S. degree in accounting and finance at Brigham Young University and his M.B.A. and Ph.D. at Louisiana State University. He is a certified public accountant in Louisiana and Utah. Dr. Herbert has been professionally active in both accounting education and in accounting practice. He has been a professor of accounting at Louisiana State University, Brigham Young University, Louisiana Tech, and Virginia Tech. He has been an adjunct professor of accounting at George Washington University and the American University. In the United States General Accounting Office in Washington, D.C., he was director of the Office of Personnel Management, deputy director of the Office of Policy and Special Studies, and director of the Office of Staff Management. In Louisiana, he was assistant state auditor and supervisor of public funds. He has also served the United Nations as a consultant to the Commission on Audit of the Republic of the Philippines and the Sahel Regional Financial Management Project of the United States as a consultant to The Gambia in West Africa.

Dr. Herbert has contributed to numerous professional journals and is the author of several books and monographs, including the recently published *Auditing the Performance of Management, A Conceptual Framework for Understanding Auditing*, and *Governmental Accounting and Control* (with Larry N. Killough and Alan W. Steiss).

LARRY N. KILLOUGH received his B.S. degree in business administration from the University of Tennessee, his M.B.A. from Temple University, and his Ph.D. from the University of Missouri. He is a professor of accounting at Virginia Polytechnic Institute and State University. Dr. Killough is a certified public accountant.

Dr. Killough has authored or coauthored numerous articles appearing in such publications as *The Accounting Review, Management Accounting, Cost and Management, Managerial Planning, Advanced Management Journal, The National Public Accountant*, and *The Woman CPA*. He has also coauthored a number of textbooks, including *Cost Accounting Concepts and Techniques for Management, Governmental Accounting and Control* (with Leo Herbert and Alan W. Steiss), and *CPA Review*.

He has considerable experience as an educator and accounting professional. Dr. Killough has over eight years of combined industrial and public accounting experience. He has been a full-time educator for sixteen years. Dr. Killough has served on several committees of major professional associations, including the American Accounting Association, American Institute of Certified Public Accountants, National Association of Accountants, and the Virginia Society of Certified Public Accountants. He is currently a member of the executive education committee of the AICPA and serves as coeditor of *The Virginia Accountant Quarterly*.

ALAN WALTER STEISS is associate provost for research and director of sponsored programs at Virginia Polytechnic Institute and State University. He received his A.B. in psychology and sociology from Bucknell University and his M.A. and Ph.D. in urban and regional planning from the University of Wisconsin. Dr. Steiss has served at Virginia Tech as director of the Center for Urban and Regional Studies, chairman of the Urban and Regional Planning and Urban Affairs Program, chairman of the Division of Environmental and Urban Systems, and associate dean for research and graduate studies of the College of Architecture and Urban Studies. He was formerly the head of statewide planning for the state of New Jersey and has served as consultant to the states of Wisconsin, New Jersey, Maryland, Virginia, South Carolina, New York, Alaska, and Hawaii, the Trust Territory of the Pacific, and the Federal-State Land Use Planning Commission for Alaska. Dr. Steiss is the author of several books, including: *Systemic Planning: Theory and Application* (with Anthony J. Catanese); *Public Budgeting and Management; Models for the Analysis and Planning of Urban Systems; Urban Systems Dynamics; Dynamic Change and the Urban Ghetto* (with Michal Harvey, John Dickey, and Bruce Phelps); *Local Government Finance: Capital Facilities Planning and Debt Administration; Performance Administration* (with Gregory A. Daneke); *Governmental Accounting and Control* (with Leo Herbert and Larry N. Killough); and *Management Control in Government*. He has contributed to numerous professional journals in the United States and abroad.

# CONTENTS

PREFACE — xix

## PART I  ACCOUNTING AND FINANCIAL REPORTING FOR GOVERNMENTAL ENTITIES — 1

### 1  Introduction to Accounting and Control for Governmental and Other Nonbusiness Organizations — 5

PUBLIC MANDATE FOR GREATER ACCOUNTABILITY — 5
    The Governmental Sector. Other Nonbusiness Sectors.
ASSUMPTIONS, STANDARDS, AND PRINCIPLES — 7
THE MEANING OF ACCOUNTING — 7
    Financial Accounting and Reporting. Management Accounting
THE ENTITY — 9
    The Accounting Entity. The Reporting Entity. Business and Nonbusiness Funds and Account Groups. Fund Accounting: Emphasis on Fiscal Control. Funds in Government. Account Groups in Government.
THE BASIC ACCOUNTING EQUATION — 17
THE BASIS OF ACCOUNTING — 18
    The Cash Basis. The Accrual Basis. The Modified Accrual Basis.
GENERALLY ACCEPTED ACCOUNTING PRINCIPLES — 20
    GAAP in Not-for-Profit Applications.
CONTROL — 21
    Internal Accounting Control. Budgetary Control. Subsidiary Ledger Control. Management Control. Auditing.
ORGANIZING FOR ACCOUNTING IN GOVERNMENT — 25
    Unified Department of Finance. The Controller's Office and the Budget Office. The Audit Function. Organizational Flexibility and Change.
SUMMARY — 28
QUESTIONS — 29
PROBLEMS — 30
NOTES — 35

## 2 Proprietary Funds—Enterprise Funds — 37

Similarities of Accounting in Proprietary Funds of Government and Business Entities. New Approaches.

PROFIT VERSUS BREAK-EVEN OPERATIONS — 39
BASIS OF ACCOUNTING — 40
Revenue and Other Sources of Financing. Expenses and Other Uses of Financial Resources.
CAPITAL EQUITY — 43
Residual Equity Transfers. Capital Grants. Retained Earnings. Other Sources.
DEBT FINANCING — 45
INTERFUND TRANSACTIONS — 46
Operating Revenues and Expenses. Operating Transfers. Residual Equity Transfers
SPECIALIZED NEEDS — 49
Budgetary Accounting in Proprietary Funds
ILLUSTRATIVE TRANSACTIONS—ENTERPRISE FUNDS — 49
The Enterprise Fund in the City of Ruthberg. Journal Entries for Transactions During the Year. Illustrative "T" Accounts. Adjusting Journal Entries. Closing Entries. After Closing "T" Accounts and Trial Balances. Worksheet of Transactions. Financial Statements. Illustrative Financial Statements.
SUMMARY — 61
QUESTIONS — 63
PROBLEMS — 64
NOTES — 69

## 3 Proprietary Funds—Internal Service Funds — 71

Cost Accounting in Internal Service Funds. Relationship of Internal Service Funds to Enterprise Funds.

ILLUSTRATIVE TRANSACTIONS—INTERNAL SERVICE FUND — 72
Transactions to Open Internal Service Fund. Establishing the Fund. Developing Costing Charges. Operating Transactions During the Period. Adjustments to Accounts at Year's End. Worksheet of Transactions. Closing Entries. Internal Service Printing Fund Financial Statements.
SUMMARY — 76
QUESTIONS — 78
PROBLEMS — 79
NOTES — 84

## 4 Governmental Funds—Introduction to Budgets and Budgetary Accounting — 85

THE PLANNING EMPHASIS IN CURRENT BUDGET PRACTICES — 85
Planning Objectives of Budgeting. The Need to Integrate Planning and Control Objectives.

| | | |
|---|---|---|
| | INTRODUCTION TO THE PRINCIPLES AND PRACTICES OF BUDGETING | 86 |
| | Purposes and Objectives of Budgeting. Objectives of the Annual Operating Budget. | |
| | THE BUDGET CYCLE | 88 |
| | The Budget Calendar. The Executive Budget. Budget and Accounting Classifications. The Budget Document. Legislative Action on the Budget. | |
| | BUDGET EXECUTION | 94 |
| | Allocations and Allotments. Expenditure Controls. Budget Adjustments. Internal and External Audits. | |
| | BUDGETARY ACCOUNTING | 98 |
| | The Accounting Equation for Governmental Funds. | |
| | ILLUSTRATIVE BUDGETARY ACCOUNTING TRANSACTIONS | 101 |
| | Budget Adoption Transactions. Encumbrance Transactions: Goods and Equipment Ordered and Received. Year-End Encumbrances. Budget Adjustments. Closing Entries. | |
| | USE OF SUBSIDIARY LEDGERS | 105 |
| | SUMMARY | 106 |
| | QUESTIONS | 106 |
| | PROBLEMS | 107 |
| | NOTES | 113 |
| 5 | **General and Special Revenue Funds—Budgetary and Revenue Transactions** | **114** |
| | BUDGETS AND BUDGETARY ACCOUNTING | 115 |
| | Allocations and Allotments | |
| | BASIS OF ACCOUNTING | 117 |
| | REVENUE ACCOUNTING | 118 |
| | Ad Valorem Taxes. Self-Assessment Taxes. Revenue Sharing and Grants. Special Problems in Revenue Accounting. | |
| | ILLUSTRATIVE TRANSACTIONS FOR THE GENERAL FUND—CITY OF RUTHBERG | 125 |
| | Beginning Balances. Budget Adoption Transactions. Revenue Transactions. Subsidiary Revenue Ledgers. Prior-Year Revenue Transactions. Worksheet of Revenue Transactions. | |
| | SUMMARY | 139 |
| | QUESTIONS | 139 |
| | PROBLEMS | 139 |
| | NOTES | 145 |
| 6 | **General and Special Revenue Funds, Continued—Expenditure Accounting, Closing Entries, and Financial Statements** | **146** |
| | EXPENDITURE ACCOUNTING | 146 |
| | Personal Services. Materials and Supplies. Contractual Services. Capital Outlay. Debt Servicing. Residual Equity Transfers. Prior Year's Reserve for Encumbrances. Adjusting Entries. | |
| | ILLUSTRATIVE TRANSACTIONS FOR THE GENERAL FUND—CITY OF RUTHBERG | 153 |

Expenditure Transactions. Expenditure Subsidiary Ledger. Prior Year's Transactions. Closing Entries. Worksheet of Transactions During the Year. Financial Statements. Budget Comparison Schedule.

| | |
|---|---|
| VARIATIONS IN PROCEDURES AND SPECIALIZED NEEDS | 170 |
| SUMMARY | 173 |
| QUESTIONS | 173 |
| PROBLEMS | 174 |
| NOTES | 184 |

## 7 Capital Projects Funds — 185

| | |
|---|---|
| SPECIAL USE OF CAPITAL PROJECTS FUNDS | 185 |
| Capital Projects Funds Financing. | |
| THE CAPITAL BUDGET | 187 |
| RELATIONSHIP BETWEEN THE CAPITAL PROJECTS FUNDS AND OTHER FUNDS AND ACCOUNT GROUPS | 188 |
| PARTIAL USE OF BUDGETARY ACCOUNTING IN CAPITAL PROJECTS FUNDS | 188 |
| BASIS OF ACCOUNTING | 191 |
| PREMIUMS, DISCOUNTS, AND ACCRUED INTEREST ON THE SALE OF BONDS | 191 |
| Accrued Interest on Sale of Bonds. Premiums and Discounts on Sale of Bonds. | |
| INVESTMENT OF EXCESS CASH | 192 |
| NEW TRANSACTIONS | 192 |
| Journal Entries Regarding Issuance of Bonds. Journal Entries Regarding Multiple Periods. Journal Entries Regarding CLosing Entries. | |
| ILLUSTRATIVE TRANSACTIONS—CITY OF RUTHBERG'S CAPITAL PROJECTS FUND | 195 |
| Initial Accounting Entries. Construction of the Building. Financial Statements—Incomplete Project. Second-Year Transactions. Final Closing Entries. Financial Statements— Completed Projects. Combining Capital Projects Funds Statements. | |
| SUMMARY | 205 |
| QUESTIONS | 205 |
| PROBLEMS | 205 |
| NOTES | 210 |

## 8 Debt Service Funds — 211

| | |
|---|---|
| SPECIAL USE OF DEBT SERVICE FUNDS | 211 |
| FINANCES FOR REPAYMENT OF DEBT | 212 |
| BASIS OF ACCOUNTING FOR DEBT SERVICE FUNDS | 212 |
| Budgetary Accounting. | |
| ILLUSTRATIVE TRANSACTIONS—DEBT SERVICE FUNDS—CITY OF RUTHBERG | 214 |
| Debt Service Fund Accounting for Serial Bonds. Financial Statements for Debt Service Funds—Serial Bonds. Debt Service Fund Accounting for Term Bonds Issued. Financial Statements. Debt Service Fund Accounting for Previously Issued Term Bonds. Combining Debt Service Fund Financial Statements. | |

|  |  |  |
|---|---|---|
| | SUMMARY | 226 |
| | QUESTIONS | 226 |
| | PROBLEMS | 228 |
| | NOTES | 233 |

## 9 Special Assessment Funds — 234

USE OF SPECIAL ASSESSMENT FUNDS — 234
    Relationship Between Special Assessment Funds and Other Funds and Account Groups. Basis of Accounting for Special Assessment Funds. Special Accounting Considerations—Special Assessment Fund.

ILLUSTRATIVE TRANSACTIONS FOR SPECIAL ASSESSMENT FUNDS — 238
    Current-Period Transactions. Statements—First Year's Operations. Transactions—Second Year. Statements—Second Year. Budgetary Accounting in Special Assessment Funds.

SUMMARY — 247
QUESTIONS — 247
PROBLEMS — 248
NOTES — 253

## 10 Fiduciary Funds — 254

PARTICULAR CHARACTERISTICS OF FIDUCIARY FUNDS — 255
BASIS OF ACCOUNTING — 255
ILLUSTRATION OF ACCOUNTING FOR EXPENDABLE AND NONEXPENDABLE TRUST FUNDS — 256
    Nonexpendable Trust Fund. Expendable Trust Fund.

ILLUSTRATIVE ACCOUNTING FOR THE PENSION TRUST FUND FOR THE CITY OF RUTHBERG — 260
    Transactions for the Pension Trust Fund. Pension Trust Fund Financial Statements.

REVENUE SHARING FUNDS — 270
AGENCY FUNDS — 272
    Payroll Tax Agency Fund—City of Ruthberg.

SUMMARY — 273
QUESTIONS — 274
PROBLEMS — 274
NOTES — 279

## 11 General Fixed Assets and General Long-Term Debt — 280

ACCOUNTING CONTROL THROUGH THE USE OF ACCOUNT GROUPS — 281
    Fixed Asset Control. Long-Term Debt Control.

SPECIAL ACCOUNTING CONSIDERATIONS FOR ACCOUNT GROUPS — 282
    Principles of Accounting for Fixed Assets. Principles of Accounting for Long-Term Debt.

ILLUSTRATIONS OF GENERAL FIXED ASSETS ACCOUNT GROUP ACCOUNTING — 284

Illustrative Transactions from the General Fund. Illustrative Transactions from the Capital Projects Fund. Illustrative Transactions from the Special Assessment Fund. Removal of Assets from the General Fixed Assets Account Group. Worksheet for the General Fixed Assets Account Group.

DEPRECIATION IN THE GENERAL FIXED ASSETS ACCOUNTS GROUP   **290**

STATEMENTS AND SCHEDULES FOR THE GENERAL FIXED ASSETS ACCOUNT GROUP   **290**

    Balance Sheet and General Fixed Assets Schedules.

ILLUSTRATIONS OF GENERAL LONG-TERM DEBT ACCOUNT GROUP ACCOUNTING   **293**

    Serial Bond Accounting. Term Bond Accounting.

STATEMENTS AND SCHEDULES FOR THE GENERAL LONG-TERM DEBT ACCOUNT GROUP   **299**

    General Long-Term Debt Account Group Financial Reporting.

OTHER LONG-TERM FINANCING   **300**

    Capital Lease Accounting. Claims, Judgments, and Compensated Leave Liability.

SUMMARY   **302**
QUESTIONS   **302**
PROBLEMS   **303**
NOTES   **308**

## 12 Interfund and Interentity Relationships and Single Audits   **309**

INTERFUND AND INTERENTITY RELATIONSHIPS AND TRANSACTIONS   **309**
ILLUSTRATIVE TRANSACTIONS   **310**

    Proprietary Funds Interfund Transactions. Governmental Funds Interfund and Interentity Transactions.

THE SINGLE AUDIT   **321**

    Single Audit Reports.

SUMMARY   **324**
QUESTIONS   **324**
PROBLEMS   **324**
NOTES   **329**
APPENDIX: CITY OF ROANOKE, VIRGINIA—SINGLE AUDIT REPORT, JUNE 30, 1984   **330**

## 13 Financial Reporting   **342**

THE REPORTING ENTITY   **342**
THE COMPREHENSIVE ANNUAL FINANCIAL REPORT   **343**

    Combined Statements. Individual Funds Statements. Combining Statements. Notes to the Financial Statements.

THE AUDITOR'S REPORT   **362**
STATISTICAL TABLES   **363**
LEGAL REQUIREMENTS AND GENERALLY ACCEPTED ACCOUNTING PRINCIPLES   **375**
SUMMARY   **376**
QUESTIONS   **378**

|  |  |  |
|---|---|---|
| | PROBLEMS | 378 |
| | NOTES | 386 |
| | APPENDIX 13-1: COMPREHENSIVE ANNUAL FINANCIAL REPORT | 387 |
| | APPENDIX 13-2: NOTES TO THE FINANCIAL STATEMENTS | 389 |
| | APPENDIX 13-3: STATISTICAL DATA | 404 |
| | APPENDIX NOTES | 412 |

## PART II  ACCOUNTING AND FINANCIAL REPORTING FOR OTHER NONBUSINESS ORGANIZATIONS      413

### 14  Voluntary Health and Welfare and Certain Nonprofit Organizations      415

|  |  |
|---|---|
| VOLUNTARY HEALTH AND WELFARE ORGANIZATIONS | 416 |
| FUND ACCOUNTING | 416 |
|     Current Unrestricted Fund. Current Restricted Fund. Land, Building, and Equipment Fund. Custodian Funds. Loan and Annuity Funds. Endowment Funds. | |
| BASIS OF ACCOUNTING | 418 |
| SPECIAL ACCOUNTING CONSIDERATIONS | 418 |
| FINANCIAL REPORTING | 418 |
| ILLUSTRATIVE TRANSACTIONS—VOLUNTARY HEALTH AND WELFARE ORGANIZATIONS | 419 |
|     Current Unrestricted Fund. Current Restricted Fund. Land, Buildings, and Equipment Fund. Financial Statements. | |
| CERTAIN NONPROFIT ORGANIZATIONS | 431 |
|     Summary of Accounting Principles and Reporting Practices. Illustrative Reports. | |
| SUMMARY | 442 |
| QUESTIONS | 452 |
| PROBLEMS | 453 |
| NOTES | 460 |

### 15  Colleges and Universities      461

|  |  |
|---|---|
| PARTICULAR CHARACTERISTICS OF COLLEGE AND UNIVERSITY ACCOUNTING | 462 |
|     Accounting Principles for Colleges and Universities. Budgetary Accounting. Similarities and Differences Between College and University and Governmental Principles of Accounting. Funds Used in College and University Accounting. Similarities and Differences Between Funds in Colleges and Universities and Funds in Government. Financial Reporting. | |
| ILLUSTRATIVE TRANSACTIONS | 466 |
|     Unrestricted Current Funds. Plant Funds. | |
| FINANCIAL REPORTING | 480 |
| SUMMARY | 480 |

| | QUESTIONS | 482 |
|---|---|---|
| | PROBLEMS | 483 |
| | NOTES | 488 |

### 16 Hospitals — 489

THE OPERATIONS OF A MODERN HOSPITAL — 490
GENERALLY ACCEPTED ACCOUNTING PRINCIPLES FOR HOSPITALS — 491
FUNDS IN HOSPITAL ACCOUNTING — 492
    Unrestricted Fund. Restricted Funds.
APPLICATION OF HOSPITAL ACCOUNTING PRINCIPLES—UNRESTRICTED FUND — 495
    Assets. Liabilities. Revenues. Expenses. Fund Balance.
APPLICATION OF ACCOUNTING PRINCIPLES—RESTRICTED FUNDS — 502
    Specific Purpose Funds. Plant Replacement and Expansion Funds. Endowment Funds.
FINANCIAL STATEMENTS — 505
    Illustrative Balance Sheet. Illustrative Statement of Revenues and Expenses—Unrestricted Fund. Illustrative Statement of Changes in Fund Balances. Illustrative Statement of Changes in Financial Position—Unrestricted Fund.
VARIATIONS IN ACCOUNTING AND SPECIALIZED NEEDS — 510
    Budgetary Accounting. Cost Accounting. Hospitals as a Part of Other Organizations. Board-Designated Funds. Hospitals Operated by Governmental Units. Malpractice Loss Contingencies.
SUMMARY — 515
QUESTIONS — 516
PROBLEMS — 517
NOTES — 522

## PART III ACCOUNTING FOR MANAGEMENT PLANNING AND CONTROL — 525

### 17 Management Accounting in the Management Process — 527

    Management Control Defined. Establishing a Basis for Comparison. Measuring Performance. Comparison and Evaluation. Corrective Action.
COMPONENTS OF ACCOUNTING — 532
    Financial Accounting. Cost Accounting. Management Accounting.
MANAGEMENT ACCOUNTING AND MANAGEMENT CONTROL — 533
    The Management Accounting Framework.
THE ROLE OF THE MANAGEMENT ACCOUNTANT — 535
    The Duties of the Controller.
COST CONCEPTS AND TERMINOLOGY — 536
    Full Costs and Partial Costs. Direct and Indirect Costs. Controllable or Noncontrollable Costs. Differential Costs. Opportunity Costs. Variable and Fixed Costs.

| | COST-ESTIMATION METHODS | 540 |
|---|---|---|
| | Initial Approach to Developing Cost Estimates. The High-Low Method. The Scattergraph Method. Regression Analysis. | |
| | SUMMARY | 543 |
| | QUESTIONS | 544 |
| | PROBLEMS | 545 |
| | NOTES | 547 |

## 18 Cost Accounting Techniques — 548

| | |
|---|---|
| AREAS IN NEED OF MANAGEMENT ACCOUNTING | 548 |
| COST MEASUREMENT AND ASSIGNMENT | 549 |
| COST ACCOUNTING SYSTEMS | 549 |
| Cost Allocation. Cost Accounting Record-keeping Procedures. Process Costing. Job-Order Cost Accounting Systems. | |
| STANDARD COSTING AND VARIANCE ANALYSIS | 561 |
| SUMMARY | 561 |
| QUESTIONS | 562 |
| PROBLEMS | 562 |

## 19 Management Accounting Techniques — 565

| | |
|---|---|
| BREAK-EVEN ANALYSIS | 565 |
| FLEXIBLE BUDGETS | 568 |
| COST-BENEFIT ANALYSIS | 568 |
| Elements of Cost-Benefit Analysis. Discounting Methods Used. Value of Cost-Benefit Analysis | |
| RESPONSIBILITY ACCOUNTING AND PERFORMANCE MEASUREMENT | 572 |
| Responsibility Accounting. Performance Measurement | |
| PROBLEMS IN CONTROLLING NONBUSINESS COSTS | 573 |
| Costs Versus Expenditures. Accounting for Department, Fund, or Program Responsibility Centers. | |
| SUMMARY | 579 |
| QUESTIONS | 580 |
| PROBLEMS | 580 |
| NOTES | 584 |

# PART IV  ADVANCED TOPICS — 585

## 20 A Strategic Management Framework — 587

| | |
|---|---|
| MANAGEMENT: THE ART OF GETTING THINGS DONE | 587 |
| THE PLANNING-CONTROL CONTINUUM | 589 |
| Strategic, Management, and Operational Planning. Strategic, Management, and Operational Control. Management Information Systems. | |

ACCOUNTING AND PROGRAM EFFECTIVENESS — 593
Strategic Planning Defined. Programs in Strategic Planning. Goal Statements. Program Objectives. How Statements: Identification of Implementation Strategies. Analysis of Program Alternatives. Program Measurement. Strategic Planning and Program Budgeting.

ACCOUNT DATA CROSSWALKS — 601
SUMMARY — 603
QUESTIONS — 604
CASE 20-1 PROGRAM CROSSWALK — 605
NOTES — 610

## 21 Management Emphasis on Performance and Accountability — 611

THE BUDGET AS A WORK PROGRAM — 611
Performance Classification Systems. Activity Classification. Performance Measures.

SERVICE DELIVERY ACCOUNTABILITY — 616
Service Level Analysis. Actionable Programs versus Fixed Expenditures. Components of Service Level Analysis. Minimum Service Levels. Ranking Service Levels. Driving Accountability Deeper into the Organization.

SUMMARY — 623
QUESTIONS — 623
CASE 21-1: UNIT COST ANALYSIS — 623
CASE 21-2: ANNUAL BUDGET BUILT ON UNIT COSTS — 625
CASE 21-3: SERVICE LEVEL ANALYSIS — 625
NOTES — 633

## 22 Control Through Performance Auditing — 635

APPROPRIATE SUPERVISORY AND MANAGERIAL TECHNIQUES — 635
Management's Accountability Function. Auditor's Responsibility.

PERFORMANCE AUDITING — 637
Types of Performance Audits. Audit Evidence and Audit Objectives.

THE PHASES OF A PERFORMANCE AUDIT — 640
Reasons for Conducting a Performance Audit

ILLUSTRATIVE PHASES OF AN EFFICIENCY AND ECONOMY AUDIT—A CONTRACT BY UNIVERSITY *A* FOR A COMPUTERIZED ACCOUNTING AND ADMINISTRATIVE RECORDS SYSTEM — 642
Preliminary Survey. A Tentative Audit Objective. Review and Testing of Management Control. A Firm Audit Objective. The Detailed Audit. The Report Development

ILLUSTRATIVE PHASES OF AN EFFECTIVENESS AUDIT—UNIVERSITY *A's* CONTRACT FOR A COMPUTERIZED ACCOUNTING AND ADMINISTRATIVE RECORDS SYSTEM — 647
Preliminary Survey and Review and Testing of Management Control. A Firm Audit Objective. The Detailed Audit. The Report Development.

| | |
|---|---|
| ACCOUNTING SYSTEMS AND PERFORMANCE AUDITING | **653** |
| SUMMARY | **653** |
| QUESTIONS | **653** |
| CASE 22-1: USER CHARGES IN THE STATE | **654** |
| CASE 22-2: THE EFFECTIVENESS OF GRANT AUDITING | **656** |
| NOTES | **658** |
| **INDEX** | **659** |

# PREFACE

In state and local governments, financial transactions are made between *funds*—accounting entities that embody a whole group of self-balancing accounts. Therefore, the central accounting focus in government and many other not-for-profit organizations is *fund accounting*.

Accounting majors often are exposed only to those aspects of fund accounting that relate to financial reporting. In many cases, this limited focus is all that is required to pass the nonbusiness part of the CPA examination. The literature of governmental and nonbusiness accounting, in general, lacks a unified approach that brings together the principles and procedures of financial accounting and reporting with those of management accounting. Students and practitioners of accounting generally receive only limited exposure to public and nonbusiness management procedures, wherein policy is reflected in financial reports, budgeting practices, and management controls.

Students of public administration, business administration, and others interested in nonbusiness organizations also are most often introduced only to accounting procedures for financial reporting. While these students may have backgrounds in the nature of public and nonbusiness policy and practice, their exposure to accounting seldom is designed to help them manage these nonbusiness organizations.

The public, however, is demanding greater efficiency, effectiveness, and accountability in the management of public and other nonbusiness entities. In response to this demand, effective accounting systems must be devised and adopted that can be used both for financial and management accounting—systems that also relate more directly to improved techniques for budgeting that have emerged in recent years.

Approximately 40 percent of all persons employed in the United States now work in public and nonbusiness service organizations. These organizations increasingly are becoming a significant employment market for accounting students. This book provides the essential background required to prepare accountants for the management of financial activities in public and nonbusiness organizations, as well as for the financial reporting requirements of these entities.

The book has two primary objectives: (1) to provide students with a thorough grounding in accounting principles and practices for financial reporting by public and nonbusiness organizations—including assisting in the preparation for the nonbusiness portion of the CPA examinations—and (2) to prepare students for managerial decision-making roles in accounting and financial management for both governmental and other nonbusiness activities.

Parts I and II of the book introduce students to the broad field of nonbusiness accounting, with special reference to financial reporting requirements of governmental units, health and welfare organizations, colleges and universities, hospitals, and other nonbusiness entities. In Part III, the techniques of management accounting are integrated with financial accounting and reporting procedures. These chapters provide the bridge between the two primary objectives of this textbook. To ensure that the bridge is built on a firm foundation at both ends, Part IV is concerned with more advanced topics in financial management, budgeting, and auditing as they apply to public and other nonbusiness organizations. The first three parts can be used by accounting majors, after completion of their first year of study. Part IV will be of particular assistance to upper-level undergraduate and graduate students in accounting, business administration, or public administration seeking a more in-depth understanding of these more advanced topics and their integration with the basic principles and practices of accounting.

Accounting textbooks usually provide short problems to assist students in the consolidation of their learning experiences. This approach has been followed in Parts I, II, and III. More extensive case-studies are used in Part IV to explore more advanced topics of nonbusiness financial management. The case-study approach is commonplace in other disciplines, especially in the field of business administration, but only recently has begun to find application in advanced undergraduate and graduate accounting textbooks. Especially in the areas of management control, understanding of complex case situations is much more important than the mere application of ''cookbook'' rules.

After first introducing the entire field of nonbusiness accounting, the historical origins of certain components of governmental accounting are discussed in Chapter 1. The generally accepted accounting principles, including those applied in fund accounting, are then described in detail.

In order to provide important linkages between the students' existing knowledge of subjects in business accounting and the unknowns of governmental accounting, proprietary funds—the profit-type funds of government—are next considered. This represents something of a departure from many textbooks on governmental accounting, which usually begin with general and special revenue funds. However, this transition from business accounting to businesslike funds seems a more natural and logical approach. Enterprise funds, covered in Chapter 2, are those in government that are most nearly related to business-type entities. Internal service funds that operate on a businesslike basis but are primarily related to government are discussed and illustrated in Chapter 3.

Budgets and budgetary accounting are then introduced in Chapter 4, and these subjects are applied to the principal not-for-profit (governmental) types of funds—the general and special revenue funds—in Chapters 5 and 6. Building on the knowledge base thus established, Chapters 7 through 13 then explain and illustrate the principles and practices of accounting and financial reporting for each of the other funds and account groups used in governmental organizations.

The chapters in Part I provide the basic foundation in fund and budgetary accounting—a foundation that is needed when approaching fund accounting for other nonbusiness entities. Other organizations, such as churches, private foundations, labor unions, colleges and universities, hospitals, and health and welfare organizations, may use fund accounting or budgetary accounting or both. Financial accounting and reporting procedures for these types of entities are developed in Part II. The accounting and reporting requirements of voluntary health and welfare organizations and certain other nonprofit entities are described and illustrated in Chapter 14; colleges and universities are covered in Chapter 15; and the accounting and financial reporting needs of hospitals are examined in Chapter 16.

Parts I and II are designed to provide students with a comprehensive understanding of the current practices of fund accounting and budgetary accounting. Mindful of the need to prepare students to pass the nonbusiness accounting section of the uniform CPA examination, many questions and problems from prior examinations are used in these chapters.

Part III seeks to integrate management accounting techniques with the principles and practices previously covered under financial accounting and reporting. Chapter 17, "Management Accounting in the Management Process," incorporates the subjects of accounting for financial reporting and management decision making and control. Building on this foundation, the concepts and procedures of cost accounting and management accounting are then fully explained and applied in Chapters 18 and 19.

In Part IV, more advanced concepts and practices of public management are examined, especially those concerning budgeting and auditing. These ideas can be readily adapted to other nonbusiness organizations as well as to public agencies. A management structure for the application of these techniques is outlined in Chapter 20. Efforts to achieve more effective program operations and goal accomplishment serve as the primary focus of these techniques, which include strategic planning, management information systems, program analysis, and program budgeting. The chapter concludes with a discussion of procedures for the conversion of accounting data (crosswalking) from one classification system to another.

Management procedures to increase performance efficiency and accountability are then addressed in Chapter 21. The use of budgets for programming and measuring work activities and techniques of service level analysis as mechanisms for greater accountability are discussed in this chapter. The case-study problems provide the students with "hands-on" experience in the application of these techniques.

Many of the available techniques and practices in budgeting and accounting that relate to the effectiveness of goal achievement and the efficiency of operations are not being used today in governmental and nonbusiness organizations. Therefore, many organizations have expanded the use auditing practices to determine their efficiency and effectiveness. In Chapter 22, the necessary background is supplied to apply performance auditing to most nonbusiness organizations. Performance auditing goes beyond financial statement or compliance auditing to examine the critical issues of the organizational efficiency (doing things right) and effectiveness (doing the right things).

In summary, the purpose of this book is twofold: (1) for students to learn the theory and procedures of nonbusiness accounting for financial reporting, including sufficient familiarity with the questions and problems given in the CPA examination pertaining to these concepts and practices; and (2) for students to become cognizant of the concepts and practices of management accounting for nonbusiness entities, including the use of contemporary planning, budgeting, and auditing techniques for these nonbusiness entities. Achievement of the first purpose should get the student of accounting across an important professional threshold. Accomplishing the second purpose should place the student firmly on a path leading to significant participation in the management decision-making processes of these organizations.

Many individuals have helped in the development of this book including: other authorities in the field who have given permission to use their prior published works, departmental officials, graduate students, secretaries, fellow faculty members, reviewers, the publishing staff, the editing staff, and practicing public administrators. We appreciate the help they have given. Without their help and cooperation, the book could not have been completed and published.

We would like to express our thanks for the useful suggestions provided by colleagues who reviewed this text during the course of its development: Paul A. Dierks, University of Texas at Arlington; Howard Jensen, University of Colorado; James Patton, University of Pittsburgh; Craig Shoulders, Virginia Polytechnic Institute and State University; and A. J. Stagliano, George Mason University.

*Leo Herbert*
*Larry N. Killough*
*Alan Walter Steiss*

# PART ONE

# ACCOUNTING AND FINANCIAL REPORTING FOR GOVERNMENTAL ENTITIES

The economic and social patterns of our society were drastically changed by the Industrial Revolution over 200 years ago. Some historians have suggested that without *accounting* these changes might never have occurred. Accounting provided the basic financial information about economic activities—the "language of business"—which was essential to support the technological advances that marked the rise of industry and commerce.

Today, other economic and social revolutions are bringing about conditions that could just as drastically affect our ways of living and means of earning our livelihood. Among the most significant of these changes is the growing importance of governmental and nonbusiness organizations in the overall economic and social fabric of society. Some economists, for example, estimate that nearly 50 percent of our gross national product (GNP) now comes from government and other nonbusiness segments of our society. At the beginning of this century—and even fifty years ago—only a relatively small percentage of the GNP could be attributed to these public and quasi-public sectors of the economy.

The tremendous economic impact of these organizations has created a rapidly growing demand from many sources for improved and expanded accounting information. Examples include:

1 the public need to hold these organizations accountable for the resources that they expend;

2 the need of the federal government to oversee the distributive resources that flow to state and local governments; and

3 the need for information for better decision making and control within these organizations.

Other third parties have also expressed great interest in improved accounting and reporting for governments at all levels. In recent years, for example, several cities and other local authorities, borrowing large amounts of money without proper accountability for those funds, have been brought to the brink of bankruptcy. As a consequence, lending institutions are now insisting that governments provide better accounting information and more effective measures of accountability.

Other nonbusiness entities—schools, hospitals, universities, labor unions, foundations, and other nonbusiness organizations—have proliferated since the end of World War II. This rapid expansion has given rise to increased interest and concern by third parties in the financial activities of these organizations.

Dramatic changes have recently occurred in governmental and nonbusiness accounting. Nevertheless, it appears that even more dramatic changes may take place in the future. Thus it should be evident why accountants, financial managers, and others involved with economic and fiscal activities in the public and other nonbusiness sectors require a broad grounding in the principles and practices of governmental and nonbusiness accounting.

## PURPOSE AND OBJECTIVES OF PART I

A basic premise of this book is that accounting systems designed to serve the broader purposes of management must be based on the concepts of accounting for information and record keeping for financial reporting. Therefore, Part I of this book provides a basic understanding of the field of financial accounting, reporting, and auditing as applied to governmental organizations. This foundation is extended to other nonbusiness organizations in Part II. In Part III, management accounting techniques are developed and their applications explained. Part IV examines the broader applications of accounting and auditing as they support the functions of planning, decision making, and management control for all nonbusiness organizations.

The first chapter in Part I establishes a foundation for the study of: (1) financial accounting and reporting, and (2) management accounting and control for governmental and nonbusiness organizations. Its purpose is to demonstrate that accounting—as an information system for an organization's financial record keeping and external reporting—*can* and *should* serve as a very valuable tool for management planning, decision making, and control. These elements are critical organizational responses to the public mandate for greater accountability.

A distinction is made in Chapter 1 between business and nonbusiness accounting practices, using the basic assumptions, standards, and principles listed below:

- The meaning of accounting
- The accounting entity
- The basic accounting equation
- The basis of accounting
- Generally accepted accounting principles
- Accounting as a control mechanism

These assumptions, standards, and principles are used throughout the book as a conceptual structure for the reader's understanding of nonbusiness accounting for both financial reporting and management control. Nonbusiness accounting is further divided into (1) accounting and financial reporting for governmental organizations and for other nonbusiness entities, such as schools, colleges and universities, hospitals, health and welfare entities, churches, labor unions, and so forth; and (2) management accounting and control for these same organizations.

A brief historical perspective of governmental accounting, budgeting, and financial reporting provides a foundation for *governmental fund accounting*. The various entities of government (funds and account groups) are defined and described, including both profit and not-for-profit funds of government. Chapter 1 concludes with a discussion of the reasons for *budgetary control* in the not-for-profit funds of government.

The *profit funds* (proprietary funds) of government are related to business accounting principles in Chapters 2 and 3. It is assumed that the reader has some knowledge of these basic accounting principles as they are applied to the development of a financial statement—the end product of the financial reporting process for a single entity that is profit oriented. Knowledge of what financial statements are intended to communicate should help in gaining an understanding of the total accounting process—from the initial data-gathering stage to reporting and disseminating information.

Budgeting for the not-for-profit funds of government (usually the general and special revenue funds) is discussed and illustrated in Chapter 4. A budget provides the legal basis for public spending and fiscal accountability. Budgeting is integrally linked to an accounting process wherein revenue and expenditure information can be organized to facilitate continuous monitoring, evaluation, and management control. The budget process makes it possible to delegate financial responsibility and authority while maintaining appropriate management controls.

Budgetary accounting principles are then applied in Chapters 5 and 6 to transactions commonly found in the *general* and *special revenue funds*, two of the most important not-for-profit funds in government. Unless some specific law, regulation, or other principle or standard requires that certain resources be accounted for in another fund, the general fund is normally considered the entity through which all operations of the governmental unit are conducted. Budgets are needed to determine the estimated revenue and expected expenditures in the general and special revenue funds. The types of financial statements that are prepared under these two funds for external financial reporting purposes are also illustrated in these chapters.

The principles of accounting and financial reporting are explained and applied to each of the other not-for-profit governmental funds in Chapters 7 through 10. *Capital projects funds* account for the resources used to acquire long-term capital assets. Such resources may include bond proceeds, grants from other levels of government, gifts from foundations or civic-minded citizens, and so forth. The accounting for the resources and expenditures of capital project funds is described and illustrated in Chapter 7. *Debt service funds* are used to gather the monies required to pay the principal and interest on long-term debt for the governmental unit. Debt service funds do not account for the debt itself or for the long-term assets acquired with the proceeds from the debt;

*account groups* are used to record these financial data. The accounting process for debt service funds is presented in Chapter 8. *Special assessment funds* account for and control resources that are used to provide capital improvements or special services to an identifiable segment of the community, rather than to all citizens. Chapter 9 describes and illustrates these funds.

Chapter 10 explains the accounting and financial reporting requirements of *fiduciary funds*—funds that may be either profit or not-for-profit. Not-for-profit trust funds—the resources of which can be spent—are accounted for in the same manner as other governmental funds. For-profit trust funds and pension funds, on the other hand, are accounted for in the same manner as proprietary or other for-profit funds. Agency funds are purely custodial and do not involve any measurement of the results of operations.

Several aspects of accounting for governmental funds (not-for-profit funds) differ significantly from the procedures and practices followed in proprietary or business-type funds in government. Accounting for *fixed assets* and, in most cases, *long-term debt*, for example, requires that separate records be kept outside the governmental fund that acquired these assets or liabilities. This requirement is in contrast to proprietary funds, in which fixed assets and long-term debts are accounted for within the fund. These separate records, called *account groups*, are discussed in Chapter 11.

Various types of *interentity transactions* are discussed in Chapter 12, with illustrations of the accounting for these types of transactions, between and among these entities, in each of the funds or account groups. Illustrative statements for what is called a *single audit* also are provided. A single audit reports upon all of the federal grants made to a given municipality or other unit of local government at a point in time, rather than preparing a separate audit for each grant. The appropriate *accounting statements* for an entire municipality, including statements of both funds and account groups, are presented in Chapter 13.

Part I is designed to provide the reader with a thorough grounding in fund and budgetary accounting, a foundation required when dealing with the financial management of the nonbusiness entities. The various chapters include numerous illustrations of the principles and practices under discussion, and each chapter concludes with a set of review questions and problems. With this basic understanding of governmental accounting procedures established, the concepts are then applied in Part II to other nonbusiness entities, such as schools, colleges and universities, hospitals, health and welfare entities, labor unions, churches, and foundations.

**CHAPTER 1**

# INTRODUCTION TO ACCOUNTING AND CONTROL FOR GOVERNMENTAL AND OTHER NONBUSINESS ORGANIZATIONS

Accounting has always been important in serving the record-keeping and fiscal control functions of governmental and other nonbusiness organizations. These accounting/control systems, for the most part, are based on double-entry accounting practices inherited from the private sector. The role of accounting in these organizations, however, is expanding. Increasing attention has been given in recent years to the need for greater economy, efficiency, and effectiveness in the operations of governmental and other nonbusiness organizations. A basic objective of this book is to demonstrate that in addition to providing a financial record-keeping and external reporting function accounting *can* and *should* serve as an invaluable tool for management planning, decision making, and control.

## PUBLIC MANDATE FOR GREATER ACCOUNTABILITY

The clamor for greater accountability in government and other nonbusiness entities, in large measure, can be traced to the growing recognition of the significant impact that these organizations have on our economy. Almost one-half of the nation's gross national product (GNP) comes from these nonbusiness sectors. In addition, the power and influence in governmental and other nonbusiness organizations sometimes is mind boggling. Consider, for example, the impact of labor unions, international foundations, churches, research organizations, and health and welfare groups on both our economic and social structures.

### The Governmental Sector

The federal government provides approximately 40 percent of the financial resources used by state and local governments. It is not surprising, therefore, that the concern for greater accountability begins at the national level. In 1972, the U.S. General Accounting Office (GAO)—the accounting principle-setting and auditing arm of Congress—issued a statement entitled *Standards for Audit of Governmental Organizations, Programs, Activities & Functions*. In these standards, the Comptroller General states:

> A fundamental tenet of a democratic society holds that governments and agencies entrusted with public resources and the authority for applying them have a responsibility to render a full accounting of their activities. This accountability is inherent in the governmental process and is not always specifically identified by legislative provision. This governmental accountability should identify not only the objects for which the public resources have been devoted but also the manner and effect of their application.[1]

The 1981 revision of these standards suggests that audits be made not only to determine whether the financial reports of a public agency are presented fairly in accordance with generally accepted accounting principles, consistently applied, but also:

1 whether the entity (agency) has complied with applicable laws and regulations,
2 whether it is managing or using its resources in an efficient and economical manner,
3 whether the desired results are being obtained from the programs established through the legislature or other authorizing body, and
4 whether there are any indications of fraud, abuse, or illegal acts.[2]

These standards underline the interest of the federal government in seeing not only that organizations follow generally accepted accounting principles consistently applied, but also that the activities of these organizations are managed efficiently, economically, effectively, and without fraud. Recognizing the need for improved accountability, other organizations and individuals have also studied the problems and have issued reports on accounting and financial reporting in the public sector.[3]

## Other Nonbusiness Sectors

The mandate for greater accountability in other nonbusiness sectors is somewhat akin to that in the public sector. The American Institute of Certified Public Accountants (AICPA) issued its *Statement of Position, 78-10* in 1978.[4] Prior to that time, however, the accounting profession had no generally accepted guidelines for the financial reporting of such nonbusiness organizations as labor unions, churches, foundations, and social clubs. However, other nonbusiness organizations (e.g., universities, hospitals, and health and welfare organizations) did have statements of accounting principles, along with audit guides affirming these principles, prior to the 1978 AICPA report. More recently, the AICPA has issued guides for use by auditors of these types of nonbusiness organizations.[5] Other groups and individuals also have provided important contributions to our understanding of the financial reporting practices of these nonbusiness organizations.[6]

Many of the resources of these nonbusiness entities come from grants provided by federal and state governments and other public organizations, as well as by private groups and individuals. While government agencies often have the resources to audit the compliance of nonbusiness organizations with the grant provisions, the individual may be unable to determine what has happened to the money that he or she has contributed. This dilemma can be resolved, however, through information from audits of financial statements that follow generally accepted accounting principles. Thus an understanding of these accounting principles is important both to accountants working for or auditing these organizations and to the financial managers of these entities.

## ASSUMPTIONS, STANDARDS, AND PRINCIPLES

The frequent prerequisite of a course in business accounting suggests that such basic accounting principles can be used as a foundation to prepare students for nonbusiness accounting. Most individuals starting the study of nonbusiness accounting have at least some familiarity with business accounting principles and practices.

Governments and other nonbusiness entities not only account for their not-for-profit activities, but, in many instances, they also must account for their profit activities. Examples of these profit activities in nonbusiness entities include public utilities, printing centers, food services, repair and maintenance facilities and so forth. Chapters 2 and 3, devoted to an examination of these profit activities in government, serve as a bridge from the more familiar business accounting practices to the principles of fund accounting.

Before undertaking this discussion, however, it is important to make a distinction between certain assumptions, standards, and principles found in business accounting and those applicable in accounting for nonbusiness entities. Only the most basic ones that achieve our purpose of making these distinctions will be discussed in this chapter. Others will be explained in later chapters as they are applied. The characteristics considered in this chapter relate to:

- The meaning of accounting
- The accounting entity
- The basic accounting equation
- The basis of accounting
- Generally accepted accounting principles
- Accounting as a control mechanism

## THE MEANING OF ACCOUNTING

Accounting often is defined as an *information system*. An accounting system accumulates and measures financial data and converts those data to information that is then communicated and applied by various groups. The users of accounting information include both those within the organization for which the data are gathered and those outside (e.g., stockholders, investors, regulatory agencies, and the general public).

This process of accumulating and measuring financial data includes recording, summarizing, and analyzing the data and then reporting—and possibly interpreting—the information derived from the data. This process is applicable to governmental and nongovernmental organizations, to business as well as nonbusiness activities, and to profit and not-for-profit entities.

### Financial Accounting and Reporting

Financial information can be useful to external users and to the internal management of an organization. The process that provides information to external users is most often called *financial accounting and reporting*. Most basic textbooks on business accounting explain financial accounting very thoroughly. Governmental accounting and other nonbusiness textbooks used in courses given primarily for students studying to pass the CPA examination emphasize the financial reporting function almost exclusively.

### Management Accounting

The process that records, summarizes, and analyzes data for internal management is called *management accounting*. Accounting procedures designed to maximize the usefulness of financial information for management are at the core of systems that integrate accounting, budgeting, and control processes. While more conventional financial accounting emphasizes the external financial reporting function, the integrated management approach shifts the focus to include several new substantive dimensions (see Exhibit 1-1).

The development of management accounting has both accompanied and contributed to better understanding of financial management and decision making within organizations. Management accounting should anticipate the questions that decision makers must resolve. The information provided in management accounting reports should be focused so as to facilitate solutions to these questions. Such information must be timely and in a form that is responsive to the decision needs of management in the formulation of policy, in programming activities, and in controlling operations. Many

---

**EXHIBIT 1-1**

MAJOR DIMENSIONS OF MANAGEMENT ACCOUNTING

- Greater emphasis is placed on the production of information for the purposes of planning, programming, and decision making.
- Management controls are added to the more traditional focus on legal compliance and fiscal accountability through the development of cost standards and the preparation of reports that highlight significant variance from such standards.
- Internal management reports supply information pertinent to the responsibilities of various levels of management within the organization.
- Emphasis on performance standards, unit costs, and full costing, wherever feasible, promotes greater cost consciousness among management personnel.
- Management accounting is linked with decision making and performance program budgeting rather than fiscal control budgets.

such decisions are current, while others—such as those involved in capital facilities planning and debt management—have longer range implications. The accounting system must supply data for proposed alternatives and for the development of cost-benefit and cost-effectiveness analyses. Following the selection and implementation of an alternative course of action, the program/activity must be monitored and evaluated in terms of intended objectives.

While parallel improvements have been made in financial management functions in the business sectors, the concept of management accounting in government and nonbusiness organizations is still in its formative stages.[7] The efficiency, effectiveness, and economy of any nonbusiness operation can be improved significantly, however, if an accounting system is built around the purposes of planning, decision making, and management control, as well as fiscal control and financial reporting.

More recent budgetary reforms in government, such as program budgeting and zero-base budgeting, have emphasized the critical functions of planning and operations control. At the same time, the financial management functions of operating efficiency, economy, and performance effectiveness have been incorporated into the audit function as it is applied to nonbusiness organizations.

Management accounting will not replace traditional financial accounting. It cannot, for traditional accounting is required for external reporting purposes. Nor is it necessary to adopt all the features of management accounting at one time. The establishment of *cost centers*—organizational units where costs can be collected and analyzed—and *responsibility centers*—organizational units where the specific responsibility for an operation can be identified—is an important first step. New processes should then be devised to collect and utilize both statistical data—performance and effectiveness measures—and cost data. Both should be linked with standards within internal management reports originating in cost centers or responsibility centers.

In general, governmental accounting textbooks do not emphasize management accounting to any extent. However, as has been noted previously, Parts III and IV of this book are concerned with the processes for providing information for internal management's planning and decision making and the control of the operations of governmental and other nonbusiness organizations.

## THE ENTITY

In providing information to both external and internal users, one of the basic assumptions of accounting is that the information should come from a particular *accounting entity*. This entity establishes the boundaries from which the data are gathered, recorded, analyzed, and for which information is provided to users.

### The Accounting Entity

One of the major differences between business and nonbusiness accounting pertains to the concept of *entity*. While the accounting entity often is related to the legal organization for both business and nonbusiness applications, the identity of the legal organization is more clearly recognized in private sector situations than in nonbusiness situations. The corporation, partnership, or individual proprietorship, for example, is the usual business entity. For financial reporting purposes, however, the city is not the accounting entity for municipal government. Neither is the college or university the accounting entity for an institution of higher education; nor is the particular health or welfare organization an accounting entity.

Within the nonbusiness unit, other entities—called *funds*—are established for the purposes of maintaining accounting records and preparing financial statements. Funds are defined as fiscal and accounting entities with self-balancing sets of accounts.

In recent years, some nonbusiness organizations have been organizing their activities into *programs* in addition to funds. A *program* is a group of closely related activities that are used to accomplish a common goal or set of objectives. Often programs overlap several funds or departments. A counseling program for juvenile delinquents, for example, may have activities in the welfare department, the police department, and even in the parks and recreation department. Programs as well as funds can be used as accounting entities. However, accounting for program entities is associated more often with management accounting than with financial accounting and reporting. Accordingly, the use of program entities will be further discussed in Part IV.

## The Reporting Entity

Not only is the accounting entity substantially different for nonbusiness than it is for business organizations, the reporting entity can also be different. In business, the organization usually is the accounting entity (e.g., the corporation, the partnership, or the individual proprietorship). For reporting purposes, many individual businesses may be part of a larger organization (i.e., the corporate entity), and the financial statements of individual business entities are usually consolidated into one financial report for the overall organization. When the financial statements are consolidated, intercompany (intracorporate) transactions are eliminated in order to show the results of one organization instead of many individual companies. For external reporting purposes, individual businesses lose their identity in the consolidated financial statements.

In nonbusiness organizations, especially government, each fund is a separate and distinct entity. Some authors maintain that the consolidation and elimination of interentity transactions might give improper information to third parties. Developers of the principles of accounting for government, for example, have stated that for purposes of reporting the overall operations of a municipality the amounts in individual accounts should determine a total for each account. The totals for each account for each fund would then be aggregated into a *combined statement*. This statement provides a *memorandum total* for each account common to all of the various funds. It also provides a total for all accounts for all funds.

This approach to financial reporting does not support the assumption that the city is a consolidated reporting entity. Furthermore, the definition criteria of the reporting entity imply that if a separate entity is under the control of the governing body of the municipality (e.g., a public service utility) the financial statement of that entity must also be included in the overall financial report of the governmental unit. Thus financial reports for governmental organizations may include financial statements for some entities (e.g., a public housing commission, a drainage district, or a transit authority) for which the elected public officials have oversight responsibility but not day-to-day control.[8] As will be discussed in further detail in the next section, the funds used to account for the transactions of these various governmental entities may exhibit quite different characteristics.

In recent years, some experimentation has been occurring in government with the use of *consolidated financial statements*. No final determination has been made as yet as to whether these statements are useful and meaningful.

### Business and Nonbusiness Funds and Account Groups

Classifying all profit organizations as business and all not-for-profit organizations as nonbusiness is a misnomer. This is especially true for some nonbusiness organizations that operate profit activities and account for these activities in profit funds. These organizations also operate not-for-profit activities and account for them in not-for-profit funds.

To clarify this distinction, profit funds often are labeled *nonexpendable funds*, because the capital equity of this type of fund remains constant over time and is not expended during any one accounting period. Not-for-profit funds, on the other hand, often are called *expendable funds*, because all of the capital equity can be expended during the accounting period. In fact, in most cases, any equity that remains in such funds at the end of the fiscal period reverts to a higher level or central account (as when budget appropriations made to specific agencies revert to the general fund at the end of the fiscal year).

Not-for-profit funds are used for the purpose of keeping records of the resource and reporting on the inflow of revenues and the outflow of expenditures. Hence, they also are called *resource outflow funds*, monitoring the flow into and out of the fund.

In this book, the fund in a government or other nonbusiness organization that is used for profit determination purposes will be called a *profit fund*. In some cases, the terms ''nonexpendable'' or ''income funds'' may also be used (especially when other authorities are referenced). *Not-for-profit funds* will be used when discussing governmental or other nonbusiness entities that can expend all of their resources during a specific accounting or fiscal period. At times, however, the term ''expendable funds'' may be used (e.g., when other authorities are cited).

Another type of accounting entity in which there is no flow of funds also must be identified and applied in government and some other nonbusiness organizations. These entities, called *account groups* in government, are used to keep records of the fixed assets or long-term debt of the not-for-profit entities of the overall organization.

Funds and account groups can be illustrated most readily in the governmental sector (see Exhibit 1-2). Funds of other classes of nonbusiness organizations will be discussed and illustrated in the chapters that pertain to these organizations.

### Fund Accounting: Emphasis on Fiscal Control

The concept of *fund accounting* emerged from the so-called *Oakley Report*, published in 1921 by the Institute for Governmental Research (now the Brookings Institution).

Fund accounting comprises a number of self-balancing sets of accounts within a particular governmental unit, instead of only one set of accounts for the entire government. A constant balance is maintained between debits and credits for each fund. Thus control of certain specific types of activities—revenues and expenditures—can be maintained for each of these funds.

The primary objective of fund accounting is *fiscal control*. All revenues in each fund usually are expended during the fiscal period, that is, there is no surplus income or earnings. Therefore, external controls must be exercised in relation to some other standards. Revenues are controlled through the *appropriation process*, and proposed expenditures are controlled through an *object-of-expenditure* budget. Expenditures from the fund for any object code (e.g., salaries, supplies and materials, travel, equipment) cannot exceed the dollar amount that the legislative body has appropriated in the budget for that particular category of expenditures. The control of each object code (or cluster of object codes) in a budget, in turn, also prevents the overexpenditure of the appropriation to a given fund entity as a whole. One of the basic principles of governmental fund accounting is that financial statements must compare the actual revenues and expenditures with those estimated in the budget.

Fund accounting, however, has a major drawback. While control of receipts and disbursements can be maintained for each activity, it is not possible to add up the receipts and expenditures for each of the funds to arrive at any meaningful total for the overall

---

**EXHIBIT 1-2**

STANDARD FUNDS AND ACCOUNT GROUPS

**Proprietary funds**

These funds account for the financing of services rendered primarily to the general public for compensation, such as the operation of a public utility.

**Governmental funds**

*General funds* account for all financial resources (and activities financed by them), which are not accounted for in some special fund. Among the revenues normally included are property taxes, licenses, fees, permits, penalties, and fines. Expenditures are authorized in the general budget.

*Special revenue funds* account for taxes and other revenues (except special assessments) that are legally restricted for a particular purpose (e.g., parks, schools, and streets).

*Debt service funds* account for the financing of interest and retirement of general long-term debt principal.

*Capital project funds* account for capital projects financed either on a "pay-as-you-go" basis or out of capital reserves, grants-in-aid, or transfers from other funds. They are limited to an accounting of receipts and expenditures on capital projects paid out of current revenues.

*Special assessment funds* account for the financing of improvements or services deemed to benefit properties against which special assessments are levied.

**Fiduciary funds**

These funds account for assets held by a governmental unit, other funds, private organizations, or individuals (e.g., employee pension funds).

**Account groups**

*General fixed assets account group* records all fixed assets—long-term resources of the governmental unit—acquired through governmental funds.

*Long-term debt account group* records general long-term liabilities assumed by the governmental unit involving the commitment of governmental funds (except for those associated with special assessment funds).

governmental unit. Dollars may be "counted" several times as they are moved from fund to fund. Such an accounting system does not indicate the total resources used during any fiscal period or what future liabilities may result from current commitments (e.g., annual leave or pension deficits). As will be discussed in further detail later in this chapter, not-for-profit records are usually kept on a different *accounting basis* than are profit funds.

Fund accounting can become fragmented. It is easy to lose track of the overall financial situation when several funds are used to finance one major activity. No one comprehensive financial statement is maintained. Rather, sets of statements are created by the governmental unit for each fund. A city's annual financial report, for example, may consist of a set of statements for the general fund (accounting for all resources not otherwise devoted to specific activities) and, in addition, sets of statements for each of the other funds maintained by the municipality. In larger cities, this annual report can run to twenty or more separate sets of financial statements.

Efforts have been made to circumvent this reporting problem through *combined* and *combining statements*. Combined statements add together the particular items for all fund statements for a given unit. When the governmental unit has more than one fund of a particular type, such as several funds for projects to build or acquire capital assets, a combining statement is prepared. Combining statements add together all of the particular items, such as cash disbursements, for each statement for each of the specific types of funds in a given category.

**Funds in Government**

Concerning governmental units as fund accounting entities, the National Council on Governmental Accounting (NCGA) has stated that: "Governmental accounting systems should be organized and operated on a fund basis." The NCGA has defined a fund as:

- a fiscal and accounting entity
- with a self-balancing set of accounts
- together with all related liabilities and residual equities or balances, and changes therein,
- which are segregated for the purposes of carrying on specific activities or attaining certain objectives
- in accordance with specific regulations, restrictions, or limitations.[9]

The NCGA goes on to suggest that: "Only the minimum number of funds consistent with legal and operating requirements should be established, however, since unnecessary funds result in inflexibility, undue complexity, and inefficient financial administration."[10]

By this definition, a fund is both a *fiscal entity* and an *accounting entity*. In governmental not-for-profit funds, as contrasted to profit (nonexpendable) funds, the use of monetary resources often is described as "funds flow"—money comes in and goes out of the fund, based on the normal flow of resources. Resources other than money can be found in certain governmental funds (e.g., taxes receivable in the general fund). However, all assets and liabilities in most not-for-profit funds are current and can be converted or paid in cash in the normal accounting cycle.[11]

Long-term and short-term assets as well as long-term and short-term liabilities can be found in the profit funds of government. Whether a profit or a not-for-profit fund, it must have the characteristics of a fiscal entity as well as an accounting entity if it is to be called a "fund."

The reasoning behind the numerous funds in government is outlined by the NCGA in *Statement 1* as follows:

> The diverse nature of governmental operations and the necessity of assuring legal compliance preclude recording and summarizing all governmental financial transactions and balances in a single accounting entity. Unlike a private business, which is accounted for as a single entity, a governmental unit is accounted for through several fund and account group entities, each accounting for designated assets, liabilities, and equity or other balances. Thus, from an accounting and financial management viewpoint, a governmental unit is a combination of several distinctly different fiscal and accounting entities, each having a separate set of accounts and functioning independently of other funds and account groups.[12]

At the present time, three major classifications are used for the funds of government: (1) proprietary funds, (2) governmental funds, and (3) fiduciary funds (see Exhibit 1-3).

*Proprietary funds* are typically the profit funds found in government. These funds generally follow the same type of accounting procedures as applied in businesses that operate for profit. Some of the activities of a local government that could be accounted for in a proprietary fund include: a water and sewer utility, an electrical utility, an automotive repair shop or motor pool, a computer service department, a swimming pool, a golf course or other recreational facility supported by user fees, and a supplies department (central stores).

Each of these activities has the following characteristics: it operates with contributed capital to provide goods or services to other governmental units or to external clientele in a manner similar to private businesses (1) on a profit basis or (2) on a cost reimbursement (break-even) basis. The first category of proprietary funds is referred to as an *enterprise fund*, while the second category is called an *internal service fund*. The primary distinction between these two categories is that the majority of users of the services of enterprise funds is from *outside* the government, while the majority of users of the services of internal service funds is from *inside* the government.

In proprietary funds, the total operating expenses for each fiscal period are recovered from the revenues collected for the services rendered. Therefore, the period costs of fixed assets (e.g., depreciation), as well as all other costs must be included in the expenses. Fixed assets are recorded in proprietary funds and are depreciated over the lifetime of the assets in order to recover the costs of those assets. This procedure, of course, is the same as is followed in a for-profit business.

*Governmental funds* follow not-for-profit accounting practices:

**1** They are not concerned with making a profit.
**2** Funds flow in and out without any permanent capital.
**3** All money received in the fiscal period can be expended.

**EXHIBIT 1-3**  SUMMARY OF FUNDS IN GOVERNMENT

| Descriptive titles | Formal classification and title |
|---|---|
| I. Profit funds | I. Proprietary funds |
|    Nonexpendable funds<br>   Business funds<br>   Income funds<br>   Commercial funds |    A. Enterprise funds<br>      Profit entity: Revenue primarily from outside the organization to carry out profit-type activities |
|    Working capital funds<br>   Intergovernmental<br>      service funds<br>   Break-even funds |    B. Internal service funds<br>      Break-even entity: Revenue primarily from other funds within the organization for the provision of service activities |
| II. Not-for-profit funds | II. Governmental funds |
|    Expendable funds |    A. General fund<br>      Basic not-for-profit fund: Revenue from general governmental sources to carry out general services |
|    Service and disposi-<br>      tion funds<br>   Nonbusiness funds<br>   Resource flow funds |    B. Special revenue funds<br>      Revenue from specific sources to provide specific services |
| |    C. Capital projects funds<br>      Revenue from bonds, grants, and transfers to buy or build capital improvement projects |
| |    D. Debt service funds<br>      Revenues transferred from other funds to service long-term debt |
| |    E. Special assessment funds<br>      Revenue from specific groups to provide services and facilities that benefit those groups on whom the assessment is levied |
| III. Trust funds | III. Fiduciary funds |
|    Agency funds |    A. Trust funds<br>      Assets held in trust for others to provide services from income or from assets of the trust |
| |    B. Agency funds<br>      Assets held in trust for others to be returned to them or to provide services for them |

Money spent for buildings or equipment—both fixed assets—is considered expenditures of a not-for-profit fund in the fiscal period in which the assets are purchased. Such expenditures are not capitalized or recorded as fixed assets in the fund. Since there is no intention of measuring the income earned, from a financial reporting perspective, there is no reason for determining the amount of depreciation on the fixed assets. The failure to include provisions for the depreciation of fixed assets in governmental funds, however, has important implications for management decision making. This point will be discussed further in Chapters 17 through 21.

Government funds may be further classified as follows:

**1** *The general fund* accounts for all financial resources except those required to be accounted for in another fund.

**2** *Special revenue funds* account for the proceeds of specific revenue sources (other than special assessments, expendable trusts, or those for major capital projects) that are legally restricted to expenditures for specific purposes.

**3** *Capital projects funds* account for financial resources used for the acquisition or construction of major capital facilities (other than those financed by proprietary funds, special assessment funds, and trust funds).

**4** *Debt service funds* account for the accumulation of resources for, and the payment of, general long-term debt principal and interest.

**5** *Special assessment funds* account for the financing of public improvements or services deemed to benefit the properties against which special assessments are levied.

Each of these funds will be further elaborated in Chapters 4 through 9.

The third classification of governmental funds is *fiduciary funds*. According to the NCGA, these funds are used "to account for assets held by a governmental unit in a trustee capacity or as an agent for individuals, private organizations, other governmental units, and/or other funds."[13] Fiduciary funds are further divided into trust funds and agency funds. *Trust funds* may have some of the characteristics of either proprietary funds or governmental funds. For example, some trust indentures provide for a distinction between principal and income. Income determination is similar to that found in a proprietary fund. When income is not determined or when the resources of the fund are expendable, then the fund would be comparable to a governmental fund.

A *pension trust fund* is a special type of trust fund that is used to account for the receipt of monies that will be invested by the governmental unit, serving as a trustee, for its employees. Eventually, both the payments received, including those from employees and the contributions from the governmental unit, and the interest earned on these monies will be used for payment of pensions to the government's employees.

*Agency funds* have no capital equity—only assets and liabilities. These funds serve as agents for others, for instance, receiving withholding taxes from each of the other governmental funds. Payments are then made from the agency fund to the appropriate governmental entity. The operations of fiduciary funds are explained in greater detail in Chapter 10.

## Account Groups in Government

Proprietary funds record fixed assets as fund resources so that these assets can be depreciated to allocate their costs for the fiscal period. Governmental funds, however, record the purchase of a fixed asset as an expenditure, and, therefore, these fixed assets are not recorded as part of the expendable resources of the fund.

Once purchased, however, fixed assets become long-term resources of the governmental unit as a whole. And unless some provision is made to inventory these assets, there will be no record in any governmental fund beyond the initial purchase. Thus, to maintain this inventory, all fixed assets acquired through governmental funds are recorded in the *general fixed assets account group*.

As with general fixed assets, general long-term liabilities are recorded in a *long-term debt account group* instead of the governmental fund in which the transactions originated. However, long-term liabilities for proprietary funds, special assessment funds, and certain trust funds are recorded in the fund incurring the debt. Concerning general long-term debt, the NCGA says:

> General long-term debt is the *unmatured principal* of bonds, warrants, notes, or other forms of noncurrent or long-term *general obligation* indebtedness that is not a specific liability of any proprietary fund, Special Assessment Fund, or Trust Fund. General long-term debt is not limited to liabilities arising from debt issuance *per se*, but may also include noncurrent liabilities on lease-purchase agreements and other commitments that are not current liabilities properly recorded in governmental funds.[14]

General long-term debt is usually secured by the full faith and credit of the governmental unit. In other words, the general revenue-raising powers of the governmental unit may be called upon to repay such debt.

## THE BASIC ACCOUNTING EQUATION

The basic accounting equation is fundamental to an understanding of double-entry accounting and financial reporting. This equation may be stated as follows:

$$\text{Assets} = \text{Liabilities} + \text{Owner's Equity} + \text{Revenue} - \text{Expenses}$$

From this equation, accountants have developed the basic concepts of debits and credits to accounts and the basic concepts of the preparation of financial statements. The relationships of debits and credits are shown in Exhibit 1-4.

The balance sheet also is derived from the balances in the portion of the basic accounting equation that deals with:

$$\text{Assets} = \text{Liabilities} + \text{Owner's Equity}$$

The income statement is derived from the account balances in the revenue *minus* expenses portion of the equation.

Much of the understanding of accounting and financial reporting for profit organizations comes from an understanding of the basic accounting equation. This basic equa-

**EXHIBIT 1-4** DEBITS AND CREDITS TO ACCOUNTS

| Debits | Credits |
| --- | --- |
| Increases in assets | Decreases in assets |
| Increases in expenses | Decreases in expenses |
| Decreases in liabilities | Increases in liabilities |
| Decreases in owner's equity | Increases in owner's equity |
| Decreases in revenue | Increases in revenue |

tion must be adapted to not-for-profit accounting and financial reporting. As used in fund accounting, the equation is:

$$\text{Assets} = \text{Liabilities} + \text{Fund Balance} + \text{Revenue} - \text{Expenditures}$$

With these adaptations, this equation can be used as a basis for understanding the debits and credits and financial statements for this newer field of accounting. Since budgets and budgetary accounting also are important parts of the accounting and reporting processes for not-for-profit entities, the basic accounting equation must be further adapted to budgetary accounts as well as actual accounts. These further modifications, detailed in Chapter 4, provide a much clearer understanding regarding the accounting for nonbusiness transactions and the financial reporting of the results of those transactions.

## THE BASIS OF ACCOUNTING

The National Council of Governmental Accounting defines the basis of accounting as "when revenues, expenditures, expenses, and transfers—and the related assets and liabilities—are recognized in the accounts and reported in the financial statements."[15] The basis of accounting determines not only when the amounts are recorded in the accounts but also what accounts should be used. The three methods used to determine when various amounts are placed in accounting records and in reports are: (1) cash basis, (2) accrual basis, and (3) modified accrual basis.

### The Cash Basis

Many smaller nonbusiness organizations still use the cash basis of accounting—that is, transactions are only recorded when cash is received or paid out. This basis is fairly easy to use and is not as elementary as it sounds. The unit's accountant can adjust the financial statements from the cash to the accrual or modified accrual basis of accounting when the financial reports are issued.

In larger units, however, it would be impractical to try to adjust all of the accounts to an accrual or modified accrual basis for transactions that occurred all during the year. This book will illustrate only the accrual basis and the modified accrual basis of accounting as they apply to specific funds of nonbusiness entities.

### The Accrual Basis

The accrual basis of accounting normally is employed in profit fund accounting and reporting. The accrual basis is used in proprietary funds and other income-producing funds of government, such as those in fiduciary funds. It also is required in several of the funds of other nonbusiness organizations.

For-profit accounting is concerned with accrual of income and expenses related not only to current assets and liabilities, but also to long-term assets and long-term liabilities as well. The accrual basis recognizes transactions in the accounts and reports the results of these transactions in the time period in which they occur, rather than in the time period in which cash is received or paid. An example is a credit sale: the asset is recorded as *accounts receivable* and the income from the sale is recognized when the sale is made, not when the cash is received. Another example is a credit purchase: the liability is recorded as *accounts payable*, and the expense generated by the purchase is recognized in the period in which the credit purchase occurs, not when the cash is paid for the purchase. A further example can be seen when a portion of a fixed asset is used: depreciation is recognized in each particular period to which the asset relates and not to the period in which cash was paid for the purchase of the asset.

**The Modified Accrual Basis**

The modified accrual basis of revenue and expenditure accounting differs from the accrual basis in several important ways. As defined for not-for-profit funds, the modified accrual basis has the following characteristics:

**1** Revenues and other nonbusiness fund financial resources are recorded as received in cash except for:
    **a** revenues susceptible to accrual (i.e., both measurable and available) and
    **b** material revenues and other nonbusiness fund financial resources that are not received at the normal time of receipt.

**2** Expenditures are recorded on an accrual basis except for:
    **a** disbursements for inventory-type items, which may be considered expenditures at the time of purchase or at the time the items are used;
    **b** prepaid expenses, which normally are not recorded; and
    **c** unmatured principal and interest on long-term debt, normally an expenditure when due.[16]

Most not-for-profit funds in nonbusiness accounting include only current assets and current liabilities (i.e., assets and liabilities that will either become cash or be paid in cash in the current operating cycle or within the fiscal year). In these types of funds, the term *expenditures* is used instead of the term *expenses*, since expenditures decrease the net working capital of the fund. Modified accrual accounting—accrued revenue and expenditure accounting—includes accruals pertaining to some current assets and current liabilities, but not to fixed assets or long-term debt. In government applications, modified accrual accounting also does not consider prepaid expenses and only partially considers inventory-type items and unmatured principal and interest on long-term debt. Pertaining to revenue, modified accrual accounting primarily operates as the cash basis except for certain items that are susceptible to accrual, such as taxes receivable and revenue from taxes receivable. When material revenue is not received at the normal time of receipt, it also should be accrued.

Using the funds of government for illustrative purposes, the basis of accounting can be summarized as follows:

- Proprietary funds should use the accrual basis to account for income, expenses, and all related assets and liabilities.

- Governmental funds should use the modified accrual basis to account for revenues and expenditures and related current assets and liabilities.

While the cash basis is not considered appropriate for accounting or financial reporting, there are some instances when:

- Fiduciary funds, involving trust indentures, require the use of this basis.

In smaller organizations, the cash basis may be used to account for transactions; however, the financial statements should be prepared on the accrual or modified accrual basis.

- Nonexpendable trust funds—being proprietary-type funds—should use the accrual basis to account for income, expenses, assets, and liabilities.

To be sure that the expenses match the income of the period, fixed assets must be recorded in proprietary-type funds and be depreciated in order to allocate the proportion of the costs of the fixed assets to the fiscal period from which income is derived. Fixed assets are recorded as expenditures in governmental funds, and the record of the fixed assets is maintained in a fixed asset account group. Long-term debt is recorded in a revenue-type account when incurred. Except for long-term liabilities in special assessment funds, the record of long-term debt in other governmental funds is kept in a long-term debt account group.

## GENERALLY ACCEPTED ACCOUNTING PRINCIPLES

Generally accepted accounting principles (GAAP) have been developed to provide an underlying structure for financial accounting and reporting. GAAP represent standards that independent auditors use when expressing opinions on the fairness of presentation of the financial statements of an organization. Profit funds of nonbusiness entities use the same principles of accounting as are applied in private business to maintain accounts and prepare financial statements.

### GAAP in Not-for-Profit Applications

Only recently, however, have principles of accounting been available for use as a basis for expressing opinions on financial statements of not-for-profit entities. Moreover, the establishment of these principles is still in the developmental stages. The Governmental Accounting Standards Board (GASB), for example, was established in April 1984 as an arm of the Financial Accounting Foundation. The GASB, in *Statement No. 1* issued in July 1984, has accepted the statements of the National Council on Governmental Accounting (NCGA) as being authoritative principles of accounting for auditors to use when auditing state and local governments. The GASB *Statement No. 1* also states:

> 2 The Governmental Accounting Standards Board (GASB) was established...to promulgate standards of financial accounting and reporting with respect to activities and transactions of state and local governmental entities. The GASB is the successor organization to the NCGA.... the NCGA's Statements and the AICPA's State and Local Government Industry

Audit Guide shall be recognized by the GASB as being in force until modified by the GASB.[17]

Certain due process procedures for the issuance by the GASB of *Statements of Governmental Accounting Standards* are set forth in chapter A, article IV-A, section 6 of the certification of incorporation and by-laws of the Financial Auditing Foundation.

Statements of the GASB, including those that incorporate the principles of the National Council on Governmental Accounting (NCGA) and the American Institute of Certified Public Accountants (AICPA), will be used in this book as the basic reference source for governmental accounting principles. In its *Audits of State and Local Governmental Units* and in its *Statement of Position 80-2*, the AICPA has likewise accepted, with minor modifications, the principles of the NCGA for use by its members. The AICPA has revised its audit guide to provide GASB statements as the basic principles for state and local government accounting.

The U.S. General Accounting Office (GAO) has the responsibility for establishing principles of accounting for federal agencies in their accounting systems and in statement preparation. Only limited references will be made in this book to the application of these federal principles, however, since few private auditors ever have need for them. Seldom, if ever, are they called upon to express an opinion on federal financial statements. Moreover, the GAO is committed to following the principles of the GASB, to the extent practicable, when auditors examine federal financial statements.

The National Association of College and University Business Officers (NACUBO) provides the most authoritative statement of accounting principles for institutions of higher education. The AICPA, in its industry audit guide, *Audits of Colleges and Universities*,[18] has affirmed the use of these principles by its members. These sources will be used in this book, therefore, for the principles of accounting applicable to colleges and universities.

The AICPA industry audit guide, *Audits of Voluntary Health and Welfare Organizations*, and its *Statement of Position 78-10, Accounting Principles and Reporting Practices for Certain Nonprofit Organizations*, provide the accounting principles for these other not-for-profit organizations to be followed in this book. Accounting principles for hospitals are provided by the American Hospital Association, the Hospital Financial Management Association, and the AICPA audit guide, *Audits of Hospitals*.

## CONTROL

Control is often defined as the assurance that acceptable standards are being or have been followed. A form of control can be seen when the independent auditor assures third parties that the financial statements of an organization are fairly presented in accordance with generally accepted accounting principles consistently applied. In the past, governmental and other nonbusiness organizations have obtained fiscal control through very specific budgetary practices. For example, the legislative body of a government may *appropriate* a specific amount to a certain executive operation for a specific activity (e.g., for employee salaries and wages) for a specific accounting period. The administrator of that operation cannot spend an amount greater than that appropriated, nor can he or she spend the appropriation for any category other than the one designated.

Five different types of control are discussed in this book:

1 Internal accounting control
2 Budgetary control
3 Subsidiary ledger control
4 Management control
5 Auditing

**Internal Accounting Control**

The basic accounting control in any organization is a double-entry set of records. Internal accounting control is the organizational plan and the practices and records concerned with safeguarding assets and providing reasonable assurance that

    **a** Transactions are executed in accordance with management's general or specific authorization.

    **b** Transactions are recorded as necessary: (1) to permit preparation of financial statements in accordance with generally accepted accounting principles or other criteria applicable to state and local governments and (2) to maintain accountability for assets.

    **c** Access to assets is permitted only in accordance with management's authorization.

    **d** The recorded accountability for assets is compared with the existing assets at reasonable intervals and appropriate action taken with respect to any differences.[19]

The primary emphasis on internal accounting controls will be discussed in Chapters 2 through 16.

**Budgetary Control**

Accounting systems for government and other nonbusiness entities were developed initially in an era in which fiscal control was a primary concern. In its landmark report in 1912, the Taft Commission recommended that governmental expenditures be classified by class of work (function), organizational unit, and character of expense (e.g., operating expenditures, capital expenditures, and debt service expenditures).[20] Early efforts to develop account classifications that reflected the various functions of government (e.g., general administration, public safety, education, etc.), however, were relatively unsuccessful. Such classifications did not provide adequate protection against possible administrative improprieties—safeguards that were a watchword during this period of governmental reform.

After some experimentation with functional accounts, most localities settled on a detailed itemization of *objects of expenditure* (e.g., salaries and wages, materials and supplies, contractual services, equipment, and other capital outlays). This object of expenditures classification was believed desirable not only "because it provides for the utilization of all the machinery of control which has been provided, but it also admits to a much higher degree of perfection than it has presently attained."[21]

Under this approach, the budget process is considered primarily as a financial control and accounting device in which expenditure estimates for various agencies are submitted and reviewed in monetary terms. These requests are supported by detailed object codes—tabulations of the myriad of items required to operate a governmental or other nonbusiness unit. Technical routines for the compilation and review of estimates and the disbursement of funds are built on these object codes. The legislative authorization to commit these funds may be "line itemized," that is, restrictions may be placed on clusters of object codes, and funds thus appropriated may not be spent outside these "line items" without the approval of the legislative body. Thus, under the object-of-expenditure approach to budgeting and accounting, administrative discretion for decision making has relatively narrow bounds.

In most of the general operations of not-for-profit organizations, a *budget* has come to represent a plan for anticipated receipts and proposed expenditures. Budgetary control is a part of the accounting system for financial reporting for most general operations of not-for-profit organizations. When budgets are adopted and recorded in the accounting system, new account formats also are introduced. For example, instead of having only revenue and expenditure accounts, budgetary accounts such as *estimated revenue* and *appropriations* (estimated expenditures) must also be used. In addition, according to GAAP, one of the required financial statements compares actual revenues and expenditures with budgeted revenues and appropriations.

When strict budgetary control is enforced within an accounting system, provisions also must be made for legal commitments for proposed expenditures during the appropriation period. Unless a portion of the appropriation is reserved or obligated for these future commitments, the budget might be overspent by the end of the budgetary year. In state and local accounting systems, these budgetary commitments are called *encumbrances*. In the federal system, they are called *obligations*. Encumbrance accounting also provides an approach to the management of governmental or nonbusiness organizations that assures program administrators that the appropriation for the current year does not revert back to its original source at the end of the year, since these resources are legally committed for the fiscal year for which they are encumbered.

## Subsidiary Ledger Control

In business accounting, subsidiary ledger controls are used primarily for accounts receivable, accounts payable, and inventories. The subsidiary ledger is a record of the details of these accounts, while the total is maintained in the general ledger. Provision must be made in the journals—whether kept by hand, machine, or computer—for posting of the details to the subsidiary ledger, while the total is posted to the general ledger. Through this method, the detailed information is readily available, while the general ledger is not cluttered with all this detail.

In nonbusiness accounting, subsidiary ledgers take on an added importance. Subsidiary ledgers concerning the budgetary and actual records for revenues and expenditures are of primary importance. In addition, the usual subsidiary ledgers pertaining to assets and liabilities (e.g., taxes receivable, inventories, and accounts payable) also are used. Subsidiary ledger controls become a very important consideration in nonbusiness accounting.

## Management Control

Management control involves the development and maintenance of standards for efficient performance and economical practices in the operations of an organization and for the overall effectiveness of goal accomplishment. The provision of such standards is as important as assurance that the accounting records have been maintained and statements have been presented in accordance with generally accepted accounting principles consistently applied. The principles and practices of management control are covered in some detail in Parts III and IV of this book.

## Auditing

Assurance that financial statements are prepared and fairly presented in accordance with generally accepted accounting principles consistently applied can be accomplished through an audit by an independent auditor. The traditional and necessary audit of financial statements is required for most governmental organizations. Such audits include the determination of fidelity, legality, and accuracy in financial records. The report and audit certification are presented in Chapter 13 to illustrate the types of audits made for governmental units by certified public accountants.

Efforts to identify opportunities in the nonbusiness sectors to reduce costs, increase efficiency, and improve program effectiveness have resulted in an extension of the accountability function from financial auditing to *performance auditing*.[22] The Comptroller General of the United States has described three types of audits included in this expanded scope:

*Financial and compliance*: determines (a) whether financial statements of an audited entity present fairly the financial position and the results of financial operations in accordance with generally accepted accounting principles and (b) whether the entity has complied with laws and regulations that may have a material effect upon the financial statements.

*Economy and efficiency*: determines (a) whether the entity is managing and utilizing its resources (such as personnel, property, space) economically and efficiently, (b) the causes of inefficiencies or uneconomical practices, and (c) whether the entity has complied with laws and regulations concerning matters of economy and efficiency.

*Program results*: determines (a) whether the desired results or benefits established by the legislature or other authorizing body are being achieved and (b) whether the agency has considered alternatives that might yield desired results at a lower cost.[23]

Although standards and criteria for performance auditing have been identified in the public sector, they are still in their developmental stages in other nonbusiness organizations. There is considerable interest, however, in this approach as a further component of the auditing system.

A number of state and local governments have adopted the principles of performance auditing as a logical extension of their program budget structure. Performance auditing in government also is linked to both program evaluation and sunset legislation. Both of these concepts have received considerable attention in various levels of government. Sunset legislation adopted in some states calls for a performance audit to be carried out periodically for the agencies or functions under review. As program evaluations examine the more tangible aspects of program performance in terms of costs and effectiveness, they assume many of the characteristics of a performance audit.

As other nonbusiness organizations adopt a program-based organization, along with a program budget, performance auditing undoubtedly will be used to evaluate program effectiveness and to determine the efficiency and economy of the operations and functions carried out by the organization.

## ORGANIZING FOR ACCOUNTING IN GOVERNMENT

The financial management activities of any organization should be under the general direction of the chief executive so as to promote the full consideration of these vital functions. The chief executive has overall responsibility for (1) the formulation of long-range plans for the entire organization, (2) the preparation and execution of the budget, (3) the maintenance of financial reporting activities, and (4) the development of related systems for measuring activity and program accomplishments. Most organizations also have a governing body (e.g., board of directors, city council, board of commissioners, etc.) that (1) determines overall fiscal policy, (2) approves the organization's budget, (3) adopts revenue and expenditure authorization measures, and (4) holds the chief executive accountable for the effectiveness of financial procedures and program results. Both the chief executive and the governing body must exercise financial stewardship in the conduct of these important financial affairs.

It is important to have a competent, well-organized accounting and financial management staff to carry out these financial responsibilities. Although good results are not necessarily guaranteed by sound organizational arrangements, past history has demonstrated that inappropriate assignments of accounting, budgeting, and control functions can create serious problems and prevent effective leadership. Local government will be used as a "model" to illustrate the staffing and organizational requirements for financial management in the public/nonbusiness sectors.

### Unified Department of Finance

The distribution of financial management responsibilities within local government may vary considerably. Organizations vary depending on the size and form of government, existing legal parameters (state and local laws and ordinances), past practices and traditions, and the management styles of those individuals with overall executive responsibility. A model organization for the financial operations of local government was first recommended by the National Municipal League in its *Model City Charter* in 1941. This "model" has remained fairly stable over the past forty years, as evidenced by its inclusion in the recent International City Management Association (ICMA) publication on the subject of municipal finance.[24] This model reflects the emphasis on the chief executive form of government (i.e., strong mayor or manager-council), with its increased centralization of management responsibilities.

All financial operations, except the independent audit function, are grouped into a single organization—a department of finance—directly responsible through its director to the chief executive (see Exhibit 1-5). Financial activities are distributed among five functional offices: controller, treasurer, assessor, purchasing agent, and the budget officer. The budget office may operate as one of the divisions of the finance department or as a separate unit directly responsible to the chief executive. The latter arrangement reflects the policy emphasis of the budget as contrasted to the line emphasis of the other divisions.

Either way, a strong functional tie should exist between the chief executive and the budget function. While the governing body holds the ultimate responsibility for the activities of government and for particular elements of the financial system (e.g., budget adoption and the financial audit), the formulation and administration of the budget should be the overall responsibility of the chief executive.

## The Controller's Office and the Budget Office

Two offices under the director of finance are directly related to the accounting function—the controller's office and the budget office. The controller's office is the basic accounting division of the governmental unit. Its responsibilities include:

**1** Maintaining the general accounts of the municipal government; prescribing all subsidiary accounts; and maintaining and supervising the cost accounting system (if one exists).

**2** Exercising preaudit controls over all receipts, commitments, and expenditures to assure that no agency/program is spending more than is authorized by the governing body.

**3** Furnishing financial data for the preparation of the budget and supplying accounting information required for budget execution and for the independent postaudit, and preparing all general financial statements.

**4** Maintaining inventory records of municipal property, and billing for taxes, special assessments, and service charges.

The budget office occupies a pivotal position in the overall financial organization of municipal government. Functional responsibilities of this office may include:

**1** Establishing the basis for fiscal policy through an analysis of current municipal finances, local and regional economic conditions, and population projections and demographic trends.

**2** Analyzing service standards and cost-conditioning factors as they relate to each program, activity, and operation performed, including: (*a*) scope and quality of services provided, (*b*) volume of activity required to render these services, (*c*) methods, facilities, and organization for performing these activities, (*d*) qualities and types of labor, materials, equipment, and other cost elements required by public programs, and (*e*) price levels of the various cost elements.

**3** Maintaining the budget calendar, scheduling procedures, instructions, and forms for compilation, review, and presentation of the budget.

**4** Developing a basis for expenditure estimates and the formulation of annual work programs and personnel requirements by agencies.

## Director of Finance

Supervises all finance activities.
Advises chief administrator on fiscal policy.
Manages retirement and other city investments.
Handles debt administration.
Makes interim and annual financial reports.

### Controller — Divisions of Accounts

- Preaudits all purchase orders, receipts, and disbursements.
- Prepares payrolls.
- Prepares and issues all checks.
- Keeps general accounting records.
- Maintains or supervises cost accounts.
- Bills property and other taxes, special assessments, and utility and other service charges.
- Maintains inventory records of all municipal property.

### Assessor — Division of Assessments

- Makes studies of property values for assessment purposes.
- Prepares and maintains property maps and records.
- Assesses property for taxation.
- Prepares assessment rolls.
- Distributes special assessments for local improvements.

### Treasurer — Treasury Division

- Collects all taxes, special assessments, utility bills, and other revenues.
- Issues licenses.
- Administers tax sales.
- Maintains custody of all city funds.
- Disburses city funds on proper vouchers or warrants.

### Purchasing Agent — Purchasing Division

- Purchases all materials, supplies, and equipment for city departments.
- Establishes standards and prepares specifications.
- Tests and inspects materials and supplies purchased by the city.
- Maintains warehouses and stores system.
- Provides certain central services such as mailing, duplicating, etc.
- Administers city's insurance program.

### Budget Officer* — Budget Division

- Makes departmental work measurement studies for development and administration of performance budget system.
- Assembles budget estimates and assists chief administrator in preparing budget document.
- Acts as agent of the chief administrator in controlling the administration of the budget by executive allotments, etc.
- Conducts studies relative to improvements in administrative organization and procedures.

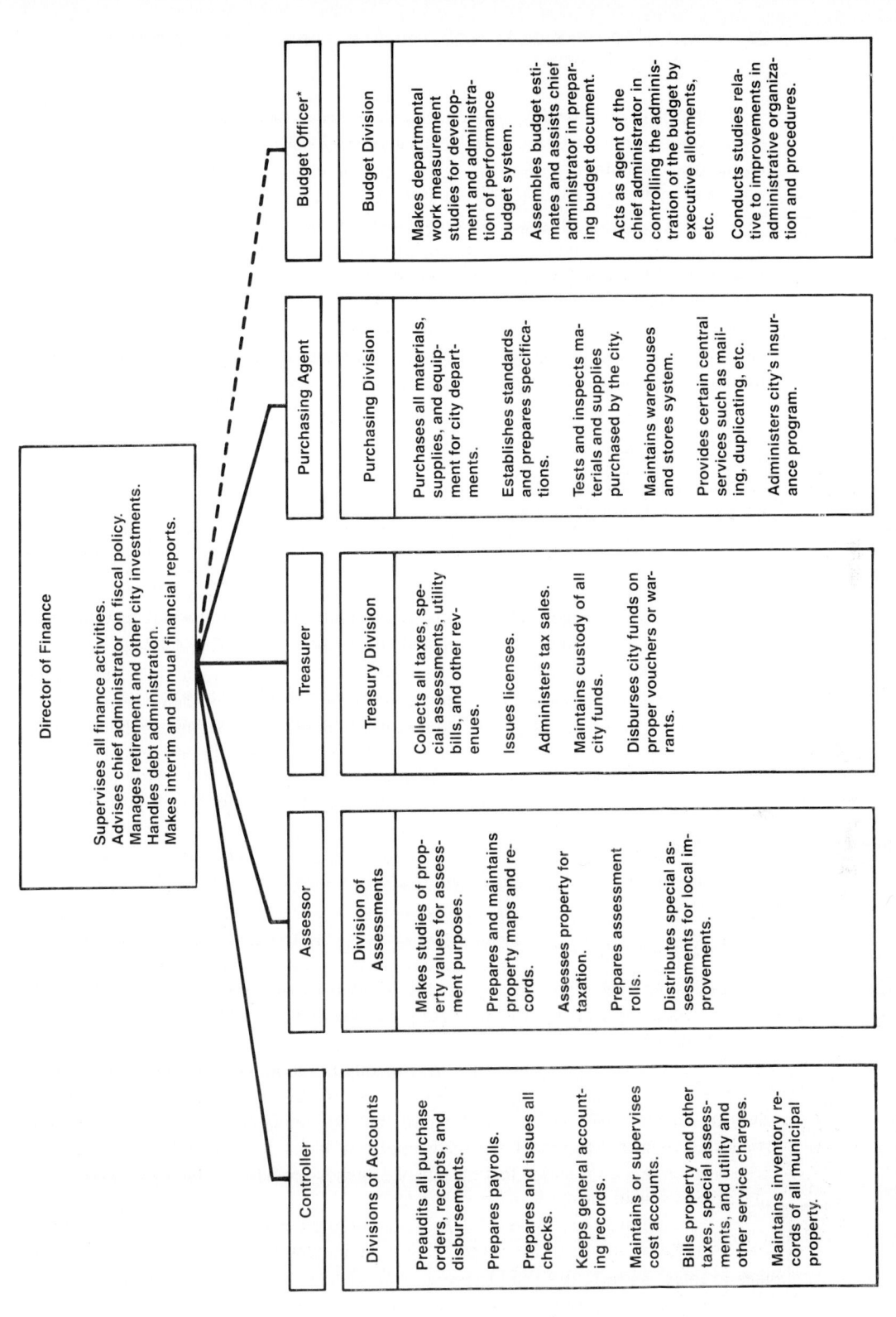

*The dotted line between the director of finance and the budget officer indicates that the latter is often primarily responsible to the chief administrator, being physically located in the finance department to prevent the duplication of records. In many cities, the finance director handles the budget job himself.

**EXHIBIT 1-5** Detailed organizational chart—department of finance.

5 Preparing revenue estimates under various fiscal policy assumptions.

6 Formulating longer range budgetary forecasts, particularly with reference to capital facilities planning.

7 Reviewing estimates and formulating recommended expenditure cuts and/or revenue increases—the traditional "balancing act" of the budget process.

8 Preparing the budget document, including the budget message, summary schedules, and detailed revenue and expenditure estimates.

9 Serving as an information resource in the budget review and adoption process.

10 Assisting in the formulation and maintenance of an allocation and allotment system, accounting and management controls, procedures for budget adjustments, and financial statement and performance reports.[25]

## The Audit Function

The audit function cannot be properly carried out by the same official who maintains the accounts showing the transactions of the organization. The controller carries out a daily check of all revenues and receipts, often called a *preaudit* because it is made prior to the payment of all claims. The independent audit, often called the *postaudit* in government, must be performed by a firm or agency strictly in the capacity of an independent reviewer outside the control of the chief administrator and preferably appointed or selected by the governing body. The independent auditor verifies and checks financial transactions and records with respect to legality, accuracy, accountability, and the application of generally accepted accounting principles. The auditor then can express an opinion on the fairness of the financial statements being presented in accordance with GAAP consistently applied. This review usually is made after the close of the fiscal year, and the findings are reported to the governing body.

## Organizational Flexibility and Change

Regardless of the organizational structure adopted, the principal objective should be to facilitate the financial management process and to direct management control for the chief executive. All too often, an organizational chart is assumed to have perpetual status. Changing concepts of management, however, often require significant changes in organization. The structure should exist so that management processes can be carried out efficiently and effectively. These processes do not exist to maintain the organizational structure.

While any organization must have the capacity to accommodate multiple processes, the importance of the financial process demands first-order consideration. The organizational structure should allow for flexibility and the maintenance of horizontal ties between the finance department and other operating units. The ties with other units are based on the service function that the finance agency provides to line departments.

## SUMMARY

This chapter has been designed to provide an introduction to the field of nonbusiness accounting. An understanding of these basic principles and practices is essential for anyone in the management of such organizations, whether serving as an accountant, providing audits, or preparing financial statements. Since approximately half of the nation's gross national product comes from government and other nonbusiness organizations, the need for accounting information for financial record keeping, external reporting, and better managerial decision making and control should be readily apparent.

Discussion in this introductory chapter focused on the public mandate for greater accountability, distinctions between business and nonbusiness accounting, and the meaning of accounting, including financial accounting and reporting and management accounting and control. An overview of fund accounting, including a discussion on each of the funds and account groups of government, was provided to further distinguish between business and nonbusiness accounting. It was noted that funds include not only profit types but also not-for-profit, nonbusiness funds. The basis of accounting for each of these types of funds was explained. The various types of control in nonbusiness accounting were identified. The chapter concluded with a brief description of the organizational "model" recommended for local government to carry out the functions of accounting, financial management, and control.

With this foundation, the reader should now be prepared to undertake an in-depth examination of each of the major components of governmental accounting for financial reporting. Such an examination is the purpose of the balance of Part I.

## QUESTIONS

1 Identify the primary functions of accounting under the traditional approaches to financial administration.
2 What organization has primary responsibility for establishing accounting principles for state and local governments?
3 Distinguish between accounting for financial reporting and management accounting.
4 Explain the entity concept as it applies to business entities and to nonbusiness entities.
5 Is there a difference between accounting entities and reporting entities? Explain this difference as it applies to business and nonbusiness accounting and reporting entities.
6 Define funds as they relate to governmental accounting.
7 List and define each of the funds classified as proprietary funds, as governmental funds, and as fiduciary funds.
8 Distinguish between expendable and nonexpendable funds.
9 Why are records of fixed assets and fixed liabilities kept in some funds and not in other funds of government? In which type of funds are fixed assets and fixed liabilities kept? In which types of funds are fixed assets and fixed liabilities not kept?
10 Explain what is meant by general fixed assets account group. What types of records are kept in this group of accounts?
11 Define the basis of accounting.
12 Do the profit funds in a nonbusiness unit follow the same set of accounting principles as applied to the not-for-profit funds?
13 What is the basis of accounting for proprietary funds? For governmental funds? For fiduciary funds?
14 What is the accrual basis of accounting? The modified accrual basis of accounting? Make a distinction between the two bases.
15 List the major responsibilities of a unified finance department as identified in the *Model City Charter*, prepared by the National Municipal League.

16 List the responsibilities of the controller's office.
17 List the responsibilities of the budget office.
18 In accounting, the word "control" may mean different things to different people. Generally, the meaning is concerned with the measurement of achievement of the goals and objectives of the organization. How does budgetary control within the accounting records fit within this definition of "control"?
19 List some of the basic differences between what can be expected in governmental accounting and what you have already learned in business accounting.

## PROBLEMS

1-1 Circle the letter for the statement that most adequately completes the statement or answers the question.[26]

1. Taxes collected and held by a municipality for a school district would be accounted for in a(n):
   a Enterprise fund
   b Internal agency fund
   c Agency fund
   d Special revenue fund

2. If a municipality established a data processing unit to service all agencies within the local government, the unit should be accounted for as a(n):
   a Capital projects fund
   b Internal service fund
   c Agency fund
   d Trust fund
   e Special revenue fund

3. In which of the following funds would it be appropriate to record the depreciation of fixed assets?
   a Capital projects fund
   b General fund
   c Internal service fund
   d Special assessment fund

4. Which fund of government would account for fixed assets in a manner similar to a business (for-profit) organization?
   a Enterprise fund
   b Capital projects fund
   c General fixed assets account group
   d General fund

5. The general fixed assets account group is used to record the fixed assets of the:
   a Special assessment fund
   b Enterprise fund
   c Nonexpendable trust fund
   d Internal service fund

6. Cash obtained from property tax revenue is transferred for the eventual payment of principal and interest on general obligation bonds. The bonds were issued when land was acquired several years ago for a city park. Upon the transfer, in which of the following should an entry be made?
   a Debt service fund
   b General fixed assets account group

    **c** General long-term debt account group
    **d** General fund
  **7** Self-supporting activities provided on a user charge basis are accounted for in a(n):
    **a** Agency fund
    **b** Enterprise fund
    **c** General fund
    **d** Special revenue fund
  **8** Which of the following is a for-profit fund?
    **a** Capital projects fund
    **b** General fund
    **c** Special revenue fund
    **d** Internal service fund
  **9** Part of the proceeds from a new issuance of a general obligation bond was used to pay for the construction of an addition to the city hall as soon as the work was completed. The remainder of the proceeds was transferred to repay the debt. Entries are needed to record these transactions in the:
    **a** General fund and general long-term debt account group
    **b** General fund, general long-term debt account group, and debt service fund
    **c** Trust fund, debt service fund, and general fixed assets account group
    **d** General long-term debt account group, debt service fund, general fixed assets account group, and capital projects fund.
  **10** The general fixed assets account group can best be described as:
    **a** A fiscal entity
    **b** An accounting entity
    **c** An integral part of the general fund
    **d** The only fund in which to properly account for fixed assets
  **11** A city should record depreciation as an expense in its:
    **a** General fund and enterprise fund
    **b** Internal service fund and general fixed assets account group
    **c** Enterprise fund and internal service fund
    **d** Enterprise fund and capital projects fund
**1-2** Circle the letter for the statement that best answers the following questions.
  **1** Which type of fund can be either not-for-profit or for-profit?
    **a** Debt service fund
    **b** Enterprise fund
    **c** Trust fund
    **d** Special revenue fund
    **e** General fund
  **2** Within a governmental unit, which three funds are accounted for in a manner similar to a for-profit entity?
    **a** General, debt service, and special assessment funds
    **b** Internal service, enterprise, and general funds
    **c** Enterprise, general, and debt service funds
    **d** Trust (nonexpendable), enterprise, and internal service
  **3** Why does a governmental unit use separate funds to account for its transactions?
    **a** Governmental units are so large that it would be unduly cumbersome to account for all transactions as a single unit.
    **b** It is necessary to segregate activities by their functional character because of the diverse nature of services offered and legal provisions regarding activities of a governmental unit.

c Generally accepted accounting principles require that not-for-profit entities report on a funds basis.
d Many activities supported by governmental units are short-lived and their inclusion in a general set of accounts could cause greater probability of error and omission.

4 Premiums received on general obligation bonds are generally transferred to what fund or account group?
a Debt service fund
b General long-term debt account group
c General fund
d Special revenue fund

5 When a truck is received by a municipality, it should be recorded in the general fund as a(n):
a Appropriation
b Encumbrance
c Expenditure
d Fixed asset

6 Which of the following funds of government uses the accrual method of accounting?
a General fund
b Internal service fund
c Special revenue fund
d Debt service fund

7 Under the modified accrual method of accounting used in local government, which of the following revenue sources would be susceptible to accrual?
a Income taxes
b Business licenses
c Property taxes
d Sales taxes

8 Which of the following funds should use the modified accrual basis of accounting?
a Enterprise fund
b Internal service fund
c Special revenue fund
d Trust (nonexpendable) fund

9 How should wages that have been earned by employees of a local government, but not paid, be recorded in the general fund?
a As an appropriation
b As an encumbrance
c As an expenditure
d As an expense

10 Under the modified accrual basis of accounting, which of the following taxes is usually recorded before it is received in cash?
a Property taxes
b Income taxes
c Gross receipts taxes
d Gift taxes

1-3 The items on page 34 were taken from the chart of accounts of a municipality. Determine if the item may be found in:

1 An enterprise fund
2 The general fund

3 A capital projects fund
4 The fixed assets account group
5 The long-term debt account group

If so, place an X in the proper column of the chart. An item may be listed under more than one category.

1-4 Using the following fund and account group titles, identify the fund or account group that should be used to account for the transactions described.

1 General fund
2 Special revenue fund
3 Capital projects fund
4 Debt service fund
5 Agency fund
6 Special assessment fund
7 Internal service fund
8 General fixed assets account group
9 General long-term debt account group

_____ The computing center of the city provides analytical services for all departments and funds in the city. The finance department purchases $15,000 in services from the computer department.

_____ The city restricts part of its school taxes for the purpose of paying the salary of the school librarian.

_____ The city receives monies from a special tax levied on one of the largest industries in Boomtown for improvement to the drainage and sewer systems adjoining the firm's property.

_____ The city receives approval to offer a new series of bonds. The proceeds from the bonds will be used to retire some old bonds that are maturing.

_____ The city received proceeds from the sale of some general obligation bonds for the purpose of building a fire station. The fire station was completed.

_____ A rapidly growing city of approximately 30,000 people received a grant from the federal government to be used for the construction of an inner-city youth center. The youth center was completed during the year.

1-5 Obtain from the department of finance at your local city or town a copy of the audited financial statements and financial reports. Can you relate some of the topics discussed in this chapter to the information shown in the financial reports? Some of those topics might include the following:

1 How is the department of finance organized? Does it include all financial operations or only one?
2 Are actual expenditures compared with budgeted appropriations?
3 How are the accounts classified in the financial statements—by objects of expenditures or by functions and activities? Can you see from the statements the differences between a function and a department?
4 In which funds are general fixed assets and general long-term debt recorded? Why do some funds keep fund assets and fund liabilities separate from the general operations of the fund?
5 Does the annual financial report include more than financial information?

1-6 The basic accounting systems for nonbusiness organizations are financial accounting and re-

|  | 1 | 2 | 3 | 4 | 5 |
|---|---|---|---|---|---|
| Cash |  |  |  |  |  |
| Inventory |  |  |  |  |  |
| Notes receivable |  |  |  |  |  |
| Appropriations |  |  |  |  |  |
| Property taxes receivable |  |  |  |  |  |
| Accounts receivable (trade) |  |  |  |  |  |
| Depreciation expense for buildings |  |  |  |  |  |
| Expenditure for equipment |  |  |  |  |  |
| Equipment |  |  |  |  |  |
| Long-term bonds payable |  |  |  |  |  |
| Income tax revenues |  |  |  |  |  |
| Estimated revenue |  |  |  |  |  |
| Merchandise inventory |  |  |  |  |  |
| Prepaid expenses |  |  |  |  |  |
| Accumulated depreciation |  |  |  |  |  |
| Buildings |  |  |  |  |  |
| Encumbrances |  |  |  |  |  |
| Repair expenses |  |  |  |  |  |
| Retained earnings |  |  |  |  |  |
| Salaries and wages payable |  |  |  |  |  |
| Office supplies |  |  |  |  |  |
| Salary and wages expenditures |  |  |  |  |  |
| Fund balance |  |  |  |  |  |
| Reserve for encumbrances |  |  |  |  |  |
| Travel expenses |  |  |  |  |  |
| Sales |  |  |  |  |  |

porting systems. These systems produce information for external users regarding the fair presentation of financial statements in accordance with generally accepted accounting principles consistently applied. A management system, designed to serve the broader management purposes of planning, decision making, and management control, must be based on the concepts found in a financial accounting and reporting system.

1. Distinguish between financial accounting and reporting and management accounting.
2. How must a financial accounting and reporting system be adapted to provide information for planning, decision making, and control? Consider these adaptations from:
   a. A costing standpoint
   b. An organizational standpoint
   c. An accounting basis standpoint

## NOTES

1. The Comptroller General of the United States, *Standards for Audit of Governmental Organizations, Programs, Activities & Functions* (Washington, D.C.: The U.S. General Accounting Office, 1974), pp. 1–2.
2. The Comptroller General of the United States, *Standards for Audit of Governmental Organizations, Programs, Activities, and Functions, 1981 Revision* (Washington, D.C.: The U.S. General Accounting Office, 1981), p. 3.
3. See Coopers & Lybrand and the University of Michigan, *Financial Disclosure Practices of the American Cities* (New York: Coopers & Lybrand, 1976); Sidney Davidson, et al., *Financial Reporting by State and Local Government Units* (Chicago: The Center for Management of Public and Nonprofit Enterprise of the Graduate School of Business, University of Chicago, 1977); Allan R. Drebin, James L. Chan, and Lovna C. Ferguson, *Objectives of Accounting and Financial Reporting for Governmental Units: A Research Study* (Chicago: National Council on Governmental Accounting, 1981); Relmond P. Van Daniker and Kay T. Pohlmann, *Preferred Accounting Practices for State Governments* (Lexington, Ky.: The Council of State Governments, 1983). Also see the reports of the American Accounting Association's committees on the public sector in 1971, 1973, and 1974.
4. American Institute of Certified Public Accountants, *Statement of Position 78-10. Accounting Principles and Practices for Certain Nonprofit Organizations* (New York: AICPA, 1978).
5. American Institute of Certified Public Accountants, *Audit and Accounting Guide: Audits of Certain Nonprofit Organizations* (New York: AICPA, 1981).
6. One of the most important studies was prepared in 1978 by Robert N. Anthony, *Financial Accounting in Non-Business Organizations: An Exploratory Study of Conceptual Issues* (Stamford, Conn.: Financial Accounting Standards Board, 1979). Four years earlier, the National Association of College and University Business Officers (NACUBO) commissioned a group of accounting professors at Brigham Young University to provide guidelines for financial reporting in institutions of higher education. See Fred Skousen, Jay M. Smith, and Leon W. Woodfield, *User Needs—An Empirical Study of College and University Financial Reporting* (Washington, D.C.: National Association of College and University Business Officers, 1975).
7. For a further discussion of these developments, see Robert G. May, Gerhard G. Muller, and Thomas H. Williams, *A Brief Introduction to the Managerial and Social Uses of Accounting* (Englewood Cliffs, N.J.: Prentice-Hall, 1975); Charles T. Horngren, *Introduction to Management Account* (Englewood Cliffs, N.J.: Prentice-Hall, 1978); Robert N. Anthony and James S. Reese, *Management Accounting: Text and Cases* (Homewood, Ill.: Richard D. Irwin, 1975); and James H. Rossell and William W. Frasure, *Managerial Accounting* (Columbus, Ohio: Charles E. Merrill, 1972).

8 See National Council on Governmental Accounting, *Statement 3. Defining the Governmental Reporting Entity* (Chicago: Municipal Finance Officers Association of the United States and Canada, 1982). For a comparative discussion of the entity issue, see Van Daniker and Pohlmann, *Preferred Accounting Practice*, pp. 36–42, 161, 164–169.

9 National Council on Governmental Accounting, *Statement 1. Governmental Accounting and Financial Reporting Principles* (Chicago: Municipal Finance Officers Association of the United States and Canada, 1979), p. 11.

10 Ibid.

11 An excellent discussion of the pros and cons of a governmental unit using funds as the basic accounting entity is provided in Van Daniker and Pohlmann, *Preferred Accounting Practices*, pp. 43–56.

12 NCGA, *Statement 1*, p. 7.

13 Ibid., p. 7.

14 Ibid., p. 7.

15 Ibid., p. 11.

16 See discussion on modified accrual basis, ibid., pp. 11–12.

17 *Statement 1 of the Governmental Accounting Standards Board, Authoritative Status of NCGA Pronouncements and AICPA Industry Audit Guide* (Stamford, Conn.: Governmental Accounting Standards Board, 1984), pp. 1–2. Copyright by Governmental Accounting Standards Board, High Ridge Park, Stamford, Connecticut 06905. Reprinted with permission. Copies of GASB documents are available upon request.

18 American Institute of Certified Public Accountants, *Industry Audit Guides: Audits of Colleges and Universities* (1975); *Audits of Voluntary Health and Welfare Organizations* (1974); and *Hospital Audit Guide* (1979).

19 American Institute of Certified Public Accountants, *AICPA Professional Standards. Volume A. U.S. Audit Standards, Section 320.28* (New York: American Institute of Certified Public Accountants, 1984), p. 246.

20 President's Commission on Economy and Efficiency, *The Need for a National Budget* (Washington, D.C.: Government Printing Office, 1912), pp. 210–213.

21 New York Bureau of Municipal Research, "Some Results and Limitations of Central Financial Control in New York City," *Municipal Research*, vol. 81 (1917), p. 67.

22 Leo Herbert, *Auditing the Performance of Management* (Belmont, Cal.: Lifetime Learning Publications, 1979).

23 Comptroller General of the United States, *Standards for Audit of Governmental Organizations, 1981 Revision*, p. 3.

24 J. Richard Aronson and Eli Schwartz (eds.) *Management Policies in Local Government Finance* (Washington, D.C.: International City Management Association, 1975).

25 Alan Walter Steiss, *Public Budgeting and Management* (Lexington, Mass.: Lexington Books—D.C. Heath and Company, 1972), chap. 8.

26 Adapted from American Institute of Certified Public Accountants, *Uniform CPA Examination Questions and Answers Unofficial* (New York: Copyright © by the American Institute of Certified Public Accountants, various dates. Adapted with permission).

# CHAPTER 2

# PROPRIETARY FUNDS— ENTERPRISE FUNDS

Chapter 1 indicated that nonbusiness accounting includes many areas, one of which is governmental accounting. The discussion in Chapter 1 also established that the governmental accounting system, if properly developed, is capable of producing reports for internal management decision making and control as well as financial statements for external users. The accounting system that produces financial statements for external users is called *financial accounting and reporting*, and the system that produces reports for internal management's decision making and control functions is called *management accounting*. The remaining chapters in Part I will focus primarily on financial accounting and reporting for governmental units.

Chapter 1 also distinguished between entities in nonbusiness accounting and business accounting: The nonbusiness unit has many entities, while the business unit usually has only one. These many entities (called *funds* and *account groups* in government) include some that are profit-making entities (similar to a business entity) and a great many *not-for-profit* entities. The profit entities in government are called *proprietary funds*, and the not-for-profit entities are called *governmental funds*. This chapter examines the enterprise funds of proprietary funds. Chapter 3 will examine the internal service funds of proprietary funds.

The persons who begin the study of nonbusiness accounting usually are junior, senior, or graduate students in colleges or universities; practitioners in government or other nonbusiness organizations; and public accountants. Generally, these people have studied business accounting but are not actively carrying out the mechanics of double-entry accounting. They often find it easier, when approaching a new subject such as governmental accounting, to visualize the newer transactions, if those transactions do not change appreciably from the ones they have previously learned.

Accounting and financial reporting for proprietary funds of government (enterprise and internal service funds) are similar to those previously learned in accounting for business organizations. As suggested in Chapter 1, an understanding of business accounting is generally required in most colleges and universities as a background for taking a course in nonbusiness accounting. Thus a vast majority of the material in Chapter 2 will be a review. Proprietary funds, their accounts, their accounting transactions, and their financial statements will be considered first in our discussions of fund accounting in government. The similarities between proprietary fund accounting in government and similar entities in business will be examined, followed by a discussion of the differences.

## Similarities of Accounting in Proprietary Funds of Government and Business Entities

The basic similarities of proprietary fund accounting in government and their counterparts in business are as follows:

**1** The basic accounting equation, discussed in Chapter 1, is the same for transactions in proprietary funds as for those in similar entities in business:

$$\text{Assets} = \text{Liabilities} + \text{Capital Equity} + \text{Income} - \text{Expenses}$$

If the basic accounting equation is the same for proprietary funds of government as for similar private business entities, then the debits and credits for transactions in both types of entities would be similar.

**2** Most of the account titles are similar, for example: cash, accounts receivable, inventories, land, buildings, accounts payable, salaries and wages, depreciation on buildings, accumulated depreciation, and so forth.

**3** The financial statements are the same as those found in any private business: the balance sheet; the statement of revenues, expenses, and changes in retained earnings; and the statement of changes in financial position.

**4** Most of the account classifications on the financial statements are similar. For example, in the balance sheet, the accounts are classified as: current assets, fixed assets, other assets (e.g., prepaid expenses), current liabilities, fixed liabilities (long-term debt), and capital equity.

**5** The basis of accounting is the same. The accrual basis of accounting is employed in both proprietary funds of governments and in business entities.

## New Approaches

However, some new transactions, account names, and financial statement titles are encountered in proprietary funds of government that are not a part of private business accounting. These new approaches will be detailed under the following headings:

**1** Profit versus break-even operations,
**2** Basis of accounting,
**3** Capital equity,
**4** Debt financing,

5 Interfund transactions, and
6 Specialized needs.

The transactions, account names, and financial statements that are similar to those in private, for-profit entities, along with any that are discussed as new types, will be illustrated by transactions for both an enterprise fund and an internal service fund for a fictitious city—the city of Ruthberg.

## PROFIT VERSUS BREAK-EVEN OPERATIONS

Some funds in government provide services to those outside of government. These include funds that provide services for a fee to residents of the governmental unit as well as to those who are nonresidents. They include, but are not limited to, water, garbage, sewer, electricity, airport service, parking, bus or subway transportation services, swimming pools, hospitals, nursing homes, public housing services, toll highway services, and liquor retailing services. From an accounting and financial reporting standpoint, the entities that provide these services in government operate them identically to those providing the same services in the private sector. These funds should receive sufficient revenue to cover all expenses and provide an appropriate amount of net income. These entities in government are called *enterprise funds*, and they will be discussed and illustrated in this chapter.

Printing, computer services, automobile repairing and servicing, automobile leasing, equipment repairing, and inventory warehousing are similar services found in both government and private business. In private business, however, these services usually are provided, for a fee sufficient to make a profit, to users outside of the business unit, and not to those who are directly related to the business. In government, these types of services generally are provided only to other funds of government and not to users outside of government. The price for these services to the other fund users is usually determined on a cost-reimbursement basis to the provider fund rather than at a price that will make a profit for the fund. So, determining the costs of operating these funds is an important consideration in these entities. This type of fund in government is called an *internal service fund*. It will be discussed and illustrated in Chapter 3.

Proprietary funds have been called *nonexpendable* because the capital equity is retained fairly permanently rather than being expended each period, as will be found in governmental funds. Capital equity usually is maintained in enterprise funds by charging for services that will not only recover costs but will also provide *retained earnings* for future use or for distribution to the general fund or other funds of the governmental unit. Capital equity in internal service funds is usually maintained by recovering any costs expended through fees for services. Through this method, the capital equity in an internal service fund should remain fairly constant.

Furthermore, one should remember that all services provided by proprietary funds can be furnished by governmental funds. For example, water or garbage services can be supplied by the general fund, which is a governmental fund, thereby using tax revenue rather than levying separate water or sewer service charges (enterprise funds). Or, each of the governmental funds can arrange for its own printing, computer, or automobile repairing service, rather than the governmental unit providing separate internal service funds to carry out these activities for all of the other funds. The governmental unit uses proprietary funds to provide more convenient services, additional revenue, or reduced costs to the overall governmental units.

## BASIS OF ACCOUNTING

The purpose of proprietary funds is to provide services or goods either to other funds or to outside users so that full costs can be recovered, along with possible net earnings for enterprise funds. Therefore, the basis of accounting must be such that all costs, including the costs of fixed assets, must be recovered. The accrual basis of accounting would be used.

The accrual basis of accounting records revenues in the period the revenue is earned, not when cash is received. For example, revenue is earned in a public utility when the electric services are provided to the customer, not when cash is received for the services. The same holds true for expenses of a proprietary fund; expenses are recognized in the period that the transaction pertaining to the use of the asset or service takes place, and not when cash is paid. Thus, when a building is purchased, the asset is recorded when purchased, but the expense of using the building is extended over the period that the building is used.

So, both long-term assets and long-term debt are recorded in proprietary funds. Transactions pertaining to the use of the fixed assets and the payment of the long-term debt, along with any financing charges, moreover, will occur in the particular proprietary fund in the proper period.

### Revenue and Other Sources of Financing

Revenue and other sources of financing needed for carrying out the operations of a proprietary fund are classified similarly to those found in a comparable business, with the exception of interfund and grant transactions. These sources can be discussed under the following headings:

1 Charges for services,
2 Operating grants,
3 Operating transfers in, and
4 Other.

**Charges for Services** Charges for services are classified as operating revenue in the statement of revenues, expenses, and changes in retained earnings. They are recorded on an accrual basis for both enterprise and internal service funds, which is very similar to their recording in any business organization.

The principles of accounting for revenue recognition in proprietary funds of government are the same for external transactions as they are in any business. One of the problems often encountered in accounting for proprietary funds of government, however, pertains to the recognition of revenue in interfund transactions. The purchase of electricity by the general fund from the utility fund (enterprise fund) is one example. A computer fund (internal service) providing services to a special revenue fund is another example. These transactions are revenue transactions when bought by external sources; therefore, they are revenue transactions when purchased by the internal funds of government. These types of transactions are called "quasi-external" transactions, because they are comparable to transactions provided to users outside of the governmental unit, even when provided to internal users.

To illustrate, if the general fund purchased $5,000 worth of electricity from the utility fund during May 19X4, the utility fund would make the following entry:

|  | Dr. | Cr. |
|---|---|---|
| Due from general fund | $5,000 |  |
|     Charges for services |  | $5,000 |

Charges for electricity sold to the general fund.

Or, if the special revenue fund used $2,000 worth of computer services during the month, the computer fund (internal service fund) would make the following entry:

|  | Dr. | Cr. |
|---|---|---|
| Due from special revenue fund | $2,000 |  |
|     Charges for services |  | $2,000 |

Charges for services to special revenue fund.

**Operating Grants** Operating grants are resources received that are equivalent to revenue. These types of grants are shown on the statements as "nonoperating revenue." The basis of accounting for operating grants in proprietary funds for both internal service and enterprise funds is the accrual basis.

Grants, entitlements, or shared revenue are often given for use in multiple years. The conditions of the grant, therefore, must be met by the fund before the grant is final. The NCGA says:

> Grants, entitlements, or shared revenues received before the revenue recognition criteria have been met should be reported as *Deferred Revenue*, a liability account. Such resources not received should be reported as a receivable if the revenue recognition criteria have been met. When such resources have not been received nor the revenue recognition criteria met, they should not be reported on the balance sheet, but may be disclosed in the notes to the financial statements.[1]

For example, suppose the revenue recognition criterion is that the city must spend an amount equal to any revenue recognized from the grant. The city has received the total amount of the grant, $100,000, from the federal government. However, only $50,000 has been spent of its own money for grant purposes during the period. Upon receiving the grant funds, the entries for these transactions would be:

|  | Dr. | Cr. |
|---|---|---|
| Cash | $100,000 |  |
|     Operating grant—deferred |  | $100,000 |

Upon expending $50,000 of the city's own money for the particular services required by the grant, $50,000 of grant revenue will be recognized. The following entries would be made:

| | | |
|---|---:|---:|
| Expenses (grant related) | $50,000 | |
|     Cash | | $50,000 |
| Operating grant—deferred | 50,000 | |
|     Operating grant revenue | | 50,000 |

**Operating Transfers** When one fund, such as the general fund, transfers to an internal service fund resources that can be used by the internal service fund to provide services to all funds, it is called an operating transfer. Operating transfers must be shown separately in the financial statements.

**Other** Interest on loans or other debt receivables are considered in this category. Interest is classified in the financial statements as nonoperating revenue. However, if the purpose of the fund is to provide revenue from interest-bearing obligations, it is an operating revenue. Rental income on property not generally considered rental property also fits the "other" classification. If rental income comes from property that is to be rented for income purposes, then the income is considered operating income.

## Expenses and Other Uses of Financial Resources

Expenses and other uses of financial resources needed for the operations of proprietary funds are classified similarly to those found in business organizations that render the same type of service being provided by a proprietary fund of government. The following headings for expenses and other types of operating uses of financial resources in proprietary funds of government can be used for discussing this subject:

1 Operating expenses,
2 Nonoperating expenses, and
3 Operating transfers.

**Operating Expenses** Operating expenses are recorded and reported on an accrual basis and include such items as personal services, other services, materials and supplies, and depreciation.

Personal services, sometimes called personnel services, include not only direct and indirect labor costs but also other costs such as pensions, insurance, and the fund's share of the costs for such items as those incurred under the Federal Insurance Contributions Act.

Materials and supplies can be shown as an expense when purchased, and an adjusting entry can be made at the end of the fiscal year for the unused amount that would be shown as inventory at the end of the accounting period. This method then accurately reflects the amount used for the period. Also, the materials and supplies can be shown as inventory when purchased, and the amount used is recorded when the actual usage takes place. Where costs of a particular service are needed, such as the cost of a particular printing job, the latter method is the one generally used.

When significant, expenses such as rent, contractual services, and transportation can be shown as individual amounts instead of being included under the "other" category. It always should be remembered that in a proprietary fund fixed assets are recorded directly in that fund as an asset and not recorded as an expense until used. When a proportionate part of the fixed asset is used, the expense is recorded as depreciation for the period. This is always an operating expense.

**Nonoperating Expenses**  Nonoperating expenses include such items as interest expense and fiscal charges. Both long-term and short-term debt are kept in proprietary funds, and the costs of those items (e.g., interest) is paid by those funds and not by the governmental unit.

**Operating Transfers**  Transfers from a proprietary fund to another fund of the governmental unit that will be used in the operations of the second fund are recorded as operating transfers and shown separately in the financial statements. Payments to other funds that are usually considered as a normal operating expense (e.g., payments to the general fund in lieu of taxes) are not considered transfers but expenses. As expenses, they are considered a normal operating expense for the period.

## CAPITAL EQUITY

Proprietary fund capital equity usually comes from one or more of four sources:

1 Residual equity transfers,
2 Capital grants,
3 Retained earnings, and
4 Other sources.

Capital equity account titles such as "capital stock," "John Jones, Partner," or "Harry Smith, Capital Account" do not exist in proprietary funds of government. Therefore, different account titles for the capital equity accounts of the proprietary funds of government must be used.

The resources that provide the capital for the proprietary funds come from various sources. The principal source is that transferred from other funds of government, primarily the general fund. These amounts transferred from the other funds of government to provide capital equity for the proprietary funds of governement are called residual equity transfers.

### Residual Equity Transfers

Many enterprise and internal service funds are started by capital generated from transfers from other funds of government. The general fund is a common source of this capital equity for proprietary funds. For example, when the general fund transfers resources to an electric utility fund for buying or constructing an electric utility system, a residual equity transfer is made. Or, when the general fund provides the resources necessary to establish a garage fund, the resources transferred from one fund to another for capital equity formation are called *residual equity transfers*.

To illustrate residual equity transfer transactions in an internal service fund, assume that $100,000 is being transferred from the general fund to a garage fund. The transfer entry in the garage fund would be:

|  | Dr. | Cr. |
|---|---|---|
| Cash | $100,000 |  |
|    Residual equity transfer from general fund |  | $100,000 |

To record receipt of capital resources from the general fund.

The garage fund would then set up the capital equity account, called "Contributed Capital," through the following entry:

| Residual equity transfer from general fund | $100,000 |  |
|---|---|---|
|    Contributed capital |  | $100,000 |

To record capital contribution from the general fund.

## Capital Grants

Capital grants are also an important source of capital equity for proprietary funds of government. Concerning grants for proprietary funds for acquisition or construction of capital assets, the NCGA says: "resources externally restricted for capital acquisition or construction are reported as contributed capital."[2]

One of the peculiarities of governmental accounting for proprietary funds is that, unlike governmental funds, the fixed assets obtained from capital grant resources are recorded in the proprietary funds and depreciated in order to determine the total costs of operation. NCGA's *Statement 2*, concerning financial statements that include depreciation on the fixed assets externally restricted by grants to fixed-asset acquisition or construction, says:

> Depreciation recognized on assets acquired or constructed through such resources externally restricted for capital acquisition may be closed to the appropriate contributed capital account and reported in the operating statement. If this option is followed, the net income (loss), adjusted by the amount of depreciation on fixed assets acquired or constructed through such resources externally restricted for this purpose is closed to Retained Earnings and reported as shown in Illustration 2.[3]

This method is optional. An alternative method is to close all depreciation on fixed assets, including depreciation on the fixed assets acquired from resources externally restricted for capital acquisition, to net income and thus to retained earnings. This second method is comparable to that normally found in business accounting.

Since the first method is somewhat different from that normally encountered in business, it will be illustrated in this chapter by reproducing a portion of Illustration 2 of NCGA's *Statement 2* (see Exhibit 2-1).[4]

**EXHIBIT 2-1**
Name of Governmental Unit
A Proprietary Fund
Statement of Revenues, Expenses,
and Changes in Retained Earnings
for the Fiscal Year Ended (date)

| | |
|---|---:|
| (Detailed information concerning revenues, expenses [including all depreciation expenses], and transfers to net income or loss). | |
| Net income (loss) | XX |
| Add depreciation on fixed assets acquired by grants, entitlements, and shared revenues externally restricted for capital acquisition and construction that reduces contributed capital (optional) | XX |
| Increase (decrease in retained earnings) | XX |
| Retained earnings—Beginning of period | XX |
| Retained earnings—End of period | $XX |

## Retained Earnings

As is true of any business organization, retained earnings would provide additional capital equity for operation of the proprietary fund.

## Other Sources

Distinguishing between operating resources and capital resources is often one of the problems in proprietary fund accounting. When a gift is given specifically for capital acquisition purposes, it obviously is contributed capital. If the gift can be used in any manner by the proprietary fund, it would follow the same basic accounting classification as would grants, usually as nonoperating income.

## DEBT FINANCING

As is true in a business enterprise, proprietary funds of government can use various types of long-term debt to finance the entity: bonds, mortgages, long-term notes, long-term leases, and advances from other funds of the governmental unit, to name only a few. Conditions concerning borrowing money and the payment of the debt to those outside of the governmental unit require much more stringent procedures to be followed than when borrowing within the governmental unit. Bond indentures, for example, often require the proprietary fund to build up resources through a sinking fund in order to have sufficient resources to pay the bonds when due. As is sometimes required in business accounting, reservations of retained earnings are often required to provide sufficient resources to pay the bonds and interest. Quite often, bond indentures require a first claim on any revenues of the fund in order to pay interest and build up a sinking fund for eventual payment of the bonds.

Since the proprietary fund is an entity within the governmental unit, lenders often require that the full faith, credit, and taxing power of the governmental unit be used as support for the issuance of bonds. Other than this particular requirement—the use of the full faith, credit, and taxing power of the governmental unit—long-term borrowing by proprietary funds is very similar to that found in long-term debt financing by a business organization. A sinking fund in a proprietary fund is a fund within a fund. Reservation of retained earnings discloses additional protection afforded the lender by restricting the proprietary fund equity in order to provide resources for eventual payment of bonds, long-term debt, or interest.

In addition, as is required by generally accepted accounting principles for businesses, long-term leases are considered long-term assets and long-term debt. Accounting and reporting for long-term leases follows those procedures normally encountered in business accounting.

Long-term loans from other governmental funds, rather than being contributed capital from those funds, are often used as a means of financing proprietary funds. These obligations are called "advances from other funds," rather than "due to the other fund." The latter is the term normally used for short-term loans from other governmental funds.

## INTERFUND TRANSACTIONS

As discussed in Chapter 1, a nonbusiness unit can be composed of many accounting entities instead of only one. In local government accounting, for example, instead of only one entity for the governmental unit, many entities called *funds* and *account groups* are employed to record the transactions and prepare the financial statements.

Since these many entities are a part of the overall governmental unit, it becomes obvious that many transactions can occur between and among the various entities. If a transaction between entities is recorded in one entity, then, to be consistent, the transaction should also be recorded in the other entity. These types of transactions are called *interentity transactions*.

Interentity transactions in proprietary funds of a local government usually are found only between governmental funds and proprietary funds. Seldom does one encounter many of the transactions between these funds and account groups. Since proprietary funds record each fund's fixed assets and each fund's long-term debt in those funds, the primary type of transactions between proprietary funds in a local government and other entities would be between funds. These types of transactions then are called *interfund transactions*.

Interfund transactions can occur between:

1 Enterprise and internal service funds and governmental funds,
2 Enterprise funds and internal service funds, and
3 Enterprise funds or internal service funds and fiduciary funds.

Interfund transactions can be considered under the following subjects:

1 Operating revenues and expenses,
2 Operating transfers, and
3 Residual equity transfers.

## Operating Revenues and Expenses

**Operating Revenues** When a proprietary fund charges another fund for services rendered or products sold that are similar to external transactions for the same product or service sold to customers outside of the governmental unit, this interfund transaction would be recorded similarly to the external transaction. However, instead of billing the other fund as an account receivable, the account title that is used is called "due from X fund." The account title used for the operating revenue received is often called "charges for services."

Other than account titles, the transactions are recorded exactly the same as those found in a similar business entity. For example, suppose a utility fund, which is an enterprise fund, charged the general fund for electricity used during the month. The journal entry in the utility fund would be:

|  | Dr. | Cr. |
|---|---|---|
| Due from general fund | $5,000 |  |
|     Charges for services |  | $5,000 |

Amount charged the general fund for electricity during the month.

When the amount was paid, the journal entry would be:

| | | |
|---|---|---|
| Cash | $5,000 | |
|     Due from general fund | | $5,000 |

Payment on account.

**Operating Expenses** Except for account titles, operating expenses are identical to those found in a similar business entity. Take for example the purchase of stationery by an enterprise fund from an internal service printing fund. The purchase of the stationery can be recorded either in an inventory account or directly as an expense. When used, the stationery expense will be an operating expense. The amount credited for the purchase of the stationery, however, would go into an account called "due to printing fund" rather than to an accounts payable account. To illustrate this operating expense transaction, assume the utility fund purchased $2,000 of stationery during the month from the printing fund. When recording this purchase directly to the expense account, the transaction would be:

|  | Dr. | Cr. |
|---|---|---|
| Supplies expense | $2,000 |  |
|     Due to printing fund |  | $2,000 |

Purchased stationery from the printing fund.

When paid, the entry would be:

| | | |
|---|---|---|
| Due to printing fund | $2,000 | |
|     Cash | | $2,000 |

Paid printing fund amount owed.

## Operating Transfers

Many operations of a governmental unit can be either *for profit*—those that result from charges for the services to customers—or *not for profit*—those carried out as a general activity of government from the general revenues of government. For example, garbage services of a city can be carried out in the general fund as a not-for-profit service of government from the tax revenues. Or the garbage service can be a for-profit operation as an enterprise fund.

Sometimes in proprietary funds of government, especially when the charges for services are insufficient to meet the operating expenses of the fund, other funds, especially the general fund, subsidize the operations. For example, civic golf courses and swimming pools, set up to operate as enterprise funds, often are subsidized from general fund revenues in order to make these recreational activities available to as many of the taxpayers as possible at a price they can afford. When the general fund gives this money to the swimming pool fund, the golf course fund, or the garbage fund, the amounts received in these funds become operating revenues. Note that the amounts received are called "operating transfers" rather than "charges for services" in order to show that the amounts were transferred from another fund, rather than being received from customers for the services received.

To illustrate an operating transfer transaction, assume that the general fund pays the swimming pool fund $25,000 in order to assure profitable operations of the fund. Upon determining that the amount is owed, the entry would be:

|  | Dr. | Cr. |
|---|---|---|
| Due from general fund | $25,000 |  |
|     Operating transfer from general fund |  | $25,000 |

To accrue operating transfer from the general fund.

Upon receiving the amount from the general fund, the entry would be:

| Cash | $25,000 |  |
|---|---|---|
|     Due from general fund |  | $25,000 |

To record payment of cash received for operating transfer.

## Residual Equity Transfers

The capital equity of an enterprise fund or an internal service fund is often provided by money or other assets from other funds. The type of transaction that provides capital equity for one fund that is given from another fund is called a residual equity transfer. For example, suppose the general fund of a municipality decided to set up an internal service fund for computer operations in order to charge each department for its use of the computer. The debit would be to the asset received (e.g., cash), while the credit would be to an account called "residual equity transfer." If $100,000 in cash was provided from the general fund to the computer fund, the entry in the computer fund would be:

|  | Dr. | Cr. |
|---|---|---|
| Cash | $100,000 | |
|     Residual equity transfer | | $100,000 |

To record receipt of resources transferred from the general fund in order to set up a computer fund.

The residual equity transfer account would then be closed at the end of the year, in order to set up the "contributed capital account" as follows:

| Residual equity transfer | $100,000 | |
|---|---|---|
|     Contributed capital | | $100,000 |

To close residual equity transfer account to contributed capital account.

Any type of asset can be contributed to a proprietary fund in order to provide the capital equity to set up that fund. Cash is ordinarily the type of asset contributed as capital for a proprietary fund. Each of these contributions would be a residual equity transfer.

## SPECIALIZED NEEDS

In some areas, governmental accounting for proprietary funds approaches accounting somewhat differently than does business accounting. This is especially true in one particular area—budgetary accounting.

### Budgetary Accounting in Proprietary Funds

Most business-type operations are such that fixed budgetary control will not work very satisfactorily. If revenues vary, then costs usually vary. If costs are held constant, then the purpose of the business-type fund seldom can be accomplished. This is especially true where the purpose relates to income measurement. Therefore, if a budget is used for proprietary funds, it is usually a flexible, managerial-type budget, in which costs vary in proportion to revenue. (Flexible budgets for proprietary funds are not discussed in this book because numerous books already are available on flexible budgeting for business-type operations.)

One of the problems in governmental accounting is that administrators do not accept that costs vary in proportion to revenue and require a fixed budget, especially in relation to the amount of cash expended. This type of budget is fully explained in Chapter 4. It applies to proprietary funds as well as to specific governmental funds, especially the general and special revenue funds.

## ILLUSTRATIVE TRANSACTIONS—ENTERPRISE FUND

According to the NCGA, the purpose of enterprise funds is:

> to account for operations (*a*) that are financed and operated in a manner similar to private business enterprises—where the intent of the governing body is that the costs (expenses, in-

cluding depreciation) of providing goods or services to the general public on a continuing basis be financed or recovered primarily through user charges; or (*b*) where the governing body has decided that determination of revenues earned, expenses incurred, and/or net income is appropriate for capital maintenance, public policy, management control, accountability, or other purposes.[5]

In enterprise funds, the costs of operations are recovered by making a charge that usually not only covers the costs of operations but also provides retained earnings for future use or for distribution to the general fund or other funds of the governmental unit. Many authorities consider this approach inappropriate because it can become a "hidden tax" to the taxpayer.

To govern these entities, many enterprise funds have independent boards or commissions to operate them (e.g., toll roads or bridges). Most, however, are governed and operated directly by the governmental unit (e.g., a sewage disposal fund).

## The Enterprise Fund in the City of Ruthberg

Several years previously, the city of Ruthberg decided to set up an enterprise fund in order to operate a bus transportation system. The federal government provided the resources to buy the buses if the city would provide for several years' operating transfers to assure the profitable operation of the bus system. The city has provided operating grants for several years to assure the profitable operations of the bus system. The bus fund has also received annual operating grants from the federal government.

The trial balance of the bus fund of the city of Ruthberg as of July 1, 19X5 is shown in Exhibit 2-2.

**EXHIBIT 2-2**
**City of Ruthberg—Bus Fund**
**Trial Balance**
**July 1, 19X5**

| Accounts | Dr. | Cr. |
|---|---|---|
| Cash | $ 10,000 | |
| Investments | 75,000 | |
| Interest receivable | 500 | |
| Grants receivable | 50,000 | |
| Inventory | 50,000 | |
| Accounts receivable | 5,000 | |
| Other current assets | 6,000 | |
| Land | 300,000 | |
| Building | 200,000 | |
| Equipment | 1,500,000 | |
| Accumulated depreciation of equipment | | $ 550,000 |
| Accounts payable | | 80,000 |
| Accrued expenses | | 10,000 |
| Due to general fund | | 40,500 |
| Contributed capital | | 1,500,000 |
| Retained earnings | | 16,000 |
| Total | $2,196,500 | $2,196,500 |

The bus fund of the city of Ruthberg depreciates its buses over seven-and-one-half years on a straight-line basis. The buses were purchased with a grant from the federal government, so for illustrative purposes, the depreciation expense each year is written off to the contributed capital account.

The building was constructed with funds that had become available from revenue, and the building was available for use at the beginning of the current year. The depreciation on the building will be written off to income each year.

## Journal Entries for Transactions During the Year

The following journal entries were made for the total of the yearly transactions during the year. The explanation of the transaction will be made prior to the transaction's journal entry.

**E1** Total cash received for bus operations during the year was $500,000.

|  | Dr. | Cr. |
|---|---|---|
| Cash | $500,000 | |
|     Charges for services | | $500,000 |

**E2** Cash received from other operations was $5,000, and from accounts receivable was $5,000—a total of $10,000.

| | | |
|---|---|---|
| Cash | $10,000 | |
|     Other operating revenue | | $5,000 |
|     Accounts receivable | | $5,000 |

**E3** An operating grant from the federal government for $445,000 was made available for operating purposes. This amount was accrued.

| | | |
|---|---|---|
| Grants receivable | $445,000 | |
|     Operating grants | | $445,000 |

**E4** Total cash received from grants during the year was $495,000.

| | | |
|---|---|---|
| Cash | $495,000 | |
|     Grants receivable | | $495,000 |

**E5** Interest receivable for the year was $1,500.

| | | |
|---|---|---|
| Interest receivable | $1,500 | |
|     Interest revenue | | $1,500 |

**E6** This and the prior year's interest receivable was paid.

| | | |
|---|---|---|
| Cash | $2,000 | |
|     Interest receivable | | $2,000 |

**E7** Incurred personnel costs of $598,000, including accrued expenditures of prior year.

| | | |
|---|---|---|
| Personnel services | $588,000 | |
| Accrued expenses | 10,000 | |
|     Accounts payable | | $598,000 |

**E8** Materials and supplies purchased during the year cost $200,000; of this amount, $20,000 was purchased from the printing fund.

| | | |
|---|---|---|
| Inventory | $200,000 | |
|     Accounts payable | | $180,000 |
|     Due to printing fund | | 20,000 |

**E9** Materials and supplies used during the year cost $190,000.

| | | |
|---|---|---|
| Materials and supplies expense | $190,000 | |
|     Inventory | | $190,000 |

**E10** Other current assets from the preceding year were received in cash.

| | | |
|---|---|---|
| Cash | $6,000 | |
|     Other current assets | | $6,000 |

**E11** Other services and charges incurred during the year amounted to $140,000; the amount due to the general fund was also paid.

| | | |
|---|---|---|
| Other services and charges | $140,000 | |
| Due to general fund | 40,500 | |
|     Accounts payable | | $140,000 |
|     Cash | | 40,500 |

**E12** Accounts payable and amounts owed to the printing fund that were paid during the year amounted to $953,000.

| | | |
|---|---|---|
| Due to printing fund | $ 20,000 | |
| Accounts payable | 933,000 | |
|     Cash | | $953,000 |

## Illustrative "T" Accounts

The preceding entries are posted to "T" accounts to illustrate balances in the accounts. Exhibit 2-3 illustrates these "T" accounts with the balances in the accounts after the yearly transactions have been posted. The balances are then summarized in a trial balance (see Exhibit 2-4) to prove the equality of the debits and credits.

**EXHIBIT 2-3**
**Illustrative "T" Accounts**
**City of Ruthberg—Bus Fund**
**Fiscal Year 19X6**

| Cash | | | | | Investments | | |
|---|---|---|---|---|---|---|---|
| B | 10,000 | E11 | 40,500 | | B | 75,000 | |
| E1 | 500,000 | E12 | 953,000 | | | | |
| E2 | 10,000 | | | | | | |
| E4 | 495,000 | | | | | | |
| E6 | 2,000 | | | | | | |
| E10 | 6,000 | | | | | | |
| | 1,023,000 | | 993,500 | | | | |
| | | B | 29,500 | | | | |
| | 1,023,000 | | 1,023,000 | | | | |
| B | 29,500 | | | | | | |

| Interest receivable | | | | | Inventory | | |
|---|---|---|---|---|---|---|---|
| B | 500 | E6 | 2,000 | | B | 50,000 | E9 | 190,000 |
| E5 | 1,500 | | | | E8 | 200,000 | | |
| | 2,000 | | 2,000 | | | 250,000 | | 190,000 |
| | | | | | | | B | 60,000 |
| | | | | | | 250,000 | | 250,000 |
| | | | | | B | 60,000 | | |

| Grants receivable | | | | | Other current assets | | |
|---|---|---|---|---|---|---|---|
| B | 50,000 | E6 | 495,000 | | B | 6,000 | E10 | 6,000 |
| E3 | 445,000 | | | | | | | |
| | 495,000 | | 495,000 | | | | | |

| Accounts receivable | | | | | Land | | |
|---|---|---|---|---|---|---|---|
| B | 5,000 | E2 | 5,000 | | B | 300,000 | |

| Building | | | | Equipment | | |
|---|---|---|---|---|---|---|
| B | 200,000 | | | B | 1,500,000 | |

| Accumulated dep. of equipment | | | | Accounts payable | | | |
|---|---|---|---|---|---|---|---|
| | | B | 550,000 | E11 | 933,000 | B | 80,000 |
| | | | | | | E7 | 598,000 |
| | | | | | | E8 | 180,000 |
| Due to printing fund | | | | | | E11 | 140,000 |
| E12 | 20,000 | E8 | 20,000 | | 933,000 | | 998,000 |
| | | | | | 65,000 | | |
| | | | | | 998,000 | | 998,000 |
| | | | | | | B | 65,000 |

**EXHIBIT 2-3**
*(continued)*

| Accrued expenses payable | | | | Due to general fund | | | |
|---|---|---|---|---|---|---|---|
| E7 | 10,000 | B | 10,000 | E11 | 40,500 | B | 40,500 |

| Contributed capital | | | Retained earnings | | |
|---|---|---|---|---|---|
| | B | 1,500,000 | | B | 16,000 |

| Charges for services | | | Other operating revenue | | |
|---|---|---|---|---|---|
| | E1 | 500,000 | | E2 | 5,000 |

| Interest revenue | | | Personnel services | | |
|---|---|---|---|---|---|
| | E5 | 1,500 | E7 | 588,000 | |

| Materials and supplies expense | | | Other services and charges | | |
|---|---|---|---|---|---|
| E9 | 190,000 | | E11 | 140,000 | |

| Operating grants | | |
|---|---|---|
| | E3 | 445,000 |

**EXHIBIT 2-4**
**City of Ruthberg—Bus Fund**
**Preadjustment Trial Balance**
**Fiscal Year 19X6**

| Accounts | Dr. | Cr. |
|---|---|---|
| Cash | $ 29,500 | |
| Investments | 75,000 | |
| Inventory | 60,000 | |
| Land | 300,000 | |
| Building | 200,000 | |
| Equipment | 1,500,000 | |
| Accumulated depreciation of equipment | | $ 550,000 |
| Accounts payable | | 65,000 |
| Contributed capital | | 1,500,000 |
| Retained earnings | | 16,000 |
| Charges for services | | 500,000 |
| Other operating revenue | | 5,000 |
| Operating grants | | 445,000 |
| Interest revenue | | 1,500 |
| Personnel services | 588,000 | |
| Material and supplies expense | 190,000 | |
| Other services and charges | 140,000 | |
| Total | $3,082,500 | $3,082,500 |

## Adjusting Journal Entries

At the end of the year, the following adjustments needed to be made to the accounts before final preparation of the financial statements:

1. A grant of $25,000, for which the revenue recognition criteria had been met, was receivable from the federal government.
2. Interest receivable at year end was $500.
3. Accrued personnel costs were $12,000.
4. Other revenue from accounts receivable was $5,000.
5. Other services and charges were $35,000.
6. Depreciation on the equipment was based on a life of seven and one-half years. Depreciation on the building was based on a twenty-year life.

|     |                                      | Dr.      | Cr.      |
| --- | ------------------------------------ | -------- | -------- |
| EA1 | Grants receivable                    | $ 25,000 |          |
|     | Operating grants                     |          | $ 25,000 |
| EA2 | Interest receivable                  | 500      |          |
|     | Interest revenue                     |          | 500      |
| EA3 | Personnel services                   | 12,000   |          |
|     | Accrued expenses payable             |          | 12,000   |
| EA4 | Accounts receivable                  | 5,000    |          |
|     | Other operating revenue              |          | 5,000    |
| EA5 | Other services and charges           | 35,000   |          |
|     | Accounts payable                     |          | 35,000   |
| EA6 | Depreciation of building             | 10,000   |          |
|     | Depreciation of equipment            | 200,000  |          |
|     | Accumulated depreciation of building |          | 10,000   |
|     | Accumulated depreciation of equipment |         | 200,000  |

## Closing Entries

Instead of closing the depreciation on the equipment to the retained earnings account, it will be closed to the contributed capital account (see Exhibit 2-1). The following journal entries are made to close the accounts:

|     |                            | Dr.      | Cr.      |
| --- | -------------------------- | -------- | -------- |
| EC1 | Contributed capital        | $200,000 |          |
|     | Depreciation of equipment  |          | $200,000 |
| EC2 | Charges for services       | $500,000 |          |
|     | Other operating revenue    | 10,000   |          |
|     | Operating grants           | 470,000  |          |
|     | Interest revenue           | 2,000    |          |
|     | Personnel services         |          | $600,000 |
|     | Other services and charges |          | 175,000  |
|     | Material and supplies      |          | 190,000  |
|     | Depreciation of building   |          | 10,000   |
|     | Retained earnings          |          | 7,000    |

## After Closing "T" Accounts and Trial Balances

After the accounts are adjusted and closed for the fiscal period, the accounts would appear as shown in Exhibit 2-5. Often a trial balance is prepared immediately after the adjusting entries are made in order to obtain the balances in the accounts that are part of the financial statements (see Exhibit 2-6). Then a postclosing trial balance is prepared in order to obtain the account balances for the start of the next period.

**EXHIBIT 2-5**
**Illustrative "T" Accounts**
**City of Ruthberg—Bus Fund**
**After Adjusting and Closing Entries**
**Fiscal Year 19X6**

| Cash | | | | | Investments | | |
|---|---|---|---|---|---|---|---|
| B | 10,000 | E11 | 40,500 | B | 75,000 | | |
| E1 | 500,000 | E12 | 953,000 | | | | |
| E2 | 10,000 | | | | | | |
| E4 | 495,000 | | | | | | |
| E6 | 2,000 | | | | | | |
| E10 | 6,000 | | | | | | |
| | 1,023,000 | | 993,500 | | | | |
| | | B | 29,500 | | | | |
| | 1,023,000 | | 1,023,000 | | | | |
| B | 29,500 | | | | | | |

| Interest receivable | | | | | Inventory | | |
|---|---|---|---|---|---|---|---|
| B | 500 | E6 | 2,000 | B | 50,000 | E9 | 190,000 |
| E5 | 1,500 | | | E8 | 200,000 | | |
| | 2,000 | | 2,000 | | 250,000 | | 190,000 |
| EA2 | 500 | | | | | B | 60,000 |
| | | | | | 250,000 | | 250,000 |
| | | | | B | 60,000 | | |

| Grants receivable | | | | | Other current assets | | |
|---|---|---|---|---|---|---|---|
| B | 50,000 | E4 | 495,000 | B | 6,000 | E10 | 6,000 |
| E3 | 445,000 | | | | | | |
| | 495,000 | | 495,000 | | | | |
| EA1 | 25,000 | | | | | | |

| Accounts receivable | | | | | Land | | |
|---|---|---|---|---|---|---|---|
| B | 5,000 | E2 | 5,000 | B | 300,000 | | |
| EA4 | 5,000 | | | | | | |

| Building | | | | | Equipment | | |
|---|---|---|---|---|---|---|---|
| B | 200,000 | | | B | 1,500,000 | | |

**EXHIBIT 2-5**
*(continued)*

| Accumulated dep. of building | | | | Accumulated dep. of equipment | | | |
|---|---|---|---|---|---|---|---|
| | | EA6 | 10,000 | | | B | 550,000 |
| | | | | | | EA6 | 200,000 |
| | | | | | | B | 750,000 |

| Accounts payable | | | | Accrued expenses payable | | | |
|---|---|---|---|---|---|---|---|
| E12 | 933,000 | B | 80,000 | E7 | 10,000 | B | 10,000 |
| | | E7 | 598,000 | | | EA3 | 12,000 |
| | | E8 | 180,000 | | | | |
| | | E11 | 140,000 | | | | |
| | 933,000 | | 998,000 | | | | |
| B | 65,000 | | | | | | |
| | 998,000 | | 998,000 | | | | |
| | | B | 65,000 | | | | |
| | | EA5 | 35,000 | | | | |
| | | B | 100,000 | | | | |

| Due to general fund | | | | Contributed capital | | | |
|---|---|---|---|---|---|---|---|
| E11 | 40,500 | B | 40,500 | EC1 | 200,000 | B | 1,500,000 |
| | | | | B | 1,300,000 | | |
| | | | | | 1,500,000 | | 1,500,000 |
| | | | | | | B | 1,300,000 |

| Retained earnings | | | | Charges for services | | | |
|---|---|---|---|---|---|---|---|
| | | B | 16,000 | EC2 | 500,000 | E1 | 500,000 |
| | | EC2 | 7,000 | | | | |
| | | B | 23,000 | | | | |

| Other operating revenues | | | | Operating grants | | | |
|---|---|---|---|---|---|---|---|
| EC2 | 10,000 | E2 | 5,000 | EC2 | 470,000 | E3 | 445,000 |
| | | EA4 | 5,000 | | | EA1 | 25,000 |
| | 10,000 | | 10,000 | | 470,000 | | 470,000 |

| Interest revenue | | | | Personnel services | | | |
|---|---|---|---|---|---|---|---|
| EC2 | 2,000 | E5 | 1,500 | E7 | 588,000 | EC2 | 600,000 |
| | | EA2 | 500 | EA3 | 12,000 | | |
| | 2,000 | | 2,000 | | 600,000 | | 600,000 |

| Materials and supplies expense | | | | Other services and charges | | | |
|---|---|---|---|---|---|---|---|
| E9 | 190,000 | EC2 | 190,000 | E11 | 140,000 | EC2 | 175,000 |
| | | | | EA5 | 35,000 | | |
| | | | | | 175,000 | | 175,000 |

| Depreciation of building | | | | Depreciation of equipment | | | |
|---|---|---|---|---|---|---|---|
| EA6 | 10,000 | EC2 | 10,000 | EA6 | 200,000 | EC1 | 200,000 |

## EXHIBIT 2-6
## City of Ruthberg—Bus Fund
## Preclosing Trial Balance
## June 30, 19X6

| Accounts | Dr. | Cr. |
|---|---:|---:|
| Cash | $ 29,500 | |
| Investments | 75,000 | |
| Interest receivable | 500 | |
| Grants receivable | 25,000 | |
| Accounts receivable | 5,000 | |
| Inventory | 60,000 | |
| Land | 300,000 | |
| Building | 200,000 | |
| Accumulated depreciation of building | | $ 10,000 |
| Equipment | 1,500,000 | |
| Accumulated depreciation of equipment | | 750,000 |
| Accounts payable | | 100,000 |
| Accrued expenses payable | | 12,000 |
| Contributed capital | | 1,500,000 |
| Retained earnings | | 16,000 |
| Charges for services | | 500,000 |
| Other operating revenue | | 10,000 |
| Operating grants | | 470,000 |
| Interest revenue | | 2,000 |
| Personnel services | 600,000 | |
| Material and supplies expense | 190,000 | |
| Other services and charges | 175,000 | |
| Depreciation of building | 10,000 | |
| Depreciation of equipment | 200,000 | |
| Total | $3,370,000 | $3,370,000 |

The postclosing trial balance from which the balance sheet can be prepared is shown in Exhibit 2-7. The balances shown in the postclosing trial balance are the accounts and amounts that are the beginning balances for the next year.

## Worksheet of Transactions

The "T" account method is a visual method of bringing together all of the accounting transactions for a particular accounting period for a particular accounting entity. This method, however, requires separate trial balance statements for the beginning of the year, after the yearly transactions, after adjustments, and after the closing entries.

A method often used by practicing accountants to visualize all of the transactions and balances for statements on a single sheet is that of a worksheet. Exhibit 2-8 is an illustration of such a worksheet. Although some problems will require the use of "T" accounts, the worksheet will be the primary method used for illustrative purposes throughout the balance of the book.

## EXHIBIT 2-7
### City of Ruthberg—Bus Fund
### Postclosing Trial Balance
### June 30, 19X6

| Accounts | Dr. | Cr. |
|---|---:|---:|
| Cash | $ 29,500 | |
| Investments | 75,000 | |
| Inventory | 60,000 | |
| Interest receivable | 500 | |
| Grants receivable | 25,000 | |
| Accounts receivable | 5,000 | |
| Land | 300,000 | |
| Building | 200,000 | |
| Accumulated depreciation of building | | $ 10,000 |
| Equipment | 1,500,000 | |
| Accumulated depreciation of equipment | | 750,000 |
| Accounts payable | | 100,000 |
| Accrued expenses payable | | 12,000 |
| Contributed capital | | 1,300,000 |
| Retained earnings | | 23,000 |
| Total | $2,195,000 | $2,195,000 |

## Financial Statements

Proprietary funds financial statements include the following:

1  A balance sheet for each enterprise fund and each internal service fund.
2  A statement of revenues, expenses, and changes in retained earnings for each enterprise fund and each internal service fund.
3  A statement of changes in financial position for each proprietary fund.

**Combined and Combining Statements**  Each individual fund must prepare the preceding statements. In addition, when the governmental unit has more than one accounting entity for each particular type of fund (e.g., more than one enterprise fund or more than one internal service fund), GAAP requires that the individual statements must be aggregated into a single statement, which is called a *combining statement*. Thus balance sheets; statements of revenue, expenses, and changes in fund balance; and statements of changes in financial position for each individual fund for those types for which more than one of each type exists, must be combined into a single total for all statements for the funds of that particular type. Combined statements are illustrated in Chapter 13.

In addition, all balance sheets of the governmental unit, in accordance with GAAP requirements, will be aggregated into one balance sheet for the governmental unit as a whole. This type of statement is called a *combined balance sheet*. It will be fully illustrated in Chapter 13. In addition to a combined statement for the balance sheets of the governmental unit, a combined statement is made of all proprietary fund types for the statement of revenues, expenses, and changes in fund equity and the statements of

## EXHIBIT 2-8
### City of Ruthberg—Bus Fund
### Worksheet for Year 19X6

| Accounts | Beginning trial balance Dr. | Cr. | No. | Transactions Dr. | No. | Cr. |
|---|---|---|---|---|---|---|
| Cash | $ 10,000 | | E1 | $ 500,000 | E11 | $ 40,500 |
| | | | E2 | 10,000 | E12 | 953,000 |
| | | | E4 | 495,000 | | |
| | | | E6 | 2,000 | | |
| | | | E10 | 6,000 | | |
| Investments | 75,000 | | | | | |
| Interest receivable | 500 | | E5 | 1,500 | E6 | 2,000 |
| Grants receivable | 50,000 | | E3 | 445,000 | E4 | 495,000 |
| Inventory | 50,000 | | E8 | 200,000 | E9 | 190,000 |
| Accounts receivable | 5,000 | | | | E2 | 5,000 |
| Other current assets | 6,000 | | | | E10 | 6,000 |
| Land | 300,000 | | | | | |
| Equipment | 1,500,000 | | | | | |
| Accumulated depreciation of equipment | | $ 550,000 | | | | |
| Building | 200,000 | | | | | |
| Accumulated depreciation of building | | | | | | |
| Contributed capital | | 1,500,000 | | | | |
| Retained earnings | | 16,000 | | | | |
| Accounts payable | | 80,000 | E12 | 933,000 | E7 | 598,000 |
| | | | | | E8 | 180,000 |
| | | | | | E11 | 140,000 |
| Due to printing fund | | | E12 | 20,000 | E8 | 20,000 |
| Accrued expenses payable | | 10,000 | E7 | 10,000 | | |
| Due to general fund | | 40,500 | E11 | 40,500 | | |
| Charges for services | | | | | E1 | 500,000 |
| Other operating revenue | | | | | E2 | 5,000 |
| Personnel services | | | E7 | 588,000 | | |
| Other services and charges | | | E11 | 140,000 | | |
| Materials and supplies expense | | | E9 | 190,000 | | |
| Depreciation: equipment | | | | | | |
| building | | | | | | |
| Operating grants | | | | | E3 | 445,000 |
| Interest revenue | | | | | E5 | 1,500 |
| Total | $2,196,500 | $2,196,500 | | $3,581,000 | | $3,581,000 |
| Retained earnings | | | | | | |

changes in financial position. If the governmental unit has more than one proprietary fund, then a combining statement is used, along with statements from fiduciary funds of the proprietary fund types, for the combined statement total. These statements also are illustrated in Chapter 13.

**Illustrative Financial Statements**

Exhibit 2-9 shows the balance sheet for the bus fund; Exhibit 2-10, the statement of revenues, expenses, and changes in retained earnings; and Exhibit 2-11, the statement of changes in financial position.

## EXHIBIT 2-8
*(continued)*

| Ending trial balance | | Adjustments | | | Operating statement | | Balance sheet | |
|---|---|---|---|---|---|---|---|---|
| Dr. | Cr. | No. | Dr. | Cr. | Dr. | Cr. | Dr. | Cr. |
| $ 29,500 | | | | | | | $ 29,500 | |
| 75,000 | | | | | | | 75,000 | |
| | | EA2 | 500 | | | | 500 | |
| | | EA1 | 25,000 | | | | 25,000 | |
| 60,000 | | | | | | | 60,000 | |
| | | EA4 | 5,000 | | | | 5,000 | |
| 300,000 | | | | | | | 300,000 | |
| 1,500,000 | | | | | | | 1,500,000 | |
| | $ 550,000 | EA6 | | 200,000 | | | | $ 750,000 |
| 200,000 | | | | | | | 200,000 | |
| | | EA6 | | 10,000 | | | | 10,000 |
| | 1,500,000 | | | | $ 200,000 | | | 1,300,000 |
| | 16,000 | | | | | | | 16,000 |
| | 65,000 | | | | | | | 100,000 |
| | | EA5 | | 35,000 | | | | |
| | | EA3 | | 12,000 | | | | 12,000 |
| | 500,000 | | | | | $ 500,000 | | |
| | 5,000 | EA4 | | 5,000 | | 10,000 | | |
| 588,000 | | EA3 | 12,000 | | 600,000 | | | |
| 140,000 | | EA5 | 35,000 | | 175,000 | | | |
| 190,000 | | | | | 190,000 | | | |
| | | EA6 | 200,000 | | 200,000 | | | |
| | | EA6 | 10,000 | | 10,000 | | | |
| | 445,000 | EA1 | | 25,000 | | | 470,000 | |
| | 1,500 | EA2 | | 500 | | | 2,000 | |
| $3,082,500 | $3,082,500 | | $287,500 | $287,500 | $1,175,000 | $1,182,000 | 2,195,000 | $2,188,000 |
| | | | | | 7,000 | | | 7,000 |
| | | | | | $1,182,000 | $1,182,000 | $2,195,000 | $2,195,000 |

## SUMMARY

Proprietary funds are classified into two types: enterprise and internal service. Enterprise funds provide goods or services for a fee, with the greater proportion of the revenue coming from fees from customers outside of the governmental unit. Internal service funds provide services or goods for a fee, also, but the primary customers are from other funds within the governmental unit.

Enterprise funds usually charge a fee sufficient not only to recover costs for the

**EXHIBIT 2-9**
**City of Ruthberg—Bus Fund**
**Balance Sheet**
**June 30, 19X6**

### Assets

| | | | |
|---|---|---|---|
| Current assets: | | | |
| Cash | | $ 29,500 | |
| Investments | | 75,000 | |
| Interest receivable | | 500 | |
| Grants receivable | | 25,000 | |
| Inventory | | 60,000 | |
| Other current assets | | 5,000 | |
| Total current assets | | | $ 195,000 |
| Fixed assets: | | | |
| Land | | 300,000 | |
| Building | $ 200,000 | | |
| Less accumulated depreciation | 10,000 | 190,000 | |
| Equipment | 1,500,000 | | |
| Less accumulated depreciation | 750,000 | 750,000 | |
| Total fixed assets | | | 1,240,000 |
| Total assets | | | $1,435,000 |

### Liabilities and Fund Equity

| | | |
|---|---|---|
| Current liabilities: | | |
| Accounts payable | $ 100,000 | |
| Accrued expenses payable | 12,000 | |
| Total current liabilities | | $ 112,000 |
| Fund equity: | | |
| Contributed capital | 1,300,000 | |
| Retained earnings | 23,000 | |
| Total fund equity | | 1,323,000 |
| Total liabilities and fund equity | | $1,435,000 |

goods or services but also to create income. Internal service funds, on the other hand, usually try to recover only costs from the charges for services.

Proprietary funds generally follow the principles of accounting related to businesses: They use accrual accounting; they record long-term assets and liabilities in the funds and depreciate the depreciable fixed assets in order to have a period expense for the assets; they prepare the same type of statements required of business-type organizations; and they usually do not have fixed-type budgets normally found in certain types of governmental funds.

Some of the principles of accounting vary from those of a normal business, however, because of the nature of government. Capital equity can come from transfers (residual equity transfers) from other funds in government. Grants for capital resources and for operations can come from other levels of government. However, the proprietary funds of government seldom sell stock to outsiders to obtain capital equity.

Debt financing, however, can come from all of the sources normally available to the business community. Bonds, mortgages, long-term leases, long-term notes, and other

**EXHIBIT 2-10**
**City of Ruthberg—Bus Fund**
**Statement of Revenues, Expenses, and Changes in Retained Earnings**
**Year Ended June 30, 19X6**

| | | | |
|---|---|---:|---:|
| Operating revenues | | | |
|   Charges for services | | $500,000 | |
|   Other operating revenue | | 10,000 | |
|     Total operating revenue | | | $ 510,000 |
| Operating expenses | | | |
|   Personnel services | | $600,000 | |
|   Other services and charges | | 175,000 | |
|   Materials and supplies expense | | 190,000 | |
|   Depreciation: | | | |
|     Building | $ 10,000 | | |
|     Equipment | 200,000 | 210,000 | |
|     Total operating expenses | | | 1,175,000 |
| Operating loss | | | (665,000) |
| Nonoperating revenues | | | |
|   Operating grants | | 470,000 | |
|   Interest revenues | | 2,000 | |
|     Total nonoperating revenues | | | 472,000 |
| Net loss | | | (193,000) |
|   Depreciation charged to contributed capital | | | 200,000 |
| Increase in retained earnings | | | 7,000 |
|   Retained earnings, July 1, 19X5 | | | 16,000 |
| Retained earnings, June 30, 19X6 | | | $ 23,000 |

sources of long-term debt are available to the proprietary funds of government as well as to business-type organizations.

Proprietary funds of government operate similarly to business organizations; therefore, the accounting is very similar. For this reason, this type of fund accounting for governmental units has been provided in Chapter 2. It will be further explored in Chapter 3 before going into the not-for-profit or nonbusiness accounting provided in Chapters 4 through 13.

## QUESTIONS

1. What type of funds in government are similar to business-type entities?
2. Describe the types of services that can be performed by an enterprise fund. To whom are these services basically provided?
3. Explain what is meant by a nonexpendable fund. Which type of funds as a class is a nonexpendable fund of government?
4. How can capital equity be generated in a proprietary fund? List and describe each of the sources of capital equity.
5. A major source of financing for a proprietary fund can come from long-term debt. List and describe the major sources of debt financing for a proprietary fund.
6. What is the basis of accounting used in proprietary funds?

## EXHIBIT 2-11
### City of Ruthberg—Bus Fund
### Statement of Changes in Financial Position
### Year Ended June 30, 19X6

| | |
|---|---:|
| Sources of financial resources | |
| Net increase in retained earnings | $ 7,000 |
| Depreciation on building not requiring financial resources | 10,000 |
| Total financial resources from operations | $17,000 |
| Uses of financial resources | |
| Increase in working capital | $17,000 |

**Net Increase in Working Capital for Year 19X6**

| | July 1 | June 30 | Increase (decrease) |
|---|---:|---:|---:|
| Current assets | | | |
| Cash | $ 10,000 | $ 29,500 | $ 19,500 |
| Investments | 75,000 | 75,000 | |
| Interest receivable | 500 | 500 | |
| Grants receivable | 50,000 | 25,000 | (25,000) |
| Inventory | 50,000 | 60,000 | 10,000 |
| Accounts receivable | 5,000 | 5,000 | |
| Other current assets | 6,000 | | (6,000) |
| Total current assets | $196,500 | $195,000 | $ (1,500) |
| Current liabilities | | | |
| Accounts payable | $ 80,000 | $100,000 | $(20,000) |
| Accrued expenses payable | 10,000 | 12,000 | (2,000) |
| Due to general fund | 40,500 | | 40,500 |
| Total current liabilities | 130,000 | 112,000 | 18,500 |
| Net increase (decrease) | 66,000 | 83,000 | 17,000 |

7 One of the problems of accounting for government is interfund transaction accounting. Why would this be a problem in accounting for government?
8 Is an operating grant an operating or nonoperating revenue?
9 In proprietary funds, to which account are the revenue and expense accounts closed at the end of each accounting period?
10 Which financial statements are prepared for proprietary funds?
11 Should the normal budgetary accounting be used in proprietary funds? If budgetary accounting is used, what is the recommended type?
12 The statement is often made that accounting for proprietary funds of government is similar to accounting for business-type entities. Why?

## PROBLEMS

2-1 Select the best answer for each of the following.
  1 In a proprietary fund, which of the following accounts are debited to close out the transactions for income and expense accounts for the period?
   a The expense accounts.
   b The revenue accounts.

**c** The asset accounts.
   **d** The liability accounts.
 **2** The accounts in the statement of revenues, expenses, and changes in retained earnings are classified in a proprietary fund generally (by)
   **a** Object of expenditures.
   **b** Activity.
   **c** Program.
   **d** Similar to the type of business the proprietary fund resembles.
 **3** In business, the organization usually consists of
   **a** Only a single accounting entity.
   **b** Multiple accounting entities.
   **c** Many related accounting entities.
   **d** None of the above.
 **4** The entities used in government to provide business-type services are:
   **a** A general fund and an internal service fund.
   **b** A general fund and an enterprise fund.
   **c** An internal service fund and an enterprise fund.
   **d** A proprietary fund and a fixed asset account group.
 **5** Accounting and financial reporting for proprietary funds of government, in relation to business-type organizations,
   **a** Are completely different.
   **b** Are basically similar.
   **c** Follow only generally accepted accounting principles for governmental funds.
   **d** None of the above.
 **6** The account classification of an enterprise fund of government on its financial statements:
   **a** Is basically the same as those for similar entities in business.
   **b** Is unrelated to business-type financial statements.
   **c** Follows the basic types of statements prepared for governmental funds.
   **d** None of the above.
**2-2** Select the best answer for each of the following.
 **1** Accounting and financial reporting for enterprise funds of government operate their activities:
   **a** Comparable to private businesses that provide similar services.
   **b** Quite differently than private businesses that provide similar services.
   **c** Using principles of accounting and reporting applicable to governmental funds.
   **d** Using principles of accounting and reporting developed for proprietary funds by the Governmental Financial Fund Accounting Board.
 **2** An entity of government that operates a for-profit activity (e.g., a utility) accounts for those operations in:
   **a** A capital projects fund.
   **b** The general fund.
   **c** A fixed asset account group.
   **d** An enterprise fund.
 **3** Fixed assets in a proprietary fund are:
   **a** Accounted for in a fixed assets account group.
   **b** Accounted for in a specific proprietary fund.
   **c** Partly accounted for in the proprietary fund and partly accounted for in the fixed assets account group.
   **d** Accounted for in the general fund.

**4** Capital grants in which resources are externally restricted for capital acquisition are shown as:
  **a** Reservations of fund balance.
  **b** Retained earnings.
  **c** Revenue.
  **d** Contributed capital.
**5** Proprietary funds account for long-term debt in the:
  **a** Long-term debt account group.
  **b** The general fund.
  **c** Specific proprietary fund.
  **d** Fixed assets account group.
**6** Interentity transactions in an enterprise fund are usually found only between:
  **a** Enterprise funds and the general fund.
  **b** Enterprise funds and the fixed assets account group.
  **c** Enterprise funds and the long-term debt account group.
  **d** Enterprise funds and private subscribers.

**2-3** The following is a partial trial balance of the Homer Township water utility fund for the year ended June 30, 19X5. Prepare the necessary closing entries based on the information provided. Accumulated depreciation at the beginning of the year was $20,000 and the supplies inventory (physical count) indicated a balance of $16,000 at year end.

|  | Dr. | Cr. |
| --- | --- | --- |
| Cash | $10,000 | |
| Accounts receivable | 40,000 | |
| Charges for services | | $150,000 |
| Accumulated depreciation | | 25,000 |
| Administrative salaries | 40,000 | |
| Supplies inventory | 20,000 | |
| Operating salaries | 60,000 | |
| Power costs | 15,000 | |

**2-4** For each of the following situations, analyze the information and prepare the necessary adjusting entry:

  **1** The enterprise fund maintains an inventory of supplies and recognizes usage by taking an inventory at year end. The balance in the inventory at the beginning of the year was $4,800. Purchases during the year amounted to $24,000, and the year end balance was $5,000.
  **2** Halfway through the year a two-year theft insurance policy was purchased for $4,000.
  **3** At the end of the year, salary expense of $450 had been earned but not paid.
  **4** At the beginning of the year, equipment costing $10,000 with a twenty-year life was purchased. Depreciation, on a straight-line basis, has not been recorded.

**2-5** Cable TV fund, an enterprise fund in the city of Douglas, was instituted by the city several years ago in order to provide adequate television service to local residents. Television reception had been very poor in the remote locality, and the city's services improved TV reception to a considerable degree.

The city had contributed $50,000 to start the fund, and for the first few years the cable TV fund needed operating transfers from the general fund to keep it operating on a profitable basis. The cable TV fund currently seems to be operating profitably without too much help from the city.

The financial statements for the preceding year, 19X6, reflect the financial condition and financial operations for the fund for that year (see Exhibits 2-12, 2-13 and 2-14).

**EXHIBIT 2-12**
**City of Douglas**
**Cable TV Fund**
**Balance Sheet**
**June 30, 19X6**

**Assets**

| | | | |
|---|---|---|---|
| Current assets: | | | |
| Cash | | $ 1,045 | |
| Accounts receivable | | 9,100 | |
| Installations and repair parts inventory | | 1,465 | |
| Prepaid insurance | | 3,100 | |
| Total current assets | | | $14,710 |
| Fixed assets: | | | |
| Land | | 4,000 | |
| Building | $48,000 | | |
| Less accumulated depreciation | 14,920 | 33,080 | |
| Equipment | 12,000 | | |
| Less accumulated depreciation | 4,000 | 8,000 | |
| Total fixed assets | | | 45,080 |
| Total assets | | | $59,790 |

**Liabilities and Fund Equity**

| | | |
|---|---|---|
| Current liabilities: | | |
| Accounts payable | $ 3,795 | |
| Inspection income—unearned | 567 | |
| Total current liabilities | | $ 4,362 |
| Fund equity: | | |
| Contributed capital | 50,000 | |
| Retained earnings | 5,428 | |
| Total fund equity | | $55,428 |
| Total liabilities and fund equity | | $59,790 |

**EXHIBIT 2-13**
**City of Douglas**
**Cable TV Fund**
**Statement of Revenues, Expenses,**
**and Changes in Retained Earnings**
**For Fiscal Year Ended June 30, 19X6**

| | | |
|---|---|---|
| Operating revenues | | |
| Charges for services | $143,000 | |
| Total operating revenue | | $143,000 |
| Operating expenses | | |
| Utility expense | 9,000 | |
| Truck expense | 7,000 | |
| Office expense | 6,000 | |
| Advertising | 5,000 | |
| Salaries and wages | 100,000 | |
| Depreciation | 5,000 | |
| Installation expense | 8,000 | |
| Insurance | 2,000 | |
| Total operating expenses | | $142,000 |
| Net operating income | | 1,000 |
| Prior year's retained earnings | | 4,428 |
| Retained earnings, June 30, 19X6 | | $ 5,428 |

**EXHIBIT 2-14**
**City of Douglas**
**Cable TV Fund**
**Statement of Changes in Financial Position**
**For Fiscal Year Ended June 30, 19X6**

| | | |
|---|---|---|
| Financial resources provided | | |
|   Net income | $1,000 | |
|   Depreciation | 5,000 | |
| Working capital provided from operations | | $6,000 |
| Financial resources applied | | |
|   Addition to equipment | | 2,400 |
| Increase in working capital | | $3,600 |

**Elements of Increase in Working Capital**

| | Current year | Prior year | Increase (decrease) |
|---|---|---|---|
| Current assets: | | | |
|   Cash | $ 1,045 | $ 4,498 | ($3,453) |
|   Accounts receivable | 9,100 | 2,000 | 7,100 |
|   Inventory | 1,465 | 1,550 | ( 85) |
|   Prepaid insurance | 3,100 | 3,200 | ( 100) |
|     Total current assets | $14,710 | $11,645 | $3,462 |
| Current liabilities: | | | |
|   Accounts payable | $ 3,795 | $ 4,500 | $ 705 |
|   Unearned income | 567 | — | ( 567) |
|     Total current liabilities | 4,362 | 4,500 | 138 |
| Increase in working capital | $10,348 | $ 7,145 | $3,600 |

The following summarized transactions took place during the fiscal year ended June 30, 19X7:

1. A capital grant of $10,000 in cash was paid by the state.
2. Purchased office furniture for $10,000 with the full amount to be paid in sixty days.
3. Billed customers for services rendered, $148,000.
4. Collected customers' accounts, $150,000.
5. Incurred the following liabilities:
   a. Miscellaneous office expenses, $6,200.
   b. Utility expenses, $8,900.
   c. Truck expenses, $7,200.
   d. Advertising, $5,200.
   e. Installation expenses, $8,500.
6. Paid salaries, wages, and other personnel costs, $102,000.
7. Paid accounts payable, $47,795.
8. The following information is needed for the end of the year adjustments:
   a. Insurance considered used during the year was $2,400.
   b. Depreciation is computed as follows: building—twenty-year life estimated; equipment—four-year life, estimated; and office furniture—ten-year life, estimated.
9. Accrued salaries at the end of the year were $500.
10. Inspection income unearned was $667.

**11** The inventory was considered to be worth $1,665. Installation and repair parts inventory is considered as installation expense when used.

**Required**:
1 Prepare journal entries for the transactions for the current year. Post to a worksheet comparable to that illustrated in the chapter.
2 Prepare adjusting and closing entries and post to the worksheet.
3 Prepare the financial statements needed for the year.

**2-6** The municipal swimming pool fund accounts for the city of Radford include the following balances at year end after adjustments.

|  | Dr. | Cr. |
|---|---|---|
| Cash | $ 80,000 |  |
| Accounts receivable | 10,000 |  |
| Prepaid expenses | 5,000 |  |
| Equipment | 160,000 |  |
| Accumulated depreciation—equipment |  | $ 60,000 |
| Accounts payable |  | 50,000 |
| Salaries payable |  | 20,000 |
| Contributed capital |  | 100,000 |
| Retained earnings |  | 5,000 |
| Charges for services |  | 125,000 |
| Salaries and wages | 60,000 |  |
| Supplies | 20,000 |  |
| Depreciation | 20,000 |  |
| Miscellaneous expenses | 5,000 |  |
|  | $360,000 | $360,000 |

**Required**:
1 Prepare a balance sheet and a statement of revenue, expenses, and changes in retained earnings.
2 Would any other statements need to be prepared? Can you prepare them?

**2-7** The city of Smithfield has several enterprise and internal service funds. Each of the following situations occurred during the year in one of the enterprise funds—the bus fund.

 1 The bus fund received a grant of $400,000 from the state to purchase new buses that are expected to last eight years.
 2 The grant was paid in full.
 3 The adjusting entry for the depreciation on the buses was made.
 4 The entries pertaining to the closing of the depreciation account on the buses was made.

**Required**:
Prepare journal entries for each of the preceding transactions. The transactions all pertain to a capital grant used to purchase buses.

# NOTES

**1** National Council on Governmental Accounting, *Statement 2. Grant Entitlement and Shared Revenue Accounting and Reporting by State and Local Governments* (Chicago: Municipal Finance Officers Association of the United States and Canada, 1979), p. 2.

2 Ibid., p. 3.
3 Ibid., p. 3.
4 Ibid., pp. 2–3.
5 National Council on Governmental Accounting, *Statement 1. Governmental Accounting and Financial Reporting Principles* (Chicago: Municipal Finance Officers Association of the United States and Canada, 1979), p. 7.

# CHAPTER 3

# PROPRIETARY FUNDS—INTERNAL SERVICE FUNDS

Internal service funds, often called revolving funds, provide services to other funds of government. This service normally can be within each of these other funds of government. Instead of each fund providing its own computer services, a central internal service fund can provide computer services for all of the funds in the governmental unit. By centralizing the computer service operations, the overall cost to each of the funds and to the governmental unit as a whole usually, but not always, is reduced.

The costs of operating the internal service fund are borne by all of the users through a cost-reimbursement user charge. The charges should recover all of the costs; therefore, the internal service fund should have no profit or no loss.

Obviously no one has such foresight to estimate exactly the total costs of operation so that total costs can be recovered in user charges. Theoretically, if the charges are such that at the end of the earnings period earnings are much more than expected, then the internal service fund should reimburse those other funds that have used the service during the period on a pro rata usage basis. The opposite would also be true. If the initial charges were low and the losses were great, then the internal service fund should recover the losses from the user funds. Practically, however, the user charge can be determined close enough that the profit or loss is a relatively insignificant amount. The rate, then, if necessary, can be adjusted and applied to charges for services during the following year, since most funds would use the services of the internal service fund year after year.

## Cost Accounting in Internal Service Funds

Cost accounting is very important in the internal service funds of government. Cost accounting for proprietary funds as well as governmental funds is fully discussed in Chapter 18 and will be discussed only as needed in this chapter.

## Relationship of Internal Service Funds to Enterprise Funds

The discussion in Chapter 2 concerning basis of accounting, capital equity, and interfund transactions applies to internal service funds as well as to enterprise funds. Both are proprietary funds.

## ILLUSTRATIVE TRANSACTIONS—INTERNAL SERVICE FUND

While most of the basic principles of accounting for proprietary funds, both enterprise funds and internal service funds, are similar, there are sufficient differences between them to warrant illustration. The illustrative case, an internal service printing fund, continues the operations of the fictitious city of Ruthberg as they pertain to an internal service fund. Chapter 2 started the operations of fund accounting in this city by explaining and illustrating the operations of an enterprise fund—the bus fund. This chapter and others will continue the discussion on particular funds of this city.

## Transactions to Open Internal Service Fund

At the beginning of the fiscal year, 19X6, the general fund of the city of Ruthberg contributed $150,000 in cash to establish an internal service printing fund. The fund's purpose is to provide printing services to all of the funds of the city government at cost. The assumption is that if the city can receive these services at cost, there will be quite a savings in printing costs by the city over that incurred when sending the printing out to private printers.

## Establishing the Fund

**I1** The entry to record the establishment of the fund is:

|  | Dr. | Cr. |
|---|---|---|
| Cash | $150,000 |  |
|     Residual equity transfer |  | $150,000 |

## Developing Costing Charges

The fund will charge actual cost for direct material and direct labor and will add on an overhead charge of two-thirds of the direct labor cost. This charge was determined from the following estimate:

|  | Direct | Indirect | Total |
|---|---|---|---|
| Labor | $30,000 | $ 4,000 | $34,000 |
| Material | 24,000 | 1,000 | 25,000 |
| Overhead, rent |  | 5,000 | 5,000 |
| Depreciation of equipment |  | 10,000 | 10,000 |
| Total | $54,000 | $20,000 | $74,000 |

For example, if the direct labor for a certain printing job was $3,000 and the material was $2,400, the overhead would be $2,000 (two-thirds of the direct labor cost of $3,000); the total cost would be $7,400.

## Operating Transactions During the Period

During the year, the following transactions, with journal entries, took place.

**12** Rented building for $5,000 per year. Paid in cash. The journal entry to record the transaction for the rental of the building is:

| | | |
|---|---|---|
| Rent expense | $5,000 | |
| Cash | | $5,000 |

**13** Purchased printing, binding, and other equipment for $120,000. The equipment is expected to last twelve years. The journal entry to record the transaction for the purchase of equipment is:

| | | |
|---|---|---|
| Equipment | $120,000 | |
| Cash | | $120,000 |

**14** Purchased materials and supplies on credit for $35,000. During the year, $32,000 was paid. The journal entry to record this transaction is:

| | | |
|---|---|---|
| Inventory | $35,000 | |
| Accounts payable | | $35,000 |
| Accounts payable | $32,000 | |
| Cash | | $32,000 |

**15** Materials used during the year amounted to: direct materials, $23,000; indirect materials, $1,000. The journal entries to record the inventory transactions are:

| | | |
|---|---|---|
| Direct materials used | $23,000 | |
| Indirect materials used | 1,000 | |
| Inventory | | $24,000 |

**16** The following labor costs were paid during the year:

| | Paid | Accrued | Total |
|---|---|---|---|
| Direct labor | $29,000 | $1,000 | $30,000 |
| Indirect labor | 3,500 | 500 | 4,000 |
| Total | $32,500 | $1,500 | $34,000 |

The journal entries to record the labor transactions are:

| | | |
|---|---|---|
| Direct labor | $29,000 | |
| Indirect labor | 3,500 | |
| Cash | | $32,500 |

**17** Billings on account during the year were:

| | |
|---|---|
| General fund | $54,000 |
| Bus fund | 20,000 |
| Total | $74,000 |

The journal entries to record this transaction are:

| | | |
|---|---|---|
| Due from general fund | $54,000 | |
| Due from bus fund | 20,000 | |
|     Charges for services | | $74,000 |

**I8** Collections on billings for services were:

| | |
|---|---|
| General fund | $50,000 |
| Bus fund | 20,000 |
| Total | $70,000 |

The journal entries to record this transaction are:

| | | |
|---|---|---|
| Cash | $70,000 | |
|     Due from general fund | | $50,000 |
|     Due from bus fund | | 20,000 |

### EXHIBIT 3-1
### City of Ruthberg—Internal Service Printing Fund
### Worksheet for Year 19X6

| Accounts | Transactions | | | | Trial balance | |
|---|---|---|---|---|---|---|
| | No. | Dr. | No. | Cr. | Dr. | Cr. |
| Cash | I1 | 150,000 | I2 | 5,000 | 30,000 | |
| | I8 | 70,000 | I3 | 120,000 | | |
| | | | I4 | 32,000 | | |
| | | | I6 | 32,500 | | |
| Due from: | | | | | | |
|   General fund | I7 | 54,000 | I8 | 50,000 | 4,000 | |
|   Bus fund | I7 | 20,000 | I8 | 20,000 | | |
| Inventory | I4 | 35,000 | I5 | 24,000 | 11,000 | |
| Equipment | I3 | 120,000 | | | 120,000 | |
| Accumulated depreciation— | | | | | | |
|   equipment | | | | | | |
| Accounts payable | I4 | 32,000 | I4 | 35,000 | | 3,000 |
| Accrued expenses | | | | | | |
| Contributed capital | | | | | | |
| Residual equity transfer | | | I1 | 150,000 | | 150,000 |
| Charges for services | | | I7 | 74,000 | | 74,000 |
| Direct labor | I6 | 29,000 | | | 29,000 | |
| Indirect labor | I6 | 3,500 | | | 3,500 | |
| Direct material used | I5 | 23,000 | | | 23,000 | |
| Indirect material used | I5 | 1,000 | | | 1,000 | |
| Rent expense | I2 | 5,000 | | | 5,000 | |
| Depreciation—equipment | | | | | | |
| | | $542,500 | | $542,500 | $227,000 | $227,000 |
| Retained earnings | | | | | | |

## Adjustments to Accounts at Year's End

At the end of the year, the following adjustments were made to correct the labor accounts and to provide for depreciation:

|  |  |  | Dr. | Cr. |
|---|---|---|---|---|
| IA1 | Direct labor | | $1,000 | |
| | Indirect labor | | 500 | |
| | Accrued expenses | | | $1,500 |
| IA2 | Depreciation—equipment | | $10,000 | |
| | Accumulated depreciation—equipment | | | $10,000 |

## Worksheet of Transactions

Instead of using "T" accounts to bring together all of the information concerning the operations of the internal service printing fund for the year, the preceding transactions are posted to a worksheet (see Exhibit 3-1).

**EXHIBIT 3-1**
*(continued)*

| | Adjustments | | Revenue and expenses | | Balance sheet | |
|---|---|---|---|---|---|---|
| No. | Dr. | Cr. | Dr. | Cr. | Dr. | Cr. |
| | | | | | 30,500 | |
| | | | | | | |
| | | | | | 4,000 | |
| | | | | | 11,000 | |
| | | | | | 120,000 | |
| IA2 | | 10,000 | | | | 10,000 |
| | | | | | 3,000 | |
| IA1 | | 1,500 | | | 1,500 | |
| IA3 | | 150,000 | | | 150,000 | |
| IA3 | 150,000 | | | | | |
| | | | | 74,000 | | |
| IA1 | 1,000 | | 30,000 | | | |
| IA1 | 500 | | 4,000 | | | |
| | | | 23,000 | | | |
| | | | 1,000 | | | |
| | | | 5,000 | | | |
| IA2 | 10,000 | | 10,000 | | | |
| | $161,500 | $161,500 | $73,000 | $74,000 | $165,500 | $164,500 |
| | | | 1,000 | | | 1,000 |
| | | | $74,000 | $74,000 | $165,500 | $165,500 |

## Closing Entries

Before closing the books, the entry concerning the residual equity transfer from the general fund to the internal service printing fund must be made to the contributed capital account. This entry is as follows:

|  |  | Dr. | Cr. |
|---|---|---|---|
| IA3 | Residual equity transfer | $150,000 |  |
|  | Contributed capital |  | $150,000 |

Closing entries for the operation of the internal service printing fund would be as follows:

|  |  | Dr. | Cr. |
|---|---|---|---|
| IC1 | Charges for services | $74,000 |  |
|  | Direct labor |  | $30,000 |
|  | Indirect labor |  | 4,000 |
|  | Direct material |  | 23,000 |
|  | Indirect material |  | 1,000 |
|  | Rent expense |  | 5,000 |
|  | Depreciation—equipment |  | 10,000 |
|  | Retained earnings |  | 1,000 |

## Internal Service Printing Fund Financial Statements

The financial statements for the internal service printing fund are the same as those for the enterprise fund: the balance sheet; the statement of revenues, expenses, and changes in retained earnings; and the statement of changes in financial position (see Exhibits 3-2, 3-3, and 3-4).

## SUMMARY

Proprietary funds are classified into two types: enterprise funds and internal service funds. Enterprise funds, as explained and illustrated in Chapter 2, provide goods or services for a fee, with the greater proportion of the revenue from the fees coming from customers outside of the governmental unit. Internal service funds, as explained and illustrated in this chapter, also provide services or goods for a fee, but the primary customers are other funds within the governmental unit. Usually, internal service funds try to recover only costs from the charges for services and do not try to make a profit.

Since these funds are business-type proprietary funds, internal service funds generally follow the principles of accounting related to businesses: they use accrual accounting; they record long-term assets and liabilities in the funds, and depreciate the assets in order to have a period expense for the assets; they prepare the same type of statements required of business-type organizations; and they usually do not have the fixed type of budgets normally found in certain types of governmental funds. However, they do need some type of cost system in order to account for the goods and services sold to

**EXHIBIT 3-2**
**City of Ruthberg—Internal Service Printing Fund**
**Balance Sheet**
**June 30, 19X6**

### Assets

| | | |
|---|---:|---:|
| Current assets: | | |
|   Cash | $ 30,500 | |
|   Due from general fund | 4,000 | |
|   Inventory | 11,000 | |
|     Total current assets | | $ 45,500 |
| Fixed assets: | | |
|   Equipment | 120,000 | |
|   Less accumulated depreciation | 10,000 | |
|     Total fixed assets | | 110,000 |
| Total assets | | $155,500 |

### Liabilities and Fund Equity

| | | |
|---|---:|---:|
| Current liabilities: | | |
|   Accounts payable | 3,000 | |
|   Accrued expenses payable | 1,500 | |
|     Total current liabilities | | $ 4,500 |
| Fund equity: | | |
|   Contributed capital (residual equity transfer) | 150,000 | |
|   Retained earnings | 1,000 | |
|     Total fund equity | | 151,000 |
| Total liabilities and fund equity | | $155,500 |

**EXHIBIT 3-3**
**City of Ruthberg—Internal Service Printing Fund**
**Statement of Revenues, Expenses,**
**and Changes in Retained Earnings**
**For Fiscal Year 19X6**

| | | |
|---|---:|---:|
| Operating revenues | | |
|   Charges for services | | $74,000 |
| Operating expenses | | |
|   Labor | $34,000 | |
|   Material | 24,000 | |
|   Rent | 5,000 | |
|   Depreciation—equipment | 10,000 | |
|     Total operating expenses | | 73,000 |
| Operating income | | 1,000 |
| Retained earnings | | |
|   Retained earnings, beginning of year | | — |
|   Retained earnings, June 30, 19X6 | | $ 1,000 |

## EXHIBIT 3-4
### City of Ruthberg—Internal Service Printing Fund
### Statement of Changes in Financial Position
### For Fiscal Year 19X6

#### Sources of Working Capital

| | | |
|---|---:|---:|
| Operating revenue | $ 1,000 | |
| Add—depreciation on equipment not requiring financial resources | 10,000 | |
| Total working capital from operations | | $ 11,000 |
| Contributed capital (cash—residual equity transfer) | | 150,000 |
| Total sources of working capital | | 161,000 |
| Uses of working capital | | |
| Purchase of equipment | | 120,000 |
| Increase in working capital | | $ 41,000 |

#### Elements of Increase in Working Capital

| | July 1 | June 30 | Increase (Decrease) |
|---|---:|---:|---:|
| Current assets: | | | |
| Cash | — | $30,500 | $30,500 |
| Due from general fund | — | 4,000 | 4,000 |
| Inventory | — | 11,000 | 11,000 |
| Total current assets | | $45,500 | $45,500 |
| Current liabilities: | | | |
| Accounts payable | — | $ 3,000 | ($ 3,000) |
| Accrued expenses | — | 1,500 | ( 1,500) |
| Total current liabilities | | 4,500 | ($ 4,500) |
| Net increase in working capital | | $41,000 | $41,000 |

the other funds of the governmental unit. Some of the principles of accounting vary from those of a normal business, however, because of the nature of government. Capital equity resulting from residual equity transfers from the general fund of the city were illustrated in this chapter, along with "quasi-external transactions" resulting from sales of services to other funds of the governmental unit.

Internal service funds of government operate similarly to business organizations; therefore, the accounting is very similar as well. In addition, they have very close relations with the governmental funds, thereby providing an excellent link between business accounting and governmental fund accounting.

## QUESTIONS

1 Describe the types of services that can be performed by an internal service fund. To whom are these services basically provided?
2 The older term for internal service funds was revolving funds. Explain why this type of fund would be called a revolving fund.

3 Distinguish between residual equity transfers and operating transfers. Explain how each is shown on the financial statements.
4 Are adjusting journal entries a normal type of entry in a proprietary fund? Explain.
5 In internal service funds, to which account are the revenue and expense accounts closed at the end of each accounting period?
6 Which financial statements are prepared for internal service funds?
7 When are combined statements prepared for internal service funds? When are combining statements prepared?
8 Are the financial statements for internal service funds different from those prepared for enterprise funds?
9 Should governmental budgetary accounting be used in internal service funds?
10 Explain why cost accounting is so important in internal service funds.
11 The statement is often made that accounting for internal service funds of government is similar to accounting for business-type entities. Explain.

**PROBLEMS**

3-1 Select the best answer for each of the following.
  1 Which of the following funds receives compensation for the services it renders primarily to other funds within the governmental unit?
    a The general fund.
    b The enterprise fund.
    c The capital projects fund.
    d The internal service fund.
  2 Which of the following funds apply the accrual basis of accounting?
    a Enterprise but not internal service.
    b Internal service but not enterprise.
    c Neither internal service nor enterprise.
    d Both internal service and enterprise.
  3 Which of the following accounts will become contributed capital of a proprietary fund?
    a Capital grants.
    b Charges for services.
    c Operating transfers.
    d Bonds.
  4 In proprietary funds, budgetary accounting can be used:
    a In internal service funds to determine costs as a basis for its charges.
    b To prepare external reporting financial statements.
    c In enterprise funds as a basis for its charges.
    d In none of the above.
  5 The costs of an internal service fund are borne by:
    a All users from other governmental funds through a cost-reimbursement charge.
    b Service fees from users from outside of government.
    c A residual equity transfer.
    d The general fund.
  6 In an internal service fund,
    a Cost accounting is a very important process.
    b Cost accounting is never used.
    c Budgetary accounting replaces cost accounting.
    d Budgetary accounting is never used.

**3-2** Select the best answer for each of the following.
  1 Through using an internal service fund:
    a Costs for a particular service to the funds of government can be reduced.
    b Costs are usually higher than outside provided services.
    c Charges to service users seldom recover all costs.
    d None of the above.
  2 An internal service fund seldom can estimate exactly the yearly costs for jobs or services in order to provide continuing services. Therefore, the internal service fund usually:
    a Adjusts the costs for services during the year.
    b Adjusts the costs for services on a year-to-year basis.
    c Does not adjust the costs.
    d Takes in jobs or services outside the government to provide additional revenue.
  3 A residual equity transaction in an internal service fund is closed to:
    a Retained earnings.
    b Revenue.
    c Expenses.
    d Contributed capital.
  4 The income and expense accounts of an internal service fund are closed to:
    a The fund balance account.
    b The retained earnings account.
    c The contributed capital account.
    d The earned surplus account.
  5 Adjusting journal entries for an internal service fund are:
    a Usually needed at the end of the fiscal year.
    b Seldom used in internal service funds.
    c Combined with closing entries.
    d None of the above.
  6 The financial statements needed for an internal service fund are (is):
    a The balance sheet; the statement of revenues, expenditures, and changes in fund balance.
    b Only a statement of revenue and expenses.
    c The balance sheet; the statement of revenues, expenses and changes in retained earnings; and the statement of changes in financial position.
    d Only a balance sheet.

**3-3** The following before and after adjustment balances for the town of Whitehurst's computer fund (internal service fund) indicate the effect of adjustments on year-end balances. For each of the items, prepare the adjusting entry that would have likely been made.

| Accounts | Balances before adjustment | Balances after adjustment |
|---|---|---|
| Supplies inventory | $6,500 | $4,200 |
| Wages payable | 2,000 | 4,000 |
| Depreciation expense | — | 6,000 |
| Prepaid insurance | 3,000 | 1,800 |

**3-4** The city of Merlot operates a central garage through an internal service fund to provide garage space and repairs for all city-owned and city-operated vehicles. The central garage fund was established by a contribution of $200,000 from the general fund on July 1, 19X4, at which time the building was acquired. The postclosing trial balance at June 30, 19X5 follows.[1]

| Accounts | Dr. | Cr. |
|---|---|---|
| Cash | $150,000 | |
| Due from general fund | 20,000 | |
| Inventory of materials and supplies | 80,000 | |
| Land | 60,000 | |
| Building | 200,000 | |
| Allowance for depreciation—building | | $ 10,000 |
| Machinery and equipment | 56,000 | |
| Allowance for depreciation—machinery and equipment | | 12,000 |
| Accounts payable | | 38,000 |
| Contribution from general fund | | 200,000 |
| Retained earnings | | 306,000 |
| | $566,000 | $566,000 |

The following information applies to the fiscal year ended June 30, 19X6:

**1** Materials and supplies were purchased on account for $74,000.

**2** The inventory of materials and supplies at June 30, 19X6, was $58,000, which agreed with the physical count taken.

**3** Salaries and wages paid to employees totaled $230,000, including related costs.

**4** A billing was received from the enterprise fund for utility charges totaling $30,000, and it was paid.

**5** Depreciation of the building was recorded in the amount of $5,000. Depreciation of the machinery and equipment amounted to $8,000.

**6** Billings to other departments for services rendered to them were as follows:

| | |
|---|---|
| General fund | $262,000 |
| Water and sewer fund | 84,000 |
| Special revenue fund | 32,000 |

**7** Unpaid interfund receivable balances at June 30, 19X6 were as follows:

| | |
|---|---|
| General fund | $ 6,000 |
| Special revenue fund | 16,000 |

**8** Accounts payable at June 30, 19X6, were $14,000.

**Required**:

1 For the period July 1, 19X5 through June 30, 19X6, prepare journal entries for the above transactions and record them on a worksheet similar to that illustrated in this chapter.
2 Prepare adjusting and closing entries for the central garage fund at June 30, 19X6.
3 Prepare the year-end financial statements needed for the fund.

**3-5** Lewisburg has a garage fund that services all of the automotive equipment for the city. During the previous year, it had the following expenses:

| | | |
|---|---:|---:|
| Direct labor | | $100,000 |
| Direct material | | 50,000 |
| Overhead: | | |
|   Indirect labor | $25,000 | |
|   Indirect material | 12,500 | 37,500 |
|     Total expenses | | $187,000 |

In September of the current year, the department of public works had all of its automobiles serviced at the garage. It received a bill from the central garage as follows:

### City of Lewisburg
### Central Garage
### Statement of Charges for September 19X7

| | | |
|---|---:|---:|
| Direct labor (repair of 16 automobiles— | | |
|   32 hours at $12 per hour) | $384 | |
| Supplies | 254 | |
|   Total direct costs | | 638 |
| Overhead | | 144 |
|   Total | | $782 |

**Required**:
Determine if the total of $782 is an appropriate amount to pay for the services from the garage based on the previous year's costs.

**3-6** The city of Frankfurt has operated a central stores fund, which is an internal service fund, for several years in order to service all stores activities for the city. The following trial balance was prepared from the accounts after all transactions for the 19X8 year had been recorded, but before adjusting and closing entries had been made.

**Required**:
Record all of the accounts shown on page 83 in "T" accounts, adjust the accounts, close the accounts, prepare appropriate trial balances, and prepare a balance sheet and an income statement for the year. Since the beginning balances are not given, a statement of changes in financial position is not necessarily appropriate, so it is not necessary to prepare this statement.

**3-7** The Silver City case is a problem that continues throughout most of Part I. It illustrates many of the principles and procedures discussed in these chapters and gives the student an opportunity to see how the operation of a single fund ties into the operations of a total city—Silver City. While the requirements that follow help in guiding the discussion of the case, many other points can be raised from the transactions given.

    Silver City began operations on July 1, 19X0. They had professional advice in the installation of their accounting system, and they intended to follow generally accepted accounting principles for governmental entities in order to receive an unqualified opinion on their audited statements for the year ended June 30, 19X1. The transactions and financial activities pertain to the various funds and account groups—in this chapter, an internal service printing fund. In your answers to the requirements, you should follow the current GASB and FASB principles and standards.

    Since this is the first year of operation for the city, there are no balances in the accounts at the beginning of the year, and comparative statements will not be made. Insofar as possible, the transactions are combined and account titles are grouped in order to save time and space.

**City of Frankfurt**
**Central Stores Fund**
**Trial Balance**
**As of June 30, 19X8**

| Accounts | Dr. | Cr. |
|---|---|---|
| Cash | $ 12,000 | |
| Due from general fund | 50,000 | |
| Due from capital projects fund | 20,000 | |
| Inventory | 100,000 | |
| Prepaid insurance | 2,000 | |
| Contributed capital | | $300,000 |
| Retained earnings | 6,000 | |
| Accounts payable | | 50,000 |
| Sales to other funds | | 200,000 |
| Purchases | 150,000 | |
| Sales returns and allowances | 2,000 | |
| Purchase returns and allowances | | 2,000 |
| Building | 200,000 | |
| Accumulated depreciation of building | | 60,000 |
| Equipment | 100,000 | |
| Accumulated depreciation of equipment | | 50,000 |
| Freight in | 1,000 | |
| Wages and salaries expenses | 15,000 | |
| Miscellaneous administrative expenses | 4,000 | |
| Total | $662,000 | $662,000 |
| Adjustments: | | |
| Depreciation of building (20-year life) | | 10,000 |
| Depreciation of equipment (10-year life) | | 10,000 |
| Insurance (4-year policy) | | 500 |
| Accrued salaries | | 1,000 |
| Inventory | | 10,000 |

The following information pertains to Silver City's garage fund, an internal service fund.

1 Received a contribution from the general fund, $50,000.

2 Rented a garage for $1,000 per month. Paid one year's rent in advance. The garage started one month after the city began operations, so the rent extended one month into the next fiscal year.

3 Bought equipment for $24,000. The equipment was expected to last six years.

4 Purchased supplies for $5,000.

5 The labor cost that was paid during the year amounted to $50,000.

6 Services rendered to the general fund amounted to $75,000.

7 Cash was received from the general fund in the amount of $70,000.

8 The inventory of supplies at the end of the year amounted to $1,000. Accrued payroll salaries, wages, and other costs amounted to $3,000. Other expenses needing adjustment should be adjusted properly.

**Required**:

1 Prepare journal entries for each of the preceding transactions in the internal service garage fund of the city.

2 Post the journalized transactions to a worksheet for the fund, comparable to that illustrated in the chapter.

3 Prepare the following financial statements:
  a A balance sheet for the fund.
  b A statement of revenue, expenses, and changes in retained earnings for the fund. Should a statement of changes in financial position be prepared for this fund? If so, prepare it.

# NOTES

1 Adapted from American Institute of Certified Public Accountants. *Uniform CPA Examination Questions and Unofficial Answers* (New York: American Institute of Certified Public Accountants, May 1981).

# CHAPTER 4

# GOVERNMENTAL FUNDS— INTRODUCTION TO BUDGETS AND BUDGETARY ACCOUNTING

Significant advances have been made over the past twenty-five years in the theory and practice of budgeting as applied in both the private and public sectors. Budgeting is a cyclical decision-making process. It requires a systematic evaluation of prior resource commitments and their consequences in terms of anticipated achievements as well as projections of future commitments to meet organizational goals and objectives. If properly applied, budgeting can make important contributions to greater efficiency, effectiveness, and accountability in the operations, programs, and activities of any organization.

## THE PLANNING EMPHASIS IN CURRENT BUDGET PRACTICES

It has long been recognized that the budget process offers the potential for periodic reevaluations of broad goals and objectives and comparisons of organizational programs and their costs in light of these longer-range objectives. The budget document can provide a common terminology for describing the plans and programs covering diverse organizational operations. This planning potential, however, was largely overshadowed until the mid-sixties by the fiscal control focus of more traditional budgeting procedures.

### Planning Objectives of Budgeting

Emphasis on planning in the budget process was first brought to full public attention in August 1965, when President Lyndon B. Johnson proclaimed that by fiscal year 1968 all federal departments would adopt the budgeting system that had been used for some years in the Department of Defense. This budget format—known as a Planning-Programming-Budgeting System (PPBS)—was an outgrowth of budget-building techniques that earlier had developed in business and industry under the concept of program budgeting.

As with many innovations introduced by dictum, however, inadequate groundwork was laid for the development of PPBS at the federal level and even less so in state and local government. PPBS was received with great enthusiasm by the proponents of a more rational and comprehensive approach to financial management and with equal skepticism by many who had earlier experiments with performance and program budgeting. What had been a fairly successful technique in the evaluation of weaponry systems in the Defense Department proved to have only limited immediate application in other public agencies.

### The Need to Integrate Planning and Control Objectives

One of the more evident shortcomings of these new budgetary formats has been a failure to fully integrate these systematic procedures with other basic components of a financial management system. In particular, these more recently developed techniques for public budgeting (e.g., program budgeting and zero-base budgeting) have not been well aligned with appropriate accounting procedures. These new budgetary formats have tended to emphasize the planning function to the near exclusion of the equally important techniques and procedures for financial control. As a result, these new techniques, in many cases, have failed to produce the desired improvements in terms of more efficient, economical, and effective governmental operations.

The introduction of these budgetary procedures in the private sector has been accompanied by parallel improvements in accounting procedures and, in particular, the fuller application of cost-management accounting techniques. Applications of cost-management accounting are still in the formative stages in government.

A secondary objective of this book is to provide readers with sufficient background in the theory and practice of budgeting as applied in government and other nonbusiness organizations so they might make some contribution to the further development of cost-management accounting applications in these organizations. A discussion of the more recent developments in budgeting will be provided in Part IV. These later chapters (Parts III and IV) will also explore the appropriate accounting procedures to provide for more efficient, economical, and effective operations of programs and activities of nonbusiness entities.

In the following chapters on governmental funds, however, our primary focus will be on the *object-of-expenditure* budget. This traditional budget format, with its detailed recording of spending requirements and subsequent commitments, serves the objectives of *financial control* most effectively. Agencies can spend their budget allocations within relatively narrow, predetermined limits. The financial accounting system—developed in parallel with the budget to emphasize fiscal control—serves these needs well.

## INTRODUCTION TO THE PRINCIPLES AND PRACTICES OF BUDGETING

It is important to recognize at the outset that a budget is much more than a fixed document presented annually for the review and approval of the governing body. A budget represents a complex decision process whereby: (1) organizational policy is formulated, (2) action programs are put into effect, and (3) both legislative and administrative controls are established. The annual cyclical nature of this process should not be misinterpreted as an inflexible routine. Budgets seldom are "set in concrete," but must have the capacity to accommodate changing needs, interests, and available technology for the delivery of organizational services.

## Purposes and Objectives of Budgeting

A budget can be defined as "the financial articulation of the activities of a governmental unit that at the local level takes the form of an ordinance or resolution which recognizes anticipated revenues, authorizes activities, and appropriates expenditures" for a specific period of time.[1] A budget provides the legal basis for spending and accountability. Budgeting, especially in the not-for-profit activities of government, is integrally linked to the accounting process, whereby revenue and expenditure information is structured to facilitate the continuous monitoring, evaluation, and control of fiscal resources. Through the budgeting/accounting process, financial authority and responsibility can be delegated throughout the organization, while appropriate central control is maintained.

Budgeting also involves decision making under conditions of uncertainty, where such decisions may have significant future consequences (i.e., require careful analysis and planning). Before a budget can be prepared, goals and objectives should be formulated, policies analyzed, and plans and programs delineated. The purposes of a budget include both *policy formulation* and *administration*. The financial commitment to organizational programs in the budget is (or should be) a clear declaration of policy. The fiscal stewardship that builds on the budget is a principal responsibility of administration. In government, budgeting also serves as the public substitute for mechanisms of the economic market system—the process by which decisions are made regarding the allocation of scarce resources—the politics of "who gets what."

## Objectives of the Annual Operating Budget

In most state and local governments, a distinction is made between the annual operating budget and the capital budget. The basic function of an *operating budget* is to justify projected resource allocations that will be expended during the coming fiscal year. The annual operating budget provides the basis upon which the governing body may adopt an ordinance or resolution that authorizes public agencies to incur obligations and to make payments for them. These obligations and payments are for such things as personal services (e.g., salaries and wages and related employee benefits), contractual services (e.g., travel, computing services, consulting services, etc.), materials and supplies, certain types of equipment, and so forth.

The *capital budget*, on the other hand, represents an estimate of expenditures to be made over a period of years to meet the public improvement needs (i.e., capital facilities) of the jurisdiction. The capital budget usually includes an identification of the means of financing these longer-term commitments for the current fiscal year. A capital budget often is supported by a *capital improvements program*, which documents improvement needs over a longer time period (usually five to six years). The capital budget is the first year of this program statement. In some jurisdictions, a *capital facilities plan* also is prepared, encompassing an even longer time horizon (fifteen to twenty years). The capital facilities plan provides an analysis of the anticipated financial resources to support debt commitments that might be incurred through the issuance of municipal bonds to finance public improvements.[2]

The operating and capital budgets usually are incorporated into one budget document and approved by the governing body at the same time. In some jurisdictions, however, the capital budget is presented separately and on a different time cycle from the annual operating budget. Different accounting principles and procedures are associated with the financial transactions generated by each of these budgets. The objectives of a capital budget and the accounting and control procedures for capital projects and debt service funds are discussed in further detail in Chapters 7 and 8.

The annual operating budget provides an estimate of expenditures that must be balanced against the recommended revenue program. Each successive level of management—especially the chief executive—is provided with information upon which to evaluate competing requirements for the limited fiscal resources. While the budget provides limits to spending, the adoption of the budget ordinance or resolution by the governing body should be viewed as a positive act. Emphasis on the control aspects of budgeting often results in a negative psychology surrounding the process, with significant adverse effects in the execution of the budget.

The operating budget can provide a basis for articulating organizational objectives and, subsequently, for measuring their degree of attainment within a given fiscal period. A budget also facilitates the scheduling of work and the coordination of personnel and nonpersonnel service requirements. Thus the budget process can enhance the understanding of the governing body and the general public as to proposed plans of operation for the ensuing fiscal year. Once the budget is approved, agencies can adjust activities planned for the upcoming fiscal year to conform to their fiscal appropriations. Finally, the budget provides a basis for a financial audit and, as appropriate, a performance evaluation both during and after the close of the fiscal year.

## THE BUDGET CYCLE

Budget making requires careful scheduling if officials are to be given adequate time and information for sound budget decisions. The budget process commonly involves four major steps:

1 Executive preparation,
2 Review, modification, and enactment by the governing body,
3 Budget execution, and
4 Postaudit and evaluation.

The steps in this process must be undertaken in a logical sequence if the required mass of detail is to be coordinated and important deadlines are to be met. Responsibility for performing each specific step must be clearly assigned. Well-designed forms should be provided to the agencies to ensure that their budget requests are submitted in as uniform and complete a manner as possible. Policies and special instructions for the preparation of the budget also should be set forth in writing (i.e., as a *budget manual*).

## The Budget Calendar

A budget calendar should be established in advance and should set forth, in chronological order, the key dates and assignments of responsibility for carrying out the preparation of the budget. At the local level, controlling dates of the budget calendar often are set by state law, city charter, or local ordinance. These dates include important deadlines such as those for submitting the budget to city council, for council's adoption of the budget, and for setting the annual property tax levy and rate.

The budget calendar suggested in Exhibit 4-1 is based on a fiscal year beginning January 1, with property taxes falling due on the same date. The actual dates, of course, will have to be adjusted to the fiscal year of the municipality (in a number of states, for example, the fiscal year runs from July 1 to June 30). The total time for the annual budget preparation cycle will vary from four to six months in large cities and from two to three months in smaller municipalities. The time intervals required for each step also will vary somewhat depending on the size of the jurisdiction, established legal requirements, and the type of budget format applied.

## The Executive Budget

The chief executive—strong mayor or manager—has primary responsibility for the preparation of budget estimates and for the development of a preliminary budget docu-

**EXHIBIT 4-1** SUGGESTED BUDGET PREPARATION CALENDAR

| Time period | Budget requirement | Responsible official |
|---|---|---|
| Feb. 1– July 15 | Preparation of long-term program services and capital improvements. | Chief administrator & dept. heads |
| Prior to July 15 | Preliminary work, including entering prior-year and current-year data on estimating forms and preliminary revenue estimates. | Chief finance officer & budget officer |
| July 15– Sept. 1 | Prepare work program and budget estimates. | Department heads |
| July 15 | Issue budget instructions and estimating forms. | Chief administrator |
| July 15– Sept. 1 | Prepare revenue estimates. | Chief finance officer & budget director |
| Aug. 15– Sept. 7 | Check mathematical accuracy of estimates; compile and summarize. | Chief finance officer |
| Sept. 1– Oct. 15 | Investigate and review requests; determine final recommendations. | Chief administrator & budget director |
| Oct. 15– Nov. 1 | Prepare budget document and submit budget to governing body. | Chief administrator, budget director & finance officer |
| Nov. 1– Nov. 21 | Legislate consideration of the budget. | Governing body |
| Nov. 7–15 | Public budget hearings. | Governing body |
| Nov. 21 | Budget adoption by enactment of appropriation and revenue ordinances. | Governing body |
| Nov. 22– Jan. 1 | Prepare and mail tax bills. | Finance dept. |
| Dec. 15– Jan. 10 | Prepare, review, and establish budget allotments. | Dept. heads & budget officer |

ment. The executive budget is then presented to the governing body for review and adoption. In large jurisdictions, the chief executive may rely on the staff of a budget office, finance department, and financial planning analysts to develop the background information and financial details necessary to support the budget document.

A *budget guidance memorandum* or similar statement should be issued to all departments and agencies, along with a set of instructions or manual for completing the requisite forms and for developing supporting information and justifications. The guidance memorandum should outline: (1) anticipated fiscal policies, (2) agreed-upon goals and objectives, and (3) performance expectations of the current administration. Statements of total public needs and demands should be presented in order to establish appropriate levels of program activity or services. These service levels, in turn, must be further structured in the agencies' submissions. Budget targets may be set forth in the memorandum, reflecting preliminary estimates of revenue potentials.

Each agency or department should complete the required budget forms to reflect a "best estimate" as to the most appropriate assignment of resources for personnel, equipment, materials and supplies, and so forth in order to carry out the programs and activities within its areas of responsibility. Departments and agencies may be called upon to further refine the broad goals and objectives identified in the guidance memorandum in order to place their specific programs into this broader perspective. Budget justifications may include various performance measures and/or measures of effectiveness (to be discussed in further detail in Part IV). Such justifications may also include a priority listing of all programs. Major policy issues or administrative problems, if any, should be identified, and the requirements for new legislation should be outlined, as appropriate.

The central budget agency must check the departmental submissions for completeness and accuracy. Agency requests are then compiled into a preliminary document to provide an overall summary of total dollar needs. The budget staff also may prepare preliminary estimates as to the impact of changes in employee compensation and benefits, develop estimates of debt service requirements and interfund transfers, and identify any policy changes inherent in agency budget requests.

## Budget and Accounting Classifications

It is important that the data presented in agency budget requests be compatible with data that are available within the accounting system. This compatibility facilitates comparisons between what has been spent in previous fiscal periods and what is proposed to be expended in the future. It also is essential for evaluation and financial reporting purposes.

Generally accepted accounting principles require that financial statements follow certain standards. One standard is that expenditures be classified by functions or programs. Another standard is that, in all cases in which a budget is used to appropriate monies to funds, there be a statement that compares *actual* revenue and expenditures with *budgeted* revenue and expenditures (see Exhibit 4-2). Therefore, whenever possible, the budget classification system should follow the accounting classification system.

**EXHIBIT 4-2** COMPARISON OF ACTUAL AND BUDGETED EXPENDITURES THROUGH EIGHT MONTHS OF THE FISCAL YEAR

Department: Financial management

| Object classifications | Budgeted | Expend. to-date | Est. annual expend. | Difference |
|---|---|---|---|---|
| Personal services | | | | |
| 1100 Salaries | 278,020 | 188,345 | 282,520 | 4,500 |
| 1120 Wages | 0 | 1,050 | 1,575 | 1,575 |
| 1130 Special payments | 0 | 0 | 0 | 0 |
| 1140 Overtime payments | 5,250 | 2,200 | 3,300 | (1,950) |
| Subtotal: Person. serv. | $283,270 | $191,595 | $287,395 | $4,125 |
| Contractual services | | | | |
| 1210 General repairs | 700 | 445 | 668 | ( 32) |
| 1220 Utility services | 3,600 | 2,500 | 3,750 | 150 |
| 1230 Motor veh. repairs | 500 | 600 | 750 | 250 |
| 1240 Travel | 2,100 | 1,400 | 2,100 | 0 |
| 1250 Professional serv. | 5,725 | 3,250 | 4,875 | ( 850) |
| 1260 Communications | 6,780 | 4,600 | 6,900 | 120 |
| 1270 Printing | 1,000 | 500 | 1,000 | 0 |
| 1280 Computing serv. | 64,725 | 44,200 | 66,300 | 1,575 |
| 1290 Other contr. serv. | 3,000 | 2,000 | 3,000 | 0 |
| Subtotal: Contract. serv. | $ 88,130 | $ 59,495 | $ 89,343 | $1,213 |
| Supplies and materials | | | | |
| 1310 Office supplies | 29,440 | 20,000 | 30,000 | 560 |
| 1320 Fuel supplies | 0 | 200 | 300 | 300 |
| 1330 Operating supplies | 1,000 | 700 | 1,050 | 50 |
| 1340 Maint. supplies | 900 | 500 | 750 | ( 150) |
| 1350 Drugs and chemicals | 0 | 0 | 0 | 0 |
| 1360 Food supplies | 0 | 75 | 110 | 110 |
| 1370 Clothing & linens | 0 | 0 | 0 | 0 |
| 1380 Ed. & recre. supp. | 0 | 50 | 50 | 50 |
| 1390 Other supplies | 1,500 | 900 | 1,350 | ( 150) |
| Subtotal: Suppl. & mat. | $ 32,840 | $ 22,425 | $ 33,610 | $ 770 |
| Subtotal: Equipment | $ 17,020 | $ 15,000 | $ 15,800 | (1,220) |
| Subtotal: Current oblg. | $ 10,940 | $ 4,000 | $ 5,600 | (5,340) |
| Subtotal: Employ. bene. | $ 27,800 | $ 18,780 | $ 28,170 | $ 370 |
| Total | $460,000 | $311,295 | $459,918 | ( 82) |

For financial accounting and reporting purposes, revenue in the budget should be classified by both *fund* and *source*, although sometimes revenue is classified by organization as well. Expenditures in the budget should be classified by object of expenditure, character of expenditure, organizational unit, activity (in program budgeting, by program and subprogram), function, and fund (see Exhibit 4-3).

The basic control device for the traditional budget is the *object of expenditure*—the fundamental elements of an organization's operations in terms of the goods and services procured. *Object codes*—three-digit or four-digit numbers—are used to budget and record expenditures in considerable detail (see Exhibit 4-2). These object codes

**EXHIBIT 4-3**    BUDGET AND ACCOUNTING CLASSIFICATIONS

| | |
|---|---|
| Functions | Broad classification of governmental responsibilities, such as public safety, education, health, welfare, recreation, and general government. |
| Program or subprogram classification | Used in program budgeting to group the activities of several organizational units for the purposes of analysis and evaluation as well as the allocation of funds. |
| Activity classifications | Provide the means for organizing expenditure data according to the responsibilities of governmental units. The police department, for example, is responsible for crime investigations, traffic control, crowd control, etc. |
| Organizational unit | The designated unit within the organization, such as the police department or department of parks and recreation, authorized to hire personnel and make expenditures. |
| Character of expenditure | Aggregates of expenditures that have certain specific qualities such as current operating expenditures, capital expenditures, and debt service. Current operating expenditures represent the aggregate of personal services, contractual services, materials and supplies, and some types of equipment expenditures. |
| Object of expenditure | The lowest level of classification. Objects of expenditure are the particular types of goods bought or services received for the expenditures. Examples include such line items as personal services (salaries and wages and related employee benefits), contractual services (e.g., travel), materials and supplies, equipment, property improvements, principal and interest payments, etc. |

can be further subdivided into subobject classifications—for example, 1200 contractual services can be broken down into: 1210 general repairs; 1220 utility services; 1230 motor vehicle repairs; 1240 travel; and so forth. These categories of contractual services can be further enumerated; for example, 1240 travel might be organized as follows:

    1241   Mileage (use of private vehicles)
    1242   Automobile rentals
    1243   Fares for airlines and other public conveyance
    1244   Tolls and parking
    1245   Subsistence and lodging
    1246   Convention & educational expenses

Objects of expenditures can be aggregated under broad expenditure characteristics such as for current operations, capital expenditures, and debt service. They also can be assigned to and recorded as the expenditures of a specific organizational unit, activity classification, program and subprogram classification, and/or function of government. For example, the following sixteen-digit code:

$$23\text{-}07\text{-}105\text{-}1245\text{-}45301$$

might be used to record a travel expenditure for meals and lodging (1245) of a staff member from the department of financial management (105) under the general government function (23) in conjunction with an audit review project (45301). The code 07 might be used to designate the funding source to which this expenditure will be charged. The project code might also be used to designate the program or subprogram (45xxx) and the activity classification (xx30x). Using such multidigit codes, accounting entries can be retrieved and sorted to meet a variety of financial management purposes. This capacity to monitor and to ''crosswalk'' expenditure data for various management purposes will be discussed in further detail in Parts III and IV.

The object of expenditure classification—being the lowest and most often applied classification in budgeting and accounting—will be used in illustrations in this text. In some instances, functional and character classifications also will be used, especially in illustrating financial reporting requirements.

A budget based on objects of expenditure is readily understood by members of the governing body. This is one important reason why this budget format has survived so long in spite of its limitations. It is relatively easy to grasp the significance of a proposed increase of 10 percent in printing, data processing, or in salaries and wages. Therefore, the governing body can review and alter the minutiae of expenditures in the budget. The larger issues of efficiency and effectiveness that should be examined through the budget process, however, often remain buried in the object detail. The object classification cannot provide a basis for assessing the performance of an agency or program, nor can the progress made in the implementation of a particular set of activities be measured.

**The Budget Document**

Balancing total requested resources for expenditures against total anticipated revenues is one of the major budgeting tasks for the chief executive and his or her staff. State laws usually prohibit a jurisdiction from making expenditure commitments that exceed expected revenues. Department heads, concerned primarily with the operations of their own units, will generally submit budget requests that, in the aggregate, exceed estimated revenues. Thus the process at this stage often is one of budget cutting to bring the total budget into line with overall fiscal constraints. At the same time, however, it may be necessary and appropriate to identify new or modified fiscal policies that will provide increased resources to meet justified program needs.

An opportunity may be provided for the department heads and other agency officials to meet with the chief executive in order to explain or defend all, or selected portions, of their budget submissions. Such conferences may be wide ranging in scope or may be restricted to a few points that require further clarification prior to the final executive decision.

The executive budget document should provide a clear picture of both the programs to be carried out and the financial basis to support these activities. The budget must be designed so that it can be readily understood by members of the governing body, administrators, reporters, and citizens, as well as financial experts. Particular attention should be given to important policy decisions that must be made. The enthusiasm of technicians for complete detail often must be curtailed in the interest of clarity and simplicity. Simplicity can be achieved, however, without omitting important facts by:

1 Presenting a well-constructed budget message,
2 Choosing summaries carefully, and
3 Using charts and tables to explain service programs and the interrelationships among various elements of proposed expenditures.

### Legislative Action on the Budget

The first step in the legislative review is for the governing body to consult with the chief executive and budget staff for detailed explanations of the proposed programs and the means of financing them. The governing body, however, should not be concerned with minor details contained within the proposed budget except as these details relate to major policies and programs.

Next, public hearings are held so that citizens may express their sentiments on the budget. These hearings should be widely publicized to ensure all citizens an adequate opportunity to present their views. Since relatively few citizens attend unless they are irate over some aspect of the budget, public hearings often prove to be dismal failures. Officials should be prepared for surprises, however, as citizens may decide to attend the hearing and public officials must be prepared to answer any and all questions.

Following the public hearing, the budget may again be discussed in executive sessions. Every effort must be made to provide the governing body with a full understanding of the budget in terms of range and scope of public services it represents. Members of the governing body should receive more than a thick document, with page after page of tables, providing little or no explanation of the services or the intent of the administration. Under such circumstances, members of the governing body may feel obliged to check details of expenditures, such as the amount requested for office supplies, publications, and so forth. Such nit-picking over details arises from the absence of any broad explanation of the programs to be undertaken. As a consequence, important policy decisions involved in determining levels of public services may never be confronted directly.

On the basis of these discussions, the governing body may amend the expenditure portion of the budget and modify the proposed revenue measures. The final product of these deliberations is reported in public session and is likely to be adopted in the form thus presented. The governing body may ''approve the budget'' by *resolution*, or it may adopt a separate *appropriation ordinance* that lists specific amounts for specific agencies by specific categories of expense. An appropriation ordinance provides a more effective bench mark for administration and postauditing. However, care must be taken not to limit the ability of agencies to adjust to changing conditions in order to implement program activities during the fiscal year.

## BUDGET EXECUTION

When the appropriation and revenue measures have been adopted for the coming fiscal year, the budget is returned to the chief executive for execution—the second half of the budget cycle. All the steps of formulating and reviewing the budget are of relatively little consequence if the financial plan is not administered properly. Budget execution is both a substantive operational process and a financial process. Accounting plays a central role in these processes, both as a mechanism of fiscal control and as a source of management information. This stage of the budget cycle involves the initiation of authorized projects and programs within an established time schedule, within monetary limits, and ideally, within standard cost limits. This stage covers the full fiscal year and is the longest in the budget cycle, overlapping both the formulation and legislative review stages of the succeeding year's budget.

## Allocations and Allotments

Patterns of budget administration vary considerably from one jurisdiction to the next. In some cases, procedures consist of little more than the establishment of appropriate accounts and the recording of expenditures as they are processed for payment. This approach essentially is a cash flow bookkeeping system that tracks the outflow of funds in accordance with predetermined item accounts.

In more advanced budgetary control systems, however, the steps in administration include: (1) allocation, (2) allotment, (3) expenditure control, and (4) adjustment. Under these procedures, the budget is viewed as both a mandate for and a limit on expenditures. The operating and accounting cycles are based in the budget. The fiscal period opens with the legal adoption of the budget; it contains estimates of revenues to be collected from various sources and anticipated expenditures in the form of *appropriations*.

In effect, appropriations represent the legal authority to spend. Such authority normally is very specific about how much and for what each agency can spend. Initial accounting entries for the operating cycle of the fiscal period formally record the budget at the level of detail specified in the appropriations.

The budget appropriation is further subdivided through an *allocation process*. Allocations may be made according to objects and/or character of expenditure, activity, organizational units, programs and/or functions. For example, the appropriation to the health department might be subdivided through the allocation process to show a stipulated amount for out-patient clinics, to segregate funds for a community mental health unit, to earmark operating funds for public health nurses, and so forth. Allocations often are made for personal services (salaries, wages, and fringe benefits) and for operations, with further subdivisions of operating allocations by major line items possible (e.g., travel, materials and supplies, fixed assets or equipment, etc.). Classifications by functions or programs are especially important because current generally accepted accounting principles suggest that, as a minimum, operating expenditures in governmental funds should be classified by function in the operating statements.

Following the process of allocation, budget administrators may determine that provision should be made for an *allotment system*. Under this system, allocations are further subdivided into *time elements*, for example, monthly or quarterly allotments for personal services or for some item or group of items in the nonpersonal service categories. An allotment system is particularly appropriate in such circumstances where expenditures are contingent upon some future events, such as the availability of grants from other levels of government or the projected opening of a new capital facility. For example, assume that provision is made in the health department's budget for utility services in a new clinic. It would be inappropriate to permit these funds to be tapped before the new clinic was completed and opened. Under such an approach, the portion of the appropriation in question is retained in the unallocated category until required for actual commitment. Thus, if the facility is not completed on schedule or the intergovernmental grant is not forthcoming, monies initially earmarked for such purposes are restricted until there is a requirement for their use as originally approved.

The basic function of the allocation and allotment processes is to assign elements of the larger budget appropriation to specific categories of expenditure in order that the funds may be reserved for that category. In some cases, specific allocations may be *encumbered*, that is, reserved from the appropriation at the outset of the fiscal year. They are then *liquidated* on an "as-billed" basis (e.g., payments for employee benefits, legal services or other consultants' fees, etc.). The purpose of an encumbrance is to ensure that these funds will be available at the time needed, that is, that they will not be spent for other purposes.

## Expenditure Controls

The accounting system plays a major role in the implementation of expenditure controls. *Budgetary accounting* supplies the principal control mechanisms for enforcing allocation, allotment, and appropriation limits through periodic internal budget reports.

An *encumbrance system* (called an obligations system in the federal government) is an important feature of the emphasis of budgetary accounting on controlling spending. In addition to recording all actual expenditures, commitments for goods and services that have been ordered but not yet received must be recorded in an encumbrance system. An encumbrance simply records the placing of a purchase order or the letting of a contract against the appropriation or allocation.

An encumbrance system protects against the creation of a "floating debt," resulting from the practice of placing orders in one fiscal period to be billed in a later fiscal period. A computing facility, for example, may be required to pay a sizeable maintenance agreement on the software and hardware that is leased from the vendor. These payments may be made in four quarterly installments. The administrator of the computing center may schedule these payments so that the final quarter can be deferred to the next fiscal year should it be necessary to do so to free some additional operating funds to meet the day-to-day expenses of the center.

Since such deferred bills would become a burden on the next period, the appropriation/allocation for that period may become exhausted prematurely, thus encouraging further deferrals. While the agency may appear to stay within its budget for any given fiscal period, eventually this accumulated debt must be funded.

Control of specific expenditures is provided to the governing body through such mechanisms as:

1 Line-item appropriations,
2 Insertion of control conditions on the use of funds,

**3** The requirement of periodic budgetary reports, and
**4** The independent audit at the close of the fiscal year.

Line-item appropriations—legislative earmarking of funds for specific, detailed spending purposes—became so commonplace in the era of fiscal control (1920s) that the budget format came to be known as a *line-item budget*. The governing body may also retain some control in the budget execution stage by requiring that proposed transfers between major appropriation items have legislative approval (usually over and above some arbitrary percentage). In some jurisdictions, the state legislature imposes mandatory expenditures upon local governments (e.g., for education), and a state supervisory authority must be satisfied that the legal aspects of budgeting have been met.

## Budget Adjustments

Few public officials are gifted with twenty-twenty foresight. Appraisals of current performance and of changing conditions often necessitate significant adjustments in the budget during the fiscal year. It is common practice to schedule mid-year reviews as well as a comprehensive review during the time that the budget for the succeeding year is being prepared. Reappraisals and revised programming, however, should occur at many points to ensure adequate flexibility in operations.

Sufficient information should be maintained—through both the accounting process and contacts with individual departments—to anticipate requirements for formal budget amendments during the fiscal year. Some amendments require immediate attention; others can be handled more efficiently through a single *omnibus amendment*, ordinarily made during the final three or four months of the fiscal year. Departmental officials should take the initiative when problems come to their attention. Regardless of the action or inaction of departmental officials, however, the central budget staff has the ultimate responsibility for recommending any actions necessary to avoid fiscal crises, such as missed paydays or the lack of funds to buy critical materials or equipment.

During the final quarter of the fiscal year, revised estimates must be made of the anticipated *closing status* of any unappropriated fund balances. Specific appropriations frequently are limited as to their fiscal year carry over, that is, unspent appropriations may revert to the general treasury at the end of the fiscal year. Year-end reversion of funds often is cited as a major shortcoming of traditional budgeting procedures, since it offers no incentive for conserving resources and, in fact, promotes year-end spending.

Some appropriations may lapse at the end of the fiscal year only if they are not encumbered. Concerning the "lapsing of appropriations," the NCGA suggests that, even if encumbered, the governmental unit may elect either to honor the contracts in progress at the end of the year or to cancel them.

> If the governmental unit intends to honor them (a) encumbrances outstanding at year end should be disclosed in the notes to the financial statements or by reservations of fund balance and (b) the subsequent year's appropriation should provide authority to complete these transactions.[3]

Thus encumbrances become estimated expenditures for the unperformed portions of existing contracts for which a comparable amount of funds must be reserved in the subsequent appropriation.

Many departments will attempt to "zero-out" their appropriations or allocations as the end of the fiscal year approaches, through either actual expenditures or encumbrances. Caution must be exercised, however, that the items of expenditure or encumbrances will withstand the test of a postaudit, that is, they are eligible items of expenditure for the agency to incur. Where appropriations do not lapse at the end of the fiscal year, or where only the unencumbered portions of the appropriation lapse:

> Encumbrances outstanding at year end should be reported as reservations of fund balance for subsequent year expenditures based on the encumbered appropriation authority carried over.[4]

## Internal and External Audits

Procedures for auditing actual performance against the budget at the close of the fiscal year will be discussed in further detail in Chapter 13. Suffice it to say at this point that there are two basic types of audits: internal and external. *Internal audits* are conducted periodically by government staff and result in reports for internal management control (see Chapter 22). The *external audit* is conducted by independent accountants after the fiscal year has been completed. This audit, normally required by state law, is submitted to the regulating state agency (e.g., the auditor of public accounts) as well as to the local governing body. The governing body, in turn, should review the audit to ensure that revenue and expenditure activities have been conducted in accordance with the intentions of the budget and appropriation ordinance.

## BUDGETARY ACCOUNTING

Budgetary accounting can be applied to any of the governmental funds. It is most appropriately used, however, in connection with general and special revenue funds, where broader accountability is required. In business accounting, the general classes of accounts are:

1 Assets and liabilities, both long-term and short-term,
2 Owner's equity,
3 Revenue, and
4 Expenses.

In accounting for governmental funds, the general classes of accounts are:

1 Short-term assets and liabilities,
2 Fund balance,
3 Revenue, and
4 Expenditures.

Since only expenditures—and not expenses—are found in governmental funds, there can be no fixed assets or long-term liabilities. Expenditures are made at the time the fixed assets are purchased. Payments are made upon the expiration of the long-term liability.

## The Accounting Equation for Governmental Funds

In governmental funds, the only *assets* are those that can be converted into cash in a relatively short period of time—no more than one year. *Liabilities* in governmental funds also are only those that would be paid in cash in a relatively short period of time. An exception to this general rule are special assessment funds, where bonds payable over an extended time period may be found.

The *fund balance* is the difference between assets and liabilities and comes from the remainder between revenues and expenditures left over from this or prior years. The fund balance may also include other resources provided, such as bond proceeds or transfers from other funds. This remaining fund balance can be used as a basis for providing resources for expenditures in this or future years.

*Revenue* is the equity in resources (other than proceeds from bond issues or transfers from other funds) that is received during the fiscal period and is available to be spent in that fiscal period. *Expenditures* are the amount of resources that were expended during the year or during the normal accounting cycle if different from the year. Thus, if the city has only a certain amount of resources available to expend during the accounting cycle, management must make certain that this amount is not overspent or overcommitted for expenditure during that fiscal period.

The basic accounting equation shown in Chapter 1 and used to explain double-entry accounting for business activities is:

$$\text{Assets} = \text{Liabilities} + \text{Owner's Equity} + \text{Revenue} - \text{Expenses}$$

From an accounting standpoint in dealing with governmental funds, the basic accounting equation must be changed to show revenue and expenditures instead of revenue and expenses. In addition, there is no owner's equity as such in governmental funds. Instead of owner's equity, the residual portion of the equation would be the fund balance.

Thus the equation pertaining to governmental funds (as contrasted to proprietary funds) would read:

$$\text{Assets (current)} = \text{Liabilities (current)} + \text{Fund Balance} + \text{Revenue} - \text{Expenditures}$$

For budgetary accounting, four new items must be added to the equation:

1 Estimated revenue,
2 Appropriations,
3 Encumbrances, and
4 Reserve for encumbrances.

Estimated revenue is the amount of revenue anticipated over and above current assets that can be used as expendable resources for the fiscal period. Appropriations are the amounts of estimated resources provided by the legislative body for expenditure during the period and would be included on the liability and fund balance side of the equation. Encumbrances are used to obligate amounts for goods and services ordered but not yet received and represent a minus from the liability and fund balance side of the equation, much as expenditures do. The reserve for encumbrance account is used to allocate a portion of the appropriations for the goods and services ordered but not yet received and represents an addition to the fund balance side of the equation.

A new equation for budgetary accounting for governmental funds can be developed by using these new budgetary terms and the accounting equation for governmental funds. To make the equation easier to follow, single letters will be used to designate actual accounting elements.

A = Assets
L = Liabilities
R = Revenue
E = Expenditures

Double letters will be used for budgetary elements or partial budgetary elements within the equation.

ER = Estimated revenue
AP = Appropriations
FB = Fund balance
EN = Encumbrances
RE = Reserve for encumbrances

The fund balance account is shown with double letters in recognition of the fact that it often will have budgetary amounts. The expanded equation then is:

$$A + ER = L + FB + R - E + AP + RE - EN.$$

Following the ideas discussed in connection with the basic accounting equation, the debit and credit conditions in governmental funds under budgetary accounting are shown in Exhibit 4-4.

**EXHIBIT 4-4** DEBITS AND CREDITS TO ACCOUNTS UNDER BUDGETARY ACCOUNTING

| Debits | Credits |
| --- | --- |
| Increases in: | Decreases in: |
|   Assets |   Assets |
|   Estimated revenue |   Estimated revenue |
|   Expenditures |   Expenditures |
|   Encumbrances |   Encumbrances |
| Decreases in: | Increases in: |
|   Liabilities |   Liabilities |
|   Fund balance |   Fund balance |
|   Revenue |   Revenue |
|   Appropriations |   Appropriations |
|   Reserve for encumbrances |   Reserve for encumbrances |

## ILLUSTRATIVE BUDGETARY ACCOUNTING TRANSACTIONS

As with business accounting, the concepts expressed in the budgetary accounting equation for not-for-profit entities likewise are essential to an understanding of double-entry fund accounting in government and other nonbusiness organizations. Abstract ideas often are difficult to grasp without concrete examples, however. The following illustrations of budgetary accounting in governmental funds give an overview of these types of transactions. They show only the double-entry concepts as applied to transactions in governmental funds that use budgetary accounting—usually general or special revenue funds. When required, actual transactions are given to illustrate the budgetary transaction. An explanation of the debits and credits also is provided. These illustrations are not intended, however, to give the reader a complete understanding of the detailed transactions one may encounter in a particular governmental fund. The details concerning these variations in accounting are given in the following chapters devoted to those funds.

### Budget Adoption Transactions

The city council, after appropriate legislative review and public hearings, adopted the following budget for the recreation department:

| | |
|---|---:|
| Budgeted revenue | $150,000 |
| Budgeted expenditures (appropriations) | 145,000 |
| Increase in fund balance | $ 5,000 |

The entry to record the transaction pertaining to these budgetary figures would be:

| | Dr. | Cr. |
|---|---:|---:|
| Estimated revenue | $150,000 | |
|     Appropriations | | $145,000 |
|     Fund balance—budgetary | | 5,000 |

To record the budgetary amounts adopted by the city council.

### Encumbrance Transactions: Goods and Equipment Ordered and Received

Materials and supplies were ordered with an estimated cost of $40,000. To assure that the appropriation is not overspent, the order is encumbered against the appropriation in the accounting records. This budgetary entry is:

| | | |
|---|---:|---:|
| Encumbrances | $40,000 | |
|     Reserve for encumbrances | | $40,000 |

To encumber the materials and supplies ordered.

The ordered materials and supplies were shipped and an invoice was received in the amount of $38,000. Note that when an actual entry is made, the budgetary entry for the encumbrance is reversed at the original amount estimated for the goods ordered. The more current amount is then used to record the actual transaction. The difference between the two amounts ($40,000 and $38,000 or $2,000) then becomes available for expenditure.

| | | |
|---|---|---|
| Reserve for encumbrances | $40,000 | |
|     Encumbrances | | $40,000 |

To reverse the original entry to encumber materials and supplies on hand.

| | | |
|---|---|---|
| Expenditures—Materials and supplies | $38,000 | |
|     Accounts payable | | $38,000 |

To record the expenditure for materials and supplies.

If the goods had been received immediately, there would have been no need for encumbering the order, and the above expenditure entry would have been the only one made.

The recreation department ordered a truck estimated to cost $25,000. When received, the truck, which is a fixed asset, will be an expenditure rather than a capitalized asset. Therefore, it is encumbered upon placing the order, the same as any other operating expenditure.

| | | |
|---|---|---|
| Encumbrances | $25,000 | |
|     Reserve for encumbrances | | $25,000 |

To encumber the order for a truck.

When the truck is received, the invoice shows that it cost $26,000. Although a long-term asset, the truck is recorded as an expenditure in a governmental fund. A related entry should be made in a separate entity called a fixed asset account group (see Chapter 11) to maintain a permanent record of the truck. When the truck and the invoice are received, the original budget entry is reversed.

| | | |
|---|---|---|
| Reserve for encumbrances | $25,000 | |
|     Encumbrances | | $25,000 |

To reverse the original entry.

To set up the liability for the truck, the entry is:

| | | |
|---|---|---|
| Expenditure—Equipment, delivery | $26,000 | |
|     Accounts payable | | $26,000 |

To set up liability for truck.

The fixed asset is recorded as an expenditure—shown as a debit—while the voucher payable, a liability (also an increase) is recorded as a credit. As with the materials and supplies, if the truck had been received immediately, no entry would have been needed for the encumbrance and only the expenditure entry would have been recorded.

## Year-End Encumbrances

Since uncommitted appropriations/allocations may revert to the general treasury at the end of the fiscal year, orders often are placed to encumber these funds as the closing of the year approaches. An order was placed by the recreation department for materials and supplies estimated to cost $5,000. This entry is:

| | | |
|---|---|---|
| Encumbrance | $5,000 | |
|     Reserve for encumbrance | | $5,000 |
| To encumber order for materials and supplies. | | |

## Budget Adjustments

At times during the fiscal year, the budget may need to be adjusted to reflect additional information concerning estimated revenues and appropriations. Suppose, for example, the estimated revenue is determined to be $158,000 instead of $150,000. Often in such situations, the increase could be reflected in the fund balance account at the end of the year, and the estimated revenue account would not need to be adjusted. However, unless the fund balance account has a sufficient amount already in it, the estimated revenue account would have to be adjusted before making any additional appropriations. Assume that the department is authorized to use a portion of the additional revenue to purchase recreational equipment worth $10,000. Under the original appropriation, only $5,000 was available; therefore, the estimated revenue would have to be increased. The entries would be:

| | | |
|---|---|---|
| Estimated revenue | $8,000 | |
|     Fund balance—budgetary | | $8,000 |
| To increase estimated revenue. | | |

| | | |
|---|---|---|
| Fund balance—budgetary | $10,000 | |
|     Appropriation | | $10,000 |
| To increase amount appropriated during the year. | | |

Note that the fund balance account now would have only $3,000 left to appropriate.

Any budgetary comparison is between the revised budget and actual figures, rather than the original budget figures. When the equipment is purchased, the transaction entries would be:

| | | |
|---|---|---|
| Expenditure | $10,000 | |
|     Accounts payable | | $10,000 |
| To record the purchase of equipment. | | |

| | | |
|---|---|---|
| Accounts payable | $10,000 | |
|     Cash | | $10,000 |
| To make payment for purchase of equipment. | | |

During the fiscal year, it may become apparent that revenues are falling short of the initial estimates. If the fund balance is insufficient to take care of the amount appropriated, it obviously would be necessary to decrease the amount appropriated. Assume that the estimate of the amount of revenue to be collected in the fiscal year is revised from $150,000 to $125,000. It then becomes necessary to revise the appropriation by the same amount. The budget adjustment would be:

| | | |
|---|---|---|
| Appropriation | $25,000 | |
|     Estimated revenue | | $25,000 |
| To revise budget. | | |

The amount that can be spent, then, would only be $120,000, instead of the original $145,000.

## Closing Entries

Closing entries are made by: (1) reversing the budget adoption transactions or (2) closing the actual revenue account to the budget revenue account (estimated revenue) and the actual expenditures account to the appropriation account. Any differences are closed to the fund balance account.

Let us assume that: (1) encumbrances do not lapse, (2) the revised budget included an increase of $8,000 in estimated revenue and increased appropriations of $10,000, (3) actual revenue for the year totaled $160,000, (4) actual expenditures against the appropriations were $150,000, and (5) $5,000 in appropriations were encumbered at the end of the year for the order of supplies.

Using the first method, the closing entry made by reversing the original budget adoption entry would be:

| | | |
|---|---|---|
| Appropriation | $155,000 | |
| Fund balance—Budgetary | 3,000 | |
|     Estimated revenue | | $158,000 |
| To close budgetary accounts. | | |

The closing entry related to actual revenue and expenditures is:

| | | |
|---|---|---|
| Revenue | $160,000 | |
|     Expenditures | | $150,000 |
|     Encumbrances | | 5,000 |
|     Fund balance | | 5,000 |
| To close the revenue, expenditures, and encumbrances accounts. | | |

An alternative approach is to reverse the original encumbrance entry and place the difference into the fund balance account. Then the reserve for encumbrance amount is set up as a reservation of the fund balance. This is illustrated as follows:

| | | |
|---|---|---|
| Reserve for encumbrance | $5,000 | |
|     Encumbrance | | $5,000 |
| To reverse encumbrance entry. | | |

| | | |
|---|---|---|
| Revenue | $160,000 | |
|     Expenditures | | $150,000 |
|     Fund balance | | 10,000 |
| To close actual accounts. | | |

| | | |
|---|---|---|
| Fund balance | $5,000 | |
|     Reserve for encumbrance | | $5,000 |

To set up a reservation of fund balance for the encumbered amount.

Using the second method of closing the accounts, revenue is closed to estimated revenue, with the difference going to the fund balance. This entry would be as follows:

| | | |
|---|---|---|
| Revenue | $160,000 | |
|     Estimated revenue | | $158,000 |
|     Fund balance | | 2,000 |

To close revenue and estimated revenue accounts.

Then the encumbrances, expenditures, and appropriations accounts are closed. The encumbrance account is closed to the appropriations account, leaving the reserve for encumbrance account open as a reservation of the fund balance. This entry is:

| | | |
|---|---|---|
| Appropriations | $5,000 | |
|     Encumbrances | | $5,000 |

To close the encumbrances account to the appropriations account.

The expenditure closing is:

| | | |
|---|---|---|
| Appropriations | $150,000 | |
|     Expenditures | | $150,000 |

To close the expenditure account to the appropriations account.

If there were any balance in the appropriations account, it also would be closed into the fund balance account. The second method of closing accounts will be used in this book.

## USE OF SUBSIDIARY LEDGERS

The city needs to maintain a running comparison of actual revenue and expenditures with budgeted revenue and expenditures. In addition to recording the above journal entries in general ledger accounts, therefore, the individual amounts would also be recorded in a subsidiary ledger. Accounts would be kept in the subsidiary ledger for the particular budgeted revenue, appropriations, actual revenue, expenditures, and encumbrances accounts.

    The city would also have to keep records in much greater detail in the subsidiary ledgers for a breakdown of classes of revenue and expenditures other than those usually shown in the general ledger. For example, licenses and permits may be of several types—automobile licenses, business licenses, dog licenses, building permits, etc. By using subsidiary accounts and ledgers, the accountant should be able to provide detail on almost any account needed. Maintaining all of the detail in the general ledger would be almost impossible, even for a small municipality (see Exhibits 5-4 and 6-3 as illustrations).

Many of the line-item expenditures would also be recorded in subsidiary ledgers. It would be almost impossible, for example, to keep track of all the necessary detail on the line items for functions, subfunctions, and departments without placing these details in subsidiary ledgers.

The Municipal Finance Officers Association in its *Governmental Accounting, Auditing, and Financial Reporting* provides an excellent statement concerning the purpose of subsidiary ledger accounts.

> The General Fund of most governments has many sources of revenue and, hence, a need for numerous general ledger revenue accounts. A great many expenditure accounts are also normally required. Excessive general ledger accounts are very inconvenient to work with. Most governments, therefore, use general ledger control accounts and subsidiary ledgers.
>
> A subsidiary ledger includes numerous detailed accounts, balances of which in total agree with the balance of a particular general ledger account. A general ledger account supported by a subsidiary ledger is called a general ledger *control* account. Through the use of subsidiary ledgers, a government can maintain a large number of individual accounts without cluttering up its general ledger.[5]

The general fund, for example, might include separate accounts for revenues from taxes, licenses and fees, intergovernmental transfers, other financing sources, and so on. A single expenditure general ledger control account often will be supported by several different expenditure subsidiary ledgers to provide multiple expenditure classifications—classifications by fund, function or program, organizational unit, activity, character, and object code.

## SUMMARY

This chapter has provided the basis for understanding the budget function and budgetary accounting in the activities of government and, in particular, in governmental funds. This understanding serves as a foundation for the accounting systems that provide financial statements and reports that can be audited in accordance with generally accepted accounting principles. This basic understanding of budgeting and budgetary accounting also is transferable to accounting procedures for other not-for-profit organizations discussed in Part II.

Budgetary and related accounting systems also can be adapted to appropriate management accounting systems useful for organizational decision making and control processes in government and other not-for-profit organizations. These adaptations are discussed in Parts III and IV.

## QUESTIONS

1. Identify the basic objectives of public budgeting in terms of the functions of planning, management, and control.
2. What major characteristics of a capital budget distinguish it from an operating budget?
3. Identify five specific objectives of an operating budget. What is the legal status of the budget in most local jurisdictions?
4. What is the purpose of a budget calendar?

5 What is the purpose of a budget guidance memorandum issued at the outset of each budget cycle?
6 If each department completes the required budget forms to reflect a "best estimate" as to the resources required to carry out the programs within its legislative mandate, why is it necessary to make significant budget cuts during the executive review?
7 Identify the basic components of the budget document as it is presented by the chief executive for review by the governing body.
8 Distinguish between budget allocations and allotments.
9 What is the purpose of requiring approval by the governing body of transfers between appropriation items in the budget?
10 Year-end reversion of funds often is cited as a major shortcoming of traditional budgeting procedures. Why?
11 What is the purpose of a budget classification system, and how are revenue and expenditures classified under this system?
12 Define object classification and its purpose.
13 Give the advantages and disadvantages of the object-of-expenditure budget format.
14 Define: estimated revenue, appropriations, encumbrances, and reserve for encumbrances.
15 What is involved in the closing process for budgetary accounting?
16 Explain the accounting equation as used in governmental fund accounting with budgetary control.
17 Explain the purpose of encumbrances in governmental accounting with budgetary control.
18 Give the journal entry for recording a budget in the accounting records.
19 Give the journal entry for recording a purchase order for supplies worth $10,000 that will be delivered in three months.
20 Give the journal entries upon delivery of these supplies, assuming that the goods cost $11,000.

## PROBLEMS

**4-1** The city of Rurbania has experienced considerable growth during the past several years. As a consequence, the city has been faced with rapidly expanding demands for new and improved public facilities and services. The impact of inflation on governmental operations, coupled with rising personnel costs, has brought the city to a critical fiscal position. There is a general reluctance among city council members to increase local taxes or to adjust fee schedules adequately to accommodate for the rising costs of government. As a result, the city's revenue base in recent years has not kept pace with the increased demand for services. The council has been able to maintain a balanced budget, however, and has not been forced to resort to deficit financing insofar as operating expenditures are concerned.

In an effort to meet these fiscal challenges, the city council has authorized the expansion of the financial management department staff to facilitate the development of improved budgeting techniques and cost-managerial accounting procedures. Bud G. Etary, director of the budget division, has developed the personnel schedule (see Exhibit 4-5) and the budget comments (see Exhibit 4-6). Nine new positions are requested for the next fiscal year. These positions include: accountant II, budget analyst II, budget analyst I, computer programmer, computer operator II, account clerk II, keypunch operator, and two clerk typists II.

Etary's first task was to accommodate these new staffing requirements in the *personnel schedule* for the next fiscal year. All new positions are to be added at the entry level of the appropriate monthly salary range. Continuing employees will receive a merit increase of 6.5 percent for supervisory personnel and 8 percent for operations personnel. Supervisory employees include those positions above the level of an administrative assistant, while the balance of the staff is in the operations category.

*Assignment 1*: The first task is to complete the salary request data for the next fiscal year to arrive at the subtotals shown in Exhibit 4-5. All operations personnel are eligible for overtime payments; 5 percent of total salary requirements for these employees forms the basis for this overtime allowance in the budget request. Calculate the overtime allowance for the next fiscal year to be shown in Exhibit 4-5. Employee benefits (retirement and pension benefits, social security contributions, federal old-age insurance, group and medical/hospitalization insurance) are calculated at 10 percent of total salaries for all employees. Calculate the benefits for the thirty-eight employees of the department and the total personal service request for the next fiscal year.

Bud G. Etary next began the incremental calculations for the various categories of operations support. Under contractual services, he estimated that the majority of the cost categories (object codes) would require an 8 percent increase over current funding levels, the exceptions being general repairs (7.85 percent), utility services (8.33 percent), and computing services (25 percent). Under supplies and materials, Etary estimated that 6 percent should be sufficient to accommodate the cost increase due to both inflation and staff expansion.

*Assignment 2*: Complete the budget data for contractual services to reach the subtotal of $106,190 for the next fiscal year (round all calculations to the nearest five-dollar increment). Complete the budget data for supplies and materials in Exhibit 4-6 (pages 110–111) to reach the subtotal of $34,805.

Equipment requests are (or should be) independent of funding in prior budget years (i.e., they are not built incrementally in terms of a percentage increase over the previous year's commitments). However, previous commitments can provide some indication of the level of funding required in requesting equipment funds. Etary decided to request $845 to provide office equipment for the new personnel and $270 for related electrical equipment (e.g., desk lamps, desk calculators, etc.). Data processing equipment is one of the few items that has been coming down in price; Etary budgeted $12,000 for five additional CRT terminals.

*Assignment 3*: Complete the budget data for equipment to reach the subtotal of $13,115 shown in Exhibit 4-6. The budget requests developed by Bud G. Etary for the final two items—current obligations and employee benefits—are shown in Exhibit 4-6. By completing the entries for personal services from the summary data in Exhibit 4-5, you should now be able to determine the total budget request for the financial management department for the next fiscal year.

**Discussion Questions:**
1 On the basis of these traditional budgeting procedures, what can the members of the city council determine regarding the expenditure requirements of the financial management department as they might relate to the functions of this agency and the programs that it is required to carry out?
2 Is adequate justification provided by these budget data for the required staff increases? How would you evaluate the requested increase in general fund support ($114,630 over the current budget) in terms of the anticipated changes in budget format and accounting procedures?
3 How do the actual expenditures during the last fiscal year relate to the current budget and to the requested funding levels for the next fiscal year?
4 Since salaries, overtime payments, and employee benefits are interrelated and account

**EXHIBIT 4-5** PERSONNEL SCHEDULE

| FUND | DEPARTMENT | FUNCTION |
|---|---|---|
| General | Financial management | General government |

The department is composed of the city treasurer's office, the budget division, the division of accounts, the data processing section, and the purchasing office. The city treasurer is responsible for all cash disbursements, maintaining cash position, administering tax collections, and managing investments. The budget division supervises the formulation and administration of the operating and capital budgets. The division of accounts directs the general accounting and payroll activities and coordinates the debt administration programs of the city. The data processing section provides management information to assist officials in their decision-making processes. The purchasing office acts as the central purchasing agent for the city.

| | Employees | | Monthly salary range | Current budget | Next fiscal year |
|---|---|---|---|---|---|
| Title | Curr. FY | Next FY | | | |
| City treasurer | 1 | 1 | $1250–1700 | $ 17,000 | $ 18,105 |
| Budget director | 1 | 1 | $1250–1700 | 16,800 | 17,890 |
| Data process. dir. | 1 | 1 | $1250–1700 | 16,500 | |
| Purchasing manager | 1 | 1 | $1100–1500 | 15,000 | |
| Systems analyst | 2 | 2 | $1050–1450 | 27,600 | 29,400 |
| Accountant III | 1 | 1 | $ 950–1250 | 13,200 | |
| Senior programmer | 1 | 1 | $ 900–1200 | 12,000 | |
| Buyer | 1 | 1 | $ 850–1125 | 11,700 | |
| Administ. analyst | 1 | 1 | $ 850–1125 | 10,800 | |
| Budget analyst II | 2 | 3 | $ 850–1125 | 21,600 | 33,205 |
| Accountant II | 1 | 2 | $ 800–1050 | 10,800 | |
| Budget analyst I | 0 | 1 | $ 750–1000 | — | |
| Programmer | 1 | 2 | $ 750–1000 | 9,600 | 19,825 |
| Administ. assist. | 1 | 1 | $ 700– 950 | 9,000 | |
| Computer operator II | 1 | 2 | $ 600– 800 | 8,400 | |
| Cashier I | 1 | 1 | $ 500– 700 | 6,600 | |
| Secretary III | 3 | 3 | $ 500– 700 | 20,400 | |
| Account clerk II | 1 | 2 | $ 500– 700 | 6,000 | |
| Bookkeep. mach. oper. | 1 | 1 | $ 470– 630 | 6,000 | |
| Key punch operator | 1 | 2 | $ 470– 630 | 6,000 | |
| Clerk typist II | 6 | 8 | $ 375– 400 | 33,020 | |
| Subtotals | 29 | 38 | | $278,020 | $363,760 |
| Add: Overtime | | | | $ 5,250 | $ |
| Benefits | | | | $ 27,800 | $ |
| Total | | | | $309,595 | $408,130 |

for over 70 percent of the total budget request for the department, is a more thorough cost analysis of other objects of expenditure really necessary? If so, why?

4-2 Select the best answer for each of the following.[6]

1 Encumbrances would not appear in which fund?
   a Capital projects
   b Special revenue
   c General
   d Enterprise

**EXHIBIT 4-6**    CURRENT AND PROJECTED BUDGET COMMITMENTS

| FUND | DEPARTMENT | FUNCTION |
|---|---|---|
| General | Financial management | General government |

**BUDGET COMMENTS**

The current budget for the financial management department is 7.14 percent (or $30,339) higher than the level of expenditure for the previous fiscal year. The projected budget request for the next fiscal year represents a 25.2% increase over the current budget. The major increases anticipated are in Personal Services (31.24%), Employee Benefits (30.86%), and Contractual Services (20.49%). Staff increases (9 new positions are requested) are required to accommodate the additional workload brought about by proposed changes in budget format and accounting procedures. These additional positions account for $61,440 (69.4%) of the $88,480 increase in salaries. The remaining increase is the result of scheduled salary adjustments. The major increase under Contractual Services is for data processing (25%). A decrease in data processing equipment costs is anticipitated, however.

| Object classifications | Last fiscal year | Current budget | Next fiscal year |
|---|---|---|---|
| Personal services | | | |
|   1100 Salaries | $257,425 | $278,020 | |
|   1120 Wages | 0 | 0 | |
|   1130 Special payments | 0 | 0 | |
|   1140 Overtime payments | 4,860 | 5,250 | |
| Subtotal: Personal services | $262,285 | $283,270 | $371,750 |
| Contractual services | | | |
|   1210 General repairs | $ 648 | $ 700 | |
|   1220 Utility services | 3,333 | 3,600 | |
|   1230 Motor vehicle repairs | 462 | 500 | |
|   1240 Travel | 1,925 | 2,100 | |
|   1250 Professional services | 5,300 | 5,725 | |
|   1260 Communications | 6,278 | 6,780 | |
|   1270 Printing | 926 | 1,000 | |
|   1280 Computing services | 53,037 | 64,725 | |
|   1290 Other contract services | 2,777 | 3,000 | |
| Subtotal: Contractual services | $ 74,686 | $ 88,130 | $106,190 |
| Supplies and materials | | | |
|   1310 Office supplies | $ 27,776 | $ 29,440 | |
|   1320 Fuel supplies | 0 | 0 | |
|   1330 Operating supplies | 944 | 1,000 | |
|   1340 Maintenance supplies | 849 | 900 | |
|   1350 Drugs & chemicals | 0 | 0 | |
|   1360 Food supplies | 0 | 0 | |
|   1370 Clothing & linens | 0 | 0 | |
|   1380 Ed. & recreation supplies | 0 | 0 | |
|   1390 Other supplies | 1,415 | 1,500 | |
| Subtotal: Supplies and materials | $ 30,984 | $ 32,840 | $ 34,805 |
| Equipment | | | |
|   1410 Office equipment | $ 713 | $ 700 | |
|   1420 Electrical equipment | 0 | 250 | |
|   1430 Motor vehicles | 4,300 | 0 | |
|   1440 Highway equipment | 0 | 0 | |
|   1450 Medical & lab equipment | 0 | 0 | |
|   1480 Data processing equipment | 20,000 | 15,000 | |
|   1490 Other equipment | 0 | 0 | |
| Subtotal: Equipment | $ 25,013 | $ 16,020 | $ 13,115 |

**EXHIBIT 4-6** (*continued*)

| | | | |
|---|---:|---:|---:|
| Current obligations | | | |
| 1510 Payments to sinking funds | 0 | 0 | 0 |
| 1520 Interest on temporary loans | 1,000 | 0 | 0 |
| 1530 Rental charges | 0 | 0 | 0 |
| 1540 Insurance | 250 | 300 | 350 |
| 1550 Dues & subscriptions | 4,000 | 5,000 | 5,300 |
| 1560 Electrostatic reproduction | 1,545 | 1,640 | 1,740 |
| 1590 Other obligations | 0 | 0 | 0 |
| Subtotal: Current obligations | $ 6,795 | $ 6,940 | $ 7,390 |
| Employee Benefits | | | |
| 1610 Retire. & pension benefits | $ 7,774 | $ 8,780 | $ 11,495 |
| 1620 Social security contrib. | 7,286 | 8,229 | 10,768 |
| 1630 Federal old-age insurance | 1,319 | 1,168 | 1,529 |
| 1640 Group insurance | 640 | 724 | 945 |
| 1650 Medical/hospital. insurance | 7,879 | 8,899 | 11,643 |
| Subtotal: Employee benefits | $ 24,898 | $ 27,800 | $ 36,380 |
| Totals | $424,661 | $455,000 | |

2 A city's general fund budget for the forthcoming fiscal year shows estimated revenue in excess of appropriations. The initial effects of recording this will result in an increase in:
   a  Taxes receivable
   b  Fund balance
   c  Reserve for encumbrances
   d  Encumbrances

3 Which of the following accounts is a budgetary account in governmental accounting?
   a  Reserve for inventory of supplies
   b  Fund balance
   c  Appropriations
   d  Estimated uncollectible property taxes

4 Which account represents the equity of a nonenterprise fund?
   a  Net assets
   b  Fund balance
   c  Reserves
   d  Unencumbered balance

5 If a credit was made to the fund balance in the process of recording a budget for a governmental unit, it can be assumed that:
   a  Estimated revenue exceeds appropriations.
   b  Estimated expenses exceed actual revenue.
   c  Actual expenses exceed estimated expenses.
   d  Appropriations exceed estimated revenue.

6 Which of the following will increase the fund balance of a governmental unit at the end of the fiscal year?
   a  Appropriations are less than expenditures and reserve for encumbrances.
   b  Appropriations are less than expenditures and encumbrances.
   c  Appropriations are more than estimated revenues.
   d  Appropriations are more than expenditures and encumbrances.

4-3 The council for the town of Boothbay is worried that the new proposition 13–type act that the state has passed will decrease its revenue substantially. Previously, property was taxed at a rate of ten mills per 50 percent of assessed value. The new state law calls for a new rate of fifteen mills but only on one-third of assessed value. Total property value in the town amounts to $56 million.

In an effort to raise additional revenue, the sales tax was raised to 6 percent. Council members expect this to provide $75,000. Licenses and permits are expected to contribute $16,000. Money from parking meters is estimated at $4,300. Aid from the state will be $50,000.

The council is being forced to cut back on expenditures due to the decrease in revenue. Salaries have been cut and some assistants have been laid off from their jobs. Appropriations have been made for salaries in the amount of $280,000, while supplies and travel have received $40,000. Capital outlays and debt servicing have received appropriations of $35,000 and $60,000, respectively.

Actual revenue from property taxes amounted to $280,000. The increased sales tax provided only $65,000 and licenses and permits provided $18,000. Revenue from the parking meters was $4,000. Aid from the state totaled $50,000.

The town's manager fully used the money in each category that had been appropriated by the council. The fund balance at the beginning of the year was $28,000.

**Required**:
1 Based upon these data, prepare the necessary journal entries, including closing entries.
2 Prepare a statement showing an analysis of the fund balance.

4-4 An appropriation was made by the town of Two Lights for supplies in the amount of $17,000. During the year, the following transactions occurred:

  1 The town ordered supplies on January 15 at an estimated cost of $4,000.
  2 The town paid $6,300 on February 20 for supplies that had been ordered the previous year and for which a reserve for encumbrance had been set up in the amount of $6,500.
  3 The town ordered supplies on May 15 at an estimated cost of $1,100.
  4 Because of a backlog of orders, the supplier was not able to deliver the goods ordered on January 15 until July 2. The actual cost of the goods was $3,650.
  5 On September 13, additional supplies estimated to cost $5,900 were ordered.
  6 Supplies ordered on May 15 were received on November 5, accompanied by an invoice for $1,100.
  7 On December 20, the town bought $5,000 worth of supplies for cash for its annual Christmas celebration.
  8 At year end, the supplies ordered on September 13 still had not been received. All other supplies ordered during the year had been paid in full, except for $300 worth of the supplies ordered on May 15 and received November 5.

**Required**:
Read all the transactions carefully. Using all the information in the chapter, prepare the necessary journal entries. Also, prepare an analysis of the supplies expenditure account.

4-5 Governmental accounting gives substantial recognition to budgets, with those budgets being recorded in the accounts of the governmental unit.[7]

**Required**:
1 What is the purpose of a governmental accounting system, and why is the budget recorded in the accounts of a governmental unit? Include in your discussion the purpose and significance of appropriations.
2 Describe when and how a governmental unit records its budget and closes it out.

**4-6** The original budget for the city of Five Miles was as follows:

| | |
|---|---|
| Estimated revenue | $500,000 |
| Fund balance | 100,000 |
| Appropriation | $600,000 |

By taking $100,000 from the fund balance account and appropriating it to the various departments, the fund balance account then became zero.

During the year, the finance department estimated that the payment of taxes and licenses would be short by at least $50,000 from the estimated amount. Thus they considered it necessary for the city council to reduce the appropriation by a like amount if the budget was to comply with state regulations. The city council then reduced the appropriation amount by $50,000.

**Required**:
1 Prepare the original budgetary accounting entry.
2 Prepare the entry needed to revise the budgetary accounts in the accounting records.

## NOTES

1 Frederick C. Mosher, *Public Budgeting* (Chicago: Public Administration Service, 1954), p. 5.
2 For a further discussion of these distinctions, see Alan Walter Steiss, *Local Government Finance: Capital Facilities Planning and Debt Administration* (Lexington, Mass.: Lexington Books—D.C. Heath and Co., 1975).
3 National Council on Governmental Accounting, *Statement 1. Governmental Accounting and Financial Reporting Principles* (Chicago: Municipal Finance Officers Association of the United States and Canada, 1979), p. 14.
4 Ibid., p. 14.
5 Municipal Finance Officers Association of the United States and Canada, *Governmental Accounting, Auditing, and Financial Reporting* (Chicago: Municipal Finance Officers Association of the United States and Canada, 1981), p. 37.
6 Adapted from American Institute of Certified Public Accountants, *Uniform CPA Examination Questions and Unofficial Answers* (New York: American Institute of Certified Public Accountants, various dates).
7 Ibid., Nov. 1981.

# CHAPTER 5

# GENERAL AND SPECIAL REVENUE FUNDS— BUDGETARY AND REVENUE TRANSACTIONS

A *general fund* accounts for all of the resources of the governmental unit except for those resources that are required—legally or administratively—to be accounted for in some other fund. *Special revenue funds* account for resources especially earmarked for a certain purpose—school and library operations, for example. In these cases, a special revenue, such as a school or library tax or a grant, is designated for that special purpose. In prior years, some municipalities used two or more general funds (e.g., a general fund for general operations and a general fund for school board operations). Presently, only one general fund is proper and that is for general operations of the municipality. The school board operations is a special revenue fund.

Accounting procedures for both the general fund and the special revenue funds are considered identical, except for the revenue sources. In this chapter, when discussing certain procedures for a general fund, those same procedures also apply to special revenue funds. Any specific differences in practices in either a general fund or a special revenue fund will be commented on separately under the specific topic being covered.

Some localities account for federal revenue-sharing money or other restricted monies in a special revenue fund, rather than going directly to the fund that eventually receives the revenue-sharing money. One advantage of this practice is that the accountant can monitor the disposal of the revenue-sharing funds fairly easily.

Current accepted principles of financial reporting require that the statements from governmental funds having several funds of a particular type (e.g., several special revenue funds) prepare combining statements. Combining statements bring together the information from the reports for two or more funds of a given type into one report. Thus a combining balance sheet and a combining statement of revenues, expenditures, and changes in fund balance would be prepared if there are two or more special revenue funds. This type of statement is illustrated in Chapter 13.

# CHAPTER 5: GENERAL AND SPECIAL REVENUE FUNDS—BUDGETARY AND REVENUE TRANSACTIONS

One of the better ways to learn a new area of accounting—in this case budgetary accounting and accounting for the general and special revenue funds of government—is by using the concepts and applying the practices of double-entry accounting. This method is used for discussing the new topics and, where applicable, for illustrative applications of the subjects, not only in this chapter but throughout the book. Discussions concerning specific topics related to general and special revenue funds will be followed by illustrative journal-entry applications of those subjects. As in Chapters 2 and 3, illustrative transactions will continue to be recorded for a fictitious city—the city of Ruthberg. Since general and special revenue funds follow the same accounting style for specific transactions, it is not necessary to illustrate a specific special revenue fund for this city.

Summary journal entries for the various types of transactions and a worksheet that brings together all of the transactions will be used to gather the information from the accounts in order to show the placement of each account in the financial statements.

In this chapter, the following subjects will be discussed and illustrated.

**1** Budgets and budgetary accounting,
**2** Basis of accounting,
**3** Revenue accounting, and
**4** Illustrative worksheet—Revenue transactions for the general fund of city of Ruthberg

## BUDGETS AND BUDGETARY ACCOUNTING

Accounting and reporting systems for general and special revenue funds should provide information concerning the accountability for revenue raised and spent to furnish services to the constituents of the governmental unit. In general and special revenue funds, the usual method to assure this accountability is through budgets and budgetary accounting. Other governmental funds also may use budgetary accounting; however, general and special revenue funds are the primary entities that use this type of control as the means of assuring accountability for the resources raised and spent for those funds.

Chapter 4 discussed the reasoning behind budgetary accounting and gave illustrative transactions pertaining to it. The transactions for the fictitious city will further discuss and illustrate budgetary accounting transactions. Two additional points concerning budgetary accounting need further discussion and illustration at this time—allocations and allotments.

### Allocations and Allotments

Allocations were defined in Chapter 4 as the reservation of budgetary appropriations for specific categories of expenditures. These appropriations were reserved in order to ensure that sufficient resources would be available when the condition concerning the expenditures from the allocation were met. Allotments were defined as the division of specific allocations of appropriations into time periods, along with the reservation of the appropriation.

To illustrate the accounting for allocations and allotments, let us suppose that the town of Smithfield receives a grant from the state government for the operation of a town library. The condition of the grant is that the town must pay for one-half of the operations before any of the grant money can be spent. The town establishes a special revenue fund—the library fund—for the purpose of receiving the grant, transferring the money from the general fund, and operating the library.

In the general fund, the normal budgetary process occurs, along with an appropriation of $100,000 to the library fund for help in operating the library. Since the money needed for operating the library will not be available unless the grant from the state is approved, the appropriation will be reserved through an allocation of the appropriation. The journal entry for this transaction is

|  | Dr. | Cr. |
|---|---|---|
| Appropriation | $100,000 |  |
|    Unallocated appropriation |  | $100,000 |

To show that the resources for the library's operations, while available, have not been allocated to the library.

Normally, these appropriations and allocations are made in the general ledger accounts of the general fund as well as in subsidiary ledgers.

The general fund administrators agreed, even though the appropriation had been made, that no payment would be made to the library fund until it was certain that the state's grant would be available. They also stipulated that the appropriation would be allotted in quarterly payments of $25,000.

The town, meanwhile, received notice that the state grant had been fully approved, and the cash was available. So all revenue-recognition criteria would be met when cash was received from the general fund. Once the general fund administrators learn that the library fund has received notice of the grant's approval, they can change the category of the appropriation from unallocated to unallotted. The following journal entry would be made:

|  | Dr. | Cr. |
|---|---|---|
| Unallocated appropriation | $100,000 |  |
|    Unallotted appropriation |  | $100,000 |

To change category of appropriation from unallocated to unallotted.

The general fund pays one-quarter of the appropriation and makes the following journal entries:

|  | Dr. | Cr. |
|---|---|---|
| Unallotted appropriation | $25,000 |  |
|    Allotted appropriation |  | $25,000 |

To allot $25,000 to the library fund.

|  |  |  |
|---|---|---|
| Operating transfer to library fund | $25,000 |  |
|    Cash |  | $25,000 |

To pay library fund amount due.

In the library fund, the following entries would be made:

| | | |
|---|---|---|
| Cash | $25,000 | |
|     Operating transfer | | $25,000 |

To establish operating transfer from general fund.

| | | |
|---|---|---|
| Cash | $25,000 | |
|     Operating grant | | $25,000 |

To record that the State grant was received.

These same procedures would be followed for the next three quarters for entries in both the general fund and the library fund. Also, entries would have to be made in both the general fund and the library fund in subsidiary ledgers for these transactions.

These transactions illustrate only the entries concerning allocations and allotments. All of the other entries would have to be made concerning the operations in both the library fund and the general fund.

## BASIS OF ACCOUNTING

In describing the *basis of accounting* for general and special revenue funds, the Municipal Finance Officers Association says:

> the focus of general and special revenue fund accounting is on sources and uses of "available spendable resources" rather than on costs of services. They are, therefore, accounted for on a spending measurement focus and using the modified accrual basis of accounting.[1]

The modified accrual basis of accounting used in general and special revenue funds recognizes revenue in the period in which it is both measurable and available. Measurable and available, according to NCGA's *Interpretation 3*, is when revenue is susceptible to accrual. Thus property taxes would be accrued if due and collected during the current period or expected to be collected within sixty days thereafter and available for expenditures during the current fiscal period.[2] Expenditures are recognized in the accounting period in which the fund liability is incurred, if measurable, except for unmatured interest on general long-term debt. This unmatured interest on general long-term debt should be recognized when due. Inventory items can be recognized either when purchased or when used. In general, prepaid expenses are not shown.[3]

One major difference between recognition of revenue and expenditures in the general and special revenue funds and income and expenses in the normal business-type enterprise can be seen in the treatment of estimated losses on receivables. Estimated losses on bad debts in business activities typically are charged as expenses. In governmental funds, since from a spending measurement focus no revenue is expended, estimated losses from taxes receivable are a deduction from revenue. For example, if taxes receivable amounted to $102,000 and estimated losses were $2,000, the entry for this transaction would be:

|  | Dr. | Cr. |
|---|---|---|
| Taxes receivable—current | $102,000 | |
|    Allowance for uncollectible | | |
|      taxes receivable—current | | $ 2,000 |
|    Revenues | | 100,000 |

If the allowance were considered an expenditure rather than a deduction from revenue, this amount would have to be provided for through an appropriation in the budget. Since no resources will be spent, it is better to provide for this transaction by deducting the estimated uncollectible from the revenue source—taxes receivable—and reducing the revenue amount rather than increasing the expenditure.

The GASB is currently studying the issues related to measurement focus and basis of accounting. Until some change is made in the basis of accounting, the method presented is in compliance with current GAAP.

## REVENUE ACCOUNTING

General fund revenue usually is derived from several different sources. Ad valorem taxes on real property and often on personal property, and self-assessment taxes on personal income, corporate income, and sales are among the more dominant revenue sources for local governments. Licenses and permits, fines and forfeits, and fees for services rendered to other governmental units (e.g., for the housing of prisoners), often called intergovernmental services, represent major sources of so-called "miscellaneous revenue." Revenue sharing and grants, either from the federal or state governments, have increasingly become important sources of revenue for local governments in recent years. Grants and gifts from private foundations and individuals represent yet another source of general fund revenue.

In addition, enterprise-type activities, such as the utility fund, the water and sewer fund, or other types of activities operating for a profit, often provide revenue for general fund operations. These transactions would be operating transfers unless they were reasonable payments, such as in lieu of taxes.

In accounting for each of these various types of revenue, some variations may be found that usually are not encountered in the accounting of for-profit enterprises. Some revenue, however, is very similar to that in business: revenue from licenses and permits, fines and forfeits, intergovernmental services, and other miscellaneous revenue is often accounted for in much the same manner as revenue from any business activity that collects money for services. Other revenue, such as ad valorem taxes, self-assessment taxes, and revenue sharing and grants need additional explanation before their accounting procedures can be illustrated.

### Ad Valorem Taxes

Ad valorem taxes are composed of two elements—a value and a rate. In a number of states, localities are now required to assess property at full market value (or as near to full value as possible), thus eliminating one of the variables in the ad valorem equation. The assessed value of property is placed on the tax rolls, usually by the tax assessor, showing the particular characteristics of the property as well as the value. The assessor applies a millage rate (a mill is one-tenth of one cent) to the assessed value to determine the taxes owed. For example, if property is assessed at 50 percent of its fair market value and the fair market value is $50,000, then the assessed value is $25,000. If the millage rate is 14 mills per dollar of assessed value, then the taxes are $350 for this particular parcel of property ($25,000 × .014 = $350). The millage rate can be stated as 14 mills per dollar, 1.4 cents per dollar, $1.40 per hundred dollars, or $14 per $1,000 of assessed value.

Tax bills are usually prepared from the tax rolls and sent to the taxpayer annually or semiannually. A taxes receivable subsidiary record is kept for each taxpayer of the governmental unit owning real property. This is similar to the record kept of accounts receivable for each credit customer of a business enterprise.

When taxes receivable are due and expected to be collected within sixty days after the close of the accounting period, revenue from the taxes is recognized as current revenue. When the taxes receivable are expected to be collected sometime after sixty days beyond the close of the current period, the revenue from the taxes is considered deferred revenue. This deferred revenue will be recognized as revenue in the accounting period in which the taxes receivable are expected to be collected.

The total of all of the taxes receivable for the accounting period, less the amounts for expected uncollectible taxes and deferred revenue, would constitute the revenue for the current accounting period from the ad valorem taxes. The estimated amount of uncollectible taxes is derived from taxes that are estimated to be uncollectible over the life of this year's taxes receivable and other unknown situations, such as errors in computing the taxes, that result in the taxes receivable never being collected.

If the taxes are not paid during the current year, they become delinquent and require additional amounts to be paid by the taxpayer for penalties and interest. Shown as interest and penalties receivable, they also should have an account showing the amounts for estimated uncollectible interest and penalties. The net amount would be shown as revenue for the current period.

Experience of most cities shows that a certain percentage of the assessed taxes are not paid during the current year but are paid in subsequent years. The amounts not paid during the current bill-paying cycle obviously would not result in current revenue, but rather deferred revenue. To illustrate the deferral of revenue from ad valorem taxes assume the following:

**1** The municipality's fiscal year is from July 1 to June 30.

**2** Tax rolls show assessed taxes of $1 million for the fiscal year ending June 30, 19X1.

**3** Taxes are assessed on July 1 and are payable before December 1, when they become delinquent. Prior years' experience shows:

    **a** Approximately 1 percent ($10,000) of the gross taxes will have to be written off as uncollectible.

    **b** About 95 percent ($950,000) of the gross taxes receivable will be collected during the current bill-paying cycle (July 1, 19X0–August 29, 19X1). Of the $950,000, $925,000 was collected before December 1, 19X0, and $25,000 was collected after December 1. Interest and penalties of $5,000 were assessed on delinquent taxes, of which $1,5000 was collected.

**c** Approximately 50 percent of the balance of the $50,000 delinquent taxes ($25,000) will be collected during the next year's bill-paying cycle (August 30, 19X1–August 29, 19X2).

**d** The balance of the delinquent taxes receivable will be collected in the following years, with either the taxpayer paying taxes plus interest and penalties, the property being sold after a tax lien has been placed on it, or the balance being written off.

The following journal entries record the transactions concerning the accrual of revenue from taxes receivable. As of July 1, 19X0:

|  | Dr. | Cr. |
|---|---|---|
| Taxes receivable—current | $1,000,000 |  |
|    Revenues |  | $950,000 |
|    Allowance for estimated losses on taxes receivable—current |  | 10,000 |
|    Deferred revenue |  | 40,000 |

Current revenue—amount estimated to be collected during the fiscal year plus sixty days—$950,000.

Estimated uncollectible current taxes—amount estimated to be written off over the life of the taxes receivable—$10,000.

Deferred revenue—amount to be received from taxes receivable in future years—$40,000.

Before December 1, 19X0:

|  | Dr. | Cr. |
|---|---|---|
| Cash | $925,000 |  |
|    Taxes receivable—current |  | $925,000 |

After December 1, 19X0 but before June 30, 19X1:

|  | Dr. | Cr. |
|---|---|---|
| Taxes receivable—delinquent | $75,000 |  |
| Allowance for estimated losses on taxes receivable—current | 10,000 |  |
|    Taxes receivable—current |  | $75,000 |
|    Allowance for estimated losses on taxes receivable—delinquent |  | 10,000 |

To transfer current taxes and allowance for estimated losses on current taxes to delinquent taxes.

|  | Dr. | Cr. |
|---|---|---|
| Cash | $25,000 |  |
|    Taxes receivable—delinquent |  | $25,000 |

Cash received on delinquent taxes within a short period after payment date:

|  | Dr. | Cr. |
|---|---|---|
| Interest and penalties on taxes receivable—delinquent | $5,000 |  |
|    Revenues |  | $5,000 |

## CHAPTER 5: GENERAL AND SPECIAL REVENUE FUNDS—BUDGETARY AND REVENUE TRANSACTIONS

Cash $1,500
    Interest and penalties on
        taxes receivable—delinquent $1,500

Setting up interest and penalties on delinquent taxes and amount collected during the year.

Additional entries concerning taxes receivable will be shown in the illustrative case in another section of this chapter. Taxes receivable that are not collected during the current year may require a lengthy legal process before being collected. Before an uncollectible taxes receivable account is written off, the allowance for estimated uncollectible taxes receivable may be transferred from taxes receivable—current to taxes receivable—delinquent, and then possibly to liens receivable.

## Self-Assessment Taxes

Presently, much of the revenue of both cities and states, as well as the federal government, comes from self-assessed taxes. Individual and corporate income taxes, sales taxes, hotel sales or bed taxes, and so forth are illustrations of such taxes.

In a self-assessment taxing system, the taxpayer does the original assessing of the taxes instead of a tax assessor. The governmental unit, then, must provide for a system of keeping an accurate record of the taxpayer, rather than keeping an accurate record of the taxpayer's property. This record must be kept on a continuing basis to assure the government that the taxpayer makes his own assessment each year. The governmental unit must also provide for audits of the self-assessment taxing system to assure accuracy and completeness of the assessment.

If the unit is on a withholding basis for self-assessment taxes and revenue is recorded at the time the withholding taxes are collected, then an account must be established to record the estimated overpayment of taxes. This type of account is commonly called a *suspense account*, since the amount in the account eventually will be distributed to revenue or other accounts. The amount that will go in this account will be deducted from the taxes received from the withholding at the time they are received.

The journal entries for the payment of the withholding taxes recorded as revenue when received is:

|  | Dr. | Cr. |
|---|---|---|
| Cash | $5,200 |  |
|   Estimated overpayment of income taxes |  | $ 200 |
|   Revenues |  | 5,000 |

This would be the entry for each of the quarterly payments—the total taxes for the year being $20,800. Assume that when the return is filed, the actual taxes are determined to be $20,500. The taxpayer claims a refund of $300. The entry would be:

|  | Dr. | Cr. |
|---|---|---|
| Estimated overpayment of income taxes | $800 |  |
|   Revenues |  | $500 |
|   Cash |  | 300 |

To illustrate this method, using a partial accrual basis for the income taxes, the entries for the entire year are shown in "T" accounts as follows:

**Estimated overpayment of income taxes**

| Dec. 15 | 800 | Feb. 15 | 200 |
|---|---|---|---|
| | | May 15 | 200 |
| | | Aug. 15 | 200 |
| | | Nov. 15 | 200 |

**Revenues**

| | | Feb. 15 | 5,000 |
|---|---|---|---|
| | | May 15 | 5,000 |
| | | Aug. 15 | 5,000 |
| | | Nov. 15 | 5,000 |
| | | Dec. 15 | 500 |

**Cash**

| Feb. 15 | 5,200 | Dec. 15 | 300 |
|---|---|---|---|
| May 15 | 5,200 | | |
| Aug. 15 | 5,200 | | |
| Nov. 15 | 5,200 | | |

As can be seen from these "T" accounts, the revenue is accrued at the date of payment. Any adjustment to revenue would come when the final return is made and the true or actual revenue is known.

Another method of accounting for withholding taxes is that the amounts received from withholding taxes may not be recorded as revenue immediately; they will be held in a suspense account—a deferred revenue account called "withholding taxes paid." The amount in this deferred revenue account will eventually be transferred to the revenue account; thus no estimated tax overpayment account is needed. The actual revenue would be known and shown in the records at the time of the filing of the tax return. At that time, the true revenue would be transferred out of the suspense account. Overpayments would also be debited to the suspense account when refunds are made to the taxpayers.

To illustrate this method, using the same payment dates and amounts previously given, the journal entries for the quarterly payments under this method would be:

**Cash**

| Feb. 15 | 5,200 | Dec. 15 | 300 |
|---|---|---|---|
| May 15 | 5,200 | | |
| Aug. 15 | 5,200 | | |
| Nov. 15 | 5,200 | | |

CHAPTER 5: GENERAL AND SPECIAL REVENUE FUNDS—BUDGETARY AND REVENUE TRANSACTIONS

| Withholding taxes paid | | | |
|---|---|---|---|
| Dec. 15  20,800 | Feb. 15 | 5,200 |
| | May 15 | 5,200 |
| | Aug. 15 | 5,200 |
| | Nov. 15 | 5,200 |

| Revenues |  |
|---|---|
| | Dec. 15   20,500 |

This method places all of the revenue in the year the final tax return is received.

## Revenue Sharing and Grants

A whole new field of local revenue availability has opened up with revenue sharing and grants. The main accounting problem with revenue sharing and grants is meeting the accounting and auditing requirements of the governmental agency providing the grants or the revenue sharing.

## Special Problems in Revenue Accounting

When dealing with revenue accounting, one often finds various problems of a specific nature, such as:

1 Taxes paid in advance,
2 Discount on taxes paid,
3 Tax anticipation notes used to obtain operating cash, and,
4 Use of an agency fund for collecting revenue.

**Taxes Paid in Advance**  When a taxpayer desires to pay his or her taxes before they are due or even before notices are sent (e.g., when the taxpayer is to be out of the country for several months), the accounting for these payments is done by using a deferred revenue account called "taxes collected in advance." To illustrate, when a taxpayer pays $1,000 on next year's taxes, the journal entry is:

|  | Dr. | Cr. |
|---|---|---|
| Cash | $1,000 | |
|    Taxes collected in advance | | $1,000 |
| To record taxes collected in advance. | | |

Entries as shown on page 120 are made when the taxes receivable and the revenue are recorded for the next period. To transfer the advance taxes paid to the current taxes receivable account, the entry is:

| | | |
|---|---|---|
| Taxes collected in advance | $1,000 | |
|     Taxes receivable—current | | $1,000 |

To transfer amount collected in advance to current account.

These types of transactions are shown in the transactions for the illustrative city, through the beginning balance accounts and entries R14 on page 131 and B5 on page 136 in this chapter.

**Discount on Taxes Paid** When a discount is allowed by the governmental unit on the taxes paid within a certain time limit, the discount on taxes should be considered a deduction from revenue rather than an expenditure. An "estimated discount on taxes" account should be set up, comparable to the "estimated losses on taxes receivable" account. When the discounts are taken, the discount can be written off to the "estimated discount on taxes" account.

**Tax Anticipation Notes Used to Obtain Operating Cash** Sometimes taxes receivable are not collected soon after the start of the fiscal period. The governmental unit, obviously, needs operating cash to pay for expenditures incurred from the start of the fiscal period until cash begins to flow from the collection of taxes. The governmental jurisdiction often borrows money, through tax anticipation notes, to obtain the cash needed to pay for current expenditures. Interest that would be paid on the note is also an expenditure and must be considered in the preparation of any appropriation for expenditures.

**1** When money is borrowed, the entry is:

| | Dr. | Cr. |
|---|---|---|
| Cash | $100,000 | |
|     Tax anticipation notes payable | | $100,000 |

Borrowed $100,000 in anticipation of taxes to be paid.

**2** When the note is paid off, the entry is:

| | | |
|---|---|---|
| Tax anticipation notes payable | $100,000 | |
| Expenditures—interest | 2,000 | |
|     Cash | | $102,000 |

To record payment of principal and interest on tax anticipation note.

**Use of Agency Funds to Collect Revenue** Agency funds often collect revenue for several taxing units. If the city and the school board are separate taxing units, for example, then an agency fund could be used to collect taxes for both. The amount that is paid to each of the units is a ratio of the total collected for each unit to the total to be collected, less an operating cost of the agency fund (see Chapter 10 for a further discussion of agency funds).

## ILLUSTRATIVE TRANSACTIONS FOR THE GENERAL FUND— CITY OF RUTHBERG

As has been said previously, the basic reasoning behind accounting for governmental funds is that the funds are expendable. If it were possible to follow this basic reasoning in practice, then, each of these funds should not have a balance in the accounts at the end of the accounting period; all revenue should have been spent. Yet, in practice, seldom is a governmental unit so capable that it can determine precisely just how much revenue will come in during the period and spend exactly that much and no more during the period. The general and special revenue funds usually have balances in several accounts at the end of each period and at the beginning of the next period.

### Beginning Balances

The trial balance for the beginning of fiscal year 19X6, for our illustrative city of Ruthberg is given in Exhibit 5-1.

The transactions during the fiscal year will affect the accounts found in this trial balance. Either the balances will remain the same, they will increase or decrease, or they will require a new account with a new balance. To show the effect of the revenue trans-

**EXHIBIT 5-1**
**City of Ruthberg**
**Trial Balance**
**Beginning of Fiscal Year, 19X6**

| Account | Dr. | Cr. |
|---|---|---|
| Cash | $ 63,090 | |
| Taxes receivable—delinquent | 14,400 | |
| Allowance for estimated losses on taxes receivable—delinquent | | $ 9,000 |
| Interest and penalties—taxes receivable | 360 | |
| Allowance for estimated uncollectible interest and penalties | | 90 |
| Due from bus fund | 40,500 | |
| Accounts receivable | 5,400 | |
| Allowance for estimated uncollectible accounts receivable | | 180 |
| Inventory | 20,000 | |
| Tax liens receivable | 5,400 | |
| Allowance for estimated uncollectible tax liens | | 180 |
| Accounts payable | | 9,000 |
| Taxes collected in advance | | 3,600 |
| Fund balance | | 62,100 |
| Reserve for encumbrances | | 45,000 |
| Reserve for inventories | | 20,000 |
| Total | $149,150 | $149,150 |

actions on the beginning balances and on the old and new accounts during the year, a worksheet (see Exhibit 5-6), will be used to record and summarize all of the transactions for the period. The reference number for these beginning balances will be shown as "0" in the worksheet.

In order for the reader to more clearly visualize the transactions for a particular type of situation, the transactions will be grouped by subject matter rather than being given in the order of occurrence (usually chronologically). The order of transactions in this chapter will be: budget adoption, revenue accounting, and accounting for the prior year's revenue transactions. In Chapter 6, the order will be: expenditure accounting, accounting for the prior year's expenditure transactions, closing-entry accounting, and financial statements.

Since many of these budgetary and revenue transactions will be found on several pages, the journal entries for all transactions pertaining to a particular subject matter with many journal entries will be summarized in a special exhibit (see Exhibit 5-3). All entries are then posted to the worksheet (see Exhibit 5-6). Thus the reader can easily follow the beginning account balances (ledger balances), the transactions during the period (journal entries), the ending account balances (ledger balances), and the amounts that are then shown on each particular statement.

## Budget Adoption Transactions

The budget adopted by the Ruthberg City Council for the fiscal year 19X6 is shown in Exhibit 5-2. Note that in this illustrative case only two budgetary classifications are shown for expenditures—object of expenditure and function classifications. For ease of presentation, only five functions are used for expenditures: general government, education, public works, public safety, and health and welfare. Also, only six objects of expenditure are used: personal services, supplies, contractual services, capital outlay, debt servicing, and a residual equity transfer classification. This classification is used for the transfer of funds from the general fund to the printing fund to establish that fund. If further accounts and classifications are needed, Exhibit 4-3 shows names for functions, activities, organizations, character of expenditures, and objects of expenditures that can be used.

Using budgetary accounts, the entry in the accounting records for the adoption of the budget would be as follows:

|   |   | Dr. | Cr. |
|---|---|---|---|
| 1 | Estimated revenues | $2,150,000 |   |
|   | Appropriations |   | $1,970,000 |
|   | Fund balance |   | 180,000 |

To record the adoption of the current budget for the year.

In addition to recording the above journal entry in the general ledger accounts (see Exhibit 5-6, entry 1), the city records individual amounts for the particular budgeted revenues and the appropriations shown in Exhibit 5-2 in subsidiary ledger accounts. (See Exhibit 5-4 for a summary of the transactions in a subsidiary revenue ledger.) A subsidiary ledger is used in order to keep a running comparison of actual revenue with budgeted revenue and appropriations with expenditures and encumbrances. The subsidiary ledger accounts normally have the budgeted amounts as well as the actual amounts in them. A comparison can then be made between actual and budgeted amounts at any point in time during the year.

**EXHIBIT 5-2**
**City of Ruthberg**
**Budget for Year 19X6**

| | | |
|---|---:|---:|
| Estimated revenues | | |
|   Real property taxes | | $ 570,000 |
|   Personal property taxes | | 80,000 |
|   Income taxes | | 290,000 |
|   Sales taxes | | 500,000 |
|   Licenses and permits | | 250,000 |
|   Fines and forfeits | | 32,000 |
|   Intergovernmental service charges | | 81,000 |
|   Revenue sharing and grants | | 310,000 |
|   Miscellaneous | | 37,000 |
|     Total estimated revenues | | $2,150,000 |
| Appropriations | | |
|   General government: | | |
|     Personal services | $160,000 | |
|     Supplies | 20,000 | |
|     Contractual services | 21,000 | |
|     Capital outlay | 80,000 | |
|     Debt servicing | 200,000 | |
|     Residual equity transfer | 150,000 | $ 631,000 |
|   Education: | | |
|     Personal services | 200,000 | |
|     Supplies | 90,000 | |
|     Contractual services | 70,000 | |
|     Capital outlay | 22,000 | 382,000 |
|   Public works: | | |
|     Personal services | 100,000 | |
|     Supplies | 180,000 | |
|     Contractual services | 65,000 | |
|     Capital outlay | 20,000 | 365,000 |
|   Public safety: | | |
|     Personal services | 120,000 | |
|     Supplies | 65,000 | |
|     Contractual services | 115,000 | |
|     Capital outlay | 12,000 | 312,000 |
|   Health and welfare: | | |
|     Personal services | 97,000 | |
|     Supplies | 82,000 | |
|     Contractual services | 61,000 | |
|     Capital outlay | 40,000 | 280,000 |
|     Total appropriations | | $1,970,000 |
| Increase in fund balance | | $ 180,000 |

## Revenue Transactions

The tax roll for real property taxes showed that taxes owed to the city of Ruthberg for general fund operations were $600,000. The finance director estimated from past experience that $30,000 of the taxes assessed would be uncollectible because of errors in the tax roll, improper assessments, and amounts that would be less than tax liens would provide. All revenue transactions are summarized in Exhibit 5-3 and posted consecutively to the worksheet (see Exhibit 5-6), using R as a prefix to the number of the entry. The journal entry to record this transaction would be:

|      |                                                      | Dr.       | Cr.       |
|------|------------------------------------------------------|-----------|-----------|
| R1   | Taxes receivable—current                             | $600,000  |           |
|      | Allowance for estimated uncollectible taxes receivable—current |           | $ 30,000  |
|      | Revenues                                             |           | 570,000   |

To record ad valorem taxes on real property.

Personal property taxes of $83,000 were collected during the period. (See entry B5 for taxes collected in advance.)

Personal property taxes can be accrued, much as real property taxes, if the tax assessor assesses the taxes; this usually is not done, however. Often the taxpayer lists his property, and the taxes become due and are recognized as revenue when paid. The following entry is thus shown as revenue when cash is received.

|      |          | Dr.      | Cr.      |
|------|----------|----------|----------|
| R2   | Cash     | $83,000  |          |
|      | Revenues |          | $83,000  |

To record amount collected on personal property taxes.

Cash collected during the year for income taxes was $308,000.

|      |          | Dr.       | Cr.       |
|------|----------|-----------|-----------|
| R3   | Cash     | $308,000  |           |
|      | Revenues |           | $308,000  |

To record amount collected during the year for income taxes.

The amount collected during the year for sales taxes amounted to $485,000.

|      |          | Dr.       | Cr.       |
|------|----------|-----------|-----------|
| R4   | Cash     | $485,000  |           |
|      | Revenues |           | $485,000  |

To record amount collected during the year for sales taxes.

During the year, the amount collected for automobile licenses and fees amounted to $240,000, and other licenses amounted to $16,000, making a total for licenses and permits of $256,000. Also the city collected $29,000 for fines and forfeits.

|      |          | Dr.       | Cr.       |
|------|----------|-----------|-----------|
| R5   | Cash     | $256,000  |           |
|      | Revenues |           | $256,000  |

To record revenues collected from licenses and permits.

| R6 | Cash | $29,000 | |
|---|---|---|---|
| | Revenues | | $29,000 |

To record revenues collected from fines and forfeits.

The federal government provided $200,000 to the city for its portion of a grant. The state also made available $110,000 to the city for its operations.

| R7 | Due from state | $110,000 | |
|---|---|---|---|
| | Due from federal government | 200,000 | |
| | Operating grants | | $310,000 |

To record amounts receivable from the state and the federal governments for grants.

Grant accounting as illustrated is that needed when the grant is recognized in the year for which the grant applies. If the grant had been received in a prior year for use during the current year, the grant revenue would have been deferred, much as that shown for taxes receivable. When the grant is recognized only after the governmental jurisdiction has made an expenditure, the revenue is recognized, and the amount due from the intergovernmental agency is shown at that time. Disallowances for expenditures are common in certain types of grants. It is impossible to determine, or even closely approximate, the amounts that will be disallowed, so these types of items are usually shown in footnotes to the financial statements rather than in accounts.

All other miscellaneous activities, including the sale of a truck for $5,000, provided $35,000 for the operations of the general fund of the city. This amount does not include interest receivable from past-due taxes and liens.

| R8 | Cash | $35,000 | |
|---|---|---|---|
| | Revenues | | $35,000 |

To record revenue from all miscellaneous activities other than interest and penalties on taxes receivable.

All of the cash entries so far recorded (R2–R6 and R8) are combined into one journal entry for ease of posting to the illustrated worksheet (see Exhibit 5-6). The journal entry is as follows:

| | Dr. | Cr. |
|---|---|---|
| Cash | $1,196,000 | |
| Revenues | | $1,196,000 |

To record revenue paid in cash.

During the year, $561,000 was collected on current taxes receivable. Of that amount, $9,000 was written off to the account called "allowance for estimated uncollectible taxes—current." The journal entry to record this transaction would be:

| R9 | Cash | $561,000 | |
|---|---|---|---|
| | Allowance for estimated | | |
| | uncollectible taxes—current | 9,000 | |
| | Taxes receivable—current | | $570,000 |

To record the collection of $561,000 and the write-off of $9,000 of taxes receivable—current.

When the time period passes for paying taxes, the unpaid taxes receivable are transferred from "taxes receivable—current" to "taxes receivable—delinquent." Also, the unused amount of "allowance for estimated uncollectible taxes—current" is transferred to the new account, "allowance for estimated uncollectible taxes—delinquent." The journal entry to record these transactions would be:

| | | | |
|---|---|---|---|
| R10 | Taxes receivable—delinquent | $26,400 | |
| | Allowance for estimated uncollectible taxes—current | 21,000 | |
| |     Taxes receivable—current | | $26,400 |
| |     Allowance for estimated uncollectible taxes receivable—delinquent | | 21,000 |

To change classification of taxes receivable and allowance for estimated uncollectibles from current to delinquent.

Once the taxes become delinquent, then interest and penalties on the delinquent taxes should be accrued. Interest and penalties of $450 accrue on the delinquent taxes, but, it is estimated that $90 of this amount will not be collectible. The entry to record this transaction is:

| | | | |
|---|---|---|---|
| R11 | Interest and penalties on taxes receivable—delinquent | $450 | |
| |     Allowance for estimated uncollectible interest and penalties—taxes receivable—delinquent | | $ 90 |
| |     Revenues | | 360 |

To record accrued interest and penalties with amount estimated to be uncollectible.

Some revenue comes into the city in the form of services performed for other governmental units. The city provided services for other governmental units in the amount of $57,640. Of this amount, $440 is estimated as being uncollectible. The amounts receivable can be shown as either accounts receivable or due from the other intergovernmental agency. Using accounts receivable, this entry would be recorded as follows:

| | | | |
|---|---|---|---|
| R12 | Accounts receivable | $57,640 | |
| |     Allowance for estimated losses on accounts receivable | | $ 440 |
| |     Revenues | | 57,200 |

To record services rendered to other governmental units.

Cash collected on the accounts receivable during the year amounted to $42,000; $210 was written off as being uncollectible. This entry would be recorded as follows:

| | | | |
|---|---|---|---|
| R13 | Cash | $42,000 | |
| | Allowance for estimated losses on accounts receivable | 210 | |
| |     Accounts receivable | | $42,210 |

To record cash received on accounts receivable and to write off uncollectible amounts.

A taxpayer paid $1,600 in advance on next year's taxes. The journal entry to record this transaction is:

| R14 | Cash | $1,600 | |
| | Taxes collected in advance | | $1,600 |
| | To record taxes collected in advance. | | |

One additional entry concerning current-year revenue accounting would have to be made to complete the revenue transactions, that is, collecting cash for the amounts due from the state and the federal government. This entry would be:

| R15 | Cash | $310,000 | |
| | Due from state | | $110,000 |
| | Due from federal government | | 200,000 |
| | To record amounts collected from the state and federal governments. | | |

All of the preceding journal entries are summarized in Exhibit 5-3.

### EXHIBIT 5-3
### Summary of Revenue Transactions
### City of Ruthberg
### Year 19X6

| No. | Transactions | Journal Entry | Dr. | Cr. |
|---|---|---|---|---|
| R1 | Accrual of revenue from ad valorem taxes on real property | Taxes receivable—Current<br>  Allowance for estimated uncollectible<br>    taxes receivable—current<br>  Revenues | $600,000 | $ 30,000<br>570,000 |
| R2 | Revenue collected for personal property taxes | Cash<br>  Revenues | 83,000 | 83,000 |
| R3 | Revenue from income tax payments | Cash<br>  Revenues | 308,000 | 308,000 |
| R4 | Revenue from sales tax payments | Cash<br>  Revenues | 485,000 | 485,000 |
| R5 | Revenue from licenses and permits | Cash<br>  Revenues | 256,000 | 256,000 |
| R6 | Revenue collected from fines and forfeits | Cash<br>  Revenues | 29,000 | 29,000 |
| R7 | Accrual of revenue from grants from the federal and state governments | Due from state<br>Due from federal government<br>  Operating grants | 110,000<br>200,000 | 310,000 |
| R8 | Revenue from miscellaneous payments | Cash<br>  Revenues | 35,000 | 35,000 |
| R9 | Cash collections on and write-off of taxes receivable | Cash<br>Allowance for estimated uncollectible<br>  taxes receivable—current<br>  Taxes receivable—current | 561,000<br><br>9,000 | <br><br>570,000 |

## EXHIBIT 5-3
*(continued)*

| No. | Transactions | Journal Entry | Dr. | Cr. |
|---|---|---|---|---|
| R10 | Current taxes receivable and estimated losses on taxes receivable reclassified to delinquent | Taxes receivable—delinquent<br>Allowance for estimated uncollectible taxes receivable—current<br>    Taxes receivable—current<br>    Allowance for estimated uncollectible taxes receivable—delinquent | 26,400<br><br>21,000 | <br><br>26,400<br><br><br>21,000 |
| R11 | Revenue from interest and penalties accrued on delinquent taxes with amount of estimated uncollectible interest and penalties on delinquent taxes | Interest and penalties on delinquent taxes<br>    Allowance for estimated uncollectible interest and penalties on delinquent taxes<br>    Revenues | 450 | <br><br><br>90<br>360 |
| R12 | Revenue from accruals for services to other governmental units | Accounts receivable<br>    Allowance for estimated losses on accounts receivable<br>    Revenues | 57,640 | <br>440<br>57,200 |
| R13 | Cash collections and write-off of accounts receivable | Cash<br>Allowance for estimated losses on accounts receivable<br>    Accounts receivable | 42,000<br><br>210 | <br><br>42,210 |
| R14 | Taxpayer paid taxes in advance | Cash<br>    Taxes collected in advance | 1,600 | 1,600 |
| R15 | Cash collected from the state and federal governments | Cash<br>    Due from state<br>    Due from federal government | 310,000 | 110,000<br>200,000 |

## Subsidiary Revenue Ledgers

In order to keep a running record of each of the various types of revenue, a subsidiary revenue ledger is usually kept. Subsidiary ledgers, discussed in Chapter 4, are used to keep a record of the detail, while the total is kept in the general ledger. When the governmental unit keeps subsidiary accounts in the subsidiary ledger, and the subsidiary ledger is in agreement with the control account in the general ledger, the balance between the estimated revenue and the actual revenue can be determined at any time during the year as a total and for each of the various types of revenue (see Exhibit 5-4).

## Prior-Year Revenue Transactions

The city collected $6,000 on delinquent taxes during the year and wrote off $8,400 of delinquent taxes. The journal entry for these transactions is:

## CHAPTER 5: GENERAL AND SPECIAL REVENUE FUNDS—BUDGETARY AND REVENUE TRANSACTIONS

|  | Dr. | Cr. |
|---|---|---|
| **B1** Cash | $6,000 | |
| Allowance for estimated uncollectible taxes—delinquent | 8,400 | |
| Taxes receivable—delinquent | | $14,400 |

To record cash collected and write-off of delinquent taxes.

The city also collected $240 of interest and penalties on taxes receivable and wrote off $120 of the interest and penalties. The journal entry for this transaction is:

|  | Dr. | Cr. |
|---|---|---|
| **B2** Cash | $240 | |
| Allowance for estimated uncollectible interest and penalties | 120 | |
| Interest and penalties on taxes receivable—delinquent | | $360 |

To record cash collected and to write off interest and penalties on taxes receivable.

The city also collected tax liens of $5,220 and wrote off $180. This journal entry is:

|  | Dr. | Cr. |
|---|---|---|
| **B3** Cash | $5,220 | |
| Allowance for estimated uncollectible tax liens | 180 | |
| Tax liens receivable | | $5,400 |

To record cash collected and write-off of tax liens during the year.

The accounts receivable from the prior year were also paid except for $400 in one of the accounts, which was written off to the "allowance for estimated losses on accounts receivable" account. The journal entry to record this transaction is:

|  | Dr. | Cr. |
|---|---|---|
| **B4** Cash | $5,000 | |
| Allowance for estimated losses on accounts receivable | 400 | |
| Accounts receivable | | $5,400 |

To record cash for accounts receivable and to write off uncollectible amount.

Note that more was written off than was estimated to be bad. Since these amounts are only estimates, a greater amount than usual would have to be estimated in future years, or an amount needed to balance the account would have to be taken from the revenues account.

Once the taxes receivable for the current year are placed in the records, then the amount paid in advance can be written off to the "taxes receivable—current" account, as follows:

## EXHIBIT 5-4
### Summary of Revenue Ledger
### City of Ruthberg
### For Fiscal Year 19X6

| Date | Account explanation | Reference | Budgeted revenue Dr. | Actual revenue Cr. | Balance Dr. | Balance Cr. | Actual to budget (over +, under −) |
|---|---|---|---|---|---|---|---|
| | *Real property taxes* | | | | | | |
| 7/1 | Estimated property taxes—budget | (1) | 570,000 | | 570,000 | | |
| | Property taxes assessed less estimated uncollectibles | R1 | | 570,000 | | | |
| | *Personal property taxes* | | | | | | |
| 7/1 | Estimated personal property taxes—budget | (1) | 80,000 | | 80,000 | | |
| | Collections during year | R2 | | 83,000 | | $ 3,000 | + $ 3,000 |
| | *Income taxes* | | | | | | |
| 7/1 | Estimated income taxes—budget | (1) | 290,000 | | 290,000 | | |
| | Collections during year | R3 | | 308,000 | | 18,000 | + 18,000 |
| | *Sales taxes* | | | | | | |
| 7/1 | Estimated sales taxes—budget | (1) | 500,000 | | 500,000 | | |
| | Collections during year | R4 | | 485,000 | 15,000 | | − 15,000 |

| Date | Account | | Ref | | | | | | |
|---|---|---|---|---|---|---|---|---|---|
| | *Licenses and permits* | | | | | | | | |
| 7/1 | Estimated licenses and permits—budget | (1) | | 250,000 | | | 250,000 | | |
| 7/1 | Collections on licenses and permits | | R5 | | 256,000 | 6,000 | | + | 6,000 |
| | *Fines and forfeits* | | | | | | | | |
| 7/1 | Estimated fines and forfeits—budget | (1) | | 32,000 | | | 32,000 | | |
| 7/1 | Collections during year | | R6 | | 29,000 | | 3,000 | − | 3,000 |
| | *Intergovernmental service* | | | | | | | | |
| 7/1 | Estimated intergovernmental service—budget | (1) | | 81,000 | | | 81,000 | | |
| 7/1 | Collections during year | | R12 | | 57,200 | | 23,800 | − | 23,800 |
| | *Operating grants* | | | | | | | | |
| 7/1 | Estimated state and federal grants—budget | (1) | | 310,000 | | | 310,000 | | |
| 7/1 | Revenue due—grants | | R7 | | 310,000 | | 310,000 | | |
| | *Miscellaneous* | | | | | | | | |
| 7/1 | Estimated miscellaneous revenue—budget | (1) | | 37,000 | | | 37,000 | | |
| | Miscellaneous revenue collections | | R8 | | 35,000 | | 2,000 | | |
| | | | R11 | | 360 | | 1,640 | − | 1,640 |
| | Totals | | | 2,150,000 | 2,133,560 | | | − | 16,440 |

| B5 | Taxes collected in advance | $3,600 | |
|---|---|---|---|
| | Taxes receivable—current | | $3,600 |

To record payments made in advance to the current taxes receivable account.

The general fund also received $40,500 from the bus fund for supplies sold during the past fiscal year. The journal entry would be as follows:

| B6 | Cash | $40,500 | |
|---|---|---|---|
| | Due from bus fund | | $40,500 |

To record receiving the amount due from the bus fund.

These transaction entries are summarized in Exhibit 5-5 and posted to the worksheet in Exhibit 5-6.

## Worksheet of Revenue Transactions

Exhibit 5-6 summarizes all of the revenue transactions for the current year in the accounts of the general fund of the city of Ruthberg. Once the expenditure transactions have been posted to the worksheet, information will be available from the accounts for the preparation of the financial statements for the general fund for the year.

### EXHIBIT 5-5
### Summary of Revenue Transactions from the Prior Year
### City of Ruthberg
### 19X6

| No. | Transaction | Journal entry | Dr. | Cr. |
|---|---|---|---|---|
| B1 | Collected $6,000 of delinquent taxes, wrote off $8,400. | Cash<br>Allowance for estimated uncollectible taxes—delinquent<br>Taxes receivable—delinquent | $ 6,000<br><br>8,400 | <br><br><br>$14,400 |
| B2 | Collected $240 of interest and penalties on delinquent taxes. Wrote off $120 of delinquent interest and penalties. | Cash<br>Allowance for estimated uncollectible interest and penalties<br>Interest and penalties on taxes receivable—delinquent | 240<br><br>120 | <br><br><br>360 |
| B3 | Collected $5,220 of tax liens and wrote off $180. | Cash<br>Allowance for estimated uncollectible tax liens<br>Tax liens receivable | 5,220<br><br>180 | <br><br>5,400 |
| B4 | Collected $5,000 on accounts receivable. Wrote off $400 of bad accounts receivable. | Cash<br>Allowance for estimated losses on accounts receivable<br>Accounts receivable | 5,000<br><br>400 | <br><br>5,400 |
| B5 | Wrote off taxes paid in advance to current taxes receivable. | Taxes collected in advance<br>Taxes receivable—current | 3,600 | <br>3,600 |
| B6 | Received payment from bus fund for supplies sold to them by the public works department the previous year. | Cash<br>Due from bus fund | 40,500 | <br>40,500 |

## EXHIBIT 5-6
### City of Ruthberg—General Fund
### Worksheet for Revenue Transactions
### Fiscal Year 19X6

| Account | Balance beginning of year Dr. | Balance beginning of year Cr. | Transactions during year No. | Transactions during year Dr. | Transactions during year No. | Transactions during year Cr. | Trial balance transactions Dr. | Trial balance transactions Cr. |
|---|---|---|---|---|---|---|---|---|
| Cash | $ 63,090 | 0 | R2–6, R8 | $1,196,000 | | | $2,190,150 | |
| | | | R9 | 561,000 | | | | |
| | | | R13 | 42,000 | | | | |
| | | | R14 | 1,600 | | | | |
| | | | R15 | 310,000 | | | | |
| | | | B1 | 6,000 | | | | |
| | | | B2 | 240 | | | | |
| | | | B3 | 5,220 | | | | |
| | | | B4 | 5,000 | | | | |
| | | | B6 | 40,500 | | | | |
| Taxes receivable—current | | | R1 | 600,000 | B5 | $ 3,600 | | |
| | | | | | R9 | 570,000 | | |
| | | | | | R10 | 26,400 | | |
| Allowance for estimated uncollectible taxes receivable—current | 0 | | | | R1 | 30,000 | | |
| Taxes receivable—delinquent | 14,400 | | R9 | 9,000 | B1 | 14,400 | 26,400 | |
| | | | R10 | 21,000 | | | | |
| Allowance for estimated uncollectible taxes receivable—delinquent | 0 | $ 9,000 | R10 | 26,400 | | | | |
| Interest and penalties—delinquent taxes | 360 | 0 | B1 | 8,400 | R10 | 21,000 | | $ 21,600 |
| Allowance for uncollected interest and penalties | 0 | 90 | B2 | 450 | B2 | 360 | 450 | |
| Due from bus fund | 40,500 | 0 | | | R11 | 90 | | 60 |
| | | | | | B6 | 40,500 | | |
| Accounts receivable | 5,400 | 0 | R12 | 57,640 | R13 | 42,210 | 15,430 | |
| | | | | | B4 | 5,400 | | |

137

**EXHIBIT 5-6** *(continued)*

| Account | Balance beginning of year Dr. | Cr. | Transactions during year No. | Dr. | No. | Cr. | Trial balance transactions Dr. | Cr. |
|---|---|---|---|---|---|---|---|---|
| Allowance for estimated losses— accounts receivable | 0 | 0 | R13 | | R12 | 440 | | 10 |
| | | | B4 | 210 | | | | |
| | | | | 400 | | | | |
| Inventory | 20,000 | | | | | | 20,000 | |
| Tax liens receivable | 5,400 | | | | B3 | 5,400 | | |
| Allowance for estimated losses— tax liens receivable | 0 | 0 | B3 | 180 | | | | |
| Due from state | | | R7 | 110,000 | R15 | 110,000 | | |
| Due from federal government | | | R7 | 200,000 | R15 | 200,000 | | |
| Accounts payable | 0 | 9,000 | | | | | | 9,000 |
| Taxes collected in advance | 0 | 3,600 | B5 | 3,600 | R14 | 1,600 | | 1,600 |
| Fund balance | 0 | 62,100 | | | 1 | 180,000 | | 242,100 |
| Reserve for encumbrances | 0 | 45,000 | | | | | | 45,000 |
| Reserve for inventory | 0 | 20,000 | | | | | | 20,000 |
| Estimated revenue | | | 1 | 2,150,000 | | | 2,150,000 | |
| Appropriations | | | | | 1 | 1,970,000 | | 1,970,000 |
| Revenues | | | | | R1 | 570,000 | | 1,823,560 |
| | | | | | R2–6, R8 | 1,196,000 | | |
| | | | | | R11 | 360 | | |
| | | | | | R12 | 57,200 | | |
| Operating grants | | | | | R7 | 310,000 | | 310,000 |
| Totals | $149,150 | $149,150 | | $5,354,960 | | $5,354,960 | $4,402,430 | $4,402,430 |

138

CHAPTER 5: GENERAL AND SPECIAL REVENUE FUNDS—BUDGETARY AND REVENUE TRANSACTIONS 139

## SUMMARY

This chapter has introduced the principles and practices of governmental fund accounting, including budgetary accounting, as they apply to general and special revenue funds. The principles and practices for general funds apply equally to special revenue funds, so only the general fund was illustrated.

Basis of accounting was discussed for general and special revenue funds, along with some special aspects of general and special revenue funds. The special features of this chapter were: (1) budgetary accounting, and (2) revenue accounting. This discussion of the basic principles and practices of general fund revenue accounting were then illustrated with transactions, journal entries, and a worksheet for a fictitious city, the city of Ruthberg.

## QUESTIONS

1. What are some of the characteristics of general and special revenue funds?
2. What is the purpose of subsidiary ledgers in the general fund?
3. What are ad valorem taxes and how are they assessed?
4. Define self-assessment taxes and give some characteristics related to this type of tax.
5. How do you account for discounts on taxes paid?
6. What is a tax anticipation note, and how is it used?
7. List the special problems in revenue accounting, and explain why they pose special problems.
8. The tax roll for city A showed that taxes owed on real property were $300,000. The finance director estimated that $4,000 of the taxes would be uncollectible. Give the journal entries necessary to record this situation.
9. How does the use of budgetary transactions facilitate control?
10. The city collected $500 on interest and penalties on taxes receivable and wrote off $80 of the interest and penalties as uncollectible. Give the necessary journal entries to record these events.
11. When is a special revenue fund required, and what is its purpose?
12. What similarities are there between accounting for the special revenue fund and accounting for the general fund?
13. What is the reasoning behind allocating resources in budgetary accounting?
14. Explain the purpose of budgetary allotments.
15. Do you believe that estimated losses on taxes receivable should be shown as an expenditure or as a deduction from revenues? Explain your reasoning.

## PROBLEMS

5-1 Circle the most appropriate answer to the following questions.[4]
1. Within a governmental unit, two funds that are accounted for in a manner similar to a for-profit entity are:
   a. General and special assessment
   b. Enterprise and internal service
   c. Internal service and general
   d. Enterprise and debt service
2. Which of the following should be accrued as revenue by the general fund of a local government?

a Sales taxes held by the state, which will be remitted to the local government
b Parking meter revenue
c Sales taxes collected by merchants
d Income taxes currently due

3 Which of the following accounts is a budgetary account in governmental accounting?
a Reserve for inventory of supplies
b Fund balance
c Appropriations
d Estimated uncollectible property taxes

4 Under the modified accrual method of accounting used by a local governmental unit, which of the following would be a revenue susceptible to accrual?
a Income taxes
b Business licenses
c Property taxes
d Sales taxes

5 In municipal accounting, both budgetary and proprietary accounts are used to account for all activities. Which of the following accounts is considered to be a budgetary account?
a Reserve for depreciation
b Expenditures
c Encumbrances
d Fund balance

6 Which of the following steps in the acquisition of goods and services occurs first?
a Appropriation
b Encumbrance
c Budget
d Expenditure

7 The accounting for special revenue funds is most similar to that for which other type of fund?
a Capital projects
b General
c Enterprise
d Special assessment

5-2 Circle the most appropriate answer.[5]

Items 1 through 3 are based on the following data:

The Board of Commissioners of Vane City adopted its budget for the year ending July 31, 19X5, comprising estimated revenues of $30,000,000 and appropriations of $29,000,000. Vane City formally integrates its budget into the accounting records.

1 What entry should be made for budgeted revenues?
a Memorandum entry only
b Debit estimated revenues receivable control, $30,000,000
c Debit estimated revenues control, $30,000,000
d Credit estimated revenues control, $30,000,000

2 What entry should be made for budgeted appropriations?
a Memorandum entry only
b Credit estimated expenditures payable control, $29,000,000
c Credit appropriations control, $29,000,000
d Debit estimated expenditures control, $29,000,000

3 What entry should be made for the budgeted excess of revenues over appropriations?

## CHAPTER 5: GENERAL AND SPECIAL REVENUE FUNDS—BUDGETARY AND REVENUE TRANSACTIONS   141

    a Memorandum entry only
    b Credit budgetary fund balance, $1 million
    c Debit estimated excess revenues control, $1 million
    d Debit excess revenues receivable control, $1 million

4 The state government provided $50,000 of revenue for Spring City through a grant. The stipulation in the grant stated that the money could only be spent to take care of food and shelter for indigent persons over sixty-five years old and it must be accounted for separately. The money received should be accounted for in:
    a The general fund
    b A special revenue fund
    c A restricted fund
    d An internal service fund

5 Taxes receivable for Spring City amounted to $1,150,000. The treasurer estimated that $50,000 would not be collected because of errors, bad debts, and so forth. The journal entry to record the transaction would be:

| | | | |
|---|---|---|---|
| a Taxes receivable | $1,150,000 | | |
|    Allowance for estimated uncollectible taxes | | $ 50,000 | |
|    Revenue | | 1,100,000 | |
| b Taxes receivable | $1,100,000 | | |
|    Revenue | | $1,100,000 | |
| c Taxes receivable | $1,150,000 | | |
|    Revenue | | $1,150,000 | |
|    Bad debts | 50,000 | | |
|      Allowance for bad debts | | 50,000 | |
| d Taxes receivable | $1,150,000 | | |
|    Revenue | | $1,150,000 | |

An adjusting entry would be made at the end of the year to enter the bad debts that had been written off.

Items 6 through 8 are based on the following data relating to Lely Township:

Printing and binding equipment used for servicing all of Lely's departments and agencies, on a cost reimbursement basis cost $100,000.

Equipment used for supplying water to Lely's residents cost $900,000.

Receivables for completed sidewalks to be paid for in installments by affected property owners were $950,000.

Cash received from the federal government earmarked for highway maintenance, which must be accounted for in a separate fund, was $995,000.

6 How much should be accounted for in a special revenue fund?
    a $995,000
    b $1,105,000
    c $1,095,000
    d $2,045,000

7 How much could be accounted for in an internal service fund?
    a $100,000
    b $900,000
    c $950,000
    d $995,000

8 How much could be accounted for in an enterprise fund?
    a $100,000

**b** $900,000
**c** $950,000
**d** $995,000

**9** When the budget of a governmental unit is adopted and the estimated revenues exceed the appropriations, the excess is
  **a** Credited to fund balance
  **b** Debited to fund balance
  **c** Credited to reserve for encumbrances
  **d** Debited to reserve for encumbrances

**10** The estimated revenues account of a governmental unit is credited when
  **a** The budget is closed out at the end of the year
  **b** The budget is recorded
  **c** Property taxes are recorded
  **d** Property taxes are collected

**5-3** The following transactions concerning the general fund occurred in the town of Camden during the year. Prepare the journal entries to record these general fund transactions.

  **1** Camden levies property taxes at the rate of 10 mills per dollar. Total assessed value of the property in Camden equals $63 million. Because of the errors in the tax roll, improper assessments, and amounts less than what tax liens would provide, the town comptroller estimates $30,000 to be uncollectible.
  **2** Personal property taxes totaling $12,000 were collected during the year.
  **3** Collections for income taxes totaled $93,000 during the year.
  **4** During the year, the town also collected:
    **a** $7,800 for automobile licenses,
    **b** $2,400 for hunting licenses,
    **c** $33,0000 for lobster and deep-sea fishing licenses,
    **d** $12,400 from parking meters; and
    **e** $8,600 for fines and forfeits.
  **5** The federal government and state provided grants of $75,000 and $25,000, respectively.
  **6** By year's end, $650,000 cash was received by the town of Camden for property taxes. This amount included $70,000 worth of taxes collected in advance. Written off was $25,000 worth of current taxes receivable. The remaining taxes receivable and estimated uncollectibles were transferred to delinquent accounts. There were no taxes collected in advance in the previous year. No discounts on taxes paid are allowed.

**5-4** From the following data, prepare a statement analyzing the changes in the taxes receivable account for the calendar year.

  **1** On January 1, the balance of current taxes receivable was $560,000 and the balance of delinquent taxes receivable was $210,000.
  **2** Additional taxes were levied for the amount of $1,850,000.
  **3** Estimated uncollectible taxes were $20,000 for current taxes and $45,000 for delinquent taxes.
  **4** Tax collections on current taxes amounted to $2,200,000. Written off was $15,000 worth of estimated uncollectibles.
  **5** Tax collections on delinquent taxes amounted to $120,000, and $30,000 of estimated uncollectibles were written off.

**5-5** The town of Jonesville kept its general fund on the modified accrual basis. The following transactions concerning the budget and actual revenue accounts took place during the year.

CHAPTER 5: GENERAL AND SPECIAL REVENUE FUNDS—BUDGETARY AND REVENUE TRANSACTIONS

1 The budget for the year was as follows:

| | |
|---|---|
| Estimated revenues | $1,000,000 |
| Appropriations | 900,000 |
| Expected budget surplus | 100,000 |

2 The actual revenues were $1,025,000.

**Required**:
Prepare the yearly journal entries for the preceding transactions.

5-6 Orange City had on its tax rolls property with a market value of $150 million. The property was assessed at 60 percent of its market value. The tax rate was $22 per $1,000 of assessed value.

Of the amount assessed, it was estimated that $18,000 would never be collected. Of the balance, $30,000 would be collected sixty days after the close of the fiscal year.

**Required**:
Prepare the journal entries to record the above transactions. Show how you calculated the amounts in the explanation to the journal entries.

5-7 The following transactions concerning the general fund and the recreation fund of Thompson City occurred during the year.

1 The recreation fund of Thompson City was promised a grant of $300,000 from their state department of recreation contingent upon the city providing an additional $150,000 for the following expenditures:

| | |
|---|---|
| Personnel costs | $125,000 |
| Supplies | 75,000 |
| Contractual services | 50,000 |
| Equipment | 200,000 |
| Total | 450,000 |

A budget for the proposed expenditures was forwarded to the general fund. The expenditures were expected to be financed as follows: general fund, $150,000; state department of recreation, $300,000.

2 An appropriation was made in the general fund budget for the recreation fund contingent upon the recreation fund receiving the $300,000 from the state.

3 The recreation fund recorded its budget in its accounts.

4 The general fund set up the amount to be paid to the recreation fund as an unallocated appropriation. The recreation fund was notified that the grant had been approved by the state. They recorded the accrued revenue for the fund.

6 The state paid the grant.

7 The general fund allotted 50 percent of the appropriation to the recreation fund. They paid the amount to the recreation fund.

8 The city allotted the balance of the amount appropriated to the recreation fund and paid the amount.

**Required**:
Prepare journal entries in both the general fund and in the recreation fund of Thompson City for the preceding transactions.

5-8 The following transactions are related to property tax revenue for the city of Gonzales.

**1** Property taxes for the city amounted to $1,225,000. Estimated uncollectibles amounted to $25,000. Taxes paid were $1,100,000, and $15,000 was written off as uncollectible.

**2** The balance of the taxes receivable were considered as delinquent. Interest and penalties were accrued at $10,000 with $1,000 estimated as being uncollectible. Collection of delinquent taxes amounted to $75,000, with $7,500 being paid in interest and penalties.

**Required**:
Prepare the journal entries for each of the preceding transactions.

**5-9** The following information was abstracted from the accounts of the general fund of the city of Rom after the books had been closed for the fiscal year ended June 30, 19X1.[6]

|  | Postclosing trial balance June 30, 19X0 | Transactions Dr. | Transactions Cr. | Postclosing trial balance June 30, 19X1 |
|---|---|---|---|---|
| Cash | $700,000 | $1,820,000 | $1,852,000 | $668,000 |
| Taxes receivable | 40,000 | 1,870,000 | 1,828,000 | 82,000 |
|  | $740,000 |  |  | $750,000 |
| Allowance for uncollectible taxes | $ 8,000 | 8,000 | 10,000 | 10,000 |
| Accounts payable | 132,000 | 1,852,000 | 1,840,000 | 120,000 |
| Fund balance: |  |  |  |  |
| Reserved for encumbrances | — | 1,000,000 | 1,070,000 | 70,000 |
| Unreserved | 600,000 | 140,000 | 60,000 |  |
|  |  |  | 30,000 | 550,000 |
|  | $740,000 |  |  | $750,000 |

The budget for the fiscal year ended June 30, 19X1 provided for estimated revenues of $2,000,000 and appropriations of $1,940,000.

**Required**:
Prepare journal entries to record the budgeted and actual transactions for the fiscal year ended June 30, 19X1.

**5-10** This Silver City case continues the one started as Problem 3-7. The general fund of Silver City will continue in Chapter 6 as well; therefore, be sure to save all of your reference material for use in future problems.

**1** The city council of Silver City approved a general fund budget as follows:

| | | |
|---|---|---|
| Estimated revenue: | | |
| Property taxes | $2,175,000 | |
| Less estimated uncollectibles | 25,000 | $2,150,000 |
| Income taxes | | 775,000 |
| Licenses and fines | | 50,000 |
| Miscellaneous revenue | | 25,000 |
| Total estimated revenue | | $3,000,000 |
| Appropriations: | | |
| Function A: | | |
| Personal services | 830,000 | |
| Materials and supplies | 70,000 | |
| Contractual services | 50,000 | |
| Equipment | 475,000 | 1,425,000 |

CHAPTER 5: GENERAL AND SPECIAL REVENUE FUNDS—BUDGETARY AND REVENUE TRANSACTIONS   **145**

| | | |
|---|---:|---:|
| Function B: | | |
|   Personal services | 670,000 | |
|   Materials and supplies | 30,000 | |
|   Contractual services | 30,000 | |
|   Equipment | 25,000 | 755,000 |
| Function C: | | |
|   Personal services | 500,000 | |
|   Materials and supplies | 35,000 | |
|   Contractual services | 50,000 | |
|   Equipment | 35,000 | |
|   Operating transfers to debt service fund | 32,000 | |
|   Operating transfers to special assessments fund | 68,000 | |
|   Residual equity transfers to garage fund | 50,000 | 770,000 |
|     Total appropriations | | $2,950,000 |

  **2** Tax bills amounting to $2,175,000 were sent out to the taxpayers.
  **3** All other revenues collected were as follows:

| | |
|---|---:|
| Income taxes | $800,000 |
| Licenses and fines | 45,000 |
| Miscellaneous revenue | 30,000 |
|   Total collected | $875,000 |

  **4** Property taxes collected amounted to $2,150,000.

**Required**:
  1 Prepare journal entries for each of the preceding transactions that pertain to the budget and revenues, and record them on a worksheet.
  2 Prepare subsidiary revenue ledgers.

## NOTES

  **1** Municipal Finance Officers Association of the United States and Canada, *Governmental Accounting, Auditing, and Financial Reporting* (Chicago: Municipal Finance Officers Association of the United States and Canada, 1981), p. 37.
  **2** National Council on Governmental Accounting, *Interpretation 3. Revenue Recognition—Property Taxes* (Chicago: Municipal Finance Officers Association of the United States and Canada, 1981).
  **3** National Council on Governmental Accounting, *Statement V. Governmental Accounting and Financial Reporting Principles* (Chicago: Municipal Finance Officers Association of the United States and Canada, 1979), pp. 11–12.
  **4** Adapted from American Institute of Certified Public Accountants, *Uniform CPA Examination Questions and Unofficial Answers* (New York: American Institute of Certified Public Accountants, various dates).
  **5** Ibid.
  **6** Ibid., Practice II, May 1981.

# CHAPTER 6

# GENERAL AND SPECIAL REVENUE FUNDS, CONTINUED— EXPENDITURE ACCOUNTING, CLOSING ENTRIES, AND FINANCIAL STATEMENTS

Chapter 6 continues the discussion on general and special revenue funds started in Chapter 5. In this chapter, expenditure accounting, closing entries, and financial statements will be the primary focus. The transactions will be illustrated using the fictitious city of Ruthberg. A worksheet that contains not only the expenditure transactions but also revenue transactions will show the closing entries for all of the fiscal year's transactions. Statements will be prepared from the worksheet for the entire year's transactions.

## EXPENDITURE ACCOUNTING

A budget is usually used in government to control expenditures in general and special revenue funds. Under stable economic conditions, actual revenues of government vary only slightly from that estimated. So the minimum and maximum expenditures that can flow from the estimated revenues can be estimated fairly closely. Under unstable economic conditions, however, revenues must be watched very closely. Expenditures must be closely controlled to keep from overexpending, under stable or unstable economic conditions, thus exceeding the available revenues.

As discussed in Chapter 5, through the use of budgets and budgetary accounting, along with accounting for actual transactions, the governmental unit has built in control. The records will show when any particular type of revenue is not approaching the estimated level or when any particular set of expenditures is beginning to exceed the appropriation for that purpose. Encumbrance accounting provides a further means of control for ensuring that appropriations are not overspent. Also, from information in subsidiary ledgers, the detail can be obtained for the control of expenditures by function, character, department, and objects of expenditure.

## Personal Services

The category of personal services (personnel services) includes not only salaries and wages but also employee benefits, that is, such items as the city's share of retirement costs. Most local and county governments also withhold the employee's share of hospitalization insurance, FICA, and so forth, as well as state and federal income taxes. An agency fund may be established to account for withholdings and retirement for all funds rather than having to account for these items in each fund, such as the general fund. Usually, there is no need to encumber salaries and wages—the amounts paid are fairly constant for the payroll period as well as for the year. However, salaries and wages can be encumbered for particular projects or activities to provide further management control.

For financial reporting purposes, salaries should be accrued if there are any working days between the last pay period and the end of the year. Many governmental units have a fifty-two-week fiscal year, and the payroll period falls within these fifty-two weeks. In this case, the budget would have no need for encumbering or accruing because the payroll period would end on the last day of the fiscal year. So the normal payroll routines would be followed, including setting up the liability for the amount owed, charging for the salary and wages expenditures, and charging for the pension and withholding provisions.

## Materials and Supplies

The National Council on Governmental Accounting states the following as an acceptable principle of accounting for inventory items.

> **2** Inventory items (e.g., materials and supplies) may be considered expenditures either when purchased (purchases method) or when used (consumption method), but significant amounts of inventory should be reported in the balance sheet.[1]

The inventory can be kept either as a perpetual inventory and shown as expenditures when consumed, or it can be shown as an expenditure when purchased. A physical inventory is taken at the end of the year to determine the amount in the inventory account. When the inventory is shown as a perpetual inventory, the inventory is debited when goods are purchased and accounts payable is credited. When goods are requisitioned from the inventory account, expenditures are debited and inventory is credited. Usually, an amount equal to the inventory is then reserved out of the fund balance account. This is done to ensure that an amount in the fund balance account, represented by the amount in the inventory account, is not used for appropriation purposes during the year.

Although reported as an expenditure when using the *consumption method*, the amount is an expense. This method is one of the contradictions to the modified accrual basis of accounting for expenditures. Most small municipalities, however, consider inventories as expenditures when purchased. Thus a debit is made to the expenditures account, and a credit is made to accounts payable. Since the inventory amount is usually small, no inventory amount is shown at the end of the year. If the amount is fairly large, however, and the inventory account is placed in the books, then at the end of the year, a comparable amount would have to be reserved out of fund balance. This entry is to assure that the assets represented by the inventory will not be appropriated out of the fund balance for other purposes. For example, if, when using the purchase method, an inventory account is set up based upon the amount of inventory found to be available, the inventory account is debited and the expenditures account is credited. At the same time, the fund balance account is debited, and a reserve for inventory account is credited for the amount of the inventory.

An example of the purchase method will be shown in our illustration of transactions in the city of Ruthberg, the next section of the chapter. To illustrate the consumption method, suppose that the municipality had a beginning inventory of $25,000, purchased $50,000 of materials and supplies during the year, and departments requisitioned $55,000 of materials and supplies. The amount consumed was $55,000, and the ending inventory would be $20,000.

In the accounts of the municipality at the beginning of the fiscal year the inventory account would have a debit of $25,000; a "reserve for inventory" account, a reservation of fund balance, would be for $25,000.

The entry for the purchase of the materials and supplies would be:

|  | Dr. | Cr. |
|---|---|---|
| Materials and supplies inventory | $50,000 |  |
|     Accounts payable (or cash) |  | $50,000 |

The entry for the materials requisitioned from the inventory would be:

| Expenditures | $55,000 |  |
|---|---|---|
|     Materials and supplies inventory |  | $55,000 |

The entry needed at the end of the year to adjust the material and supplies inventory account and the reserve for inventory account would be:

| Reserve for inventory | $5,000 |  |
|---|---|---|
|     Fund balance |  | $5,000 |

At the end of the year, expenditures would be $55,000; the inventory account would be $20,000; and the reserve for inventory account would be $20,000. The preceding entries can be further illustrated using "T" accounts as follows:

| Inventory | | | |
|---|---|---|---|
| Bal. | 25,000 | Expend. | 55,000 |
| Purch. | 50,000 | Bal. | 20,000 |
|  | 75,000 |  | 75,000 |
| Bal. | 20,000 |  |  |

## CHAPTER 6: EXPENDITURE ACCOUNTING, CLOSING ENTRIES, AND FINANCIAL STATEMENTS

**Reserve for inventory**

| Adj. | 5,000 | Bal. | 25,000 |
|---|---|---|---|
| Bal. | 20,000 | | |
| | 25,000 | | 25,000 |
| | | Bal. | 20,000 |

**Accounts payable**

| | | Purch. | 50,000 |
|---|---|---|---|

**Fund balance**

| | | Inv. Res. | 5,000 |
|---|---|---|---|

**Expenditures**

| Expend. | 55,000 | | |
|---|---|---|---|

In this method, the expenditures directly relate to the amount of inventory used, not to the amount of goods purchased.

Encumbrances accounting can be used in both methods of accounting for inventories; in both methods the encumbrance is made when the order is placed. In the consumption method, the materials are unencumbered when the goods and invoice are received and placed in the inventory; in the purchases method, the materials are unencumbered when the goods and invoice are received and recorded as an expenditure.

## Contractual Services

Contractual services include contracts to repair machinery, to maintain the buildings, to pay for travel, and to purchase insurance policies. Prepaid expenses are usually not shown when using the modified accrual basis. Therefore, multiyear insurance policies and any of the other multiple-year contractual services will be considered an expenditure during the first year of the contract. No adjustment is necessary for the annual use of the contractual service. While not often shown as prepaid assets, significant amounts for contractual services can be accrued at the time a contract is made and then shown as a prepaid asset at the end of the year. The prepaid asset would then be shown as an expenditure during the fiscal period it is used.

## Capital Outlay

Capital outlays in general funds and special revenue funds are for such items as the purchase of machinery and equipment, capital expansion to existing buildings, repairs of a capital nature, and land. All of these capital outlays are considered expenditures during the year of purchase in general funds and special revenue funds and are not recorded in these funds as fixed assets. However, they are recorded as fixed assets in the general fixed assets account group. For example, if a typewriter is purchased during the year for $900, the journal entry to record this type of transaction is:

|  | Dr. | Cr. |
|---|---|---|
| Expenditures—capital outlay | $900 | |
|     Cash (accounts payable) | | $900 |

To record the purchase of a typewriter.

## Debt Servicing

The resources used for servicing debt—that is, paying off the long-term liabilities and interest—are usually provided by the general fund and transferred to the debt service fund, the fund out of which the debt is paid. As a general rule, only one department, usually the finance department under the general government function, is appropriated the required amount. The amounts can be encumbered but often are only allotted to the department when the amounts are fairly well known and payments need to be made.

To illustrate this type of transaction, suppose that $25,000 is transferred to the debt service fund for paying off $10,000 worth of bonds and $15,000 of interest. The journal entry is:

|  | Dr. | Cr. |
|---|---|---|
| Operating transfer to debt service fund | $25,000 | |
|     Cash (or due to debt service fund) | | $25,000 |

Transferred to debt service fund to pay off $10,000 principal on bonds and $15,000 of interest.

Note that instead of calling this type of transaction an expenditure it is called an *operating transfer. Operating transfers* are those for which the resources will be used to finance expenditures in another fund. Transactions between funds that are similar to those involving external organizations are revenues or expenditures not transfers.

Also note that instead of using an accounts payable account, the account used is called "due to debt service funds." Numerous interfund transactions of this and similar types occur during the year. The subject of interfund transactions, that is, transactions between and among funds, was discussed in Chapter 2 and will be further illustrated in Chapter 12.

## Residual Equity Transfers

Since a *residual equity transfer* is a nonrecurring type transaction, it often is set up as a separate line item in the budget. This type of transaction is classified as a separate line item in our illustrative city. The receiving of a residual equity transfer was fully discussed in Chapter 2, and the transferring of the residual equity transfer to the printing fund will be illustrated in the city of Ruthberg transactions in this chapter.

### Prior Year's Reserve for Encumbrances

Regarding encumbrance accounting, the Municipal Finance Officers Association in its 1980 statement on governmental accounting, auditing, and financial reporting says:

> The extent to which a formal encumbrance system must be employed is a matter of professional judgment in light of prevailing circumstances. It is critical under any circumstances, however, that appropriate budgetary control be maintained over all government expenditures.
>
> Encumbrance accounting is an appropriate and useful financial management tool. The controversy which has surrounded it in recent years relates, not to its proper role in helping to control government spending activities during the year, but to the appropriate treatment of encumbrances outstanding at year end in annual GAAP financial statements.[2]

Encumbrances may or may not lapse at the end of the year. If they do not lapse, the encumbrances account is closed to the appropriations account, which is closed to the fund balance account. The reserve for encumbrance account remains open as a reservation of the fund balance. Encumbrances are not shown as expenditures, and the reserve for encumbrances is not shown as a liability but as a reservation of the fund balance.

If the encumbrances lapse and are reappropriated in the next year's budget, usually, the encumbrances and reserve for encumbrances accounts are both closed at the end of the year and reopened at the beginning of the next year.

Current generally accepted accounting principles require that, in addition to the normal financial statements, when a budget is used, one of the statements must show a comparison between the budgeted and the actual amounts. If the budget is on the encumbrance basis, then the statement of revenue, expenditures, and changes in fund balance would have to show not only the current year's expenditures, less the prior year's expenditures against the reserve for encumbrances, but would have to include the amount outstanding in the reserve for encumbrances account. This method is shown in the illustrative statements in this chapter. If the budget is on the modified accrual basis, then actual expenditures, including any related to prior-year encumbrances, are compared to this modified-accrual-based budget.

### Adjusting Entries

Under ordinary circumstances, it is not necessary to make adjusting entries under a modified accrual basis in governmental fund accounting. However, many small municipalities keep their books and records during the fiscal year on the cash basis. At the end of the year, the accounts are adjusted to the modified accrual basis for statement purposes. Other units keep their salaries account on a cash basis during the year and for statement purposes, adjust it to the modified accrual basis at the end of the year. Another example is that, under the purchases method, of goods being ordered and received but not yet paid for. An adjusting entry would be made, debiting expenditures for the outstanding amounts owed on the goods and crediting accounts payable.

Through this method of adjusting the accounts at the end of the year before statement preparation, the small municipality can keep the general accounts on the cash basis or other budgetary basis and then, for financial reporting purposes, prepare the statements on the modified accrual basis.

To illustrate adjusting entries to accrue certain expenditures in a small town that keeps its accounting system on a cash basis, assume the following information:

|  | | Adjustments | |
| --- | --- | --- | --- |
|  | Paid | Beginning amounts | Ending amounts due |
| Personal services | | | |
|   Salaries and wages | $25,000 | $1,500 | $2,000 |
|   Retirement | 2,500 | 150 | 200 |
| Supplies | | | |
|   Purchases | 12,000 | 1,000 | 1,500 |
| Contractual services | | | |
|   Travel | 1,000 | 200 | 150 |
| Capital outlay | | | |
|   Automotive equipment | 15,000 | 2,000 | 100 |

The adjustments needed are shown below and in the following partial worksheet, Exhibit 6-1.

|  |  | Dr. | Cr. |
| --- | --- | --- | --- |
| 1 | Expenditures: | | |
|  |   Salaries and wages | $2,000 | |
|  |   Retirement | 200 | |
|  |     Salaries and wages payable | | $2,000 |
|  |     Retirement payable | | 200 |
|  | To set up expenditures and payables. | | |
|  | Salaries and wages payable | 1,500 | |
|  | Retirement | 200 | |
|  |   Expenditures: | | |
|  |     Salaries and wages | | 1,500 |
|  |     Retirement | | 150 |
|  | To reverse the prior year's entries. | | |
| 2 | Expenditures—supplies | 1,500 | |
|  |   Accounts payable | | 1,500 |
|  | To set up expenditures and payables. | | |
|  | Accounts payable | 1,000 | |
|  |   Expenditures—supplies | | 1,000 |
|  | To reverse the prior year's entry. | | |
| 3 | Expenditures—travel | 150 | |
|  |   Accounts payable | | 150 |
|  | To set up expenditures. | | |
|  | Accounts payable | 200 | |
|  |   Expenditures—travel | | 200 |
|  | To reverse accounts. | | |

## CHAPTER 6: EXPENDITURE ACCOUNTING, CLOSING ENTRIES, AND FINANCIAL STATEMENTS

```
4  Expenditures—automotive equipment      100
      Accounts payable                             100
   To set up expenditures and payable.
   Accounts payable                      2,000
      Expenditures—automotive
        equipment                                2,000
   To reverse prior year's accounts.
```

## ILLUSTRATIVE TRANSACTIONS FOR THE GENERAL FUND—CITY OF RUTHBERG

### Expenditure Transactions

**Personal Services Transactions** In this illustration, the city pays approximately 7.54 percent of salaries and wages into a retirement fund, and the employee pays the same amount. The employees' share of retirement cost, as well as federal and state withholding taxes amounting to 15 percent of the salaries and wages (approximately 13.1 percent federal and 1.9 percent state), is withheld from the employees' salaries or wages. The city is on a fifty-two-week fiscal year for personal services. So, from a personal services standpoint, no work days are accrued for payroll purposes.

During the year, $610,000 in wages and salaries were incurred and paid. Pension costs of $46,000 were incurred by the city. The employees' share of the pension costs was also $46,000. Taxes withheld during the year were $91,500—$80,000 for federal and $11,500 for the state. These costs by function are:

**EXHIBIT 6-1**
**Illustrative Partial Worksheet**
**to Adjust from Cash to Accrual Basis**

| Accounts | Balances | | Adjustments | | | | Balances | |
|---|---|---|---|---|---|---|---|---|
| | Dr. | Cr. | No. | Dr. | No. | Cr. | Dr. | Cr. |
| Expenditures: | | | | | | | | |
| Salaries and wages | $25,000 | | 1 | $2,000 | 1 | $1,500 | $25,500 | |
| Retirement | 2,500 | | 1 | 200 | 1 | 150 | 2,550 | |
| Supplies | 12,000 | | 2 | 1,500 | 2 | 1,000 | 12,500 | |
| Travel | 1,000 | | 3 | 150 | 3 | 200 | 950 | |
| Automotive equipment | 15,000 | | 4 | 100 | 4 | 2,000 | 13,100 | |
| Accrued Liabilities: | | | | | | | | |
| Salaries and wages payable (prior year) | | $1,500 | 1 | 1,500 | 1 | 2,000 | | $2,000 |
| Retirement payable (prior year) | | 150 | 1 | 150 | 1 | 200 | | 200 |
| Accounts payable | | 1,000 | 2 | 1,000 | 2 | 1,500 | | 1,500 |
| | | 200 | 3 | 200 | 3 | 150 | | 150 |
| | | 2,000 | 4 | 2,000 | 4 | 100 | | 100 |

|  | Incurred and paid | Budget |
|---|---|---|
| Total personal services | $656,000 | $677,000 |
| General government | 155,000 | 160,000 |
| Education | 197,000 | 200,000 |
| Public works | 93,000 | 100,000 |
| Public safety | 115,000 | 120,000 |
| Health and welfare | 96,000 | 97,000 |

A journal entry normally would be made each time the salaries and wages are paid. A summary journal entry, equivalent to the sum of the individual entries for the year would be:

|  |  | Dr. | Cr. |
|---|---|---|---|
| E1 | Expenditures—personal services | $656,000 |  |
|  | Accounts payable |  | $472,500 |
|  | Due to agency fund |  | $ 91,500 |
|  | Due to pension trust fund |  | $ 92,000 |

To record total personal services paid during the year including:

|  |  |  |
|---|---|---|
| Salaries and wages |  | $610,000 |
| Pension costs |  | 46,000 |
|    Total personal services |  | $656,000 |
| Salaries and wages |  | $610,000 |
| Less: |  |  |
|   Employees' pension | $46,000 |  |
|   Withholding taxes— |  |  |
|     to agency fund | 91,500 | $137,500 |
|     Total salaries payable |  | $472,500 |
| Employees' pension | $46,000 |  |
| City's share pension | 46,000 |  |
|   Due to pension trust fund |  | $ 92,000 |

These amounts would be posted to both the general and subsidiary ledgers. The general ledger amounts are first summarized in Exhibit 6-2 and then are posted to the worksheet in Exhibit 6-6, while the detail is posted to a subsidiary ledger. A summary of the subsidiary ledger accounts is shown in Exhibit 6-3. Detail information on salaries and wages is usually kept for the amounts of withholding for each employee so that at year end, W-2 forms can be prepared. Permanent information concerning pensions and retirement can be transferred to the pension trust fund.

Payments of the amounts to employees, to the pension trust fund, and to the agency fund during the year would be recorded as follows:

|  |  |  |  |
|---|---|---|---|
| E2 | Accounts payable | $472,500 |  |
|  | Due to pension trust fund | 92,000 |  |
|  | Due to agency fund | 91,500 |  |
|  |   Cash |  | $656,000 |

To record payment of cash for salaries, wages, pension costs, and withholdings.

## CHAPTER 6: EXPENDITURE ACCOUNTING, CLOSING ENTRIES, AND FINANCIAL STATEMENTS

**Materials and Supplies Transactions** Materials and supplies transactions are on the purchase method. The total amount appropriated for supplies for the year was $457,000. The beginning inventory balance was $20,000. During the year, orders were placed, goods were received with invoices, and payments were made. Each time an order was placed, the accountant would debit encumbrances for the expected amount of the order and credit the reserve for encumbrance account. The journal entries for the encumbrances for the entire year are:

| | | | |
|---|---|---|---|
| E3 | Encumbrances | $420,000 | |
| | Reserve for encumbrances | | $420,000 |
| | To encumber orders placed. | | |

When the goods are received—in this case, $410,000 of the encumbered goods are received at an actual cost of $407,000—the encumbrances are reversed and the actual amounts placed in the accounts. Supplies of $54,000 were purchased from the printing fund.

| | | | |
|---|---|---|---|
| E4 | Reserve for encumbrances | $410,000 | |
| | Encumbrances | | $410,000 |
| | To reverse encumbrances. | | |
| E5 | Expenditures | $407,000 | |
| | Accounts payable | | $353,000 |
| | Due to printing fund | | 54,000 |
| | To set up liability for supplies received. | | |

It can be seen that $10,000 of encumbrances, with the appropriate reserve for encumbrances, is still outstanding at the end of the year.

Of this year's accounts, $400,000 was paid during the year; $350,000 to accounts payable and $50,000 of the amount due to the printing fund.

| | | | |
|---|---|---|---|
| E6 | Accounts payable | $350,000 | |
| | Due to printing fund | 50,000 | |
| | Cash | | $400,000 |
| | To pay accounts payable and amount due to the printing fund for the year. | | |

As related to the budget, the supplies expenditures by functions would be as follows:

| Function | Budget | Expenditures | Encumbered | Over or under(–) |
|---|---|---|---|---|
| Total | $437,000 | $407,000 | $10,000 | –20,000 |
| General government | 20,000 | 19,000 | 1,000 | |
| Education | 90,000 | 80,000 | 2,000 | – 8,000 |
| Public works | 180,000 | 171,000 | 4,000 | – 5,000 |
| Public safety | 65,000 | 60,000 | 1,500 | – 3,500 |
| Health and welfare | 82,000 | 77,000 | 1,500 | – 3,500 |

In some years, the public works department provides the bus fund with operating supplies, such as fuel for the buses. The department is reimbursed for the cost of the supplies. The bus fund had purchased $40,500 of these supplies during the previous year and owed the general fund this amount at the end of the year.

This type of transaction has no effect on the amount of the expenditures for the department for the year. The total expenditures would be increased by $40,500, and the sale of the supplies would decrease the amount in the account by $40,500. Therefore, the net amount would be the same. For example, when the supplies were sold to the bus fund, the entry would be:

|  | Dr. | Cr. |
|---|---|---|
| Due from bus fund | $40,500 |  |
|     Expenditures |  | $40,500 |

When the purchase was made for the additional supplies, the entry would be:

| | | |
|---|---|---|
| Expenditures | $40,500 | |
|     Accounts payable | | $40,500 |

The debit of $40,500 and the credit of $40,500 to the expenditure account nets out to a balance of zero. The amount received from the bus fund for the payment of the purchase of supplies is shown in Chapter 5, transaction B5.

The supplies transactions are posted to the worksheet (see Exhibit 6-6) and to the summary subsidiary expenditure ledger (see Exhibit 6-3). An inventory is taken at the end of the year of all the supplies in all departments and is found to total $25,000. An entry is made to adjust the inventory account as follows:

| | | | |
|---|---|---|---|
| E7 | Inventory | $5,000 | |
| |     Reserve for inventory | | $5,000 |

Note that even though the inventory is shown under the purchase method, the inventory has no effect on the amount of expenditures for the year since the modified accrual basis of accounting will continue to be used.

**Contractual Services Transactions** Encumbered contractual services during the year amounted to $318,000, of which $4,900 was still encumbered at the end of the year. Contractual services by function, as shown in the expenditure ledger, is as follows:

| Function | Budget | Expenditures | Encumbered | Over or under(−) |
|---|---|---|---|---|
| Total | $332,000 | $313,100 | $4,900 | −14,000 |
|   General government | 21,000 | 19,700 | 500 | − 800 |
|   Education | 70,000 | 66,300 | 1,200 | − 2,500 |
|   Public works | 65,000 | 59,500 | 700 | − 4,800 |
|   Public safety | 115,000 | 109,000 | 2,000 | − 4,000 |
|   Health and welfare | 61,000 | 58,600 | 500 | − 1,900 |

## CHAPTER 6: EXPENDITURE ACCOUNTING, CLOSING ENTRIES, AND FINANCIAL STATEMENTS

The journal entries needed to bring about the above results and posted to the worksheet (Exhibit 6-6) and subsidiary expenditure ledger (Exhibit 6-3) are:

| | | | |
|---|---|---|---|
| E8 | Encumbrances | $318,000 | |
| | Reserve for encumbrances | | $318,000 |
| | To set up encumbrances. | | |
| E9 | Reserve for encumbrances | $313,100 | |
| E10 | Expenditures | 313,100 | |
| | Encumbrances | | $313,100 |
| | Accounts payable | | 313,100 |
| | To reverse encumbrances and set up liability for contractual services. | | |
| E11 | Accounts payable | $310,000 | |
| | Cash | | $310,000 |
| | To pay contractual services vouchers. | | |

This year was the final year of a three-year insurance policy. Contractual payments normally are expenditures when the insurance policy is purchased the first year. Prepaid expenses need not be shown when using the modified accrual basis. Therefore, no entry is made during this year or the preceding year.

**Capital Outlay Transactions** These outlays, in relation to the appropriations and summarized by functions, are considered to be the following:

| Object of expenditure by function | Budget | Expenditures | Encumbered | Over or under(−) |
|---|---|---|---|---|
| General government: | | | | |
| Land | $ 50,000 | $ 40,000 | $10,000 | |
| Equipment | 30,000 | 20,000 | 10,000 | |
| Total | 80,000 | 60,000 | 20,000 | |
| Education: | | | | |
| Equipment | 22,000 | 20,000 | 2,000 | |
| Public works: | | | | |
| Equipment | 20,000 | 19,000 | 1,000 | |
| Public safety: | | | | |
| Land | 2,000 | 2,000 | — | |
| Equipment | 5,000 | 3,500 | 1,500 | |
| Improvements other than buildings | 5,000 | 5,000 | | |
| Total | 12,000 | 10,500 | 1,500 | |
| Health and welfare: | | | | |
| Land | 10,000 | 10,000 | | |
| Equipment | 30,000 | 27,000 | 3,000 | |
| | 40,000 | 37,000 | 3,000 | |
| Totals | $174,000 | $146,500 | $27,500 | |

The journal entries to record these summarized transactions and posted to the worksheet in Exhibit 6-6 are:

| E12 | Encumbrances | $174,000 | |
| --- | --- | --- | --- |
| |     Reserve for encumbrances | | $174,000 |
| | To set up encumbrances for capital outlay. | | |
| E13 | Reserve for encumbrances | $146,500 | |
| | Expenditures | 146,500 | |
| |     Encumbrances | | $146,500 |
| |     Accounts payable | | 146,500 |
| | To reverse encumbrances and set up liability for capital outlay. | | |

Upon payment of the vouchers, assuming that $140,000 of the vouchers were paid, the entry would be:

| E14 | Accounts payable | $140,000 | |
| --- | --- | --- | --- |
| |     Cash | | $140,000 |
| | To pay vouchers for capital outlay. | | |

**Debt-Servicing Transactions** During the year, the city needed $180,000 to pay for all debt servicing. The entries to record the transactions pertaining to debt servicing and posted to the worksheet in Exhibit 6-6 are:

| E15 | Operating transfers—principal and interest | $180,000 | |
| --- | --- | --- | --- |
| |     Due to debt service fund | | $180,000 |
| | Payment to debt service funds for current debt obligations. | | |
| E16 | Due to debt service fund | $180,000 | |
| |     Cash | | $180,000 |
| | To pay amount to debt service fund. | | |

Note that the account debited is operating transfers instead of expenditures. Current principles of accounting require that all interfund operating transfers be classified separately from revenues or residual equity transfers and expenditures and shown separately on the statements. Interfund operating transfers include all transactions except loans or advances, quasi-external transactions, residual equity transfers, or reimbursements.

**Residual Equity Transfers** An appropriation had been made to the general government function to provide a residual equity transfer to the printing fund to set up that fund (see Exhibit 5-2 and transaction I1 in Chapter 3).

The journal entry for this transaction would be:

| E17 | Residual equity transfer | $150,000 | |
| --- | --- | --- | --- |
| |     Cash | | $150,000 |

All of the journal entries for the expenditure transactions have been summarized in Exhibit 6-2 and have been recorded in the worksheet (in Exhibit 6-6).

**EXHIBIT 6-2**
**Summary of Expenditure Transactions**
**City of Ruthberg**
**Year 19X6**

| No. | Transactions | Journal entry | Dr. | Cr. |
|---|---|---|---|---|
| | Personal services: | | | |
| E1 | Salaries and wages, $610,000 plus pension costs of $46,000 | Expenditures—personal services<br>    Accounts payable<br>    Due to agency fund<br>    Due to pension trust fund | $656,000 | $472,500<br>91,500<br>92,000 |
| E2 | Payment for salaries, wages, pension costs, and withholdings | Accounts payable<br>Due to agency fund<br>Due to pension trust fund<br>    Cash | 472,500<br>91,500<br>92,000 | 656,000 |
| | Materials and supplies: | | | |
| E3 | Encumbered ordered goods | Encumbrances<br>    Reserve for encumbrances | 420,000 | 420,000 |
| E4 | Goods and invoices received; encumbrances reversed for amount of original encumbrances, $410,000 of the original $420,000 | Reserve for encumbrances<br>    Encumbrances | 410,000 | 410,000 |
| E5 | Expenditures recorded for cost of goods and liability accrued, $407,000; $353,000 accounts payable; $54,000 due to printing fund | Expenditures—materials and supplies<br>    Accounts payable<br>    Due to printing fund | $407,000 | 353,000<br>54,000 |
| E6 | Paid $350,000 on accounts payable and $50,000 on due to printing fund related to materials and supplies transactions | Accounts payable<br>Due to printing fund<br>    Cash | 350,000<br>50,000 | 400,000 |
| E7 | To set up ending inventory of $25,000 | Inventory<br>    Reserve for inventory | 5,000 | 5,000 |
| | Contractual services: | | | |
| E8 | Set up encumbrances for contractual services, $318,000 | Encumbrances<br>    Reserve for encumbrances | 318,000 | 318,000 |
| E9 | Reversed portion of encumbrances | Reserve for encumbrances<br>    Encumbrances | 313,100 | 313,100 |
| E10 | Liability for expenditure for contractual services | Expenditures—contractual services<br>    Accounts payable | 313,100 | 313,100 |
| E11 | Paid accounts payable of $310,000 | Accounts payable<br>    Cash | 310,000 | 310,000 |
| | Capital outlay: | | | |
| E12 | Encumbrances for capital outlay | Encumbrances<br>    Reserve for encumbrances | 174,000 | 174,000 |
| E13 | Reversed encumbrances for portion when setting up liability for capital outlay | Reserve for encumbrances<br>Expenditures<br>    Encumbrances<br>    Accounts payable | 146,500<br>146,500 | 146,500<br>146,500 |

## EXHIBIT 6-2
*(continued)*

| No. | Transactions | Journal entry | Dr. | Cr. |
|---|---|---|---|---|
| E14 | Paid portion of accounts payable | Accounts payable<br>    Cash | 140,000 | 140,000 |
| E15 | Debt servicing:<br>Accrued amount payable for principal and interest to debt service fund | Operating transfers—principal and interest<br>    Due to debt service fund | 180,000 | 180,000 |
| E16 | Paid amount due to debt service fund for principal and interest | Due to debt service fund<br>    Cash | 180,000 | 180,000 |
| E17 | Residual equity transfer:<br>Transferred amount needed to set up printing fund | Residual equity transfer<br>    Cash | 150,000 | 150,000 |

## Expenditure Subsidiary Ledger

As was done with individual revenue transactions, individual types of expenditure transactions—by line item, budget and actual, and so forth—are brought together in a subsidiary ledger, and the total is controlled in a control account in the general ledger. The expenditure transactions from the subsidiary ledgers have been summarized in Exhibit 6-3.

## Prior Year's Transactions

**Transactions for Prior Year's Reserve for Encumbrances** When encumbrances do not lapse at the end of the fiscal year, the accounting for the prior year's reserve for encumbrances can be prepared in either of two ways: (1) add the prior year's reserve for encumbrances to the current year's appropriation and set up the encumbrances as if they were current-year encumbrances; or (2) keep the prior year's reserve for encumbrances open, and charge all expenditures against the reserve for encumbrances as expenditures against the prior year's reserve for encumbrances.

An illustration of each of these methods is as follows:

*Illustration 1* The prior year's reserve is added to current year's appropriation. At the beginning of the current year, make the following entries:

| | Dr. | Cr. |
|---|---|---|
| Reserve for encumbrances (19X5) | $45,000 | |
|     Appropriations (19X6) | | $45,000 |
| Encumbrances | $45,000 | |
|     Reserve for encumbrances | | $45,000 |

When the goods and invoice are received, the expenditures are shown at the actual cost and the encumbrances and reserve for encumbrances are reversed at the estimated cost. Assuming that the goods cost $42,000, the entries would be:

## CHAPTER 6: EXPENDITURE ACCOUNTING, CLOSING ENTRIES, AND FINANCIAL STATEMENTS

**EXHIBIT 6-3**
**Summary of Expenditures Ledger**
**City of Ruthberg**
**Fiscal Year 19X6**

|  | Budget Cr. | Expenditure Spent Dr. | Encumbered Dr. | Over (+) or under(−) |
|---|---|---|---|---|
| Personal service |  |  |  |  |
| Total | 677,000 | 656,000 |  | 21,000 |
| General government | 160,000 | 155,000 |  | 5,000 |
| Education | 200,000 | 197,000 |  | 3,000 |
| Public works | 100,000 | 93,000 |  | 7,000 |
| Public safety | 120,000 | 115,000 |  | 5,000 |
| Health and welfare | 97,000 | 96,000 |  | 1,000 |
| Supplies |  |  |  |  |
| Total | 437,000 | 407,000 | 10,000 | 20,000 |
| General government | 20,000 | 19,000 | 1,000 |  |
| Education | 90,000 | 80,000 | 2,000 | 8,000 |
| Public works | 180,000 | 171,000 | 4,000 | 5,000 |
| Public safety | 65,000 | 60,000 | 1,500 | 3,500 |
| Health and welfare | 82,000 | 77,000 | 1,500 | 3,500 |
| Contractual services |  |  |  |  |
| Total | 332,000 | 313,100 | 4,900 | 14,000 |
| General government | 21,000 | 19,700 | 500 | 800 |
| Education | 70,000 | 66,300 | 1,200 | 2,500 |
| Public works | 65,000 | 59,500 | 700 | 4,800 |
| Public safety | 115,000 | 109,000 | 2,000 | 4,000 |
| Health and welfare | 61,000 | 58,600 | 500 | 1,900 |
| Capital outlay |  |  |  |  |
| Total | 174,000 | 146,500 | 27,500 |  |
| General government | 80,000 | 60,000 | 20,000 |  |
| Education | 22,000 | 20,000 | 2,000 |  |
| Public works | 20,000 | 19,000 | 1,000 |  |
| Public safety | 12,000 | 10,500 | 1,500 |  |
| Health and welfare | 40,000 | 37,000 | 3,000 |  |
| Debt servicing |  |  |  |  |
| Total | 200,000 | 180,000 |  | 20,000 |
| General government | 200,000 | 180,000 |  | 20,000 |
| Residual equity transfer |  |  |  |  |
| Total | 150,000 | 150,000 |  |  |
| General government | 150,000 | 150,000 |  |  |
| Totals | $1,970,000 | $1,852,600 | $42,400 | $75,000 |

|  | Dr. | Cr. |
|---|---|---|
| Reserve for encumbrances | $45,000 |  |
|     Encumbrances |  | $45,000 |
| Expenditures | $42,000 |  |
|     Accounts payable |  | $42,000 |

*Illustration 2* The prior year's reserves remain open. Expenditures are charged to "Expenditures against 19X5 reserve for encumbrances." (This method will be used in

the illustrative entries in order to keep the actual expenditures in mind when preparing the current year's statement comparing budget with actual.)

Assuming that the actual cost of the goods was only $42,000, for which the reserve for encumbrances for 19X5 was $45,000, the following entry would be made (entries B1–B6 appear in Chapter 5):

| | | | |
|---|---|---|---|
| B7 | Expenditures against 19X5 reserve for encumbrances | $42,000 | |
| | Accounts payable | | $42,000 |

To record expenditures encumbered against 19X5 appropriations: general government, supplies, $30,000; education, equipment (truck), $12,000.

When this is done and all expenditures for the year have been recorded, the expenditure against the 19X5 reserve for encumbrances account would then be closed to the 19X5 reserve for encumbrances account, with the difference going to fund balance as follows:

| | | | |
|---|---|---|---|
| B8 | Reserve for encumbrances—19X5 | $45,000 | |
| | Expenditures against 19X5 reserve for encumbrances | | $42,000 |
| | Fund balance | | $ 3,000 |

To close 19X5 appropriations by closing 19X5 expenditures and reserve for encumbrances accounts to fund balance.

Through this method of recording the transactions, the city is able to prepare statements that show total expenditures for the year and also is able to match current year's expenditures and encumbrances against the current year's appropriation. This will be shown in the illustration of general fund statements at the end of the chapter.

The entries for Illustration 2 are posted to the worksheet in Exhibit 6-6.

**Other Prior-Year Balances** The accounts payable for the prior year of $9,000, along with $42,000 worth of goods that were encumbered and became expenditures, total $51,000. The entry to record the payment of these accounts is:

| | | | |
|---|---|---|---|
| B9 | Accounts payable | $51,000 | |
| | Cash | | $51,000 |

To pay accounts of the prior year and account for encumbered goods received this year.

These transaction entries are summarized in Exhibit 6-4 and posted to the worksheet in Exhibit 6-6.

## Closing Entries

When budgetary transactions are recorded in the records, they become just as important a part of the accounting information as the actual transactions. When the budget was adopted, as seen in journal entry 1 in Chapter 5 (page 126), the accountant records

CHAPTER 6: EXPENDITURE ACCOUNTING, CLOSING ENTRIES, AND FINANCIAL STATEMENTS   163

**EXHIBIT 6-4**
**Summary of Prior Year's Expenditure Transactions**
**Fiscal Year 19X6**

| No. | Transactions | Journal entry | Dr. | Cr. |
|---|---|---|---|---|
|  | Prior year's reserve for encumbrances: |  |  |  |
| B7 | Received goods and invoices for previous year's encumbered order—$42,000 total cost: supplies $30,000; equipment $12,000 | Expenditures against 19X5 reserve for encumbrances<br>Accounts payable | 42,000 | 42,000 |
| B8 | Closed 19X5 reserve for encumbrances account | Reserve for encumbrances, 19X5<br>Expenditures against 19X5 reserve for encumbrances<br>Fund balance | 45,000 | 42,000<br>3,000 |
|  | Other prior-year balances: |  |  |  |
| B9 | Paid prior year's accounts | Accounts payable<br>Cash | 51,000 | 51,000 |

both the appropriations and the estimated revenues in the records. The difference between the estimated revenues and the appropriations, as seen in this journal entry, is $180,000, which goes to the fund balance account. This $180,000 is now available for current or future appropriations.

When closing the books for the fiscal year, the budgetary transactions are considered just as important as the actual transactions. To close the books for the fiscal year, as a general rule, actual transactions are closed against budgetary transactions. For example, revenues usually are closed against estimated revenues, and expenditures and encumbrances are closed against the appropriations. These can be individual entries or a compound entry. While the general rule is to close actual accounts against budgetary accounts, no accounting principle states this rule. Therefore, budgetary accounts (estimated revenues, appropriations, and encumbrances) can be closed against each other, and actual accounts (revenues and expenditures) can be closed against each other, with the balances going to fund balance.

To illustrate the closing entries for the city of Ruthberg, the estimated revenues (including the operating grants) were $2,150,000. The actual revenues, including the operating grants of $310,000, were $2,133,560. The journal entry to close these items would be:

|  |  | Dr. | Cr. |
|---|---|---|---|
| C1 | Revenues | $1,823,560 |  |
|  | Operating grants | 310,000 |  |
|  | Fund balance | 16,440 |  |
|  | Estimated revenues |  | $2,150,000 |

To close revenues and estimated revenues accounts with the difference going to fund balance.

The journal entries to close out the encumbrances account (C2) and the transfers and expenditures accounts (C3) are:

| | | | |
|---|---|---|---|
| C2 | Appropriations | $42,400 | |
| | Encumbrances | | $42,400 |
| | To close out encumbrances to appropriations. | | |
| C3 | Appropriations | $1,927,600 | |
| | Operating transfers | | $180,000 |
| | Residual equity transfer | | 150,000 |
| | Expenditures | | 1,522,600 |
| | Fund balance | | 75,000 |
| | To close out appropriations, operating transfers, residual equity transfers, and expenditures to fund balance. | | |

These transactions are summarized in Exhibit 6-5.

The total of the two amounts going to the fund balance account—a $16,440 debit from the revenues transactions and a $75,000 credit from the expenditures, encumbrances, and transfers transactions—net $58,560. Along with the $180,000 credit coming from the original budgetary transactions and the $3,000 credit from the prior year's reserve for encumbrance transaction, the fund balance account would be increased during the period by $241,560. With the original balance of $62,100 and the above yearly increase, the ending balance is $303,660. Obviously, $42,400 remaining in the reserve for encumbrance account and $25,000 in the reserve for inventory account could also be reservations of the fund balance. The amounts in these two reserve accounts, however, could not be appropriated as a part of next year's unappropriated surplus. A reserve account is set up from the fund balance account in order to assure that the resources that are contra to these accounts will not be appropriated.

## Worksheet of Transactions During the Year

Exhibit 6-6, the worksheet of transactions for the city of Ruthberg, reflects all of the transactions discussed in this chapter and in Chapter 5. It also brings together, from the statement columns of the worksheet, the information that is used to prepare the financial statements.

### EXHIBIT 6-5
### Summary of Closing Entries
### City of Ruthberg
### Fiscal Year 19X6

| No. | Transaction | Journal entry | Dr. | Cr. |
|---|---|---|---|---|
| C1 | Budgeted and actual revenue closings | Revenues | $1,823,560 | |
| | | Operating grants | 310,000 | |
| | | Fund balance | 16,440 | |
| | | Estimated revenue | | $2,150,000 |
| C2 | Appropriations and encumbrances closings | Appropriations | 42,400 | |
| | | Encumbrances | | 42,400 |
| C3 | Appropriations, transfers, and expenditures closings | Appropriations | 1,927,600 | |
| | | Operating transfers | | 180,000 |
| | | Residual equity transfers | | 150,000 |
| | | Expenditures | | 1,522,600 |
| | | Fund balance | | 75,000 |

## Financial Statements

The general and special revenue funds should have three financial statements shown for each governmental fund for which a budget has been adopted:

1 A balance sheet, with any necessary schedules or notes to show compliance with related legal and contractual provisions (see Exhibit 6-7).

2 A statement of revenues, expenditures, and changes in fund balance (see Exhibit 6-8).

3 A statement (or schedule if budget is not on GAAP basis) of revenues, expenditures, and changes in fund balance, budget and actual. When budgets are used but are not on the GAAP (modified accrual) basis, see Exhibit 6-9. When budgets are used that are on the GAAP basis, see Exhibit 13-5.

Comparative statements for at least two years are generally provided to the public, although not required by GAAP. All information is not available for this type of an illustration, so statements for only one year are shown. In Exhibit 6-8 encumbrances are not shown as expenditures, and in Exhibit 6-7 the reserve for encumbrances is shown as a reservation of fund balance and not a liability. Note that the expenditures against the prior year's reserve for encumbrances must be added to this year's expenditures to obtain the total expenditures for the year.

Control within the city is usually through the line-item elements of the budget; yet, when comparing the budget to the actual, it is by functions and by character of expenditure. General fund expenditures for capital outlay are usually shown as current operating expenditures and not as capital outlay in the combined statement (see Exhibit 13-8).

By reference to the summarized revenues and expenditures subsidiary ledgers, the detail concerning revenues, expenditures (whether by objects or by functions), and encumbrances (including the increase or decrease in the reserve for encumbrances) can be obtained for the revenue statements.

## Budget Comparison Schedule

The National Council on Governmental Accounting states that "encumbrances outstanding at year end do not constitute expenditures or liabilities."[3] When closing expenditure and appropriation accounts, the amount encumbered against the appropriation is not considered as an expenditure for the current year to be included in the financial statements. However, when the appropriation is on the encumbrance basis, rather than on the GAAP modified accrual basis, the encumbrances for the year end as well as those at the beginning of the year must be known. This is necessary in order to compare the expenditures and encumbrances for the year with the appropriation. This schedule, a comparison of the budget with the actual, is a necessary statement if generally accepted accounting principles are followed. It is called the combined statement of revenues, expenditures, and changes in fund balances—budget and actual—general and special revenue fund types (and similar governmental fund types for which annual budgets have been legally adopted).[4]

In accepting the National Council on Governmental Accounting's *Statement 1* as a

**EXHIBIT 6-6**
**City of Ruthberg, General Fund**
**Fiscal Year 19X6**
**Worksheet**

| Account | Balance beginning of year Dr. | Balance beginning of year Cr. | Transactions during year Dr. | | Transactions during year Cr. | |
|---|---|---|---|---|---|---|
| Cash | 0  63,090 | | B1 | 6,000 | B9 | 51,000 |
| | | | B2 | 240 | | |
| | | | B3 | 5,220 | E2 | 656,000 |
| | | | B4 | 5,000 | E6 | 400,000 |
| | | | R2–R6, R8 | 1,196,000 | E11 | 310,000 |
| | | | R9 | 561,000 | | |
| | | | R13 | 42,000 | E14 | 140,000 |
| | | | R14 | 1,600 | E16 | 180,000 |
| | | | R15 | 310,000 | E17 | 150,000 |
| | | | B6 | 40,500 | | |
| Taxes receivable—current | | | R1 | 600,000 | B5 | 3,600 |
| | | | | | R9 | 570,000 |
| | | | | | R10 | 26,400 |
| Allowance for estimated uncollectible taxes—current | | | R9 | 9,000 | R1 | 30,000 |
| | | | R10 | 21,000 | | |
| Taxes receivable—delinquent | 0  14,400 | | R10 | 26,400 | B1 | 14,400 |
| Allowance for estimated uncollectible taxes—delinquent | | 0  9,000 | B1 | 8,400 | R10 | 21,000 |
| Due from bus fund | 0  40,500 | | | | B6 | 40,500 |
| Interest and penalties—delinquent taxes | 0  360 | | R11 | 450 | B2 | 360 |
| Allowance for uncollectible interest and penalties—delinquent taxes | | 0  90 | B2 | 120 | R11 | 90 |
| Accounts receivable | 0  5,400 | | R12 | 57,640 | B4 | 5,400 |
| | | | | | R13 | 42,210 |
| Allowance for estimated losses—accounts receivable | | 0  180 | B4 | 400 | R12 | 440 |
| | | | R13 | 210 | | |
| Tax liens receivable | 0  5,400 | | | | B3 | 5,400 |
| Allowance for estimated uncollectible tax liens receivable | | 0  180 | B3 | 180 | | |
| Due from state | | | R7 | 110,000 | R15 | 110,000 |
| Due from federal government | | | R7 | 200,000 | R15 | 200,000 |
| Inventory | 0  20,000 | | E7 | 5,000 | | |
| Accounts payable | | 0  9,000 | B9 | 51,000 | B7 | 42,000 |
| | | | E2 | 472,500 | E1 | 472,500 |
| | | | E6 | 350,000 | E5 | 353,000 |
| | | | E11 | 310,000 | E10 | 313,100 |
| | | | E14 | 140,000 | E13 | 146,500 |
| Due to printing fund | | | E6 | 50,000 | E5 | 54,000 |
| Due to agency fund | | | E2 | 91,500 | E1 | 91,500 |
| Due to pension trust fund | | | E2 | 92,000 | E1 | 92,000 |

**EXHIBIT 6-6**
*(continued)*

|  Trial balance end of year  || Revenues and expenditures statement || Balance sheet ||
|---|---|---|---|---|---|
| Dr. | Cr. | Dr. | Cr. | Dr. | Cr. |
| 343,650 |  |  |  | 343,650 |  |
|  |  |  |  |  |  |
| 26,400 |  |  |  | 26,400 |  |
|  | 21,600 |  |  |  | 21,600 |
| 450 |  |  |  | 450 |  |
|  | 60 |  |  |  | 60 |
| 15,430 |  |  |  | 15,430 |  |
|  | 10 |  |  |  | 10 |
|  |  |  |  |  |  |
| 25,000 |  |  |  | 25,000 |  |
|  | 12,600 |  |  |  | 12,600 |
|  |  |  |  |  |  |
|  | 4,000 |  |  |  | 4,000 |

## EXHIBIT 6-6
*(continued)*

| Account | Balance beginning of year Dr. | Balance beginning of year Cr. | Transactions during year Dr. | | Transactions during year Cr. | |
|---|---|---|---|---|---|---|
| Taxes collected in advance | 0 | 3,600 | B5 | 3,600 | R14 | 1,600 |
| Fund balance | 0 | 62,100 | | | B8 | 3,000 |
| | | | | | 1 | 180,000 |
| Due to debt service fund | | | E16 | 180,000 | E15 | 180,000 |
| Reserve for encumbrances—19X5 | 0 | 45,000 | B8 | 45,000 | | |
| Reserve for encumbrances—19X6 | | | E4 | 410,000 | E3 | 420,000 |
| | | | E9 | 313,100 | E8 | 318,000 |
| | | | E13 | 146,500 | E12 | 174,000 |
| Reserve for inventory | 0 | 20,000 | | | E7 | 5,000 |
| Expenditures against 19X5 reserve for encumbrances | | | B7 | 42,000 | B8 | 42,000 |
| Estimated revenues | | | 1 | 2,150,000 | | |
| Revenues | | | | | R1 | 570,000 |
| | | | | | R2–R6, R8 | 1,196,000 |
| | | | | | R11 | 360 |
| | | | | | R12 | 57,200 |
| Operating grant | | | | | R7 | 310,000 |
| Appropriations | | | | | 1 | 1,970,000 |
| Expenditures | | | E1 | 656,000 | | |
| | | | E5 | 407,000 | | |
| | | | E10 | 313,100 | | |
| | | | E13 | 146,500 | | |
| Operating transfers | | | E17 | 180,000 | | |
| Residual equity transfer | | | E17 | 150,000 | | |
| Encumbrances | | | E3 | 420,000 | E4 | 410,000 |
| | | | E8 | 318,000 | E9 | 313,100 |
| | | | E12 | 174,000 | E1 | 146,500 |
| Totals | $149,150 | $149,150 | | $10,818,160 | | $10,818,160 |
| Fund balance | | | | | | |
| Totals | | | | | | |

basis for generally accepted accounting principles for state and local governments, the American Institute of Certified Public Accountants says:

> Accounting and reporting of encumbrances should follow the approach recommended in *Statement 1*: Encumbrances outstanding at year-end should not be reported as expenditures or liabilities. The budgetary comparison statement (paragraph .04c), however, should present comparisons of the legally adopted budget with actual data on the budgetary basis, which may include encumbrances or other differences from generally accepted accounting principles.[5]

CHAPTER 6: EXPENDITURE ACCOUNTING, CLOSING ENTRIES, AND FINANCIAL STATEMENTS  169

**EXHIBIT 6-6**
*(continued)*

| Trial balance end of year | | Revenues and expenditures statement | | Balance sheet | |
|---|---|---|---|---|---|
| Dr. | Cr. | Dr. | Cr. | Dr. | Cr. |
|  | 1,600 |  |  |  | 1,600 |
|  | 245,100 |  |  |  | 245,100 |
|  | 42,400 |  |  |  | 42,400 |
|  | 25,000 |  |  |  | 25,000 |
| 2,150,000 |  | 2,150,000 |  |  |  |
|  | 1,823,560 |  | 1,823,560 |  |  |
|  | 310,000 |  | 310,000 |  |  |
|  | 1,970,000 |  | 1,970,000 |  |  |
| 1,522,600 |  | 1,522,600 |  |  |  |
| 180,000 |  | 180,000 |  |  |  |
| 150,000 |  | 150,000 |  |  |  |
| 42,400 |  | 42,400 |  |  |  |
| $4,455,930 | $4,455,930 | 4,045,000 | 4,103,560 | 410,930 | 352,370 |
|  |  | 58,560 |  |  | 58,560 |
|  |  | $4,103,560 | $4,103,560 | $410,930 | $410,930 |

All expenditures for the year have been shown in Exhibit 6-8—the statement of revenues, expenditures, and changes in fund balance. To obtain meaningful figures for comparing the budgeted appropriations with budget expenditures, expenditures related to the prior year's appropriation must be eliminated and this year's encumbrances must be added. This information is usually shown in a separate schedule (see Exhibit 6-9).

Note in Exhibit 6-9 that expenditures against the prior year's reserve of encumbrances, which have been included as expenditures in this year's statement of revenue and expenditures, must be deducted from actual expenditures and this year's encum-

## EXHIBIT 6-7
### City of Ruthberg—General Fund
### Balance Sheet
### June 30, 19X6

#### Assets

| | | | |
|---|---|---|---|
| Cash | | | $343,650 |
| Taxes receivable—delinquent | | $26,400 | |
| Less allowance for estimated uncollectibles | | 21,600 | 4,800 |
| Interest and penalties—delinquent taxes | | 450 | |
| Less allowance for estimated uncollectible interest and penalties | | 60 | 390 |
| Accounts receivable | | 15,430 | |
| Less allowance for estimated losses | | 10 | 15,420 |
| Inventory | | | 25,000 |
| Total assets | | | $389,260 |

#### Liabilities and Fund Balance

| | | | |
|---|---|---|---|
| Liabilities: | | | |
|   Accounts payable | | 12,600 | |
|   Due to printing fund | | 4,000 | |
|   Taxes collected in advance | | 1,600 | |
| Total liabilities | | | 18,200 |
| Fund balance (June 30, 19X6): | | | |
|   Unappropriated | | 303,660 | |
|   Appropriated: | | | |
|     Reserve for encumbrances | $42,400 | | |
|     Reserve for inventories | 25,000 | 67,400 | 371,060 |
| Total liabilities and fund balance | | | $389,260 |

brances added to the actual expenditures in order to analyze whether the appropriations have been overspent. This addition and deduction column does not need to be shown in the schedule; only the columns for budget, actual on budgetary basis, and variance are necessary. If not shown in the schedule, however, it should be shown in the notes to the financial statements.

## VARIATIONS IN PROCEDURES AND SPECIALIZED NEEDS

The accounting needs for smaller governmental organizations often can best be met by varying some of the procedures that have been discussed in this chapter. For example, smaller organizations can keep their accounting records during the year on the cash basis and adjust their statements to the modified accrual basis at the end of the year. In addition, the cash for several funds can be kept in one bank account, with the records for each fund providing the detail concerning the amount for each fund. As long as

## EXHIBIT 6-8
### City of Ruthberg—General Fund
### Statement of Revenues, Expenditures, and Changes in Fund Balance
### Year Ended June 30, 19X6

| | | | | |
|---|---|---|---|---|
| Revenues | | | | |
| Real property taxes | | | $570,000 | |
| Personal property taxes | | | 83,000 | |
| Income taxes | | | 308,000 | |
| Sales taxes | | | 485,000 | |
| Licenses and permits | | | 256,000 | |
| Fines and forfeits | | | 29,000 | |
| Intergovernmental services | | | 57,200 | |
| Operating grants | | | 310,000 | |
| Miscellaneous | | | 35,360 | |
| Total revenues | | | | $2,133,560 |
| Expenditures and other uses of financial resources | | | | |
| General government | | | $283,700 | |
| Education | | | 375,300 | |
| Public works | | | 342,500 | |
| Public safety | | | 294,500 | |
| Health and welfare | | | 268,600 | |
| Total expenditures | | | | 1,564,600 |
| Excess of revenues over expenditures | | | | 568,960 |
| Transfers | | | | |
| Operating transfer to debt service fund for payments of principal and interest | | | 180,000 | |
| Residual equity transfer to start printing fund | | | 150,000 | |
| Total transfers | | | | 330,000 |
| Excess of revenues over expenditures and other uses of financial resources | | | | $ 238,960 |
| Fund balance, July 1, 19X5 | | | | |
| Unappropriated | | | 62,100 | |
| Reserved: | | | | |
| Reserved for encumbrances | | $45,000 | | |
| Reserved for inventories | 20,000 | | | |
| Increase for year | 5,000 | 25,000 | 70,000 | 132,100 |
| Fund balance June 30, 19X6 | | | | 371,060 |
| Fund balance June 30, 19X6 | | | | |
| Unappropriated | | | 303,660 | |
| Reserved: | | | | |
| Reserved for encumbrances | | 42,400 | | |
| Reserved for inventories | | 25,000 | 67,400 | |
| Fund balance June 30, 19X6 | | | | $ 371,060 |

## EXHIBIT 6-9
### City of Ruthberg—General Fund
### Statement of Revenues, Expenditures, and Changes in Fund Balance—Budget and Actual
### Year Ended June 30, 19X6

|  | Budget | Actual (GAAP basis) | Encumbrances (−) prior year (+) current year | Actual (budgetary basis) | Variances (+) favorable (−) unfavorable |
|---|---|---|---|---|---|
| Revenues |  |  |  |  |  |
| Real property taxes | $ 570,000 | $ 570,000 |  | $ 570,000 |  |
| Personal property taxes | 80,000 | 83,000 |  | 83,000 | $+ 3,000 |
| Income taxes | 290,000 | 308,000 |  | 308,000 | +18,000 |
| Sales taxes | 500,000 | 485,000 |  | 485,000 | −15,000 |
| Licenses and permits | 250,000 | 256,000 |  | 256,000 | + 6,000 |
| Fines and forfeits | 32,000 | 29,000 |  | 29,000 | − 3,000 |
| Intergovernmental services | 81,000 | 57,200 |  | 57,200 | −23,800 |
| Operating grants | 310,000 | 310,000 |  | 310,000 |  |
| Miscellaneous | 37,000 | 35,360 |  | 35,360 | − 1,640 |
| Total revenues | 2,150,000 | 2,133,560 |  | 2,133,560 | −16,440 |
| Expenditures and other uses of financial resources |  |  |  |  |  |
| Expenditures: |  |  |  |  |  |
| General government | 281,000 | 283,700 | −30,000 +21,500 | 275,200 | + 5,800 |
| Education | 382,000 | 375,300 | −12,000 + 5,200 | 368,500 | +13,500 |
| Public works | 365,000 | 342,500 | + 5,700 | 348,200 | +16,800 |
| Public safety | 312,000 | 294,500 | + 5,000 | 299,500 | +12,500 |
| Health and welfare | 280,000 | 268,600 | + 5,000 | 273,600 | + 6,400 |
| Total expenditures | 1,620,000 | 1,564,600 | + 400 | 1,565,000 | +55,000 |
| Operating transfers | 200,000 | 180,000 |  | 180,000 | +20,000 |
| Residual equity transfers | 150,000 | 150,000 |  | 150,000 |  |
| Total expenditures and transfers | 1,970,000 | 1,894,600 | + 400 | 1,895,000 | +75,000 |
| Excess of revenue over expenditures and other uses of financial resources | 180,000 | 238,960 | + 400 | 238,560 | +58,560 |
| Increase in fund balance | 132,100 | 132,100 |  | 132,100 |  |
| Fund balance, 6/30/19X6 | $ 312,100 | $ 371,060 | + 400 | $ 370,660 | $+58,560 |

statements can be prepared in accordance with GAAP, the procedures used in the accounting records can be varied according to the needs of the user.

The procedures discussed in this chapter are principally for financial reporting purposes. Variation in accounting procedures and the use of information from the accounting system that can be used for managerial decision making will be discussed in Parts III and IV of this book. Therefore, management accounting procedures have not been considered in this chapter.

## SUMMARY

This chapter has dealt with the principles and practices of expenditures, closing entries, and financial statements for general and special revenue funds. As was stated in Chapter 5, the principles and practices for general funds apply equally to special revenue funds, so only general fund expenditures, closing entries, and financial statements were illustrated in this chapter.

The special features of this chapter showed the accounting entries for expenditures transactions by function and by object of expenditure. Five functions—general government, education, public works, public safety, and health and welfare—were employed to illustrate the accounting for general and special revenue funds. Six objects of expenditure—personal services, material and supplies, contractual services, capital outlay, debt servicing, and residual equity transfers—were employed as expenditure categories in the continuation of our illustrative city of Ruthberg.

The information in Chapters 5 and 6 on general and special revenue funds is the foundation for understanding the other governmental funds of governmental units.

## QUESTIONS

1. What are some of the characteristics of expenditures in general and special revenue funds?
2. Materials and supplies were ordered with an estimated cost of $28,000. The materials and supplies were shipped and an invoice in the amount of $32,000 was received. Give the necessary journal entries to record these transactions.
3. Assume that there were appropriations of $250,000 and that the actual expenditures for the year were $210,000. Also, there was an encumbered appropriation of $15,000 for a truck that had been ordered but not received. The actual revenue for the year was $265,000. The estimated revenue was $260,000. Give all necessary closing journal entries.
4. What is the purpose of subsidiary expenditure ledgers in the general fund?
5. How does budgetary information facilitate control of expenditure transactions?
6. How are expenditures classified?
7. Salaries and wages for the pay period ending June 30 19X1 were $120,000, 20 percent of which was withheld for taxes. The city contributed 10 percent for pensions, and the employee contributed the other 10 percent. The fiscal year for this city begins on July 1. Give the related journal entries.
8. What are the two methods for accounting for inventory items? How are the two methods handled differently in the accounts?
9. At the end of 19X1, there was $50,000 in inventory still available. The prior year's statement showed only $45,000. Give the necessary journal entries to set up this inventory account.
10. The city signed contracts with local contractors totaling $35,000 for maintenance of the city hall. Earlier in the budgetary process, they had figured $38,000 would be needed for maintenance of the building. Payments during the year for these contracts totaled $32,000. What journal entries are needed to record these events?
11. What is the difference between "expenditures" and "transfers"? What are the two types of transfers?
12. The city received $75,000 from federal revenue sharing that was originally recorded in a special revenue fund and immediately transferred to the general fund. The general fund im-

mediately contracted for improvements to the city park. The estimated contract cost was $67,000. Give the journal entries for the special revenue fund as well as for the general fund that will be used to account for these transactions.

13  A new automobile, ordered for department B in function C, on January 31, 19X1, was expected to cost $10,000. The automobile was received on April 1, 19X1 and cost $10,700. Record these transactions.

14  Which financial statements are prepared for a city's general and special revenue funds?

15  Two employees of a city were to attend a meeting in early April. In the latter part of March, they requested permission to attend that meeting, and funds were encumbered to provide for their travel. Record this transaction. The expected costs were $750.

16  Salaries of $50,000 were to be paid for the payroll period ending December 31, 19X0. Withholdings for taxes were 10 percent; pension costs were 6 percent on the employee and 6 percent on the city. Record this transaction.

17  Explain the preparation of budgetary comparison schedules when the budgets are not on a GAAP basis.

## PROBLEMS

**6-1** Circle the most appropriate answer to the following questions.[6]

1  One of the differences between accounting for a governmental (not-for-profit) unit and a commercial (for-profit) enterprise is that a governmental (not-for-profit) unit should
   a  Not record depreciation expense in any of its funds
   b  Always establish and maintain complete self-balancing accounts for each fund
   c  Use only the cash basis of accounting
   d  Use only the modified accrual basis of accounting

2  What type of account is used to earmark the fund balance to liquidate the contingent obligations of goods ordered but not yet received?
   a  Appropriations
   b  Encumbrances
   c  Expenditures
   d  Reserve for encumbrances

3  When fixed assets purchased from general fund revenues were received, the appropriate journal entry was made in the general fixed assets account group. What account, if any, should have been debited in the general fund?
   a  No journal entry should have been made in the general fund
   b  Expenditures
   c  Fixed assets
   d  Due from general fixed assets account group

4  Repairs that have been made for a governmental unit, and for which a bill has been received, should be recorded in the general fund as an
   a  Appropriation
   b  Encumbrance
   c  Expenditure
   d  Expense

5  An expenditure account appears in
   a  The general fixed assets account group
   b  The general long-term debt account group

c A specific revenue fund
d An internal service fund

6 Which of the following steps in the acquisition of goods and services occurs first?
a Appropriation
b Encumbrance
c Budget
d Expenditure

7 Which of the following expenditures is normally recorded on the accrual basis in the general fund?
a Interest
b Personal services
c Inventory items
d Prepaid expenses

8 Authority granted by a legislative body to make expenditures and to incur obligations during a fiscal year is the definition of an
a Appropriation
b Authorization
c Encumbrance
d Expenditure

9 The initial transfer of cash from the general fund in order to establish an internal service fund would require the general fund to credit cash and debit
a Accounts receivable—internal service fund
b Residual equity transfer to internal service fund
c Reserve for encumbrances
d Appropriations

6-2 Circle the most appropriate answer to the following.[7]

1 Which of the following terms refers to an actual cost rather than an estimate?
a Expenditure
b Appropriation
c Budget
d Encumbrances

2 What journal entry should be made at the end of the fiscal year to close out encumbrances for which goods and services have not been received?
a Debit reserve for encumbrances and credit encumbrances
b Debit reserve for encumbrances and credit fund balance
c Debit fund balance (appropriation) and credit encumbrances
d Debit encumbrances and credit reserve for encumbrances

3 Which of the following accounts is closed out at the end of the fiscal year?
a Fund balance
b Expenditures
c Accounts payable
d Reserve for encumbrances

4 The following financial statement is prepared for the special revenue funds for the city of New Caledonia.
a A statement of revenues and expenses
b A combined statement of revenues and expenditures
c A statement of changes in retained earnings
d A combining balance sheet

The following information applies to questions number 5 through 7. The following balances in the accounts of the town of Brunswick are those that can be involved in closing entries at the end of the fiscal year:

| | |
|---|---:|
| Estimated revenues | $2,000,000 |
| Appropriations | 1,975,000 |
| Fund balance | 25,000 |
| Revenues | 2,010,000 |
| Expenditures | 1,887,000 |
| Encumbrances | 25,000 |
| Reserve for encumbrances | 25,000 |

**5** The following entry should be made to close the revenue accounts:

    **a** Fund balance      $ 25,000
        Appropriations      1,975,000
           Estimated revenues      $2,000,000
    **b** Fund balance      $ 10,000
        Estimated revenues      2,000,000
           Revenues      $2,010,000
    **c** Revenues      $2,010,000
           Estimated revenues      $2,000,000
           Fund balance      10,000
    **d** Estimated revenues      $2,000,000
           Appropriations      $1,975,000
           Fund balance      25,000

**6** The following entry should be made to close expenditures.

    **a** Encumbrances      $ 25,000
        Expenditures      1,887,000
           Reserve for encumbrances      $ 25,000
           Appropriations      1,887,000
    **b** Expenditures      $25,000
           Encumbrances      $25,000
    **c** Appropriations      $1,812,000
           Expenditures      $1,812,000
    **d** Appropriations      $1,925,000
           Expenditures      $1,887,000
           Fund balance      38,000

**7** The entry to record the closing of the encumbrance account is:

    **a** Appropriations      $25,000
           Encumbrances      $25,000
    **b** Reserve for encumbrances      $25,000
           Encumbrances      $25,000
    **c** Encumbrances      $25,000
           Reserve for encumbrances      $25,000
    **d** Expenditures      $25,000
           Reserve for encumbrances      $25,000

**6-3** The city of Happy Hollow has engaged a CPA to examine its financial statements for the year ended December 31, 19X9. The CPA finds that a budget was approved by the city council and was recorded at the beginning of the year, but all transactions during the year have been recorded on the cash basis. The city was incorporated as a municipality and began operations on January 1, 19X9. The bookkeeper provided the CPA an operating fund trial balance.[8]

**City of Happy Hollow**
**Trial Balance**
**December 31, 19X9**

|  | Operating trial balance |
|---|---|
| **Debits** | |
| Cash | $238,900 |
| Expenditures | 72,500 |
| Estimated revenues | 114,100 |
| Encumbrances | |
| Taxes receivable | |
| Inventories | |
| Totals | $425,500 |
| **Credits** | |
| Appropriations | $102,000 |
| Revenues | 108,400 |
| Bonds payable | 200,000 |
| Premium on bonds payable | 3,000 |
| Fund balance | 12,100 |
| Estimated uncollectible taxes | |
| Reserve for encumbrances | |
| Reserve for inventories | |
| Accounts payable | |
| Totals | $425,500 |

**1** Examination of the appropriation-expenditure ledger revealed the following information:

|  | Budgeted | Actual |
|---|---|---|
| Personal services | $ 45,000 | $38,500 |
| Supplies | 19,000 | 11,000 |
| Equipment | 38,000 | 23,000 |
| Totals | $102,000 | $72,500 |

**2** Supplies and equipment in the amounts of $4,000 and $10,000, respectively, had been received, but the vouchers had not been paid at December 31.

**3** At December 31, outstanding purchase orders for supplies and equipment not yet received were $1,200 and $3,800, respectively.

**4** The inventory of supplies on December 31 was $1,700 by physical count. A city ordinance required that expenditures are to be based on purchases, not on the basis of usage.

**5** Examination of the revenue subsidiary ledger revealed the following information:

|  | Budgeted | Actual |
|---|---|---|
| Property taxes | $102,600 | $ 96,000 |
| Licenses | 7,400 | 7,900 |
| Fines | 4,100 | 4,500 |
| Totals | $114,100 | $108,400 |

It was estimated that 5 percent of the property taxes would not be collected. Accordingly, property taxes were levied in an amount so that collections would yield the budgeted amount of $102,600.

6 On November 1, 19X9, Happy Hollow issued 8 percent general obligation term bonds with $200,000 face value for a premium of $3,000. Interest is payable each May 1 and November 1 until the maturity date of November 1, 19Z9. The city council ordered that the cash from the bond premium be set aside and restricted for the eventual retirement of the debt principal. The bonds were issued to finance the construction of a city hall, but no contracts had been let as of December 31, 19X9.

**Required**:

1 Prepare a worksheet showing journal entries to adjust the general fund accounts in conformity with generally accepted accounting principles applicable to governmental entities.
2 Identify the financial statements that should be prepared for the general fund. (You are not required to prepare those statements.)
3 Draft closing entries for the general fund. (Hint: Not all of the above transactions are recorded in the general fund.)

**6-4** The following summary of transactions was taken from the accounts of the Annaville School District, a special revenue fund, before the books had been closed for the fiscal year ended June 30, 19X3.[9]

|  | Postclosing balances 6/30/X2 | Preclosing balances 6/30/X3 |
|---|---|---|
| Cash | $400,000 | $ 700,000 |
| Taxes receivable | 150,000 | 170,000 |
| Allowance for estimated uncollectible taxes | (40,000) | (70,000) |
| Estimated revenues | — | 3,000,000 |
| Expenditures | — | 2,842,000 |
| Encumbrances | — | 91,000 |
|  | $510,000 | $6,733,000 |
| Accounts payable | $ 80,000 | $ 408,000 |
| Due to other funds | 210,000 | 142,000 |
| Reserve for encumbrances | 60,000 | 91,000 |
| Fund balance | 160,000 | 182,000 |
| Revenues from taxes | — | 2,800,000 |
| Miscellaneous revenues | — | 130,000 |
| Appropriations | — | 2,980,000 |
|  | $510,000 | $6,733,000 |

1 The estimated taxes receivable for the year ended June 30, 19X3, were $2,870,000, and taxes collected during the year totaled $2,810,000.

2 An analysis of the transactions in the accounts payable account for the year ended June 30, 19X3, follows:

|  | Debit (Credit) |
|---|---|
| Current expenditures | $(2,700,000) |
| Expenditures for prior year | ( 58,000) |
| Vouchers for payment to other funds | ( 210,000) |
| Cash payments during the year | $ 2,640,000 |
| Net change | ( 328,000) |

**3** During the year, the fund was billed $142,000 for services performed on its behalf by other city funds. These amounts were for such items as utilities, printing, and normal service activities.

**4** On May 2, 19X3, commitment documents were issued for purchase of new textbooks at a cost of $91,000.

**Required**:

Based upon the data presented above, reconstruct the original detailed journal entries that were required to record all transactions for the fiscal year ended June 30, 19X3, including the recording of the current year's budget. Do not prepare closing entries at June 30, 19X3.

**6-5** The following transactions represent practical situations frequently encountered in accounting for the general fund.

**1** The city council of Bar Harbor adopted a budget for the general operations of the government during the new fiscal year. Revenue was estimated at $575,000. Legal authorizations for budgeted expenditures were $540,000.

**2 a** On August 18, office supplies estimated to cost $2,390 were ordered for the city manager's office of Bar Harbor.

**b** The supplies ordered August 18 were received August 31 accompanied by an invoice for $2,500.

**3** On November 3, the general fund made a payment to the debt service fund of $106,000 for current debt obligations.

**4** On November 22, the city paid $115,000 out of the general operations for a central garage to service its vehicles. The estimated cost had been $107,000.

**Required**:

Prepare the necessary journal entries to record the transactions in the general fund.

**6-6** The following financial activities affecting Judbury City's general fund took place during the year ended June 30, 19X1.[10]

**1** The following budget was adopted:

| | |
|---|---|
| Estimated revenues: | |
|   Property taxes | $4,500,000 |
|   Licenses and permits | 300,000 |
|   Fines | 200,000 |
|     Total | $5,000,000 |
| Appropriations: | |
|   General government | $1,500,000 |
|   Police services | 1,200,000 |
|   Fire department services | 900,000 |
|   Public works services | 800,000 |
|   Acquisition of fire engines | 400,000 |
|     Totals | $4,800,000 |

**2** Property tax bills totaling $4,650,000 were mailed. It was estimated that $300,000 of this amount will be delinquent and $150,000 will be uncollectible.

**3** Property taxes totaling $3,900,000 were collected. The $150,000 previously estimated to be uncollectible remained unchanged, but $630,000 was reclassified as delinquent. It is estimated that delinquent taxes will be collected soon enough after June 30, 19X1 to make these taxes available to finance obligations incurred during the year ended June 30, 19X1. There was no balance of uncollected taxes at July 1, 19X0.

**4** Tax anticipation notes in the face amount of $300,000 were issued.

**5** Other cash collections were as follows:

| | |
|---|---:|
| Licenses and permits | $270,000 |
| Fines | 200,000 |
| Sale of public works equipment (original cost, $75,000) | 15,000 |
| Total | $485,000 |

**6** The following purchase orders were executed:

| | Total | Outstanding at 6/30/X1 |
|---|---:|---:|
| General government | $1,050,000 | $ 60,000 |
| Police services | 300,000 | 30,000 |
| Fire department services | 150,000 | 15,000 |
| Public works services | 250,000 | 10,000 |
| Fire engines | 400,000 | — |
| Totals | $2,150,000 | $115,000 |

No encumbrances were outstanding at June 30, 19X0.

**7** The following accounts were approved for payment:

| | |
|---|---:|
| General government | $1,440,000 |
| Police services | 1,155,000 |
| Fire department services | 870,000 |
| Public works services | 700,000 |
| Fire engines | 400,000 |
| Total | $4,565,000 |

**8** Accounts totaling $4,600,000 were paid.

**Required**:

Prepare journal entries to record the foregoing financial activities in the general fund. Omit explanations. Ignore interest accruals.

**6-7** The accounting system of the municipality of Kemp is organized and operated on a fund basis. Among the types of funds used are: a general fund, a special revenue fund, and an enterprise fund.[11]

**Required**:

1 Explain the basic differences in revenue recognition between the accrual basis of accounting and the modified accrual basis of accounting as it relates to governmental accounting.

2 What basis of accounting should be used for the general fund? The special revenue fund? The enterprise fund? Why?

**6-8** The following is the general fund trial balance of the city of Solna at December 31, 19X2.[12]

| | Dr. | Cr. |
|---|---:|---:|
| Cash | $ 62,000 | |
| Taxes receivable—delinquent | 46,000 | |
| Estimated uncollectible taxes—delinquent | | $ 8,000 |
| Stores inventory—program operations | 18,000 | |

| | | |
|---|---|---|
| Accounts payable | | 28,000 |
| Fund balance reserved for stores inventory | | 18,000 |
| Fund balance reserved for encumbrances | | 12,000 |
| Unreserved undesignated fund balance | | 60,000 |
| | $126,000 | $126,000 |

Collectible delinquent taxes are expected to be collected within sixty days after the end of the year. Solna uses the purchases method to account for stores inventory. The following data pertain to the 19X3 general fund operations:

1 Budget adopted:

| | |
|---|---|
| Revenues and other financing sources | |
| Taxes | $220,000 |
| Fines, forfeits, and penalties | 80,000 |
| Miscellaneous revenues | 100,000 |
| Share of bond issue proceeds | 200,000 |
| | $600,000 |
| Expenditures and other financing uses | |
| Program operations | $300,000 |
| General administration | 120,000 |
| Stores—program operations | 60,000 |
| Capital outlay | 80,000 |
| Periodic transfer to special assessment fund | 20,000 |
| | $580,000 |

2 Taxes were assessed at an amount that would result in revenues of $220,800, after deduction of 4 percent of the tax levy as uncollectible.

3 Orders placed but not received:

| | |
|---|---|
| Program operations | $176,000 |
| General administration | 80,000 |
| Capital outlay | 60,000 |
| | $316,000 |

4 The city council designated $20,000 of the unreserved undesignated fund balance for possible future appropriation for capital outlay.

5 Cash collections and transfer:

| | |
|---|---|
| Delinquent taxes | $ 38,000 |
| Current taxes | 226,000 |
| Refund of overpayment of invoice for purchase of equipment | 4,000 |
| Fines, forfeits, and penalties | 88,000 |
| Miscellaneous revenues | 90,000 |
| Share of bond issue proceeds | 200,000 |
| Transfer of remaining fund balance of a discontinued fund | 18,000 |
| | $664,000 |

**6** Cancelled encumbrances:

|  | Estimated | Actual |
|---|---|---|
| Program operations | $156,000 | $166,000 |
| General administration | 84,000 | 80,000 |
| Capital outlay | 62,000 | 62,000 |
|  | $302,000 | $308,000 |

**7** Additional accounts payable:

| Program operations | $188,000 |
|---|---|
| General administration | 38,000 |
| Capital outlay | 18,000 |
| Transfer to special assessment fund | 20,000 |
|  | $264,000 |

**8** Albert, a taxpayer, overpaid his 19X3 taxes by $2,000. He applied for a $2,000 credit against his 19X4 taxes. The city council granted his request.

**9** Accounts paid amounted to $580,000.

**10** Stores inventory on December 31, 19X3 amounted to $12,000.

**Required**:

Prepare journal entries to record the effects of the foregoing data. Omit explanations.

**6-9** The following isolated transactions took place during the fiscal year ending June 30, 19X8 in the general fund of the city of Jamesburg. Prepare the journal entries to reflect the transactions. The city is on the encumbrance basis.

**1** A truck, estimated to cost $12,000, was ordered on July 15.

**2** On September 1, the truck was received along with an invoice for $12,500. The invoice was paid.

**3** Salaries and wages paid during the year were $250,000. At the end of the year $8,000 for wages and salaries earned were still unpaid. Of the payroll costs, 7 percent of the costs were withheld for pensions, and the city provided an additional 7 percent. The pensions were accounted for in a pension trust fund. Withholdings for federal taxes were 15 percent; state taxes were 5 percent. These amounts were handled in the general fund and were paid directly to the proper authorities.

**4** A three-year insurance policy on the equipment was purchased for $3,000 and paid for on October 1.

**5** Supplies were kept on the purchase method. The beginning inventory, reflected in the books, was $10,000; purchases amounted to $50,000; and the ending inventory was $8,000.

**6-10** This problem continues the case of Silver City, also discussed in Problems 3-7 and 5-10. It concerns the Silver City general fund expenditure transactions, adjusting and closing entries, and financial statements. The material from Chapter 5 is needed for the completion of the case in this chapter.

**5** During the year, expenditures and transfers were paid as follows:

## CHAPTER 6: EXPENDITURE ACCOUNTING, CLOSING ENTRIES, AND FINANCIAL STATEMENTS

| | | |
|---|---:|---:|
| Function A: | | |
|   Personal services | $830,000 | |
|   Materials and supplies | 70,000 | |
|   Contractual services | 50,000 | |
|   Equipment | 450,000 | |
|   Total function A | | $1,400,000 |
| Function B: | | |
|   Personal services | 670,000 | |
|   Materials and supplies | 25,000 | |
|   Contractual services | 30,000 | |
|   Equipment | 25,000 | |
|   Total function B | | 750,000 |
| Function C: | | |
|   Personal services | 500,000 | |
|   Materials and supplies | 25,000 | |
|   Contractual services | 40,000 | |
|   Equipment | 35,000 | |
|   Transfer to debt service fund | 32,000 | |
|   Transfer to special assessment fund | 68,000 | |
|   Transfer to garage fund | 50,000 | |
|   Total function C | | 750,000 |
| Total expenditures and transfers (Cash) | | $2,900,000 |

**6** Encumbrances at year end were as follows:

| | |
|---|---:|
| Function A, equipment | $15,000 |
| Function C, materials and supplies | 10,000 |
| Total encumbrances | $25,000 |

**7** At the year end, liabilities not shown in the above cash expenditures were:

| | | |
|---|---:|---:|
| Owed to garage fund by the general fund | | |
|   Function C, contractual services | | $ 5,000 |
| Owed to other creditors: | | $10,000 |
|   Function A, equipment | $5,000 | |
|   Function B, materials and supplies | 5,000 | |

**Required**:

1. Prepare journal entries for the transactions given, including adjusting and closing entries.
2. Post the journalized transactions to the worksheet started in Chapter 5. Use the illustrations in both Chapters 5 and 6 as models.
3. Prepare the following financial statements:
   a. A balance sheet
   b. A statement of revenues, expenditures, and changes in fund balances.
   c. A statement of revenues, expenditures, and changes in fund balances, budget and actual.

## NOTES

1. National Council on Governmental Accounting, *Statement 1. Governmental Accounting and Financial Reporting Principles* (Chicago: Municipal Finance Officers Association of the United States and Canada, 1979), p. 11.
2. Municipal Finance Officers Association of the United States and Canada, *Governmental Accounting, Auditing, and Financial Reporting* (Chicago: Municipal Finance Officers Association of the United States and Canada, 1981), p. 18.
3. See NCGA, *Statement 1*, p. 14.
4. Ibid., p. 21.
5. American Institute of Certified Public Accountants, *Statement of Position 80-2* (New York: Copyright © 1980 by the American Institute of Certified Public Accountants. Reprinted with permission).
6. Adapted from American Institute of Certified Public Accountants, *Uniform CPA Examination Questions and Unofficial Answers* (New York: American Institute of Certified Public Accountants, various dates).
7. Ibid.
8. Ibid., Nov. 1972.
9. Ibid., Nov. 1976.
10. Ibid., Nov. 1981.
11. Ibid., Nov. 1984.
12. Ibid., Nov. 1984.

CHAPTER 7

# CAPITAL PROJECTS FUNDS

Capital projects funds are set up to account for: (1) resources obtained to build or buy specific capital projects, (2) the construction or purchase of those projects, and (3) the dissolving of the fund. The resources to build or buy the capital projects come from the issuance of bonds or other long-term obligations, from grants from other governmental units, or from transfers from other funds within the governmental unit.

## SPECIAL USE OF CAPITAL PROJECTS FUNDS

Within a governmental unit, major capital acquisitions may take place in at least five different types of funds: (1) proprietary funds, (2) general and special revenue funds, (3) special assessment funds, (4) trust funds, and (5) capital projects funds.

Proprietary funds build or buy capital assets for their own use. Along with resources provided from operations of these funds, proprietary funds may also obtain resources with which to buy or build capital assets from the proceeds of long-term debt, such as bonds or long-term notes. All of the transactions concerning debt issuance, building or buying the capital assets, keeping a record of the fixed assets and long-term debt, paying off the interest on the long-term debt annually, and retiring the long-term debt take place within the proprietary fund.

General or special revenue funds usually acquire short-lived capital assets, such as machinery and equipment, but occasionally purchase or build a major capital asset, such as a bridge, highway, or, infrequently, a building. Money used to finance the acquisition of capital assets in the general or special revenue funds is from general or special revenue fund resources. All of the transactions concerning the acquisition of the asset take place in the general fund or special revenue fund. The fixed asset record, however, is kept in the general fixed assets account group.

Special assessment funds obtain resources from a special group of citizens within the limits of the governmental unit. With these resources, and other resources obtained from grants from other governmental units and operating transfers from funds within the governmental unit, these funds can be used to acquire capital assets for the primary use of the special group of citizens. Sidewalks and streets are illustrations of the types of capital assets acquired from special assessments on this special group of citizens. Often, the fund obtains resources with which to immediately acquire the capital assets from the issuance of long-term debt. While the capital assets upon acquisition are recorded in the general fixed assets account group, the record of the long-term debt, including the payment of interest and the principal and the record of these payments, is kept in the special assessments fund.

Seldom do trust funds build or buy capital assets; they do acquire the assets, however, usually through gifts. The assets can be accounted for either similarly to proprietary funds or in the general fixed assets account group.

## Capital Projects Fund Financing

Until recently, most state, county, and local governments financed their capital construction in capital project funds by issuing *general obligation bonds* (i.e., bonds backed by "the full faith, credit, and taxing power" of the issuing jurisdiction) or on a "*pay-as-you-go*" basis. Internal improvement laws in a number of states had provisions that prohibited or severely limited the level of indebtedness that local jurisdictions could assume. Current revenues, usually, were needed to support annual operating commitments. Thus, many needed capital improvements often were deferred (sometimes causing reduced public services and increased costs when the project was eventually started).

Most local and county governments currently finance the acquisition of capital assets from several sources: bonds, grants, transfers, gifts, leases, and other types of long-term debt. Although bonds are still an important source, localities also receive additional resources from grants from other levels of government (state and federal), from transfers from other funds, and from gifts by foundations or civic-minded citizens. Long-term leasing is also a modern means of financing long-term capital acquisition. In addition to general obligation bonds, other long-term debt issues, such as *revenue bonds* and *long-term notes*, now are commonly used. Thus, in addition to the proceeds of bonds, all of the resources used to acquire long-term capital assets, except for long-term leases, now are accounted for in a *capital projects fund*.

Capital projects funds account for the monies received from various sources that are used to acquire one or several particular long-term assets. It is possible, therefore, for the governmental unit to have several capital projects funds in operation at the same time. The use of individual funds for each project assures the unit that the proceeds received from each of the various sources are expended for the purposes intended and are properly accounted for.

In the past, the priority of capital expenditures was often determined by the best political argument for the public improvement. More recently, however, some jurisdictions have begun to make capital budgeting decisions on somewhat different grounds.

In these jurisdictions, it has been decided that the best expenditure of resources in the long run is that which produces the most benefits to the jurisdiction for the same or lesser expenditures—that is, the project with the most favorable cost-benefit ratio.[1]

## THE CAPITAL BUDGET

One of the most appropriate means for planning for capital projects is the capital budget, supported by a capital improvements program. Long-range capital facilities planning has lagged significantly behind other developments in the field of state and local financial administration. It is very difficult to achieve maximum returns from public investments for long-term assets if capital decisions are made on a year-to-year basis. To ensure the proper balance of revenues and expenditures, it is necessary to develop a sound long-range *capital facilities plan*. Such a plan must include estimates of governmental expenditures both for the operation and maintenance of public services and for capital improvements. These estimates can then be compared with estimates of revenues from taxes, borrowing, and other sources necessary to finance these expenditures. To be effective, a capital facilities plan must be developed for a relatively long period. It must allow flexibility for adjustment as new conditions arise and must be based upon an overall strategic or comprehensive plan that includes a long-range program for the providing of public services.

The terms *capital facility* or *capital improvement* refer to projects of relatively large size, nature, and/or long life (usually a minimum of fifteen to twenty years). Such projects involve expenditures of a nonrecurring nature and are designed to provide new or additional governmental facilities for public services. Thus funds allocated for the design and construction of a new health clinic would be considered a capital expenditure. Monies appropriated to sustain the operations of such a facility, in terms of salaries, supplies, and equipment replacement (except as such replacement might constitute a significant outlay of funds), would be more properly considered an operating expenditure to be included in the annual budget request.

One test of a capital outlay is whether it adds substantially to the value of the fixed assets of government. Equipment required at the time of acquisition or construction of a facility often is included as part of the capital improvements program. However, expenditures for minor equipment acquisitions and most repair and maintenance work should not be included as part of the capital budget.

Illustrations of capital outlays that would be considered fixed assets rather than operating expenditures are such items as: major additions to the present fixed assets; acquired long-term assets including improvements needed to bring the assets to a good operating condition; and improvements, such as a modern energy-efficient heating system that replaces an outmoded one.

Since the objective is to provide major public facilities that have a relatively long life within the limits of available public resources, capital budgeting must involve planning, programming, and financing considerations. The *planning* phase begins with the formulation of policies (goals and objectives) as to the desired levels of public service to be provided. These goals and objectives must be related to population and economic trends and projections to ascertain future demands for public services and facilities. By comparing needs with the capacity of existing facilities, it is possible to determine the magnitude of additional supply necessary to meet the anticipated demand.

The need for *programming* capital improvements arises from the limited fiscal resources available to any level of government. Programming should be based on a system of priorities tied to the goals and objectives set forth in the planning phase. It should also include procedures for the continuous evaluation of public services and facilities. Planning reveals needs; programming provides the basis for ordering the sequence in which these needs can be met most effectively.

The *financing* phase relates to any analysis of the sources of funds to be drawn upon and how the payments are to be made. There are a number of ways in which capital facilities can be financed—on a pay-as-you-go basis (i.e., from current revenues), from capital reserve funds, from long-term leasing, and through long-term or short-term borrowing. These methods must be evaluated in terms of the overall fiscal capacity and in light of the particular capital improvement needs.

## RELATIONSHIP BETWEEN THE CAPITAL PROJECTS FUNDS AND OTHER FUNDS AND ACCOUNT GROUPS

The results of accounting entries and other information that comes from selling bonds or receiving other revenue, constructing or purchasing a capital project, as well as any resources that may be left over, do not remain in the capital projects fund. The capital projects fund is terminated upon completion of the capital project. Thus the accounting results are transferred to other funds or account groups—the *debt service fund* and the general *long-term debt* and general *fixed assets account groups*.

The general fixed assets account group will account for the assets constructed or purchased through resources of the capital projects fund. This account group will keep a permanent record of the fixed assets and the eventual disposition of them.

Since no record is kept in the capital projects fund of the long-term debt, other means of tracking these obligations must be developed so as to: (1) acquire and account for resources to pay off the debts and (2) keep a record of the long-term debt. Normally, the bond indenture requires, and good financial management and other management standards dictate, that the city use a debt service fund for the first purpose. Thus a debt service fund is used to account for acquiring the resources and for paying off the interest and principal of the long-term debt for each capital projects fund. For the second purpose, a long-term debt account group will provide a record of the debt.

A close accounting relationship exists between the capital projects fund and the debt service fund. The debt service fund, therefore, will be discussed in the next chapter.

## PARTIAL USE OF BUDGETARY ACCOUNTING IN CAPITAL PROJECTS FUNDS

City officials often must go through a laborious and time-consuming process for obtaining approval before initiating a capital project and opening a capital projects fund. This process often requires a public referendum, and bond buyers often stipulate in the bond indenture that certain conditions must be adhered to. This process must be followed for each formal authorization for a capital project; and, in any local government unit, several concurrent capital projects funds are possible.

From an accounting control standpoint, the equivalent of a budget is made when approval is received (e.g., through a referendum) to issue bonds, receive transfers, and obtain grants to build a project. Proposed bond proceeds, grants, and transfers from another fund are equivalent to estimated revenues. And the proposed cost of the project is an amount in the capital projects fund equivalent to the amount appropriated in general and special revenue funds. So, there is usually no need for formal budgetary accounting in a capital projects fund. For all practical purposes, this was accomplished when the authority was given to issue bonds or obtain other resources in order to build the project. When the project has received official approval, however, a memo entry is often made in the fund's accounting records to show the amount available for expenditures for capital acquisition.

While there is no need to adopt a formal budget for estimated revenues and proposed expenditures, assurance must be provided to those who have provided the funds that the managers of the project do not obligate or spend more than is available. While there is no need in the capital projects fund for accounts equivalent to "estimated revenue" and "appropriations," encumbrances and reserve for encumbrances accounts are important control tools. In addition, capital projects of any magnitude usually extend beyond one fiscal year. Thus the reserve for encumbrances and the encumbrances accounts must apply to the life of the project, rather than only to the year of approval for the project. As such, encumbrances do not lapse at the end of the year, as is possible in general and special revenue funds budgetary accounting.

If a budget is adopted, however, the capital projects fund follows the same basic pattern for budgetary accounting that has previously been illustrated in the general fund. For example, assume that during the current year a capital project will be started and completed. The project will be financed as follows: (1) bond proceeds, $1,000,000; (2) state grant, $200,000; and (3) operating transfer from the general fund, $100,000. The following journal entries would be made in relation to the budget:

**1** On adoption of the budget for a capital project:

|  | Dr. | Cr. |
|---|---|---|
| Estimated revenue from state grant | $ 200,000 | |
| Estimated proceeds from bonds | 1,000,000 | |
| Estimated operating transfers from general fund | 100,000 | |
| Appropriations | | $1,300,000 |

To record adoption of the budget for capital project estimated to cost $1,300,000.

**2** Upon accrual of grant and transfers:

| | | |
|---|---|---|
| Due from state | $200,000 | |
| Due from general fund | $100,000 | |
| Revenue | | $200,000 |
| Operating transfer | | 100,000 |

To record accrual of state grant and operating transfer from the general fund.

**3** Upon sale of bonds:

| | | |
|---|---|---|
| Cash | $1,000,000 | |
|     Proceeds from bonds | | $1,000,000 |

To record cash received from sale of bonds.

**4** Cash received from grant and operating transfer:

| | | |
|---|---|---|
| Cash | $300,000 | |
|     Due from state | | $200,000 |
|     Due from general fund | | 100,000 |

To record cash received from the grant from the state and from the operating transfer from the general fund.

**5** When expenditures are accrued for the capital project:

| | | |
|---|---|---|
| Expenditures | $1,300,000 | |
|     Accounts payable | | $1,300,000 |

To accrue amounts due for construction of project.

**6** When accounts payable are paid:

| | | |
|---|---|---|
| Accounts payable | $1,300,000 | |
|     Cash | | $1,300,000 |

To pay accounts.

**7** When closing accounts (revenue, proceeds, and operating transfers):

| | | |
|---|---|---|
| Revenue | $ 200,000 | |
| Operating transfer from general fund | 100,000 | |
| Proceeds from bonds | 1,000,000 | |
|     Estimated revenue state grant | | $ 200,000 |
|     Estimated operating transfer from general fund | | 100,000 |
|     Estimated proceeds from bonds | | 1,000,000 |

To close revenue, operating transfers, and proceeds from bonds and estimated revenue accounts.

**8** When closing accounts (expenditures):

| | | |
|---|---|---|
| Appropriations | $1,300,000 | |
|     Expenditures | | $1,300,000 |

To close expenditure accounts.

If the revenue from the state grant was not paid until the project incurred expenditures, then the capital projects fund would not accrue the revenue until after expenditures had been made. Likewise, if the project was for two years instead of one, and the grant was to be paid in two installments, one each year, then the total amount would be shown as due from the state, but the revenue would be separated into this year's revenue and next year's revenue. Next year's revenue would be shown as deferred revenue.

Comparable to accounting without an adopted budget, the bonds issued would be recorded in the general long-term debt account group and the fixed assets recorded in the general fixed assets account group.

## BASIS OF ACCOUNTING

As is true of other governmental funds, the modified accrual basis of accounting is also the basis used in capital projects funds. The account used to record the resources provided from grants or gifts is called revenues, the same as that found in the general fund. The amounts received from the sale of bonds are recorded in an account called *proceeds from bonds*. And the amounts transferred to or from other funds are called *transfers*. Transfers related to operations of both the giving and receiving funds are called *operating transfers*. Transfers related to the capital equity of both the giving and receiving funds are called *residual equity transfers*. Both types of transfers will be illustrated in this chapter. All of the resources—revenue, transfers, and proceeds—are recorded at the monetary value at the time of receipt. Gifts other than cash, however, are recorded at fair market value.

Comparable to the general fund, all capital acquisitions are called *expenditures*. As is found in modified accrual accounting, expenditures are recorded when the fund liability is incurred and not when the expenditure of cash takes place. Yet, to control the possible overexpenditure of available resources, an encumbrance is recorded when the obligation for an expenditure is made, as is done in the general fund.

## PREMIUMS, DISCOUNTS, AND ACCRUED INTEREST ON THE SALE OF BONDS

There often is a time-lag between the date of issuance of long-term debt and the time of obtaining the money to be spent. As a consequence, three special characteristics of accounting for bonds and other long-term liabilities frequently are encountered: (1) accrued interest on sale of bonds, (2) premiums and discounts on the sale of bonds, and (3) investment of excess cash from the sale of the bonds or from other money received from grants or other funds.

### Accrued Interest on Sale of Bonds

Bonds often are not sold on the same date as their date of issue. For example, if bonds with an issue date of July 1, 19X0 are sold on September 1, 19X0, then the owner of the bonds on the semi-annual interest payment date (i.e., January 1, 19X1) will receive interest on the bonds from the issue date (July 1, 19X0), not the date of purchase. Therefore, when the bonds are sold, the issuer collects interest from the buyer for the period from the issue date to the date of purchase.

Any accrued interest received on the sale of the bonds cannot be used to pay for construction in the capital projects fund. It must be transferred to the debt service fund to be used as part of the resources for the first interest payment. The accrued interest received upon the sale of the bonds will be a partial offset to the amount it needs from the general fund for the first interest payment. Therefore, the general fund will have to transfer to the debt service fund only sufficient money to pay the interest from the purchase date to the interest payment date. Journal entries for this type of transaction are illustrated in the section entitled "New Transactions."

## Premiums and Discounts on Sale of Bonds

It often is difficult to determine, at the time the bond authorization is developed, exactly what the interest rate will be on the date the bonds are sold, since the actual date of sale for the bonds seldom can be accurately predicted. The possibility always exists that the bonds will be sold for either a premium or a discount (i.e., above or below the face value) and that some interest will accrue on bonds.

The way bond premiums and discounts must be accounted for is often determined by bond indentures or state statutes. Some state laws, for example, do not permit the issuance of bonds at a discount. This prohibition automatically eliminates the accounting problem of recording bond discount. It may create a greater problem for the issuing government or authority, however, by forcing the bonds to be reissued at a higher interest rate in order to ensure their sale. When a bond discount is allowed, the project authorized, nevertheless, must have the face value of bonds to complete the project. To complete the project, then, the general fund, and sometimes the debt service fund, must make up the difference between the face value of the bonds and the amount received from the bonds.[2]

When bonds are sold at a premium, the difference between par and the premium usually is transferred to the debt service fund and used with other resources to pay off the bonds. Journal entries for this type of transaction are illustrated in the New Transactions section of this chapter.

## INVESTMENT OF EXCESS CASH

The capital projects fund often receives proceeds from the sale of bonds or transfers of monies from other governmental agencies before these resources are needed to acquire the capital assets. The city should invest these resources in order to obtain additional revenue. This can be done by each individual fund; however, most governments use a central fund that invests the idle cash from all of the individual funds. Revenue from the investment of the idle resources of the capital projects funds is transferred to the debt service fund for payment of the principal or interest of the debt.

## NEW TRANSACTIONS

Three types of transactions in the capital projects fund have not already been illustrated in the chapters on general and special revenue funds or in the chapter on proprietary funds. These transactions are concerned with (1) the issuance of bonds, (2) multiple periods, and (3) closing entries.

## Journal Entries Regarding Issuance of Bonds

To build a fire station, the city of Harrisonburg issued twenty-year term bonds dated July 1, 19X8. The bonds had a face value of $500,000 and an interest rate of 10 percent to be paid semiannually on December 31 and June 30. On September 30, 19X8, the bonds were sold for a premium of 1 percent. The cash received from the sale of the bonds would be:

| | |
|---|---:|
| Face value | $500,000 |
| Interest accrued | 12,500 |
| Premium | 5,000 |
| Total | $517,500 |

The journal entry to record this transaction is:

| | | Dr. | Cr. |
|---|---|---|---|
| Sept. 30 | Cash | $517,500 | |
| | Due to debt service fund | | $ 17,500 |
| | Proceeds from bonds | | 500,000 |
| | To record sale of bonds. | | |

The amount received for the interest accrued—$12,500 from July 1 to September 30—is collected and remitted to the debt service fund. It will be used as an offset against the total amount of interest that would be paid on December 31, 19X8. The premium on the sale of the bonds—$5,000—also would be paid to the debt service fund. The amount for the premium would be invested and eventually used, with all other amounts paid to the fund, for the retirement of the bonds. The only amount that can be used for construction of the project is the $500,000—the face value of the bonds.

The entry to transfer the premium and interest to the debt service fund is:

| | | Dr. | Cr. |
|---|---|---|---|
| Sept. 30 | Due to debt service fund | $17,500 | |
| | Cash | | $17,500 |
| | To pay debt service fund for premium and accrued interest on bonds. | | |

The entries in the debt service fund are illustrated in Chapter 8. An alternate approach to premiums and accrued interest is given in the illustrative case.

When it is legally permissible for the local unit to sell bonds at a discount, the difference between the face value of the bonds and the amount received would have to be paid from the general fund or the debt service fund. Suppose the above bonds were sold at a 1 percent discount rather than at a premium. The receipts from the sale of the bonds would be:

| | | |
|---|---:|---:|
| Face value of bonds | $500,000 | |
| Less discount on bonds | 5,000 | |
| Amount received from sale of bonds | | $495,000 |
| Interest accrued | | 12,500 |
| Total received | | $507,500 |

If the general fund is to make up the difference between the face value of the bonds and the discount, the entry to record this transaction would be:

| | | Dr. | Cr. |
|---|---|---:|---:|
| Sept. 30 | Cash | $507,500 | |
| | Due from general fund | 5,000 | |
| | Due to debt service fund | | $ 12,500 |
| | Bond proceeds | | 495,000 |
| | Operating transfer from general fund | | 5,000 |
| | To record sale of bonds. | | |

The receipt from and the payment to the other funds by the capital projects fund would need the following transactions:

| | | Dr. | Cr. |
|---|---|---:|---:|
| Sept. 30 | Cash | $ 5,000 | |
| | Due from general fund | | $ 5,000 |
| | To record amount from general fund for discount. | | |
| | Due to debt service fund | $12,500 | |
| | Cash | | $12,500 |
| | To record payment to debt service fund. | | |

Assume that a contract was executed for the construction of a building for $495,000. The building was completed during the year, with a retained percentage (5 percent) of the contract being withheld until final approval of the project. All payments were made. The journal entries would be as follows:

| | Dr. | Cr. |
|---|---:|---:|
| Encumbrances | $495,000 | |
| Reserve for encumbrances | | $495,000 |
| To encumber the contract. | | |
| Reserve for encumbrances | 495,000 | |
| Encumbrances | | 495,000 |
| Expenditures | 495,000 | |
| Accounts payable | | 470,250 |
| Retained percentages payable | | 24,750 |
| To unencumber the contract and set up liability for contract less the retained percentage. | | |
| Accounts payable | 470,250 | |
| Cash | | 470,250 |
| Retained percentages payable | 24,750 | |
| Cash | | 24,750 |
| To pay retained percentages. | | |

## Journal Entries Regarding Multiple Periods

The entries on pages 199 to 202 for the city of Ruthberg illustrate transactions for the second year that overlap two periods. Additional illustrations, therefore, are not necessary at this time. In general though, while the revenues, proceeds, expenditures, and encumbrances accounts are closed each year, the encumbrances account is reopened the next year in order to control the total of expenditures. If fixed assets are in the process of being constructed, the amount of construction in process will also be recorded in the general fixed assets account group. The final year will have no balance sheet, since there will be no assets, liabilities, or fund balance. A statement of revenues, expenditures, and changes in fund balance may be necessary if any transactions occur in these accounts during the second year. Otherwise, only a statement of changes in fund balance is prepared.

## Journal Entries Regarding Closing Entries

Closing entries for a capital project fund that runs for only a single period not only close out the bond proceeds, revenue, operating transfers, and expenditures accounts but also close the fund by transferring any balance to the debt service fund. The balance is a residual equity transfer. The following are the necessary closing entries if resources are obtained only from bond proceeds:

|  | Dr. | Cr. |
|---|---|---|
| Residual equity transfer out | $ 5,000 |  |
|     Due to debt service fund |  | $ 5,000 |
| Bond proceeds | 500,000 |  |
|     Expenditures |  | 495,000 |
|     Residual equity transfer out |  | 5,000 |
| Due to debt service fund | 5,000 |  |
|     Cash |  | 5,000 |

These are the basic new entries, other than for multiple periods, needed to open a capital projects fund, sell the bonds, construct the project, and close the fund. The following illustration for the city of Ruthberg's capital projects fund expands these basic illustrations. Additional entries are also needed in the general long-term debt account group and the general fixed assets account group for the issuance of the bonds and the construction of the fixed assets (see Chapter 11).

## ILLUSTRATIVE TRANSACTIONS—CITY OF RUTHBERG'S CAPITAL PROJECTS FUND

All of the formalities to provide the resources to buy land and construct a new administration building for the city of Ruthberg were accomplished during the prior fiscal year. Grants of $200,000 from the state and $500,000 from the federal government were approved on the condition that the city provides $800,000 for the $1,500,000 project. Through a referendum, taxpayers approved the city's issuing $800,000 of bonds to meet its share of financing the project. A memo entry stating that the construction has been authorized can be made at the beginning of the city's fiscal year beginning July 1, 19X5.

## Initial Accounting Entries

The state and federal governments approved grants for the project to be paid during the current year, so these amounts will be accrued.

**P1** July 1, 19X5

|  | Dr. | Cr. |
|---|---|---|
| Due from state | $200,000 | |
| Due from federal government | 500,000 | |
|     Revenue | | $700,000 |

To record accrual for grants from the state and federal governments.

Various methods of payment are used to transfer money from one governmental unit to another. In this case, the results are the same—the capital projects fund receives cash from the granting agency. The entry to record the payment of the grants, assuming they are paid upon the setting up of the fund, is:

**P2** July 5, 19X5

| | | |
|---|---|---|
| Cash | $700,000 | |
|     Due from state | | $200,000 |
|     Due from federal government | | 500,000 |

Receipt of cash for grants from the state and federal governments.

The city purchased land for the site of the building. All land owners, except one, agreed upon a price of $75,000. The one land owner, who could not obtain an agreement from the city for his desired price, had his land condemned. The price for the land was judged to be $50,000. These transactions were not encumbered because of the short time interval between the purchase and the payment.

In governmental fund accounting, capital assets are recorded as expenditures and not as fixed assets. This is what is done in capital projects funds. However, fixed assets will be recorded in the general fixed assets account group and are shown in Chapter 11. The journal entry to record this transaction in the capital projects fund is:

**P3** Aug. 15, 19X5

| | | |
|---|---|---|
| Expenditures | $125,000 | |
|     Accounts payable | | $75,000 |
|     Judgments payable | | 50,000 |

To record purchases of land.

Payment for the land is recorded as:

**P4** Sept. 1, 19X5

| | | |
|---|---|---|
| Accounts payable | $75,000 | |
| Judgments payable | 50,000 | |
|     Cash | | $125,000 |

Payment of accounts and judgments on land.

To complete the project, $800,000 will be needed from the sale of bonds. The bonds were dated July 1, 19X5 and were issued as twenty-year general obligation bonds with an interest rate of 5 percent, payable semiannually on December 31 and June 30. For illustrative purposes, it will be assumed that the general obligation bonds were issued as "term bonds." Interest on term bonds is paid on the full amount of principal over the twenty-year period to maturity.

On September 30, the bonds were sold at a premium of 2 percent, or $16,000, with an additional amount for accrued interest of $10,000. Total receipts of $826,000 were recorded in the capital projects fund from the sale of the bonds, the premium, and the accrued interest. An alternative method to record these transactions is as follows:

**P5**  Sept. 30, 19X5

| | | |
|---|---:|---:|
| Cash | $826,000 | |
| Operating transfer to debt service fund | 16,000 | |
|     Due to debt service fund | | $ 26,000 |
|     Proceeds from bonds | | 816,000 |

To record proceeds from sale of bonds, $826,000 including premium of $16,000; accrued interest of $10,000; and the amount due to debt service fund for premium and accrued interest.

This method shows the amount of premium as the operating transfer to the debt service fund rather than only showing it as a liability to the debt service fund. The amount for accrued interest and premium on the sale of the bonds is transferred to the debt service fund. These transactions are illustrated in Chapter 8. The entry in the capital projects fund is:

**P6**  Sept. 30, 19X5

| | | |
|---|---:|---:|
| Due to debt service fund | $26,000 | |
|     Cash | | $26,000 |

To record payment to debt service fund for accrued interest and premium on bonds.

If not used immediately, the available idle cash should be invested, and any revenue from this investment should be transferred to the debt service fund.

## Construction of the Building

A contract was used for the construction of the building. The architects said that a few improvements to the plans might be necessary before completion of the building. They designed the building to be built for $1,200,000 in order to accommodate any necessary plan changes to the maximum of $100,000.

The public works department, in accordance with the architect's suggestions, was designated to make any improvements to the land and landscape the grounds at an estimated cost of $75,000. The contract called for the completion of the building by November 1, 19X6.

Upon opening the bids, the city found that the lowest bid was from the Jones Construction Company for $1,200,000 — the estimated cost of the building. Since the contract given to the Jones Construction Company for $1,200,000 is a long-term amount, it should be encumbered. The entry for this encumbrance is:

**P7**  Oct. 1
  Encumbrances                          $1,200,000
    Reserve for encumbrances                        $1,200,000
  To encumber contract.

The construction company was to receive payments from the city on the basis of percentage of completion of the building and approval by the construction supervisor; quarterly payments were to be made on December 31, March 31, June 30, and September 30. For this fiscal year, the construction supervisor approved for payment the following invoices submitted by the company:

| | |
|---|---|
| Dec. 31, | $350,000 |
| March 31, | 225,000 |
| June 30, | 225,000 |
| | $800,000 |

Individual entries would be made to unencumber each of these amounts when the invoices were received. A summary entry for all invoices received and approved for payment is:

**P8**  Reserve for encumbrances          $800,000
    Encumbrances                                  $800,000
  To reverse the encumbered amounts.

To record the liability on the dates due, the total of each of these three invoices is:

**P9**  Expenditures                       $800,000
    Accounts payable                              $800,000

An entry for the assets provided from the construction is also made in the general fixed assets account group. This entry is shown on page 287 of Chapter 11.

Only $550,000 of the accounts payable were paid during the year. The following entry is made for paying the $550,000 liability:

**P10**  Accounts payable                 $550,000
    Cash                                          $550,000

Closing entries are made at the end of the year to close out the revenue, the proceeds, and the expenditures accounts for the year. The following entry is necessary at June 30, 19X6:

|  |  | Dr. | Cr. |
|---|---|---|---|
| PC1 | Proceeds from bonds | $816,000 | |
| | Revenue | 700,000 | |
| | Expenditures | | $925,000 |
| | Operating transfer to debt service fund | | 16,000 |
| | Encumbrances | | 400,000 |
| | Fund balance | | 175,000 |

While the encumbrances account is closed at the end of the first year, it will be reopened at the beginning of the second year (see entry P2-1).

The trial balance after closing out the preceding accounts (see the worksheet in Exhibit 7-1) is

### City of Ruthberg
### Capital Projects Fund—Trial Balance
### For Fiscal Year Ended June 30, 19X6

| Account | Dr. | Cr. |
|---|---|---|
| Cash | $825,000 | |
| Accounts payable | | $250,000 |
| Reserve for encumbrances | | 400,000 |
| Fund balance | | 175,000 |
| Total | $825,000 | $825,000 |

## Financial Statements—Incomplete Projects

Statements needed for the incomplete project for the year ended June 30, 19X6 are a balance sheet (see Exhibit 7-2) and a statement of revenue, expenditures, and changes in fund balance (see Exhibit 7-3).

## Second-Year Transactions

At the start of the second fiscal year (i.e., July 1, 19X6) in which the project will have transactions, the fund still has $825,000 in cash. This amount is offset by accounts payable of $250,000, a fund balance of $175,000, and reserve for encumbrances of $400,000. Transactions continue for the life of the project rather than only for the fiscal year. So, it is usually easier to reverse the encumbrances and reserve for encumbrances accounts each time an actual transaction is made rather than to have to place an appropriate amount from the reserve for encumbrances account back into the fund balance each time. A reversing entry for the encumbrances account is usually made at the start of the second year as follows:

|  |  | Dr. | Cr. |
|---|---|---|---|
| P2-1 | Encumbrances | $400,000 | |
| | Fund balance | | $400,000 |

## EXHIBIT 7-1
### Worksheet
### City of Ruthberg
### Capital Projects Fund
### Fiscal Years Ending June 30, 19X6 and 19X7

| Accounts | \multicolumn{4}{c}{Transactions during fiscal 19X6} | \multicolumn{2}{c}{Account balance June 30, 19X6} |
|---|---|---|---|---|---|---|
|  | No. | Dr. | No. | Cr. | Dr. | Cr. |
| Cash | P2 | 700,000 | P4 | 125,000 | 825,000 |  |
|  | P5 | 826,000 | P6 | 26,000 |  |  |
|  |  |  | P10 | 550,000 |  |  |
| Due from state | P1 | 200,000 | P2 | 200,000 |  |  |
| Due from federal government | P1 | 500,000 | P2 | 500,000 |  |  |
| Proceeds from bonds | PC1 | 816,000 | P5 | 816,000 |  |  |
| Revenue | PC1 | 700,000 | P1 | 700,000 |  |  |
| Accounts payable | P4 | 75,000 | P3 | 75,000 |  | 250,000 |
|  | P10 | 550,000 | P9 | 800,000 |  |  |
| Due to general fund |  |  |  |  |  |  |
| Fund balance |  |  | PC1 | 175,000 |  | 175,000 |
| Judgments payable | P4 | 50,000 | P3 | 50,000 |  |  |
| Due to debt service fund | P6 | 26,000 | P5 | 26,000 |  |  |
| Operating transfers to debt service fund | P5 | 16,000 | PC1 | 16,000 |  |  |
| Expenditures | P3 | 125,000 | PC1 | 925,000 |  |  |
|  | P9 | 800,000 |  |  |  |  |
| Residual equity transfer |  |  |  |  |  |  |
| Retained percentage—contracts payable |  |  |  |  |  |  |
| Encumbrances | P7 | 1,200,000 | P8 | 800,000 |  |  |
|  |  |  | PC1 | 400,000 |  |  |
| Reserve for encumbrances | P8 | 800,000 | P7 | 1,200,000 |  | 400,000 |
|  |  | $7,384,000 |  | $7,384,000 | $825,000 | $825,000 |

A contract change was made that increased the contract from $1,200,000 to $1,250,000. The journal entry to record this contract change would be:

| P2-2 | Encumbrances | $50,000 |  |
|---|---|---|---|
|  | Reserve for encumbrances |  | $50,000 |

In addition, agreement was reached with the public works department to landscape the grounds and do any additional work on driveways and sidewalks for $75,000. The entry needed to be made for this transaction at this time is:

| P2-3 | Encumbrances | $75,000 |  |
|---|---|---|---|
|  | Reserve for encumbrances |  | $75,000 |

**EXHIBIT 7-1**
*(continued)*

| Transactions during fiscal 19X7 | | | | | Balance before closing 19X7 and closing entries | | | |
|---|---|---|---|---|---|---|---|---|
| No. | Dr. | No. | Cr. | | Dr. | | Cr. | |
| | | P2-5 | 550,000 | B | 65,000 | P2-C3 | 65,000 | |
| | | P2-9 | 50,000 | | | | | |
| | | P2-8 | 160,000 | | | | | |
| P2-5 | 550,000 | P2-4 | 300,000 | | | | | |
| P2-8 | 100,000 | P2-6 | 100,000 | | | | | |
| P2-8 | 60,000 | P2-7 | 60,000 | | | | | |
| | | P2-1 | 400,000 | P2-C1 | 510,000 | B | 575,000 | |
| | | | | P2-C2 | 65,000 | | | |
| | | | | P2-C3 | 65,000 | P2-C2 | 65,000 | |
| P2-4 | 300,000 | | | B | 510,000 | P2-C1 | 510,000 | |
| P2-7 | 60,000 | | | | | | | |
| P2-6 | 150,000 | | | | | | | |
| | | | | P2-C2 | 65,000 | P2-C2 | 65,000 | |
| P2-9 | 50,000 | P2-6 | 50,000 | | | | | |
| P2-1 | 400,000 | P2-4 | 300,000 | | | | | |
| P2-2 | 50,000 | P2-6 | 150,000 | | | | | |
| P2-3 | 75,000 | P2-7 | 75,000 | | | | | |
| P2-4 | 300,000 | P2-2 | 50,000 | | | | | |
| P2-6 | 150,000 | P2-3 | 75,000 | | | | | |
| P2-7 | 75,000 | | | | | | | |
| | $2,320,000 | | $2,320,000 | | $1,280,000 | | $1,280,000 | |

On September 30, 19X6, the percentage of project completion that was approved for payment was $300,000. These entries are:

P2-4    Sept. 30
    Reserve for encumbrance    $300,000
        Encumbrance                             $300,000

    Sept. 30
    Expenditures                      $300,000
        Accounts payable                        $300,000

The journal entry to record the payment of the accounts, including those from the prior year, is:

## EXHIBIT 7-2
### City of Ruthberg
### Capital Projects Fund
### Balance Sheet (Incomplete Project)
### June 30, 19X6

Assets
  Cash                                                                $825,000

Liabilities and fund balance
  Accounts payable                                                    $250,000
  Reserve for encumbrances                        $400,000
  Fund balance                                     175,000             575,000
    Total liabilities and fund balance                                $825,000

|  |  | Dr. | Cr. |
|---|---|---|---|
| P2-5 | Accounts payable | $550,000 | |
|  | Cash | | $550,000 |

The project was not completed until December 1, 19X6 because of the addition to the contract. At that time, an invoice was received for the balance of the contract. On this project, the retained percentage was a little over 4 percent of the contract price, or $50,000. The journal entry to record the transactions concerning the completion of the contract and the retained percentage of the payment would be:

## EXHIBIT 7-3
### City of Ruthberg
### Capital Projects Fund
### Statement of Revenues, Expenditures, and Changes in Fund Balance
### (Incomplete Project)
### For Year Ended June 30, 19X6

Revenue and other sources of financing:
  Proceeds from sale of bonds                                    $  816,000
  Revenue from state grant                                          200,000
  Revenue from federal grant                                        500,000
    Total                                                        $1,516,000
Expenditures:
  For land purchases                            $125,000
  For contract                                   800,000
    Total                                        925,000
  Operating transfers to debt
    service fund                                  16,000         $  941,000
  Excess of revenue and other sources
    of financing over expenditures                               $  575,000
Changes in fund balance:
  Fund balance, 7/1/X5                                                    0
  Fund balance, 6/30/X6                                          $  575,000

| P2-6 | Dec. 1, 19X6 | | |
|---|---|---|---|
| | Reserve for encumbrances | $150,000 | |
| |     Encumbrances | | $150,000 |
| | Expenditures | $150,000 | |
| |     Accounts payable | | $100,000 |
| |     Retained percentage— | | |
| |       contracts payable | | 50,000 |

The public works department completed its work, and the cost was only $60,000 of the $75,000 encumbered. The payment for the work done by the public works department, a part of the land costs, is accrued as follows:

| P2-7 | Dec. 19X6 | | |
|---|---|---|---|
| | Reserve for encumbrances | $75,000 | |
| |     Encumbrances | | $75,000 |
| | Expenditures | $60,000 | |
| |     Due to general fund | | $60,000 |

The entry for the payment to the general fund and for the accounts is:

| P2-8 | Dec. 19X6 | | |
|---|---|---|---|
| | Accounts payable | $100,000 | |
| | Due to general fund | 60,000 | |
| |     Cash | | $160,000 |

On February 28, 19X7 any corrections to the project needed for final approval were made by the contractors, and the project was approved. The retained percentage was then paid.

| P2-9 | Feb. 28, 19X7 | | |
|---|---|---|---|
| | Retained percentage— | | |
| |     contracts payable | $50,000 | |
| |     Cash | | $50,000 |

## Final Closing Entries

The closing entries for the second year and the final completion of the projects follow.

| P2-C1 | Feb. 28, 19X7 | | |
|---|---|---|---|
| | | Dr. | Cr. |
| | Fund balance | $510,000 | |
| |     Expenditures | | $510,000 |

The fund balance account is then closed and the balance of cash on hand transferred to the debt service fund. This transferred fund balance is a residual equity transfer from the capital projects fund to the debt service fund. The entries are as follows:

| | | | |
|---|---|---|---|
| P2-C2 | Feb. 28, 19X7 | | |
| | Residual equity transfer | $65,000 | |
| |     Due to debt service fund | | $65,000 |
| | Fund balance | 65,000 | |
| |     Residual equity transfer | | 65,000 |
| | | | |
| P2-C3 | Due to debt service fund | $65,000 | |
| |     Cash | | $65,000 |

## Financial Statements—Completed Projects

A worksheet for all of the transactions for the two years is shown in Exhibit 7-1. After the closing entries for the second year, the fund has no account with a balance in it. Thus there could be no balance sheet for the second year. Yet, transactions took place in the fund during the second year, culminating in the completion of the project and the closing of the fund. The result of these transactions is a statement of revenues, expenditures, and changes in fund balance as shown in Exhibit 7-4.

## Combining Capital Projects Funds Statements

When there are several capital projects funds, the statements from each of the funds are combined into one statement that shows individually and collectively all of the capital projects in operation. This statement, usually shown in columnar form, is called a "combining funds statement." The amounts expended are classified in the combining statements and also in the combined statements, as capital assets rather than being classified by function or object expenditures. Illustrative combining funds statements are shown in Chapter 13.

**EXHIBIT 7-4**
**City of Ruthberg**
**Capital Projects Fund**
**Statement of Revenues, Expenditures, and Changes in Fund Balance**
**For Fiscal Year 19X7 (Project Completed)**

| | | |
|---|---|---|
| Revenues and other sources of financing | | — |
| Expenditures | | $510,000 |
| Expenditures over revenue and other sources of financing | | ($510,000) |
| Fund balances beginning of year: | | |
|   Reserve for encumbrances | $400,000 | |
|   Unencumbered balances | 175,000 | 575,000 |
| Fund balance at completion of project | | 65,000 |
| Residual equity transfer | | 65,000 |
| Fund balance | | 0 |

# CHAPTER 7: CAPITAL PROJECTS FUNDS

## SUMMARY

This chapter provides a discussion of accounting and financial reporting for capital projects funds. Capital projects funds provide the accounting and financial reporting for (1) the obtaining of resources to construct or build specific capital projects, (2) the building or buying of those projects, and (3) the dissolving of the fund.

The processes of obtaining resources and the building or buying of long-term assets are examined here. The resources obtained include receiving grants from other political subdivisions and issuing bonds or other long-term liabilities. The accounting is for expenditures to build the project until it is completed. Once the project is completed, the fund is dissolved. This entire process is explained and illustrated through journal entries, accounts, and financial statements.

## QUESTIONS

1. What sources currently provide funds for most capital acquisitions?
2. What is usually done with the premium from the sale of bonds for a project?
3. What do capital projects funds account for?
4. What is the objective of the long-range capital facilities plan? What is needed to carry out such a plan?
5. Give some of the characteristics of a capital facility or capital improvement.
6. Discuss the functions of capital budgeting.
7. What is the relationship between the capital projects fund and other funds and account groups such as the debt service fund, the general long-term debt account group, and the general fixed asset account group?
8. Why is there no need for formal budgetary accounting on a current basis for the capital projects fund?
9. What is the difference in the nature of the encumbrances and reserve for encumbrances accounts in the capital projects fund and the general fund?
10. What is the difference between proceeds and operating transfers?
11. How are bond discounts and premiums handled when they originate from bond issues?
12. How are idle funds usually handled by most governments?
13. The city issued ten-year term bonds with a face value of $300,000 and a 7 percent interest rate. The date of issue was March 31, 198X, with interest paid on June 30 and December 31. The bonds were dated January 1, 198X and were issued at a premium of 1/2 percent. Give the journal entries necessary to record this transaction.
14. Assume that instead of a 2 percent premium, the bonds in entry P5 (see page 197) were issued for 2 percent discount. All other facts remain the same. Give the journal entries necessary to record this event.
15. What statements are made in a capital projects fund if the project is incomplete? If the project is complete?

## PROBLEMS

7-1 Circle the correct answer to each question.[3]
   1 Premiums received on general obligation bonds are generally transferred to what fund or account group?
      a Debt service

    **b** General long-term debt
    **c** General
    **d** Special revenue
**2** When Brockton City realized $1,020,000 from the sale of a $1,000,000 bond issue, the entry in its capital projects fund was:

| | | |
|---|---|---|
| Cash | $1,020,000 | |
|     Proceeds from bonds | | $1,000,000 |
|     Due to debt service fund | | 20,000 |

Recording the transaction in this manner indicates that:
    **a** The $20,000 cannot be used for the designated purpose of the fund but must be transferred to another fund.
    **b** The full $1,020,000 can be used by the capital projects fund to accomplish its purpose.
    **c** The nominal rate of interest on the bonds is below the market rate for bonds of such term and risk.
    **d** A safety factor is being set aside to cover possible contract defaults on the construction.
**3** Proceeds from the issuance of general obligation bonds sold to finance the construction of a new city hall should be recorded in a:
    **a** Debt service fund
    **b** Capital projects fund
    **c** Revolving interest fund
    **d** Special revenue fund
    **e** None of the above
**4** A capital projects fund of a municipality is an example of what type of fund?
    **a** Internal service
    **b** Governmental
    **c** Proprietary
    **d** Fiduciary
**5** The amount received for accrued interest paid upon the sale of bonds to construct a capital facility is:
    **a** Used to help pay for the construction of the capital facility
    **b** Transferred to the general fund to help pay for the interest during the year.
    **c** Transferred to the general fixed assets account group
    **d** Transferred to the debt service fund to be used in paying for the current year's interest
**6** When investments are made in a capital projects fund, the earnings from the investments:
    **a** Are remitted to the sources that provided the amounts to buy or construct the capital facility
    **b** Are used to help pay for the construction costs
    **c** Are paid to the general fund
    **d** Are transferred to the debt service fund
**7** The financial statements of several capital projects of a local governmental unit are usually prepared in a particular form for the annual financial report. This type of form is called:
    **a** Combining statements
    **b** Individual statements
    **c** Consolidated statements
    **d** Not prepared annually, only when the project is completed

7-2 Identify the correct answer.
   1 In preparing the capital budget, a city must determine the meaning of a capital asset. An illustration of a capital asset is:
      a Repairs to an existing building
      b Resources needed to sustain the operation of a new health-care center
      c Equipment required at the time of acquisition or construction of a building
      d Minor equipment acquisition
   2 The objective of a capital budget is to provide public facilities having a relatively long life within the limits of available resources. Therefore, capital budgeting must involve:
      a Planning, programming, and financing considerations
      b Planning, operations, and control considerations
      c PPBS considerations
      d Operating considerations
   3 The records of the assets purchased or constructed in a capital projects fund:
      a Remain in the fund
      b Are transferred to the debt service fund
      c Are transferred to the general fixed assets account group
      d Are depreciated annually in order to recover the costs of the assets
   4 In a capital projects fund,
      a Full budgetary accounting is always used.
      b Partial budgetary accounting can be used.
      c Budgetary accounting is never used.
      d Actual results accounting is the only method used.
   5 The basis of accounting in capital projects funds is:
      a Modified accrual basis
      b Accrual basis
      c Cash basis
      d Project fund accounting basis
   6 The term "proceeds" is used in a capital projects fund:
      a To record the amount received as premium on the sale of bonds
      b To record the amount received from the sale of bonds
      c To record the amount received from transfers from the general fund
      d To record the amount received from other governmental agencies
   7 The entity theory of accounting requires that all capital projects:
      a Be accounted for separately
      b Be accounted for jointly with other capital projects funds
      c Be consolidated with the general fund
      d Be combined with the debt service fund
7-3 Record the journal entries for the following transactions.
   1 The proceeds from the sale of general obligation bonds issued by the town of Greensboro to finance the acquisition of capital facilities was $1,025,000. The face amount of the bond issue was $1,000,000, of which $10,000 represented interested accrued on the bonds to date of sale. Record the journal entry for the sale of bonds.
   2 The city of South Portland received approval for the construction of a civic area. The city issued $5,000,000 in bonds to finance the project and also received notice from the federal and state governments that they would grant $2,000,000 and $1,000,000, respectively, for the project. Record the journal entries for (a) the authorization for the construction, (b) the accrual of the government grants, and (c) the receipt of cash from the grants and the bonds.

**7-4** The city of Lewiston began the work of expanding its sewer system to be financed by a bond issue supplemented by state and federal grants. Estimated total cost of the project was $1,600,000—$800,000 of which was to come from the bond issue, $600,000 from a federal grant, and the balance from a state grant. Transactions for the year are as follows:

1 A $25,000 loan was supplied from the general fund.
2 The money from the federal and state governments was accrued.
3 A contract was let to Reynolds Construction Company for the major part of the project on a bid of $1,450,000.
4 A bill was received from the city's stores and services fund for supplies provided to this fund in the amount of $20,000.
5 An accounts payable was recorded for a $1,680 billing from a suit for damages to an individual's house.
6 A billing of $480,000 was received from Reynolds for work completed to date.
7 Preliminary planning and engineering costs of $19,500 were paid to the Kopfle Engineering Company. The bill was paid upon presentation.
8 Actual proceeds for the year were $800,000 from the sale of bonds at par. $300,000 was received from the federal government and $100,000 from the state government.
9 The amount due to the stores and services fund was paid.
10 The amount billed by the contractor was paid, less a 5 percent retaining.
11 Temporary investments were purchased at a cost of $675,000, of which $1,500 was for accrued interest purchased.

**Required:**
1 Prepare journal entries for the transactions.
2 Prepare closing entries for the end of the year.
3 Prepare a year-end balance sheet.
4 Prepare a statement of revenue, proceeds, expenditures, and changes in fund balance.

**7-5** This problem contains the second-year transactions for the city of Lewiston (see Problem 7-4).

Transactions for the year are:

1 Received balance of amounts from the state and federal governments.
2 Paid amount due to general fund.
3 Received $31,500 interest for six months on the investments.
4 Sold investments for $673,000 plus $1,500 accrued interest.
5 Project was completed and a billing from Reynolds Construction was received for $970,000.
6 Paid amount of construction costs, less 5 percent retained for final inspection and approval of the contract.
7 Paid amounts due to debt service fund.
8 Paid $125,000 for landscaping and extra work on the project.
9 Paid balance of amount of retained contracts payable upon acceptance of work on the project.
10 Transferred balance of cash to the debt service fund and closed the capital projects fund.

**Required:**
1 Prepare journal entries for the year.
2 Post the entries to a worksheet and complete worksheet.
3 Prepare the financial statements needed for the year.

**7-6** The following transactions took place in the town of Rockingham in year 2. The balance sheet and analysis of change in fund balance for year 1 are:

**Town of Rockingham**
**Balance Sheet—Capital Projects Fund**
**December 31, Year 1**

| Assets | | Fund balance | |
|---|---|---|---|
| Cash | $115,000 | Reserve for encumbrances | $ 65,000 |
| | | Unencumbered fund balance | 50,000 |
| Total assets | $115,000 | Fund balance | $115,000 |

**Analysis of Change in Fund Balance—Year 1**

| | | |
|---|---|---|
| Project authorization | | $120,000 |
| Fund balance, 1/1/1 | | -0- |
| Add: proceeds of bond issue | | 120,000 |
| Total | | 120,000 |
| Less: expenditures | | 5,000 |
| Fund balance | | $115,000 |
| Fund balance: | | |
| Reserve for encumbrances | $65,000 | |
| Unencumbered fund balance | 50,000 | |
| | | $115,000 |

The following transactions took place during year 2:

1 Materials ordered in year 1 at an estimated cost of $65,000 were received with an invoice for $65,000.

2 Salaries and wages amounting to $40,100 were paid.

3 Materials were paid.

4 The project was completed and the accounts closed. The remaining balance in the capital projects fund was to be transferred to the debt service fund.

**Required**:

1 Prepare all journal entries, including closing entries for year 2.
2 Post the entries to "T" accounts.
3 Prepare a statement of revenue, expenditures, and changes in fund balance for year 2.

7-7 In a special election held on May 1, 19A7, the voters of the city of Nicknar approved a $10,000,000 issue of 6 percent general obligation bonds maturing in twenty years. The proceeds of this sale will be used to help finance the construction of a new civic center. The total cost of the project was estimated at $15,000,000. The remaining $5,000,000 will be financed by an irrevocable state grant that has been awarded. A capital projects fund was established to account for this project and was designated the civic center construction fund. The formal project authorization was appropriately recorded in a memorandum entry.[4]

The following transactions occurred during the fiscal year beginning July 1, 19A7 and ending June 30, 19A8.

1 On July 1, the general fund loaned $500,000 to the civic center construction fund for defraying engineering and other expenses.

2 Preliminary engineering and planning costs of $320,000 were paid to Akron Engineering Company. There had been no encumbrance for this cost.

3 On December 1, the bonds were sold at 101 percent of par. The premium on bonds was transferred to the debt service fund.

4 On March 15, a contract for $12,000,000 was entered into with Candu Construction Company for the major part of the project.

**5** Orders were placed for materials estimated to cost $55,000.
**6** On April 1, a partial payment of $2,500,000 was received from the state.
**7** The materials that were previously ordered were received at a cost of $51,000 and paid.
**8** On June 15, a progress billing of $2,000,000 was received from Candu Construction for work done on the project. As per the terms of the contract, the city will withhold 6 percent of any billing until the project is completed.
**9** The general fund was repaid the $500,000 previously loaned.

**Required**:
1 Prepare journal entries to record the transactions in the civic center construction fund for the period July 1, 19A7, through June 30, 19A8, and the appropriate closing entries at June 30, 19A8.
2 Prepare a balance sheet of the civic center construction fund as of June 30, 19A8.

**7-8** This problem continues the case of Silver City, also discussed in problems 3-7, 5-10, and 6-10. It concerns the Silver City capital projects fund. Retain the material you develop here for future references.

**1** A capital projects fund was approved for a project that was estimated to cost $800,000. A bond authorization for $500,000 was approved for the project. The state also approved a grant for $300,000. The bonds issued were $500,000, 8 percent term bonds, with interest of 8 percent payable semiannually. The bonds were sold at 102. Cash received was $510,000.
**2** The state paid their share of the project—$300,000.
**3** Land for the building was purchased for $50,000.
**4** A contract was let to construct the building for $700,000.
**5** Bills to pay for the construction that was completed were received for $500,000.
**6** The progress payment bills were paid.
**7** The premium on the sale of the bonds was transferred to the debt service fund.

The building was not completed until the following year. All transactions for the current year are shown above.

**Required**:
1 Prepare journal entries for the transactions given, including adjusting and closing entries.
2 Post the journal entries to a worksheet and complete the worksheet.
3 Prepare the financial statements needed for the year.

# NOTES

**1** For a further discussion of these procedures, see Alan Walter Steiss, *Local Government Finance: Capital Facilities Planning and Debt Administration* (Lexington, Mass.: Lexington Books—D.C. Heath and Co., 1975).
**2** The bond underwriters, acting as agents for the issuing jurisdiction, will usually develop an optimum mix of bonds in large bond issues, to be issued at a discount, at par, and at a premium to provide the locality with the required funds to undertake the capital improvement.
**3** Adapted from American Institute of Certified Public Accountants, *Uniform CPA Examination Questions and Unofficial Answers* (New York: American Institute of Certified Public Accountants, various dates).
**4** Ibid., May 1979.

# CHAPTER 8

# DEBT SERVICE FUNDS

Debt service funds are used to account for and manage the resources needed to pay off the interest and the principal on general long-term obligations, such as bonds issued in the capital projects fund. The primary resources in this fund usually come from operating transfers from the general or special revenue funds. Earnings on investments purchased from resources transferred to the funds are invested and eventually are secondary resources used for retirement of the long-term obligations.

## SPECIAL USE OF DEBT SERVICE FUNDS

Most long-term debt for a municipality is issued on behalf of capital projects funds, special assessment funds, or proprietary funds. Proprietary and special assessment funds service their own debt requirements. Accounting for debt servicing for the proprietary funds has been previously discussed (see Chapter 2). Accounting for special assessment funds will be discussed in Chapter 9.

Debt service funds are used to: (1) account for the accumulation of resources from which the principal and interest on general long-term debt of the governmental unit is paid and (2) account for the investment and expenditures of those resources. Thus debt service funds account for the resources needed to pay interest and principal on all long-term debt incurred by capital projects funds. However, they do not account for the proceeds from issuance of the debt or the record keeping of the debt. The proceeds are accounted for in the capital projects fund (discussed in Chapter 7), and the record keeping of the debt will be accounted for in the general long-term debt account group (to be discussed in Chapter 11).

Long-term debt can be classified into two types: term and serial debt. With *serial debt*, a proportion of the debt matures each year over a period of years, and the interest is paid on the unmatured portion each year. Most debt currently being issued is serial debt. With *term debt*, all of the debt matures at a specified maturity date; the interest on the total debt, however, is paid each year. The principles of long-term debt accounting apply to all types of long-term indebtedness. The illustrations, therefore, will be of only long-term bond debt.

Theoretically, a debt service fund should be created for each separate long-term debt issuance. Practically, however, as many debt issuances as possible should be accounted for in a single fund, whenever possible; the fewer the number of debt service funds, the less complicated the accounting for long-term debt. One fund needs only one set of financial statements; many funds need many sets of financial statements.

## FINANCES FOR REPAYMENT OF DEBT

The money needed for the repayment of debt, as well as the interest on the bonds, can come from several sources. If the locality or authority earmarks a special revenue source for the repayment of bonds, then a special revenue fund is set up to collect and transfer the money to the debt service fund (such bonds often are called ''revenue bonds''). Generally, though, the general fund collects the revenue from various sources and transfers it to the debt service fund. Occasions can arise when the debt service fund is used to account for the collection of revenue, such as a special revenue fund, rather than having another fund collect the money that is then transferred to the debt service fund. Revenue collected in either the general or special revenue funds and transferred to the debt service fund is shown as *operating transfers out* in these funds and as *operating transfers in* in the debt service fund. Thus transfers are not shown as expenditures or as revenue.

Many bond indentures require that the money needed for the servicing of the bonds is a first claim on the general revenue of the governmental unit. In this case, the general fund is the primary source of the money needed for the funds.

Since the resources needed to service the principal and interest on serial bonds is received and expended each year, there is no collection of resources on which earnings can be made. The resources needed to service the principal on term bonds, however, is not needed until the debt matures. Resources are, however, currently needed to pay for the interest. Resources received in the debt service fund for the payment of the principal can be invested, with income being earned each year. Thus the assets and the fund balance annually increase to provide an amount that will eventually be used for the payment of the debt.

## BASIS OF ACCOUNTING FOR DEBT SERVICE FUNDS

Generally accepted accounting principles for debt service funds require the use of the modified accrual basis of accounting, with one major exception. The National Council on Governmental Accounting states:

> The major exception to the general rule of expenditure accrual relates to unmatured principal and interest on general obligation long-term debt. Financial resources usually are appro-

priated in other funds for transfer to a Debt Service Fund in the period in which maturing debt principal and interest must be paid. Such amounts thus are not current liabilities of the Debt Service Fund as their settlement will not require expenditure of existing fund assets. Further, to accrue the Debt Service Fund expenditure and liability in one period but record the transfer of financial resources for debt service purposes in a later period would be confusing and would result in overstatement of Debt Service Fund expenditures and liabilities and understatement of the fund balance. Thus, disclosure of subsequent year debt service requirements is appropriate, but they usually are appropriately accounted for as expenditures in the year of payment. On the other hand, if Debt Service Fund resources have been provided during the current year for payment of principal and interest due early in the following year, the expenditure and related liability may be recognized in the Debt Service Fund and the debt principal amount removed from the General Long-Term Debt Account Group.[1]

Since financial resources for the payment of debt in the debt service fund are usually appropriated in the general or a special revenue fund, then the liability for the debt in the debt service fund and the liability in the general fund for the amount to be paid to the debt service fund should be recorded in the year it is budgeted in the general or special revenue fund. For example, $40,000 is due to the debt service fund from the general fund before July 15, 19X5 in order to pay the semiannual interest of $15,000; and $25,000 is due to pay the principal due on ten-year serial bonds of $500,000 at an interest rate of 6 percent. The amount for this liability normally would be shown as an appropriation in the 19X6 budget. So, no accruals would be made in either the general fund or the debt service fund. One can easily see the problems that would occur if the debt service fund accrued the expenditure during the current fiscal year and the general fund did not recognize a liability and, therefore, did not make an appropriation to the debt service fund until the following fiscal year.

## Budgetary Accounting

As explained in Chapter 4, budgets are used for control purposes. And, as explained in the previous chapter concerning capital projects funds, if some other method that is akin to budgeting control is provided, there is no need for budgetary control. If certain provisions of budgetary accounting are needed for control, such as encumbrances in the capital projects funds, then they are used. Since the amounts to be transferred to the debt service fund are usually included in the budget for the general fund and since there is no need for a special control of expenditures in the debt service fund, budgetary accounting, including encumbrance accounting, typically is not needed or required in debt service funds.

In their *Governmental Accounting, Auditing, and Financial Reporting*, the Municipal Finance Officers Association says:

> Debt Service Fund spending is controlled primarily through bond indenture provisions. Accordingly, budgetary accounts are often not formally integrated into their general ledger, and budgetary comparisons for them need to be included in GAAP financial reports only if annual budgets are legally adopted.[2]

## ILLUSTRATIVE TRANSACTIONS—DEBT SERVICE FUNDS—CITY OF RUTHBERG

### Debt Service Fund Accounting for Serial Bonds

Serial debt, as previously explained, consists of bonds or other long-term debt whose principal matures and is paid in periodic installments over the life of the debt. Each year the general fund or other financing source (e.g., a special revenue fund) must provide sufficient resources to pay a proportionate share of the principal as well as the interest on this year's remaining portion of the debt.

Assume that $800,000 in serial bonds were issued with a twenty-year maturity and a 6 percent interest rate. Each year, $40,000 of the bonds were retired. At the end of ten years, $400,000 in principal remains. The current year's interest is $24,000 (i.e., 6 percent of $400,000). Therefore, $64,000 will have to be transferred from the general fund to the debt service fund to pay for servicing the principal and interest on these bonds in the tenth year. The title used in the debt service fund for monies transferred from the general fund is "operating transfers" and not "revenue." Budgetary entries are not required to record the estimated transfers and the appropriations for the year, since they are recognized in the general fund budget.

The modified accrual basis is used in this fund. The entry to accrue these amounts is:

|   |   | Dr. | Cr. |
|---|---|---|---|
| **D1** | Due from general fund | $64,000 | |
|   | Operating transfers (from the general fund) | | $64,000 |

Upon payment of the money, the entry made is:

|   |   | Dr. | Cr. |
|---|---|---|---|
| **D2** | Cash | $64,000 | |
|   | Due from general fund | | $64,000 |

The entry to record the accrual of the bonds payable is:

|   |   | Dr. | Cr. |
|---|---|---|---|
| **D3** | Expenditures | $40,000 | |
|   | Matured bonds payable | | $40,000 |

For the interest due, the accrual entry is:

|   |   | Dr. | Cr. |
|---|---|---|---|
| **D4** | Expenditures | $24,000 | |
|   | Interest payable | | $24,000 |

The entry to record the payment of the principal and interest is:

|   |   | Dr. | Cr. |
|---|---|---|---|
| **D5** | Matured bonds payable | $40,000 | |
|   | Interest payable | 24,000 | |
|   | Cash | | $64,000 |

At the end of the year, the transfers and expenditures accounts are closed with the following entries:

|     |                                         | Dr.      | Cr.      |
| --- | --------------------------------------- | -------- | -------- |
| DC1 | Operating transfers (from the general fund) | $64,000 |          |
|     | Expenditures                            |          | $64,000  |

Since the transfers equal expenditures, no fund balance would arise. If there were any differences, the amount would go to a fund balance account. In the following year, the interest payment would be $21,600, since the principal has been reduced to $360,000. Entries to illustrate the payment of the bonds are shown in Chapter 11.

## Financial Statements for Debt Service Funds—Serial Bonds

Exhibit 8-1 shows all of the preceding entries recorded on a worksheet. Since all balance sheet amounts are closed, there is no balance sheet at the end of the period. A statement of revenues, expenditures, and changes in fund balance, however, would have to be prepared (not shown).

## Debt Service Fund Accounting for Term Bonds Issued

When accounting for term bonds, a debt service fund not only receives tax revenue and transfers from other funds; it also receives revenue from earnings on investments. These differing types of revenue, transfers, and earnings must be specifically shown. "Revenue" is used for earnings from investments and for resources received from taxes or outside sources. The term "operating transfers" is used to designate resources

**EXHIBIT 8-1**
**City of Ruthberg**
**Debt Service Fund**
**Serial Bonds—Twenty Year, 6 Percent**
**For Year Ended June 30, 19X6**

|                             | Transactions |          |     |          | Closing entries |         |     |         |
| --------------------------- | ------------ | -------- | --- | -------- | --------------- | ------- | --- | ------- |
| Account                     | No.          | Dr.      | No. | Cr.      | No.             | Dr.     | No. | Cr.     |
| Cash                        | D2           | 64,000   | D5  | 64,000   |                 |         |     |         |
| Due from general fund       | D1           | 64,000   | D2  | 64,000   |                 |         |     |         |
| Interest payable            | D5           | 24,000   | D4  | 24,000   |                 |         |     |         |
| Matured bonds payable from the general fund | D5 | 40,000 | D3 | 40,000 |          |         |     |         |
| Operating transfers         |              |          | D1  | 64,000   | DC1             | 64,000  |     |         |
| Expenditures                | D3           | 40,000   |     |          |                 |         | DC1 | 64,000  |
|                             | D4           | 24,000   |     |          |                 |         |     |         |
|                             |              | $256,000 |     | $256,000 |                 | $64,000 |     | $64,000 |

received from the general fund that are earmarked for a *sinking fund*. The sinking fund is built up for the eventual payment of the principal as well as for payment of interest.

Management of a sinking fund requires that annual contributions be made to a segregated account. When combined with the return from the investment of these account monies, an amount will be provided sufficient to cover the required principal payments when the bonds reach maturity. A sinking fund provides the mechanism for spreading the cost of repayment over the life of the bond issue. In this way, large, irregular demands will not be made on the local government's annual budget.

The amount earmarked each year for the sinking fund should be determined by: (1) the dollar value of bonds to be retired, (2) the number of payments to be made into the account, and (3) the anticipated rate of earnings on the invested funds. Given these three factors, the annual amount ($N$) that must be placed (generally at the end of the year) at compound interest ($r$) for a term of years ($n$) to create a sinking fund ($S$) can be computed by applying the following formula:

$$N = S \frac{r}{(1 + r)^n - 1}$$

For example, a municipality seeking to pay off $2,000,000 at the end of ten years, with funds invested at 6 percent compound interest, would be required to make ten annual payments of $151,736 to a sinking fund. Early payments to the debt service fund or payments in semiannual or quarterly installments, of course, would increase sinking fund earnings and reduce the total requirements to be raised from taxes.

Sinking fund requirements should be recomputed on an annual basis. It may be possible to lower future requirements should a surplus in excess of actuarial requirements develop. It is sound debt management practice, however, to absorb any significant surplus gradually over several tax periods rather than achieving a large reduction in payments in a single year. Should a deficit arise in the sinking fund (i.e., should it fall behind actuarial requirements), adjustments should be made as soon as possible by increasing the level of payment into the fund. At the same time, new investment opportunities that will produce a greater return should be sought.

The previous illustration of bonds issued in the capital projects fund will also be used to illustrate the operation for term bonds in the debt service fund. Remember that the capital projects fund issued $800,000 worth of 5 percent, twenty-year bonds at a premium of $16,000, with accrued interest of $10,000 (see p. 197). The entry in the debt service fund for the amounts transferred is:

| | | | |
|---|---|---|---|
| D6 | Due from capital projects fund | $26,000 | |
| | Expenditures | | $10,000 |
| | Operating transfer from capital projects fund | | 16,000 |
| | Cash | $26,000 | |
| | Due from capital projects fund | | $26,000 |

The amount needed each year for interest payments would be:

| | |
|---|---|
| Dec. 31 (2.5 percent of $800,000) | $20,000 |
| June 30 (2.5 percent of $800,000) | 20,000 |
| Annually | $40,000 |

The bonds were sold three months after the issue date, so only $10,000 would be needed for the first payment. The other $10,000, for the total payment of $20,000, would come from the accrued interest received upon the sale of the bonds. This $10,000 is originally recorded as a credit to the expenditures account in order to have the correct amount of expenditures for interest paid for the year.

The estimated amounts needed each year to build up a sinking fund will come from operating transfers from the general fund, from taxes, from other revenue, or from earnings from investment. The estimated amount needed to be transferred from the general fund or from other funds and an estimate of the earnings required can be developed from an annuity table or from an annuity formula as previously shown. For example, the total amount needed to pay off the bonds is $800,000. If the fund can earn 8 percent each year on its investments, then an annuity table shows that one dollar invested annually for twenty years at 8 percent will return $45.762. It takes $17,481.75 added to the fund each year and invested at 8 percent to equal $800,000 at the end of twenty years ($800,000 ÷ $45.762 = $17,481.75). Exhibit 8-2 shows the estimated annual transfer requirements for the twenty-year life of the bonds. The premium received on the sale of the bonds is used to take care of part of the amount needed as a transfer from the general fund for the first year.

If the fiscal agent charges $300 each year for paying the interest to the bondholders, the general fund needs to transfer each year to the debt service fund the following amounts.

| | | |
|---|---|---|
| *For the first year:* | | |
| Annual transfer for interest payment | $40,000.00 | |
| Less accrual payment for interest for first year | 10,000.00 | |
| Total for interest | $30,000.00 | |
| Fiscal agent's charges | 300.00 | |
| Total transfers needed first year for interest | | $30,300.00 |
| Annual transfers for sinking fund | 17,481.75 | |
| Less premium on bonds | 16,000.00 | |
| Total transfers needed first year for sinking fund | | 1,481.75 |
| Total transfers needed first year from general fund for interest payments and for sinking fund | | $31,781.75 |

**EXHIBIT 8-2**
**City of Ruthberg**
**Debt Service Fund**
**Sinking Fund Reqirements**
**To Retire Twenty-year, $800,000 Bonds**

| Year number | Transfers for bond payment from capital projects | Estimated transfers for bond payment from general fund | Estimated fund earnings | Estimated yearly fund balance increase | Estimated year-end fund balance |
|---|---|---|---|---|---|
| 1 | $16,000 | $ 1,481.75 | | 17,481.75 | 17,481.75 |
| 2 | | 17,481.75 | 1,398.54 | 18,880.29 | 36,362.04 |
| 3 | | 17,481.75 | 2,908.96 | 20,390.71 | 56,752.75 |
| 4 | | 17,481.75 | 4,540.22 | 22,021.97 | 78,774.72 |
| 5 | | 17,481.75 | 6,301.98 | 23,783.73 | 102,558.45 |
| 6 | | 17,481.75 | 8,204.68 | 25,686.43 | 128,244.88 |
| 7 | | 17,481.75 | 10,259.59 | 27,741.34 | 155,986.22 |
| 8 | | 17,481.75 | 12,478.90 | 29,960.64 | 185,946.87 |
| 9 | | 17,481.75 | 14,875.75 | 32,357.50 | 218,304.37 |
| 10 | | 17,481.75 | 17,464.35 | 34,946.10 | 253,250.47 |
| 11 | | 17,481.75 | 20,260.04 | 37,741.79 | 290,992.26 |
| 12 | | 17,481.75 | 23,279.38 | 40,761.13 | 331,753.39 |
| 13 | | 17,481.75 | 26,540.27 | 44,022.02 | 375,775.41 |
| 14 | | 17,481.75 | 30,062.03 | 47,543.78 | 423,319.19 |
| 15 | | 17,481.75 | 33,865.53 | 51,347.29 | 474,666.48 |
| 16 | | 17,481.75 | 37,973.32 | 55,455.07 | 530,121.55 |
| 17 | | 17,481.75 | 42,409.72 | 59,891.47 | 590,013.02 |
| 18 | | 17,481.75 | 47,201.04 | 64,682.79 | 654,695.81 |
| 19 | | 17,481.75 | 52,375.66 | 69,857.41 | 724,553.22 |
| 20 | | 17,482.52* | 57,964.26* | 75,446.78 | 800,000.00 |
| | $16,000 | $333,635.78 | $450,364.22 | $800,000.00 | |

*Indicates rounding.

Assumption: Transfer from capital projects fund reduces first-year contribution from general fund. If 8 percent is earned on investments, then $1 invested annually in an annuity for 20 years @ 8 percent = $45.7620; and $17,481.75 invested annually in an annuity for 20 years = $800,000.

$$\text{Annuity formula: } N = S \frac{r}{(1 + r)^n - 1},$$

where $S$ = principal,
 $r$ = rate of return on investment and
 $n$ = number of years to maturity

$$N = \$800,000 \frac{.08}{(1.08)^{20} - 1}$$

$$N = \$800,000 (0.02185) = \$17,481.75$$

*For each additional year:*

|  |  |  |
|---|---:|---:|
| Annual transfer for interest payments | $40,000.00 | |
| Fiscal agent's charges | 300.00 | |
| Total transfers needed each additional year for interest | | $40,300.00 |
| Annual transfers for sinking fund | | 17,481.75 |
| Total transfers needed each additional year from general fund for interest payments and for sinking fund | | $57,781.75 |

The accounting entry for the amounts from the general fund is:

|  |  | Dr. | Cr. |
|---|---|---:|---:|
| D7 | Due from general fund | $31,781.75 | |
|  | Operating transfers from general fund | | $31,781.75 |

The journal entry for the receipt of cash from the general fund is:

|  |  | | |
|---|---|---:|---:|
| D8 | Cash | $31,781.75 | |
|  | Due from general fund | | $31,781.75 |

The payment of the interest and fiscal agent charges, although made in two entries during the year, would total the following:

|  |  | | |
|---|---|---:|---:|
| D9 | Expenditures for interest | $40,300.00 | |
|  | Cash | | $40,300.00 |

The payment as an annuity, generally, is at the end of the year. Therefore, no investments could be purchased during the year in this sinking fund because the money was not received until the end of the year. The closing entries are:

|  |  | Dr. | Cr. |
|---|---|---:|---:|
| DC2 | Operating transfers from general fund | $31,781.75 | |
|  | Fund balance | | $ 1,481.75 |
|  | Expenditures for interest | | 30,300.00 |

The balances as shown on the worksheet (see Exhibit 8-3) are: cash of $17,481.75 and fund balance of $17,481.75. During the second year and all succeeding years, the fund will invest the transfers from the general fund for the sinking fund as well as any earnings made on the investments. Also, the operating transfer from the capital projects fund must be made.

EXHIBIT 8-3
City of Ruthberg
Debt Service Fund—Term Bonds
Worksheet Transactions for 19X6 and 19X7
Years Ended June 30, 19X6 and 19X7

| Accounts | Transactions and closing entries 19X6 | | | | Balance June 30, 19X6 | | Transactions 19X7 | | | |
|---|---|---|---|---|---|---|---|---|---|---|
| | No. | Dr. | No. | Cr. | Dr. | Cr. | No. | Dr. | No. | Cr. |
| Cash | D6 | 26,000.00 | D9 | 40,300.00 | 17,481.75 | | D2-3 | 20,150.00 | D2-1 | 17,480.00 |
| | D8 | 31,781.75 | | | | | D2-5 | 1,325.00 | D2-4 | 20,150.00 |
| | | | | | | | D2-6 | 37,631.75 | D2-7 | 20,150.00 |
| | | | | | | | D2-8 | 65,000.00 | | |
| Investments | | | | | | | D2-1 | 17,480.00 | | |
| Due from capital projects fund | D6 | 26,000.00 | D6 | 26,000.00 | | | | | | |
| Premium on investments | | | | | | | D2-1 | 80.00 | | |
| Discounts on investments | | | | | | | | | D2-1 | 105.00 |
| Due from general fund | D7 | 31,781.75 | D8 | 31,781.75 | | | D2-2 | 57,781.75 | D2-3 | 20,150.00 |
| | | | | | | | | | D2-6 | 37,631.75 |
| Operating transfers from general fund | DC2 | 31,781.75 | D7 | 31,781.75 | | | | | D2-2 | 57,781.75 |
| Operating transfers from capital projects | DC3 | 16,000.00 | D6 | 16,000.00 | | | | | | |
| Revenue from investments | | | | | | | D2-1 | 25.00 | D2-5 | 1,325.00 |
| Expenditures for interest | D9 | 40,300.00 | D6 | 10,000.00 | | | D2-4 | 20,150.00 | | |
| | | | DC2 | 30,300.00 | | | D2-7 | 20,150.00 | | |
| Fund balance | | | DC3 | 16,000.00 | | 17,481.75 | | | D2-8 | 65,000.00 |
| | | | DC2 | 1,481.75 | | | | | | |
| Interest receivable | | | | | | | | | | |
| | | $203,645.25 | | $203,645.25 | $17,481.75 | $17,481.75 | | $239,773.50 | | $239,773.50 |

DC3  Operating transfers from
        capital projects fund        $16,000
            Fund balance                            $16,000

**Second-Year Transactions** At the beginning of the second year, the cash received during the preceding year would be invested. Investments purchased during the year amount to $17,480. On these investments, the seller of the securities received $25 for interest already earned. On the interest payment date, the total interest for the period would be received, and this $25 would be an offset to interest earned during the year. In addition, discounts on investments amounted to $105, and premiums on other investments were $80. The total payment was $17,480. Note that the investments are for the purpose of producing revenue for the eventual partial payment of these bonds. These amounts, pertaining to revenue-producing investments, would all be accounted for on the full accrual basis rather than the modified accrual basis. Premiums and discount on the purchased bonds would be written off to investment earnings over the life of the investments. Writing off premiums and discounts on bond investments over the life of the bonds shows the effective interest earned each year rather than the cash received. This method is used for bond investments in the debt service fund but not for bonds issued at a premium or discount.

**EXHIBIT 8-3**
(*continued*)

| Trial balance | | Adjusting and closing entries | | | | Balance—June 30, 19X7 | |
|---|---|---|---|---|---|---|---|
| Dr. | Cr. | No. | Dr. | No. | Cr. | Dr. | Cr. |
| 83,808.50 | | | | | | 83,808.50 | |
| 17,480.00 | | | | | | 17,480.00 | |
| 80.00 | 105.00 | D2-A2 | 17.50 | D2-A2 | 16.00 | 64.00 | 87.50 |
| | 57,781.75 | D2-C1<br>D2-C2 | 17,481.75<br>40,300.00 | | | | |
| 40,300.00 | 1,300.00 | D2-C3 | 1,331.50 | D2-A1<br>D2-A2<br>D2-C2 | 30.00<br>1.50<br>40,300.00 | | |
| | 82,481.75 | D2-A1 | 30.00 | D2-C1<br>D2-C3 | 17,481.75<br>1,331.50 | 101,295.00<br>30.00 | |
| $141,668.50 | $141,668.50 | | $59,160.75 | | $59,160.75 | $101,382.50 | $101,382.50 |

The entry to record this transaction is:

|  |  | Dr. | Cr. |
|---|---|---|---|
| D2-1 | Investments | $17,480.00 | |
| | Revenue from investments | 25.00 | |
| | Premiums on investments | 80.00 | |
| |     Discounts on investments | | $ 105.00 |
| |     Cash | | 17,480.00 |

The entry to record the amount due from the general fund is:

| D2-2 | Due from general fund | $57,781.75 | |
|---|---|---|---|
| |     Operating transfers from<br>    general fund | | $57,781.75 |

The entry for the cash received from the general fund for the semiannual interest payment and the fiscal agent's charges is recorded as:

| D2-3 | Cash | $20,150.00 | |
|---|---|---|---|
| |     Due from general fund | | $20,150.00 |

The entry for the payment of interest and the fiscal agent's charges as of December 31, 19X6 is:

| | | | |
|---|---|---|---|
| **D2-4** | Expenditures | $20,150.00 | |
| | Cash | | $20,150.00 |

Earnings received during the year amounted to $1,325.00. This entry is:

| | | | |
|---|---|---|---|
| **D2-5** | Cash | $1,325.00 | |
| | Revenue from investments | | $1,325.00 |

It may be noted in Exhibit 8-3, in the transactions for the second year, that the true earnings will only be $1,300, since $25 was paid for the interest on the original purchase of the securities.

The general fund transfers the amount needed for both the contribution to the sinking fund and the second interest payment. The entry to record this transaction is:

| | | | |
|---|---|---|---|
| **D2-6** | Cash | $37,631.75 | |
| | Due from general fund | | $37,631.75 |

The second payment for interest during the year is recorded as follows:

| | | | |
|---|---|---|---|
| **D2-7** | Expenditures | $20,150.00 | |
| | Cash | | $20,150.00 |

During the second year, the capital projects fund is closed, and the $65,000 fund balance is transferred to the debt service fund. Obviously, this would require a correction to the annuity table (see Exhibit 8-2) concerning the amount needed to be transferred to the debt service fund from the general fund for the sinking fund.

The journal entry to record the receipt of the capital projects fund balance is:

| | | | |
|---|---|---|---|
| **D2-8** | Cash | $65,000 | |
| | Fund balance | | $65,000 |
| | To record the residual equity transfers from the debt service fund. | | |

The investment portion of a debt service fund is accounted for on a comparable basis to any other profit-type activity. For example, assume that interest receivable on the investments is $30. The adjusting entry for this interest is:

| | | Dr. | Cr. |
|---|---|---|---|
| **D2-A1** | Interest receivable | $30.00 | |
| | Revenue from investments | | $30.00 |

The premiums and discounts on the bonds purchased for investment would have to be written off annually to earnings until exhausted. Assuming that the discount expires in six years and the premium in five years, the accountant writes off $17.50 of discount each year and $16 of premium. The following entries then are made:

| | | Dr. | Cr. |
|---|---|---|---|
| D2-A2 | Discount on investments | $17.50 | |
| | Premium on investments | | $16.00 |
| | Revenue from investments | | 1.50 |

To close the transfer, revenue, and expenditure accounts for the year, the following entries are made:

| | | Dr. | Cr. |
|---|---|---|---|
| D2-C1 | Operating transfers from general fund | $17,481.75 | |
| | Fund balance | | $17,481.75 |
| D2-C2 | Operating transfers from general fund (for interest) | $40,300.00 | |
| | Expenditures | | $40,300.00 |
| D2-C3 | Revenue from investments | $ 1,331.50 | |
| | Fund balance | | $ 1,331.50 |

It should also be noted that in accordance with current GAAP unmatured principal and interest on general obligation long-term debt should not be accrued. NCGA's *Statement 1* says that:

> Financial resources usually are appropriated in other funds for transfer to a Debt Service Fund in the period in which maturing debt principal and interest must be paid. Such amounts thus are not current liabilities of the Debt Service Fund as their settlement will not require expenditure of existing fund assets.[3]

## Financial Statements

The statements shown in the balance sheet (see Exhibit 8-4) and the statement of operations (see Exhibit 8-5) are illustrative of the types of statements needed for a debt service fund. Statements for the second year are shown for illustrative purposes only.

## Debt Service Fund Accounting for Previously Issued Term Bonds

The previous illustration concerning term bonds considered only those transactions that deal with bonds issued during one year and carried over to the second year. The serial bond illustration considered bonds that were issued in prior years.

The general fund amount for servicing long-term debt was $180,000. In addition to the above two bonds, obviously, there are other bonds. The current year's debt servicing amount, then, may be assumed to include service requirements for the following bonds:

### EXHIBIT 8-4
### City of Ruthberg—Debt Service Fund
### Balance Sheet
### June 30, 19X7

| | | |
|---|---:|---:|
| Assets | | |
| Cash | | $ 83,808.50 |
| Investments | $17,480.00 | |
| Plus premium | 64.00 | |
| | $17,544.00 | |
| Less discounts | 87.50 | 17,456.50 |
| Interest receivable | | 30.00 |
| Total assets | | $101,295.00 |
| Fund balance | | $101,295.00 |

*Serial Bonds*: $800,000 of 6 percent, twenty-year bonds, with only $400,000 left to pay at the start of this year. Debt-servicing requirements for the year are $40,000 for principal and $24,000 for interest, for a total of $64,000.

*Term Bonds*: Issued this year, $800,000 at 5 percent for twenty years. Debt-servicing requirements are: interest, $40,000 per year; principal, $17,481.75; total, $57,481.75.

### EXHIBIT 8-5
### City of Ruthberg—Debt Service Fund
### Statement of Revenues, Expenditures, and Changes in Fund Balance
### Fiscal Year 19X7

**Revenues and Other Sources of Financing**

| | | |
|---|---:|---:|
| Revenues: | | |
| From investments | | $ 1,331.50 |
| Other sources of financing: | | |
| Operating transfers from general fund | | |
| For interest | $40,300.00 | |
| For sinking fund | 17,481.75 | 57,781.75 |
| Total revenues and other sources of financing | | 59,113.25 |

**Expenditures**

| | | |
|---|---:|---:|
| For interest | | 40,300.00 |
| Excess of revenues and other sources of financing over expenditures | | 18,813.25 |
| Changes in fund balance | | |
| Beginning fund balance | 17,481.75 | |
| Residual equity transfer from capital projects fund | 65,000.00 | 82,481.75 |
| Fund balance, June 30, 19X7 | | $101,295.00 |

The bonds were issued late, so the interest accrued is $10,000.00. Also, since the bonds were sold at a premium of $16,000, the first year's transfers from the general fund to the debt service fund is $26,000 less than budgeted. The total amount, with the fiscal agent's charge of $300, that would be transferred is $31,781.75.

*Term Bonds*: Issued seven years previously for $750,000 at 9 percent for twenty years. Computations show that $16,718.25 has to be transferred from the general fund to the debt service fund for sinking fund payments, if an average interest rate of approximately 9 percent was earned on the investments, in order to accumulate sufficient resources to retire the bonds in twenty years. Transfers from the general fund for interest payments would have to be $67,500 annually.

For the bonds issued seven years previously, the amount accumulated in the sinking fund was $149,121.75. Expected earnings of $13,612.17 along with the transfer from the general fund of $16,718.25 are needed during this fiscal year to continue building up the sinking fund in accordance with expectations. Assume that there are no premiums or discounts on investments and all cash is invested when received; then the trial balance at the beginning of the year would show:

| | | |
|---|---|---|
| Investments | $149,121.75 | |
| Fund balance | | $149,121.75 |

Assuming that the transfers and the earnings were exactly equal to the estimated amounts, the following entries would be made:

| | | Dr. | Cr. |
|---|---|---|---|
| D10 | Cash | $97,830.42 | |
| | Operating transfers from general fund | | $84,218.25 |
| | Revenue from investments | | 13,612.17 |

Cash received from operating transfers from general fund for interest and sinking fund and from earnings.

When the interest is paid and the investments are purchased, the following entries are made:

| | | Dr. | Cr. |
|---|---|---|---|
| D11 | Expenditures | $67,500.00 | |
| | Investments | 30,330.42 | |
| | Cash | | $97,830.42 |

Expenditures for interest and purchases of investments.

The following entries are made to close the accounts:

| | | Dr. | Cr. |
|---|---|---|---|
| DC4 | Revenue from investments | $13,612.17 | |
| | Operating transfers | 84,218.25 | |
| | Expenditures | | $67,500.00 |
| | Fund balance | | 30,330.42 |

The balances at the end of the year in this particular debt service fund are:

| | |
|---|---|
| Investments (Dr.) | $179,452.17 |
| Fund balance (Cr.) | $179,452.17 |

The illustrative transactions are summarized in Exhibit 8-6 in order to see the overall fund operations for the sinking fund. An illustrative balance sheet for the fund is shown in Exhibit 8-7, and an illustrative statement of revenues, transfers, expenditures, and changes in fund balance is shown in Exhibit 8-8.

### Combining Debt Service Fund Financial Statements

When a particular governmental fund classification, such as debt service funds, includes more than one fund, present GAAP require that individual statements from each of the separate funds be combined into what is called a *combining statement*. Combining statements for the balance sheet and for the statement of revenues, expenditures, and changes in fund balances are needed. Combining statements are illustrated in Exhibits 13-14 through 13-20.

## SUMMARY

This chapter provides a discussion on accounting and financial reporting for debt service funds. Debt service funds provide the accounting and financial reporting needed to obtain, invest, and manage the resources needed to pay off the principal and interest on general long-term debt, such as that incurred by capital projects funds to obtain resources needed to build or buy capital projects.

This discussion concerns the obtaining, investing, expending, and accounting for the resources to pay off long-term debt and the annual interest. When the debt is paid, the fund is closed.

Financial statements for external financial reporting for debt service funds are provided from information from the illustrative transactions.

## QUESTIONS

1. What are the two major functions of the debt service fund?
2. What is the relationship between the capital projects fund and the debt service fund?
3. Generally accepted accounting principles for debt service funds suggest the use of the modified accrual or accrual basis of accounting with one exception. What is that exception, and why is it made?
4. Actual amounts received in a debt service fund for the second year were: transfers from the general fund for bond sinking fund, $11,500; for bond interest, $28,000; and for earnings, $800. Make the journal entries to record the closing entries at the end of the year.
5. What statements are needed at the end of each year for the debt service funds?
6. What are the main types of long-term debt? Discuss each.
7. Should a debt service fund be created each time a long-term debt is issued?

**EXHIBIT 8-6**
**City of Ruthberg**
**Debt Service Fund Transactions**
**$750,000 Twenty Year, 6 Percent Term Bonds**
**For Year Ended June 30, 19X6**

| Account | Balance June 30, 19X5 | | | Transactions | | | | Balance June 30, 19X6 | |
|---|---|---|---|---|---|---|---|---|---|
| | Dr. | | Cr. | No. | Dr. | No. | Cr. | Dr. | Cr. |
| Cash | $149,121.75 | | | D10 | $ 97,830.42 | D11 | $ 97,830.42 | | |
| Investments | | | | D11 | 30,330.42 | | | $179,452.17 | |
| Fund balance | | B | $149,121.75 | | | DC4 | 30,330.42 | | $179,452.17 |
| Operating transfers— general fund | | | | DC4 | 84,218.25 | D10 | 84,218.25 | | |
| Revenues | | | | DC4 | 13,612.17 | D10 | 13,612.17 | | |
| Expenditures | | | | D11 | 67,500.00 | DC4 | 67,500.00 | | |
| | $149,121.75 | | $149,121.75 | | $293,491.26 | | $293,491.26 | $179,452.17 | $179,452.17 |

**EXHIBIT 8-7**
**City of Ruthberg**
**Debt Service Fund**
**Balance Sheet**
**June 30, 19X6**

| Assets | | Fund Balance | |
|---|---|---|---|
| Investments | $179,452.17 | Fund balance | $179,452.17 |
| Total assets | $179,452.17 | Total fund balance | $179,452.17 |

8  From what sources does the money come for the payment of principal and interest on long-term debt?
9  Describe the differences between serial bonds and term bonds.
10  Is the liability for long-term debt recorded in the debt service fund? Discuss.
11  Explain the reasoning behind why long-term debt principal and interest are not accrued.
12  Is budgetary accounting normally used in debt service funds?
13  What basis of accounting is used in debt service funds?
14  Do debt service funds have a perpetual life? Explain.

## PROBLEMS

8-1  Choose the correct answer for each of the following questions.[4]
  1  Premiums received on general obligation bonds are generally transferred to what fund or account group?
   a  Debt service
   b  General long-term debt
   c  General
   d  Special revenue
  2  In order to provide for the retirement of general obligation bonds, the city of Osborn invests a portion of its receipts from general property taxes in marketable securities. This investment activity should be accounted for in:
   a  A capital projects fund
   b  A debt service fund
   c  A trust fund
   d  The general fund
  3  Several years ago a city provided for the establishment of a sinking fund to retire an issue of general obligation bonds. This year the city made a $50,000 contribution to the sinking fund from general revenues and realized $15,000 in revenue from securities in the sinking fund. The bonds due this year were retired. These transactions require accounting recognition in:
   a  The general fund
   b  A debt service fund and the general long-term debt account group
   c  A debt service fund, the general fund, and the general long-term debt account group
   d  A capital projects fund, a debt service fund, the general fund, and the general long-term debt account group
   e  None of the above
  4  Two classifications of long-term debt discussed in the chapter are:
   a  Long-term debt and short-term debt

**EXHIBIT 8-8**
**City of Ruthberg**
**Debt Service Fund**
**Statement of Revenues, Expenditures, and Changes in Fund Balance**
**For Year Ended June 30, 19X6**

### Revenues and Other Sources of Financing

| | | |
|---|---:|---:|
| Revenues: | | |
|   From investments | | $ 13,612.17 |
| Operating transfers from general fund: | | |
|   For interest | $67,500.00 | |
|   For sinking fund | 16,718.25 | |
|     Total transfers | | 84,218.25 |
| Total revenues and other sources of financing | | 97,830.42 |

### Expenditures

| | |
|---|---:|
| For interest payments | 67,500.00 |
| Net increase in fund balance | 30,330.42 |
| Changes in fund balance | |
|   Beginning fund balance, July 1, 19X5 | 149,121.75 |
|   Ending fund balance, June 30, 19X6 | $179,452.17 |

  **b** Fixed and current liabilities
  **c** Bonds and mortgages
  **d** Serial and term debt
**5** The resources needed to repay bonds and interest on long-term debt usually come from:
  **a** Transfers from the capital projects funds
  **b** Interest earned on the sinking fund
  **c** Transfers from the long-term debt account group
  **d** Transfers from the general fund
**6** The basis of accounting in the debt service funds is:
  **a** Modified accrual
  **b** Accrual
  **c** Cash
  **d** A combination of cash and accrual
**7** A debt service fund is classified as a(n):
  **a** Enterprise fund
  **b** Governmental fund
  **c** Long-term debt fund
  **d** Agency fund
**8** Cash from premiums on bonds sold and recorded in the debt service funds usually originate in:
  **a** The general fund
  **b** The debt service fund
  **c** The capital projects fund
  **d** An agency fund

8-2 Choose the most appropriate answer for each question.
1. One major deviation from the modified accrual basis of accounting in a debt service fund is:
   a. Transfers from the general fund
   b. Accrual of unmatured principal and interest
   c. Recording of assets from the capital projects fund
   d. Recording of debt owed
2. Budgetary accounting in debt service funds:
   a. Is always used as a means of control
   b. Is never used as a means of control
   c. Uses some provisions of budgetary accounting
   d. Uses variable budgeting as a means of control
3. Serial debt means:
   a. The principal is paid off in periodic installments along with the interest on the balance of the principal.
   b. Payments are serially made to a sinking fund to pay off the debt.
   c. The debt is issued periodically.
   d. Interest on the debt is paid periodically.
4. Term debt means that:
   a. The principal is paid off in periodic installments along with any interest on the balance of the principal.
   b. The debt is issued in term installments.
   c. Interest is paid in a lump sum when the debt matures.
   d. The principal is paid in a lump sum after a term of years when the debt matures.
5. The estimated amounts needed to pay off the principal on term bonds usually comes from:
   a. Transfers from the general fund at the end of the term
   b. Periodic transfers from the general fund along with interest earned on the investments purchased from the resources transferred
   c. An amount developed from an annuity table or from an annuity formula
   d. Estimated amounts developed from past experience
6. The journal entry in the debt service fund to pay bonds that have matured is:
   a. Expenditures                              xxxx
         Matured bonds payable                        xxxx
      Matured bonds payable                    xxxx
         Cash                                         xxxx
   b. Matured bonds payable                    xxxx
         Expenditures                                 xxxx
      Cash                                     xxxx
         Matured bonds payable                        xxxx
   c. Expenditures                              xxxx
         Cash                                         xxxx
   d. Cash                                      xxxx
         Matured bonds payable                        xxxx
7. Investments often are acquired in a debt service fund to earn income that will be used, along with the amounts originally transferred, to retire the term bonds. The basis of accounting for the income earned on the investments in the sinking fund is:
   a. The cash basis

b The accrual basis
  c The modified accrual basis
  d A combination of the above
8-3 For the first half of this problem, assume that a debt service fund for the town of Old Orchard is set up to account for a ten-year serial bond issue of $500,000 at 4 percent interest. Amounts to pay for the principal and interest are to be provided from the general fund.

**Required**:
Prepare the necessary journal entries in the debt service fund to:
1 Record the amount due from the general fund for the first year's payment
2 Record the receipt of cash
3 Record the liability for the first annual payment and
4 Record the payment
5 Close the accounts

For this section of Problem 8-3, assume that a debt service fund for the town of Kennebunkport is set up to account for a ten-year term bond issue of $500,000, 3 percent interest. The first payment is scheduled to be made at the end of year 1, with further payments being made until the bonds are retired. Assume the funds can be invested at 4 percent.

**Required**:
Prepare the necessary journal entries to:
1 Record the receivable due from the general fund for year 1
2 Record the receipt of cash
3 Record the payment of interest for year 1
4 Close the accounts for year 1
5 Record all resulting transactions in year 2 (Hint: record earnings on investments)

8-4 You have been asked to prepare a schedule comparing sinking fund additions and earnings with the requirements of the year for the debt service fund of the town of Gorham. Use the following data to prepare the statement.

   1 Required additions for current year, $20,000
   2 Required earnings, $30,000
   3 Actual additions, $20,000
   4 Interest earned, $29,000
   5 Amortization of discounts, $550
   6 Amortization of premiums, $2,300

8-5 A debt service fund was set up to service the bonds issued by the town of Greensville. The bonds issued were dated July 1, 19X1. They had a $1,000,000 face value, were twenty-year, 6 percent serial bonds, and sold for $1,025,000. The bonds were sold on September 1, 19X1. Interest paid in advance by the purchaser was $10,000, and the premium paid was $15,000. The interest was paid on January 2 and July 2 of each year. The general fund transfers sufficient resources each year to service the bonds. The fiscal year for the town is from July 1, 19X1 to June 30, 19X2.

**Required**:
Prepare the journal entries in the general fund and in the debt service fund for
1 The current year
2 The second year
3 The third year

**8-6** Refer to Problem 8-5 concerning the issuance of $1,000,000 worth of 6 percent serial bonds. However, for this problem, assume that instead of being serial bonds, they are twenty-year term bonds dated July 1, 19X1 and are sold on September 1, 19X1 for $1,025,000. This includes prepaid interest of $10,000 and a premium of $15,000. Interest of 10 percent can be earned on any investments in the debt service fund's sinking fund. Assume that a full year's earnings can be made on any amount in the prior year's sinking fund and that principal payments are made at the end of each year, including the first year.

**Required**:
Make the journal entries in the general fund and in the debt service fund for:
1 The current year
2 The second year
3 The third year

**8-7** A debt service fund was set up to service the bonds issued by the city of Portland's capital projects fund. The bonds issued were $5,000,000 worth of twenty-five-year, 8 percent serial bonds. The bonds were issued on January 1; the city's fiscal year ended on December 31. The bonds were sold at a premium of $5,000. The city transfers sufficient resources to pay for the principal and interest on the day the bonds become due.

**Required**:
Prepare the journal entries in the general fund and in the debt service fund for:
1 The current year
2 The second year
3 The third year

**8-8** Instead of the bonds issued by the city of Portland's capital projects fund being serial bonds (see Problem 8-7), for this problem, assume they are term bonds. The face value of the bonds was $5,000,000. They were twenty-five-year term bonds sold at a premium of $5,000 on the day of issuance, January 1, 19X1. The interest rate on the bonds was 8 percent. It was assumed that 10 percent could be earned on any investments in the debt service fund's sinking fund.

The capital projects fund completed the project during the second year and transferred the $25,000 remaining in the fund to the debt service fund and closed out the fund.

**Required**:
Prepare any journal entries pertaining to the debt service fund made in the capital projects fund, the general fund, and in the debt service fund for:
1 The current year
2 The second year
3 The third year

**8-9** The city of Keenland had issued $1,500,000 of twenty-year 4 percent serial bonds to construct a sewerage system for the city. Exactly one-half of the bonds had been paid off in the previous ten years. Interest is paid semiannually on December 31 and June 30. The proportionate amount of bonds is retired each year on December 31. The city's fiscal year ends on December 31.

**Required**:
Prepare journal entries for both the general fund and the debt service fund for the current fiscal year.

**8-10** This problem continues the case of Silver City, also discussed in 5-10, 6-10, and 7-8. It concerns the Silver City debt service fund. Retain your solutions of this problem for use in future chapters.

**1** The general fund paid to the debt service fund the following amounts:

| | |
|---|---|
| To pay the semiannual interest | $20,000 |
| To contribute to principal payment | 12,000 |
| Total | $32,000 |

**2** The premium received from the sale of the bonds, $10,000, was received from the capital projects fund.

**3** Paid the semiannual interest of $20,000.

**4** Purchased investments at par for $20,000. (Assume that no material amounts of interest had accrued at the end of the year.)

**Required**:

1 Prepare journal entries for the transactions for the debt service fund, including the adjusting and closing entries.
2 Post the journalized transactions to a worksheet from which the proper statements can be made.
3 Make the proper statements for the year.

## NOTES

1 National Council on Governmental Accounting, *Statement 1. Governmental Accounting and Financial Reporting Principles* (Chicago: Municipal Finance Officers Association of the United States and Canada, 1979), p. 12.
2 Municipal Finance Officers Association of the United States and Canada, *Governmental Accounting, Auditing, and Financial Reporting* (Chicago: Municipal Finance Officers Association of the United States and Canada, 1980), p. 43.
3 NCGA, *Statement 1*, p. 12.
4 Adapted from American Institute of Certified Public Accountants, *Uniform CPA Examination Questions and Unofficial Answers* (New York: American Institute of Certified Public Accountants, various dates).

# CHAPTER 9

# SPECIAL ASSESSMENT FUNDS

Special assessment funds are used to account for and control the resources used to provide capital improvements or special services to a selected segment of a locality rather than to all citizens. The prime beneficiaries of the improvement or service finance the major part of the project or program by charges called "special assessments" to that identifiable segment of residents. Transfers also may be made from other governmental funds that may receive some benefits from the improvements or services.

## USE OF SPECIAL ASSESSMENT FUNDS

Special assessments in the past have been limited to such areas as sewer and water improvements, special recreational facilities (e.g., where user fees are collected and applied toward facility improvements or the acquisition of additional facilities), and other similar projects where the direct beneficiaries can be readily identified. Representing about 15 percent of the total municipal bond issues in any given year, special assessment bond issues are relatively small in dollar value (averaging $500,000 or less) and, in order to attract investors, often carry a higher interest rate than general obligation bonds. Rising costs in recent years have resulted in the vast majority of special assessment bonds also being secured by a pledge of full faith and credit of the municipality, making them, for all practical purposes, general obligation bonds.

As a result of increased fiscal austerity faced by many localities, the special assessment approach has come into wider use to augment limited general fund revenues to provide public improvements for particular segments of the community. In response to Proposition 13 limits on local property taxes, some California municipalities, for example, have developed, a "uniform services" budget. This budget provides that any services or improvements beyond a given uniform level applicable to the community as a whole must be financed through special assessments. When residents of a neighborhood petition for more fire hydrants (to reduce their fire insurance rates) or improved street lighting, these improvements can be provided above the uniform service level only if the residents pay for them through special assessments. As a consequence of such budget innovations, it may be anticipated that special assessment funds will find more widespread use in local government finance.

## Relationship Between Special Assessment Funds and Other Funds and Account Groups

Accounting for special assessment funds is a mixture of features found in special revenue funds, capital projects funds, debt service funds, and the long-term debt account group (discussed in Chapter 11). Exhibit 9-1 illustrates the relationship of these features among the various funds and account groups. Many of the accounting principles and practices of special assessment funds, therefore, are the same as those already discussed and illustrated in previous chapters. The similarities to the long-term debt account group, however, will be seen in Chapter 11. Transactions in special assessment funds are comparable to transactions in all of those other funds and account groups,

**EXHIBIT 9-1** ACCOUNTING AND CONTROL FEATURES FROM OTHER FUNDS FOUND IN THE SPECIAL ASSESSMENT FUND

| Goods or services provided | Fund or account group used when service is provided to all citizens | Fund or account group used when goods or services are provided to selected citizens |
|---|---|---|
| 1. Special service provided from a special revenue | Special revenue fund is used when a special tax provides revenue for a special service (e.g., a library service for all citizens) | Special assessment fund is used when special assessments provide funds for special service (e.g., street lighting for a selected group of citizens) |
| 2. Capital assets provided by using proceeds from bond issues, transfers from other funds, or revenue from grants | Capital projects fund is used when a capital project is built for the use of all citizens | Special assessment fund is used when a capital project is constructed for the primary benefit of a selected group of citizens |
|   a. Issuance of bonds | Capital projects fund | Special assessment fund |
|   b. Taxing for revenue to pay principal and interest on bonds | Debt service fund, agency fund, special revenue fund, or general fund | Special assessment fund (or may come to an agency fund and then be transferred to a special assessment fund) |
|   c. Servicing of bond principal and interest | Debt service fund | Special assessment fund |
|   d. Accounting for long-term debt | General long-term debt account group | Special assessment fund |
|   e. Accounting for fixed assets | General fixed assets account group | General fixed assets account group |

but they are kept in one fund. Therefore, several basic differences in the accounting practices in special assessment funds will be discussed and illustrated in this chapter.

## Basis of Accounting for Special Assessment Funds

It is sometimes assumed that the life of the special assessment fund can be compared to that of the capital projects fund, since both deal with capital projects. The special assessment fund, however, is concerned not only with the construction of a project, as is the capital projects fund, but also with the record and payment of the debt from which the construction was financed. Thus an annual reporting period, rather than the life of the project, becomes the rational time period to measure the activities of special assessment funds.

As a general rule, the modified accrual basis of accounting—the basic principle used in most governmental funds—is also used in the special assessment funds. Under the modified accrual basis of accounting, revenue is recognized when measurable and available; expenditures are recognized when the fund liability is incurred.

## Special Accounting Considerations—Special Assessment Fund

Budgetary accounting can be used in the special assessment funds both for capital construction and for annual revenues and expenditures. Yet, since the equivalent of a budgetary process is employed to obtain the bonds and pay off the indebtedness, there is little need for budgetary accounts. The encumbrance method, however, is often used in the capital construction part of the fund in order to ensure the administrators of the fund that the total money available for construction is not overspent.

Another variation in special assessment funds is that long-term debt is accounted for in those funds rather than in the general long-term debt account group. Therefore, bonds payable are recorded in the special assessment fund, and from this fund interest is paid periodically. The principal is also paid from the special assessment fund either periodically, as serial bonds, or through an accumulation of resources paid as term bonds. Note also that principal retirement in the special assessment fund reduces the long-term fund liability and does not result in recognized expenditures, as is the case in debt service funds when general long-term debt principal matures. Once all long-term liabilities are paid, the fund can be dissolved. The capital assets constructed or acquired through the special assessment fund are accounted for in the general fixed assets account group. Thus the payments for buying or building capital assets are recorded in the special assessment fund as expenditures, while the fixed assets are recorded in the general fixed assets account group.

Unlike taxes assessed in a general or special revenue fund, special assessments are levied against the owners of property for the total capital goods to be acquired (or improvement to be made) rather than making an annual levy. The assessment can be paid in one installment (without interest charges) or annually over some period of years (with interest). When paid over a period of years, the total assessments are recorded as *special assessments deferred*. The interest receivable, however, is recorded annually. Since bonds payable are recorded in special assessment funds, the account "special assessments deferred'' serves as an offset to the bonds payable account for bonds that are issued.

Some authorities recommend that the revenue from the deferred assessments be placed in the books as deferred revenue and considered as current revenue only when the annual assessments are placed in the records—that is, when deferred assessments are transferred to current assessments. This type of accounting usually results in a deficit in the fund balance account equal to the deferred revenue until the final collection of all of the assessments receivable. Some financial administrators do not consider this approach an acceptable method.

When assessments are levied after construction is completed, other authorities recommend that revenue from the deferred assessments be placed in the records as current revenue upon completion of all costs of construction. These authorities reason that revenue is earned, measurable, and available when all costs of construction have been incurred. And still other authorities suggest that, since the special assessments are a total assessment rather than an annual levy, revenue is earned, measurable, and available when the assessments are levied. This latter approach is the one taken in this book.

So-called "special assessment bonds" often are considered revenue bonds—the security for the debt service comes from those who receive the benefits of the improvement rather than from general tax revenues. To illustrate the idea of revenue coming from special assessments, consider the extension of sewer lines to new residential areas. These extensions are often funded by one-time special assessments (often called a "tap-on" or "availability" fee). Major improvements to streets, curbs and gutters, and sidewalks in a residential subdivision may be funded by a bond issue that will be paid by special assessments spread over several years.

When accounted for in separate funds (e.g., the capital projects and debt service funds), similarly titled accounts in the special assessment fund would have three or four account titles. For example, for the cash account, you would have cash for construction, cash for principal payments, cash for interest payments, and so forth. Separate accounts can be kept for these individual accounts in the debt service fund, since the cash is restricted to particular uses. However, current governmental accounting principles do not require this segregation of resources in any fund as was the case at one time.

Our illustrations of transactions in the special assessment fund are restricted to those transactions that specifically show the operations of the fund. For example, special assessment levies, as do general fund tax levies, often become delinquent. The fund, therefore, must apply the same processes as are applicable in the general fund or special revenue fund (described and illustrated in Chapter 5) for recovering the resources needed to pay for the operations of the fund. While the process of accounting for the delinquencies, recoveries, and sales of property for unpaid assessments is generally the same as it is for general taxes, the process in the special assessment fund must provide for the recovery of the total assessment plus costs, rather than for only the annual taxes plus costs. For instance, assume that the balance of the special assessments levied against a certain taxpayer was $15,000, and the annual payment was $3,000 plus 10 percent interest each year on the balance. In this case, this year's interest would be $1,500. When the taxpayer is in default in his or her payments, he or she would owe the total of $15,000 plus the current year's interest of $1,500, not the $3,000 plus whatever costs were involved.

The reader should take special notice of the methods of accounting for long-term debt, since long-term debt for special assessments is recorded in that fund. These methods in this fund should be compared with those in the long-term debt account group, for the overall liability of the governmental unit, as discussed in the next chapter. Note, also that, as discussed previously, the purchase and construction of fixed assets are recorded as expenditures in this fund, while the record of the fixed asset is kept in the general fixed assets account group.

## ILLUSTRATIVE TRANSACTIONS FOR SPECIAL ASSESSMENT FUNDS

The residents of the southeast section of the city of Ruthberg have petitioned for various street improvements, to be financed through a special assessment, that will upgrade the street paving, including curbs, gutters, and so forth. Estimated to cost $700,000, these improvements will be financed partially through a federal grant and a state grant; the balance will be assessed against the local group of taxpayers. The federal government will grant $200,000 and the state highway commission will grant $175,000, if the neighborhood residents served by the improvements are assessed $325,000. Of the $325,000, $50,000 will be a current assessment, and the balance of $275,000 will come from ten-year serial bonds. The bonds will have a 7 percent interest rate, with one-tenth of the bonds paid annually. The residents would be assessed a sum sufficient each year for the next ten years to cover the annual principal payments and the interest on the outstanding bonds—on a decreasing basis.

All of the preliminaries for the issuance of the bonds and the agreements concerning the payments from the state and the federal government, as well as for the payments of principal and interest on the bonds, were completed prior to July 1, 19X5. The engineers expect the construction to be completed during the fiscal year. Because of the grants and the first year's assessments, the bond money will not be needed until December 31, 19X5.

### Current-Period Transactions

A current levy of special assessment taxes to be used for construction purposes is made against the owners of the property on July 1 to be paid on or before September 30. In addition, the state and the federal governments committed the funds necessary to pay for their share of the improvements. The accrual for these actions would be:

S1  July 1, 19X5

| | Dr. | Cr. |
|---|---|---|
| Assessments receivable—current | $ 50,000 | |
| Due from federal government | 200,000 | |
| Due from state | 175,000 | |
|    Revenue from special assessments | | $ 50,000 |
|    Revenue from federal government | | 200,000 |
|    Revenue from state | | 175,000 |

The balance of the assessments is placed on the books at this time, because the original assessment is for the total improvements authorized rather than being only an annual assessment. The balance of the assessments that are deferred and will be paid annually in order to cover the principal of the bonds is recorded as:

S2  July 1, 19X5
    Assessments receivable—deferred      $275,000
        Revenue from special assessments          $275,000

On September 30, 19X5, several transactions take place: (1) the cash is received from the federal grant and from the state; (2) cash is received from the current assessments; and (3) a contract is let for the improvements for the estimated price. When the contract is let, a journal entry is made to encumber the revenue available for construction. The entries to record the transactions, with explanations, are:

S3  Sept. 30, 19X5
    Cash      $425,000
        Due from federal government          $200,000
        Due from state          175,000
        Assessments receivable—current          50,000
    To record cash for construction received from the federal government, the state, and from current assessments.

S4  Sept. 30, 19X5
    Encumbrances      $700,000
        Reserve for encumbrances          $700,000
    To encumber contracts.

On January 2, 19X6, the bonds were sold at their face value of $275,000. Any premium or discount on bonds or any accrued interest that is received is recorded in the special assessment fund rather than being transferred to the debt service fund. Any premiums, discounts, or interest received in advance are a part of the interest transactions and not a part of the construction transactions. The bonds are dated January 2, 19X6 and sold on that date for par, so there would be no premium or discount on the bonds or accrued interest. Interest will be paid annually on January 2. The entry to record this transaction on January 2 is:

S5  Jan. 2, 19X6
    Cash      $275,000
        Bonds payable          $275,000

Since the bonds are to be serviced from the special assessment fund, the bonds payable account must be entered in this fund rather than in the general long-term debt account group. The eventual offset to the bonds payable account, as has been stated, is the assessments receivable deferred account.

On March 15, 19X6, the project was completed. The amount of $42,000 was retained in the fund until final approval of the construction. An accounts payable was set up for the balance, and it was paid. These entries would be:

**S6** Mar. 15, 19X6

| | | |
|---|---|---|
| Reserve for encumbrances | $700,000 | |
|     Encumbrances | | $700,000 |
| To reverse encumbrances. | | |
| Expenditures (construction) | $700,000 | |
|     Accounts payable | | $658,000 |
|     Retained percentage of contract payable | | 42,000 |
| To record liability for contract expenditure and to set up liability for retained percentage. | | |
| Accounts payable | $658,000 | |
|     Cash | | $658,000 |
| To pay liability for construction, except for retained percentage. | | |

The retained percentage is kept as a liability until the project is completed according to specifications. The approval of the project was not accomplished until November 1, 19X6. So, at the close of the fiscal year, these amounts are still in the books.

The closing entries at the end of the fiscal year include closing the revenue and expenditure accounts to fund balance. In this case, there is no balance to go in the fund balance account. These entries are:

**SC1** June 30, 19X6

| | Dr. | Cr. |
|---|---|---|
| Revenue from special assessments | $325,000 | |
| Revenue from federal government | 200,000 | |
| Revenue from state | 175,000 | |
|     Expenditures for construction | | $700,000 |
| To close out revenue and expenditure accounts for the fiscal year. | | |

Note that the interest for six months, the end of the period, is not accrued even though it will be paid on January 2, 19X6. Note also that the revenue to pay this interest will not be available until the next year and will not be accrued. Special assessment funds follow the modified accrual basis of accounting except when concerning interest earnings and interest expenditures. According to the NCGA, "When interest expenditures on special assessment indebtedness are approximately offset by interest earnings on special assessment levies, both may be recorded when due rather than being accrued."[1]

## Statements—First Year's Operations

At the close of the fiscal year, the only balances in the accounts, as shown in the worksheet (see Exhibit 9-2), include a debit in the cash (for construction) account of $42,000 and a debit in the deferred assessments receivable account of $275,000. The offsetting credits are $275,000 for bonds payable and $42,000 for the retained percentage of the contracts payable. The needed statements for the first year's operations are shown in Exhibits 9-3 and 9-4.

Special assessment funds usually carry over from year to year, until the long-term debt is extinguished. If any fund balance for construction existed after the completion of the improvement, then this amount would go into the fund balance account. Any excess cash available would be paid back proportionally to the fund contributors. No payment would be returned to the participants, however, until it was fairly certain that all assessments would be paid. Then, either the assessments can be reduced to avoid overassessments, or the payment can be returned upon completion of all payments.

## Transactions—Second Year

Our illustrative transactions of the special assessment fund are made to enable the reader to grasp the concepts of this fund rather than to provide detailed procedures for the operation of the fund. Most of the procedures have been adequately illustrated from the transactions in other funds.

The amount needed for the interest payment during the second year is $19,250 (7 percent of $275,000). The third year's amount for the interest payment is $17,325 (7 percent of $247,500). Each year the amount of the interest payment declines by $1,925, because $27,500 worth of bonds are retired each year.

No transactions are shown for delinquent assessments, since the accounting procedures for these types of transactions have already been explained in Chapter 5. Delinquencies may have a significant effect on the amount available for the payment of the principal and interest, so adequate additional assessments will have to be made to take care of any losses arising from delinquencies, errors, or uncollectible amounts.

At the time this year's assessments become due, an amount is transferred from the assessments receivable deferred account to the assessments receivable current account. On July 1, 19X6, the assessments receivable for the year are levied to be paid before September 30, 19X6. This entry is:

|  |  | Dr. | Cr. |
|---|---|---|---|
| S2-1 | Assessments receivable—current | $27,500 |  |
|  | Assessments receivable—deferred |  | $27,500 |

To record amount transferred from deferred to current assessments.

The interest receivable on the deferred assessments also becomes due on September 30. The entry to record the interest is:

| S2-2 | July 1, 19X6 |  |  |
|---|---|---|---|
|  | Interest receivable | $19,250 |  |
|  | Interest revenue |  | $19,250 |

To record interest revenue receivable on assessments.

As has been stated, the cash sometimes is kept separate in the records, but this is not required. The entries to record the payment to the fund for the assessment and the interest are:

## EXHIBIT 9-2
### City of Ruthberg
### Worksheet for Transactions in Special Assessment Fund
### For Fiscal Years 19X6 and 19X7

|  | Transactions fiscal year 19X6 | | | |
|---|---|---|---|---|
|  | No. | Dr. | No. | Cr. |
| Cash | S3 | 425,000 | S6 | 658,000 |
|  | S5 | 275,000 |  |  |
| Due from state | S1 | 175,000 | S3 | 175,000 |
| Due from federal government | S1 | 200,000 | S3 | 200,000 |
| Assessments receivable— current | S1 | 50,000 | S3 | 50,000 |
| Assessments receivable— deferred | S2 | 275,000 |  |  |
| Interest receivable |  |  |  |  |
| Retained percentage of contract payable |  |  | S6 | 42,000 |
| Bonds payable |  |  | S5 | 275,000 |
| Accounts payable | S6 | 658,000 | S6 | 658,000 |
| Interest revenue |  |  |  |  |
| Revenue from special assessments | SC1 | 325,000 | S1 | 50,000 |
|  |  |  | S2 | 275,000 |
| Revenue from federal government | SC1 | 200,000 | S1 | 200,000 |
| Revenue from state | SC1 | 175,000 | S1 | 175,000 |
| Encumbrances | S4 | 700,000 | S6 | 700,000 |
| Reserve for encumbrances | S6 | 700,000 | S4 | 700,000 |
| Expenditures (construction) | S6 | 700,000 | SC1 | 700,000 |
| Expenditures (interest) |  |  |  |  |
|  |  | $4,858,000 |  | $4,858,000 |

**S2-3** Sept. 30, 19X6

| | | |
|---|---|---|
| Cash | $46,750 | |
|     Assessments receivable— current | | $27,500 |
|     Interest receivable | | 19,250 |

To record cash received for payment of principal and interest.

On November 1, 19X6, the retained percentage was paid to the contractor.

**S2-4** Nov. 1, 19X6

| | | |
|---|---|---|
| Retained percentage of contracts payable | $42,000 | |
|     Cash (for construction) | | $42,000 |

To pay balance of contract retained for final approval.

On January 2, 19X7, the first of the serial bonds are retired and interest is paid on all of the bonds. The entries for these transactions are:

**EXHIBIT 9-2**
(*continued*)

| Balance June 30, 19X6 | | Transactions fiscal year 19X7 | | | | Balance June 30, 19X7 | |
|---|---|---|---|---|---|---|---|
| Dr. | Cr. | No. | Dr. | No. | Cr. | Dr. | Cr. |
| 42,000 | | S2-3 | 46,750 | S2-4 | 42,000 | | |
| | | | | S2-5 | 46,750 | | |
| | | S2-1 | 27,500 | S2-3 | 27,500 | | |
| 275,000 | | | | S2-1 | 27,500 | 247,500 | |
| | | S2-2 | 19,250 | S2-3 | 19,250 | | |
| | 42,000 | S2-4 | 42,000 | | | | |
| | 275,000 | S2-5 | 27,500 | | | | 247,500 |
| | | S2-C1 | 19,250 | S2-2 | 19,250 | | |
| | | S2-5 | 19,250 | S2-C1 | 19,250 | | |
| $317,000 | $317,000 | | $201,500 | | $201,500 | $247,500 | $247,500 |

**S2-5** Jan. 2, 19X7

| | Dr. | Cr. |
|---|---|---|
| Bonds payable | $27,500 | |
| Expenditures (interest) | 19,250 | |
|     Cash | | $46,750 |

To record payment of principal and interest on bonds.

The closing entries for the second fiscal year are those that pertain to the interest revenue and interest expense for the year. The revenue account is closed to the expense account, such as:

**S2-C1** June 30, 19X7

| | Dr. | Cr. |
|---|---|---|
| Interest revenues | $19,250 | |
|     Expenditures (interest) | | $19,250 |

## EXHIBIT 9-3
### City of Ruthberg
### Special Assessment Fund
### for Southeast Street Improvements
### Balance Sheet
### June 30, 19X6

| | | |
|---|---:|---:|
| Assets | | |
| Cash (for construction) | $ 42,000 | |
| Assessments receivable—deferred | 275,000 | |
| Total assets | | $317,000 |
| Liabilities and fund balance | | |
| Retained percentage—contracts payable | $ 42,000 | |
| Bonds payable | 275,000 | |
| Total liabilities | | $317,000 |
| Fund balance | | — |
| Total liabilities and fund balance | | $317,000 |

After closing the accounts for the year, the balances in the accounts refer only to the liability and the means of paying the liability (see Exhibit 9-2).

## Statements—Second Year

The city again prepares a balance sheet and a statement of revenues, expenditures, and changes in fund balance from the accounts summarized from the transactions for the year (see Exhibits 9-5 and 9-6). A statement of cash receipts and disbursements is sometimes shown, as illustrated in Exhibit 9-7.

## EXHIBIT 9-4
### City of Ruthberg
### Special Assessment Fund
### for Southeast Street Improvements
### Statement of Revenue, Expenditures, and Changes
### in Fund Balance
### For Fiscal Year 19X6

| | | |
|---|---:|---:|
| Revenues and other financing sources | | |
| Revenue from assessments for construction | $325,000 | |
| Revenue from federal government | 200,000 | |
| Revenue from state | 175,000 | |
| Total revenue | | $700,000 |
| Expenditures | | |
| For construction | $700,000 | |
| Total expenditures | | $700,000 |
| Excess of revenue over expenditures | | 0 |
| Fund balance, 6/30/19X6 | | 0 |

**EXHIBIT 9-5**
**City of Ruthberg**
**Special Assessment Fund**
**for Southeast Street Improvements**
**Balance Sheet**
**June 30, 19X7**

| | |
|---|---|
| Assets | |
|   Assessments receivable—deferred | $247,500 |
| Liabilities | |
|   Bonds payable | $247,500 |

## Budgetary Accounting in Special Assessment Funds

Budgetary accounting generally is not used in special assessment funds. A memo entry is usually made in the records to indicate that all of the preliminaries have been accomplished for the issuance of the bonds. If used, however, the following types of budgetary entries, other than for encumbrances, would be made:

| | Dr. | Cr. |
|---|---|---|
| Estimated revenue from special assessments | $325,000 | |
| Estimated revenue from the state | 175,000 | |
| Estimated revenue from the federal government | 200,000 | |
|   Appropriations | | $700,000 |

The budgetary entry for construction includes estimated revenues from special assessments, both current and deferred, from the state, and from the federal government. The appropriations are for the estimated costs of construction.

    The actual entries would be the same as those illustrated in this chapter. The closing entries would be:

**EXHIBIT 9-6**
**City of Ruthberg**
**Special Assessment Fund**
**for Southeast Street Improvements**
**Statement of Revenues, Expenditures, and Changes**
**in Fund Balance**
**For Fiscal Year 19X7**

| | | |
|---|---|---|
| Revenue | | |
|   For interest payments | $19,250 | |
|     Total revenue | | $19,250 |
| Expenditures | | |
|   For interest | $19,250 | |
|     Total expenditures | | $19,250 |
|     Excess of revenue over expenditures | | 0 |
| Fund balance, 7/1/X6 | | 0 |
| Fund balance, 7/1/X7 | | 0 |

## EXHIBIT 9-7
### City of Ruthberg
### Special Assessment Fund
### for Southeast Street Improvements
### Statement of Receipts and Disbursements
### For Fiscal Year 19X7

|  | Construction | Bonds | Interest |
|---|---|---|---|
| Balance on hand |  |  |  |
|   Cash for construction | $42,000 | — | — |
| Receipts |  |  |  |
|   For bond payments |  | $27,000 |  |
|   For interest payment |  |  | $19,250 |
| Total cash available | $42,000 | $27,000 | $19,250 |
| Expenditures |  |  |  |
|   For balance of construction costs | $42,000 |  |  |
|   For payment of serial bond |  | $27,000 |  |
|   For payment of interest |  |  | $19,250 |
| Total expenditures | $42,000 | $27,000 | $19,250 |
| Balance on hand | 0 | 0 | 0 |

|  |  |  |
|---|---|---|
| Revenue from special assessments | $325,000 |  |
| Revenue from the state | 175,000 |  |
| Revenue from the federal government | 200,000 |  |
|   Estimated revenue from special assessments |  | $325,000 |
|   Estimated revenue from the state |  | 175,000 |
|   Estimated revenue from the federal government |  | 200,000 |
| Appropriations | $700,000 |  |
|   Expenditures |  | $700,000 |

Any differences between the actual and estimated revenue accounts and the actual expenditures and appropriations accounts would go to the fund balance account.

Under the method of accounting used in this book for special assessment funds, there would be no need for annual budgetary revenue and appropriation amounts for bond payments. The budgetary accounts for these amounts were used during the year the bonds were sold when the estimated revenue from the special assessments deferred account and appropriations account were recorded (see previous entry). All that is needed during each year is the annual estimated revenue for interest payments along with the amount appropriated. These transactions for the interest for the second year would be recorded as follows:

|  |  |  |
|---|---|---|
| Estimated revenue (interest) | $19,250 |  |
|   Appropriations (interest) |  | $19,250 |

The closing entries would then be:

| | | |
|---|---:|---:|
| Appropriations (interest) | $19,250 | |
| Revenue (interest) | 19,250 | |
|     Estimated revenue (interest) | | $19,250 |
|     Expenditures (interest) | | 19,250 |

## SUMMARY

Special assessment funds have many accounting similarities found in a general fund, special revenue funds, capital projects funds, debt service funds, and the long-term debt account group. However, there are many differences. Instead of the assessment being an annual tax, it is for the total amount needed to be paid by the taxpayer. If paid in yearly installments, interest on the balance of the assessment must also be paid.

Fixed assets of the special assessment fund are recorded in the general fixed assets account group. The long-term liabilities, however, are recorded and serviced in the special assessment fund. One of the major differences in the basis of accounting for special assessment funds is that the interest receivable, or interest revenue, on the long-term debt is not accrued for the next operating cycle, but is recorded when matured.

With the shortage of resources needed for the general operation of local governmental units becoming more acute each year, special assessment funds may be used more often in the future than they have been in the past. Special assessment districts may be formed to obtain the resources needed for special long-term assets or services that cannot be obtained from the general taxes of the local governmental unit.

## QUESTIONS

1. What are special assessment funds used for?
2. What other funds are comparable to special assessment funds from an accounting and control standpoint?
3. Since the special assessment fund has many of the features of accounting and control found in other funds, what are some of the distinguishing features that apply especially to the special assessment fund?
4. Is there an estimated revenue account in the special assessment fund? Why or why not?
5. Bonds were issued for the improvements to be made to sewers and drainage in District X of the county of Franklin. One-tenth of the 10-year bonds for $250,000 at 5 percent would be retired each year plus the interest. They were issued at par. Prepare the entries for the transactions for the issuance of the bonds.
6. A $225,000 contract was let for the improvements described in question 4. Make the journal entry needed at that time.
7. Servicing for bond principal and interest for special assessment funds is done in that fund. The balance sheet, then, would show the bonds payable owed at the end of each year as a liability. Is there a particular asset account that is an offset to that liability?
8. Is there a need for budgetary controls each year for the special assessment funds?

9 Is there a need for segregation of the types of assets that normally go in each of these funds as well as of the fund balances for the special assessment funds?
10 The basis of accounting for the special assessment fund is the modified accrual basis. There is one item that does not follow this basis. What is it, and how does it differ?

## PROBLEMS

9-1 Circle the most appropriate answer to the following.[2]
  1 Brockton City has approved a special assessment project in accordance with applicable laws. Total assessments of $500,000, including 10 percent for the city's share of the cost, have been levied. The levy will be collected from property owners in ten equal, annual installments commencing with the current year. Recognition of the approval and levy will result in entries of:
    a $500,000 in the special assessment fund and $50,000 in the general fund
    b $450,000 in the special assessment fund and $50,000 in the general fund
    c $50,000 in the special assessment fund and $50,000 in the general fund
    d $50,000 in the special assessment fund and no entry in the general fund
  2 The liability for special assessment bonds that carry a secondary pledge of a municipality's general credit should be recorded in:
    a An enterprise fund
    b A special revenue fund and general long-term debt account group
    c A special assessment fund and the general long-term debt account group
    d A special assessment fund and disclosed in a footnote in the statement of general long-term debt
    e None of the above
  3 The activities of a street improvement project that is being financed by requiring each owner of property facing the street to pay a proportionate share of the total cost should be accounted for in the:
    a Capital projects fund
    b General fund
    c Special assessment fund
    d Special revenue fund
  4 The city of Rover has two special assessment funds. In the preparation of the statement of financial position for these funds as of the end of the fiscal year, these funds may be reported on:
    a A combining basis that shows the total for both funds and has separate columns to present account balances for each fund
    b A consolidated basis after eliminating the effects of interfund transactions
    c A combining basis that shows the total for both funds and has the separate columns to present the account balance for each fund
    d A separate basis, but never together in the same statement
    e A consolidated basis with the general fund after eliminating the effects of interfund transactions
  5 The basic use of special assessment funds is:
    a To provide the local governmental unit with additional resources not currently available from the general fund
    b To provide the capital projects fund with additional capital projects
    c To provide capital improvements or services for a selected segment of a local governmental unit

**d** To provide an accounting entity for goods and services not available from any other source

**6** Present fiscal austerity programs in local governmental units may tend to:
  **a** Use special assessment funds to augment limited general fund revenues
  **b** Use capital projects funds instead of special assessment funds
  **c** Record capital assets acquired in special assessment funds in the general fund rather than in the general fixed assets account group
  **d** Record long-term debt in the general long-term debt account group rather than in the special assessment fund.

**9-2** Choose the correct answer for each of the following.
  **1** The long-term debt of special assessment funds is:
    **a** Recorded in the special assessment fund
    **b** Recorded in the long-term debt account group
    **c** Not recorded in any fund or account group
    **d** Explained in a footnote to the financial statements
  **2** Revenue to finance special assessments can come from:
    **a** Grants, long-term borrowing, and the long-term debt account group
    **b** Grants, long-term borrowing, and special assessments
    **c** Long-term borrowing, fixed assets account group, and special assessments
    **d** The general fund, the long-term debt account group, and the special revenue fund
  **3** Special assessment funds have certain characteristics of each of the following:
    **a** General funds, capital projects funds, and fixed assets account groups
    **b** Special revenue funds, fixed assets account group, and capital projects funds
    **c** Agency funds, fixed assets account group, and long-term debt account group
    **d** Debt service funds, long-term debt account group, and capital projects funds
  **4** The term of life of a special assessment fund is:
    **a** In perpetuity
    **b** Until construction is completed
    **c** Until construction is completed and debt is paid off
    **d** Until all citizens involved have paid their annual assessments
  **5** Premiums on bonds sold for resources needed to construct the special assessment project are:
    **a** Used for the payment of the bonds
    **b** Used for the construction of the project
    **c** Transferred to the debt service fund
    **d** Transferred to the long-term debt account group
  **6** Long-term debt of a special assessment fund is accounted for in:
    **a** The special assessment fund
    **b** The long-term debt account group
    **c** A fiduciary account
    **d** A special revenue account

**9-3** In 19Y4, the citizens of Reedville initiated a program of street curb improvements and sidewalk construction. Project 88 was to use special assessment financing, with the city government contributing $50,000. The total estimated cost of the project was $750,000.

During 19Y4, the following transactions occurred:

  **1** The governmental unit's share of cost was recorded.
  **2** The assessments receivable of $100,000 from the citizens involved were recorded as currently due, and $600,000 was set up as deferred.
  **3** A contract was awarded in the amount of $710,000.

**4** Serial bonds in the amount of $630,000 par value, 5 percent were sold at a net price of $637,000. Equal amounts of the bonds mature each year for ten years.

**5** Engineering and other early-stage costs were paid in the amount of $10,000.

**6** An invoice for $100,000 was received from the contractor for work completed and was recorded as a liability.

**7** Temporary investments were made in the amount of $550,000 cash, of which $5,000 was paid for the purchase of accrued interest.

**8** Interest payable of $31,500 was due in the first quarter of the next year, and $63,000 worth of the bonds mature at the same time.

**9** Accrued interest available at year end on temporary investments was $30,000.

**Required**:

**1** Record all of the above transactions for 19Y4 on a worksheet comparable to the one illustrated in this chapter.

**2** Prepare a balance sheet as of December 31, 19Y4.

**3** Prepare a statement of revenues, expenditures, and changes in fund balance for the period ending December 31, 19Y4.

**9-4** During 19Y5, the sidewalk construction special assessment fund—Project 88 (see Problem 9-3) continued operations. The following transactions took place during the year.

**1** The current year's portion of the assessments receivable ($63,000) became due along with the interest ($31,500) and were paid.

**2** The contract was completed and the contractor submitted an invoice for $610,000.

**3** The temporary investments were sold at the price paid ($545,000). Interest received on the temporary investments was $35,000.

**4** The current year's portion of interest ($31,500) and this year's redemption of bonds ($63,000) were paid.

**5** The amount due the contractor was paid except for $35,500 retained until final inspection was made to approve the project.

**6** Additional expenditures of $40,000 were made to beautify the project area.

**7** The balance of the amount owed to the contractor was paid.

**8** The fund closed its books for the year and prepared annual financial statements.

**Required**:

**1** Prepare the journal entries for the transactions for the year.

**2** Post the journal entries to a worksheet.

**3** Prepare the financial statements for the year.

**9-5** The city of New Bern authorized a sewer project. Property owners were to be assessed 80 percent of the estimated cost of construction, with the balance to be made available by the city. The project was estimated to cost $1,000,000, and a bond issue of $800,000 was authorized. During 19Y1, the following transactions occurred:

**1** Five-year, $750,000 par value serial bonds were issued with a 6 percent coupon rate. The net proceeds were $750,000; $700,000 of the proceeds were invested in certificates yielding 10 percent.

**2** A contract was awarded to Drake Construction Company in the amount of $850,000.

**3** The city's contribution toward the project was collected.

**4** The full assessment was levied, the first of five assessments of the property owners was due, and $189,000 was collected.

**5** A bill for $150,000 was received from Drake Construction Company for construction completed to date.

**6** Supervisory engineering expenses of $20,000 were paid.
**7** The delinquent assessments were collected with fines of 5 percent added on.
**8** The first six-month bond interest payment date occurred, and interest was paid.
**9** Interest for six months was received on the $700,000 invested in certificates.
**10** As of December 31, accrued interest receivable on investments was $20,000.
**11** Interest payable accrued amounted to $15,720.

**Required**:
**1** Record the above transactions in general journal form, and post them to a worksheet.
**2** Prepare a balance sheet as of December 31, 19Y1.
**3** Prepare a statement of revenues, expenditures, and changes in fund balance for the year.

**9-6** The special assessment fund for the city of New Bern continued its operations in the year 19Y2 (see Problem 9-5). During the year, the following transactions took place:

**1** The city paid $135,000 to the Drake Construction Company. It retained 10 percent of the billing cost until final review of the project.
**2** The current year's assessment of $150,000 and interest of $45,000 became due and was paid.
**3** Bonds of $150,000 were redeemed, and interest of $45,000 became due and was paid.
**4** The contract with the Drake Construction Company was amended to include an additional $50,000 of work.
**5** The contract was completed, and a bill for $750,000 was submitted.
**6** The amount of the bill submitted by the contractor was paid except for $75,000 retained until the final inspection of the project.
**7** The fund closed its books for the year and prepared statements.

**Required**:
**1** Record the transactions in journal entries.
**2** Post the entries to a worksheet for the year.
**3** Prepare financial statements for this year.

**9-7** In the city of Jonesville, the following transactions occurred during the fiscal year ended June 30, 19Z2. Each group of transactions can be separate and distinct from or related to one or more of the other groups.

**1** On November 1, 19Z1, the city issued $360,000 of 5 percent special assessment serial bonds at par to finance a street improvement project estimated to cost $425,000. The project is to be paid by $25,000 from the city's general fund and a levy of $400,000 against the property owners who will benefit from the project. The levy against the taxpayers will be paid in five equal, annual installments beginning October 1, 19Z1. The levy was made on July 1, 19Z1, and a $425,000 contract was let for the project on July 2, 19Z1. The project was completed during the fiscal year.

**2** On October 1, 19Z1 the city issued $400,000 in thirty-year, 6 percent general obligation term bonds at par to finance the construction of a public health center. A $395,000 contract was let for the construction of the project. The project was completed, inspected, and approved during the year. An additional $3,000 was spent for landscaping the grounds—the work was done by the public works department.

**3** For the health center bonds, the city sets aside general fund revenues sufficient to pay interest on September 30, and March 31. It also pays $5,000 to the debt service fund annually, which together with the interest earned on the annual investment will provide sufficient funds to retire the bonds. Assume the annual investment will earn 6 percent each year after the first fiscal year.

**Required**:

Record the information in journal entry form in the special assessment fund, the general fund, the capital projects fund, and the debt service fund for the fiscal years 19Z2 and 19Z3.

**9-8** The town of Dexter was recently incorporated and began financial operations on July 1, 19X3, the beginning of its fiscal year.[3]

The following transactions occurred during this first fiscal year, July 1, 19X3 to June 30, 19X4:

**1** The town council adopted a budget for general operations during the fiscal year ending June 30, 19X4. Revenues were estimated at $400,000. Legal authorizations for budgeted expenditures were $390,000.

**2** Property taxes were levied in the amount of $390,000; it was estimated that 2 percent of this amount would prove to be uncollectible. These taxes are available as of the date of levy to finance current expenditures.

**3** The town decided to install lighting in the town park, and a special assessment project was authorized to install the lighting at a cost of $75,000.

**4** The assessments were levied for $72,000, with the town contributing $3,000 out of the general fund. All assessments were collected during the year, including the town's contribution.

**5** A contract for $75,000 was let for the installation of the lighting. As of June 30, 19X4, the contract was completed but not approved. The contractor was paid all but 5 percent, which was retained to ensure compliance with the terms of the contract.

**6** Cash collections recorded by the general fund during the year were as follows:

| | |
|---|---|
| Property taxes | $386,000 |
| Licenses and permits | 7,000 |

**7** The town council decided to build a town hall at an estimated cost of $500,000 to replace a space occupied in rented facilities. The town does not record project authorizations. It was decided that general obligation bonds bearing interest at 6 percent would be issued. On June 30, 19X4, the bonds were issued at their face value of $500,000, payable twenty years later on June 30. No contracts have been signed for this project, and no expenditures have been made.

**8** A fire truck was purchased for $15,000. The voucher was approved and paid by the general fund. This expenditure was previously encumbered for $15,000.

**Required**:

Prepare journal entries to properly record each of the above transactions in the appropriate fund of the town of Dexter for the fiscal year ended June 30, 19X4. Use the following funds: (1) the general fund, (2) the capital projects fund, and (3) the special assessment fund.

Each journal entry should be numbered to correspond with the transactions described in the preceding numbered list. Do not prepare closing entries for any fund.

Your answer sheet should be organized as follows:

| Transaction no. | Fund | Account title and explanation | Amounts Debit | Credit |
|---|---|---|---|---|

**9-9** This problem continues the case of Silver City, also discussed in prior chapters, and it concerns the Silver City special assessment fund.

  **1** A special assessment fund was authorized for the construction of streets and sidewalks and to beautify the area bounded by the streets and sidewalks in a particular residential area of the city. The general fund portion of the cost for these improvements was approved in the general fund budget, and $68,000 was appropriated. This appropriation was contingent upon the assessment of a special tax levy in the amount of $320,000 against the property owners in the benefited area. Thus the authorized improvements were estimated to be $388,000. The property owners would be allowed to pay their share immediately or pay the principal and interest on the needed bonds over a ten-year period.

  **2** Special assessment bonds were issued to provide funds for the project. The bonds were ten-year, 8 percent bonds issued at par. The interest payable was due annually on the issue date. Cash received was $320,000.

  **3** A contract for the improvements authorized was granted for $350,000.

  **4** The project was completed by the contractor, and a bill for $350,000 was received. The city retained 5 percent of the price of the contract to be assured that the contract was performed properly. The balance of the bill was paid.

  **5** Payments on the principal and interest on the bonds would be paid on the fifteenth of the second month after the close of the fiscal year in order to pay the interest on the bonds and provide sufficient resources to eventually pay the principal on the bonds when due.

  **6** Just before the close of the fiscal year, a contract was let for beautifying the area around the street improvements at a cost of $30,000.

**Required:**
1 Prepare journal entries for the transactions in the special assessment fund, including any closing entries.
2 Post the journal entries to a worksheet from which the proper statements can be prepared.
3 Prepare the needed statements for the year.

# NOTES

1 National Council on Governmental Accounting, *Statement 1. Governmental Accounting and Financial Reporting Principles* (Chicago: Municipal Finance Officers Association of the United States and Canada, 1979), p. 12.
2 American Institute of Certified Public Accountants, *Uniform CPA Examination Questions and Unofficial Answers* (New York: American Institute of Certified Public Accountants, various dates).
3 Ibid., May 1980.

**CHAPTER 10**

# FIDUCIARY FUNDS

The purpose of this chapter is to explain the principles and practices of accounting for trust and agency funds in government—the two basic types of fiduciary funds. Concerning fiduciary funds, the National Council on Governmental Accounting states:

> *Trust and Agency Funds*—To account for assets held by a governmental unit in a trustee capacity or as agent for individuals, private organizations, other governmental units, and/or other funds. These include (a) Expendable Trust Funds, (b) Nonexpendable Trust Funds, (c) Pension Trust Funds, and (d) Agency Funds.[1]

Trust funds are those entities in which resources are held for others—some of these resources can be spent and some cannot. Nonexpendable trust funds are comparable to proprietary, profit, or business-type funds—the income typically can be spent, but the capital (trust principal) cannot. Expendable trust funds are comparable to governmental or nonprofit funds—any capital remaining from prior years and any revenue for the period can be spent during the current period. So, in the classification of trust funds, both the governmental or expendable funds and the proprietary or nonexpendable funds are found. As illustrations, resources from private donors that can be entirely spent are considered expendable funds; grants and gifts that must be invested and only the income spent are a combination of expendable and nonexpendable trust funds.

Agency funds act as an agent to others, such as when a county treasurer's office takes temporary custody of the taxes collected for other jurisdictions in the area (e.g., a school board or a recreation district). In addition to merely collecting the taxes for other jurisdictions, the agency fund may also withhold sufficient amounts to pay for the costs of fund operations.

An agency fund operation is not required for all agency-type activity. For example, the general fund can act as the agent for the federal and state governments and often does. The general fund can do more than temporarily hold custody of the assets for federal and state withholding taxes from salaries and wages of the general fund employees; it also can act as an agent for receiving the money for tax withholdings from other funds, paying the state and federal governments, and keeping the records.

However, if several funds of the governmental unit must withhold taxes and pension payments, it is less expensive to have one agency fund handle all of the record keeping for all of the funds, rather than to have each fund go through that detailed process. In this manner, the records for withholdings and the resultant W–2-type forms would be handled by one fund rather than several funds.

## PARTICULAR CHARACTERISTICS OF FIDUCIARY FUNDS

The main accounting problems of trust funds involve distinguishing between *income* and *principal* (or corpus) of the nonexpendable and expendable portions of the fund. Legal requirements must be followed for trust activities of a governmental unit just as with any other form of trustee. If the law requires that the principal must remain intact while the income is spent, then the accounting must clearly indicate the separation of the principal and the income, so that the legal requirement can be met.

Many pension funds of local governments are also being used as investment agencies for pension investments that are not subject to income tax payments until the retirement date. This practice will probably increase to a great extent in the future.

Pension trust funds, in contrast, take on some of the characteristics of both a trust fund and an agency fund. When an employee contributes to a pension trust fund, he or she gains certain rights. These include:

**1** A right to the amount paid into the fund during the period of employment, either with or without interest.

**2** If reemployed, (if the employee terminated employment before obtaining a vested interest in a pension) a right to pay back sums that previously were withdrawn from the fund to obtain a vested right in a pension.

**3** A vested right in a retirement amount after a certain period of employment with the governmental unit. This includes a vested right to a retirement amount that includes the amounts paid in by the government as well as the amounts paid in by the employee.

Our illustrations provide examples of a right to a deceased employee's estate as a result of the employee not working a sufficient period to have a vested interest in a pension. Some heirs in a vested right could have been paid a retirement amount after the employee's death. We also illustrate an employee's withdrawal of payments from the fund, when he or she stops working for the city before gaining a vested right. Usually, the amounts paid by employers remain in the fund. Pensions are only paid to retired employees who have a vested right to a pension.

## BASIS OF ACCOUNTING

In our discussions of proprietary and governmental funds, it was stated that, as a general rule, proprietary funds follow the accrual basis of accounting, while governmental funds follow the modified accrual basis of accounting. Thus nonexpendable trust funds and pension trust funds generally follow the accrual method of accounting, while expendable trust funds follow the modified accrual basis of accounting.

In agency funds, there is no revenue or expenditure measurement as such, so neither the accrual or modified accrual basis of accounting needs to be considered—for there is no income measurement—only the value of the assets and liabilities with no fund balance. There is no need for a measurement basis—either accrual or modified accrual—unless the fund is an income-earning or revenue-expenditure-type fund.

The rule is that governmental units should follow the accrual basis of accounting for nonexpendable trust funds. However, some jurisdictions are not allowed to follow accrual accounting in a trust fund unless the indenture creating the trust requires accrual accounting. State law concerning trusts is sometimes very restrictive as to what is income and what is principal. For example, if a building is given as rental property to the city, the trust indenture may state that gross income, less expenses, may or may not consider depreciation as an expense to determine net income. Yet, if the principal is not replaced through depreciation, it will eventually dissipate through payment to the city of additional amounts of income each year that ordinarily would be reduced through depreciation. Persons giving depreciable assets to a city, if they desire, should suggest in their trust indentures that the fixed assets should remain constant through depreciation with the balance of the income available for expenditure.

While there are some distinctions in the accounting methods for fiduciary funds, they are basically the same as have been illustrated for both the proprietary and governmental funds. Specific types of accounting transactions, therefore, will be shown only in the illustrations of the particular type of agency or trust fund. Ordinarily, there is no need for budgetary accounting for control purposes in either trust or agency accounts.

## ILLUSTRATION OF ACCOUNTING FOR EXPENDABLE AND NONEXPENDABLE TRUST FUNDS

### Nonexpendable Trust Fund

This first illustration shows a combined expendable and nonexpendable trust fund. The trust was created by a certain Ed Parker, who died and left to the city of Ruthberg certain assets. The provisions of the will stated that the principal of the trust is to remain intact, while the income is to be used to provide scholarships to needy qualified students who are residents of the city and who attend any of the state universities. As of July 1, 19X5, the city received the following property:

**City of Ruthberg**
**Trust Fund for University Scholarships**
**Estate of Ed Parker**
**July 1, 19X5**

|  | Appraised value | Face value |
|---|---|---|
| Cash | $30,000 | $ 30,000 |
| Undeveloped land | 10,000 | — |
| 10 percent JFK Company bonds | 95,000 | 100,000 |
| 4 percent city of Y bonds | 35,000 | 30,000 |

Thus two types of trust funds are needed for this particular illustration—a nonexpendable trust fund and an expendable trust fund—a trust fund for the principal and one for the income. These two funds may be accounted for in one fund. If this is done, however, the city must keep the various types of assets and the various types of capital separated.

The entry to record the gift to the city, entered at appraised value in the principal fund, is:

T1  July 1, 19X5

|  | Dr. | Cr. |
|---|---|---|
| Cash | $ 30,000 | |
| Land | 10,000 | |
| Investments | 130,000 | |
|   Ed Parker trust fund | | |
|     balance—principal | | $170,000 |

To record assets donated to city for scholarship fund principal.

The purpose of the fund is to have maximum income for use as scholarships. Therefore, the administrators of the fund should sell the land and invest the proceeds in income-producing properties. The land was sold on July 1 for $12,000. This entry is:

T2  Cash                  $12,000
    Ed Parker trust fund
      balance—principal                  $ 2,000
    Land                                10,000

To record sale of land with gain on sale based on reevaluation of appraisal amount.

Private investors often invest in municipal bonds for tax purposes, so the income is often less than what they could receive from private company bonds. Since the city could receive more income from corporate bonds, they decided to sell the municipal bonds and invest in bonds that have a higher interest rate. The 4 percent city of Y bonds were sold on July 1 for the appraised value. On the same date, 12 percent bonds of the ABC Company were purchased for $35,000; 10 percent bonds of the Kearney Company were also purchased for $42,000, the face value, from the cash provided by the sale of the land along with the original cash.

The journal entries to record these transactions would be:

T3  Cash                  $35,000
    Investments                       $35,000

To record sale of 4 percent city of Y bonds.

T4  Investments        $77,000
    Cash                                 $77,000

To record purchase of 12 percent ABC Company bonds for $35,000 and 10 percent Kearney Company bonds for $42,000.

## Expendable Trust Fund

Assuming that all of the interest on each of the bonds was paid during the year, the income fund would receive cash income of $18,400. This assumption is made if the fund immediately sells the land for $12,000 and the city of Y's 4 percent bonds are immediately sold for $35,000. The interest on the bonds had been paid on June 30, so there is no accrued interest. The 12 percent bonds of the ABC Company and the 10 percent Kearney Company bonds were immediately purchased. Both the Kearney Company and the ABC Company pay interest on their bonds on December 31 and June 30. Half the scholarships were paid on December 31, and the rest were paid on June 30, upon receipt of the income from the bonds.

The income can be computed as follows:

| | |
|---|---|
| 10 percent JFK Company bonds—$100,000 | $10,000 |
| 10 percent Kearney Company bonds—$42,000 | 4,200 |
| 12 percent ABC Company bonds—$35,000 | 4,200 |
| Total income | $18,400 |

This amount of income is recorded in the income fund rather than in the principal fund, as follows:

| T5 | Cash | $18,400 | |
|---|---|---|---|
| | Interest income | | $18,400 |

To record income earned on investments during the year.

In the income fund during the year, eight scholarships of $2,100 each were made, for total expenditures of $16,800. This entry is:

| T6 | Expenditures | $16,800 | |
|---|---|---|---|
| | Cash | | $16,800 |

To record expenditures for scholarships.

The income accounts are closed at the end of the year by the following entry:

| T7 | Interest income | $18,400 | |
|---|---|---|---|
| | Expenditures | | $16,800 |
| | Ed Parker trust fund balance—income | | 1,600 |

To close income and expenditure accounts to fund balance.

You may notice that the fund balance for the principal remains constant for the year, except for the $2,000 increase arising from the sale of the land. This increase is more a reevaluation of the appraised value of the land rather than income. Meanwhile, the net income for the year in the income fund has almost been spent, a balance remaining in the fund balance-income account of only $1,600. This is in accordance with the terms of the bequest to the city. This information is illustrated in Exhibits 10-1 and 10-2.

Year-end statements needed are: (1) a statement of revenues, expenditures, and changes in fund balance for the income fund, including a statement of changes in fund

**EXHIBIT 10-1**
**City of Ruthberg**
**Transactions—Principal Trust Fund for University Scholarships**
**Estate of Ed Parker**
**Fiscal Year 19X6**

| Accounts | Beginning balances | | | | Transactions | | | | Ending balances | |
|---|---|---|---|---|---|---|---|---|---|---|
| | No. | Dr. | No. | Cr. | No. | Dr. | No. | Cr. | Dr. | Cr. |
| Cash—principal | T1 | $ 30,000 | | | T2 | $ 12,000 | T4 | $ 77,000 | | |
| | | | | | T3 | 35,000 | | | | |
| Land | T1 | 10,000 | | | | | T2 | 10,000 | | |
| Investments | T1 | 130,000 | | | T4 | 77,000 | T3 | 35,000 | $172,000 | |
| Ed Parker trust fund—principal | | | T1 | $170,000 | | | T2 | 2,000 | | $172,000 |
| | | $170,000 | | $170,000 | | $124,000 | | $124,000 | $172,000 | $172,000 |

## EXHIBIT 10-2
### City of Ruthberg
### Transactions—Income Trust Fund for College Scholarships
### Estate of Ed Parker
### Fiscal Year 19X6

| | Transactions | | | | Ending balances | |
|---|---|---|---|---|---|---|
| Accounts | No. | Dr. | No. | Cr. | Dr. | Cr. |
| Income—cash | T5 | $18,400 | T6 | $16,800 | $1,600 | |
| Interest income | T7 | 18,400 | T5 | 18,400 | | |
| Expenditures | T6 | 16,800 | T7 | 16,800 | | |
| Ed Parker trust fund—income | | | T7 | 1,600 | | $1,600 |
| | | $53,600 | | $53,600 | $1,600 | $1,600 |

balance for the principal fund, and (2) a balance sheet for each of the funds. These statements are not shown for they can easily be determined from Exhibits 10-1 and 10-2.

## ILLUSTRATIVE ACCOUNTING FOR THE PENSION TRUST FUND FOR THE CITY OF RUTHBERG

In pension trust funds, resources are gathered, invested, and then spent, usually several years later, for pensions for those who have placed their money in the fund. Both employees and employers can contribute to the pension trust fund. When both contribute, it is called a contributory pension fund; when only the employer contributes, the fund is called a noncontributory pension fund. Our illustration of accounting and control for a pension trust fund shows contributions from both employees and employer, so it is a contributory pension fund.

To be actuarially sound, contributions to the pension trust fund from both the employer and the employee, along with the earnings from the investments purchased from the contributions, should be sufficient to pay pensions to all of the contributors to the fund when they retire. If sufficient contributions and earnings are not received, then there is an actuarial deficit in the operations of the fund. This deficit should be shown in the statements for the current period. All of the requirements for eventual payments from the fund are reservations from the fund balance, and the entries for the reservations are made each period.

There is a fund balance only when contributions are greater than all needs, and this seldom happens. The fund usually has a deficit, because it does not have sufficient resources, on an actuarial basis, to pay for all of the future pensions.

Sometimes a pension trust fund includes all of the employees of the city; sometimes it only includes employees from certain funds. Our illustration includes only the pension accounting for the employees from the general fund. The information on the pension deductions for the general fund is shown in Chapter 6, pages 153–154.

## Transactions for the Pension Trust Fund

The employees of the general fund of the city of Ruthberg contributed approximately 7.54 percent of their salaries for a pension. The city matched this amount. During the year, the employee pension contributions were $46,000. With the city matching this amount, the total paid to the pension trust fund was $92,000. Assuming the fund had been in operation for several years, the account balances are:

**City of Ruthberg**
**Pension Trust Fund**
**Trial Balance**
**June 30, 19X5**

|  | Dr. | Cr. |
|---|---|---|
| Cash | $ 42,000 | |
| Interest receivable | 3,000 | |
| Investments | 1,400,000 | |
| Premiums on investments | 3,000 | |
| Discounts on investments | | 5,000 |
| Payable to resigned employees | | 4,000 |
| Payable to deceased employee estates | | 16,000 |
| Annuities payable | | 6,000 |
| Reserve for employee contributions | | 520,000 |
| Reserve for employer contributions | | 530,000 |
| Reserve for retiree annuities | | 367,000 |
| Reserve for actuarial deficiency | | 240,000 |
| Fund balance (deficit) | 240,000 | |
| Total | $1,688,000 | $1,688,000 |

One of the major problems associated with pension funds is that the total collections and earnings over the life of the fund may not balance out to the need for pension payments. The fund employs actuaries to determine the actuarial soundness of the fund. And the actuarial deficiency determined by the actuary is recorded in the fund to show that the fund needs additional resources in order for it to be actuarially sound. Or it may show what the fund is capable of paying off in the way of future liabilities for pensions over the life of the fund.

During the fiscal year, the general fund pays into the pension trust fund the amounts collected from the employees as well as the amounts the city paid as its share. Since we have assumed that no accruals were necessary for salaries in the general fund, likewise no accruals are necessary in the pension trust fund. This entry, over the year, is:

|  | Dr. | Cr. |
|---|---|---|
| P1  Due from general fund | $92,000 | |
|     Employee contributions | | $46,000 |
|     Employer contributions | | 46,000 |

To set up receivable for employer and employee contributions to the pension trust fund.

When the cash is transferred from the general fund to the pension trust fund, these entries are summarized as follows:

**P2**  Cash $92,000
  Due from general fund $92,000
  To record cash received from general fund.

Often, a pension trust fund allows the employee to have a vested interest in the fund, if he or she remains employed for a certain period of time (e.g., five years). When resigning after only short periods of employment, the employee may take out of the fund whatever he or she has invested. In addition, if an employees dies before retirement, interest in the fund may be given to the employee's estate. Some pension trusts pay a retirement to the widow if the employee has been with the fund for a certain length of time.

During the preceding year, some employees, without a vested interest in a pension, had died and others had left the employ of the city. An accrual had been made for these actions, leaving a liability of $16,000 for those who had died and $4,000 for those who had terminated employment. The entry to pay off these liabilities is:

**P3**  Payable to deceased employees'
    estates $16,000
  Payable to resigned employees 4,000
    Cash $20,000
  To pay liabilities for deceased and terminated employees.

The annuities payable at the end of the previous year were also paid. This entry would be:

**P4**  Annuities payable $6,000
    Cash $6,000
  To pay annuities due at year end.

Several employees retired during the year and made applications for their pensions. Expected pension benefits of $58,000 to the employees would be taken from the reserve accounts representing the contributions from both the employee and the employer. This entry is:

**P5**  Reserve for employee contributions $27,000
  Reserve for employer contributions 31,000
    Reserve for retiree annuities $58,000
  To set up reserve for retiree annuities.

The amount paid for annuities for the year is $74,000. The liability for these annuities is recorded as follows:

| P6 | Expenses—annuities | $74,000 | |
|---|---|---|---|
| | Annuities payable | | $74,000 |
| | To set up liabilities for annuities. | | |

During the year, investments having a face value of $74,000 are purchased for the fund. Accrued interest on some fund investments amounted to $2,000, and some bonds were purchased at a discount of $3,000. This entry is recorded as follows:

| P7 | Investments | $74,000 | |
|---|---|---|---|
| | Interest receivable | 2,000 | |
| | Discount on investments | | $ 3,000 |
| | Cash | | 73,000 |
| | To record bonds purchased at a discount of $3,000, interest receivable of $2,000, and a face value of $74,000. | | |

During the year, the fund received earnings on the investments of $117,000. A part of the cash received included the accrued interest paid on investments purchased during the year. This entry would be:

| P8 | Cash | $117,000 | |
|---|---|---|---|
| | Interest receivable | | $ 3,000 |
| | Interest income | | 114,000 |
| | To record interest earned during the year. | | |

The bond discount and premium could be written off when the interest is received. It would seem better, however, to wait until the end of the year and figure the discounts and premiums on all of the bonds. In this way, they can be written off all at one time, since these write-offs would be an adjustment of the interest income received during the year.

Of the liabilities set up for the payment of the annuities, only $68,000 is paid during the year. This entry is:

| P9 | Annuities payable | $68,000 | |
|---|---|---|---|
| | Cash | | $68,000 |
| | To record payment for annuities. | | |

During the year, the fund should keep as much of its cash invested as possible, in order to earn the maximum interest. Additional investments of $60,000 were made during the year. This entry is:

| P10 | Investments | $60,000 | |
|---|---|---|---|
| | Cash | | $60,000 |
| | To record purchase of investments. | | |

## EXHIBIT 10-3
### City of Ruthberg—Pension Trust Fund
### Worksheet
### Fiscal Year 19X6

| Accounts | Beginning balance Dr. | Beginning balance Cr. | Transactions No. | Transactions Dr. | Transactions No. | Transactions Cr. |
|---|---|---|---|---|---|---|
| Cash | $ 42,000 | | P2 | $ 92,000 | P3 | $ 20,000 |
| | | | P8 | 117,000 | P4 | 6,000 |
| | | | | | P7 | 73,000 |
| | | | | | P9 | 68,000 |
| | | | | | P10 | 60,000 |
| Due from general fund | | | P1 | 92,000 | P2 | 92,000 |
| Interest receivable | 3,000 | | P7 | 2,000 | P8 | 3,000 |
| Investments | 1,400,000 | | P7 | 74,000 | | |
| | | | P10 | 60,000 | | |
| Premiums on investments | 3,000 | | | | | |
| Discounts on investments | | 5,000 | | | P7 | 3,000 |
| Payable to resigned employees | | 4,000 | P3 | 4,000 | | |
| Payable to deceased employees' estates | | 16,000 | P3 | 16,000 | | |
| Annuities payable | | 6,000 | P4 | 6,000 | P6 | 74,000 |
| | | | P9 | 68,000 | | |
| Reserve for employee contributions | | 520,000 | P5 | 27,000 | | |
| Reserve for employer contributions | | 530,000 | P5 | 31,000 | | |
| Reserve for retiree annuities | | 367,000 | | | P5 | 58,000 |
| Reserve for actuarial deficiency | | 240,000 | | | | |
| Fund balance | 240,000 | | | | | |
| Employer contributions | | | | | P1 | 46,000 |
| Employee contributions | | | | | P1 | 46,000 |
| Expenses—annuities | | | P6 | 74,000 | | |
| Interest income | | | | | P8 | 114,000 |
| Expenses—deceased employee claims | | | | | | |
| Expenses—resigned employee claims | | | | | | |
| | $1,688,000 | $1,688,000 | | $663,000 | | $663,000 |

All of the preceding entries have been recorded on the worksheet for the pension trust fund (see Exhibit 10-3). The original balances are recorded in columns 1 and 2, the entries for the period in columns 3 and 4, and the balances before any adjustments are shown in columns 5 and 6. Some adjusting entries would have to be made in order to have the correct balances to place in the statements. The temporary accounts then are closed to start a new fiscal year.

EXHIBIT 10-3
(continued)

| Trial balance | | Adjustments and closings | | | | Ending balance | |
|---|---|---|---|---|---|---|---|
| Dr. | Cr. | No. | Dr. | No. | Cr. | Dr. | Cr. |
| $ 24,000 | | | | | | $ 24,000 | |
| 2,000 | | P11 | 3,000 | | | 5,000 | |
| 1,534,000 | | | | | | 1,534,000 | |
| 3,000 | | | | P11 | 400 | 2,600 | |
| | 8,000 | P11 | 500 | | | | 7,500 |
| | | | | P12 | 9,000 | | 9,000 |
| | | | | P12 | 3,000 | | 3,000 |
| | 6,000 | | | | | | 6,000 |
| | 493,000 | P15 | 12,000 | P13 | 46,000 | | 568,000 |
| | | | | P16 | 41,000 | | |
| | 499,000 | | | P13 | 46,000 | | 586,000 |
| | | | | P16 | 41,000 | | |
| | 425,000 | P14 | 74,000 | P16 | 35,100 | | 386,100 |
| | 240,000 | P17 | 15,000 | | | | 225,000 |
| 240,000 | | | | P17 | 15,000 | 225,000 | |
| | 46,000 | P13 | 46,000 | | | | |
| | 46,000 | P13 | 46,000 | | | | |
| 74,000 | | | | P14 | 74,000 | | |
| | 114,000 | P16 | 117,100 | P11 | 3,100 | | |
| | | P12 | 3,000 | P15 | 3,000 | | |
| | | P12 | 9,000 | P15 | 9,000 | | |
| $1,877,000 | $1,877,000 | | $329,600 | | $329,600 | $1,790,600 | $1,790,600 |

**Adjusting Entries** Often, the expense of operating a pension trust fund is borne by the city, as is the case for all other trust funds. If the city determines that it should have correct information on the operations of the pension trust fund, then, all costs should be included. Thus an entry for the accrual, for the cost borne by the general fund, could be made at the end of the year. This entry is:

| | | |
|---|---|---|
| Employee costs | xxxx | |
| Administrative costs | xxxx | |
|     Due to general fund | | xxxx |

In this illustration, these costs are not considered; therefore, the primary adjustments would be those concerned with interest earnings for the year. Interest due but not collected at the end of the year amounted to $3,000, the bond discount to be written off was $500, and the bond premium to be written off was $400. This entry is:

| | | | |
|---|---|---|---|
| P11 | Interest receivable | $3,000 | |
| | Discount on bond investments | 500 | |
| |     Premium on bond investments | | $ 400 |
| |     Interest income | | 3,100 |
| | To adjust interest earnings for year. | | |

Claims by estates of several deceased former members of the city's retirement system and resigned employees were accrued as follows:

| | |
|---|---|
| Claims by deceased member's estates | $ 3,000 |
| Claims by former members who were employees | 9,000 |
|     Total | $12,000 |

The journal entries to record these liabilities are as follows:

| | | | |
|---|---|---|---|
| P12 | Expenses—deceased employee claims | $3,000 | |
| | Expenses—resigned employee claims | 9,000 | |
| |     Payable to deceased employee estates | | $3,000 |
| |     Payable to resigned employees | | 9,000 |
| | To set up claims by resigned employees and deceased employees' estates. | | |

**Closing Entries**   Each of the temporary accounts would be closed to the appropriate fund balance reserve account. The contributions from the employees and employers would go to the reserves for those accounts, and the expenses would be closed to the reserve for retiree annuities. These entries would be:

| | | | |
|---|---|---|---|
| P13 | Employee contributions | $46,000 | |
| | Employer contributions | 46,000 | |
| |     Reserve for employee contributions | | $46,000 |
| |     Reserve for employer contributions | | 46,000 |
| | To close out temporary accounts. | | |
| P14 | Reserve for retiree annuities | $74,000 | |
| |     Expenses—annuities | | $74,000 |
| | To close expense account. | | |

To close out the accounts pertaining to resigned employees and deceased employees' estates, the journal entry is:

| | | |
|---|---|---|
| P15 Reserve for employee contributions | $12,000 | |
|     Expenses—deceased employee claims | | $3,000 |
|     Expenses—resigned employee claims | | 9,000 |

The gross earnings for the year are closed not only to the current retiree's reserve accounts but also to the future retiree's reserve accounts. After adjustment, the income account shows a balance of $117,100. This balance is closed proportionately or, if legally mandated otherwise, to the appropriate reserve accounts. The amounts to be distributed to the various reserve accounts are:

| | |
|---|---|
| Reserve for employee contributions | $ 41,000 |
| Reserve for employer contributions | 41,000 |
| Reserve for retiree annuities | 35,100 |
|     Total | $117,000 |

The entry to record this transaction is:

| | | |
|---|---|---|
| P16 Interest income | $117,100 | |
|     Reserve for employee contributions | | $41,000 |
|     Reserve for employer contributions | | 41,000 |
|     Reserve for retiree annuities | | 35,100 |
| To close interest income account. | | |

At the end of the year, because of increased earnings possible over the next several years, the actuarial assumption is that there is only a shortage of $225,000 for the entire fund, to be paid by employer contributions.

The entry for this transaction is:

| | | |
|---|---|---|
| P17 Reserve for actuarial deficiency | $15,000 | |
|     Fund balance (deficit) | | $15,000 |
| To adjust fund balance for actuarial deficiency. | | |

By posting these entries to the worksheet in Exhibit 10-3, the net results of all of the transactions for the current year can readily be seen.

## Pension Trust Fund Financial Statements

The statements needed for the pension trust fund are: the balance sheet, the statement of revenues, expenses, and changes in reserve accounts and fund balance, and the statement of changes in financial position (see Exhibits 10-4, 10-5 and 10-6). An alternative method of presenting the changes in reserves and fund balance is given in Exhibit 10-7. In summarizing *Statement 6* in their *Pension Accounting and Financial Reporting: Public Employee Retirement Systems and State and Local Government Employers*, the NCGA states:

The statement calls for public employee retirement systems (PERS) financial statement presentations to include: 1) investments at cost or amortized cost with parenthetical disclosures

**EXHIBIT 10-4**
**City of Ruthberg**
**Pension Trust Fund**
**Balance Sheet**
**June 30, 19X6**

| | | |
|---|---:|---:|
| **Assets** | | |
| Cash | | $ 24,000 |
| Interest receivable | | 5,000 |
| Investments | | 1,529,100 |
|    Net investment at amortized cost | | |
|      (market value—$1,540,000) | | |
|    Total assets | | $1,558,100 |
| **Liabilities** | | |
| Annuities payable | | $ 6,000 |
| Payable to deceased employee estates | | 3,000 |
| Payable to resigned employees | | 9,000 |
|    Total liabilities | | 18,000 |
| **Fund balance*** | | |
| Reserve for employee contribution | $ 568,000 | |
| Reserve for employer contribution | 586,000 | |
| Reserve for retiree annuities | 386,100 | |
| | | 1,540,100 |
| Reserve for actuarial deficiency | 225,000 | |
| Fund balance (deficit) | (225,000) | 0 |
| Total liabilities and fund balance | | $1,558,100 |

*\*NCGA Statement 6, effective June 15, 1982, changed the method of presenting the fund balance section of the balance sheet. NCGA Interpretation 8 extended indefinitely the effective date of NCGA Statement 6. This extension was given to allow the NCGA (now GASB) and FASB members to reconcile differences. (See Exhibit 10-7 for presentation of the fund balance section of the pension trust fund balance sheet that is in accordance with NCGA Statement 6.)*

of market value, 2) current liabilities, 3) the actuarial present value of credited projected benefits and 4) the unfunded actuarial present value of credited projected benefits. Employer financial statements are to include the same asset and current liability amounts with the difference shown as reserved fund balance. The information on actuarial present value of credited projected benefits is to be disclosed in the notes to the financial statements of the employer. The employer must report as pension expenditure/expense an amount determined in accordance with an acceptable actuarial cost method, regardless of whether such amount is actually contributed to the PERS. In preparing comprehensive annual financial reports, PERS and employers are required to disclose in the statistical section of those reports historical trend information intended to enhance understanding of PERS financial activity. The statement outlines conditions under which it is acceptable, in accounting for the exchange of debt securities, for the PERS to use the amortization and deferral or the cost pass-through approach. The emphasis throughout the statement is on disclosure of information needed for fair presentation of PERS and employer financial position on a going-concern basis.[2]

The actuarial values for the past and current years are not shown in the statements for the following reason. The requirement to be followed in NCGA's *Statement 6. Pen-*

**EXHIBIT 10-5**
**City of Ruthberg**
**Pension Trust Fund**
**Statement of Revenues, Expenses, and Changes in Reserve Accounts and Fund Balance**
**July 1, 19X5–June 30, 19X6**

### Operating Revenues

| | | |
|---|---:|---:|
| Contributions: | | |
|   Employees | $ 46,000 | |
|   Employers | 46,000 | $ 92,000 |
| Interest | | 117,100 |
| Total operating revenues | | 209,100 |

### Operating Expenses

| | | |
|---|---:|---:|
| Deceased employee claims | 9,000 | |
| Refunds to terminated employees | 3,000 | 12,000 |
| Benefit payments | | 74,000 |
| Net operating expense | | 86,000 |
| Operating income | | 123,100 |

### Distribution of Operating Income

| | | |
|---|---:|---:|
| To reserve for employee contributions: | | |
|   Contributions | $ 46,000 | |
|   Earnings | 41,000 | |
| Less expenses for claims to resigned employees and deceased employees' estates | 87,000 | |
| | 12,000 | 75,000 |
| To reserve for employer contributions: | | |
|   Contributions | 46,000 | |
|   Earnings | 41,000 | 87,000 |
| To reserve for retiree annuities: | | |
|   Earnings | 35,100 | |
|   Payments | (74,000) | (38,900) |
| Total | | $123,100 |
| To fund balance | | — |
| Beginning fund balance (deficit) | (240,000) | |
| Decrease in reserve for actuarial deficiency | 15,000 | |
| Fund balance, June 30, 19X6 | (225,000) | |
| Reserve for actuarial deficiency | 225,000 | |
| Fund balance | | — |

*sion Accounting and Financial Reporting: Public Employee Retirement Systems and State and Local Government Employers*, issued in June 1983, was to be effective for fiscal years beginning after June 15, 1982, but the effective date requirement was changed to June 15, 1985 in the preface of *Statement 6*. NCGA *Interpretation 8*, issued in November 1983, extended the effective date indefinitely "to allow NCGA and FASB members to conduct discussions aimed at reconciling the material differences between *Statement 6* and SFAS 35."[3]

**EXHIBIT 10-6**
**City of Ruthberg**
**Pension Trust Fund**
**Statement of Changes in Financial Position**
**For Year Ended June 30, 19X6**

| | | | |
|---|---|---|---|
| Sources of funds | | | |
|   Contributions: | | | |
|     Employees | | $ 46,000 | |
|     Employers | | 46,000 | $ 92,000 |
|   Interest | | | 117,100 |
| | | | $209,100 |
| Application of funds | | | |
|   Increase in investments | | $131,100 | |
|   Refunds: | | | |
|     Death | $ 9,000 | | |
|     Resignation | 3,000 | 12,000 | |
|   Benefit payments | | 74,000 | 217,100 |
|   Decrease in working capital | | | $( 8,000) |

**Schedule of Changes in Net Current Assets**

| | Beginning of year | End of year | Working capital increase (decrease) |
|---|---|---|---|
| Current assets | | | |
|   Cash | $42,000 | $24,000 | $(18,000) |
|   Interest receivable | 3,000 | 5,000 | 2,000 |
| | $45,000 | $29,000 | $(16,000) |
| Current liabilities | | | |
|   Payable to deceased employees' estates | 16,000 | 3,000 | 13,000 |
|   Payable to resigned employees | 4,000 | 9,000 | ( 5,000) |
|   Annuities payable | 6,000 | 6,000 | — |
| | $26,000 | $18,000 | $ 8,000 |
| | $19,000 | $11,000 | $( 8,000) |

Notes to the statements concerning the historical trend information are not available but would have to be obtained and presented as a footnote to the financial statements.

## REVENUE SHARING FUNDS

Originally the State and Local Fiscal Assistance Act of 1972 as amended, commonly known as the Revenue Sharing Act, stated that "a recipient government which receives entitlement funds shall: Establish a trust fund and deposit all entitlement funds received and all interest earned thereon in that trust fund." The act also said that: "the governmental unit receiving the monies should use, obligate, or appropriate such funds within 24 months from the end of the entitlement period to which the entitlement payment is applicable."[4]

Another important section of the Revenue Sharing Act stated that

**EXHIBIT 10-7**
**Balance Sheet***
**City of Ruthberg**
**Pension Trust Fund**
**June 30, 19X6**

| | |
|---|---:|
| Total assets (Exhibit 10-4) | $ 1,558,100 |
| Total liabilities (Exhibit 10-4) | 18,000 |
| Net assets available for benefits | $ 1,540,100 |

**Fund Balance**

| | |
|---|---:|
| Actuarial present value of projected benefits to current retirants and beneficiaries | $ 373,741 |
| Actuarial present value of projected benefits payable to terminated vested participants | 68,766 |
| Actuarial present value of credited projected benefits to active employees | |
|     Member contributions | 650,882 |
|     Employer financial portion | 676,711 |
| Total actuarial present value of credited projected benefits | $ 1,765,100 |
| Unfunded actuarial present value of credited projected benefits | ( 225,000) |
| Fund balance | $ 1,540,100 |

*This balance sheet is in accordance with NCGA's *Statement 6*. The figures used are those from Exhibit 10-4, but they have been revised.

each recipient government must have an independent audit of its financial statements. This audit would be conducted for the purpose of determining compliance with the provisions of the act, in accordance with generally accepted auditing standards, not less often than once every three years.[5]

Record keeping for revenue sharing purposes, then, is no different from any other trust fund. Current regulations, however, do not require the use of a trust fund. Therefore, some municipalities meet their legal obligations for proper accounting for these funds by placing them in special revenue funds or in agency-type accounts in the general fund. Since this segment of the law has recently been changed, the accountant must make sure that the fund is kept in accordance with the revenue sharing law and that it is auditable in accordance with the law and regulations.

Current regulations pertaining to revenue sharing state that accounting for these funds shall employ the same procedures as are used for expenditures from revenues derived from the recipient government's own sources. Thus budgetary procedures, encumbrances, and cash control should be the minimum necessary for these types of funds. In respect to grant, entitlement, and shared revenue accounting, the NCGA says:

> In some instances, it may be necessary or desirable to record grant, entitlement, or shared revenue transactions in an Agency Fund in order to provide an audit trail and/or to facilitate

the preparation of special purpose financial statements. The transactions are recorded as they occur in the Agency Fund utilizing "memoranda" revenue and expenditure accounts coded in accordance with specialized needs. The same transactions are subsequently recorded as revenues or contributed capital and expenditures or expenses, as appropriate, in conformity with GAAP in the fund(s) financed.[6]

## AGENCY FUNDS

Each fund in governmental accounting is considered a separate accounting entity. Therefore, there are many transactions in government for which the same type of entry might be made in each of many funds. When each of the funds has employees, for example, the transactions for withholdings for pensions and taxes are similar and are accounted for separately in each of the funds. The accounting for these types of transactions can be simplified by creating an agency fund. In another example, taxes are collected by the county for the city, the school board, recreation districts, street lighting districts, or other special assessment districts. The agency fund collects the taxes for the entire city, the county, and other jurisdictions, distributing them proportionally to each of the funds. In a further illustration, idle cash resources from several funds of a city need to be invested. A pooled fund, as an agency fund, can make investments for the entire governmental unit, instead of each fund having to make its own investments.

Since the agency fund acts as agent for the original fund, movement of resources between these types of funds is not considered a "transfer" between funds. For example, if an agency fund collects funds for two or three other funds, the agency fund, then, can consider the payment to the other funds as a share of the money collected rather than as an expenditure or transfer. Only a liability needs to be shown as an offset to the assets received. The receiving fund will consider the taxes as revenue when they receive them from the agency fund. The taxes received are assets and liabilities only when they are a part of the operations of the agency fund. The financial statement of the agency fund would be a statement of changes in assets and liabilities—not a balance sheet—and a statement of revenue, expenditures, and changes in fund balance.

### Payroll Tax Agency Fund—City of Ruthberg

The illustration in Chapter 6 included only wages and salaries for the general fund. Special revenue funds, such as a school board, often have withholdings for taxes as well as pensions. The capital projects fund, instead of contracting for buildings, roads, or other work done, often uses city employees for such work. Therefore, the capital projects fund can have paid employees, and, thus, withholdings. Records must be kept in those funds of the total wages and salaries and also of the amount withheld from each employee's earnings. The employee must receive a statement at the end of each year, not only of the total withholdings but the total wages or salary as well.

Using the general fund as an illustration, the withholding for taxes amounted to $91,500 during the year—$11,500 for state withholding and $80,000 for federal withholding. The law concerning federal and state withholdings must be followed in regard to payment of the liability—either payment to the governmental unit or deposits must be made in the bank to the account of the unit.

The entry in the agency fund to show the accrual for what is owed and the receipt of cash from the general fund for the taxes is:

|  |  | Dr. | Cr. |
|---|---|---|---|
| G1 | Due from general fund | $91,500 |  |
|  | Due to the state |  | $11,500 |
|  | Due to the federal government |  | 80,000 |
|  | To set up liability for withholding taxes. |  |  |
| G2 | Cash | $91,500 |  |
|  | Due from general fund |  | $91,500 |

Acting as an agent for the general fund, the agency fund also keeps a detailed record, usually in a subsidiary ledger, of the withholdings for the individual employees. At the end of the year, a statement can be provided to the employees for the amount withheld—state and federal—and the total withheld during the year.

The payment for the taxes is accounted for by the following entry:

| G3 | Due to the state | $11,500 |  |
|---|---|---|---|
|  | Due to the federal government | 80,000 |  |
|  | Cash |  | $91,500 |
|  | Payment of withholding taxes. |  |  |

The same type of entries and records would be made for other employee withholdings from other funds. The type of statement for this fund is shown in Exhibit 10-8.

## SUMMARY

Normal business accounting principles and practices are used for accounting and reporting for nonexpendable trust funds, except when specific legal requirements must be followed. Expendable trust funds follow the same basic principles and practice as illustrated for any expendable governmental fund.

Pension trust funds combine some of the accounting principles and practices of both governmental-type funds and proprietary-type funds. Eventually, all of the principal and income will be spent. However, to provide payments to all pensioners in the long

**EXHIBIT 10-8**
**City of Ruthberg**
**Payroll Tax Agency Fund**
**For Fiscal Year Ended June 30, 19X6**

| Assets | Balance July 1, 19X5 | Addition | Deduction | Balance June 30, 19X6 |
|---|---|---|---|---|
| Cash | — | 91,500 | 91,500 | — |

run, the fund must be actuarially sound at all times. This actuarial soundness is reflected in the records and the statements for each year.

Revenue sharing trust funds often are accounted for in a trust fund, in the general fund, in a special revenue fund, as an agency fund, or in an agency account in the general fund.

Agency funds are often used to provide for efficient operations of a special activity found in several funds, such as tax collecting, various types of withholding, and investments of excess revenues.

## QUESTIONS

1 Can a trust fund be both a profit fund and a not-for-profit fund? Explain.
2 Make a distinction between pension trust funds and regular trust funds.
3 Make a distinction between an agency fund and a trust fund.
4 What happens in a nonexpendable trust fund if the trust indenture does not allow accrual accounting?
5 What is a contributory-type pension trust fund?
6 Should a pension trust fund be actuarially sound? If so, how is actuarial soundness determined and accounted for?
7 What type of account is the reserve for employer contributions? Reserve for employee contributions? Reserve for retiree annuities?
8 In a pension trust fund, to which accounts do you close the income earned during a year?
9 Does the Revenue Sharing Act have an impact on the use of trust and agency funds?
10 State the purpose of a trust fund.
11 State the purpose of an agency fund.
12 What type of a trust fund results from gifts?
13 Is the question of accounting for pension trust funds for local governments fully settled at the present time?

## PROBLEMS

10-1 Circle the best answer for the following questions or statements.[8]

1 Transactions originating in a fund in which principal cannot be spent but that provides resources for another fund in which principal can be spent requires accounting recognition in:
  a The general fund
  b A debt service fund
  c An agency fund
  d An enterprise fund
  e None of the above

2 The monthly remittance to an insurance company of the lump sum of hospital-surgical insurance premiums collected as payroll deductions from employees should be recorded in:
  a The general fund
  b An agency fund
  c A special revenue fund
  d An internal service fund
  e None of the above

3 Activities of a central print shop offering printing service at a cost to various city departments should be accounted for in:

a The general fund
b An internal service fund
c A special revenue fund
d A special assessment fund
e An agency fund

4 Sanders County collects property taxes for the benefit of the state government and the local school districts, and the county periodically remits collections to these units. These activities should be accounted for in:
a An agency fund
b The general fund
c An internal service fund
d A special assessment fund

5 Transactions of a central purchasing and stores department organized to serve all municipal departments should be recorded in:
a An enterprise fund
b An internal service fund
c An agency fund
d The general fund
e An expendable trust fund

6 The activities of a municipal swimming pool that receives three-fourths of its total revenue from an endorsement created in the will of Harry Frazier should be accounted for in:
a An internal service fund
b The general fund
c A trust fund
d A special revenue fund
e None of the above

7 The transactions of a municipal police retirement system should be recorded in:
a The general fund
b A special revenue fund
c A trust fund
d An internal service fund

8 Activities supported by income from a trust fund are accounted for in what fund?
a An agency fund
b An enterprise fund
c An internal service fund
d A special revenue fund
e An expendable trust fund

**10-2** Circle the best answer for the following questions or statements.
1 Expendable trust funds are most comparable to:
a Internal service funds
b Enterprise funds
c Fixed asset account group
d Governmental funds

2 Nonexpendable trust funds are most comparable to:
a Internal service funds
b General funds
c Fixed asset account group
d Capital projects fund

3 Agency funds are most comparable to:

a Internal service funds
b General funds
c General fixed assets account group
d Capital projects funds
e None of the above

4 A pension trust fund takes on the characteristics of:
a Both a trust and an agency fund
b A general fund and a special revenue fund
c A capital projects and a debt service fund
d A general long-term debt account group and a fixed assets account group.

5 In fiduciary fund accounting, the basis of accounting is:
a Accrual accounting in an agency fund
b Accrual accounting in a nonexpendable trust fund
c Accrual accounting in an expendable trust fund
d Modified accrual accounting in a nonexpendable trust fund

6 Depreciation accounting is sometimes recognized in:
a A trust fund
b An agency fund
c A special revenue fund
d A capital projects fund

7 The cash basis of accounting is sometimes required in:
a A trust fund
b An agency fund
c A special revenue fund
d A capital projects fund

**10-3** A citizen, Henry Smith, contributed the following assets to a city to be used as a continuing memory of his relationship to the city. Prepare the journal entries to record these transactions.

| Assets | Cost | Fair market |
|---|---|---|
| Land | $ 75,000 | $145,000 |
| Building | 1,500,000 | 900,000 |
| Allowance for depreciation | 750,000 | |
| Cash | 10,000 | 10,000 |
| Stocks: | | |
| Henry Smith Company—1,000 common shares at $90 par | 90,000 | 150,000 |

**10-4** The city of Richlands uses an agency fund to account for payroll withholdings and taxes related to payroll withholdings. The following table identifies each of these taxes.

City of Richlands
Taxes—Withholdings

| Fund | Payroll | State income | Federal income | Employee | F.I.C.A. employer |
|---|---|---|---|---|---|
| General | $4,500,000 | $135,000 | $ 810,000 | $270,000 | $270,000 |
| Special revenue | 1,800,000 | 54,000 | 324,000 | 108,000 | 108,000 |
| Capital projects | 700,000 | 21,000 | 126,000 | 42,000 | 42,000 |
| Total | $7,000,000 | $210,000 | $1,260,000 | $420,000 | $420,000 |

**Required**:

Prepare the necessary entries for each of the funds involved.

**10-5** Prepare the journal entries for the following transactions of the town of Glen Burnie's retirement fund.

    **1** Contributions of $60,000 came from the general fund and of $30,000 from the capital projects fund. Contributions were evenly divided between employer and employee.

    **2** The amounts were paid by the respective funds.

    **3** During the year, the town incurred a liability of $18,000 to estates for workers who had died and a liability of $4,300 to people who had acquired new jobs.

    **4** The annuities payable at year end were paid in the amount of $8,000.

    **5** For employees retiring during the year, the expected benefits to be taken from the fund are $40,000, split evenly between employer and employee contributions.

    **6** A liability for annuities paid during the year is $50,000. All were paid.

    **7** Close the temporary accounts.

**10-6** The city of Tampa's pension fund conducted the following activities. Prepare the journal entries required to record the transactions.

    **1** The fund purchased $40,000 par value securities for $41,000.

    **2** More securities were acquired for $22,500, including a premium of $450 and accrued interest of $50.

    **3** Interest was received in the amount of $1,050.

    **4** Premiums were amortized at year's end in the amount of $145.

    **5** Interest receivable at year's end amounted to $750.

**10-7** John Williams died and left the city $500,000. The city received the money on July 1, 19X0 and immediately invested the money in $300,000 worth of 14 percent Johnson Company bonds and $200,000 worth of 12 percent Excelsior Company bonds. Both bonds pay interest on July 2 and January 2 of each year. The bonds were purchased immediately after the semiannual interest had been paid, so there was no accrued interest. In addition, the bonds were purchased at par.

The cash received from the investments is to be used for improving recreation, especially in the inner city. The city determined that it would have no income from the gift that could be appropriated during fiscal 19X1 but would have $70,000 to be appropriated during fiscal year 19X2.

**Required:**

Prepare journal entries, including closing entries, for transactions in each of the funds involved in this situation for the fiscal years 19X1 and 19X2.

**10-8** The city of New Arnheim has engaged you to examine the following balance sheet, which was prepared by the city's bookkeeper.[9]

**City of New Arnheim**
**Balance Sheet**
**June 30, 19X9**

**Assets**

| | |
|---|---:|
| Cash | $ 159,000 |
| Taxes receivable—current | 32,000 |
| Supplies on hand | 9,000 |
| Marketable securities | 250,000 |
| Land | 1,000,000 |
| Fixed assets | 7,000,000 |
|     Total | $8,450,000 |

|  | Liabilities | |
|---|---|---|
| Accounts payable | | $ 42,000 |
| Reserve for supplies inventory | | 8,000 |
| Bonds payable | | 3,000,000 |
| Fund balance | | 5,400,000 |
| Total | | $8,450,000 |

Your audit disclosed the following information:

**1** An analysis of the fund balance account:

| | | |
|---|---|---|
| Balance, June 30, 19X8 | | $2,100,000 |
| Add: | | |
|   Donated land | $ 800,000 | |
|   Federal grant-in-aid | 2,200,000 | |
|   Creation of endowment fund | 250,000 | |
|   Excess of actual tax revenue over estimated revenue | 24,000 | |
|   Excess of appropriations closed out over expenditures and encumbrances | 20,000 | |
|   Net income from endowment funds | 10,000 | 3,304,000 |
| | | 5,404,000 |
| Deduct: | | |
|   Excess of cultural center operating expenses over income | | 4,000 |
| Balance, June 30, 19X9 | | $5,400,000 |

**2** In July 19X8, land appraised at a fair market value of $800,000 was donated to the city for a cultural center that was opened on April 15, 19X9. Building construction expenditures for the project were financed from a federal grant-in-aid of $2,200,000 and from an authorized ten-year $3,000,000 issue of 6 percent general obligation bonds sold at par on July 1, 19X8. Interest is payable on December 31 and June 30. The fair market value of the land and the cost of the building are included respectively in the land and fixed assets accounts.

**3** The cultural center receives no direct state or city subsidy for current operating expenses. A cultural center endowment fund was established by a gift of marketable securities having a fair market value of $250,000 at date of receipt. The endowment principal is to be kept intact. Income is to be applied to any operating deficit of the center.

**4** Other data:

  **a** It is anticipated that $7,000 of the 19X8–X9 tax levy is uncollectible.

  **b** The physical inventory of supplies on hand at June 30, 19X9 amounted to $12,500.

  **c** Unfilled purchase orders for the general fund at June 30, 19X9 totaled $5,000.

  **d** On July 1, 19X8, an all-purpose building was purchased for $2,000,000. Of the purchase price, $200,000 was allotted to the land. The purchase had been authorized under the budget for the year ended June 30, 19X9.

**Required:**

Prepare a worksheet to record the transactions as they relate to the general fund and the endowment fund. Number the adjusting entries. Prepare appropriate financial statements for each of the funds as of June 30, 19X9.

**10-9** This problem continues the case of Silver City, which has been discussed in preceding chapters, and it concerns the Silver City Trust Fund.

   **1** The city received $200,000 from a wealthy citizen for a trust fund under terms that required the contribution to be invested and the revenue to be used to finance cultural events in the city.
   **2** The cash was invested.
   **3** Interest income amounting to $10,000 was received.
   **4** Expenditures for cultural events paid from the income amounted to $9,000.

**Required:**
   **1** Prepare the journal entries needed to record the transactions for the year in the proper fund or funds.
   **2** Post the entries to a worksheet or worksheets from which the statements can be prepared.
   **3** Prepare the statements.

# NOTES

**1** National Council on Governmental Accounting, *Statement 1. Governmental Accounting and Financial Reporting Principles* (Chicago: Municipal Finance Officers Association of the United States and Canada, 1979), p. 7.
**2** National Council on Governmental Accounting, *Statement 6. Pension Accounting and Financial Reporting: Public Employee Retirement Systems and State and Local Government Employers* (Chicago: Municipal Finance Officers Association of the United States and Canada, 1983), p. 1. Also see NCGA, *Interpretation 8* (Chicago: National Council on Governmental Accounting, 1982).
**3** NCGA, *Statement 6*, p. 2. Also see NCGA, *Interpretation 8*, p. 2.
**4** State and Local Fiscal Assistance Act of 1972, *U.S. Statutes at Large, Volume 86, Public Law 92-512* (Washington, D. C.: U.S. Government Printing Office, 1972), pp. 919–947.
**5** Ibid.
**6** National Council on Governmental Accounting, *Statement 2. Grant, Entitlement, and Shared Revenue Accounting and Reporting by State and Local Governments* (Chicago: Municipal Finance Officers Association of the United States and Canada, 1979), p. 2.
**7** Ibid., p. 2.
**8** Adapted from American Institute of Certified Public Accountants, *Uniform CPA Examination Questions and Unofficial Answers* (New York: American Institute of Certified Public Accountants, various dates).
**9** Ibid., Nov. 1966.

# CHAPTER 11

# GENERAL FIXED ASSETS AND GENERAL LONG-TERM DEBT

This chapter discusses accounting for two types of entities not concerned with fiscal transactions. These entities are concerned only with the record keeping of the fixed assets and long-term debt of the governmental unit as a whole. Remember that in the proprietary funds—enterprise and internal service funds—fixed assets purchased and long-term debt incurred become assets and liabilities of those entities. They are not a part of the long-term assets and debts of the governmental unit as a whole. In governmental funds—the general and special revenue funds, the capital projects funds, and the special assessment funds—all of the purchases or construction of long-term assets are recorded as expenditures and not shown as fixed assets in those funds. And, in the capital projects fund, all of the receipts from long-term debt are shown as proceeds and not recorded as long-term debts in that fund. In the special assessment fund, on the other hand, the long-term debt is recorded in that fund. In order to have a record of the fixed assets and long-term debt of governmental funds, other than the long-term debt of special assessment funds, a record must be kept of those items in an account group outside of the fund in which the original transaction took place. The purpose of the account groups, then, is to keep a record of the fixed assets and long-term debt that are not accounted for in a particular fund.

Concerning the relationship between funds and account groups, the National Council on Governmental Accounting states:

> General fixed assets do not represent financial resources available for expenditure, but are items for which financial resources have been used and for which accountability should be maintained. They are not assets of any fund but of the governmental unit as an instrumentality. Their inclusion in the financial statements of a governmental fund would increase the fund balance, which could mislead users of the fund balance sheet.[1]

Long-term liabilities are classified in the general long-term debt account group as: term bonds, serial bonds, long-term notes, and other general long-term commitments. Since no asset accounts are shown in the general long-term debt account groups, offset accounts to the long-term liability accounts—the debits to the long-term liability credits—are the following: (1) accounts that show the amounts in the debt service funds that are currently available for the payment of debt principal and (2) accounts that show the amounts that must be provided in future years for payment of debt principal.

*Fixed assets* in the general fixed assets account group are classified as: land, buildings, improvements other than buildings (e.g., streets, sidewalks, tunnels, etc.), capital equipment (e.g., desks, typewriters, office copiers, automobiles, trucks, earth-moving equipment, etc.), and construction in progress (e.g., uncompleted projects in the capital projects fund at the end of the fiscal year). And, since no liability or capital accounts are shown in the general fixed asset account group, the offset accounts to the general fixed assets accounts—the credits to the asset debits—are those accounts that show the investment in general fixed assets by revenue source and not by fund.

## ACCOUNTING CONTROL THROUGH THE USE OF ACCOUNT GROUPS

Unless some form of record is kept of them, a governmental unit could permanently lose some of its long-term assets. Employees or others could remove them from the possession of the government and possibly could use them for personal purposes. Without this record, the governmental unit would have no way of knowing whether the assets had been misplaced or stolen. In addition, without this record, the government would not have information from which it could determine costs for planning purposes. Protecting the government from loss, theft, or improper use of the fixed assets is one of the major purposes of the general fixed assets account group. This chapter shows the use of information from the fixed assets records only for ownership information and financial reporting. Later chapters will discuss the use of information from the fixed asset records for management planning and decision making.

General long-term debt records are maintained for two general purposes:

**1** Accurate record keeping. This includes the maintenance of records of the identity, purpose, and amount of all long-term debts, including the principal and interest payments made. This information is needed for the short-term fiscal operations of government.

**2** Financial planning. Principal and interest requirements must be available (a) to determine the financial capacity to meet future capital construction requirements, and (b) to plan the retirement schedule for any new borrowing.

### Fixed Asset Control

Subsidiary records are kept on each individual asset, in addition to the control account for each general ledger classification. Key information concerning these individual assets is kept, and an inventory is taken periodically of those assets to make sure that they are still the possession of the governmental unit and are being used for the intended purposes. Lost, discarded, junked, or sold assets are removed from the records by reversing the entry originally made (see pages 289 and 290 for illustrations).

## Long-Term Debt Control

Comparable to the records kept in the general and subsidiary ledgers for the fixed assets, long-term debt can be controlled best through the use of a subsidiary ledger, such as a *bond and interest register*, in addition to the general ledger. Being a special journal and a subsidiary ledger, entries are made in the bond and interest ledger that allow management to trace the complete history of each bond issue. The register collects in one place all pertinent information regarding individual bond issues, assists in establishing a schedule of debt service requirements, and collects information for posting to the general ledger, bonded debt ledger, and interest payable ledger.

A subsidiary *bonded debt ledger* contains a sheet for each bond issue, showing the amount of bonds originally outstanding, the amount retired to date, and the balance outstanding. In an *interest payable ledger*, a separate sheet is maintained for the interest payable on each bond issue. As interest payments come due, they are entered in the "credit" and "balance" columns; as payments are made, the amount is entered in the "debit" column, and the balance payable is reduced by a corresponding sum.

Bonds and interest paid from general revenue sources must be kept separate from bonds and interest paid from special assessment and proprietary fund revenue sources. The record of the amount of unmatured bonded debt payable from general revenues is carried in a separate self-balancing group of accounts independent of any municipal funds. *General obligation bonds* are totally dependent on each year's revenue collections, even though funds are collected in the debt service funds through transfers from the general fund, for current payment of interest, current payment of serial bonds, and eventual payment of term bonds.

## SPECIAL ACCOUNTING CONSIDERATIONS FOR ACCOUNT GROUPS

When fixed assets are purchased or constructed by a governmental fund, the fund acquiring those assets records them as an expenditure—as an expenditure against either: (1) the current year's appropriations, (2) a prior year's encumbered appropriation, or (3) a legal proposition that is comparable to an appropriation. The cash or liability transaction concerned with the buying or selling of the asset is not recorded in the general fixed asset account group. This transaction is only recorded in the fund acquiring the fixed asset or receiving any revenue from the sale or disposition of the fixed asset. The general fixed assets account group only keeps a record of the asset; no funds flow through the account group.

The same type of accounting consideration holds for long-term debt as for long-term assets—no buying or selling is recorded in the account group. Yet, when other funds acquire resources for retirement of the bonds, this type of transaction is considered in the account group in order to show the amounts that need to be provided and the amounts available for the payment of the bonds.

## Principles of Accounting for Fixed Assets

In the general fixed assets account group, all fixed assets purchased, constructed, or obtained by contract are recorded *at cost*. Fixed assets obtained by gift are recorded at the fair market value when donated. Assets obtained through foreclosure are recorded in the account group at the lower of the appraised value of the property and the total taxes or assessments plus costs.

Depreciation is not recorded in the general fixed assets account group for external reporting purposes. However, depreciation should be recorded in supplemental records for internal costing purposes. Concerning depreciation in the accounts, the NCGA says:

> The recommendation that depreciation not be recorded in the governmental fund accounts neither denies its existence nor precludes calculating depreciation to determine total and/or unit costs (expenses) of all or certain governmental activities and/or programs. The Council encourages use of cost accounting systems or cost finding analyses for such activities—e.g., vehicle operation, garbage collection, and data processing services—either routinely, in the process of "make or buy" or "do or contract for" decision analyses, or for such purposes as determining reimbursable costs under grant provisions, establishing fee schedules, or analyzing activity or program cost. Maintaining governmental fund and account group records in the manner recommended facilitates such calculations.
>
> Recording accumulated depreciation in the General Fixed Assets Account Group is optional. When it is recorded, the entry should increase the Accumulated Depreciation account(s) and decrease the Investment in General Fixed Assets account(s).[2]

The subject of depreciation of fixed assets for cost and management accounting purposes will be discussed in further detail in Parts III and IV, Chapters 17 through 21. Depreciation for management purposes should be kept separate from the normal records for financial reporting purposes so that it will not be shown in the financial statements for external users.

A fully developed, double-entry accounting system for the general fixed assets account group, then, needs only to have an equity-type balancing account to be credited when the asset account is debited. To illustrate, when a truck is purchased in the general fund for $7,500, the entry in that fund is:

|  | Dr. | Cr. |
|---|---|---|
| Expenditures | $7,500 | |
|     Cash (or accounts payable) | | $7,500 |

The entry in the general fixed assets account group is:

| | | |
|---|---|---|
| Equipment | $7,500 | |
|     Investment in fixed assets— | | |
|         general fund revenues | | $7,500 |

The credit balance account, *investment in fixed assets—general fund revenue*, is an equity type account that describes the source of the funding for the fixed asset rather than describing the fund from which the asset came. It is the credit account for the debit to the asset. Funding sources other than from general fund revenues are gifts, grants, general obligation bonds, and special assessments. Each of these funding sources is added to the title, "investment in fixed assets."

Assets sold, destroyed, or otherwise becoming valueless are removed from the account group by reversing the above entry—that is, debit the investment in fixed assets account for the original amount recorded and credit the particular fixed asset. Additional improvements to the asset require an entry comparable to the original entry, but only for the amount of the improvement. General repairs, to keep the asset in the same operating condition, are not considered as improvements and should not be added to the value of the fixed asset in the account group.

### Principles of Accounting for Long-Term Debt

Long-term debt consists of both serial and term bonds, long-term notes, and other long-term liabilities. In addition to recording long-term liabilities from debt issuance in the long-term debt account group, such debt as long-term commitments arising from lease or purchase agreements should also be recorded in this account group. All governmental funds, except special assessment funds, use the long-term debt account group to keep a record of the long-term debt for those funds. The special assessment funds keep their own records of their long-term debt. Proprietary and profit-type fiduciary funds also keep their own records of their long-term debt. Short-term debt of one year or less, on the other hand, is kept in each of the various funds—governmental, proprietary, and fiduciary—and not in the general long-term debt account group.

Material vested amounts that may arise from such items as vacation and sick leave of employees that would extend longer than that normally considered as a current liability are also long-term liabilities. While not arising from debt issuance and not recorded in the general long-term debt account group, these liabilities should be disclosed in the footnotes to the financial statements.[3] In addition, certain other contingent liabilities such as those not requiring accrual and arising from long-term debt in funds other than those that record these long-term liabilities in the long-term debt account group, should be disclosed in the notes to the financial statements.[4]

### ILLUSTRATIONS OF GENERAL FIXED ASSETS ACCOUNT GROUP ACCOUNTING

The transactions concerning the acquisition of fixed assets, described in the preceding chapters on the general and special revenue funds, the capital projects funds, and the special assessment funds, are used to illustrate the entries found in the general fixed assets account group. Certain transactions in governmental-type fiduciary funds will also be assumed. The balances in the general fixed assets account group, as of June 30, 19X5, are:

## CHAPTER 11: GENERAL FIXED ASSETS AND GENERAL LONG-TERM DEBT

**City of Ruthberg**
**Trial Balance**
**General Fixed Assets Account Group**
**June 30, 19X5**

| Account | Dr. | Cr. |
|---|---|---|
| Land | $ 200,000 | |
| Buildings | 2,250,000 | |
| Improvements other than buildings | 1,300,000 | |
| Equipment | 950,000 | |
| Construction in progress | — | |
| Investments in general fixed assets: | | |
|   General fund revenues | | $ 800,000 |
|   General obligation bonds | | 1,150,000 |
|   Federal grants | | 1,250,000 |
|   State grants | | 900,000 |
|   Special assessments: | | |
|     Taxpayer assessments | | 450,000 |
|     City's share | | 75,000 |
|   Gifts | | 75,000 |
| | $4,700,000 | $4,700,000 |

These balances (B) are entered on our illustrative worksheet (see Exhibit 11-1).

## Illustrative Transactions from the General Fund

Chapter 6, on accounting for expenditures in the general and special revenue funds, shows the total expenditures for capital outlays for the fiscal year from the city's general fund appropriations were:

| | | |
|---|---|---|
| General government: | | |
|   Land | $40,000 | |
|   Equipment | 20,000 | $ 60,000 |
| Education: | | |
|   Equipment | | 20,000 |
| Public works: | | |
|   Equipment | | 19,000 |
| Public safety: | | |
|   Land | 2,000 | |
|   Equipment | 3,500 | |
|   Improvements other than buildings | 5,000 | 10,500 |
| Health and welfare: | | |
|   Land | 10,000 | |
|   Equipment | 27,000 | 37,000 |
| Total expenditures for capital outlay | | $146,500 |

The entry in the general fund to record these expenditures, as shown in Chapter 6, entry E13, was as follows:

| | Dr. | Cr. |
|---|---|---|
| **E13** Expenditures | $146,500 | |
|     Accounts payable | | $146,500 |

The entry to record these expenditures from the general fund for capital outlays in the general fixed assets account group is:

|  |  | Dr. | Cr. |
|---|---|---|---|
| F1 | Land | $52,000 | |
| | Improvements other than buildings | 5,000 | |
| | Equipment | 89,500 | |
| | Investments in fixed assets— general fund revenues | | $146,000 |

To record investments in fixed assets by the various functions in the general fund.

The city must keep individual fixed asset subsidiary records by functions and departments, as well as by type of asset. When the time comes for inventorying the assets, the exact location of the asset must be known, as must be the particular type, model, description, and other characteristics of the asset.

Fixed asset transactions of the general fund, as discussed in Chapter 6 under the heading "Prior Year Transactions," included an amount for a truck for the year ended June 30, 19X5 in the reserve for encumbrances account. The truck had been ordered at the end of the year and encumbered for $12,000 against last year's appropriation. The entry for the payment for this truck in the current fiscal year, as shown in Chapter 6, entry B7, was:

| B7 | Expenditures against 19X5 reserve for encumbrances | $12,000 | |
|---|---|---|---|
| | Accounts payable | | $12,000 |

This was only a part of the total entry for the amount of $42,000 spent from last year's appropriation and included in the reserve for encumbrances—19X5 account.

The entry to record this equipment purchase in the general fixed assets account group would be:

| F2 | Equipment | $12,000 | |
|---|---|---|---|
| | Investments in fixed assets— general fund revenues | | $12,000 |

Notice that no fixed asset is recorded in the account group until either cash is paid or an accrual for a liability is recorded. Thus no entry is made in the general fixed assets account group when a possible expenditure is denoted through an encumbrance entry.

These entries from the transactions in the general fund are posted to the worksheet in Exhibit 11-1.

## Illustrative Transactions from the Capital Projects Fund

**First-Year Transactions** Entries from the capital projects fund (see Chapter 7) are somewhat different from those in the general fund because of the sources of revenue used to obtain the assets. Since procurement of assets in the capital projects fund extends beyond one year, both years are shown in transaction form, although only one year is posted to the worksheet.

It may be remembered that the sources of funds used to procure the fixed assets in the capital projects fund came from the federal government, from the state, and from the proceeds of a bond issue. The fixed assets obtained from these resources must be divided proportionally among these investment sources. Therefore, the account "investment in fixed assets" for each of these amounts would be credited with its proportionate share. For example, the entry for the buying of land in the capital projects fund was as follows:

| | | | |
|---|---|---|---|
| P4 | Expenditures | $125,000 | |
| | Accounts payable | | $75,000 |
| | Judgments payable | | 50,000 |

The accounts payable and the judgment payable would be paid from the cash obtained from the three sources: the state, the federal government, and the proceeds from the sale of the bonds. The entry to record this transaction in the fixed assets account group would be:

| | | | |
|---|---|---|---|
| F3 | Land | $125,000 | |
| | Investments in fixed assets: | | |
| | State grants | | $16,667 |
| | Federal grants | | 41,667 |
| | General obligation bonds | | 66,666 |

To record purchase of land by the capital projects fund proportionately from the following:

| | | | |
|---|---|---|---|
| State grants | $ 200,000 | 2/15 | $ 16,667 |
| Federal grants | 500,000 | 5/15 | 41,667 |
| General obligation bonds | 800,000 | 8/15 | 66,666 |
| Total | $1,500,000 | 15/15 | $125,000 |

Payments of $800,000 for construction in progress were made from the capital projects fund during the fiscal year 19X6. These payments were accumulated into one entry in that fund. The entry was:

| | | | |
|---|---|---|---|
| P9 | Expenditures | $800,000 | |
| | Accounts payable | | $800,000 |

The work has not been completed; therefore, the asset is shown as "construction in progress" in the records of the fixed assets account group. The entry to record this transaction in this account group would be:

| | | | |
|---|---|---|---|
| F4 | Construction in progress | $800,000 | |
| | Investments in fixed assets: | | |
| | General obligation bonds | | $426,666 |
| | State grants | | 106,667 |
| | Federal grants | | 266,667 |

To record payments for construction work in progress in the capital projects fund in the following proportions:

| | | | |
|---|---|---|---|
| State grants | $ 200,000 | 2/15 | $106,667 |
| Federal grants | 500,000 | 5/15 | 266,667 |
| General obligation bonds | 800,000 | 8/15 | 426,666 |
| Total | $1,500,000 | 15/15 | $800,000 |

In order to record these accounts in a ledger, the above transactions have been posted to the worksheet in Exhibit 11-1.

**Second-Year Transactions** Only two transactions in the capital projects fund that have a major effect on the accounts in the general fixed assets account group occur during the second year:

1 Improvements to the land at a cost of $60,000.
2 Completion of the building, including:
 a Elimination of the construction in progress, and
 b Capitalization of the completed building.

The entry in the capital projects fund to record the amount incurred for the improvements to the land given in entry P2-7 in Chapter 7 was:

| | | | |
|---|---|---|---|
| P2-7 | Expenditures | $60,000 | |
| | Due to general fund | | $60,000 |

Since the money obtained for the payment of this debt has come from several sources, the investment in the fixed asset is distributed proportionally to those sources. The entry is:

| | | | |
|---|---|---|---|
| F2-1 | Land | $60,000 | |
| | Investment in fixed assets: | | |
| |   General obligation bonds | | $32,000 |
| |   Federal grants | | 20,000 |
| |   State grants | | 8,000 |

To record payment for land in the following proportions:

| | | | |
|---|---|---|---|
| General obligation bonds | $ 800,000 | 8/15 | $32,000 |
| Federal grants | 500,000 | 5/15 | 20,000 |
| State grants | 200,000 | 2/15 | 8,000 |
| Total | $1,500,000 | 15/15 | $60,000 |

When the contractor completed the construction of the building, the combined entries to record these transactions would be:

| | | | |
|---|---|---|---|
| P2-4 | Expenditures | $450,000 | |
| P2-6 | Accounts payable | | $400,000 |
| | Retained percentage—contract payable | | 50,000 |

With the $800,000 that had been considered construction in progress at the end of the preceding year and the amounts expended during this year, the total cost of the building is $1,250,000. The entry to record this information in the general fixed assets account group is:

| | | | |
|---|---|---|---|
| F2-2 | Buildings | $1,250,000 | |
| | Construction in progress | | $800,000 |
| | Investment in fixed assets: | | |
| |    General obligation bonds | | 240,000 |
| |    State grants | | 60,000 |
| |    Federal grants | | 150,000 |

To record construction costs of building during this year as well as to transfer cost of construction in progress upon completion of building.

Since all of the transactions concerning fixed assets for all funds are not shown for the second year, no entries for the second year are shown on the worksheet.

### Illustrative Transactions from the Special Assessment Fund

Fixed assets of special assessment funds are recorded only in the general fixed assets account group, although special assessment fund long-term liabilities are recorded in special assessment funds. The fixed assets are not recorded in the special assessment funds because, for all practical purposes, those assets become the property of the local government. We will use the transactions in Chapter 9 to illustrate the accounting for fixed assets of special assessment funds in the general fixed assets accounts group.

The money to pay for the $700,000 worth of improvements in the special assessment fund came from three sources: (1) assessments of $325,000 on the residents who receive direct benefits from the improvements, (2) payment by the state of $175,000, and (3) payment by the federal government of $200,000. The city also may make payments to special assessment funds and, if so, the city would be included as a source of fixed assets.

These fixed assets include such items as sidewalks, lighting, and street improvements; as such, they are improvements other than buildings. The entry in the general fixed assets account group is:

| | | | |
|---|---|---|---|
| F5 | Improvements other than buildings | $700,000 | |
| | Investment in fixed assets: | | |
| |    Taxpayer assessments | | $325,000 |
| |    Federal grants | | 200,000 |
| |    State grants | | 175,000 |

To record improvements for special assessment funds proportionally to amounts paid from fund.

### Removal of Assets from the General Fixed Assets Account Group

Assets are removed from the account group when sold, abandoned or worn out, or discarded. For example, assume a truck in the equipment account was purchased for

$6,000 and sold for $750. The entry for the receipt of this amount was recorded in the general fund in the miscellaneous revenue account as follows:

| R8 | Cash | $750 | |
|---|---|---|---|
| | Revenues | | $750 |

To record receipt of cash for truck sold.

The entry in the general fixed assets account group to remove this truck is:

| F6 | Investment in fixed assets— general fund revenues | $6,000 | |
|---|---|---|---|
| | Equipment | | $6,000 |

To remove fixed asset as a result of the sale of the asset.

## Worksheet for the General Fixed Assets Account Group

Exhibit 11-1 summarizes all of the transactions for the general fixed assets account group, from which the balance sheet can be prepared.

## DEPRECIATION IN THE GENERAL FIXED ASSETS ACCOUNT GROUP

In general, depreciation is not recorded in governmental funds. The purchase of an asset is recorded in these funds as an expenditure, and the asset is recorded in the general fixed assets account group. However, when calculating unit costs for the purpose of determining operating costs, depreciation can be determined and shown in the fixed assets account group. When calculated and shown in the fixed assets account group, the credit entry would be to an accumulated depreciation account and the debit entry for the depreciation would be to the investment in general fixed assets accounts. If depreciation accounting is used, the net fixed assets and investment in general fixed assets can be shown in the financial statements. The use of cost accounting—hence the need for knowing the amount of depreciation expense rather than capital expenditures—is discussed more fully in Chapters 17 through 21.

## STATEMENTS AND SCHEDULES FOR THE GENERAL FIXED ASSETS ACCOUNT GROUP

No funds flow in the general fixed assets account group; therefore, the only statement needed is a balance sheet. A detailed schedule of the assets is also provided.

A complete picture of the assets of the governmental unit as a whole is shown in the combined balance sheet of all funds and account groups. This statement shows the amounts, normally found in the balance sheet, relative to the assets and investments in fixed assets (see illustrative combined balance sheet, Exhibit 13-2).

### Balance Sheet and General Fixed Assets Schedules

All of the transactions for fixed assets during the year concern the recording or removal of fixed assets from the general fixed assets account group. Therefore, the only

EXHIBIT 11-1
City of Ruthberg
General Fixed Assets
Transactions 19X6

| Accounts | Balance June 30, 19X5 Dr. | | Cr. | No. | Transactions 19X6 Dr. | No. | Cr. | Balance June 30, 19X6 Dr. | Cr. |
|---|---|---|---|---|---|---|---|---|---|
| Land | B | $ 200,000 | | F1 | $ 52,000 | | | $ 377,000 | |
| | | | | F3 | 125,000 | | | | |
| Buildings | B | 2,250,000 | | F1 | 5,000 | | | 2,250,000 | |
| Improvements other than buildings | B | 1,300,000 | | F5 | 700,000 | | | 2,005,000 | |
| Equipment | B | 950,000 | | F2 | 12,000 | F6 | $ 6,000 | 1,045,500 | |
| | | | | F1 | 89,500 | | | | |
| Construction in progress | | | | F4 | 800,000 | | | 800,000 | |
| Investment in general fixed assets: | | | | | | | | | |
| General fund revenues | B | | $ 800,000 | F6 | 6,000 | F1 | 146,500 | | $ 952,500 |
| | | | | | | F2 | 12,000 | | |
| General obligation bonds | B | | 1,150,000 | | | F3 | 66,666 | | 1,643,332 |
| | | | | | | F4 | 426,666 | | |
| Federal grants | B | | 1,250,000 | | | F3 | 41,667 | | 1,758,334 |
| | | | | | | F4 | 266,667 | | |
| | | | | | | F5 | 200,000 | | |
| State grants | B | | 900,000 | | | F3 | 16,667 | | 1,198,334 |
| | | | | | | F4 | 106,667 | | |
| | | | | | | F5 | 175,000 | | |
| Special assessments: | | | | | | | | | |
| Taxpayer assessments | B | | 450,000 | | | F5 | 325,000 | | 775,000 |
| City's share | B | | 75,000 | | | | | | 75,000 |
| Gifts | B | | 75,000 | | | | | | 75,000 |
| | | $4,700,000 | $4,700,000 | | $1,789,500 | | $1,789,500 | $6,477,500 | $6,477,500 |

## EXHIBIT 11-2
### City of Ruthberg
### Balance Sheet—General Fixed Assets
### June 30, 19X6

| | |
|---|---:|
| General fixed assets | |
| Land | $ 377,000 |
| Buildings | 2,250,000 |
| Improvements other than buildings | 2,055,000 |
| Equipment | 1,045,500 |
| Construction in progress | 800,000 |
| Total | $6,527,500 |
| Sources of investments in general fixed assets | |
| General fund revenues | $ 952,500 |
| General obligation bonds | 1,323,331 |
| Federal grants | 1,968,334 |
| State grants | 1,333,335 |
| Special assessments: | |
|   Taxpayer assessments | 800,000 |
|   City's share | 75,000 |
| Gifts | 75,000 |
| Total | $6,527,500 |

statement needed is that concerning the amount of the fixed assets and the corresponding investments in fixed assets. A schedule of changes in fixed assets may also be given. The balance sheet reflects the total of all the assets at the balance sheet date. In addition, assets schedules are also made by department, by functions, or by activities, including a schedule showing the changes in the fixed assets for the year (see Exhibits 11-2 and 11-3).

## EXHIBIT 11-3
### City of Ruthberg
### Statement of Changes in General Fixed Assets
### For Fiscal Year Ended June 30, 19X6
### Additions from Revenue Source

| Accounts | Beginning balance | General fund revenues | General obligation bonds |
|---|---:|---:|---:|
| General fixed assets: | | | |
| Land | $ 200,000 | $ 52,000 | $ 66,666 |
| Buildings | 2,250,000 | | |
| Improvements other than buildings | 1,300,000 | 5,000 | |
| Equipment | 950,000 | 101,500 | |
| | | (6,000) | |
| Construction in progress | | | 426,666 |
| Totals | $4,700,000 | $152,500 | $493,332 |

## ILLUSTRATIONS OF GENERAL LONG-TERM DEBT ACCOUNT GROUP ACCOUNTING

Chapter 8, which discusses debt service funds, shows that the long-term debt owed by the city of Ruthberg as of July 1, 19X5 consisted of the following general obligation bonds:

1 Serial bonds:

| Original issue | Paid | Balance 7/1/X5 | Rate | Terms |
|---|---|---|---|---|
| $800,000 | $400,000 | $400,000 | 6 percent | 20 years |

2 Term bonds:

| Original issue | Balance in sinking fund | Rate | Terms |
|---|---|---|---|
| $750,000 | $149,121.75 | 9 percent | 20 years |

These balances are shown in Exhibits 11-4 and 11-5 for the general long-term debt account group. As discussed earlier, the asset-type accounts used as the contra to the bonds payable account are: "amount to be provided" and "amount available" for payment of the bonds. The amounts that go into these accounts come from the debt service funds.

During the current year, the capital projects fund issued $800,000 worth of term bonds with an interest rate of 5 percent for a period of twenty years. This information is to be recorded during this year (see entry L3).

### Serial Bond Accounting

Serial bonds worth $400,000 were still outstanding on July 1, 19X5, and $40,000 worth of the bonds were paid during the year (see entries D3, D4, and D5 in Chapter

**EXHIBIT 11-3**
*(continued)*

| | | Special assessments | | | |
|---|---|---|---|---|---|
| Federal government | State government | Taxpayer assessments | City's share | Gifts | Ending balance |
| $ 41,667 | $ 16,667 | | | | $ 377,000 |
| | | | | | 2,250,000 |
| 200,000 | 175,000 | $325,000 | | | 2,005,000 |
| | | | | | 1,045,500 |
| 266,667 | 106,667 | | | | 800,000 |
| $508,334 | $298,334 | $325,000 | | | $6,477,500 |

**EXHIBIT 11-4**
**City of Ruthberg**
**General Long-term Debt**
**July 1, 19X5**

| | |
|---|---:|
| Amount to be provided for payment of serial bonds | $ 400,000.00 |
| Amount available for payment of term bonds | 149,121.75 |
| Amount to be provided for payment of term bonds | 600,878.25 |
| Total | $1,150,000.00 |
| General obligation bonds payable: | |
|   Serial bonds | $ 400,000.00 |
|   Term bonds | 750,000.00 |
| | $1,150,000.00 |

8). The amount shown as balances for the serial bonds in the worksheet (see Exhibit 11-6) is:

| | | Dr. | Cr. |
|---|---|---|---|
| B | Amount to be provided for payment of serial bonds | $400,000 | |
| |   Bonds payable—serial | | $400,000 |

The entry to record the transactions for this year's payment (also shown in Exhibit 11-6) is:

| | | Dr. | Cr. |
|---|---|---|---|
| L1 | Bonds payable—serial | $40,000 | |
| |   Amount to be provided for payment of serial bonds | | $40,000 |
| | To record the transaction for this year's payment. | | |

A subsidiary ledger containing a detailed record of the serial bonds outstanding would continue to be kept in order to know exactly those redeemed and those still outstanding.

The balances in the accounts at the end of the year are:

| | Dr. | Cr. |
|---|---|---|
| Amount to be provided for payment of serial bonds | $360,000 | |
|   Bonds payable—serial | | $360,000 |

Notice that the account "amount to be provided for payment of serial bonds" offsets the bonds payable account in order to have a balancing set of records.

The only amounts provided for payment of serial bonds would be the current amount available to pay the debt, as reflected in the debt service fund. Since no current liabilities are shown in the account groups, there would be no reason for an entry in the accounts for this type of transaction.

CHAPTER 11: GENERAL FIXED ASSETS AND GENERAL LONG-TERM DEBT   295

**EXHIBIT 11-5**
**City of Ruthberg**
**Schedule of Principal and Interest Payments**
**For Year 19X6**

| Bond type | Balance | Principal payment | Interest payment | Total payment |
|---|---|---|---|---|
| Serial bonds—20 yrs., June 30, 19X5: 6% $800,000 paid $400,000 | $400,000 | $40,000.00 | $24,000 | $ 64,000.00 |
| Term bonds—20 yrs., $750,000 at 9%. | 750,000 | 16,718.25 | 67,500 | 84,218.25 |
| 19X6 serial bonds 800,000 5% bonds | 800,000 | 17,481.75 | 40,000 | |
| Premium on bonds, prepaid interest | | 16,000.00 | 10,000 | |
| Net | | 1,481.75 | 30,000 | |
| Fiscal agents' charges | | | 300 | |
| Amount to be paid this year | | 1,481.75 | 30,300 | $ 31,781.75 |
| Total amount needed for principal and interest | | | | $180,000.00 |

### Term Bond Accounting

With term bonds, an accumulation is made each year in the debt service fund for the actual retirement of the bonds. This accumulation in the debt service fund becomes the amount available for the payment of the bonds in the account group. Each year the amount available for the payment of bonds increases, while the amount to be provided decreases.

**Term Bonds Outstanding**   For the $750,000 worth of twenty-year, 9 percent term bonds, there is an accumulation of $149,121.75 at the beginning of the year, leaving an amount to be provided of $600,878.25. A long-term debt statement at the beginning of the year for both the serial and term bonds is shown in Exhibit 11-4.

The balances for the term bonds in the worksheet (see Exhibit 11-6) as of the beginning of the fiscal year for the long-term debt account group is:

| | Dr. | Cr. |
|---|---|---|
| B  Amount available for payment of term bonds | $149,121.75 | |
| Amount to be provided for payment of term bonds | 600,878.25 | |
| Bonds payable—term | | $750,000 |

The debt service fund received $16,718.25 (see entry D10, Chapter 6—$84,218.25 − $67,500.00 = 16,718.25) from the general fund during the year as a contribution to the sinking fund for those bonds issued prior to this year. The investments of the fund also earned $13,612.17. Thus the amount available for the payment of the bonds increased by $30,330.42 (see entry D11, Chapter 8), and the amount to be provided decreased by the same amount. The entry to record this transaction is:

## EXHIBIT 11-6
### City of Ruthberg
### Long-term Debt Account Groups
### Transactions for 19X6

|  |  | Balance July 1, 19X5 |  |  |
|---|---|---|---|---|
| Accounts |  | Dr. |  | Cr. |
| Amount to be provided for payment of serial bonds | B | $ 400,000.00 |  |  |
| Amount to be provided for payment of term bonds (prior year's) | B | 600,878.25 |  |  |
| Amount available for payment of term bonds (prior year's) | B | 149,121.75 |  |  |
| Amount to be provided for payment of term bonds—19X5 |  |  |  |  |
| Amount available for payment of term bonds—19X5 |  |  |  |  |
| Bonds payable—serial |  |  | B | $ 400,000.00 |
| Bonds payable—term (prior year's) |  |  | B | 750,000.00 |
| Bonds payable—term (issue 19X5) |  |  |  |  |
|  |  | $1,150,000.00 |  | $1,150,000.00 |

L2  Amount available for payment
    of term bonds                  $30,330.42
      Amount to be provided for
        payment of term bonds                     $30,330.42

Therefore, $179,452.17 is available for the payment of the bonds. Generally, this amount is the amount shown as investments in the debt service fund. The "amount to be provided for payment of term bonds" account also is reduced from $600,878.25 to $570,547.83.

**Term Bonds Issued This Year** The capital projects fund issued new term bonds for $800,000 during the year. When the bonds are issued, the following journal entry is made in the long-term debt account group.

L3  Amount to be provided for
    payment of term bonds        $800,000
      Bonds payable—term                    $800,000
    To record the new issue of 5 percent, twenty-year term bonds.

The capital projects fund transferred to the debt service fund $16,000 for the premium on the issuance of the bonds. The general fund then transferred to the debt service fund the $1,481.75 needed to equal the first year's contribution to the sinking fund of $17,481.75. This information has been recorded in the accounts in the debt service fund by entries D6, D7, and D8 in Chapter 8. Thus $17,481.75 is now the amount

**EXHIBIT 11-6**
*(continued)*

| | Transactions | | | Balance June 30, 19X6 | |
|---|---|---|---|---|---|
| No. | Dr. | No. | Cr. | Dr. | Cr. |
| | | L1 | $ 40,000.00 | $ 360,000.00 | |
| | | L2 | 30,330.42 | 570,547.83 | |
| L2 | $ 30,330.42 | | | 179,452.17 | |
| L3 | 800,000.00 | L4 | 17,481.75 | 782,518.25 | |
| L4 | 17,481.75 | | | 17,481.75 | |
| L1 | 40,000.00 | | | | $ 360,000.00 |
| | | | | | 750,000.00 |
| | | L3 | 800,000.00 | | 800,000.00 |
| | $887,812.17 | | $887,812.17 | $1,910,000.00 | $1,910,000.00 |

available for the payment of the bonds and recorded in the general long-term debt account groups through the following journal entry:

| | | | |
|---|---|---|---|
| L4 | Amount available for payment of term bonds | $17,481.75 | |
| | Amount to be provided for payment of term bonds | | $17,481.75 |

**Payment of Bonds**   Over the years, the debt service fund would build its sinking fund by transfers from the general fund and interest on investments to an amount equal to that needed to pay off the bonds. Let us use the amounts determined in the debt service fund as that amount needed to pay off the $750,000 worth of twenty-year, 9 percent term bonds issued seven years previously (see page 225). The bonds would have to be paid off twelve years after this year.

At the end of the last year, investments in the fund should equal $733,281.75. With the transfer from the general fund at the end of the year of $16,718.25 for payment of principal, the total amount available would be $750,000. Transfer of $67,500 for the payment of interest would also be needed.

Before receiving the last payment for the principal in the debt service fund, assuming the interest earned has already been recorded, the amounts shown in the long-term debt account group would be:

| | |
|---|---|
| Amount available for payment of bonds | $733,281.75 |
| Amount to be provided for payment of bonds | 16,718.25 |
| Total bonds payable | $750,000.00 |

The entry in the debt service fund for the transfer from the general fund for payment of principal and interest would be:

|  | Dr. | Cr. |
|---|---|---|
| Cash | $84,218.25 | |
|    Operating transfer from the general fund—principal | | $16,718.25 |
|    Operating transfer from the general fund—interest | | 67,500.00 |

From the sale of investments, $733,281.75 cash was received. This entry would be:

| | | |
|---|---|---|
| Cash | $733,281.75 | |
|    Investments | | $733,281.75 |

For interest to be paid, the entry would be:

| | | |
|---|---|---|
| Expenditures—interest | $67,500 | |
|    Interest payable | | $67,500 |

For the principal to be paid, the entry would be:

| | | |
|---|---|---|
| Expenditures—principal | $750,000 | |
|    Matured bonds payable | | $750,000 |

For the payment of principal and interest, the entries would be:

| | | |
|---|---|---|
| Interest payable | $ 67,500 | |
| Matured bonds payable | 750,000 | |
|    Cash | | $817,500 |

The closing entry for interest would be:

| | | |
|---|---|---|
| Operating transfers from the general fund—interest | $67,500 | |
|    Expenditures—interest | | $67,500 |

The debt service fund closing entry for the principal would be:

| | | |
|---|---|---|
| Operating transfer from the general fund—principal | $ 16,718.25 | |
|    Fund balance | | $ 16,718.25 |
| Fund balance | $750,000 | |
|    Expenditures—principal | | $750,000 |

If there were any amounts left over from the assets needed to pay off the bonds, this amount would be transferred to the general fund.

In the general long-term debt account group, the following entries are needed.

**1** Upon transfer of annual sinking funds requirement to the debt service fund:

| | | |
|---|---|---|
| Amount available for payment of bonds | $16,718.25 | |
|     Amount to be provided for payment of bonds | | $16,718.25 |

**2** Upon recording the matured bonds payable in the debt service fund:

| | | |
|---|---|---|
| Bonds payable—term | $750,000 | |
|     Amount available for payment of bonds | | $750,000 |

The debt service fund for this bond issuance would be closed out, and the amounts in the general long-term debt account group would also be closed.

## STATEMENTS AND SCHEDULES FOR THE GENERAL LONG-TERM DEBT ACCOUNT GROUP

No funds flow in the long-term debt account group, so the only statement needed is a balance sheet. Supporting schedules are also provided. Similar to the fixed assets, a complete picture of the long-term debts of the governmental unit as a whole can be seen in the combined statement of all funds and account groups. Also, the changes in general long-term debt should be shown in a separate schedule or in the notes to the financial statements.

### General Long-Term Debt Account Group Financial Reporting

As with the general fixed assets account group, only a balance sheet can be prepared as a financial statement. However, much more information on long-term debt is needed.

Financial analysts of governmental financial statements often say that the development of annual financial reports concerning public debt is a weak point in governmental financial management. Such reports are important to the basic credit rating of the governmental unit. Bondholders have a great deal of interest in these reports, as do public officials and citizens. Through adequate debt records, the preparation of such reports becomes a relatively simple procedure.

Annual financial reports concerning debt cover three categories of information:

**1** A listing of all outstanding debt by type of issue (i.e., general obligation, special assessment, or revenue bonds). For each bond issue, the following information should be provided: date of issue, original amount, date of maturity, coupon (interest) rate, total interest, amount of principal and interest presently outstanding, and amount carried in sinking funds, if any.

**2** The overlapping debt of the jurisdiction. What portion of the debt is that of the school district, county, township, or special districts payable from taxes levied by the reporting jurisdiction?

**3** The jurisdiction's legal borrowing capacity. A computation of the status must be shown.

Debt arising from the issuance of revenue bonds in proprietary funds must be shown, including complete and factual information covering the facilities that support such debt. Revenue bond indentures often require an annual report by an independent certified public accountant. Supplemental information, such as average daily supply and consumption, storage capacity, number of customers, consumption per customer, method of billing, legal provisions, and so forth, should be shown for revenue bonds for such activities as water or sewer facilities. Special assessment bonds guaranteed by the municipality are also shown in the schedule of debt.

Accurate and complete financial reporting on public debt develops confidence on the part of investors and the general public as to the management of the jurisdiction's financial affairs. The relatively small amount of time and expense used in the preparation of such reports is often repaid many times over through lower interest rates.

See Chapter 13 for illustrations of the type of statements and exhibits needed for fully informing third parties concerning the long-term debt of a municipality.

## OTHER LONG-TERM FINANCING

Several other methods are used for long-term financing. One of the ways to obtain capital assets is through long-term leases, rather than through borrowing or purchasing.

### Capital Lease Accounting

Practically, some lease financing provides the equivalent of an installment purchase of an asset and is often called a *capital lease*. Consequently, both the asset and long-term debt should be recorded.

To illustrate capital lease accounting, assume the general fund makes a capital lease for computer equipment. Using a present value table, assuming an interest rate of 10 percent and a life of ten years, the following table of principal and interest payments could be developed.

| Year | Capital lease payment | Annual interest | Reduction of capital lease | Balance of capital lease debt |
|------|----------------------|-----------------|----------------------------|-------------------------------|
| 0    |                      |                 |                            | $30,725.00**                  |
| 1    | $5,000               | $3,072.50       | $1,927.50                  | 28,797.50                     |
| 2    | 5,000                | 2,879.75        | 2,120.25                   | 26,677.25                     |
| 3    | 5,000                | 2,667.73        | 2,332.27                   | 24,344.98                     |
| 4    | 5,000                | 2,434.50        | 2,565.50                   | 21,779.48                     |
| 5    | 5,000                | 2,177.95        | 2,822.05                   | 18,957.43                     |
| 6    | 5,000                | 1,895.74        | 3,104.26                   | 15,853.17                     |
| 7    | 5,000                | 1,585.32        | 3,414.68                   | 12,438.49                     |
| 8    | 5,000                | 1,243.85        | 3,756.15                   | 8,682.34                      |
| 9    | 5,000                | 868.23          | 4,131.77                   | 4,550.57                      |
| 10   | 5,000                | 449.43*         | 4,550.57                   |                               |

*Cumulative rounding errors.
**Present value table: 10 periods at 10 percent = 6.145; $5,000 × 6.145 = $30,725.

In the year in which the long-term lease is entered into, the following entry would be made in the general fund:

| | | |
|---|---|---|
| Expenditures | $30,725 | |
|    Other financing sources—increases | | |
|       in obligations under capital lease | | $30,725 |

In the first year of payment, the following entry would be made in the general fund:

| | | |
|---|---|---|
| Expenditures—lease and interest payable | $5,000 | |
|    Cash (or accounts payable) | | $5,000 |

Lease payable is $1,927.50; interest is $3,072.50.

Also, in the year in which the long-term lease is entered into, the following entry would be made in the general fixed assets account group:

| | | |
|---|---|---|
| Equipment | $30,725 | |
|    Investment in fixed assets—general | | |
|       fund revenue | | $30,725 |

In the long-term debt account group, the following entry would be made in the year in which the lease was entered into:

| | | |
|---|---|---|
| Amount to be provided for payment of lease | $30,725 | |
|    Capital lease debt | | $30,725 |

Somewhat similar to payments for serial bonds, but emanating from the general fund rather than the debt service fund, would be the transaction each year to reduce the amount of the capital lease debt. The entry for the principal payment for each year would vary, since the amount of interest from the payment of $5,000 would vary for each year depending upon the amount of the balance of the debt. As shown, the amounts for the entry for the first year for interest and principal would be: lease payable, $1,927.50; interest, $3,072.50. So, in the long-term debt account group, the entry for the first payment is:

| | | |
|---|---|---|
| Capital lease debt | $1,927.50 | |
|    Amount to be provided for | | |
|       payment of lease | | $1,927.50 |

Each year after the first year's payment, the amount of lease principal write-off in the long-term debt account group would vary in accordance with the previous table that shows the annual reduction of the capital lease.

The amount in the general fixed assets account group would remain constant after the first year's entry, until the asset wore out, was destroyed, or was exchanged for a new capital asset.

## Claims, Judgments, and Compensated Leave Liability

Current principles of accounting also suggest that claims, judgments, and compensated leave liability should be shown in the long-term debt account or in the notes to the financial statements. (See notes to financial statements, Appendix 13-2, VI, long-term debt, and XIII, contingent liabilities, in our illustrative financial statements in Chapter 13.)

## SUMMARY

This chapter is concerned with accounting for general fixed assets and general long-term debt rather than fiscal accounting. No funds flow through these types of entities; only a record is kept of the general fixed assets and general long-term debt of the overall governmental organization.

General fixed assets include only those fixed assets considered as expenditures in the general fund, special revenue funds, capital projects fund, special assessment funds, and expendable trust funds. Fixed assets of proprietary funds and nonexpendable trust funds are considered as fixed assets of those funds and not as general fixed assets of the governmental unit.

General long-term debt includes those long-term liabilities issued by the general fund, special revenue funds, capital projects funds, debt service funds, and expendable trust funds. Long-term debt of proprietary funds, nonexpendable trust funds, and special assessment funds are debts of those funds and not general long-term debts of the governmental unit.

Since there is no funds flow, all that is needed for double-entry accounting in the account groups, for both fixed assets and long-term debt, is an offset equity-type account for the assets and an offset asset-type account for the debt.

The offset equity in the general fixed assets account group is called "investment in general fixed assets." These equity accounts are classified by the revenue source from which the general fixed assets were acquired. An illustration is "investment in fixed assets from general fund revenue." The offset accounts in the general long-term debt account group are called "amount to be provided" and "amount available" to pay the debt.

Financial reporting for the fixed assets and long-term debt is shown in the combined balance sheet of the governmental unit. Supporting schedules of both the fixed assets and long-term debt and changes in the general fixed assets and long-term debt are also shown.

## QUESTIONS

1. Are records of fixed assets for proprietary-type funds kept in the general fixed assets account group? Why or why not?
2. How are long-term assets classified in the general fixed assets account group?
3. What titles are given to the capital-type accounts in the general fixed assets account group?
4. Do you show "investments in general fixed assets" as investments from revenue sources of the assets or from fund sources of the assets?
5. Is accumulated depreciation shown as a deduction from the fixed assets in the fixed assets account group?
6. Does any other accounting entity in governmental accounting keep records of long-term debt other than the long-term debt account group? If so, which ones and why?

7 What is the major distinction between keeping records for serial bonds and keeping records for term bonds in the long-term debt account group?
8 Bonds payable are shown as the liability in the general long-term debt account group. What are the asset-type accounts?
9 Describe the statements needed for the account groups.
10 In addition to the financial statements, what schedules are needed for the account groups?
11 What entries are needed in which funds and account groups when term bonds are paid off?
12 Is depreciation normally recorded in the account groups as an expense? Why or why not?
13 Is there funds flow in account groups? Discuss.
14 When are assets in the account groups recorded at appraised value? At cost? At fair market value?
15 Is a fixed asset recorded in the account group when an encumbrance to purchase a truck is recorded in the general fund?
16 How are the amounts determined when an increase is made in the "amounts available for payment of bonds" account and a decrease is made in the "amount to be provided for payment of bonds" account?

## PROBLEMS

**11-1** Choose the best answer to the following questions.
1 In accounting for general fixed assets in the general fixed assets account group for governmental fund types, the investment in fixed assets account represents
   a An asset-type account
   b A description of the fund from which the asset came
   c A description of the revenue source from which the fixed asset was obtained
   d An expenditure by the fixed assets account group
2 Under which of the following circumstances would a general fixed asset definitely be recorded in the general fixed assets account group at fair market value?
   a The asset is purchased.
   b The asset is obtained by gifts.
   c The asset is built by the governmental unit.
   d The asset arises as a result of the expansion of an original building.
3 Which of the following is most accurate for a general fixed asset of a governmental fund recorded in the general fixed assets account group?
   a Depreciation should be recorded for both external and internal reporting purposes.
   b Depreciation should be recorded for external reporting purposes but not for internal reporting purposes.
   c Depreciation should not be recorded at all.
   d Depreciation can be recorded for internal reporting purposes but should not be for external reporting purposes.
4 Which of the following bond issues would *not* be kept in the general long-term debt account group?
   a A bond issue to finance a capital project
   b A bond issue for a special assessment
   c General obligation bonds
   d General serial bonds
5 The entry in the general long-term debt account group to record a contribution by the general fund to the debt service fund's sinking fund to repay term bonds is:
   a Debit term bonds payable; credit sinking fund

**b** Debit amount to be provided for payment of term bonds; credit term bonds payable
   **c** Debit sinking fund cash; credit term bonds payable
   **d** Debit amount available for payment of term bonds; credit amount to be provided for payment of term bonds
  **6** The reason governmental accounting has a general fixed assets account group is:
   **a** To have a record of the general fixed assets not recorded in another particular fund
   **b** To have a record of the fixed assets and fixed liabilities in one fund
   **c** To provide detailed information on expenses for the general fund
   **d** To provide a subsidiary record of the fixed assets of the governmental unit
  **7** The entry to record a fixed asset in the account groups is:
   **a** Debit investment in fixed assets; credit the particular fixed asset
   **b** Debit depreciation on fixed assets; credit allowance for depreciation
   **c** Debit the particular fixed asset; credit investment in fixed assets by revenue source
   **d** Debit expenditures; credit investment in fixed assets

**11-2** Choose the best answer for the following questions.
  **1** A fixed asset was sold for $500; its cost was $5,000. The entry to remove the fixed asset from the account group is:
   **a** Debit fixed asset (market value); credit investment in fixed asset (market value)
   **b** Debit cash (amount received); credit fixed asset (amount received)
   **c** Debit investment in fixed asset (market value); credit fixed asset (market value)
   **d** Debit loss on sale of fixed asset (cost); credit fixed asset
  **2** A financial statement needed for the fixed asset account group is:
   **a** A balance sheet
   **b** A statement of revenues and expenditures
   **c** A statement of changes in financial position
   **d** A statement of changes in fund balance
  **3** An account not used in a general fixed asset account group is:
   **a** Cash
   **b** Investment in fixed assets, general fund revenue
   **c** Equipment
   **d** Land
  **4** The offset accounts (asset accounts) to the liability account for serial bonds payable in the long-term debt account group is called:
   **a** Fixed assets
   **b** Amount to be provided for payment of serial bonds
   **c** Amount to be provided for payment of term bonds
   **d** Serial bonds payable
  **5** In addition to the long-term debt account group, long-term debt is also recorded in:
   **a** Enterprise funds and capital projects funds
   **b** Internal service funds and special assessment funds
   **c** General fund and capital projects funds
   **d** Debt service funds and capital projects funds
  **6** A financial statement needed for a general long-term debt account group is:
   **a** A balance sheet
   **b** A statement of revenues and expenditures
   **c** A statement of changes in financial position
   **d** A statement of changes in fund balance
  **7** An account not used in a general long-term debt account group is:
   **a** Bonds payable

**b** Cash
   **c** Amount available for payment of term bonds
   **d** Mortgages payable
**8** When a $500,000 term bond is paid, the journal entry needed in the long-term debt account group is:
   **a** Debit bonds payable; credit cash
   **b** Debit bonds payable; credit investments
   **c** Debit cash; credit bonds payable
   **d** Debit bonds payable; credit amount available for payment of term bonds.

**11-3** A beginning-of-the-year statement, July 1, 19X0, of the general fixed assets of the city of South Portland consisted of the following items:

| | |
|---|---:|
| Land | $ 480,000 |
| Buildings (finished) | 1,375,000 |
| Buildings (unfinished) | 255,000 |
| Equipment | 962,900 |
| Investment in land, buildings, and equipment—utility fund | $2,222,200 |
| Total | $5,295,100 |

Additional information regarding the city's general fixed assets includes:

   **1** Land on which the unfinished buildings are being built was purchased and recorded at the cost of $220,000. The fair market value of the land is $300,000.

   **2** Additional land was donated to the city for general use. An appraiser valued the land at $125,000. It was recorded at a value of $100,000, which was the amount it originally cost the purchaser.

   **3** The unfinished buildings were completed. The total cost of the entire project of erecting the buildings was $600,000. Proceeds to build consisted of:
      **a** Proceeds of $300,000 from sale of general obligation bonds
      **b** Proceeds from a federal grant of $200,000
      **c** Proceeds from a state grant of $100,000

   **4** Equipment originally recorded at a cost of $153,000 was sold for its salvage value of $13,000. The useful life of the equipment was seven years, and depreciation is by the straight-line method. However, no depreciation had ever been recorded, and the sale has not been recorded as yet.

**Required**:
Make the necessary adjustments to the accounts in the general fixed assets account group, and prepare a balance sheet of the fixed assets account group for the year's end, June 30, 19X1.

**11-4** At the beginning of the year, debt owed by the city of Albanca consisted of the following general obligation bonds:

   **1** Serial bonds:

| Bond | Original issue | Paid | Balance 7/01/X0 | Rate | Term |
|---|---|---|---|---|---|
| A | $280,000 | $112,000 | $168,000 | 8.5% | 10 years |
| B | 750,000 | 150,000 | 600,000 | 7.0% | 25 years |

**2** Term bonds:

| Bond | Original issue | Balance in sinking fund | Rate | Term |
|---|---|---|---|---|
| A | $300,000 | $98,625 | 6.5% | 15 years |
| B | 550,000 | -0- | 8.0% | 15 years |

Additional information regarding the city's general obligation bonds includes:

 **1** During the year, $28,000 worth of A serial bonds were repaid, along with the interest on the bonds.
 **2** During the year, $30,000 of B serial bonds were repaid, along with the interest on the bonds.
 **3** The debt service fund received $12,000 for issue A and $20,000 for issue B from the general fund as a contribution to the sinking fund as well as a sufficient amount to pay the interest, and $8,500 was also earned during the year on investments.
 **4** The city had not used a long-term debt account group to record its long-term debt.

**Required:**
**1** Make journal entries, with explanations, to set up a long-term debt account group for the city at the beginning of the year to record both the serial and term bonds.
**2** Make journal entries, with explanations, in the long-term debt account group for the transactions during the year.
**3** Make journal entries in the debt service fund for the amounts received from the general fund for the payment of the principal and interest on the serial bonds.
**4** Make journal entries in the debt service fund for the amounts received for issues A and B term bonds for the sinking fund and the payment of interest on the bonds.

**11-5** The following financial activities affecting Judbury City's general fund and the fixed assets account group occurred during the year ended June 30, 19X1.[5]

 **1** The following budget was adopted:

| | |
|---|---|
| Estimated revenues: | |
|   Property taxes | $4,500,000 |
|   Licenses and permits | 300,000 |
|   Fines | 200,000 |
|   Total | $5,000,000 |
| Appropriations: | |
|   General government | $1,500,000 |
|   Police services | 1,200,000 |
|   Fire department services | 900,000 |
|   Public works services | 800,000 |
|   Acquisition of fire engines | 400,000 |
|   Total | $4,800,000 |

 **2** Property tax bills totaling $4,650,000 were mailed. It was estimated that $300,000 of this amount will be delinquent, and $150,000 will be uncollectible.
 **3** Property taxes totaling $3,900,000 were collected. The $150,000 previously estimated to be uncollectible remained unchanged, but $630,000 was reclassified as delinquent. It is estimated that delinquent taxes will be collected soon enough after June

30, 19X1 to make these taxes available to finance obligations incurred during the year ended June 30, 19X1. There was no balance of uncollected taxes at July 1, 19X0.

4  Tax anticipation notes in the face amount of $300,000 were issued.

5  Other cash collections were as follows:

| | |
|---|---|
| Licenses and permits | $270,000 |
| Fines | 200,000 |
| Sale of public works equipment (original cost, $75,000) | 15,000 |
| Total | $485,000 |

6  The following purchase orders were executed:

| | Total | Outstanding at 6/30/X1 |
|---|---|---|
| General government | $1,050,000 | 60,000 |
| Police services | 300,000 | 30,000 |
| Fire department services | 150,000 | 15,000 |
| Public work services | 250,000 | 10,000 |
| Fire engines | 400,000 | — |
| Totals | $2,150,000 | $115,000 |

No encumbrances were outstanding as of June 30, 19X0.

7  The following accounts were approved for payment:

| | |
|---|---|
| General government | $1,440,000 |
| Police services | 1,155,000 |
| Fire department services | 870,000 |
| Public works services | 700,000 |
| Fire engines | 400,000 |
| Total | $4,565,000 |

8  Accounts totaling $4,600,000 were paid.

**Required:**
Prepare journal entries to record the foregoing financial activities in the general fund and the fixed assets account group. Omit explanations. Ignore interest accruals.

**11-6** During the year, the city of York entered into a ten-year lease agreement with a computer company for the lease-purchase of computer equipment. The capital lease payments were to be $10,000 per year for ten years. (The current interest rate is 12 percent per year, and the present value of $1 a year at 12 percent is $5.650.)

**Required:**
Prepare the journal entries in the general fund and in the account groups to record these transactions for each of the next three years, that is, for years 1, 2, and 3.

**11-7** This problem continues the case of Silver City, which has been discussed in previous problem sections, and concerns the general fixed assets and general long-term debt accounts. Keep the material you have developed in order to prepare the statements and schedules in Chapter 13.

**Required**:

Prepare the journal entries, record the transactions on a worksheet, and prepare the needed statements or schedules for the general fixed assets and the general long-term debt account groups for the transactions as they have occurred in the case presented in each of the funds in Chapters 3, 5, 6, 7, 8, 9, and 10.

## NOTES

1 The National Council on Governmental Accounting, *Governmental Accounting and Financial Reporting Principles, Statement 1* (Chicago: Municipal Finance Officers Association, 1979, p. 9).
2 Ibid., p. 10.
3 Ibid., p. 9.
4 Ibid., p. 9.
5 Adapted from American Institute of Certified Public Accountants, *Uniform CPA Examination Questions and Unofficial Answers* (New York: American Institute of Certified Public Accountants, November 1981).

CHAPTER **12**

# INTERFUND AND INTERENTITY RELATIONSHIPS AND SINGLE AUDITS

In previous chapters concerning financial accounting, we have seen that governmental units are not a single accounting entity. Rather, they are a complex of entities that make up the overall governmental unit. So, many accounting transactions will not only be with individuals and organizations outside of the governmental unit, but also will be between the entities within the governmental unit. For example, the general fund—a governmental fund—must use electricity made and sold by the city utility—a proprietary fund. The debt service funds pay the principal and interest on the city's indebtedness from money transferred from the general fund. And the record of the assets and the long-term debts, which are assets and obligations of the governmental unit rather than of any particular governmental fund, are kept in account groups rather than in the fund that purchased the asset or incurred the debt.

In this chapter, we will first discuss the various types of interfund transactions that may occur between entities within the governmental unit. Then, we will review the many interfund transactions given in the illustrative case, the city of Ruthberg. Single audits, a rather new process within local governmental units, will be discussed and illustrated. When a governmental unit obtains grants from the federal government—no matter to which fund the grant goes—it is required to have a "single audit" of all of the grants obtained, rather than an audit of each individual grant. Thus, the audits of the grants received by the governmental unit will be a single audit instead of multiple audits.

## INTERFUND AND INTERENTITY RELATIONSHIPS AND TRANSACTIONS

As discussed in previous chapters on the individual funds and account groups, a transaction in one fund can result in a transaction in another fund or account group. One of the problems that may be created through this interfund relationship is that if a transaction is accrued in one fund, it should be accrued in the other. Thus, if the utility fund charges the general fund for sales of electricity, the amount of the charge should be recorded in each of the funds on the same basis. For example, if the utility fund charges the general fund for sales of electricity, the amount of the charge should be recorded in the utility fund as a debit to "due from the general fund" and a credit to "sales of electricity." Then the general fund should debit "expenditures" and credit "due to utility fund." Note that this transaction is an expenditure in the general fund rather than a transfer of funds from the general fund to the utility fund, because it is equivalent to a transaction with an outside entity. These transactions are known as *quasi-external transactions* and are recorded similarly to external transactions. Any student of fund accounting should become sufficiently familiar with interfund and interentity transactions to be able to prepare entries in each of the funds or account groups that the transaction affects.

## ILLUSTRATIVE TRANSACTIONS

Transactions used in each of the preceding chapters to illustrate the various fund and account group activities will be used to show the journal entries needed for the various interfund and interentity transactions. No explanations will be given to the journal entries that have been given previously. The reference number for the illustrative transactions will be the same number given in the chapter in which the transaction first appeared. A 0 will be used as a reference number for transactions not previously given.

## Proprietary Funds Interfund Transactions

**Bus Fund Interfund Transactions** (See Chapter 2.) In the previous year, the bus fund purchased $40,500 of supplies from the general fund. The following interfund entries would have been made.

1 Bus fund entry for the purchase of $40,500 of supplies from the general fund (0 is used as the reference number for the entry last year):

|   |   | Dr. | Cr. |
|---|---|---|---|
| 0 | Inventory (supplies) | $40,500 |   |
|   | Due to general fund |   | $40,500 |

2 Bus fund entries for payment for purchase of supplies:

| E11 | Due to general fund | $40,500 |   |
|---|---|---|---|
|   | Cash |   | $40,500 |

3 General fund entry for the sale during the previous year of supplies to the bus fund (0 is used as the reference number for the entry last year):

|   |                      | Dr.      | Cr.      |
|---|----------------------|----------|----------|
| 0 | Due from bus fund    | $40,500  |          |
|   | Expenditures (supplies) |       | $40,500  |

4 General fund entry for receipt of payment for last year's sale of supplies:

|    |                   | Dr.     | Cr.     |
|----|-------------------|---------|---------|
| B6 | Cash              | $40,500 |         |
|    | Due from bus fund |         | $40,500 |

**Printing Fund Interfund Transactions—Residual Equity Transfer** The general fund transferred to the printing fund $150,000 to set up an internal service printing fund. The entry in the printing fund to record this was:

|    |                                              | Dr.      | Cr.      |
|----|----------------------------------------------|----------|----------|
| I1 | Cash                                         | $150,000 |          |
|    | Residual equity transfer (from general fund) |          | $150,000 |

The entry in the general fund was:

|     |                                            | Dr.      | Cr.      |
|-----|--------------------------------------------|----------|----------|
| E17 | Residual equity transfer (to printing fund) | $150,000 |          |
|     | Cash                                       |          | $150,000 |

**Printing Fund Interfund Service Transactions** (See Chapter 3.) During the year, the general fund purchased $54,000 worth of supplies from the printing fund and the bus fund purchased $20,000 worth. The general fund paid $50,000 and the bus fund paid $20,000, leaving a balance of $4,000 owed to the printing fund. The entries for these interfund transactions were:

|    |                       |         |         |
|----|-----------------------|---------|---------|
| I7 | Due from general fund | $54,000 |         |
|    | Due from bus fund     | 20,000  |         |
|    | Charges for service   |         | $74,000 |

For the payments of these charges, the entries in the printing fund would be:

|    |                       |         |         |
|----|-----------------------|---------|---------|
| I8 | Cash                  | $70,000 |         |
|    | Due from general fund |         | $50,000 |
|    | Due from bus fund     |         | 20,000  |

The interfund entry in the bus fund for the purchase of supplies was:

|    |                     |         |         |
|----|---------------------|---------|---------|
| E8 | Inventory           | $20,000 |         |
|    | Due to printing fund|         | $20,000 |

For the payment to the printing fund, the entry was:

| E12 | Due to printing fund | $20,000 | |
|---|---|---|---|
| | Cash | | $20,000 |

For the purchase of the supplies, the interfund entry in the general fund was:

| E5 | Expenditures | $54,000 | |
|---|---|---|---|
| | Due to printing fund | | $54,000 |

For the partial payment of the supplies, the interfund entry in the general fund was:

| E6 | Due to printing fund | $50,000 | |
|---|---|---|---|
| | Cash | | $50,000 |

## Governmental Funds Interfund and Interentity Transactions

**General Fund Interfund Transactions** (See Chapter 6.) Several interfund transactions, in addition to those already illustrated, occurred in the general fund during the year; salaries and wages were earned by the employees during the year, from which were deducted payroll taxes and pension costs. A part of the pension costs was also paid by the general fund. The amounts for withholding taxes and pension costs were paid to the agency fund and to the pension trust fund. Also, capital assets were purchased and transfers were made to the debt service fund for payment of principal and interest on indebtedness.

**1** General fund payroll withholding entries (see Chapter 6):

| | | Dr. | Cr. |
|---|---|---|---|
| E1 | Expenditures | $656,000 | |
| | Accounts payable | | $472,500 |
| | Due to agency fund | | 91,500 |
| | Due to pension trust fund | | 92,000 |
| E2 | Accounts payable | $472,500 | |
| | Due to agency fund | 91,500 | |
| | Due to pension trust fund | 92,000 | |
| | Cash | | $656,000 |

**2** Agency fund entries for tax withholdings (see Chapter 10):

| | | | |
|---|---|---|---|
| G1 | Due from general fund | $91,500 | |
| | Due to state | | $11,500 |
| | Due to federal government | | 80,000 |
| G2 | Cash | $91,500 | |
| | Due from general fund | | $91,500 |

**3** Pension trust fund entries for employee pension withholdings and city's share of pension costs (see Chapter 10):

| | | | |
|---|---|---|---|
| P1 | Due from general fund | $92,000 | |
| | Employee contributions | | $46,000 |
| | Employer contributions | | 46,000 |
| P2 | Cash | $92,000 | |
| | Due from general fund | | $92,000 |

**4** General fund capital outlay entries for land, $52,000; improvements other than buildings, $5,000; and equipment $89,500; and partial payment of invoice for equipment, $12,000, from last year's reserve for encumbrances (see Chapter 6):

| | | | |
|---|---|---|---|
| E13 | Expenditures | $146,500 | |
| | Accounts payable | | $146,500 |
| E14 | Accounts payable | $140,000 | |
| | Cash | | $140,000 |
| B7 | Expenditures—against 19X5 reserve for encumbrances | $12,000 | |
| | Accounts payable | | $12,000 |
| B9 | Accounts payable | $12,000 | |
| | Cash | | $12,000 |

**5** Fixed asset account group entries (see Chapter 11):

| | | | |
|---|---|---|---|
| F1 | Land | $52,000 | |
| | Improvements other than buildings | 5,000 | |
| | Equipment | 89,500 | |
| | Investments in general fixed assets: | | |
| | General fund revenues | | $146,500 |
| F2 | Equipment | $12,000 | |
| | Investment in general fixed assets: | | |
| | General fund revenues | | $12,000 |

**6** General fund debt service entries for principal and interest payments (see Chapter 6):

| | | | |
|---|---|---|---|
| E15 | Operating transfers—principal and interest | $180,000 | |
| | Due to debt service fund | | $180,000 |
| E16 | Due to debt service fund | $180,000 | |
| | Cash | | $180,000 |

**7** Individual debt service fund entries from general fund transfers for principal and interest payments (see Chapter 8):

| | | | |
|---|---|---|---|
| D1 | Due from general fund | $64,000 | |
| | Operating transfers from general fund | | $64,000 |
| D2 | Cash | $64,000 | |
| | Due from general fund | | $64,000 |

| | | |
|---|---|---|
| **D7** Due from general fund | $31,781.75 | |
|     Operating transfer from general fund | | $31,781.75 |
| **D8** Cash | $31,781.75 | |
|     Due from general fund | | $31,781.75 |
| **D10** Cash | $84,218.25 | |
|     Operating transfers from general fund | | $84,218.25 |

**Capital Projects Funds Interfund and Interentity Transactions** (See Chapter 7.) The capital projects funds are primarily involved in interfund transactions with the debt service funds, the long-term debt account group, and the fixed assets account group, although sometimes an interfund entry can be found with the general fund.

**1** Capital projects fund entries for sale of term bonds at a premium of $16,000 and accrued interest of $10,000 (see Chapter 7):

| | Dr. | Cr. |
|---|---|---|
| **P5** Cash | $826,000 | |
|     Operating transfer to debt service fund | 16,000 | |
|         Due to debt service fund | | $26,000 |
|         Proceeds from bonds | | 816,000 |
| **P6** Due to debt service fund | $26,000 | |
|     Cash | | $26,000 |

**2** Debt service fund entries for premium, $16,000, and accrued interest, $10,000 (see Chapter 8):

| | | |
|---|---|---|
| **D6** Due from capital projects fund | $26,000 | |
|     Expenditures | | $10,000 |
|     Operating transfers | | 16,000 |
|     Cash | $26,000 | |
|         Due from capital projects fund | | $26,000 |

**3** Long-term debt account group entries for sale of $800,000 of term bonds (see Chapter 11):

| | | |
|---|---|---|
| **L3** Amount to be provided for payment of term bonds | $800,000 | |
|     Bonds payable—term | | $800,000 |
| **L4** Amount available for payment of term bonds | $17,481.75 | |
|     Amount to be provided for payment of term bonds | | $17,481.75 |

(Note: The $16,000 for premium on bonds plus the $1,481.75 transferred from the general fund for the sinking fund contribution would equal the amount available for the payment of these bonds for the first year.)

**4** Fixed assets account group entries from capital projects fund for acquiring or constructing fixed assets (see Chapter 11). The capital projects fund acquired land at a cost of $125,000 and had construction in progress of $800,000. For the land acquisition, the journal entry was:

| | | | |
|---|---|---|---|
| P3 | Expenditures | $125,000 | |
| | Accounts payable | | $75,000 |
| | Judgment payable | | 50,000 |

The entry in the fixed assets account group was:

| | | | |
|---|---|---|---|
| F3 | Land | $125,000 | |
| | Investment in fixed assets: | | |
| | State grants | | $16,667 |
| | Federal grants | | 41,667 |
| | General obligation bonds | | 66,666 |

The journal entry in the capital projects fund for the work in progress was:

| | | | |
|---|---|---|---|
| P9 | Expenditures | $800,000 | |
| | Accounts payable | | $800,000 |

The entry in the fixed assets account group was:

| | | | |
|---|---|---|---|
| F4 | Construction in progress | $800,000 | |
| | Investment in fixed assets: | | |
| | State grants | | $106,667 |
| | Federal grants | | 266,667 |
| | General obligation bonds | | 426,666 |

**Debt Service Fund Interentity Transactions** (See Chapter 8.) The debt service fund paid the principal on the serial bonds of $40,000. For the previously issued term bonds, the amount in the fund balance was increased by $30,330.42, through revenue from investments and an operating transfer from the general fund.

**1** Debt service fund entry for the payment of the serial bonds:

| | | Dr. | Cr. |
|---|---|---|---|
| D3 | Expenditures | $40,000 | |
| | Matured bonds payable | | $40,000 |

**2** Long-term debt account group entry for payment of the serial bonds:

| | | | |
|---|---|---|---|
| L1 | Bonds payable—serial | $40,000 | |
| | Amount to be provided for payment of serial bonds | | $40,000 |

**3** Debt service fund entry for the increase in the fund balance for the previously issued term bonds:

**316** PART I: ACCOUNTING AND FINANCIAL REPORTING FOR GOVERNMENTAL ENTITIES

| | | | |
|---|---|---|---|
| DC4 | Revenue from investments | $13,612.17 | |
| | Operating transfers | 16,718.25 | |
| | Fund balance | | $30,330.42 |

**4** Long-term debt account group entry for the transfer from account "amount to be provided" to account "amount available for payment" of term bonds:

| | | | |
|---|---|---|---|
| L2 | Amount available for payment of term bonds | $30,330.42 | |
| | Amount to be provided for payment of term bonds | | $30,330.42 |

**Special Assessment Fund Interfund and Interentity Transactions**  (See Chapter 9.) The primary interfund relationship is between the special assessment fund and the fixed assets account group, although transactions can occur between the special assessment fund and any of the other funds.

**1** Special assessment fund entries:

| | | Dr. | Cr. |
|---|---|---|---|
| SC1 | Revenue from special assessments | $325,000 | |
| | Revenue from the federal government | 200,000 | |
| | Revenue from the state government | 175,000 | |
| | Expenditures for construction | | $700,000 |

**2** Fixed assets account group entries:

| | | | |
|---|---|---|---|
| F5 | Improvements other than buildings | $700,000 | |
| | Investments in fixed assets: | | |
| | Taxpayer assessments | | $325,000 |
| | Federal grants | | 200,000 |
| | State grants | | 175,000 |

**Fixed Assets Account Group Interentity Transactions**  (See Chapter 11.) Only one type of interentity transaction could originate in the fixed assets account group—the sale of property. This occurred when a truck, originally costing $6,000, was sold for $750. This property came from general fund revenue, so the entry concerning the receipt of the money for the sale would be recorded in the general fund as a miscellaneous receipt.

**1** Fixed asset account group entry:

| | | Dr. | Cr. |
|---|---|---|---|
| F6 | Investments in fixed assets: | | |
| | General fund revenues | $6,000 | |
| | Equipment | | $6,000 |

**2** General fund entry for revenue from sale of truck:

| R8 | Cash | $750 | |
|---|---|---|---|
| | Revenue (miscellaneous) | | $750 |

These illustrative interfund and interentity transactions are only a small portion of the numerous transactions that could occur between the various funds and account groups. Exhibit 12-1 summarizes these transactions for ease of reference.

**EXHIBIT 12-1**
**City of Ruthberg**
**Summary of Interfund and Interentity Transactions**
**For Fiscal Year 19X6**

| No. | Fund | Transaction | Journal entry | Dr. | Cr. |
|---|---|---|---|---|---|
| | | | **Proprietary Funds** | | |
| 0 | Bus | Prior year's purchase of supplies from general fund | Inventory (supplies)<br>Due to general fund | $ 40,500 | $ 40,500 |
| E11 | Bus | Paid amount owed to general fund for purchase of supplies | Due to general fund<br>Cash | 40,500 | 40,500 |
| I1 | Printing | Transfer from general fund of capital equity for printing fund | Cash<br>Residual equity transfer from general fund | 150,000 | 150,000 |
| I7 | Printing | Charges for services to general and bus funds | Due from general fund<br>Due from bus fund<br>Charges for services | 54,000<br>20,000 | 74,000 |
| I8 | Printing | Received payment from general and bus funds for services | Cash<br>Due from general fund<br>Due from bus fund | 70,000 | 50,000<br>20,000 |
| E8 | Bus | Purchases of supplies from printing fund | Inventory<br>Due to printing fund | 20,000 | 20,000 |
| E5 | General | Purchases of supplies from printing fund | Expenditures<br>Due to printing fund | 54,000 | 54,000 |
| E12 | Bus | Full payment to printing fund | Due to printing fund<br>Cash | 20,000 | 20,000 |
| E6 | General | Partial payment to printing fund | Due to printing fund<br>Cash | 50,000 | 50,000 |
| 0 | General | Previous year's sale of supplies to bus fund | Due from bus fund<br>Expenditures (supplies) | 40,500 | 40,500 |
| B6 | General | Payment by bus fund for previous year's sale of supplies | Cash<br>Due from bus fund | 40,500 | 40,500 |
| E17 | General | Transfer of cash to printing fund—residual equity transfer | Residual equity transfer to printing fund<br>Cash | 150,000 | 150,000 |

## EXHIBIT 12-1
*(continued)*

| No. | Fund | Transaction | Journal entry | Dr. | Cr. |
|---|---|---|---|---|---|
| | | | **Governmental Funds** | | |
| E1 | General | Payroll costs for period | Expenditures<br>  Accounts payable<br>  Due to agency fund<br>  Due to pension trust fund | $656,000 | $472,500<br>91,500<br>92,000 |
| E2 | General | Paid accounts:<br>accounts payable, $472,500;<br>due to agency fund, $91,500;<br>and due to pension trust fund, $92,000 | Accounts payable<br>Due to agency fund<br>Due to pension trust fund<br>  Cash | 472,500<br>91,500<br>92,000 | 656,000 |
| G1 | Agency | Agency fund entry for tax withholdings | Due from general fund<br>  Due to state<br>  Due to federal government | 91,500 | 11,500<br>80,000 |
| G2 | Agency | General fund paid agency fund amount due | Cash<br>  Due from general fund | 91,500 | 91,500 |
| P1 | Pension trust | Employee and employer amounts for pensions | Due from general fund<br>  Employee contributions<br>  Employer contributions | 92,000 | 46,000<br>46,000 |
| P2 | Pension trust | Cash received from general fund for employer and employee shares of pension annuities | Cash<br>  Due from general fund | 92,000 | 92,000 |
| E13 | General | Expenditures: land, $52,000; improvements other than buildings, $5,000; and equipment, $89,500 | Expenditures<br>  Accounts payable | 146,500 | 146,500 |
| E14 | General | Paid for capital outlay purchases | Accounts payable<br>  Cash | 140,000 | 140,000 |
| B7 | General | Expenditures for previous year's equipment | Expenditures—against 19X5 reserve for encumbrances<br>  Accounts payable | 12,000 | 12,000 |
| B9 | General | Paid equipment part of accounts payable | Accounts payable<br>  Cash | 12,000 | 12,000 |
| F1 | General fixed assets account group | Record of general fund new fixed assets acquisitions | Land<br>Improvements other than buildings<br>Equipment<br>  Investment in general fixed assets—general fund revenues | 52,000<br>5,000<br>89,500 | 146,500 |
| F2 | General fixed assets account group | Equipment purchased from prior year's reserve for encumbrances | Equipment<br>  Investment in general fixed assets: general fund revenues | 12,000 | 12,000 |

## EXHIBIT 12-1
*(continued)*

| No. | Fund | Transaction | Journal entry | Dr. | Cr. |
|---|---|---|---|---|---|
| E15 | General | Transfers to debt service fund for principal and interest payments | Operating transfers—principal and interest<br>  Due to debt service fund | 180,000 | 180,000 |
| E16 | General | Payment to debt service fund | Due to debt service fund<br>  Cash | 180,000 | 180,000 |
| D1 | Debt service | Debt service fund entry for transfer of $40,000 principal and $24,000 interest from general fund | Due from general fund<br>  Operating transfers from general fund | 64,000 | 64,000 |
| D2 | Debt service | Received payment for transfer of principal and interest on serial bonds | Cash<br>  Due from general fund | 64,000 | 64,000 |
| D7 | Debt service | Debt service fund entry for newly issued term bonds: interest, $30,300; principal, $1,481.75 | Due from general fund<br>  Operating transfer from general fund | 31,781.75 | 31,781.75 |
| D8 | Debt service | Receipt of payment for principal and interest | Cash<br>  Due from general fund | 31,781.75 | 31,781.75 |
| D10 | Debt service | Operating transfer from general fund for principal and interest payments on previously issued term bonds | Cash<br>  Operating transfers from general fund | 84,218.25 | 84,218.25 |
| P5 | Capital projects | Sale of bonds for premium of $16,000 and accrued interest of $10,000 | Cash<br>Operating transfer to debt service fund<br>  Due to debt service fund<br>  Proceeds from bonds | 826,000<br>16,000 | 26,000<br>816,000 |
| P6 | Capital projects | Payment of premium and accrued interest to debt service fund | Due to debt service fund<br>  Cash | 26,000 | 26,000 |
| D6 | Debt service | Amount accrued for premiums, $16,000, and accrued interest, $10,000, on sale of bonds by capital projects fund | Due from capital projects fund<br>  Expenditures<br>  Operating transfers | 26,000 | 10,000<br>16,000 |
| D6 | Debt service | Payment of cash from capital projects fund | Cash<br>  Due from capital projects fund | 26,000 | 26,000 |
| L3 | Long-term debt account group | To set up liability for bonds in long-term debt account group | Amount to be provided for payment of term bonds<br>  Bonds payable—term | 800,000 | 800,000 |
| L4 | Long-term debt account group | Amount in debt service fund available for principal payment | Amount available for payment of term bonds<br>  Amount to be provided for payment of term bonds | 17,481.75 | 17,481.75 |

## EXHIBIT 12-1
*(continued)*

| No. | Fund | Transaction | Journal entry | Dr. | Cr. |
|---|---|---|---|---|---|
| P3 | Capital projects | Expenditures for land: accounts payable, $75,000; judgments payable, $50,000 | Expenditures<br>  Accounts payable<br>  Judgments payable | 125,000 | 75,000<br>50,000 |
| F3 | Fixed assets account group | To capitalize land in proportion to revenue source | Land<br>  Investments in general<br>    fixed assets:<br>      State grants<br>      Federal grants<br>      General obligation<br>        bonds | 125,000 | 16,667<br>41,667<br><br>66,666 |
| P9 | Capital projects | Expenditures for work in progress in capital projects fund | Expenditures<br>  Accounts payable | 800,000 | 800,000 |
| F4 | Fixed assets account group | To capitalize work in progress in proportion to revenue source | Construction in progress<br>  Investment in fixed assets:<br>    State grants<br>    Federal grants<br>    General obligation<br>      bonds | 800,000 | 106,667<br>266,667<br><br>426,666 |
| D3 | Debt service | Payment of this year's portion of serial bonds | Expenditures<br>  Matured bonds payable<br>Matured bonds payable<br>  Cash | 40,000<br><br>40,000 | 40,000<br><br>40,000 |
| L1 | Long-term debt account group | To show portion of long-term debt retired | Bonds payable—serial<br>  Amount to be provided for<br>    payment of serial bonds | 40,000 | 40,000 |
| DC4 | Debt service | To close earnings and transfers to fund balance | Revenues from investments<br>Operating transfers<br>  Fund balance | 13,612.17<br>16,718.25 | 30,330.42 |
| L2 | Long-term debt account group | To show amount currently available for payment of term bonds | Amount available for payment<br>  of term bonds<br>    Amount to be provided for<br>      payment of term bonds | 30,330.42 | 30,330.42 |
| SC1 | Special assessments | To close amount for construction in special assessment fund | Revenue from special<br>  assessments<br>Revenue from the federal<br>  government<br>Revenue from the state<br>  government<br>    Expenditures for construction | 325,000<br><br>200,000<br><br>175,000 | <br><br><br><br><br><br>700,000 |
| F5 | Fixed assets account group | To capitalize fixed assets from special assessment fund | Improvements other than<br>  buildings<br>  Investments in fixed<br>    assets:<br>      Taxpayer assessments<br>      Federal grants<br>      State grants | 700,000 | <br><br><br><br>325,000<br>200,000<br>175,000 |

## EXHIBIT 12-1
*(continued)*

| No. | Fund | Transaction | Journal entry | Dr. | Cr. |
|-----|------|-------------|---------------|-----|-----|
| F6 | Fixed assets account group | Sale of truck for $750; originally purchased for $6,000 from general fund revenue | Investments in fixed assets: general fund revenues<br>    Equipment | 6,000 | 6,000 |
| R8 | General | Receipt of cash, $750, from sale of truck | Cash<br>    Revenue (miscellaneous) | 750 | 750 |

## THE SINGLE AUDIT

As has been stated previously, the proportion of resources needed for running state and local governments, as well as other nonbusiness organizations, that comes from the federal government has been increasing from year to year. In the past, most of these resources from grants were audited by both independent auditors and federal auditors on a grant-by-grant basis to determine whether the agency receiving the grant had complied with the grant provisions.

However, since 1979 the federal Office of Management and Budget (OMB), as stated in *OMB Circular 102, Attachment P*, has determined that audits of federal funds granted to state and local governments and to other nonbusiness organizations will be done by independent auditors on a "single audit" basis. This means that the audit will cover all activities carried out by the agency that are funded through federal grants and not on a grant-by-grant basis.

The single audit concept, however, has gone beyond the OMB. In 1984, Congress passed legislation that makes the single audit a law (Single Audit Act of 1984, Public Law 98-502). The *Government Accountants Journal* in addressing the provisions of the single audit says:

> Essentially, the single audit was to have the following characteristics:
> 
> - conducted on an organization-wide basis rather than on a grant-by-grant basis;
> - include financial and compliance audits, but not efficiency or effectiveness audits;
> - satisfy the audit needs of all levels of government;
> - performed by independent grantee or grantee-designated auditors;
> - conducted at least once every two years;
> - monitored by designated federal "cognizant" audit agency;
> - follow standard guidelines; and
> - issue audit reports using standard requirements.[1]

Thus, independent auditors making audits of an agency receiving federal monies will have to understand government audit standards for auditing governmental organizations, programs, activities, and functions, in addition to the AICPA audit standards. Government audit standards state that auditors must follow the AICPA audit standards with these additional standards:

1. Planning shall include consideration of the requirements of all levels of government.
2. A review is to be made of compliance with applicable laws and regulations.

**3** A written record of the auditors' work shall be retained in the form of working papers.

**4** Auditors shall be alert to situations or transactions that could be indicative of fraud, abuse, and illegal expenditures and acts and if such evidence exists, extend audit steps and procedures to identify the effect on the entity's financial statements.

**5** Written audit reports are to be submitted to the appropriate officials of the organization audited and to the appropriate officials of the organizations requiring or arranging for the audits unless legal restrictions or ethical considerations prevent it. Copies of the reports should also be sent to other officials who may be responsible for taking actions and to others authorized to receive such reports. Unless restricted by law or regulation, copies should be made available for public inspection.

**6** A statement in the auditors' report that the examination was made in accordance with generally accepted government auditing standards for financial and compliance audits will be acceptable language to indicate that the audit was made in accordance with these standards. (The AICPA requires that public accountants state that the examination was made in accordance with generally accepted auditing standards. They should also state that their examination was performed in accordance with those additional standards and requirements set forth in this chapter.)

**7** Either the auditors' report on the entity's financial statements or a separate report shall contain a statement of positive assurance on those items of compliance tested and negative assurance on those items not tested. It shall also include material instances of noncompliance and instances or indications of fraud, abuse, or illegal acts found during or in connection with the audit.

**8** The auditors shall report on their study and evaluation of internal accounting controls made as a part of the financial and compliance audit. They shall identify as a minimum: (1) the entity's significant internal accounting controls, (2) the controls identified that were evaluated, (3) the controls identified that were not evaluated (the auditor may satisfy this requirement by identifying any significant classes of transactions and related assets not included in the study and evaluation), and (4) the material weaknesses identified as a result of the evaluation.

**9** Either the auditors' report on the entity's financial statements or a separate report shall contain any other material deficiency findings identified during the audit not covered in 7 above.

**10** If certain information is prohibited from general disclosure, the report shall state the nature of the information omitted and the requirement that makes the omission necessary.[2]

Resources for making the single audit usually come from the grants that were received from the federal government. Auditors making these types of audits must be sure they follow the governmental audit standards, not only the AICPA standards. While no great number of single audits has been made at the present time, estimates place the number of audits that need to be made under this law at approximately 50,000 a year. The appendix to this chapter shows the single audit report for the city of Roanoke, Virginia for the period ending June 30, 1984.[3]

The Office of Management and Budget has issued *Circular No. A-128* explaining the audit requirements for state and local governments that receive federal aid. The OMB also has issued a supplement to *Circular No. A-128* that sets forth the major compliance requirements that should be considered in an organizationwide audit of state and local governments that receive federal assistance. Called "Compliance Supplement for Single Audits of State and Local Governments" and revised in April 1985, this supplement is divided into two parts. The first part contains those generally applicable requirements that should be considered in financial and compliance audits. The second part provides requirements that are specific to sixty-two programs that provide over 90 percent of the federal aid to state and local governments.[4]

A single audit is to be made when a governmental unit receives more than $25,000 a year. Special provisions apply to the unit that receives between $25,000 and $100,000. Over $100,000, the full provisions of the act apply. Federal funding includes grants, contracts, cooperative agreements, loans or loan guarantees, property, interest subsidies, insurance, and awards passed through state or other local governments.

A local governmental unit defined under the act includes:

1 Counties
2 Cities
3 Towns
4 Townships
5 Special districts
6 School districts
7 Parishes
8 Local public authorities
9 Intrastate districts
10 Council of governments
11 Other public authorities, such as:
   a Electric authorities
   b Hospital or health care commissions
   c Transportation authorities
   d Water and sewer authorities
   e Planning districts
   f Community service boards[5]

## Single Audit Reports

The general rule is that the auditor who makes the financial statement audit will also make the single audit. Therefore, his or her single audit report will make reference to the audit that is made in accordance with generally accepted audit standards and that is presented in accordance with generally accepted accounting principles consistently applied. In addition, the report must state that the internal controls provide reasonable assurance that the federal financial assistance is managed in accordance with laws and regulations pertaining to the money received. The report also must assure its recipient that the operations resulting from the financial resources received must be in compliance with laws or regulations that may have a material effect on the program.

The appendix presents a single audit report for the city of Roanoke, Virginia. It shows the total receipts and expenditures for each grant/contract and relates the expenditures to those shown in the audited financial statements in Exhibit 13-5 and Exhibit 13-6 in the next chapter. The report also specifically identifies internal control effectiveness and compliance with specific laws and regulations.

**324** PART I: ACCOUNTING AND FINANCIAL REPORTING FOR GOVERNMENTAL ENTITIES

## SUMMARY

Chapter 12 is concerned with two specific subjects: (1) interfund and interentity relationships and (2) single audits. To understand governmental accounting you must understand the numerous transactions between and among the various funds and account groups of government. This chapter examines the reasoning behind interfund and interentity transactions and shows how interfund and interentity transactions apply in governmental operations as a whole. Bringing together all of the interfund and interentity transactions for an entire city should help you understand this important subject.

A new subject in governmental accounting that applies to most state and local governmental units because of federal grants is that of "single audits." In order to comply with the requirements of the numerous grants that state and local governmental units receive for the operation of those units, current federal law now requires that all grants be audited as a single operation, rather than having numerous auditors auditing each grant. Single audits are illustrated in this chapter's appendix through a single audit report for the city of Roanoke, Virginia.

## QUESTIONS

1. What is meant by the "single audit"?
2. In the "single audit" report for the city of Roanoke, does the report contain a listing of each of the federal grants received by the city? Explain.
3. Can the "single audit" report include the audit of grants other than federal grants?
4. Does the Single Audit Act require the disclosure of indications of fraud, abuse, or illegal acts? If your answer is "yes," where is the standard for this type of disclosure found?
5. The Single Audit Act requires that the audit be made in accordance with governmental audit standards. Are these standards for the governmental audit the same as those required for the audit and report of a business organization?
6. What type of governmental organization is included in the requirements for a single audit? Would this include a private, nonprofit organization, such as a nursing home for mentally retarded children, organized for the purpose of receiving grants from a city for this purpose? The city receives more than $100,000 a year from the federal government in grants for this purpose, and the nursing home receives more than $25,000 of this money.
7. Why is a knowledge of interfund and interentity transactions so important in governmental accounting?
8. What is the distinction between an interentity transaction and an interfund transaction?
9. Interfund transactions often require a knowledge of the distinction between expenditures and transfers out and revenues and transfers in. Explain that distinction.
10. Interfund transactions also require a knowledge of the distinction between an operating transfer and a residual equity transfer. Explain that distinction.

## PROBLEMS

**12-1** Choose the best answer for each of the following questions.[6]

1. Which of the following accounts of a governmental unit is credited when taxpayers are billed for property taxes?

a Estimated revenues
b Revenues
c Appropriations
d Reserve for encumbrances

2 Which of the following funds of a governmental unit uses the modified accrual basis of accounting?
a General
b Enterprise
c Internal service
d Nonexpendable trust

3 Which of the following funds of a governmental unit would account for depreciation in the accounts of the fund?
a General
b Internal service
c Capital projects
d Special assessment

4 Which of the following funds of a governmental unit uses the same basis of accounting as the special revenue fund?
a Internal service
b Expendable trust
c Nonexpendable trust
d Enterprise

5 Which of the following funds of a governmental unit would account for long-term liabilities in the accounts of the fund?
a Special assessment
b Special revenue
c Capital projects
d Debt service

6 Which of the following accounts would be included in the assets section of the combined balance sheet of a governmental unit for the general long-term debt account group?

|   | Amount available in debt service funds | Amount to be provided for retirement of general long-term debt |
|---|---|---|
| a | Yes | Yes |
| b | Yes | No |
| c | No | Yes |
| d | No | No |

7 Revenues of a municipality should be recognized in the accounting period in which they become available and measurable for a

|   | Governmental fund | Proprietary fund |
|---|---|---|
| a | Yes | No |
| b | Yes | Yes |
| c | No | Yes |
| d | No | No |

**8** Revenues of a special revenue fund of a governmental unit should be recognized in the period in which the
   **a** Revenues become available and measurable
   **b** Revenues become available for appropriation
   **c** Revenues are available for billing
   **d** Cash is received

**12-2** Choose the best answer for each of the following questions.

**1** Which of the following funds of a governmental unit would use the general long-term debt account group to account for unmatured general long-term liabilities?
   **a** Special assessment
   **b** Capital projects
   **c** Trust
   **d** Internal service

**2** Which of the following funds of a governmental unit uses the same basis of accounting as an enterprise fund?
   **a** Special revenue
   **b** Internal service
   **c** Expendable trust
   **d** Capital projects

**3** A capital projects fund of a municipality is an example of what type of fund?
   **a** Internal service
   **b** Proprietary
   **c** Fiduciary
   **d** Governmental

**4** Which of the following accounts could be included in the balance sheet of an enterprise fund?

|   | Reserve for encumbrances | Revenue bonds payable | Retained earnings |
|---|---|---|---|
| **a** | No  | No  | Yes |
| **b** | No  | Yes | Yes |
| **c** | Yes | Yes | No  |
| **d** | No  | No  | No  |

**5** Which of the following accounts would be included in the combined balance sheet for the long-term debt account group?
   **a** Amount to be provided for retirement of general long-term debt
   **b** Unreserved fund balance
   **c** Reserve for encumbrances
   **d** Cash

**6** Customers' meter deposits that cannot be spent for normal operating purposes would be classified as restricted cash in the balance sheet of which fund?
   **a** Internal service
   **b** Trust
   **c** Agency
   **d** Enterprise

**7** For state and local governmental units, the full accrual basis of accounting should be used for what type of fund?

a Special revenue
b General
c Debt service
d Internal service

8 Which of the following will increase the fund balance of a governmental unit at the end of the fiscal year?

a Appropriations are less than expenditures and reserve for encumbrances.
b Appropriations are less than expenditures and encumbrances.
c Appropriations are more than expenditures and encumbrances.
d Appropriations are more than estimated revenues.

12-3 The internal service computer fund of Barsto City had the following individual transactions for the year 19X9:

1 The computer fund received $500,000 from the general fund in order to purchase equipment, supplies, and start operations of the fund.

2 Computer and related equipment worth $200,000 was purchased.

3 Services to other funds were provided as follows:

| | |
|---|---|
| General fund | $100,000 |
| Special revenue fund | 25,000 |
| Capital projects fund | 60,000 |
| | $185,000 |

4 Payments for services were received as follows:

| | |
|---|---|
| General fund | $ 95,000 |
| Special revenue fund | 25,000 |
| Capital projects fund | 55,000 |
| | $175,000 |

**Required**:

1 Prepare the original journal entry to record the transaction in the computer fund. All journal entries are not given.

2 Prepare any interentity or interfund journal entries that may be needed.

3 If interfund or interentity transactions are not required, explain why not.

12-4 The general fund of the city of Phoenix had the following transactions as a part of the total operations of the city. The city's fiscal year is from July 1 to June 30.

1 On July 15, a truck that was expected to cost $25,000 was ordered for the city.

2 On August 31, the general fund transferred $63,500 to the debt service fund to provide $13,500 for semiannual interest and $50,000 for principal on a ten-year, 6 percent $500,000 serial bond issue. The debt service fund paid the principal and interest.

3 On September 10, the truck ordered by the general fund on July 15 was received, along with an invoice for $24,500.

4 On September 30, the invoice for the truck was paid.

5 On January 15, office equipment was purchased for cash for $10,000.

6 On February 28, transferred semi-annual interest to debt service fund, $12,000.

7 On June 15, an order was placed: $10,000 for supplies, $25,000 for personal computers, and $15,000 for an automobile.

8 On June 30, the personal computers were received with an invoice for $25,000.

**Required:**

1. Prepare the original journal entries to record the transactions in the city's general fund. Label these entries as general fund entries. Be sure and place the appropriate dates on the journal entries.
2. Prepare any interfund or interentity journal entries that may be required as a result of the general fund journal entries. Identify the fund or account group that is involved. Use the appropriate dates for the entries.
3. If an interfund or interentity journal entry is not required for the transaction, explain why.

**12-5** The capital projects fund for the city of Newcastle during the year 19X5 had the following transactions as a part of the total operations of the fund. The fund was opened for the purpose of constructing an additional bridge over the river that separates the two sections of the city.

The fund expected to finance the construction of the bridge from the following financing sources:

| | |
|---|---:|
| Transfer from the general fund | $ 100,000 |
| State grant | 200,000 |
| Federal grants | 300,000 |
| Ten-year, eight percent serial bonds | 900,000 |
| Total | $1,500,000 |

1. The bonds were sold for $925,000. The $25,000 difference was for $15,000 premium on the sale of the bonds and accrued interest of $10,000. Paid the debt service fund the premium and accrued interest.
2. Amounts due from the general fund, the state, and the federal government were accrued.
3. Cash was received from the general fund and the state and federal governments.
4. Land for the site of the bridge was purchased for $250,000. Condemnation proceedings were necessary to obtain judgments on the balance of the land needed for $125,000. These amounts were paid to the landowners.
5. A contract was let to the Smith Construction Company for the preparation of the land, the construction of the bridge, and the beautification of the project area for $1,100,000.
6. The contractor completed all of the work on the contract and submitted an invoice for $1,100,000.
7. The bill for the contract was paid except for 5 percent retained until final approval was received.
8. All bills were paid, excess funds transferred, and the capital projects fund was closed.

**Required:**

1. Prepare the journal entries for the preceding transactions that took place during the year in the bridge construction capital projects fund.
2. Prepare any journal entries that would be interfund or interentity as a result of the transactions that took place in the capital projects fund.
3. If no interfund or interentity journal entries are made, explain why not.

**12-6** The "single audit" is a rather new requirement of governmental auditing and reporting.

**Required**:
1 Explain the purpose of the single audit.
2 What requirements are necessary to ensure that the single audit figures agree with the annual financial statement figures?
3 What provisions for reporting on the single audit go beyond those for the audit of financial statements?

12-7 Single audits are made in compliance with governmental audit standards. These standards require, in addition to other standards, the following:

   1 A review is to be made of compliance with applicable laws and regulations.
   2 The auditors shall report on their study and evaluation of internal accounting controls made as a part of the financial and compliance audit. They shall identify as a minimum: (a) the entity's significant internal accounting controls, (b) the controls identified that were evaluated, (c) the controls identified that were not evaluated (the auditor may satisfy this requirement by identifying any significant classes of transactions and related assets not included in the study and evaluation), and (d) the material weaknesses identified as a result of the evaluation.[7]

**Required**:
1 Refer to the appendix and identify the report's reference to compliance with applicable laws and regulations.
2 Refer to the appendix and identify the report's reference to significant internal accounting controls.

12-8 This problem continues the case of Silver City with reference to resources received from federal grants.

**Required**:
1 Review the case in each chapter and identify the situations that can be identified as providing resources from the federal government.
2 Is it necessary to have a single audit of the federal grant funds received by Silver City?

# NOTES

1 Chuck Hamilton, "SIS10: The Uniform Single Financial Audit Bill," *The Government Accountants Journal* 32(3):1, 1983.
2 The Comptroller General of the United States, *Standards for Audit of Governmental Organizations, Programs, Activities, and Functions. 1981 Revision* (Washington, D.C.: United States General Accounting Office, 1981), pp. 24–31.
3 City of Roanoke, Virginia, "Single Audit Report," June 30, 1984.
4 See Executive Office of the President, Office of Management and Budget, *Circular No. A-128. Audits of State and Local Governments. April 1985* (Washington, D.C.: U.S. Government Printing Office, 1985).
5 The Comptroller General of the United States, pp. 25, 29.
6 Adapted from American Institute of Certified Public Accountants, *Uniform CPA Examination Questions and Unofficial Answers* (New York: American Institute of Certified Public Accountants, various dates).
7 See Hamilton. "SIS10: The Uniform Single Financial Audit Bill."

## APPENDIX: City of Roanoke, Virginia— Single Audit Report, June 30, 1984

### TABLE OF CONTENTS

Accountants' Report—Single Audit
   Schedule of Grant Activity
   Reconciliation of Grant Expenditures to Combined
      Financial Statement Expenditures
Accountants' Report—Single Audit Internal Accounting Control
Accountants' Report—Single Audit Compliance

**Peat, Marwick, Mitchell & Co.**
Certified Public Accountants
213 South Jefferson Street
Roanoke, Virginia 24011

The Honorable Members of City Council
City of Roanoke, Virginia:

Under date of September 28, 1984 we have reported on the combined financial statements of the City of Roanoke, Virginia and the combining financial statements of the City as of and for the year ended June 30, 1984 and rendered our opinion thereon. Our examination of such financial statements was made in accordance with generally accepted auditing standards and, accordingly, included such tests of the accounting records and such other auditing procedures as we considered necessary in the circumstances.

The examination referred to above was made for the purpose of forming an opinion on the combined financial statements of the City of Roanoke, Virginia and the combining financial statements of the City taken as a whole. The schedule of federal grant activity and reconciliation of grant expenditures to combined financial statement expenditures for the year ended June 30, 1984 are presented for purposes of additional analysis and are not a required part of the basic financial statements. Such information has been subjected to the auditing procedures applied in the examination of the basic financial statements and, in our opinion, is stated fairly in all material respects in relation to the basic financial statements taken as a whole.

*Peat, Marwick, Mitchell & Co.*

September 28, 1984

CITY OF ROANOKE, VIRGINIA
Schedule of Federal Grant Activity
June 30, 1984

| Grant title | Grant number | Budget |
|---|---|---|
| Department of Housing & Urban Development: | | |
|   Community Development Block Grant | B-78-MC-51-0020 | $ 2,028,851 |
|   Community Development Block Grant | B-79-MC-51-0020 | 2,673,467 |
|   Community Development Block Grant | B-80-MC-51-0020 | 2,727,370 |
|   Community Development Block Grant | B-81-MC-51-0020 | 2,873,768 |
|   Community Development Block Grant | B-82-MC-51-0020 | 2,315,857 |
|   Community Development Block Grant | B-83-MC-51-0020 | 2,784,732 |
|   CDBG Jobs Act | B-83-MJ-51-0020 | 575,000 |
|   Urban Development Action Grant: | | |
|     Cultural Center & Williamson Road Parking Garages | B-80-AA-51-0116 | 5,286,213 |
|     Roanoke Center for Industry and Technology—Cooper Industries | B-82-AA-51-0172 | 3,974,102 |
|     Wometco Coca-Cola Bottling Co. of Roanoke, Inc. | B-83-AA-51-0179 | 4,000,000 |
|     Wometco Coca-Cola Bottling Co. of Roanoke, Inc., Section 108 Loan | B-83-MC-51-0020 | 3,015,000 |
|   Total | | |
| Department of Interior: | | |
|   Parks Rehabilitation Study | 51CTY2100-81-01 | 298,500 |
|   Neighborhood Park Rehabilitation | 51CTY2100-83-03 | 287,000 |
|   Total | | |
| Small Business Administration: | | |
|   Landscaping Grant | 51-30037 | 24,420 |
|   Total | | |
| Federal Emergency Management Agency: | | |
|   Civil Defense | VA-80-011 | 36,052 |
|   Total | | |
| Department of Transportation: | | |
|   Capital Equipment Grant | VA-05-0011 | 1,248,520 |
|   Intermodal Transportation Center (UMTA) | VA-03-0023 | 3,669,810 |
|   Urban Mass Transportation Act | VA-05-4057 | 1,168,058 |
|   Urban Mass Transportation Act | VA-05-4066 | 1,365,768 |
|   Airport Development Aid Project | 651004506 | 720,000 |
|   Airport Development Aid Project | 651004507 | 185,000 |
|   Airport Development Aid Project | 651004512 | 563,535 |
|   Airport Development Aid Project | 651004513 | 3,727,750 |
|   Airport Improvement Program | 3-51-0045-01 | 7,188,098 |
|   Airport Improvement Program | 3-51-0045-03 | 264,000 |
|   Airport Improvement Program | 3-51-0045-04 | 83,771 |
|   Safety First 81–82 (School) | SB801101018 | 17,600 |
|   Total | | |
| Department of Education: | | |
|   Chapter I Winter 84–1 (School) | 124-84-1 | 1,249,459 |
|   Chapter I Carryover 83–3 (School) | 124-83-3 | 341,403 |
|   Chapter I Carryover (School) | 124-83-1 | 826,472 |
|   Chapter I Summer 83–2 (School) | 124-83-2 | 80,249 |
|   Chapter I Summer 84–2 (School) | 124-84-2 | 107,058 |
|   Title IV C CPC 82–83 (School) | 124-A-82-2 | 8,200 |
|   Chapter II 83–84 (School) | 124-C2-84 | 131,386 |
|   Language Learning Center | 124-8283 | 4,930 |
|   Chapter II 82–83 (School) | 124-C2-83 | 188,112 |
|   Career Education 82–83 (School) | 124-82-83-CEF | 3,000 |
|   Refugee Children 1983 (School) | 5077 (0-9) | 3,737 |
|   Flow Through 81–82 (School) | 124-8182FT | 441,140 |
|   Flow Through 83–84 (School) | 124-8384FT | 449,293 |
|   Refugee Children Transition 82–83 (School) | 124-174-02 | 7,305 |
|   Transitional Services 81–82 (School) | 124-80-313C | 6,000 |
|   Transitional Services 83–84 (School) | 124-83-313C | 6,000 |
|   Pre-School Incentive Mini-Grant (School) | 828-3IG-124 | 4,182 |
|   Project SOS 83–84 | DE84-6-58006 | 45,887 |
|   Flow Through 82–83 (School) | 124-8283FT | 408,702 |

|  | Receipts | | | | | Disbursements | | | Cumulative receivable (payable) June 30, 1984 |
| --- | --- | --- | --- | --- | --- | --- | --- | --- | --- |
| Cumulative June 30, 1983 (1) | Current year (2) | Local match | State match | Cumulative June 30, 1984 (1) | Cumulative June 30, 1983 | Current year | Cumulative June 30, 1984 | | |
| 2,033,931 | (5,080) | — | — | 2,028,851 | 2,028,851 | — | 2,028,851 | — |
| 2,668,387 | 5,080 | — | — | 2,673,467 | 2,469,082 | 161,480 | 2,630,562 | (42,905) |
| 2,727,370 | — | — | — | 2,727,370 | 2,527,901 | 46,303 | 2,574,204 | (153,166) |
| 2,566,385 | 307,383 | — | — | 2,873,768 | 2,279,592 | 311,672 | 2,591,264 | (282,504) |
| 885,841 | 1,430,016 | — | — | 2,315,857 | 1,726,048 | 257,323 | 1,983,371 | (332,486) |
| — | 211,014 | — | — | 211,014 | — | 879,282 | 879,282 | 668,268 |
| — | 165,287 | — | — | 165,287 | — | 500,793 | 500,793 | 335,506 |
| 4,818,259 | 366,317 | 87,268 | — | 5,271,844 | 5,052,683 | 219,161 | 5,271,844 | — |
| 187,021 | 2,351,164 | 1,352,618 | — | 3,890,803 | 672,799 | 3,218,004 | 3,890,803 | — |
| — | — | — | — | — | — | 2,148,375 | 2,148,375 | 2,148,375 |
| 15,887,194 | 4,831,181 | 1,439,886 | — | 22,158,261 | 16,756,956 | 7,742,393 | 24,499,349 | 2,341,088 |
| 202,980 | 47,868 | — | 44,267 | 295,115 | 295,232 | (117) | 295,115 | — |
| — | — | 4,249 | — | 4,249 | — | 28,328 | 28,328 | 24,079 |
| 202,980 | 47,868 | 4,249 | 44,267 | 299,364 | 295,232 | 28,211 | 323,443 | 24,079 |
| — | 22,435 | 1,983 | — | 24,418 | — | 24,418 | 24,418 | — |
| — | 22,435 | 1,983 | — | 24,418 | — | 24,418 | 24,418 | — |
| — | 36,052 | — | — | 36,052 | — | 36,052 | 36,052 | — |
| — | 36,052 | — | — | 36,052 | — | 36,052 | 36,052 | — |
| 1,264,510 | 7,450 | 186 | 1,676 | 1,273,822 | 1,264,510 | 9,312 | 1,273,822 | — |
| 1,146,435 | 1,165,036 | 14,566 | 250,188 | 2,576,225 | 1,003,915 | 1,456,296 | 2,460,211 | (116,014) |
| 1,161,191 | 6,867 | — | 56,448 | 1,224,506 | 1,129,416 | 95,090 | 1,224,506 | — |
| — | 559,913 | 367,358 | 262,220 | 1,189,491 | — | 1,139,780 | 1,139,780 | (49,711) |
| 704,583 | 14,050 | — | — | 718,633 | 718,635 | (2) | 718,633 | — |
| 166,734 | 5,920 | 386 | 461 | 173,501 | 165,777 | 7,724 | 173,501 | — |
| 55,438 | 450,000 | 1,847 | 56,250 | 563,535 | 554,380 | 9,155 | 563,535 | — |
| 3,472,431 | 193,356 | 50,580 | — | 3,716,367 | 3,619,491 | 101,876 | 3,721,367 | 5,000 |
| 586,484 | 2,752,067 | 114,731 | 105,964 | 3,559,246 | 771,161 | 2,590,627 | 3,361,788 | (197,458) |
| 52,800 | 211,200 | — | — | 264,000 | 264,000 | — | 264,000 | — |
| — | — | 1,655 | — | 1,655 | — | 16,551 | 16,551 | 14,896 |
| 17,570 | (84) | — | — | 17,486 | 16,973 | 247 | 17,220 | (266) |
| 8,628,176 | 5,365,775 | 551,309 | 733,207 | 15,278,467 | 9,508,258 | 5,426,656 | 14,934,914 | (343,553) |
| — | 480,442 | — | — | 480,442 | — | 797,416 | 797,416 | 316,974 |
| — | 341,403 | — | — | 341,403 | — | 341,403 | 341,403 | — |
| 420,856 | 291,454 | — | — | 712,310 | 710,678 | 1,632 | 712,310 | — |
| — | 66,281 | — | — | 66,281 | 24 | 66,257 | 66,281 | — |
| — | — | — | — | — | — | 2,315 | 2,315 | 2,315 |
| 412 | 7,164 | 668 | — | 8,244 | 5,794 | 2,450 | 8,244 | — |
| — | 95,444 | — | — | 95,444 | — | 131,124 | 131,124 | 35,680 |
| 4,930 | (321) | — | — | 4,609 | 4,608 | 1 | 4,609 | — |
| 149,887 | 38,097 | — | — | 187,984 | 182,593 | 5,517 | 188,110 | 126 |
| — | 2,675 | — | — | 2,675 | 1,862 | 813 | 2,675 | — |
| — | 3,446 | — | — | 3,446 | — | 3,737 | 3,737 | 291 |
| 441,140 | — | — | — | 441,140 | 439,919 | 1,221 | 441,140 | — |
| — | 245,149 | — | 93,568 | 338,717 | — | 432,147 | 432,147 | 93,430 |
| 3,881 | 3,424 | — | — | 7,305 | 4,823 | 2,482 | 7,305 | — |
| 5,869 | 129 | — | — | 5,998 | 5,869 | 129 | 5,998 | — |
| — | 731 | — | — | 731 | — | 1,760 | 1,760 | 1,029 |
| — | 3,107 | — | — | 3,107 | — | 3,107 | 3,107 | — |
| — | 3,922 | 4,950 | — | 8,872 | — | 36,972 | — | 28,100 |
| 282,962 | 125,740 | — | — | 408,702 | 362,441 | 46,160 | 408,601 | (101) |

## Schedule of Federal Grant Activity (continued)

| Grant title | Grant number | Budget |
|---|---|---|
| Transitional Services 82–83 (School) | 124-81-313C | 5,069 |
| Project Aware (School) | SB82-00-006 | 11,787 |
| ABE/DIAL 83–84 (School) | 124-8384 | 78,840 |
| Impact Aid 83–84 (School) | 56-VA-84-1803 | 16,419 |
| ABE/DIAL 82–83 (School) | 124-8283 | 74,311 |
| Low Rent Housing PL 874 (School) | 56-VA-81-E | 138,967 |
| Refugee Children 81–82 (School) | 174-02-1E002226 | 10,318 |
| Refugee Child Transition 1984 | 50771 | 4,400 |
| Nutrition Services (School) | — | 2,557,096 |
| ESAA Special Arts 81–82 (School) | 124-8182 | 17,394 |
| Title VI 81–82 (School) | G008001958 | 227,427 |
| Total | | |
| **National Endowment for the Humanities:** | | |
| Artists in Schools (School) | 124-82-320 | 12,400 |
| Artists in Education 82–83 (School) | 124-83-067 | 10,600 |
| Artists in Education 83–84 (School) | 124-84-310 | 12,996 |
| Total | | |
| **Department of the Treasury:** | | |
| Revenue Sharing | 47-2-128-001 Entitlement 14 | 2,745,953 |
| Revenue Sharing | 47-2-128-001 Entitlement 15 | 2,682,098 |
| Total | | |
| **National Endowment of Arts:** | | |
| National Endowment of Arts | 12-4250-255 | 19,190 |
| Total | | |
| **Economic Development Administration:** | | |
| Mini-Mall | 01-01-02308 | 765,000 |
| Total | | |
| **Environmental Protection Agency:** | | |
| Norfolk Avenue Sewer Project | C510-510 | 2,261,780 |
| Vinton Connection Facility | C510-442 | 655,245 |
| Total | | |
| **Department of Social Services:** | | |
| Food Stamps | — | 368,335 |
| Social Services—Administration, Services and Income Maintenance | — | 3,034,559 |
| Aid to Dependent Children, Aid to Dependent Children—Foster Care, and Emergency Assistance | — | 617,199 |
| Other Purchased Services | — | 839,876 |
| Indochinese Resettlement Assistance | — | 7,994 |
| Blind and Blind Purchased Services | — | 6,697 |
| Fuel Assistance | — | 88,298 |
| Total | | |
| **Virginia State Library:** | | |
| Virginia State Library Grant | — | 14,914 |
| Total | | |
| **Department of Corrections:** | | |
| Juvenile Detention Home 83–84 | — | 801 |
| Total | | |
| Grand Total | | |
| Increase in accrued grant revenues | | |
| Increase in deferred grant revenues | | |
| **Virginia Department of Corrections** | | |
| Youth Services Grant* | 82-I-5 | 34,511 |
| Youth Services Grant | 83-I-5 | 37,098 |

*This State grant was subjected to testing at the request of the City of Roanoke.
(1)Includes federal grant award, state and local match, and program income.
(2)Includes federal grant receipts and program income.

## Schedule of Federal Grant Activity (continued)

| Cumulative June 30, 1983 (1) | Receipts | | | | | Disbursements | | | Cumulative receivable (payable) June 30, 1984 |
|---|---|---|---|---|---|---|---|---|---|
| | Current year (2) | Local match | State match | Cumulative June 30, 1984 (1) | Cumulative June 30, 1983 | Current year | Cumulative June 30, 1984 | |
| 1,328 | 3,741 | — | — | 5,069 | 4,339 | 730 | 5,069 | — |
| 6,607 | 4,607 | — | — | 11,214 | 7,944 | 3,641 | 11,585 | 371 |
| — | 48,014 | 19,000 | — | 67,014 | — | 60,001 | 60,001 | (7,013) |
| — | 40,584 | — | — | 40,584 | — | 26,207 | 26,207 | (14,377) |
| 75,279 | — | 6,268 | — | 81,547 | 81,547 | — | 81,547 | — |
| 153,076 | (14,297) | — | — | 138,779 | 138,396 | 383 | 138,779 | — |
| 10,118 | — | — | — | 10,118 | 10,318 | — | 10,318 | 200 |
| — | — | — | — | — | — | 2,630 | 2,630 | 2,630 |
| — | 1,377,040 | 1,085,030 | 103,209 | 2,565,279 | — | 2,475,369 | 2,475,369 | (89,910) |
| 12,808 | — | 2,298 | — | 15,106 | 14,432 | 674 | 15,106 | — |
| 227,427 | — | — | — | 227,427 | 221,183 | 1,274 | 222,457 | (4,970) |
| 1,796,580 | 3,167,976 | 1,118,214 | 196,777 | 6,279,547 | 2,196,770 | 4,447,552 | 6,644,322 | 364,775 |
| | | | | | | | | |
| 12,400 | — | — | — | 12,400 | 12,161 | 15 | 12,176 | (224) |
| 10,060 | 540 | — | — | 10,600 | 9,290 | 890 | 10,180 | (420) |
| — | 2,550 | 9,996 | — | 12,546 | — | 11,735 | 11,735 | (811) |
| 22,460 | 3,090 | 9,996 | — | 35,546 | 21,451 | 12,640 | 34,091 | (1,455) |
| | | | | | | | | |
| 2,059,261 | 686,692 | — | — | 2,745,953 | 1,372,569 | 1,373,384 | 2,745,953 | — |
| — | 2,011,572 | — | — | 2,011,572 | — | 1,341,049 | 1,341,049 | (670,523) |
| 2,059,261 | 2,698,264 | — | — | 4,757,525 | 1,372,569 | 2,714,433 | 4,087,002 | (670,523) |
| | | | | | | | | |
| — | 19,190 | — | — | 19,190 | 19,190 | — | 19,190 | — |
| — | 19,190 | — | — | 19,190 | 19,190 | — | 19,190 | — |
| | | | | | | | | |
| 18,225 | 369,749 | 86,347 | — | 474,321 | 91,122 | 402,998 | 494,120 | 19,799 |
| 18,225 | 369,749 | 86,347 | — | 474,321 | 91,122 | 402,998 | 494,120 | 19,799 |
| | | | | | | | | |
| 1,999,830 | — | — | — | 1,999,830 | 2,261,780 | — | 2,261,780 | 261,950 |
| 177,550 | 259,900 | 71,719 | — | 509,169 | 558,348 | 29,052 | 587,400 | 78,231 |
| 2,177,380 | 259,900 | 71,719 | — | 2,508,999 | 2,820,128 | 29,052 | 2,849,180 | 340,181 |
| | | | | | | | | |
| — | 164,749 | 80,556 | 164,749 | 410,054 | — | 402,781 | 402,781 | (7,273) |
| — | 1,175,136 | 572,180 | 1,175,136 | 2,922,452 | — | 2,860,902 | 2,860,902 | (61,550) |
| | | | | | | | | |
| — | 305,466 | — | 230,439 | 535,905 | — | 617,199 | 617,199 | 81,294 |
| — | 602,833 | 125,981 | 200,944 | 929,758 | — | 839,876 | 839,876 | (89,882) |
| — | 9,341 | — | — | 9,341 | — | 7,994 | 7,994 | (1,347) |
| — | 2,712 | 1,339 | 181 | 4,232 | — | 6,697 | 6,697 | 2,465 |
| — | 38,083 | — | 38,083 | 76,166 | — | 83,236 | 83,236 | 7,070 |
| — | 2,298,320 | 780,056 | 1,809,532 | 4,887,908 | — | 4,818,685 | 4,818,685 | (69,223) |
| | | | | | | | | |
| — | 21,133 | — | — | 21,133 | — | 21,133 | 21,133 | — |
| — | 21,133 | — | — | 21,133 | — | 21,133 | 21,133 | — |
| | | | | | | | | |
| — | 801 | — | — | 801 | — | 801 | 801 | — |
| — | 801 | — | — | 801 | — | 801 | 801 | — |
| $30,792,256 | 19,141,734 | 4,063,759 | 2,783,783 | 56,781,532 | 33,081,676 | 25,705,024 | 58,786,700 | 2,005,168 |
| | 93,108 | | | | | | | |
| | (532,329) | | | | | | | |
| | $18,702,513 | | | | | | | |
| | | | | | | | | |
| 34,511 | — | — | — | 34,511 | 33,301 | 1,210 | 34,511 | — |
| — | — | 9,358 | 27,740 | 37,098 | — | 36,764 | 36,764 | (334) |
| 34,511 | — | 9,358 | 27,740 | 71,609 | 33,301 | 37,974 | 71,275 | (334) |

## CITY OF ROANOKE, VIRGINIA
### Reconciliation of Grant Expenditures to Combined Financial Statements Expenditures
### Year Ended June 30, 1984

|  | Federal grant expenditures* | Expenditures on non-federal grant programs** | Non-grant expenditures | Expenditures per combined financial statements |
|---|---|---|---|---|
| Governmental fund type |  |  |  |  |
| Expenditures (Exhibit 13-3): |  |  |  |  |
| General government | $ — | — | 4,567,405 | 4,567,405 |
| Judicial | — | — | 1,503,621 | 1,503,621 |
| Public safety | 2,750,485 | — | 11,285,260 | 14,035,745 |
| Public works | — | 8,726 | 11,586,936 | 11,595,662 |
| Health and welfare | 4,819,486 | 37,974 | 3,315,988 | 8,173,448 |
| Education | 4,460,439 | 206,812 | 36,809,792 | 41,477,043 |
| Parks, recreation, and cultural | 73,762 | — | 1,867,232 | 1,940,994 |
| Community development | — | — | 481,309 | 481,309 |
| Non-departmental | — | — | 7,403,107 | 7,403,107 |
| Debt service | — | — | 7,744,355 | 7,744,355 |
| Major capital outlay | 8,145,391 | — | 5,886,566 | 14,031,957 |
| Total | 20,249,563 | 253,512 | 92,451,571 | 112,954,646 |
| Proprietary fund type |  |  |  |  |
| Expenditures (Exhibits 13-5 & 13-6): |  |  |  |  |
| Operating expenses | 4,211,279 | — | 10,461,883 | 14,673,162 |
| Acquisition of fixed assets | 1,244,182 | — | 3,716,601 | 4,960,783 |
| Total | 5,455,461 | — | 14,178,484 | 19,633,945 |
| Grand total | $25,705,024 | 253,512 | 106,630,055 | 132,588,591 |

*Includes expenditures of federal funds as well as expenditures of state and local matching funds related to federal programs.
**Does not include state and local matches of federal funds.

**Peat Marwick**

**Peat, Marwick, Mitchell & Co.**
Certified Public Accountants
213 South Jefferson Street
Roanoke, Virginia 24011

The Honorable Members of City Council
City of Roanoke, Virginia

We have examined the combined financial statements of the City of Roanoke, Virginia and the combining financial statements of the City as of and for the year ended June 30, 1984 and have issued our report thereon dated September 28, 1984. As part of our examination, we made a study and evaluation of the City's system of internal accounting control to the extent we considered necessary to evaluate the system as required by generally accepted auditing standards, the standards for financial and compliance audits contained in the U.S. General Accounting Office's Standards for Audit of Governmental Organizations, Programs, Activities and Functions (1981 Revision), Office of Management and Budget Circular A-102, Uniform Requirements for Assistance to State and Local Governments, Attachment P, Audit Requirements, and the Specifications for Audit of Counties, Cities, and Towns (1983) issued by the Auditor of Public Accounts of the Commonwealth of Virginia. For the purpose of this report, we have classified the significant internal accounting controls in the following categories:

- Revenue Cycle
    Cash Receipts
    Accounts Receivable
- Purchasing Cycle
    Cash Disbursements
    Accounts Payable
- Payroll System

The purpose of our study and evaluation was to determine the nature, timing and extent of the auditing procedures necessary for expressing an opinion on the City's financial statements. Our study and evaluation was more limited than would be necessary to express an opinion on the system of internal accounting control taken as a whole or on any of the categories of controls identified above.

The management of the City of Roanoke, Virginia is responsible for establishing and maintaining a system of internal accounting control. In fulfilling this responsibility, estimates and judgments by management are required to assess the expected benefits and related costs of control procedures. The objectives of a system are to provide management with reasonable, but not absolute, assurance that assets are safeguarded against loss from unauthorized use or disposition, and that transactions are executed in accordance with management's authorization and recorded properly to permit the preparation of financial statements in accordance with generally accepted accounting principles.

Because of inherent limitations in any system of internal accounting control, errors or irregularities may nevertheless occur and not be detected. Also, projection of any evaluation of the system to future periods is subject to the risk that procedures may become inadequate because of changes in conditions or that the degree of compliance with the procedures may deteriorate.

Our study and evaluation made for the limited purpose described in the first paragraph would not necessarily disclose all material weaknesses in the system. Accordingly, we do not express an opinion on the system of internal accounting control of the City of Roanoke, Virginia taken as a whole. However, our study and evaluation disclosed no condition that we believe to be a material weakness.

Because of inherent limitations in any system of internal accounting control, errors or irregularities may nevertheless occur and not be detected. Also, projection of any evaluation of the system to future periods is subject to the risk that procedures may become inadequate because of changes in conditions or that the degree of compliance with the procedures may deteriorate.

This report is intended solely for the use of the City of Roanoke, Virginia and the cognizant and other Federal and state audit agencies. This restriction is not intended to limit the distribution of this report which, upon acceptance by the cognizant and other Federal audit agencies, is a matter of public record.

*Peat, Marwick, Mitchell & Co.*

September 28, 1984

**PEAT MARWICK**

Peat, Marwick, Mitchell & Co.
Certified Public Accountants
213 South Jefferson Street
Roanoke, Virginia 24011

The Honorable Members of City Council
City of Roanoke, Virginia

We have examined the combined financial statements of the City of Roanoke, Virginia and the combining financial statements of the City as of and for the year ended June 30, 1984 and have issued our report thereon dated September 28, 1984. The schedule of grant activity for the year ended June 30, 1984 has been prepared as a separate report for purposes of additional analysis and we have issued our report thereon dated September 30, 1984 in relation to the basic financial statements of the City taken as a whole. Our examination was made in accordance with generally accepted auditing standards; the provisions of <u>Standards for Audit of Governmental Organizations, Programs, Activities and Functions</u>, promulgated by the Comptroller General, which pertain to financial and compliance audits; the Office of Management and Budget's <u>Major Compliance Features and Programs Administered by State and Local Governments</u> (the approved compliance supplement) and, provisions Office of Management and Budget (OMB) Circular A-102, <u>Uniform Administrative Requirements for Grants-in-Aid to State and Local Governments</u>, Attachment P, <u>Audit Requirements</u> and the <u>Guidelines for Financial and Compliance Audits of Federally Assisted Programs</u>, and, accordingly, included such tests of the accounting records and such other auditing procedures as we considered necessary in the circumstances.

In connection with the examination referred to above, a representative number of charges to Federal awards were selected to determine if (1) Federal funds are being expended in accordance with the terms of applicable agreements and those provisions of Federal law or regulations that could have a material effect on the financial statements or on the awards tested and (2) Federal financial reports accurately present the underlying financial data of the Federal grants of the City of Roanoke, Virginia.

The results of our tests indicate that for the items tested, except as described in the following paragraphs, the City of Roanoke, Virginia complied with the material terms and conditions of the Federal award agreements and that Federal financial reports accurately present the underlying financial data of the Federal grants of the City. Further, for the items not tested, based on our examination and the procedures referred to above, nothing came to our attention, except as noted in the following paragraphs, to indicate that the City of Roanoke, Virginia had not complied with the significant compliance terms and conditions of the awards referred to above.

Civil Rights

At June 30, 1984, five civil rights cases against the City of Roanoke were in litigation. These cases include charges of discrimination based on age, sex, race, and equal pay. Four additional civil rights discrimination charges have been filed with the Equal Employment Opportunity Commission. The City of Roanoke respectfully denies any violation of civil rights, and at the date of this letter, no determination has been made as to whether the City violated the civil rights of these employees.

Davis-Bacon Act

Compliance with the Davis-Bacon Act (the Act) is required on all federally funded construction programs. Grant recipients are responsible for developing a system to monitor applicable contractors and subcontractors for compliance with wage standards under the Act. The

City has established a system to monitor compliance with the Act for construction programs under the Community Development Block Grant, Urban Development Action Grant (UDAG), Airport Development Aid Program and Airport Improvement Project. Our review of contractor labor files indicated that an insufficient number of interviews were performed by the City in order to verify the accuracy of contractor payroll listings. In addition, reviews of payroll listings for UDAG were not performed.

We recommend that management review the City's system of monitoring compliance with the Act to satisfy itself that all federally funded construction programs are included. Weekly or other timely payroll listings from all contractors and subcontractors on these construction programs should be reviewed for compliance with wage standards under the Act and the review should be documented by the reviewer's initials on the payroll listings.

We understand that the interviewing of contractors' personnel on a regular basis in order to verify the accuracy of payroll listings submitted by the contractors is costly and time consuming. We recommend that the City periodically verify the job descriptions and pay rates of a sample of personnel included in contractors' listings by mail confirmation with the selected persons. We have been advised by City Engineering personnel that this is a feasible method of verifying the accuracy of these listings.

The City has established a grant compliance department as of August 1984. We understand this department will be responsible for monitoring compliance with the Act.

Errors and Omissions on Federal Financial Reports

The Federal Revenue Sharing Use Reports as of June 30, 1982 and June 30, 1983 contained amounts that were not in agreement with the respective financial statements and supplemental schedules. Differences noted included calculation errors, exclusion of certain amounts, and inconsistent treatment of similar transactions between years.

The preparers of Federal financial reports should maintain sufficient working papers documenting the reconciliation of financial data per the reports to City financial data. We noted that this procedure is being performed for other filings of grant related reports. We recommend that the same procedure be applied to Revenue Sharing. The City should prepare an index listing the expenditures per the financial statements and schedules that are included in each line item of the use report. This procedure would ensure consistent treatment over the years.

The City has shifted responsibilities for preparation of these reports and expects to have this situation corrected.

Other Items

With regard to the Nutrition Services Program, we noted certain discrepancies in the individual schools' calculations of families' annual income. These discrepancies were due to mathematical errors. Although these miscalculations would not have resulted in a change of student status under the free and reduced meal guidelines, they could have potentially resulted in changes in student eligibility. We recommend that a policy be implemented to ensure the accuracy of the eligibility determinations.

The School Board will strengthen its review policy at the school level to examine and correct errors made in the completion of applicant forms.

\* \* \* \* \*

This report is intended solely for the use of the City of Roanoke, Virginia and the cognizant and other Federal and state audit agencies. This restriction is not intended to limited the distribution of this report which, upon acceptance by the cognizant and other Federal or state audit agencies, is a matter of public record.

*Peat, Marwick, Mitchell & Co.*

September 28, 1984

CHAPTER 13

# FINANCIAL REPORTING

When it comes to reporting, the financial reports for the governmental unit should consider not only the operations and resources of a particular fund, but all of the assets, liabilities, operations, and fund balances of the overall unit. This reporting consideration should not be a consolidation of all of the activities of the unit; rather, the report should reflect a combination of all of the resources and equities that were available and were used for the rendering of services to the citizens of the unit. When it comes to reporting, therefore, the governmental unit must go through the process of combining funds and preparing statements, schedules, and notes. This combination will show all of the funds and account groups, and even entities for which the governmental unit does not keep records but over which it does have control. For information purposes, all of the results, resources, and equities of all of the entities should be included.

In this chapter, the various types of statements, schedules, and notes prepared for external reporting purposes by the governmental unit will be discussed. This will be done (1) by individual funds and account groups and (2) by combined units, with an overall report for all governmental units. As a final section, you will see the independent accountant's opinion, which is offered when the financial statements of the overall governmental unit are audited to determine whether or not those statements are presented in accordance with generally accepted accounting principles consistently applied. An actual report of the city of Roanoke, Virginia, with the accompanying statements, notes, and schedules, is included to illustrate financial reporting.

## THE REPORTING ENTITY

For accounting purposes, there is no such thing as a single entity of government. Funds and account groups, along with boards, authorities, districts, and so forth, make up the numerous accounting entities. In trying to bring together all of the accounting entities that represent the numerous activities of government into a reporting entity, the National Council on Governmental Accounting says:

> The NCGA concludes that the basic—but not the only—criterion for including a governmental department, agency, institution, commission, public authority, or other governmental organization in a governmental unit's reporting entity for general purpose financial reports is the exercise of oversight responsibility over such agencies by the governmental unit's elected officials. Oversight responsibility is derived from the governmental unit's power and includes, but is not limited to, financial interdependency, selection of governing authority, designation of management, ability to significantly influence operations and accountability for fiscal matters. Oversight responsibility implies that a governmental unit is dependent on another and the dependent unit should be reported as part of the other.[1]

Using this criterion, many organizations not necessarily considered a part of the governmental unit's normal operations might be included in the financial reports. For examples, independent school districts controlled by a city council might be included in the city's financial reports; an urban renewal public benefit corporation, whose governing board is appointed by the city council, might be included in a city's financial reports; and a county flood control district, whose governing body is the same as the county's, might be included in the county's financial reports.[2]

## THE COMPREHENSIVE ANNUAL FINANCIAL REPORT

Prior to 1980 the only financial statements needed in a governmental unit's financial reports were those of the individual funds, since each fund was considered to be an accountable entity. When these statements were shown together (e.g., in the annual financial report), no total was given. This was done to keep from conveying the impression that the governmental unit could be considered as one accounting entity.

In terms of current annual financial reporting, the NCGA states:

> A comprehensive annual financial report covering all funds and account groups of the reporting entity—including introductory section; appropriate combined, combining and individual fund statements; notes to the financial statements; schedules; narrative explanations; and statistical tables—should be prepared and published. The reporting entity is the oversight unit and all other component units combined in accordance with NCGA principles.[3]

The NCGA uses a pyramidal chart (see Exhibit 13-1) to illustrate the present types of financial reporting appropriate to local governments. Appendix 13-1, the table of contents for the Comprehensive Annual Financial Report for the city of Roanoke, Virginia for the year ended June 30, 1984, presents the information customarily found in a comprehensive annual financial report.

Accounting principles for external financial reporting currently suggest that all of the funds and component units of a governmental unit should be "combined" into a single statement, with a separate column for each major fund classification. The total for all of the funds and account groups is provided, for information purposes. This statement should not be viewed as a combination of all of the funds into a total for the entire government. In addition, particular types of funds that may have more than one

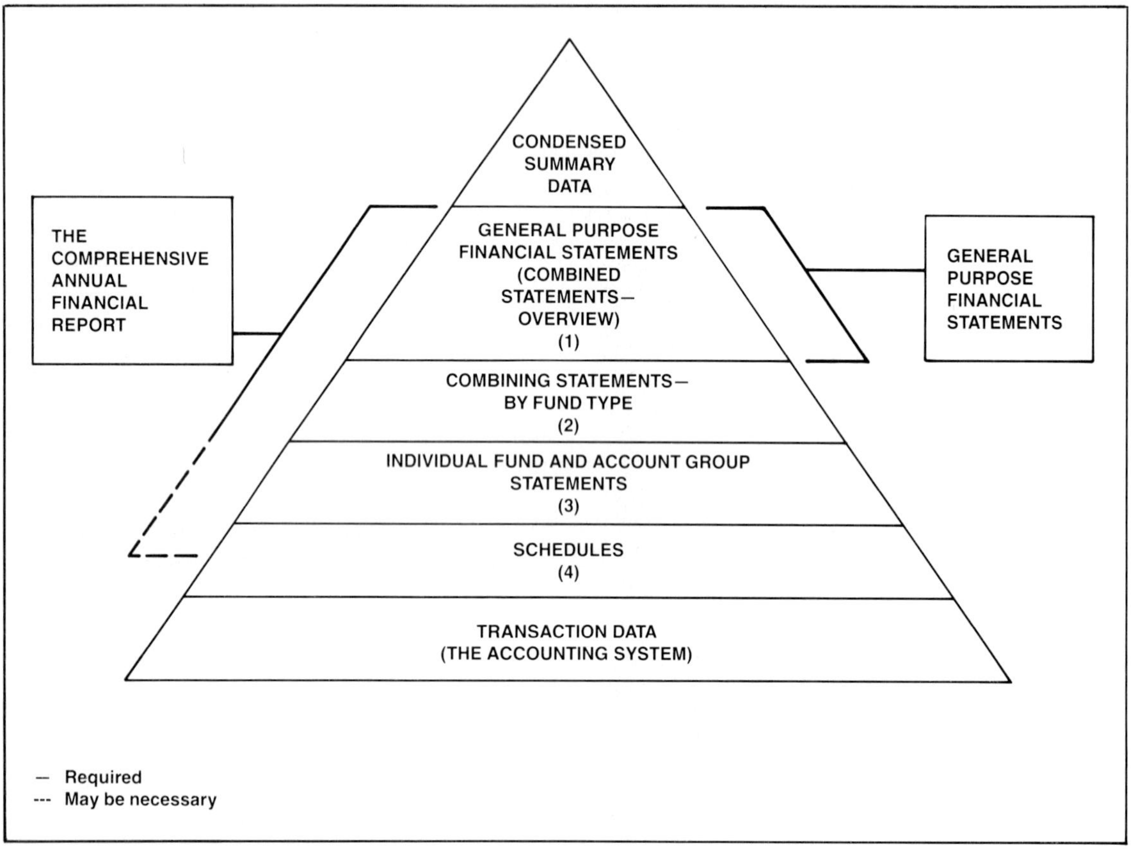
CONDENSED
SUMMARY
DATA
GENERAL PURPOSE
FINANCIAL STATEMENTS
(COMBINED
STATEMENTS—
OVERVIEW)
(1)
COMBINING STATEMENTS—
BY FUND TYPE
(2)
INDIVIDUAL FUND AND ACCOUNT GROUP
STATEMENTS
(3)
SCHEDULES
(4)
TRANSACTION DATA
(THE ACCOUNTING SYSTEM)
THE
COMPREHENSIVE
ANNUAL
FINANCIAL
REPORT
GENERAL
PURPOSE
FINANCIAL
STATEMENTS
— Required
--- May be necessary

**EXHIBIT 13-1** The financial reporting "pyramid."[4]

fund under that type should show these funds combined under what are called "combining funds statements."

Let us consider a governmental unit's financial statements under four basic headings: (1) combining statements, (2) individual fund and account group statements, (3) combined statements and, (4) notes to the financial statements. *Combining funds statements* present totals for each fund of a particular type, such as special revenue funds or capital projects funds. The balance sheets of all of the funds and account groups of the governmental unit are shown together and combined into a memorandum total in what is called a "*combined balance sheet*." Individual statements can be determined from combining statements when they are used. When there is only one fund of a particular type, combining statements are not used; rather, individual statements must be shown.

Statements for a governmental unit, usually are not consolidated. But there is no prohibition against interfund and similar eliminations being made in the combining or combined balance sheets for all fund types or in the combined statement of revenues, expenditures, and changes in fund balances for all. The totals, however, must be labeled "memorandum only," and a statement must be placed in the notes indicating that the total is not a consolidated total. Thus, in external financial reporting, interfund and similar eliminations must be disclosed, either in the headings or in the notes to the financial statements.

There are both proponents and opponents to the use of consolidated financial statements for governmental reporting. Opponents to consolidating the statements are currently in the majority, but have relinquished their fund entity reporting views sufficiently to allow the use of combined statements. Originally, their belief was to keep the financial statements of each entity separate and distinct from any other entity. The *1968 Governmental Accounting and Financial Reporting Principles Statement* followed the idea of separate entities and did not combine the entities. The GASB, from the NCGA's *Statement 1*, the 1979 edition of GAAP, and the AICPA's *Statement of Position 80-2*, now require combined and combining financial statements, but leave the consolidated statement to an individual governmental unit's choice.[5]

## Combined Statements

The statements from the annual financial report, year ended June 30, 1984, for the city of Roanoke, Virginia, are used to illustrate these required combined statements, a listing of which follows:

**1** A combined balance sheet composed of all fund types and account groups. These statements are grouped by: (a) governmental fund types, (b) proprietary fund types, (c) fiduciary fund types, (d) account groups, and (e) total (memorandum only). (See Exhibit 13-2.)[6]

**2** A combined statement of revenues, expenditures, and changes in fund balances for all governmental fund types. (See Exhibit 13-3.)[7]

**3** Fiduciary funds may be of the governmental type (expendable funds on the modified accrual basis). Then those governmental-type fiduciary funds may be combined with the other governmental funds. (Not shown.)

**4** A combined statement of revenues, expenditures, and changes in fund balance for all governmental fund types that have annual budgets is prepared that compares the budget with actual revenues and expenditures for the year. Only the general fund is shown in this illustration. (See Exhibit 13-4.)[8]

**5** A combined statement of revenues and expenses, along with a statement of changes in retained earnings, is also needed for all proprietary fund types. (See Exhibit 13-5.)[9]

**6** A combined statement of changes in financial position is needed for all proprietary fund types. Fiduciary-type funds that are similar to proprietary-type funds, that is, accrual basis entities that are nonexpendable, may be combined with the combined statement of revenues and expenses of all proprietary funds. (See Exhibit 13-6.)[10]

## Individual Funds Statements

When a local governmental unit has only one fund of a particular type, the statements for those funds are usually presented separately.

The statements for the following individual funds are shown for:

**1** The general fund (see Exhibits 13-7, balance sheet;[11] 13-8, statement of revenue, budget and actual;[12] and 13-9, statement of expenditures, budget and actual, non-GAAP budgetary basis[13]).

**2** Debt service fund (see Exhibits 13-10, balance sheet;[14] and 13-11, statement of revenues, expenditures, and changes in fund balance[15]).

**3** Capital projects fund (see Exhibits 13-12, balance sheet;[16] and 13-13, statement of revenues, expenditures, and changes in fund balance[17]).

## Combining Statements

Concerning combining statements, the National Council on Governmental Accounting states:

**EXHIBIT 13-2**
**City of Roanoke, Virginia**
**Combined Balance Sheet**
**All Fund Types and Account Groups**
**June 30, 1984**

|  | Governmental fund types | | |
|---|---|---|---|
|  | General | Debt service | Capital projects |
| **Assets and Other Debits** | | | |
| Cash | $ 2,910,271 | $ 11,337 | $ 79,801 |
| Investments | 8,932,781 | 5,775,000 | 12,900,000 |
| Interest and dividends receivable | 67,214 | 45,045 | 109,330 |
| Due from other governments | 2,724,920 | — | 2,682,142 |
| Due from other funds | 49,711 | — | 423,423 |
| Taxes receivable | 2,010,080 | — | — |
| Accounts receivable | 402,298 | — | 246,105 |
| Allowance for uncollectible receivables | (810,995) | — | — |
| Inventories | 934,973 | — | — |
| Other assets | — | — | — |
| Land | — | — | — |
| Buildings and structures | — | — | — |
| Equipment and other fixed assets | — | — | — |
| Accumulated depreciation | — | — | — |
| Construction in progress | — | — | — |
| Amount available in debt service fund | — | — | — |
| Amount to be provided for retirement of general long-term debt | — | — | — |
| Total assets | $17,221,253 | $5,831,382 | $16,440,801 |

Where a governmental unit has more than one fund of a given type (e.g., Special Revenue Funds), combining statements for all funds of that type should be presented in a columnar format. The total columns of these combining statements should agree with the amounts presented in the GPFS. (In some instances, disclosure sufficient to meet CAFR reporting objectives may be achieved at this level: in other cases, these statements "link" the GPFS and the individual fund statements).[18]

Thus combining statements bring together, into one statement, the statements for all funds of a particular type. Proprietary funds statements that follow the combining pattern are: (1) the balance sheet for all proprietary funds (see Exhibit 13-14[19] for enterprise funds and Exhibit 13-17[20] for internal service funds); (2) the statement of revenues, expenses, and changes in retained earnings (or equity) for all proprietary funds (see Exhibit 13-15[21] for enterprise funds and Exhibit 13-18[22] for internal service funds); and (3) the statement of changes in financial position for all proprietary funds (see Exhibit 13-16[23] for enterprise funds and Exhibit 13-19[24] for internal service

**EXHIBIT 13-2**
(continued)

| Proprietary fund types | | Fiduciary fund type | Account groups | | Memorandum only totals | |
|---|---|---|---|---|---|---|
| Enterprise | Internal service* | Trust and agency | General fixed assets | General long-term debt | June 30, 1984 | June 30, 1983 |
| $ 431,882 | $ 71,024 | $ 202,194 | $ — | $ — | $ 3,706,509 | $ 2,052,688 |
| 8,910,671 | 600,000 | 48,470,643 | — | — | 85,589,095 | 83,480,781 |
| 78,725 | 1,481 | 609,101 | — | — | 910,896 | 946,809 |
| 414,640 | — | — | — | — | 5,821,702 | 5,538,063 |
| — | — | 162,828 | — | — | 635,962 | 476,534 |
| — | — | — | — | — | 2,010,080 | 2,198,849 |
| 651,500 | — | 160,723 | — | — | 1,460,626 | 1,155,857 |
| | | | | | (810,995) | (680,097) |
| — | — | — | — | — | 1,515,022 | 1,389,607 |
| 580,049 | — | — | — | — | 24,301 | 41,434 |
| 20,889 | — | 3,412 | — | — | 18,794,185 | 18,236,739 |
| 7,686,664 | — | — | 11,107,521 | — | 134,582,235 | 133,232,873 |
| 68,590,189 | — | — | 65,992,046 | — | 44,544,522 | 41,308,667 |
| 27,385,452 | 1,582,326 | — | 15,576,744 | — | (36,171,244) | (33,309,409) |
| (35,776,564) | (394,680) | — | — | — | 37,068,784 | 29,473,231 |
| 13,423,960 | — | — | 23,644,824 | — | | |
| — | — | — | — | 5,803,854 | 5,803,854 | 5,750,166 |
| — | — | — | — | 48,149,547 | 48,149,547 | 52,585,754 |
| $92,398,057 | $1,860,151 | $49,608,901 | $116,321,135 | $53,953,401 | $353,635,081 | $343,878,546 |

**EXHIBIT 13-2**
(*continued*)

|  | Governmental fund types | | |
|---|---|---|---|
|  | General | Debt service | Capital projects |
| **Liabilities and Fund Equity** | | | |
| Liabilities: | | | |
|   Warrants payable | $ 6,313,172 | $ — | $ 664,041 |
|   Accounts payable and accrued expenses/expenditures | 2,935,927 | — | — |
|   Due to other governments | — | — | — |
|   Due to other funds | 141,043 | — | — |
|   Deferred revenue | 1,504,068 | — | — |
|   Other liabilities | — | — | — |
|   Matured bonds and interest payable | — | 27,528 | — |
|   Revenue bonds payable | — | — | — |
|   General obligation debt payable | — | — | — |
|   Total liabilities | 10,894,210 | 27,528 | 664,041 |
| Fund equity: | | | |
|   Investment in general fixed assets | — | — | — |
|   Contributed capital | — | — | — |
|   Retained earnings | — | — | — |
|   Fund balances: | | | |
|     Reserved for encumbrances | 1,674,452 | — | 6,647,316 |
|     Reserved for employee retirement benefits | — | — | — |
|     Unreserved: | | | |
|       Designated for worker's compensation | 108,503 | — | — |
|       Designated for subsequent year's expenditures | 670,524 | — | — |
|       Designated for debt service | — | 5,803,854 | — |
|       Designated for capital equipment | 3,027,463 | — | — |
|       Designated for future capital projects | — | — | 8,304,547 |
|       Undesignated | 846,101 | — | 824,897 |
|   Total fund equity | 6,327,043 | 5,803,854 | 15,776,760 |
| Total liabilities and fund equity | $17,221,253 | $5,831,382 | $16,440,801 |

*See note 2 in notes to the financial statements, Appendix 13-2.

funds). Statements that follow the combining pattern in governmental funds include: (1) the balance sheet and (2) the statement of revenues, expenditures, and changes in fund balance. Statements for fiduciary fund types that include more than one of each type, may be included with the governmental funds, the proprietary funds, or may be shown separately. The agency funds are usually combined separately from other fiduciary funds (see Exhibits 13-20,[25] 13-21,[26] 13-22,[27] and 13-23[28]).

## EXHIBIT 13-2
*(continued)*

| Proprietary fund types | | Fiduciary fund type | Account groups | | Memorandum only totals | |
|---|---|---|---|---|---|---|
| Enterprise | Internal service* | Trust and agency | General fixed assets | General long-term debt | June 30, 1984 | June 30, 1983 |
| $ 332,240 | $ 175,249 | $ 145,077 | $ — | $ — | $ 7,629,779 | $ 8,645,231 |
| 589,366 | 291,895 | 139,352 | — | — | 3,956,540 | 4,272,385 |
| 177,562 | — | 1,193 | — | — | 178,755 | 32,799 |
| 59,788 | 435,131 | — | — | — | 635,962 | 476,534 |
| — | — | — | — | — | 1,504,068 | 1,807,865 |
| 234,822 | — | — | — | — | 234,822 | 137,496 |
| — | — | — | — | — | 27,528 | 29,017 |
| 4,745,000 | — | — | — | — | 4,745,000 | 5,291,000 |
| 564,510 | — | — | — | 53,953,401 | 54,517,911 | 58,973,710 |
| 6,703,288 | 902,275 | 285,622 | — | 53,953,401 | 73,430,365 | 79,666,037 |
| — | — | — | 116,321,135 | — | 116,321,135 | 110,126,028 |
| 57,680,325 | 690,543 | — | — | — | 58,370,868 | 54,886,693 |
| 28,014,444 | 267,333 | — | — | — | 28,281,777 | 25,746,912 |
| — | — | — | — | — | 8,321,768 | 8,696,855 |
| — | — | 49,323,279 | — | — | 49,323,279 | 44,556,606 |
| — | — | — | — | — | 108,503 | 94,919 |
| — | — | — | — | — | 670,524 | 686,692 |
| — | — | — | — | — | 5,803,854 | 5,750,166 |
| — | — | — | — | — | 3,027,463 | 2,470,189 |
| — | — | — | — | — | 8,304,547 | 9,969,016 |
| — | — | — | — | — | 1,670,998 | 1,228,433 |
| 85,694,769 | 957,876 | 49,323,279 | 116,321,135 | — | 280,204,716 | 264,212,509 |
| $92,398,057 | $1,860,151 | $49,608,901 | $116,321,135 | $53,953,401 | $353,635,081 | $343,878,546 |

## Notes to the Financial Statements

In addition to financial statements, a great deal of information concerning the statements can be included in *notes to financial statements*. Appendix 13-2, the notes to the financial statements for the city of Roanoke, Virginia, shows: (1) a summary of significant accounting policies, (2) internal service funds, (3) due from other governmental funds, (4) property taxes, (5) fund equity balances, (6) long-term debt, (7) interfund

EXHIBIT 13-3
City of Roanoke, Virginia
Combined Statement of Revenues, Expenditures, and Changes in Fund Balance
All Governmental Fund Types
Year Ended June 30, 1984

| | Governmental fund types | | | Memorandum only totals | |
| --- | --- | --- | --- | --- | --- |
| | | | | Year ended | |
| | General | Debt service | Capital projects | June 30, 1984 | June 30, 1983 |
| **Sources of Financial Resources** | | | | | |
| Revenues: | | | | | |
| Local taxes | $ 54,850,470 | $ — | $ — | $ 54,580,470 | $ 50,678,835 |
| Permits, fees, and licenses | 359,348 | — | — | 359,348 | 337,510 |
| Fines and forfeitures | 475,635 | — | — | 475,635 | 425,737 |
| Rents and interest | 991,940 | 466,107 | 1,375,250 | 2,833,297 | 2,757,312 |
| Intergovernmental | 40,706,223 | — | 7,786,291 | 48,492,514 | 43,499,068 |
| Charges for services | 4,891,791 | — | — | 4,891,791 | 6,571,280 |
| Miscellaneous | 895,284 | — | 226,201 | 1,121,485 | 1,125,345 |
| Total revenues | 103,170,691 | 466,107 | 9,387,742 | 113,024,540 | 105,395,087 |
| Other sources: | | | | | |
| Bond proceeds | — | — | — | — | 11,000,000 |
| Transfers from general fund | — | 7,331,935 | 2,463,968 | 9,795,903 | 7,700,682 |
| Total sources of financial resources | 103,170,691 | 7,798,042 | 11,851,710 | 122,820,443 | 124,095,769 |
| **Uses of Financial Resources** | | | | | |
| Expenditures: | | | | | |
| Current: | | | | | |
| General government | 4,567,405 | — | — | 4,567,405 | 4,384,589 |
| Judicial | 1,503,621 | — | — | 1,503,621 | 1,399,792 |
| Public safety | 14,035,745 | — | — | 14,035,745 | 12,452,196 |
| Public works | 11,595,662 | — | — | 11,595,662 | 13,041,841 |
| Health and welfare | 8,173,448 | — | — | 8,173,448 | 7,670,434 |
| Education | 41,477,043 | — | — | 41,477,043 | 37,926,364 |
| Parks, recreation, and cultural | 1,940,994 | — | — | 1,940,994 | 1,891,030 |
| Community development | 481,309 | — | — | 481,309 | 389,917 |
| Nondepartmental | 7,418,667 | — | — | 7,418,667 | 7,677,411 |
| Debt service | — | 7,744,355 | — | 7,744,355 | 7,010,165 |
| Major capital outlay | — | — | 14,031,957 | 14,031,957 | 17,225,340 |
| Total expenditures | 91,193,894 | 7,744,355 | 14,031,957 | 112,970,206 | 111,069,079 |
| Other uses: | | | | | |
| Transfers to governmental fund types | 9,795,903 | — | — | 9,795,903 | 7,700,682 |
| Transfers to proprietary fund types | 949,194 | — | — | 949,194 | 865,602 |
| Total uses of financial resources | 101,938,991 | 7,744,355 | 14,031,957 | 123,715,303 | 119,635,363 |
| Net increase (decrease) in fund balances | 1,231,700 | 53,687 | (2,180,247) | (894,860) | 4,460,406 |
| Fund balances—July 1* | 5,095,343 | 5,750,167 | 17,957,007 | 28,802,517 | 24,435,865 |
| Fund balances—June 30 | $ 6,327,043 | $5,803,854 | $15,776,760 | $ 27,907,657 | $ 28,896,271 |

*See note 2 in notes to financial statements, Appendix 13-2.

**EXHIBIT 13-4**
**City of Roanoke, Virginia**
**Statement of Revenues, Expenditures, and Changes in Fund Balance**
**Budget (Non-GAAP Budgetary Basis) and Actual**
**General Fund**
**Year Ended June 30, 1984**

|  | Revised budget | Actual | Variance— favorable (unfavorable) |
|---|---|---|---|
| **Sources of Financial Resources** | | | |
| Fund balance, July 1, 1983* | $ 5,095,343 | $ 5,095,343 | — |
| Revenues: | | | |
|   Local taxes | 53,416,521 | 54,850,470 | $1,433,949 |
|   Permits, fees, and licenses | 387,500 | 359,348 | (28,152) |
|   Fines and forfeitures | 437,000 | 475,635 | 38,635 |
|   Rents and interest | 816,100 | 991,940 | 175,840 |
|   Intergovernmental | 40,232,540 | 40,706,223 | 473,683 |
|   Charges for services | 4,877,728 | 4,891,791 | 14,063 |
|   Miscellaneous | 910,907 | 895,284 | (15,623) |
|     Total revenues | 101,078,296 | 103,170,691 | 2,092,395 |
|     Total sources of financial resources | 106,173,639 | 108,266,034 | 2,092,395 |
| **Uses of Financial Resources** | | | |
| Expenditures: | | | |
|   General government | 4,749,907 | 4,567,405 | 182,502 |
|   Judicial | 1,549,686 | 1,503,621 | 46,065 |
|   Public safety | 14,496,372 | 14,199,236 | 297,136 |
|   Public works | 13,152,973 | 12,757,117 | 395,856 |
|   Health and welfare | 8,445,753 | 8,173,448 | 272,305 |
|   Education | 41,852,801 | 41,826,549 | 26,252 |
|   Parks, recreation, and cultural | 1,987,852 | 1,940,994 | 46,858 |
|   Community development | 497,829 | 481,309 | 16,520 |
|   Nondepartmental | 7,710,719 | 7,418,667 | 292,052 |
|     Total expenditures | 94,443,892 | 92,868,346 | 1,575,546 |
| Other uses: | | | |
|   Transfers to governmental fund types | 9,795,903 | 9,795,903 | — |
|   Transfers to proprietary fund types | 1,023,329 | 949,194 | 74,135 |
|     Total other uses | 10,819,232 | 10,745,097 | 74,135 |
|     Total uses of financial resources | 105,263,124 | 103,613,443 | 1,649,681 |
| Fund balance, June 30, 1984** | $ 910,515 | $ 4,652,591 | $3,742,076 |

*See note 2 in notes to financial statements, Appendix 13-2.
**See note 1-D in notes to financial statements, Appendix 13-2.

## EXHIBIT 13-5
### City of Roanoke, Virginia
### Combined Statement of Revenues, Expenses, and Changes in Retained Earnings/Fund Balance
### All Proprietary Fund Types and Similar Trust Fund
### Year Ended June 30, 1984

|  | Proprietary fund types | | Fiduciary fund type | Memorandum only totals | |
|---|---|---|---|---|---|
|  | | | | Year ended | |
|  | Enterprise | Internal service* | Pension trust | June 30, 1984 | June 30, 1983 |
| **Operating revenues** | | | | | |
| Charges for services | $13,067,045 | $4,710,282 | $ — | $17,777,327 | $12,552,014 |
| Contributions | — | — | 4,499,002 | 4,499,002 | 4,076,835 |
| Interest and dividends | — | — | 3,735,509 | 3,735,509 | 3,393,948 |
| Gain on sale of securities | — | — | 17,748 | 17,748 | 1,042,946 |
| Other | 132,838 | — | — | 132,838 | 75,410 |
| Total operating revenue | 13,199,883 | 4,710,282 | 8,252,259 | 26,162,424 | 21,141,153 |
| **Operating expenses** | | | | | |
| Benefit payments | — | — | 3,027,440 | 3,027,440 | 2,855,937 |
| Personal services | 3,780,660 | 2,954,803 | — | 6,735,463 | 3,578,457 |
| Other services and charges | 7,385,199 | 1,051,871 | 392,314 | 8,829,384 | 7,747,696 |
| Materials and supplies | 1,040,150 | 359,916 | — | 1,400,066 | 1,083,020 |
| Depreciation | 2,467,153 | 394,680 | — | 2,861,833 | 2,397,342 |
| Loss on sale of securities | — | — | 65,831 | 65,831 | — |
| Total operating expenses | 14,673,162 | 4,671,270 | 3,485,585 | 22,920,017 | 17,662,452 |
| Operating income (loss) | (1,473,279) | (50,988) | 4,766,674 | 3,242,407 | 3,478,701 |
| **Nonoperating revenues (expenses)** | | | | | |
| Operating grants | 1,001,989 | — | — | 1,001,989 | 945,759 |
| Interest revenue | 701,064 | 20,491 | — | 721,555 | 425,182 |
| Interest expense | (292,716) | — | — | (292,716) | (325,815) |
| Total nonoperating revenues (expenses) | 1,410,337 | 20,491 | — | 1,430,828 | 1,045,126 |
| Income (loss) before operating transfers | (62,942) | (30,497) | 4,766,674 | 4,673,235 | 4,523,827 |
| **Operating transfers** | | | | | |
| Transfers from general fund | 892,823 | 56,371 | — | 949,194 | 865,602 |
| Net income | 829,881 | 25,874 | 4,766,674 | 5,622,429 | 5,389,429 |
| Depreciation charged to contributed capital | 1,437,651 | 241,459 | — | 1,679,110 | 1,420,983 |
| Increase in retained earnings/fund balance | 2,267,532 | 267,333 | 4,766,674 | 7,301,539 | 6,810,412 |
| Retained earnings/fund balance— July 1 | 25,746,912 | — | 44,556,605 | 70,303,517 | 63,493,105 |
| Retained earnings/fund balance— June 30 | $28,014,444 | $ 267,333 | $49,323,279 | $77,605,056 | $70,303,517 |

*See note 2 in notes to financial statements, Appendix 13-2.

## EXHIBIT 13-6
## City of Roanoke, Virginia
## Combined Statement of Changes in Financial Position
## All Proprietary Fund Types and Similar Trust Fund
## Year Ended June 30, 1984

|  | Proprietary fund types | | Fiduciary fund type | Memorandum only totals | |
|---|---|---|---|---|---|
|  | | | | Year ended | |
|  | Enterprise | Internal service* | Pension trust | June 30, 1984 | June 30, 1983 |

### Sources of Financial Resources

|  | Enterprise | Internal service* | Pension trust | June 30, 1984 | June 30, 1983 |
|---|---|---|---|---|---|
| Operations: | | | | | |
| Net increase in retained earnings/fund balance during the year | $2,267,532 | $ 267,333 | $4,766,674 | $ 7,301,538 | $ 6,810,412 |
| Expenses not requiring current outlay of financial resources—depreciation | 1,029,502 | 153,221 | — | 1,182,723 | 976,359 |
| Total financial resources from operations | 3,297,034 | 420,554 | 4,766,674 | 8,484,262 | 7,786,771 |
| Contributed capital | 4,231,285 | 932,002 | — | 5,163,287 | 6,135,836 |
| Total sources of financial resources | 7,528,319 | 1,352,556 | 4,766,674 | 13,647,548 | 13,922,607 |

### Uses of Financial Resources

|  | Enterprise | Internal service* | Pension trust | June 30, 1984 | June 30, 1983 |
|---|---|---|---|---|---|
| Acquisition of fixed assets | 4,960,783 | 1,582,326 | — | 6,543,109 | 6,004,817 |
| Retirement of bonds payable | 608,280 | — | — | 608,280 | 608,280 |
| Total uses of financial resources | 5,569,063 | 1,582,326 | — | 7,151,389 | 6,613,097 |
| Net increase (decrease) in working capital | $1,959,256 | $ (229,770) | $4,766,674 | $ 6,496,159 | $ 7,309,510 |

### Elements of Net Increase (Decrease) in Working Capital

|  | Enterprise | Internal service* | Pension trust | June 30, 1984 | June 30, 1983 |
|---|---|---|---|---|---|
| Cash | $ 76,673 | $ 71,024 | $ (20) | $ 147,677 | $ (211,309) |
| Investments | 2,757,671 | 600,000 | 3,222,638 | 6,580,309 | 6,330,109 |
| Interest and dividends receivable | 52,442 | 1,481 | 54,653 | 108,576 | (126,817) |
| Due from other governments | (1,308,805) | — | — | (1,308,805) | 141,489 |
| Due from other funds | — | — | 31,990 | 31,990 | 8,199 |
| Accounts receivable | 12,847 | — | 160,723 | 173,570 | (187,201) |
| Inventory | 17,466 | — | — | 17,466 | 474,436 |
| Other assets | (13,412) | — | (3,721) | (17,134) | (4,020) |
| Warrants payable | 459,741 | (175,249) | 187,577 | 472,069 | (40,531) |
| Accounts payable and accrued expenses | 88,744 | (291,895) | 1,112,834 | 909,683 | 622,605 |
| Due to other funds | 79,777 | (435,131) | — | (355,354) | 188,547 |
| Due to other governments | (177,562) | — | — | (177,562) | — |
| Other liabilities | (97,326) | — | — | (97,326) | 114,003 |
| Current maturities of long-term debt | 11,000 | — | — | 11,000 | — |
| Net increase (decrease) in working capital | $1,959,256 | $ (229,770) | $4,766,674 | $ 6,496,159 | $ 7,309,510 |

*See note 2 in notes to financial statements, Appendix 13-2.

**EXHIBIT 13-7**
**City of Roanoke, Virginia**
**General Fund**
**Balance Sheet**
**June 30, 1984**
**(With Comparative Totals for June 30, 1983)***

**Assets**

|  | 1984 | 1983 |
|---|---|---|
| Cash | $ 2,910,271 | $ 1,533,402 |
| Investments | 8,932,781 | 8,644,775 |
| Interest receivable | 67,214 | 17,448 |
| Due from other governments | 2,724,920 | 3,151,899 |
| Due from other funds | 49,711 | 345,696 |
| Taxes receivable | 2,010,080 | 2,198,849 |
| Accounts receivable | 402,298 | 383,444 |
| Allowance for uncollectible receivables | (810,995) | (680,097) |
| Inventory | 934,973 | 827,024 |
| Total assets | $17,221,253 | $16,422,440 |

**Liabilities and Fund Equity**

| Liabilities: | | |
|---|---|---|
| Warrants payable | $ 6,313,172 | $ 6,886,525 |
| Accounts payable and accrued expenses | 2,935,927 | 2,383,377 |
| Due to other governments | — | 32,799 |
| Due to other funds | 141,043 | 122,777 |
| Deferred revenue | 1,504,068 | 1,807,865 |
| Total liabilities | 10,894,210 | 11,233,343 |
| Fund equity: | | |
| Fund balances: | | |
| Reserved for encumbrances | 1,674,452 | 1,610,001 |
| Unreserved: | | |
| Designated for worker's compensation | 108,503 | 94,919 |
| Designated for subsequent year's expenditures | 670,524 | 686,692 |
| Designated for capital equipment | 3,027,463 | 2,470,189 |
| Undesignated | 846,101 | 327,296 |
| Total fund equity | 6,327,043 | 5,189,097 |
| Total liabilities and fund equity | $17,221,253 | $16,422,440 |

*See notes to financial statements, Appendix 13-2.

receivables and payables, (8) changes in general fixed assets, (9) construction in progress and contract commitments, (10) pension plan, (11) segment information for enterprise funds, (12) joint ventures, and (13) contingent liabilities. Note that quite a bit of detailed information is given in these footnotes, along with information required by generally accepted accounting principles, such as segment information for the enterprise funds.

## EXHIBIT 13-8
### City of Roanoke, Virginia
### Statement of Revenue, Budget and Actual
### General Fund
### Year Ended June 30, 1984
### (With Comparative Totals for June 30, 1983)*

| Revenue source | 1984 Revised budget | 1984 Actual | 1984 Variance—favorable (unfavorable) | 1983 |
|---|---:|---:|---:|---:|
| Local taxes: | | | | |
| 1985 real estate | $ — | $ 6,846 | $ 6,846 | $ — |
| 1984 real estate | 20,630,000 | 20,825,759 | 195,759 | 2,830 |
| 1983 real estate | 270,000 | 379,989 | 109,989 | 19,937,827 |
| 1982 real estate | 120,000 | 197,328 | 77,328 | 233,554 |
| 1981 real estate | 75,000 | 72,972 | (2,028) | 60,134 |
| 1980 real estate | 110,000 | 114,263 | 4,263 | 87,632 |
| 1979 real estate | — | — | — | 86,818 |
| Delinquent real estate | 60,000 | 91,823 | 31,823 | 85,769 |
| 1984 personal property | 6,811,366 | 7,321,161 | 509,795 | — |
| 1983 personal property | 140,000 | 132,638 | (7,362) | 6,295,853 |
| 1982 personal property | 3,500 | 3,702 | 202 | 136,524 |
| 1981 personal property | — | — | — | 852 |
| Tax judgments | 1,600 | 549 | (1,051) | 1,615 |
| Delinquent personal property | 3,000 | 1,086 | (1,914) | 4,689 |
| Public service | 2,420,000 | 2,416,753 | (3,247) | 2,346,590 |
| Penalties and interest | 290,000 | 365,513 | 75,513 | 269,443 |
| Sales tax 1% | 8,150,000 | 8,378,391 | 228,391 | 7,287,463 |
| Utility consumer tax | 6,346,000 | 6,430,235 | 84,235 | 5,888,956 |
| Cigarette tax | 260,000 | 285,963 | 25,963 | 265,325 |
| Recordation and probate tax | 190,000 | 235,942 | 45,942 | 174,360 |
| Business and occupational license | 5,400,000 | 5,458,028 | 58,028 | 5,330,945 |
| Transient room tax | 450,000 | 403,601 | (46,399) | 401,102 |
| Admissions tax | 85,000 | 110,506 | 25,506 | 82,712 |
| Motor vehicle license | 1,100,000 | 1,102,049 | 2,049 | 1,055,914 |
| Franchise taxes | 501,055 | 515,373 | 14,318 | 641,928 |
| Total local taxes | 53,416,521 | 54,850,470 | 1,433,949 | 50,678,835 |
| Permits, fees, and licenses: | | | | |
| Dog licenses | 32,000 | 23,319 | (8,681) | 27,045 |
| Permits and fees | 355,500 | 336,029 | (19,471) | 310,465 |
| Total permits, fees, and licenses | 387,500 | 359,348 | (28,152) | 337,510 |
| Fines and forfeitures: | | | | |
| General district court | 290,000 | 304,513 | 14,513 | 279,045 |
| Circuit court | 12,000 | 35,081 | 23,081 | 13,114 |
| J & D relations court | 10,000 | 6,653 | (3,347) | 8,054 |
| Parking tickets | 125,000 | 129,388 | 4,388 | 125,524 |
| Total fines and forfeitures | 437,000 | 475,635 | 38,635 | 425,737 |
| Rents and interest: | | | | |
| Interest on investments | 300,000 | 453,021 | 153,021 | 377,147 |
| Market rents | 43,000 | 15,693 | (27,307) | 27,798 |
| Stadium and athletic field | 24,100 | 21,970 | (2,130) | 19,448 |
| Rental of miscellaneous properties | 111,000 | 123,972 | 12,972 | 99,543 |
| Sale of materials and equipment | 35,000 | 54,101 | 19,101 | 10,032 |
| Municipal parking garage | 303,000 | 323,183 | 20,183 | 304,595 |
| Total revenue from use of money and property | $ 816,100 | $ 991,940 | $ 175,840 | $ 838,563 |

## EXHIBIT 13-8
*(continued)*

|  | 1984 | | | |
|---|---|---|---|---|
| Revenue source | Revised budget | Actual | Variance—favorable (unfavorable) | 1983 |
| Intergovernmental revenues: | | | | |
| General fund uses: | | | | |
| Alcoholic beverage control tax | $ 360,000 | $ 352,068 | $ (7,932) | $ 357,996 |
| Wine tax | 67,000 | 59,212 | (7,788) | 57,820 |
| Boxing and wrestling | 3,500 | — | (3,500) | — |
| Sales and use tax—mobile homes | 12,000 | 9,036 | (2,964) | 12,343 |
| Rolling stock tax | 6,500 | 8,128 | 1,628 | 6,241 |
| Rental car tax | 86,000 | 91,004 | 5,004 | 81,734 |
| Commonwealth's attorney | 227,741 | 262,258 | 34,517 | 268,386 |
| Sheriff | 665,838 | 618,101 | (47,737) | 607,356 |
| Commissioner of revenue | 133,511 | 149,752 | 16,241 | 150,655 |
| Treasurer | 147,956 | 176,063 | 28,107 | 165,904 |
| Medical examiner | 11,000 | 5,920 | (5,080) | 6,760 |
| Registrar | 25,600 | 27,012 | 1,412 | 25,878 |
| Public assistance | 4,626,853 | 4,550,285 | (76,568) | 4,376,911 |
| Food stamp authorization | 354,941 | 321,674 | (33,267) | 309,266 |
| Hospitalization of indigents | 135,000 | 129,016 | (5,984) | 99,872 |
| Indo-Chinese refugee program | 15,684 | 9,341 | (6,343) | 10,354 |
| Fuel assistance | 109,426 | 76,166 | (33,260) | 98,289 |
| Employment services—ADC | 263,005 | 248,396 | (14,609) | — |
| Employment services—food stamp recipients | 52,955 | 44,218 | (8,737) | — |
| Prevention of placement of neglected children | 40,797 | 34,411 | (6,386) | — |
| Emergency food and shelter | 26,627 | 26,627 | — | — |
| Social services to the unemployed | 116,075 | 111,499 | (4,576) | — |
| Street construction and maintenance | 3,547,870 | 3,550,493 | 2,623 | 3,296,591 |
| City jail | 1,500,574 | 1,517,529 | 16,955 | 1,523,057 |
| Juvenile facilities block grant | 811,287 | 807,533 | (3,754) | 770,246 |
| Juvenile probation house | 2,400 | 3,100 | 700 | 7,866 |
| Juvenile detention home | 7,455 | 10,566 | 3,111 | 14,020 |
| Crisis intervention | 4,050 | 5,677 | 1,627 | 8,722 |
| Library | 155,824 | 137,380 | (18,444) | 156,757 |
| Law enforcement | 1,862,146 | 1,848,581 | (13,565) | 1,794,446 |
| Revenue sharing transfers | 2,743,508 | 2,698,264 | (45,244) | 2,701,311 |
| Federal aid to libraries | 14,914 | 21,133 | 6,219 | 28,356 |
| Civil defense | 86,129 | 79,936 | (6,193) | 40,590 |
| Special purpose grants | 24,119 | 24,119 | — | 92,342 |
| Other | — | — | — | 5,760 |
| Total general fund use | $18,248,285 | $18,014,498 | $ (233,787) | $17,075,829 |

**EXHIBIT 13-8**
(*continued*)

|  | 1984 | | | |
| --- | --- | --- | --- | --- |
| Revenue source | Revised budget | Actual | Variance favorable (unfavorable) | 1983 |
| Education: | | | | |
| State school funds | $ 13,818,846 | $ 13,843,350 | $ 24,504 | $12,474,682 |
| State sales tax | 4,580,278 | 5,264,402 | 684,124 | 4,282,896 |
| Federal school funds | 1,441,396 | 1,440,238 | (1,158) | 1,390,044 |
| State and federal grants | 2,143,735 | 2,143,735 | — | 1,920,493 |
| Total education | 21,984,255 | 22,691,725 | 707,470 | 20,068,115 |
| Total intergovernmental revenues | 40,232,540 | 40,706,223 | 473,683 | 37,143,944 |
| Charges for current services | | | | |
| Other school revenue | 1,335,200 | 1,355,257 | 20,057 | 1,298,627 |
| Court cost | 336,400 | 437,968 | 101,568 | 365,895 |
| Commonwealth's attorney's fees | 2,500 | 2,786 | 286 | 2,533 |
| Streets and sidewalks | 7,000 | 3,645 | (3,355) | 5,660 |
| Parking meters | 50,000 | 39,135 | (10,865) | 40,721 |
| Sanitation charges | 24,000 | 21,590 | (2,410) | 18,908 |
| Bulk garbage collection | 50,000 | 42,756 | (7,244) | 47,880 |
| City home Medicaid payments | 622,000 | 674,801 | 52,801 | 691,269 |
| City home patient payments | 135,000 | 169,993 | 34,993 | 138,280 |
| Food stamp issuance | 48,000 | 43,018 | (4,982) | 47,217 |
| Title XX receipts | — | — | — | 66,664 |
| Recreation fees | 77,500 | 76,437 | (1,063) | 76,517 |
| Library fees | 28,500 | 19,648 | (8,852) | 24,929 |
| Burglar alarm fees | 22,000 | 19,305 | (2,695) | 18,710 |
| Damages to city property | 3,000 | 7,659 | 4,659 | 2,204 |
| Central services | 553,743 | 553,743 | — | 441,388 |
| Billing and collection fees | 360,000 | 360,000 | — | 360,000 |
| Fire safety services | 360,000 | 345,101 | (14,899) | 338,103 |
| Interfund services | 862,885 | 718,949 | (143,936) | 2,585,775 |
| Total charges for current services | 4,877,728 | 4,891,791 | 14,063 | 6,571,280 |
| Miscellaneous revenue: | | | | |
| Payments in lieu of taxes | 532,000 | 526,748 | (5,252) | 655,951 |
| Insurance recoveries | — | — | — | 11,318 |
| Contributions | — | — | — | 12,357 |
| Reimbursements | 220,821 | 220,821 | — | 259,332 |
| Sale of property | 60,200 | 84,101 | 23,901 | 1,700 |
| Miscellaneous | 97,886 | 63,614 | (34,272) | 43,398 |
| Total miscellaneous | 910,907 | 895,284 | (15,623) | 984,056 |
| Total sources of revenue | $101,078,296 | $103,170,691 | $2,092,395 | $96,979,925 |

*See notes to financial statements, Appendix 13-2.

EXHIBIT 13-9
City of Roanoke, Virginia
Statement of Expenditures, Budget and Actual
Non-GAAP Budgetary Basis
General Fund
Year Ended June 30, 1984
(With Comparative Totals for June 30, 1983)*

|  | 1984 | | | |
|---|---:|---:|---:|---:|
|  | Revised budget | Actual | Variance—favorable (unfavorable) | 1983 |
| **General government** | | | | |
| Council | $ 101,855 | $ 99,530 | $ 2,325 | $ 97,890 |
| City clerk | 177,703 | 175,525 | 2,178 | 121,846 |
| City manager | 230,181 | 226,665 | 3,516 | 205,107 |
| Budget and systems | 73,678 | 73,596 | 82 | 59,362 |
| Citizens' request | 57,169 | 55,474 | 1,695 | 47,974 |
| City attorney | 302,013 | 296,743 | 5,270 | 229,941 |
| Director of finance | 672,232 | 656,949 | 16,283 | 415,871 |
| Division of billings and collections | 538,111 | 538,111 | — | 384,541 |
| Commissioner of revenue | 406,026 | 382,907 | 23,119 | 302,789 |
| City treasurer | 546,086 | 525,248 | 20,838 | 295,226 |
| Real estate valuation | 430,249 | 365,817 | 64,432 | 355,116 |
| Board of equalization | 16,430 | 14,039 | 2,391 | 25,571 |
| General services | 333,610 | 330,372 | 3,238 | — |
| Municipal auditing | 218,731 | 214,343 | 4,388 | 188,628 |
| Director of utilities and operations | 87,616 | 84,028 | 3,588 | 72,919 |
| Director of administration and public safety | 56,650 | 56,402 | 248 | 55,455 |
| Personnel | 263,313 | 245,585 | 17,728 | 219,881 |
| Director of human resources | 78,804 | 77,862 | 942 | 75,659 |
| Director of public works | 41,299 | 40,430 | 869 | 45,298 |
| Board of elections | 117,151 | 107,779 | 9,372 | 77,005 |
| Total general government | 4,749,907 | 4,567,405 | 182,502 | 3,276,079 |
| **Judicial administration** | | | | |
| Circuit court | 50,014 | 47,364 | 2,650 | 47,450 |
| Clerk of circuit court | 451,088 | 441,908 | 9,180 | 415,908 |
| General district court | 33,273 | 32,128 | 1,145 | 22,741 |
| Juvenile and domestic relations court | 24,172 | 24,172 | — | 29,592 |
| Juvenile and domestic relations court clerk | 13,550 | 10,474 | 3,076 | 9,180 |
| Sheriff | 633,815 | 612,100 | 21,715 | 552,959 |
| Law library | 49,082 | 48,880 | 202 | 45,596 |
| Commonwealth's attorney | 294,692 | 286,595 | 8,097 | 276,361 |
| Total judicial administration | 1,549,686 | 1,503,621 | 46,065 | 1,399,787 |
| **Public safety** | | | | |
| Police administration | 110,813 | 105,247 | 5,566 | 94,370 |
| Police investigation | 1,011,431 | 957,928 | 53,503 | 842,203 |
| Police patrol | 3,792,873 | 3,752,239 | 40,634 | 3,542,589 |
| Police services | 963,890 | 887,979 | 75,911 | 548,139 |
| Police training | 88,830 | 83,584 | 5,246 | 77,190 |
| Fire administration | 63,489 | 59,358 | 4,131 | 59,452 |
| Fire prevention | 214,529 | 207,839 | 6,690 | 148,740 |
| Fire suppression | 5,042,462 | 4,998,563 | 43,899 | 4,609,058 |

## EXHIBIT 13-9
*(continued)*

|  | 1984 | | | 1983 |
|---|---|---|---|---|
|  | Revised budget | Actual | Variance—favorable (unfavorable) |  |
| Fire training | $ 25,895 | $ 24,157 | $ 1,738 | $ 21,159 |
| Contribution to rescue squads | 77,500 | 77,500 | — | 98,500 |
| Jail | 1,629,717 | 1,606,782 | 22,935 | 1,512,826 |
| Juvenile detention home | 361,854 | 357,798 | 4,056 | 374,895 |
| Outreach detention | 88,572 | 87,644 | 928 | 84,016 |
| Juvenile probation house | 214,258 | 206,997 | 7,261 | 183,097 |
| Crisis intervention | 235,003 | 234,273 | 730 | 232,771 |
| Inspections | 308,719 | 302,491 | 6,228 | 273,644 |
| Emergency services | 148,638 | 145,258 | 3,380 | 86,673 |
| Animal control | 117,899 | 103,599 | 14,300 | 103,672 |
| Medical examiner | — | — | — | 8,350 |
| Total public safety | 14,496,372 | 14,199,236 | 297,136 | 12,901,344 |
| **Public works** | | | | |
| Engineering | 648,931 | 644,935 | 3,996 | 651,017 |
| Public works general services | 157,507 | 154,454 | 3,053 | 112,050 |
| Communications | 560,656 | 558,554 | 2,102 | 535,881 |
| Street maintenance | 1,722,753 | 1,602,566 | 120,187 | 2,642,763 |
| Building maintenance | 1,940,907 | 1,876,562 | 64,345 | 1,616,551 |
| Custodial services | 594,428 | 589,887 | 4,541 | 461,591 |
| Grounds maintenance | 1,982,814 | 1,918,222 | 64,592 | 852,435 |
| Street paving | 1,822,228 | 1,822,227 | 1 | 1,628,534 |
| Snow removal | 109,466 | 92,755 | 16,711 | 108,186 |
| Street lighting | 686,498 | 685,573 | 925 | 531,399 |
| Signals and alarms | 446,175 | 442,496 | 3,679 | 389,188 |
| Refuse collection | 2,471,884 | 2,360,160 | 111,724 | 1,762,525 |
| Special purpose grants | 8,726 | 8,726 | — | 8,731 |
| Total public works | 13,152,973 | 12,757,117 | 395,856 | 11,300,851 |
| **Health and welfare** | | | | |
| Health department | 737,659 | 734,244 | 3,415 | 665,175 |
| Mental health and retardation | 218,147 | 218,147 | — | 213,113 |
| Citizens' service committee | 259,079 | 259,079 | — | 247,085 |
| Social services—administration | 566,889 | 536,495 | 30,394 | 279,920 |
| Food stamp authorization | 314,463 | 302,916 | 11,547 | 298,633 |
| Income maintenance | 2,082,379 | 1,947,951 | 134,428 | 2,128,013 |
| Social services—services | 2,777,715 | 2,748,716 | 28,999 | 2,756,883 |
| Fuel assistance | 90,959 | 70,398 | 20,561 | 84,931 |
| Employment services—ADC | 228,276 | 222,045 | 5,871 | 9,446 |
| Employment services—food stamp recipients | 42,890 | 36,051 | 6,839 | 2,399 |
| Prevention of placement of neglected children | 40,797 | 30,649 | 10,148 | 9,203 |
| Emergency food and shelter | 26,627 | 26,627 | — | — |
| Emergency needs services | 116,075 | 111,511 | 4,564 | — |
| Hospitalization of indigents | 180,000 | 176,789 | 3,211 | 175,851 |
| Burial of indigents | 885 | (445) | 1,330 | (291) |
| Nursing home | 724,939 | 713,941 | 10,998 | 691,659 |
| Special purpose grants | 37,974 | 37,974 | — | 38,062 |
| Title XX services | — | — | — | 70,352 |
| Total health and welfare | 8,445,753 | 8,173,448 | 272,305 | 7,670,434 |

**EXHIBIT 13-9**
*(continued)*

|  | 1984 | | | 1983 |
|---|---|---|---|---|
|  | **Revised budget** | **Actual** | **Variance— favorable (unfavorable)** |  |
| Education | | | | |
|   Administration | $ 592,660 | $ 591,392 | $ 1,268 | $ 599,169 |
|   Instruction | 22,931,410 | 22,931,306 | 104 | 21,392,074 |
|   Attendance and health services | 191,185 | 191,185 | — | 193,616 |
|   Pupil transportation | 1,299,658 | 1,296,546 | 3,112 | 1,039,817 |
|   Food services | 2,483,795 | 2,483,101 | 694 | 2,339,149 |
|   Maintenance of school plant | 4,871,770 | 4,868,787 | 2,983 | 4,531,170 |
|   Fixed charges | 6,298,238 | 6,280,147 | 18,091 | 5,495,618 |
|   State and federal grants | 2,172,731 | 2,172,731 | — | 1,927,493 |
|   Capital outlay | 982,221 | 982,221 | — | 525,258 |
|   Internal services | 29,133 | 29,133 | — | — |
|     Total education | 41,852,801 | 41,826,549 | 26,252 | 38,043,364 |
| Parks, recreational and cultural | | | | |
|   Parks and recreation | 861,361 | 831,593 | 29,768 | 777,554 |
|   Armory | 36,950 | 36,136 | 814 | 42,239 |
|   Stadium and athletic field | 41,605 | 37,826 | 3,779 | 40,670 |
|   City market | 10,480 | 9,861 | 619 | 16,113 |
|   Contributions—cultural | 27,750 | 27,750 | — | 27,500 |
|   Library | 985,405 | 973,527 | 11,878 | 934,891 |
|   Special purpose grants | 24,301 | 24,301 | — | 52,063 |
|     Total parks, recreational and cultural | 1,987,852 | 1,940,994 | 46,858 | 1,891,030 |
| Community development | | | | |
|   Community planning | 162,317 | 161,637 | 680 | 137,898 |
|   Economic development and grants | 84,714 | 84,104 | 610 | 100,463 |
|   Grants compliance | 21,210 | 20,863 | 347 | — |
|   Regional economic development agency | 50,994 | 50,110 | 884 | — |
|   Board of zoning appeals | 4,568 | 3,701 | 867 | 3,555 |
|   Parking garage | 96,945 | 83,953 | 12,992 | 75,691 |
|   Contributions to VPI & SU | 59,256 | 59,256 | — | 57,256 |
|   Contributions to community college | 3,579 | 3,579 | — | 3,539 |
|   Community education | 14,246 | 14,106 | 140 | 11,515 |
|     Total community development | 497,829 | 481,309 | 16,520 | 389,917 |
| Nondepartmental | | | | |
|   Fringe benefits | 7,315,020 | 7,067,249 | 247,771 | 6,525,243 |
|   Miscellaneous | 395,699 | 351,418 | 44,281 | 1,152,168 |
|     Total nondepartmental | 7,710,719 | 7,418,667 | 292,052 | 7,677,411 |
| Transfers to other funds | | | | |
|   Transit company | 335,928 | 261,793 | 74,135 | 207,647 |
|   Water fund | 918 | 918 | — | — |
|   Sewage fund | 2,808 | 2,808 | — | — |
|   Airport fund | 432 | 432 | — | — |
|   Civic center fund | 626,872 | 626,872 | — | 657,955 |
|   City information systems fund | 11,148 | 11,148 | — | — |
|   Materials control fund | 10,289 | 10,289 | — | — |
|   Management services fund | 10,081 | 10,081 | — | — |

## EXHIBIT 13-9
(*continued*)

|  | 1984 | | | 1983 |
|---|---|---|---|---|
|  | Revised budget | Actual | Variance—favorable (unfavorable) |  |
| Utility line services fund | $ 13,101 | $ 13,101 | $ — | $ — |
| Motor vehicle maintenance fund | 11,752 | 11,752 | — | — |
| Capital projects fund | 2,463,968 | 2,463,968 | — | 570,548 |
| Debt service fund | 7,331,935 | 7,331,935 | — | 7,130,134 |
| Total transfers to other funds | 10,819,232 | 10,745,097 | 74,135 | 8,566,284 |
| Total general fund | $105,263,124 | $103,613,443 | $1,649,681 | $93,116,501 |

### Reconciliation of Expenditures to GAAP Basis

| | |
|---|---|
| Total expenditures per exhibit | $103,613,443 |
| Less encumbrances included in expenditures | (1,674,452) |
| Total expenditures (see Exhibit 13-3) | $101,938,991 |

*See notes to financial statements, Appendix 13-2.

## EXHIBIT 13-10
### City of Roanoke, Virginia
### Debt Service Fund
### Balance Sheet
### June 30, 1984
### (With Comparative Totals for June 30, 1983)*

|  | 1984 | 1983 |
|---|---|---|
| **Assets** | | |
| Cash | $ 11,337 | $ 2,836 |
| Investments | 5,775,000 | 5,735,000 |
| Interest receivable | 45,045 | 41,963 |
| Total assets | $5,831,382 | $5,779,799 |
| **Liabilities** | | |
| Warrants payable | $ — | $ 616 |
| Matured bonds and interest payable | 27,528 | 29,016 |
| Total liabilities | 27,528 | 29,632 |
| **Fund equity** | | |
| Unreserved: | | |
| Designated for debt service | 5,803,854 | 5,750,167 |
| Total fund equity | 5,803,854 | 5,750,167 |
| Total liabilities and fund equity | $5,831,382 | $5,779,799 |

*See notes to financial statements, Appendix 13-2.

**EXHIBIT 13-11**
**City of Roanoke, Virginia**
**Debt Service Fund**
**Statement of Revenues, Expenditures,**
**and Changes in Fund Balance**
**Year Ended June 30, 1984**
**(With Comparative Totals for June 30, 1983)***

|  | 1984 | 1983 |
|---|---|---|
| Sources of financial resources |  |  |
| Revenues: |  |  |
|   Interest on investments | $ 466,107 | $ 304,529 |
|   Miscellaneous | — | 76,289 |
|   Total revenues | 466,107 | 380,818 |
| Other sources: |  |  |
|   Transfers from general fund | 7,331,935 | 7,130,134 |
|   Total sources of financial resources | 7,798,042 | 7,510,952 |
| Uses of financial resources |  |  |
| Expenditures: |  |  |
|   Debt service | 7,744,355 | 7,010,165 |
|   Total uses of financial resources | 7,744,355 | 7,010,165 |
|   Net increase in fund balance | 53,687 | 500,787 |
| Fund balance, July 1 | 5,750,167 | 5,249,380 |
| Fund balance, June 30 | $5,803,854 | $5,750,167 |

*See notes to financial statements, Appendix 13-2.

## THE AUDITOR'S REPORT

The American Institute of Certified Public Accountants says:

> The objective of the ordinary examination of financial statements by the independent auditor is the expression of an opinion on the fairness with which they present financial position, results of operations, and changes in financial position in conformity with generally accepted accounting principles. The auditor's report is the medium through which he expresses his opinion or, if circumstances require, disclaims an opinion. In either case, he states whether his examination has been made in accordance with generally accepted auditing standards. These standards require him to state whether, in his opinion, the financial statements are presented in conformity with generally accepted accounting principles and whether such principles have been consistently applied in the preparation of the financial statements of the current period in relation to those of the preceding period.[29]

The record keeping necessary to prepare statements in conformity with generally accepted principles of accounting has been shown in Part I. The statements given are those presented in accordance with generally accepted accounting principles consistently applied. And, when audited by an independent accountant, an unqualified opinion can be expressed that the statements are in accordance with GAAP consistently

## EXHIBIT 13-12
## City of Roanoke, Virginia
## Capital Projects Fund
## Balance Sheet
## June 30, 1984
### (With Comparative Totals for June 30, 1983)*

|  | 1984 | 1983 |
|---|---:|---:|
| **Assets** | | |
| Cash | $ 79,801 | $ 60,150 |
| Investments | 12,900,000 | 17,600,000 |
| Interest receivable | 109,330 | 306,667 |
| Due from other governments | 2,682,142 | 553,884 |
| Due from other funds | 423,423 | — |
| Accounts receivable | 246,105 | 133,760 |
| Total assets | $16,440,801 | $18,654,461 |
| **Liabilities and fund equity** | | |
| Liabilities: | | |
| Warrants payable | $ 664,041 | $ 697,454 |
| Total liabilities | 664,041 | 697,454 |
| Fund equity: | | |
| Reserved for encumbrances | 6,647,316 | 7,086,854 |
| Unreserved: | | |
| Designated for future capital projects | 8,304,547 | 9,969,016 |
| Undesignated | 824,897 | 901,137 |
| Total fund equity | 15,776,760 | 17,957,007 |
| Total liabilities and fund equity | $16,440,801 | $18,654,461 |

*See notes to financial statements, Appendix 13-2.

applied. When the statements are not in accordance with GAAP, the auditor may give a qualified opinion. In other cases, an adverse opinion may be rendered, or the auditor may state that he or she is unable to give an opinion. Exhibit 13-24[30] shows the auditor's opinion for the financial statements for the city of Roanoke, Virginia.

## STATISTICAL TABLES

In addition to financial statements, the comprehensive annual financial report (CAFR) should also include various statistical tables. The NCGA says:

> Statistical tables differ from financial statements because they usually cover more than two fiscal years and may present nonaccounting data. Statistical tables reflect social and economic data, financial trends, and the fiscal capacity of the government.[31]

The following statistical tables should be included in the CAFR unless clearly inapplicable in the circumstances:

**EXHIBIT 13-13**
**City of Roanoke, Virginia**
**Capital Projects Fund**
**Statement of Revenues,**
**Expenditures, and Changes in Fund Balance**
**Year Ended June 30, 1984**
**(With Comparative Totals for June 30, 1983)***

|  | 1984 | 1983 |
|---|---:|---:|
| **Sources of Financial Resources** | | |
| Revenues: | | |
|   Interest on investments | $ 1,375,250 | $ 1,614,220 |
|   Intergovernmental | 7,786,291 | 6,355,124 |
|   Miscellaneous | 226,201 | 65,000 |
|     Total revenues | 9,387,742 | 8,034,344 |
| Other sources: | | |
|   Bond sale proceeds | — | 11,000,000 |
|   Transfers from general fund | 2,463,968 | 570,548 |
|     Total sources of financial resources | 11,851,710 | 19,604,892 |
| **Uses of Financial Resources** | | |
| Expenditures: | | |
|   General government | 3,951,366 | 4,437,630 |
|   Urban redevelopment | 4,318,332 | 3,225,828 |
|   Fire protection | 38,213 | 138,930 |
|   Mass transit facilities | 697,203 | 96,422 |
|   Other buildings | 1,069,269 | 4,761,588 |
|   Recreational | 390,010 | 313,323 |
|   Educational | 989,157 | 601,673 |
|   Streets and bridges | 916,696 | 1,185,578 |
|   Sanitation projects | 1,578,793 | 2,452,950 |
|   Traffic engineering | 82,918 | 11,418 |
|     Total uses of financial resources | 14,031,957 | 17,225,340 |
|     Net increase (decrease) in fund balance | (2,180,247) | 2,379,552 |
| Fund balance, July 1 | 17,957,007 | 15,577,455 |
| Fund balance, June 30 | $15,776,760 | $17,957,007 |

*See notes to financial statements, Appendix 13-2.

1 General governmental expenditures by function, last ten fiscal years
2 General revenues by source, last ten fiscal years
3 Property tax levies and collections, last ten fiscal years
4 Assessed and estimated actual value of taxable property, last ten fiscal years
5 Property tax rates, all overlapping governments, last ten fiscal years
6 Special assessment collections, last ten fiscal years
7 Ratio of net general bonded debt to assessed value and net bonded debt per capita, last ten fiscal years

**EXHIBIT 13-14**
**City of Roanoke, Virginia**
**Combining Balance Sheet**
**Enterprise Funds**
**June 30, 1984**
**(With Comparative Totals for June 30, 1983)***

## Assets

|  | Transit company | Water | Sewage treatment | Airport | Civic center | Totals June 30, 1984 | Totals June 30, 1983 |
|---|---:|---:|---:|---:|---:|---:|---:|
| Current assets: | | | | | | | |
| Cash | $ 6,643 | $ 110,073 | $ 62,866 | $ 89,143 | $ 163,157 | $ 431,882 | $ 355,209 |
| Investments | 210,671 | 2,750,000 | 2,500,000 | 2,950,000 | 500,000 | 8,910,671 | 6,153,000 |
| Interest receivable | — | 21,039 | 14,001 | 39,144 | 4,541 | 78,725 | 26,283 |
| Due from other governments | 74,459 | — | 340,181 | — | — | 414,640 | 1,723,445 |
| Accounts receivable | 13,785 | 103,825 | 310,885 | 204,853 | 18,152 | 651,500 | 638,653 |
| Inventory | 115,171 | — | 464,878 | — | — | 580,049 | 562,583 |
| Other assets | 4,457 | — | — | — | 16,432 | 20,889 | 34,301 |
| Total current assets | 425,186 | 2,984,937 | 3,692,811 | 3,283,140 | 702,282 | 11,088,356 | 9,493,474 |
| Fixed assets: | | | | | | | |
| Land | 603,302 | 1,810,642 | 458,537 | 3,667,624 | 1,146,559 | 7,686,664 | 7,616,703 |
| Buildings and structures | — | 4,945,238 | 37,534,994 | 14,191,660 | 11,918,297 | 68,590,189 | 68,564,422 |
| Equipment and other fixed assets | 3,170,557 | 20,481,041 | 1,730,264 | 329,999 | 1,673,591 | 27,385,452 | 26,046,723 |
| Accumulated depreciation | (1,563,947) | (15,157,502) | (7,910,478) | (7,271,341) | (3,873,296) | (35,776,564) | (33,309,409) |
| Construction in progress | 1,886,393 | 329,036 | 4,764,875 | 6,443,656 | — | 13,423,960 | 9,897,634 |
| Net fixed assets | 4,096,305 | 12,408,455 | 36,578,192 | 17,361,598 | 10,865,151 | 81,309,701 | 78,816,073 |
| Total assets | $4,521,491 | $15,393,392 | $40,271,003 | $20,644,738 | $11,567,433 | $92,398,057 | $88,309,547 |

## EXHIBIT 13-14
*(continued)*

### Liabilities and Fund Equity

| | Transit company | Water | Sewage treatment | Airport | Civic center | Totals June 30, 1984 | Totals June 30, 1983 |
|---|---|---|---|---|---|---|---|
| **Current liabilities:** | | | | | | | |
| Warrants payable | $ — | $ 100,708 | $ 155,654 | $ 38,712 | $ 37,166 | $ 332,240 | $ 791,981 |
| Accounts payable and accrued expenses | 90,139 | 165,058 | 187,689 | 55,402 | 91,078 | 589,366 | 678,110 |
| Current maturities of long-term debt | — | 200,000 | 335,000 | 73,280 | — | 608,280 | 619,280 |
| Due to other funds | 49,711 | 2,695 | 4,467 | 1,274 | 1,641 | 59,788 | 139,565 |
| Due to other governments | — | — | — | 177,562 | — | 177,562 | — |
| Other liabilities | 48,736 | 186,086 | — | — | — | 234,822 | 137,496 |
| Total current liabilities | 188,586 | 654,547 | 682,810 | 346,230 | 129,885 | 2,002,058 | 2,366,432 |
| **Long-term liabilities:** | | | | | | | |
| Revenue bonds payable | — | 1,400,000 | 3,345,000 | — | — | 4,745,000 | 5,291,000 |
| General obligation bonds payable | — | — | — | 564,510 | — | 564,510 | 637,790 |
| Less current maturities | — | (200,000) | (335,000) | (73,280) | — | (608,280) | (619,280) |
| Total long-term liabilities | — | 1,200,000 | 3,010,000 | 491,230 | — | 4,701,230 | 5,309,510 |
| Total liabilities | 188,586 | 1,854,547 | 3,692,810 | 837,460 | 129,885 | 6,703,288 | 7,675,942 |
| **Fund equity:** | | | | | | | |
| Contributed capital | 4,148,890 | 353,940 | 26,063,181 | 16,828,009 | 10,286,305 | 57,680,325 | 54,886,693 |
| Retained earnings | 184,015 | 13,184,905 | 10,515,012 | 2,979,269 | 1,151,243 | 28,014,444 | 25,746,912 |
| Total fund equity | 4,332,905 | 13,538,845 | 36,578,193 | 19,807,278 | 11,437,548 | 85,694,769 | 80,633,605 |
| Total liabilities and fund equity | $4,521,491 | $15,393,392 | $40,271,003 | $20,644,738 | $11,567,433 | $92,398,057 | $88,309,547 |

*See notes to financial statements, Appendix 13-2.

**EXHIBIT 13-15**
**City of Roanoke, Virginia**
**Combining Statement of Revenues, Expenses, and Changes in Retained Earnings**
**Enterprise Funds**
**Year Ended June 30, 1984**
(With Comparative Totals for June 30, 1983)*

| | Transit company | Water | Sewage treatment | Airport | Civic center | Totals Year ended June 30, 1984 | Totals Year ended June 30, 1983 |
|---|---|---|---|---|---|---|---|
| Operating revenues | | | | | | | |
| Charges for services | $ 796,279 | $ 3,440,858 | $ 6,371,639 | $1,660,008 | $ 798,261 | $13,067,045 | $12,552,014 |
| Other | 11,428 | 90,997 | 25,691 | — | 4,722 | 132,838 | 75,295 |
| Total operating revenues | 807,707 | 3,531,855 | 6,397,330 | 1,660,008 | 802,983 | 13,199,883 | 12,627,309 |
| Operating expenses | | | | | | | |
| Personal services | 1,271,023 | 626,823 | 1,100,052 | 287,080 | 495,682 | 3,780,660 | 3,578,457 |
| Other services and charges | 419,743 | 2,404,847 | 2,757,665 | 1,074,158 | 728,786 | 7,385,199 | 7,398,237 |
| Materials and supplies | 388,841 | 103,688 | 501,595 | 13,967 | 32,059 | 1,040,150 | 1,083,020 |
| Depreciation | 247,289 | 563,977 | 763,668 | 581,396 | 310,823 | 2,467,153 | 2,397,342 |
| Total operating expenses | 2,326,896 | 3,699,335 | 5,122,980 | 1,956,601 | 1,567,350 | 14,673,162 | 14,457,056 |
| Operating income (loss) | (1,519,189) | (167,480) | 1,274,350 | (296,593) | (764,367) | (1,473,279) | (1,829,747) |
| Nonoperating revenues (expenses) | | | | | | | |
| Operating grants | 1,001,989 | — | 159,989 | 205,861 | — | 1,001,989 | 945,759 |
| Interest revenue | 19,921 | 284,616 | — | — | 30,677 | 701,064 | 425,182 |
| Interest expense | — | (65,000) | (197,240) | (30,476) | — | (292,716) | (325,815) |
| Total nonoperating revenues (expenses) | 1,021,910 | 219,616 | (37,251) | 175,385 | 30,677 | 1,410,337 | 1,045,126 |
| Income (loss) before operating transfers | (497,279) | 52,136 | 1,237,099 | (121,208) | (733,690) | (62,942) | (784,621) |
| Operating transfers from general fund | 261,793 | 918 | 2,808 | 432 | 626,872 | 892,823 | 865,602 |
| Net income (loss) | (235,486) | 53,054 | 1,239,907 | (120,776) | (106,818) | 829,881 | 80,981 |
| Depreciation charged to contributed capital | 244,384 | 9,778 | 530,368 | 355,291 | 297,830 | 1,437,651 | 1,420,983 |
| Increase (decrease) in retained earnings | 8,898 | 62,832 | 1,770,275 | 234,515 | 191,012 | 2,267,532 | 1,501,964 |
| Retained earnings—July 1 | 175,117 | 13,122,073 | 8,744,737 | 2,744,754 | 960,231 | 25,746,912 | 24,244,948 |
| Retained earnings—June 30 | $ 184,015 | $13,184,905 | $10,515,012 | $2,979,269 | $1,151,243 | $28,014,444 | $25,746,912 |

*See notes to financial statements, Appendix 13-2.

**EXHIBIT 13-16**
**City of Roanoke, Virginia**
**Combining Statement of Changes in Financial Position**
**Enterprise Funds**
**Year Ended June 30, 1984**
**(With Comparative Totals for June 30, 1983)***

|  | Transit company | Water | Sewage treatment | Airport | Civic center | Totals Year ended June 30, 1984 | Totals Year ended June 30, 1983 |
|---|---|---|---|---|---|---|---|
| *Sources of Financial Resources* | | | | | | | |
| Operations: | | | | | | | |
| Net increase (decrease) in retained earnings during the year | $ 8,898 | $ 62,832 | $1,770,275 | $ 234,515 | $191,012 | $2,267,532 | $1,501,964 |
| Expenses not requiring current outlay of financial resources—depreciation | 2,905 | 554,199 | 233,300 | 226,105 | 12,993 | 1,029,502 | 976,359 |
| Total financial resources from operations | 11,803 | 617,031 | 2,003,575 | 460,620 | 204,005 | 3,297,034 | 2,478,323 |
| Contributed capital | 1,544,667 | 11,428 | 29,054 | 2,646,136 | — | 4,231,285 | 6,135,836 |
| Total sources of financial resources | 1,556,470 | 628,459 | 2,032,629 | 3,106,756 | 204,005 | 7,528,319 | 8,614,159 |

**Uses of Financial Resources**

|  |  |  |  |  |  |  |
|---|---|---|---|---|---|---|
| Acquisition of fixed assets | 1,434,583 | 523,994 | 186,784 | 2,765,046 | 50,376 | 4,960,783 | 6,004,817 |
| Retirement of bonds payable | — | 200,000 | 335,000 | 73,280 | — | 608,280 | 608,280 |
| Total uses of financial resources | 1,434,583 | 723,994 | 521,784 | 2,838,326 | 50,376 | 5,569,063 | 6,613,097 |
| Net increase (decrease) in working capital | $ 121,887 | $(95,535) | $1,510,845 | $ 268,430 | $153,629 | $1,959,256 | $2,001,062 |

**Elements of Net Increase (Decrease) in Working Capital**

|  |  |  |  |  |  |  |  |
|---|---|---|---|---|---|---|---|
| Cash | $ (29,417) | $ 45,480 | $ (38,793) | $ 67,422 | $ 31,981 | $ 76,673 | $ (211,149) |
| Investments | 52,671 | (75,000) | 1,750,000 | 930,000 | 100,000 | 2,757,671 | 1,728,000 |
| Interest receivable | (1,215) | 5,575 | 11,403 | 33,814 | 2,865 | 52,442 | (49,776) |
| Due from other governments | (34,940) | — | (302,567) | (971,298) | — | (1,308,805) | 141,489 |
| Accounts receivable | 3,622 | (1,296) | (25,319) | 40,419 | (4,579) | 12,847 | (187,201) |
| Inventory | 16,888 | — | 578 | — | — | 17,466 | 474,436 |
| Other assets | (8,844) | — | — | — | (4,568) | (13,412) | (298) |
| Warrants payable | — | (25,554) | 114,859 | 353,096 | 17,340 | 459,741 | (94,064) |
| Accounts payable and accrued expenses | 90,065 | (6,582) | 1,414 | (7,050) | 10,897 | 88,744 | (102,925) |
| Due to other funds | 81,793 | (568) | (730) | (411) | (307) | 79,777 | 188,547 |
| Due to other governments | — | — | — | (177,562) | — | (177,562) | — |
| Other liabilities | (48,736) | (48,590) | — | — | — | (97,326) | 114,003 |
| Current maturities of long-term debt | — | 11,000 | — | — | — | 11,000 | — |
| Net increase (decrease) in working capital | $ 121,887 | $ (95,535) | $1,510,845 | $ 268,430 | $153,629 | $1,959,256 | $2,001,062 |

*See notes to financial statements, Appendix 13-2.

**EXHIBIT 13-17**
**City of Roanoke, Virginia**
**Combining Balance Sheet**
**Internal Service Funds***
**June 30, 1984**

## Assets

| | City information systems | Materials control | Management services | Utility line services | Motor vehicle maintenance | Total June 30, 1984 |
|---|---|---|---|---|---|---|
| Current assets: | | | | | | |
| Cash | $ 3,801 | $ 6,926 | $ 6,188 | $ 37,569 | $ 17,260 | $ 71,024 |
| Investments | 26,000 | 58,000 | 54,000 | 315,000 | 147,000 | 600,000 |
| Interest receivable | 64 | 143 | 133 | 778 | 363 | 1,481 |
| Total current assets | 29,145 | 65,069 | 60,321 | 353,347 | 164,623 | 672,505 |
| Fixed assets: | | | | | | |
| Equipment | 833,345 | 19,093 | 60,739 | 535,595 | 133,554 | 1,582,326 |
| Accumulated depreciation | (172,669) | (4,326) | (12,889) | (175,589) | (29,207) | (394,680) |
| Net fixed assets | 660,676 | 14,767 | 47,850 | 360,006 | 104,347 | 1,187,646 |
| Total assets | $689,821 | $79,836 | $108,171 | $713,353 | $268,970 | $1,860,151 |

## Liabilities and Fund Equity

| | City information systems | Materials control | Management services | Utility line services | Motor vehicle maintenance | Total June 30, 1984 |
|---|---|---|---|---|---|---|
| Current liabilities: | | | | | | |
| Warrants payable | $ 4,975 | $29,283 | $ 14,984 | $ 7,606 | $118,401 | $ 175,249 |
| Accounts payable and accrued expenses | 47,883 | 19,231 | 1,881 | 145,846 | 77,054 | 291,895 |
| Due to other funds | 425,384 | 559 | 160 | 5,745 | 3,283 | 435,131 |
| Total current liabilities | 478,242 | 49,073 | 17,025 | 159,197 | 198,738 | 902,275 |
| Total liabilities | 478,242 | 49,073 | 17,025 | 159,197 | 198,738 | 902,275 |
| Fund equity: | | | | | | |
| Contributed capital | 115,688 | 14,767 | 47,850 | 414,289 | 97,949 | 690,543 |
| Retained earnings (deficit) | 95,891 | 15,996 | 43,296 | 139,867 | (27,717) | 267,333 |
| Total fund equity | 211,579 | 30,763 | 91,146 | 554,156 | 70,232 | 957,876 |
| Total liabilities and fund equity | $689,821 | $79,836 | $108,171 | $713,353 | $268,970 | $1,860,151 |

*See note 2 in notes to financial statements, Appendix 13-2.

**EXHIBIT 13-18**
**City of Roanoke, Virginia**
**Combining Statement of Revenues, Expenses, and Changes in Retained Earnings**
**Internal Service Funds***
**Year Ended June 30, 1984**

| | City information systems | Materials control | Management services | Utility line services | Motor vehicle maintenance | Total for year ended June 30, 1984 |
|---|---|---|---|---|---|---|
| Operating revenues | | | | | | |
| Charges for services | $1,067,004 | $157,973 | $244,098 | $1,935,603 | $1,305,604 | $4,710,282 |
| Total operating revenue | 1,067,004 | 157,973 | 244,098 | 1,935,603 | 1,305,604 | 4,710,282 |
| Operating expenses | | | | | | |
| Personal services | 532,643 | 134,047 | 37,488 | 1,437,881 | 812,744 | 2,954,803 |
| Other services and charges | 275,674 | 17,578 | 50,689 | 189,119 | 518,811 | 1,051,871 |
| Materials and supplies | 27,154 | 1,327 | 123,767 | 190,257 | 17,411 | 359,916 |
| Depreciation | 172,669 | 4,326 | 12,889 | 175,589 | 29,207 | 394,680 |
| Total operating expenses | 1,008,140 | 157,278 | 224,833 | 1,992,846 | 1,378,173 | 4,761,270 |
| Operating income (loss) | 58,864 | 695 | 19,265 | (57,243) | (72,569) | (50,988) |
| Nonoperating revenues | | | | | | |
| Interest revenue | 4,641 | 686 | 1,061 | 8,420 | 5,683 | 20,491 |
| Total nonoperating revenues | 4,641 | 686 | 1,061 | 8,420 | 5,683 | 20,491 |
| Income (loss) before operating transfers | 63,505 | 1,381 | 20,326 | (48,823) | (66,886) | (30,497) |
| Operating transfers | | | | | | |
| Transfers from general fund | 11,148 | 10,289 | 10,081 | 13,101 | 11,752 | 56,371 |
| Net income (loss) | 74,653 | 11,670 | 30,407 | (35,722) | (55,134) | 25,874 |
| Depreciation charged to contributed capital | 21,238 | 4,326 | 12,889 | 175,589 | 27,417 | 241,459 |
| Increase (decrease) in retained earnings | 95,891 | 15,996 | 43,296 | 139,867 | (27,717) | 267,333 |
| Retained earnings—July 1 | — | — | — | — | — | — |
| Retained earnings—June 30 | $ 95,891 | $ 15,996 | $ 43,296 | $ 139,867 | $ (27,717) | $ 267,333 |

*See note 2 in notes to financial statements, Appendix 13-2.

**EXHIBIT 13-19**
**City of Roanoke, Virginia**
**Combining Statement of Changes in Financial Position**
**Internal Service Funds***
**Year Ended June 30, 1984**

| | City information systems | Materials control | Management services | Utility line services | Motor vehicle maintenance | Total Year ended June 30, 1984 |
|---|---|---|---|---|---|---|
| **Sources of financial resources** | | | | | | |
| Operations: | | | | | | |
| Net increase (decrease) in retained earnings during the year | $ 95,891 | $15,996 | $ 43,296 | $139,867 | $ (27,717) | $ 267,333 |
| Expenses not requiring current outlay of financial resources—depreciation | 151,431 | — | — | — | 1,790 | 153,221 |
| Total financial resources from operations | 247,322 | 15,996 | 43,296 | 139,867 | (25,927) | 420,554 |
| Contributed capital | 136,926 | 19,093 | 60,739 | 589,878 | 125,366 | 932,002 |
| Total sources of financial resources | 384,248 | 35,089 | 104,035 | 729,745 | 99,439 | 1,352,556 |
| **Uses of financial resources** | | | | | | |
| Acquisition of fixed assets | 833,345 | 19,093 | 60,739 | 535,595 | 133,554 | 1,582,326 |
| Total uses of financial resources | 833,345 | 19,093 | 60,739 | 535,595 | 133,554 | 1,582,326 |
| Net increase (decrease) in working capital | $(449,097) | $15,996 | $ 43,296 | $194,150 | $ (34,115) | $ (229,770) |
| **Elements of net increase (decrease) in working capital** | | | | | | |
| Cash | $ 3,081 | $ 6,926 | $ 6,188 | $ 37,569 | $ 17,260 | $ 71,024 |
| Investments | 26,000 | 58,000 | 54,000 | 315,000 | 147,000 | 600,000 |
| Interest receivable | 64 | 143 | 133 | 778 | 363 | 1,481 |
| Warrants payable | (4,975) | (29,283) | (14,984) | (7,606) | (118,401) | (175,249) |
| Accounts payable and accrued expenses | (47,883) | (19,231) | (1,881) | (145,846) | (77,054) | (291,895) |
| Due to other funds | (425,384) | (559) | (160) | (5,745) | (3,283) | (435,131) |
| Net increase (decrease) in working capital | $(449,097) | $15,996 | $ 43,296 | $194,150 | $ (34,115) | $ (229,770) |

*See note 2 in notes to financial statements, Appendix 13-2.

**EXHIBIT 13-20**
**City of Roanoke, Virginia**
**Combining Balance Sheet**
**All Fiduciary Fund Types**
**June 30, 1984**
**(With Comparative Totals for June 30, 1983)***

| | Pension trust fund | Agency fund | Memorandum only totals | |
| --- | --- | --- | --- | --- |
| | Employees retirement system | Fifth district employment and training consortium | June 30, 1984 | June 30, 1983 |
| **Assets** | | | | |
| Current assets: | | | | |
| Cash | $ 28 | $202,166 | $ 202,194 | $ 101,091 |
| Investments | 48,470,643 | — | 48,470,643 | 45,348,006 |
| Interest and dividends receivable | 609,101 | — | 609,101 | 554,448 |
| Unsettled securities trades receivable | 160,723 | — | 160,723 | — |
| Employer contributions receivable | 162,828 | — | 162,828 | 130,838 |
| Due from other governments | — | — | — | 108,835 |
| Prepaid expenses | 3,412 | — | 3,412 | 7,133 |
| Total current assets | $49,406,735 | $202,166 | $49,608,901 | $46,250,351 |
| **Liabilities and Fund Equity** | | | | |
| Current liabilities: | | | | |
| Warrants payable | $ — | $145,077 | $ 145,077 | $ 268,655 |
| Accounts payable and accrued expenses | 83,456 | 55,896 | 139,352 | 94,674 |
| Unsettled securities trades payable | — | — | — | 1,116,224 |
| Due to other funds | — | — | — | 214,192 |
| Due to other governments | — | 1,193 | 1,193 | — |
| Total current liabilities | 83,456 | 202,166 | 285,622 | 1,693,745 |
| Fund equity: | | | | |
| Reserved for employees' retirement system | 49,323,279 | — | 49,323,279 | 44,556,606 |
| Total liabilities and fund equity | $49,406,735 | $202,166 | $49,608,901 | $46,250,351 |

*See notes to financial statements, Appendix 13-2.

  **8** Computation of legal debt margin (if not presented in the GPFS)
  **9** Computation of overlapping debt (if not presented in the GPFS)
 **10** Ratio of annual debt service for general bonded debt to total general expenditures, last ten fiscal years
 **11** Revenue bond coverage, last ten fiscal years
 **12** Demographic statistics

**EXHIBIT 13-21**
**City of Roanoke, Virginia**
**Statement of Revenues, Expenses, and Changes in Fund Balance**
**Employees' Retirement System Trust Fund**
**Year Ended June 30, 1984**
**(With Comparative Totals for June 30, 1983)***

|  | Year ended | |
|---|---|---|
|  | 1984 | 1983 |
| Operating revenues | | |
|   Contributions | $ 4,499,002 | $ 4,076,950 |
|   Interest and dividends | 3,735,509 | 3,393,948 |
|   Gain on sale of investments | 17,748 | 1,042,946 |
|     Total operating revenues | 8,252,259 | 8,513,844 |
| Operating expenses | | |
|   Benefit payments | 3,027,440 | 2,855,937 |
|   Loss on sale of investments | 65,831 | — |
|   Administrative expense | 100,142 | 86,667 |
|   Commissions | 292,172 | 262,792 |
|     Total operating expenses | 3,485,585 | 3,205,396 |
|     Net income | 4,766,674 | 5,308,448 |
| Fund balance—July 1 | 44,556,605 | 39,248,157 |
| Fund balance—June 30 | $49,323,279 | $44,556,605 |

*See notes to financial statements, Appendix 13-2.

13 Property value, construction, and bank deposits, last ten fiscal years
14 Principal taxpayers
15 Miscellaneous statistics

Appendix 13-3 shows the type of statistical data presented in the annual financial report for the city of Roanoke, Virginia. This appendix includes: Table 1, General fund revenues by source, last ten fiscal years; Table 2, General fund expenditures and other uses by function, last ten fiscal years; Table 3, Local tax revenues by source, last ten fiscal years; Table 4, General property tax levies and collections, last ten years; Table 5, Assessed and estimated actual value of taxable property, last ten years; Table 6, Property tax rates and tax levies, last ten years; Table 7, Ratio of net general bonded debt to total assessed value and net bonded debt per capita, last ten fiscal years; Table 8, Computation of legal debt margin, June 30, 1984; Table 9, Ratio of annual debt service expenditures for general long-term debt to total general fund expenditures, last ten fiscal years; Table 10, Revenue bond coverage, water and sewage treatment bonds, last ten fiscal years; Table 11, Summary of bonded debt requirements to maturity, June 30, 1984; Table 12, Demographic statistics, last ten fiscal years; Table 13, Construction and bank deposits, last ten fiscal years; and Table 14, Principal property taxpayers, June 30, 1984.

**EXHIBIT 13-22**
City of Roanoke, Virginia
Statement of Changes in Financial Position
Employees' Retirement System Trust Fund
Year Ended June 30, 1984
(With Comparative Totals for June 30, 1983)*

|  | Year ended | |
|---|---|---|
|  | 1984 | 1983 |
| Sources of financial resources | | |
| Operations: | | |
| Net increase in fund balance | $4,766,674 | $5,308,448 |
| Total sources of financial resources | 4,766,674 | 5,308,448 |
| Uses of financial resources | | |
| Net increase in working capital | $4,766,674 | $5,308,448 |
| Elements of net increase (decrease) in working capital | | |
| Cash | $ (20) | $ (160) |
| Investments | 3,222,638 | 4,602,109 |
| Interest and dividends receivable | 54,653 | (77,041) |
| Due from other funds | 31,990 | 8,199 |
| Accounts receivable | 160,723 | — |
| Other assets | (3,721) | (3,722) |
| Warrants payable | 187,577 | 53,533 |
| Accounts payable and accrued expenses | 1,112,834 | 725,530 |
| Net increase in working capital | $4,766,674 | $5,308,448 |

*See notes to financial statements, Appendix 13-2.

## LEGAL REQUIREMENTS AND GENERALLY ACCEPTED ACCOUNTING PRINCIPLES

In most cases, generally accepted accounting principles—the formal and specific rules, conventions, and procedures for the practice of accounting and financial reporting in both the governmental and private profit entities—have been set by private organizations. Governmental jurisdictions, however, can establish—by law or regulation—their own accounting requirements, principles, and standards. For example, some states give an agency the right to state the funds, the account titles, and even the account codes of the jurisdiction's accounting system. The Virginia auditor of public accounts, for instance, has set principles and standards for accounting for counties and municipalities for the commonwealth of Virginia.

Legal requirements for accounting and reporting in a governmental unit, obviously, must be followed. The certified public accountant, however, when acting as the independent auditor and attester of the funds of government, must report to third parties

**EXHIBIT 13-23**
**City of Roanoke, Virginia**
**Statement of Changes in Assets and Liabilities**
**Fifth District Employment and Training Consortium Agency Fund**
**Year Ended June 30, 1984***

|  | Balance July 1, 1983 | Additions | Deductions | Balance June 30, 1984 |
|---|---|---|---|---|
| **Assets** | | | | |
| Cash | $101,043 | $2,755,860 | $2,654,737 | $202,166 |
| Investments | 100,000 | — | 100,000 | — |
| Due from U.S. Department of Labor | 108,835 | — | 108,835 | — |
| Total assets | $309,878 | $2,755,860 | $2,863,572 | $202,166 |
| **Liabilities** | | | | |
| Warrants payable | $ 81,078 | $2,718,736 | $2,654,737 | $145,077 |
| Due to other funds | 214,192 | 75,000 | 289,192 | — |
| Due to U.S. Department of Labor | — | 1,193 | — | 1,193 |
| Accounts payable | 14,608 | 59,767 | 18,479 | 55,896 |
| Total liabilities | $309,878 | $2,854,696 | $2,962,408 | $202,166 |

*See notes to financial statements, Appendix 13-2.

that the statements were prepared in accordance with generally accepted accounting principles consistently applied, if an unqualified opinion is desired. When the statements are prepared following legal requirements that differ from GAAP, the CPA must explain the reason for the differences or qualify his or her opinion on the statements. In some cases, public organizations might have to prepare their statements using two different sets of accounting principles—GAAP and the legal requirements—in order to obtain a "clean" opinion from the auditor and the state. Or, perhaps, GAAP statements can be prepared with schedules demonstrating legal compliance. If financial statements that are only on the legal basis are attested to by an independent auditor, they are considered "special reports." CPAs preparing these reports must follow generally accepted auditing standards concerned with special reports.

Whenever possible, those involved in setting governmental accounting and financial reporting principles should strive to have the legal requirements agree with generally accepted accounting principles. By doing so, costs will be reduced and the financial reporting will be improved.

## SUMMARY

Financial reports bring together the results of the financial accounting for the period. Third parties seldom understand the way records are kept and how the information in the records is brought together into financial statements. This chapter examines all of the statements, schedules, notes, and other information found in a city's comprehensive annual financial report.

**PEAT MARWICK**

Peat, Marwick, Mitchell & Co.
Certified Public Accountants
213 South Jefferson Street
Roanoke, Virginia 24011

The Honorable Members of City Council
City of Roanoke, Virginia:

We have examined the combined financial statements of the City of Roanoke, Virginia and the combining and individual fund financial statements of the City as of and for the year ended June 30, 1984, as listed in the financial section of the table of contents. Our examination was made in accordance with generally accepted auditing standards, the financial and compliance elements of the Standards for Audit of Governmental Organizations, Programs, Activities and Functions (1981 Revision) issued by the Comptroller General of the United States, and Specifications for Audit of Counties, Cities and Towns (1983) issued by the auditor of Public Accounts of the Commonwealth of Virginia and, accordingly, included such tests of the accounting records and such other auditing procedures as we considered necessary in the circumstances.

In our opinion, the aforementioned combined financial statements present fairly the financial position of the city of Roanoke, Virginia at June 30, 1984, and the results of its operations and the changes in financial position of its proprietary fund types for the year then ended, in conformity with generally accepted accounting principles applied on a basis consistent with that of the preceding year. Also, in our opinion, the aforementioned combining and individual fund financial statements present fairly the financial position of the individual funds of the City of Roanoke, Virginia at June 30, 1984, and the results of operations of such funds and the changes in financial position of individual proprietary funds for the year then ended, in conformity with generally accepted accounting principles applied on a basis consistent with that of the preceding year.

We did not examine the statistical data listed in the statistical section of the accompanying table of contents and, therefore, express no opinion thereon.

*Peat, Marwick, Mitchell & Co.*

September 28, 1984

**EXHIBIT 13-24**  The auditor's opinion for the financial statements of the city of Roanoke, Virginia.

In addition to the annual financial statements audited by an independent accountant, the comprehensive annual financial report includes various schedules and can include summary data concerning the city, along with any description of the accounting system that will be useful (see Exhibit 13-1). This chapter illustrates the numerous statements, schedules, and other pertinent data found in the comprehensive annual financial report of the city of Roanoke, Virginia.

## QUESTIONS

1. What is preferred in external financial reporting, generally accepted accounting principles or legal requirements?
2. What is a combined statement?
3. What is a combining statement?
4. A comprehensive annual financial report (CAFR) encompasses what statements, exhibits, and statistical data?
5. Refer to Exhibit 13-2. From the column "proprietary fund types," can you tell how many proprietary funds there are in the city of Roanoke?
6. Explain how combining statements can be used when preparing combined statements.
7. Refer to Exhibit 13-23. In an agency fund, what sort of fund balance is used?
8. Explain how encumbered appropriations are carried over from one year to the next by the city of Roanoke, Virginia.

## PROBLEMS

**13-1** Choose the best answer for the following questions.[32]

1. A state governmental unit should use which basis of accounting for each of the following types of funds?

    | | Governmental | Proprietary |
    |---|---|---|
    | a | Cash | Modified accrual |
    | b | Modified accrual | Modified accrual |
    | c | Modified accrual | Accrual |
    | d | Accrual | Accrual |

2. Which of the following accounts of a governmental unit is (are) closed out at the end of the fiscal year?

    | | Estimated revenues | Fund balance |
    |---|---|---|
    | a | No | No |
    | b | No | Yes |
    | c | Yes | Yes |
    | d | Yes | No |

3. Which of the following accounts of a governmental unit is credited when a purchase order is approved?
    a. Reserve for encumbrances
    b. Encumbrances
    c. Vouchers payable
    d. Appropriations

4. Repairs that have been made for a governmental unit, and for which a bill has been received, should be recorded in the general fund as a debit to an

a Expenditure
   b Encumbrance
   c Expense
   d Appropriation
5 A debt service fund of a municipality is an example of which of the following types of funds?
   a Fiduciary
   b Governmental
   c Proprietary
   d Internal service
6 At the end of the fiscal year of a governmental unit, the excess of expenditures and encumbrances over appropriations
   a Increases the fund balance
   b Decreases the fund balance
   c Increases the reserve for encumbrances
   d Decreases the reserve for encumbrances
7 Which of the following accounts of a governmental unit is closed out at the end of the fiscal year?
   a Fund balance
   b Reserve for encumbrances
   c Appropriations
   d Vouchers payable
8 The encumbrance account of a governmental unit is debited when
   a A purchase order is approved
   b Goods are received
   c A voucher payable is recorded
   d The budget is recorded
9 Which of the following funds of a governmental unit recognizes revenues and expenditures under the same basis of accounting as the general fund?
   a Debt service
   b Enterprise
   c Internal service
   d Nonexpendable pension trust
10 Which of the following funds of a governmental unit would include retained earnings in its balance sheet?
   a Expendable pension trust
   b Internal service (intragovernmental service)
   c Special revenue
   d Capital projects

**13-2** The following balances appeared in the city of Reedsbury's general fund at June 30, 19X1. Items 1 and 2 are based on this information.

| Account | Balance Dr. (Cr.) |
|---|---|
| Encumbrances—current year | $ 200,000 |
| Expenditures: | |
|   Current year | 3,000,000 |
|   Prior year | 100,000 |
| Fund balance reserved for encumbrances: | |
|   Current year | (200,000) |
|   Prior year | None |

Reedsbury maintains its general fund books on a legal budgetary basis, requiring revenues and expenditures to be accounted for on a modified accrual basis. In addition, the sum of current-year expenditures and encumbrances cannot exceed current-year appropriations.

1  What total amount of expenditures (and encumbrances, if appropriate) should Reedsbury report in the general fund column of its combined statement of revenues, expenditures, and changes in fund balance for the year ended June 30, 19X1?
   a  $3,000,000
   b  $3,100,000
   c  $3,200,000
   d  $3,300,000

2  What total amount of expenditures (and encumbrances, if appropriate) should Reedsbury report in the general fund "actual" column of its combined statement of revenues, expenditures, and changes in fund balance—budget and actual—for the year ended June 30, 19X1?
   a  $3,000,000
   b  $3,100,000
   c  $3,200,000
   d  $3,300,000

Items 3 and 4 are based on the following information:

During the year ended December 31, 19X1, Leyland City received a state grant of $500,000 to finance the purchase of buses and an additional grant of $100,000 to aid in the financing of bus operations in 19X1. Only $300,000 of the capital grant was used in 19X1 for the purchase of buses, but the entire operating grant of $100,000 was spent in 19X1.

3  If Leyland City's bus transportation system is accounted for as part of the city's general fund, how much should Leyland City report as grant revenues for the year ended December 31, 19X1?
   a  $100,000
   b  $300,000
   c  $400,000
   d  $500,000

4  If Leyland City's bus transportation system is accounted for as an enterprise fund, how much should the city report as grant revenues for the year ended December 31, 19X1?
   a  $100,000
   b  $300,000
   c  $400,000
   d  $500,000

5  Ariel Village issued the following bonds during the year ended June 30, 19X1:

| | |
|---|---:|
| Revenue bonds to be repaid from admission fees collected by the Ariel zoo enterprise fund | $200,000 |
| General obligation bonds issued for the Ariel water and sewer enterprise fund, which will service the debt | 300,000 |

How much of these bonds should be accounted for in Ariel's general long-term debt account group?
   a  $0
   b  $200,000
   c  $300,000
   d  $500,000

Items 6 and 7 are based on the following information:

On December 31, 19X1, Madrid Township paid a contractor $2,000,000 for the total cost of a new firehouse built in 19X1 on township-owned land. Financing was by means of a $1,500,000 general obligation bond issue sold at face amount on December 31, 19X1, with the remaining $500,000 transferred from the general fund.

**6** What should be reported on Madrid's 19X1 financial statements for the capital projects fund?
  a Revenues, $1,500,000; expenditures, $1,500,000
  b Revenues, $1,500,000; other financing sources, $500,000; expenditures, $2,000,000
  c Revenues, $2,000,000; expenditures, $2,000,000
  d Other financing sources, $2,000,000; expenditures, $2,000,000

**7** What should be reported on Madrid's 19X1 financial statements for the general fund?
  a Expenditures, $500,000
  b Other financing uses, $500,000
  c Revenues, $1,500,000; expenditures, $2,000,000
  d Revenues, $1,500,000; other financing uses, $2,000,000

**13-3** The bookkeeper of the city of Three-Mile has prepared the following balance sheet. Rearrange the elements included in the balance sheet into a properly prepared combined balance sheet.

**City of Three-Mile**
**Balance Sheet**
**June 30, 19XX**

**Assets**

Current assets:
  Cash (including: general fund, $380,000;
    special revenue fund, $60,000;
    debt service fund, $55,000;
    capital projects fund, $35,000;
    public utility fund, $48,000;
    internal service fund, $19,000; and
    trust fund, $120,000)                                      $ 717,000
  Taxes receivable                                               370,000
  Due from public utility fund                                    60,000
  Accounts receivable (including:
    general fund, $80,000;
    special revenue fund, $20,000;
    public utility fund, $163,000; and
    internal service fund, $26,000)                              289,000
  Inventories (including:
    general fund, $23,000;
    public utility fund, $159,000;
    internal service fund, $30,000)                              212,000
  Due from state government (including:
    general fund, $51,000;
    special revenue fund, $39,000)                                90,000
Fixed assets:
  Investments (including:
    debt service fund, $285,000;
    trust fund, $125,000)                                        410,000
  Land (including:
    public utility fund, $98,000;
    fixed assets account group, $273,000)                        371,000

| | | |
|---|---:|---:|
| Buildings (including: | | |
|   public utility fund, $126,000; | | |
|   fixed assets account group, $390,000 | | 516,000 |
| Equipment (including: | | |
|   public utility fund, $102,000; | | |
|   fixed assets account group, $98,000) | | 200,000 |
|     Total assets | | $3,235,000 |

**Liabilities**

| | | |
|---|---:|---:|
| Current liabilities | | |
|   Accounts payable (including: | | |
|     general fund, $480,000; | | |
|     public utility fund [including amount | | |
|     owed to general fund] $223,000; | | |
|     internal service fund, $35,000; | | |
|     trust fund, $78,000; | | |
|     special revenue fund, $76,000) | | $ 892,000 |
| Fixed liabilities: | | |
|   Bonds payable—general | $600,000 | |
|   Unamortized premium on bonds | 2,000 | 602,000 |
| Fund balances: | | |
|   General fund | | 484,000 |
|   Special revenue fund | | 43,000 |
|   Debt service fund | | 340,000 |
|   Capital projects fund | | 35,000 |
|   Public utility fund | | 410,000 |
|   Internal service fund | | 30,000 |
|   Trust fund | | 167,000 |
|   Account group fund | | 159,000 |
| Retained earnings: | | |
|   Public utility fund | | 63,000 |
|   Internal service fund | | 10,000 |
|     Total liabilities and fund balance | | $3,235,000 |

The following information was found by discussing the balance sheet with the bookkeeper:

**1** The internal service fund was a garage fund and was started by a $30,000 contribution from the general fund.

**2** The public utility fund received a $410,000 contribution from the general fund as a basis for starting the utility. All earnings above approximately 50 percent of those remaining are given to the general fund for general operations of the city.

**3** Encumbrances that have been carried over from the current year in order to have resources to pay for them when the goods are delivered amount to $80,000 in the general fund.

**4** A $2,000 amount had been transferred to the debt service fund from the capital projects fund upon sale on bonds at a $2,000 premium.

**13-4** The bookkeeper in the city of Bayport keeps all of its governmental type funds—the general fund, a trust fund, and a special assessment fund—in one ledger. The following is a partial trial balance of these ledger accounts.

## City of Bayport
### Trial Balance (Partial)
### For the Period Ending June 30, 19XX

|  | Debits | Credits |
|---|---|---|
| Revenues |  |  |
| Property taxes—general fund |  | $ 58,000 |
| Licenses and fines—general fund |  | 13,000 |
| Interest revenues—special assessment fund |  | 9,750 |
| Transfers—to special assessment from general fund |  | 6,310 |
| Interest—general fund |  | 1,890 |
| Interest—trust fund |  | 100 |
| Sales of excess property—special assessment fund |  | 8,200 |
| Expenditures |  |  |
| Administrative—general fund | $ 15,800 |  |
| Administrative—special assessment fund | 5,150 |  |
| Protective services—general fund | 14,500 |  |
| Welfare services—general fund | 12,400 |  |
| Other expenditures—special assessment fund | 2,500 |  |
| Capital expenditures—general fund | 17,000 |  |
| Capital expenditures—special assessment fund | 6,000 |  |
| Interest expenditures—special assessment fund | 8,650 |  |
| Operating transfers |  |  |
| To special assessment from general fund | 6,310 |  |
| Totals | $ 88,310 | $ 97,250 |
| Fund balances |  |  |
| General fund |  | 17,000 |
| Trust fund |  | 1,500 |
| Special assessment fund |  | 2,000 |
| Net assets | 29,440 |  |
| Total | $117,750 | $117,750 |

Additional information obtained from the records and from other sources needed to prepare the required statements is:

1 Budgetary information:

| Estimated revenues (general fund) | $75,000 |
|---|---|
| Appropriations (general fund) | 72,500 |

2 Encumbrance information:

Prior year's reserve for encumbrances (general fund):

| | |
|---|---|
| Administration | $ 800 |
| Protective services | 600 |
| Welfare services | 400 |
| Capital outlay | 500 |
| Total | $2,300 |

Current year's reserve for encumbrances (general fund):

| | |
|---|---|
| Administration | $ 500 |
| Protective services | 700 |
| Welfare services | 500 |
| Capital outlay | 500 |
| Total | $2,200 |

**3** Budgetary appropriations by functions (general fund):

| | |
|---|---|
| Administration | $16,000 |
| Protective services | 16,000 |
| Welfare services | 16,000 |
| Capital outlay | 18,000 |
| Transfers to special assessment fund | 6,500 |
| Total | $72,500 |

**Required**:

1 Separate the revenues, expenditures, and fund balances into their proper funds, and prepare a combined statement of revenue, expenditures, and fund balances for all governmental fund types.

2 Prepare a statement of revenues, expenditures, and fund balances for the general fund, budget and actual.

**13-5** You have been engaged by the town of Nihill to examine its June 30, 19X4 balance sheet. You are the first CPA to be engaged by the town, and you find that acceptable methods of municipal accounting have not been employed. The town clerk stated that the books had been closed and presented the following balance sheet:[33]

**Town of Nihill**
**Balance Sheet**
**June 30, 19X4**

| | |
|---|---|
| Assets | |
| Cash | $ 36,200 |
| Taxes receivable | 21,900 |
| Accounts receivable | 9,000 |
| Investments | 84,200 |
| Prepaid expenses | 21,000 |
| Fixed assets | 245,400 |
| Total | $417,700 |
| Liabilities | |
| Accounts payable | $ 6,500 |
| Bonds payable | 200,000 |
| Fund balance | 211,200 |
| Total | $417,700 |

The town of Nihill was formed as a separate political unit on July 1, 19X2. The town was formerly a real estate development within the township of Hamton. Your audit disclosed the following information:

**1** On July 1, 19X3, the town received a bequest of $50,000 in cash and a house with a fair market value of $40,000. The house was recorded on the books as an investment at its fair market value at July 1, 19X3. The bequest arose under the terms of a will that provided that the house would be used as a public library and the $50,000 would be established as a nonexpendable trust fund whose income would be used to buy library books. Securities costing $49,200 were purchased in July 19X3, by the town for the trust fund, and in June 19X4, securities with a cost of $5,000 were sold for $6,800. The trust fund had dividend and interest income of $2,100 during the year, of which $1,900 was expended. In addition the town expended from general funds $9,000 for conversion of the house to library purposes and $19,000 for books; these last amounts were charged to expenditures. The town has no other investments. The decision was made to account for the library trust earnings in a separate fund.

**2** Taxes levied for the year amounted to $84,300, of which $62,400 was collected and $800 has been identified as being illegal and requiring abatement. In addition, it is anticipated that $1,400 of the remaining 19X3–X4 levy will prove uncollectible.

**3** The water company that had been formed by the developer to service the real estate development was purchased by the town on July 1, 19X3. The seller accepted 5 percent general obligation bonds in settlement. Details of the sales contract follow:

| | | |
|---|---:|---:|
| Plant and equipment | | $108,000 |
| Assets and liabilities assumed: | | |
|   Prepaid expenses (inventories) | $19,000 | |
|   Accounts receivable | 8,000 | |
|   Total | $27,000 | |
| Accounts payable | 5,000 | 22,000 |
| Sales price | | $130,000 |

Cash arising from the operation of the water plant, except for a $1,000 working fund, is used for the general purposes of the town. At June 30, 19X4, the following accounts pertain solely to the operation of the water plant: accounts receivable, prepaid expenses, and accounts payable.

**4** A $300,000 issue of 5 percent general obligation bonds was authorized on July 1, 19X3. In addition to the settlement for the purchase of the water company, bonds in the amount of $70,000 were sold at 100 on that date, and $65,400 of the proceeds had been used up to June 30, 19X4 to obtain other equipment for the town. Interest is payable on June 30 and December 31; no interest payments are in arrears. Commencing June 30, 19X5, bonds in the amount of $10,000 are to be retired each June 30.

**5** A shipment of supplies for the water plant was received in June 19X4 and included in prepaid expenses, but the invoice for $700 was recorded in July. An order was placed in June with a printer for stationery to be used by the town's governing body. The stationery was delivered in July and cost $500. The remaining composite life of the water company plant and equipment at July 1, 19X3 was estimated at thirty years.

**Required**:
Fill out a worksheet to adjust the accounts with the following worksheet headings: account; balance per books; adjustments, Dr., and Cr.; general fund; endowment fund; library fund; fixed assets account group; enterprise fund; capital projects fund; and long-

term debt account group. Distribute the amounts to the proper funds or account groups. Prepare the necessary journal entries.

**13-6** This problem concludes the illustrative case of Silver City that has continued throughout the book. It will be necessary to have the working papers for each of the problems previously worked in order to complete the requirements for this final problem.

**Required**:

1 Prepare the following financial statements:
  a A combined balance sheet for all funds and account groups.
  b A combined statement of revenues, expenditures, and changes in fund balances for all governmental funds.
  c A combined statement of revenues, expenses, and fund balance (equity or retained earnings) for the proprietary fund. Should a statement of changes in financial position be prepared for this fund? If so, prepare it.
  d A statement of revenues, expenditures, and changes in fund balance—budget and actual—for the general fund.
  e Combining statements where appropriate or when they can be prepared. If none are appropriate, explain the reason why you should not prepare them.
  f Individual statements or schedules for funds or account groups where appropriate information is not available in either a combined or combining funds statement.

# NOTES

1 National Council on Governmental Accounting, *Statement 3, Defining the Governmental Reporting Entity* (Chicago: National Council on Governmental Accounting, 1981), p. 2.
2 National Council on Governmental Accounting, *Interpretation 7. Clarification as to the Application of the Criteria in NCGA Statement 3. Defining the Governmental Reporting Entity* (Chicago: National Council on Governmental Accounting, 1983).
3 National Council on Government Accounting, *Statement 1. Governmental Accounting and Financial Reporting Principles* (Chicago: Municipal Finance Officers Association of the United States and Canada, 1979), p. 4.
4 Ibid., p. 20.
5 For an excellent discussion on the pros and cons of both combined and combining versus consolidated financial statements, see Richard P. Van Daniker and Kay T. Pohlmann, *Preferred Accounting Practices for State Governments* (Lexington, Kentucky: The Council of State Governments, 1983), pp. 164–168.
6 City of Roanoke, Virginia, *Comprehensive Annual Financial Report, City of Roanoke, Virginia, Year Ended June 30, 1984* (Roanoke, Virginia: City of Roanoke, Virginia, 1984), pp. 20–21.
7 Ibid., p. 22.
8 Ibid., p. 23.
9 Ibid., p. 24.
10 Ibid., p. 25.
11 Ibid., p. 39.
12 Ibid., pp. 40–42.
13 Ibid., pp. 43–47.
14 Ibid., p. 49.
15 Ibid., p. 49.

16 Ibid., p. 51.
17 Ibid., p. 52.
18 NCGA, *Statement 1*, pp. 20–21.
19 City of Roanoke, p. 55.
20 Ibid., p. 59.
21 Ibid., p. 56.
22 Ibid., p. 60.
23 Ibid., p. 57.
24 Ibid., p. 61.
25 Ibid., p. 65.
26 Ibid., p. 66.
27 Ibid., p. 67.
28 Ibid., p. 68.
29 American Institute of Certified Public Accountants, *AICPA Professional Standards, Volume A. U.S. Auditing Standards* (New York: American Institute of Certified Public Accountants, 1985), AU par. 110.01, p. 61.
30 City of Roanoke, p. 18.
31 NCGA, *Statement 1*, p. 24.
32 Adapted from American Institute of Certified Public Accountants, *Uniform CPA Examination Questions and Unofficial Answers* (New York: American Institute of Certified Public Accountants, various dates).
33 Ibid., May 1965, (adapted).

# APPENDIX 13-1: Comprehensive Annual Financial Report[34]

## INTRODUCTORY SECTION

Letter of Transmittal
Certificate of Conformance
Director—Principal Officials
Organizational Chart

## FINANCIAL SECTION

### General Purpose Financial Statements

Accountant's Opinion (Exhibit 13-24)

| | |
|---|---|
| Exhibit 13-2 | Combined Balance Sheet—All Fund Types and Account Groups |
| Exhibit 13-3 | Combined Statement of Revenues, Expenditures, and Changes in Fund Balance—All Governmental Fund Types |
| Exhibit 13-4 | Statement of Revenues, Expenditures, and Changes in Undesignated Fund Balance—Budget and Actual—General Fund |
| Exhibit 13-5 | Combined Statement of Revenues, Expenses and Changes in Retained Earnings/Fund Balance—All Proprietary Fund Types and Similar Trust Fund |
| Exhibit 13-6 | Combined Statement of Changes in Financial Position—All Proprietary Fund Types and Similar Trust Fund |

Notes to Financial Statements (Appendix 13-2)

## Combining and Individual Financial Statements

*General Fund:*
Exhibit 13-7   Comparative Balance Sheet
Exhibit 13-8   Comparative Statement of Revenue, Budget and Actual
Exhibit 13-9   Comparative Statement of Expenditures, Budget and Actual

*Debt Service Fund:*
Exhibit 13-10   Comparative Balance Sheet
Exhibit 13-11   Comparative Statement of Revenues, Expenditures, and Changes in Fund Balance

*Capital Projects Fund:*
Exhibit 13-12   Comparative Balance Sheet
Exhibit 13-13   Comparative Statement of Revenues, Expenditures, and Changes in Fund Balance

*Enterprise Funds:*
Exhibit 13-14   Combining Balance Sheet
Exhibit 13-15   Combining Statement of Revenues, Expenses, and Changes in Retained Earnings
Exhibit 13-16   Combining Statement of Changes in Financial Position

*Internal Service Funds:*
Exhibit 13-17   Combining Balance Sheet
Exhibit 13-18   Combining Statement of Revenues, Expenses, and Changes in Retained Earnings
Exhibit 13-19   Combining Statement of Changes in Financial Position

*Fiduciary Funds:*
Exhibit 13-20   Combining Balance Sheet
Exhibit 13-21   Comparative Statement of Revenues, Expenses, and Changes in Fund Balance—Employees' Retirement System Trust Fund
Exhibit 13-22   Statement of Changes in Financial Position—Employees' Retirement System Trust Fund
Exhibit 13-23   Statement of Changes in Assets and Liabilities—Fifth District Employment and Training Consortium Agency Fund

## STATISTICAL SECTION (APPENDIX 13-3)

Table 1   General Fund Revenues By Source
Table 2   General Fund Expenditures and Other Uses By Function
Table 3   Local Tax Revenues By Source
Table 4   General Property Tax Levies and Collections
Table 5   Assessed and Estimated Actual Value of Taxable Property
Table 6   Property Tax Rates and Tax Levies
Table 7   Ratio of Net General Bonded Debt to Total Assessed Value and Net Bonded Debt Per Capita
Table 8   Computation of Legal Debt Margin
Table 9   Ratio of Annual Debt Service Expenditures for General Long-Term Debt to Total General Fund Expenditures

Table 10    Revenue Bond Coverage—Water and Sewage Treatment Bonds
Table 11    Summary of Bonded Debt Principal Requirements to Maturity
Table 12    Demographic Statistics
Table 13    Construction and Bank Deposits
Table 14    Principal Property Taxpayers
Table 15    Miscellaneous Data

# APPENDIX 13-2: Notes to Financial Statements[35]

**I** Summary of Significant Accounting Policies:

The accounting policies of the City of Roanoke, Virginia conform to generally accepted accounting principles as applicable to governments.

**A** Reporting Entity

The City's financial statements include the accounts of all City operations and those of separately administered organizations that are controlled by or dependent on the City. Control or dependence is determined by financial interdependency, selection of governing board, and ability to significantly influence operations.

Based on the foregoing criteria, the following entities are included in the accompanying financial statements:

Roanoke City School Board—City Council appoints the members of the School Board and levies taxes for the Board's operation. It also issues debt for capital projects. The operations of the School Board are reported as a category within the General Fund, the Capital Projects Fund, and the account groups.

Greater Roanoke Transit Company—The Greater Roanoke Transit Company is a public service bus company organized to provide mass transportation services to the Roanoke Valley. The Company is owned by the City of Roanoke with City Council acting as its board of directors. The Company's operations are reported as an Enterprise Fund, a Proprietary Fund Type.

The following organizations are not part of the City of Roanoke and are excluded from the accompanying financial statements for the reasons stated below:

Roanoke Valley Regional Solid Waste Management Board—The Board operates a regional sanitary landfill jointly owned by the City of Roanoke, the Town of Vinton, and the County of Roanoke. City Council appoints three members of the six-member board. The Board has the authority to finance by use of long-term borrowing, which is not an obligation of the City. Its operations are financed entirely by user fees. See note 12.

Industrial Development Authority of the City of Roanoke—The authority is a political subdivision of the State created by City Council to induce industrial, governmental, and commercial enterprises to locate or remain in Roanoke. To this end, the Authority issues low-interest, tax-free industrial revenue bonds to acquire and improve property and equipment which is then sold or leased to the enterprise at terms necessary to retire the financing. This debt is not an obligation of the City. Board members of the Authority are appointed by City Council. The Authority obtains and expends its financial resources independent of the City.

Roanoke Redevelopment and Housing Authority—The Authority is a political subdivision of the State created to provide low-income and subsidized housing. It can issue bonds and other obligations which are not liabilities of the City. Commissioners to the Housing Authority are appointed by City Council. Although overall housing plans require the approval of City Council, the Authority has administrative control of its affairs without requiring the approval of the City. Its operations are financed primarily by federal government subsidies and rents.

**B** Financial Statement Presentation

The accounts are organized on the basis of fund types and account groups, each of which is considered to be a separate accounting entity. The operation of each fund is accounted for by providing a separate set of self-balancing accounts that comprise its assets, liabilities, fund equity, revenues and expenditures or expenses, as appropriate.

Government resources are allocated to and accounted for in individual funds based upon the purposes for which they are to be spent and the means by which spending activities are controlled. The various funds are grouped, in the financial statements in this report, into seven generic fund types, three broad fund categories and two account groups as follows:

- Governmental Fund Types account for the expendable financial resources, other than proprietary fund types. The governmental fund measurement focus is upon determination of financial position and changes in financial position, rather than upon income determination. The governmental fund types are:

    **General Fund**—Accounts for all revenues and expenditures which are not accounted for in other funds. It finances the regular day-to-day operations of the City.

    **Debt Service Fund**—Accounts for the accumulation of resources for, and the payment of, general long-term debt principal, interest, and fiscal charges.

    **Capital Projects Fund**—Accounts for financial resources to be used for the acquisition or construction of major capital facilities, other than those financed by proprietary funds.

- Proprietary Fund Types account for operations that are financed and operated in a manner similar to private business enterprises. The proprietary fund measurement focus is upon determination of net income, financial position, and changes in financial position. The proprietary fund types are:

    **Enterprise Funds**—Accounts for the financing of services to the general public where all or most of the operating expenses involved are recovered in the form of charges to users of such services. Included in this category are the water, sewer, civic center, airport, and transit company funds.

**Internal Service Funds**—Accounts for the financing of goods or services provided by one department primarily or solely to other departments within the City government. Funds included in this category are City Information Systems, Management Services, Motor Vehicle Maintenance, Materials Control, and Utility Line Services.

- Fiduciary Fund Types account for assets held by the City in a trustee capacity or as an agent for individuals, other governmental units, and other funds. The fiduciary fund types are:

    **Pension Trust Fund**—Accounts for the operations of the City's pension fund. It is accounted for in the same manner as a proprietary fund type, measurement focus is upon determination of net income, financial position, and changes in financial position.

    **Agency Fund**—Accounts for the assets and liabilities of the Fifth District Employment and Training Consortium. The fund is custodial in nature and does not involve measurement of results of operations.

- Account Groups are used to establish accounting control and accountability for the general fixed assets and the unmatured principal of its general obligation long-term debt. These account groups are not funds since they represent only an accountability for the general fixed assets and general long-term debt.

C  Basis of Accounting

Basis of accounting refers to when revenues and expenditures or expenses are recognized in the accounts and reported in the financial statements. Basis of accounting relates to the timing of the measurements made, regardless of the measurement focus applied.

All governmental funds and the agency fund are accounted for using the modified accrual basis of accounting. Their revenues are recognized when they become measurable and available as net current assets. General Property Taxes (less an allowance for uncollectible receivables), interest income and intergovernmental receivables (state and federal grants to the extent of allowable expenditures) are considered susceptible to accrual. General property taxes are considered susceptible to accrual as determined to be measurable and available, not exceeding 60 days, as defined by NCGA *Statement 1* and further clarified by NCGA *Interpretation 3*. Expenditures are generally recognized under the modified accrual basis of accounting when the related fund liability is incurred. Exceptions to the general rule include: (1) accumulated unpaid vacation and sick leave amounts which are not accrued and (2) principal and interest on general long-term debt which is recognized when due.

All proprietary funds and the Pension Trust Fund are accounted for using the accrual basis of accounting. Their revenues are recognized when they are earned, and their expenses are recognized when they are incurred. Unbilled

Water and Sewer Fund utility service receivables are not recorded since such amounts are not significant.

**D** Budgets and Budgetary Accounting

The City follows these procedures in establishing the budgetary data reflected in the financial statements (Exhibit 13-4):

1 Proposal—At least sixty days prior to June 30, the City Manager submits to the City Council a proposed operating budget for the fiscal year commencing July 1. The operating budget includes proposed expenditures and the means of financing them.

2 Projects—The capital budget is prepared on a project length basis under which the total outlay for each project is estimated for the length of the project. A capital budget on an annual period basis is not legally enacted so that a budgetary comparison for the Capital Projects Fund is not presented in the budgetary statement (Exhibit 13-4).

3 Adoption—Public hearings are conducted to obtain citizen comments on the proposed budget. Prior to May 15, the budget is legally adopted at the departmental level through passage of an appropriation ordinance by City Council.

4 Amendment—The City Manager is authorized to transfer amounts not exceeding $5,000 between departments within any fund. All other transfers or supplemental appropriations must be enacted by City Council. During the year $7,286,400 in supplemental appropriations were enacted by City Council. The Statement of Revenues, Expenditures, and Changes in Fund Balance—Budget and Actual—General Fund—reflects these revisions.

5 Integration—Formal budgetary integration is employed as a management control device during the year for the General and Capital Projects Funds. Formal budgetary integration is not employed for the Debt Service Fund because effective budgetary control is alternatively achieved through general obligation bond indenture provisions.

6 Compliance—"Actual" expenditures and operating transfers out may not legally exceed "budget" appropriations for each of the nine functional classifications which are shown in the budgetary statement (Exhibit 13-4). Budgetary control is maintained at the departmental level.

The General Fund budget is adopted on a basis consistent with generally accepted accounting principles except for the recognition of encumbrances. The following is a reconciliation of the actual General Fund expenditures presented on the budgetary basis in Exhibit 13-4 to the actual General Fund expenditures presented in Exhibit 13-3 in accordance with generally accepted accounting principles:

| | |
|---|---:|
| Total general fund expenditures, Exhibit 13-4 | $103,613,443 |
| Less encumbrances at June 30, 1984 | 1,674,452 |
| Total general fund expenditures, Exhibit 13-3 | $101,938,991 |

The following is a reconciliation of the fund balance of the General Fund presented on the budgetary basis in Exhibit 13-4, to the actual fund balance presented in Exhibits 13-2 and 13-3, in accordance with generally accepted accounting principles:

| | |
|---|---|
| Fund balance of general fund, Exhibit 13-4 | $4,652,591 |
| Encumbrances at June 30, 1984 | 1,674,452 |
| Fund balance of general fund, Exhibits 13-2 & 13-3 | $6,327,043 |

**E** Encumbrances

Encumbrance accounting, under which purchase orders, contracts, and other commitments for the expenditure of monies are recorded in order to reserve that portion of the applicable appropriation, is employed as an extension of formal budgetary integration in the General Fund. Encumbrances outstanding at year-end are reported as reservations of fund balances since they do not constitute expenditures or liabilities. An appropriation equal to the outstanding year-end encumbrance is required in the succeeding year. Unspent appropriations lapse at year end.

**F** Investments

Investments are stated at cost. The investments of governmental and proprietary fund types consist of security repurchase agreements with financial institutions and certificates of deposit, which represent market value. The market value of the Employees' Retirement System (Pension Trust) was $45,725,696 as of June 30, 1984. Investments of the Employees' Retirement System (Pension Trust) consist of cash equivalents, bonds and common stock.

**G** Inventories

Inventories are valued at cost determined principally on the moving weighted average method. Inventory consists of materials and supplies held for consumption and is adjusted to actual based on an annual physical count. The cost is recorded as an expenditure or expense at the time individual inventory items are used.

**H** Pension Plan

The City's policy is to fund pension costs, which include both normal costs and amortization of prior service costs.

**I** Fixed Assets

Fixed assets acquired or constructed for general governmental use are recorded as expenditures in the governmental fund type accounts and then recorded at cost in the General Fixed Asset Account Group upon completion of the project. Infrastructures (i.e., bridges, curbs and gutters, streets and sidewalks, etc.) normally are immovable and are of value only to the governmental unit. Therefore, these assets are not recorded in the General Fixed Assets. Gifts or contributions are recorded at fair market value when received. Depreciation on General Fixed Assets is not required and has not been recorded.

Fixed assets of the proprietary fund types are recorded at cost or estimated cost. Depreciation is taken on a straight-line basis over the estimated useful life of each asset. Depreciation on assets acquired with contributed capital is accounted for as an operating expense and as a reduction of contributed capital instead of retained earnings. The estimated useful lives of the Proprietary funds' fixed assets are as follows:

|  | Buildings and structures | Equipment |
|---|---|---|
| Transit company | — | 5–15 yrs. |
| Water fund | 40 yrs. | 10 yrs. |
| Sewage treatment fund | 55 yrs. | 20 yrs. |
| Airport fund | 30 yrs. | 10 yrs. |
| Civic center fund | 50 yrs. | 10 yrs. |
| Internal service funds | — | 5–10 yrs. |

**J** Accumulated Vacation and Sick Pay

Employees earn vacation and sick leave in varying amounts based on length of service.

Upon termination City employees are paid for a maximum of 240 hours of vacation at their normal rate of pay. They are not paid for their accumulated sick leave.

School Board employees are paid upon termination at their normal rate of compensation for vacation leave up to 36 days.

School Board employees are paid for their accumulated sick pay at the rate of $10 per day up to a maximum of $1,000 upon termination.

Vacation and sick pay are reflected as an expenditure in the General Fund when paid. The non-current portion of accrued vacation and sick pay is recorded in the General Long-Term Debt Account group. At June 30, 1984 this liability amounted to $4,210,457.

Proprietary Funds accrue unpaid vacation pay in accordance with Statement 43 of the Financial Accounting Standards Board. This liability was $204,216 for the Enterprise Funds, and $247,916 for the Internal Service Funds at June 30, 1984.

**K** Comparative Data

Comparative total data for the prior year have been presented in the accompanying financial statements in order to provide an understanding of changes in the City's financial position and operations. However, comparative (i.e., presentation of prior year totals by fund type) data have not been presented in each of the statements since their inclusion would make the statements unduly complex and difficult to read.

**L** Total Columns on Combined Statements

Total columns on the Combined Statements are captioned Memorandum Only to indicate that they are presented only to facilitate analysis. Data in these columns do not present financial position, results of operations, or changes in financial position in conformity with generally accepted accounting principles. Neither is such data comparable to a consolidation. Interfund eliminations have not been made in the aggregation of this data.

**M** Warrants Payable

A warrant is an instrument promising to pay a specified amount to a named payee upon demand. It circulates in the same manner as a bank check. The

City Treasurer reimburses each bank by check for the amount of the warrants cleared daily. The balance in the warrants payable account represents the amount of warrants which are outstanding or for which the City has not yet reimbursed the paying bank.

**II** Internal Service Funds

During fiscal year 1984, the City established internal service funds for City Information Systems (data processing), Management Services (print shop and mail room), Materials Control (warehouse), Motor Vehicle Maintenance, and Utility Line Services. These funds were reported in the prior year as part of the General Fund and General Fixed Assets Account Group. Effective July 1, 1983 fixed assets, valued at estimated cost, and General Fund equity of $93,754 were transferred to the respective internal service funds as follows:

|  | **Contributed capital** |
|---|---|
| City information systems | $ 136,926 |
| Management services | 60,739 |
| Materials control | 19,093 |
| Motor vehicle maintenance | 125,366 |
| Utility line services | 589,878 |
| Total | $ 932,002 |
| General fund balance as reported June 30, 1983 | $5,189,097 |
| Less transfer of reserve for encumbrances | (93,754) |
| General fund balance July 1, 1983 per Exhibits 13-3 & 13-4 | $5,095,343 |

This transaction has been reported as a residual equity transfer from the General Fund. The transfer of fixed assets has been reported as a reduction of general fixed assets and accordingly presented as contributed capital in the respective internal service funds. The fiscal year 1983 General Fund expenditures shown on Exhibit 13-9 do not include the above departments in order to facilitate comparability.

**III** Due From Other Governmental Units

|  | **General fund** | **Capital projects fund** | **Enterprise funds** |
|---|---|---|---|
| Commonwealth of Virginia |  | $ | $ |
| Welfare funds | $ 932,094 |  |  |
| School funds | 256,757 |  |  |
| Shared expenses | 218,025 |  |  |
| Transit company subsidy |  |  | 74,459 |
| Other |  | 9 |  |
| Sports complex |  | 39,292 |  |
| Industrial access grant—RCIT |  | 260,000 |  |
| Federal government |  |  |  |
| School funds | 629,766 |  |  |
| Revenue sharing funds | 670,524 |  |  |
| Public safety grant | 17,754 |  |  |
| Transportation center grant |  | 19,799 |  |

|  | General fund | Capital projects fund | Enterprise funds |
|---|---|---|---|
| Sewage project grants |  |  | 307,000 |
| Community development block grant |  | 192,713 |  |
| Wometco |  | 2,148,375 |  |
| Park rehabilitation |  | 21,954 |  |
| Other localities |  |  |  |
| Town of Vinton—Sewage project |  |  | 33,181 |
|  | $2,724,920 | $2,682,142 | $414,640 |

## IV Property Taxes

Property Taxes are assessed annually as of January 1. Personal property tax is due on or before May 31 and real estate tax is payable in two equal installments on or before October 5 and April 5. The City bills and collects taxes and recognizes such as revenue when levied to the extent that they result in current receivables.

The annual assessment for real estate is based on 100% of the assessed fair market value. A penalty of 10% of the unpaid tax is due for late payment. At July 1, 1984, interest on unpaid taxes is the maximum annual rate authorized by the Internal Revenue Code section 6621(b) which is currently 12%. The tax rates are established annually, without limitation by City Council. The tax rates for the year ended June 30, 1984, for real estate and personal property were $1.33 and $3.70, respectively, per $100 of assessed value.

## V Fund Equity Balances

The fund equity balances have been classified to reflect the limitations and restrictions placed on the respective funds as follows:

- Investment in General Fixed Assets—Represents the investment in City-owned general fixed assets which have been capitalized.
- Contributed Capital—Includes capital contributions to Enterprise funds and Internal Services funds from customers, City, State and Federal governments; net of accumulated depreciation on assets purchased. The following is a summary of contributed capital transactions:

|  | 1984 | 1983 |
|---|---|---|
| Contributed capital—July 1 | $54,886,693 | $50,171,835 |
| From other governments | 4,205,104 | 4,986,103 |
| From general fund | 946,753 | 1,149,998 |
| Sale or donation of assets | — | (260) |
| From customers | 11,428 | — |
| Current year depreciation | (1,679,110) | (1,420,983) |
| Contributed capital—June 30 | $58,370,868 | $54,886,693 |

- Retained Earnings—Represents the remainder of the City's equity in Enterprise funds.
- Fund Balance—Reserved—Represents those portions of fund balances which are not available for expenditure or are legally segregated for a specific future use.

- Fund Balance—Unreserved—Available for management designation.
- Fund Balances—Designated—Indicates tentative plans for financial resource utilization in a future period.
- Fund Balances—Undesignated—Represents the remainder of the City's equity in governmental type funds.

## VI Long-Term Debt

The general long-term debt of the City is recorded in a separate, self-balancing group of accounts. Long-term debt obligations of the Sewage Treatment Fund, Water Fund, and Airport Fund are reported as liabilities of the respective Enterprise Fund.

The fund balance of the Debt Service Fund of $5,803,854 is for future retirement of long-term debt.

The City legal debt margin at June 30, 1984 is $111,203,715. The City has no overlapping debt.

Outstanding long-term debt at June 30, 1984 comprises the following:

| | |
|---|---:|
| $ 8,000,000   1958 public school series KK serial bonds due in annual installments of $180,000 through September 15, 1988; and one annual installment of $100,000 December 1, 1989; interest at 3.50% | $ 1,000,000 |
| $ 7,000,000   1970 civic center series A-1 serial bonds due in annual installments of $400,000 through September 1, 1985; interest at 3.0% to 5.6% | 800,000 |
| $ 3,500,000   1970 public improvement series A-2 serial bonds due in annual installments of $300,000 through September 1, 1985; interest at 3.0% to 5.6% | 600,000 |
| $ 4,400,000   1971 public improvement series A-3 serial bonds due in annual installments of $220,000 through March 1, 1991; interest at 3.0% to 4.7% | 1,540,000 |
| $ 9,000,000   1971 public improvement series A-4 serial bonds due in annual installments of $450,000 through September 1, 1991; interest at 3.5% to 4.9% | 3,600,000 |
| $10,000,000   1975 public improvement series A-5 serial bonds due in annual installments of $500,000 through April 15, 1995; interest at 4.5% to 6.5% | 5,500,000 |
| $ 5,500,000   1976 parking facility series A-6 serial bonds due in annual installments of $275,000 through August 1, 1996; interest at 4.5% to 6.5% | 3,575,000 |
| $ 6,000,000   1976 jail facility series A-7 serial bonds due in annual installments of $300,000 through August 1, 1996; interest at 4.5% to 6.5% | 3,900,000 |
| $10,815,000   1976 public school series A-8 serial bonds due in annual installments of $540,000 through August 1, 1995 and one annual installment of $555,000 August 1, 1996; interest at 4.5% to 6.5% | 7,035,000 |
| $ 8,000,000   1980 public building series 1980A serial bonds due in annual installments of $335,000 to $815,000 through July 1, 1995; interest at 5.0% to 6.6% | 6,975,000 |
| $ 4,500,000   1980 public improvement series 1980A serial bonds due in annual installments of $190,000 to $460,000 through July 1, 1995; interest at 5.0% to 6.6% | 3,925,000 |

| | |
|---|---:|
| $11,000,000 1982 public improvement series 1982 bonds due in annual installments of $200,000 to $1,500,000 through December 15, 1994; interest at 7.75% to 8.25% | 11,000,000 |
| Total General Bonded Debt | $49,450,000 |
| Annexation debt per provisions of the annexation decrees of the Circuit Court of Roanoke County effective December 31, 1946, 1968, and 1976. Annual installments from $399,426 to $1,804 through December 8, 1994; interest at 3.0% to 6.0% | 857,454 |
| Accumulated vacation and sick leave liability for employees of the General Fund | 4,210,457 |
| Total General Long-Term Debt | $54,517,911* |
| $ 4,000,000 1971 water series WW-4 serial bonds due in annual installments of $200,000 through March 1, 1991; interest at 3.0% to 4.7% | 1,400,000 |
| $ 1,700,000 1971 sewage series ST-2 serial bonds due in annual installments of $85,000 through March 1, 1991; interest at 3.0% to 4.7% | 595,000 |
| $ 5,000,000 1975 sewage series ST-3 serial bonds due in annual installments of $250,000 through April 15, 1995; interest at 4.5% to 6.5% | 2,750,000 |
| Total Sewage Treatment Long-Term Debt | $ 3,345,000 |
| | $59,262,911 |

*4.90% of series A-2, A-3, A-4, and 5.15% of series A-5 are being repaid by the Airport Fund and are shown as liability (bonds payable) in the fund.

| | |
|---|---:|
| General | $53,953,401* |
| Water | 1,400,000 |
| Sewage treatment | 3,345,000 |
| Airport | 564,510* |
| | $59,262,911 |

*4.90% of series A-2, A-3, A-4 and 5.15% of series A-5 are being repaid by the Airport Fund and are shown as a liability (bonds payable) in the fund.

The annual requirements to amortize all debt outstanding as of June 30, 1984, including interest payments of $19,432,357 are as follows:

| Fiscal year | General obligation serial bonds(1) | General obligation revenue serial bonds(2) | Annexation debt | Total |
|---|---:|---:|---:|---:|
| 1984–85 | $6,874,066 | $775,825 | $388,441 | $8,038,332 |
| 1985–86 | 7,084,657 | 746,430 | 245,271 | 8,076,358 |
| 1986–87 | 6,688,578 | 719,035 | 106,200 | 7,513,813 |
| 1987–88 | 6,482,374 | 691,390 | 109,180 | 7,282,944 |
| 1988–89 | 6,270,460 | 663,495 | 27,170 | 6,961,125 |
| 1989–90 | 6,070,978 | 635,350 | 12,058 | 6,718,386 |
| 1990–91 | 5,873,170 | 611,800 | 11,728 | 6,496,698 |
| 1991–92 | 5,520,369 | 303,250 | 8,060 | 5,831,679 |
| 1992–93 | 4,961,331 | 288,000 | 1,966 | 5,251,297 |
| 1993–94 | 4,747,600 | 272,500 | 1,912 | 5,022,012 |
| 1994–95 | 3,095,725 | 261,250 | 1,858 | 3,358,833 |

| Fiscal year | General obligation serial bonds(1) | General obligation revenue serial bonds(2) | Annexation debt | Total |
|---|---|---|---|---|
| 1995–96 | 2,508,013 | — | — | 2,508,013 |
| 1996–97 | 1,155,425 | — | — | 1,155,425 |

(1) Debt service principal on $564,510 of outstanding general obligation serial bonds is included, but is being paid from the Airport Fund and shown only as a liability (Bonds Payable) in such Fund.

(2) Debt service principal on $4,745,000 of outstanding general obligation Water and Sewage Treatment Fund revenue serial bonds is being paid from the respective Enterprise Fund.

### Changes in General Long-Term Debt

| | June 30, 1983 | Additions | Deletions | June 30, 1984 |
|---|---|---|---|---|
| Amount available in debt service fund | $ 5,750,166 | $7,798,042 | $(7,744,354) | $ 5,803,854 |
| Amount to be provided for retirement of general long-term debt | 52,585,754 | 207,568 | (4,643,775) | 48,149,547 |
| Total available and to be provided | $58,335,920 | | | $53,953,401 |
| General obligation debt payable: | | | | |
| Serial bonds | $52,552,211 | $ — | $(3,666,721) | $48,885,490 |
| Annexation debt | 1,256,879 | — | (399,425) | 857,454 |
| Group medical insurance deficit | 339,575 | — | (339,575) | — |
| Employee leave payable | 4,187,255 | 207,568 | (184,366) | 4,210,457 |
| Total general obligation debt payable | $58,335,920 | | | $53,953,401 |

**VII** Interfund Receivables and Payables

Individual fund interfund receivable and payable balances at June 30, 1984 are as follows:

| Fund | Interfund receivables | Interfund payables |
|---|---|---|
| General | $ 49,711 | $141,043 |
| Transit company | — | 49,711 |
| Water | — | 2,695 |
| Sewage treatment | — | 4,467 |
| Airport | — | 1,274 |
| Civic center | — | 1,641 |
| City information systems | — | 425,384 |
| Materials control | — | 559 |
| Management services | — | 160 |
| Utility line services | — | 5,745 |
| Motor vehicle maintenance | — | 3,283 |
| Capital projects | 423,423 | — |
| Pension trust | 162,828 | — |
| | $635,962 | $635,962 |

## VIII Changes in General Fixed Assets

### General Fixed Assets

|  | June 30, 1983 | Additions | Deletions | June 30, 1984 |
|---|---|---|---|---|
| Cost: |  |  |  |  |
|   Land | $ 10,620,036 | $ 500,985 | $ 13,500 | $ 11,107,521 |
|   Buildings and structures | 64,668,451 | 1,498,853 | 175,258 | 65,992,046 |
|   Equipment | 15,261,944 | 2,129,052 | 1,814,252 | 15,576,744 |
|   Construction in progress | 19,575,597 | 6,521,325 | 2,452,098 | 23,644,824 |
|     Total cost | $110,126,028 |  |  | $116,321,135 |
| Investments in general fixed assets: |  |  |  |  |
|   From capital projects | $ 76,357,629 | $1,606,164 | $ 306,918 | $ 77,656,875 |
|   From bonds | 10,809,712 | 1,626,058 | — | 12,435,770 |
|   From gifts and grants | 8,883,761 | 3,463,785 | 145,655 | 12,201,891 |
|   From general revenues | 14,074,926 | 774,122 | 822,449 | 14,026,599 |
|     Total investment in general fixed assets | $110,126,028 |  |  | $116,321,135 |

## IX Construction in Progress and Contract Commitments

A summary of construction in progress by function and contract commitments (encumbrances) at June 30, 1984 is as follows:

### General Fixed Assets

|  | Project authorizations | Expended to June 30, 1984 | Contract commitments (encumbrances) | Required future financing |
|---|---|---|---|---|
| Function: |  |  |  |  |
|   General government | $16,578,425 | $14,215,774 | $2,201,915 | None |
|   Fire prevention and protection | 60,642 | 37,572 | 15,587 | None |
|   Education | 1,299,737 | 1,063,508 | 101,827 | None |
|   Recreation | 2,176,727 | 1,026,685 | 424,720 | None |
|   Other public buildings | 8,447,809 | 7,301,285 | 349,186 | None |
|     Subtotal | $28,563,340 | $23,644,824 | $3,093,235 | None |
|   Infrastructure projects | 16,847,998 | 8,420,131 | 3,554,082 | None |
|     Total | $45,411,338 | $32,064,955 | $6,647,317 | None |

### Enterprise funds

|  | Project authorizations | Expended to June 30, 1984 | Contract commitments (encumbrances) | Required future financing |
|---|---|---|---|---|
| Fund: |  |  |  |  |
|   Transit company | $ 3,633,112 | $ 1,886,393 | $ 365,313 | None |
|   Water | 968,703 | 329,036 | 16,228 | None |
|   Sewage treatment | 5,403,267 | 4,764,875 | 106,808 | None |
|   Airport | 11,570,983 | 6,443,656 | 4,527,277 | None |
|     Total | $21,576,065 | $13,423,960 | $5,015,626 | None |

## X Pension Plans

The City maintains the Employees' Retirement System (Pension Trust) as a separate trust fund covering substantially all of its employees except the professional School Board employees, who are eligible for the Virginia Supplemental Retirement System. The total pension expense was $4,499,002 for the year ended June 30, 1984, which includes amortization of prior service cost over the next 21 years. The City's policy is to fund accrued pension cost.

Actuarial and net asset information of the Employees' Retirement System, based on the most recent data available, follows:

| | |
|---|---|
| Actuarial present value of accumulated plan benefits as of June 30, 1983 | $50,452,193 |
| Actuarial present value of vested plan benefits, as of June 30, 1983 | $44,587,314 |
| Net assets available for benefits, as of June 30, 1983 at fair value | $46,962,727 |

Accumulated plan benefits are those benefits attributable under the provisions of the System's authorizing ordinance to employees for service rendered to June 30, 1983. Vested plan benefits are those accumulated plan benefits that are not contingent on an employee's future service. The actuarial present value of accumulated plan benefits and vested plan benefits are determined by the Plan's actuary, George B. Buck Consulting Actuaries, Inc., and are those amounts that resulted from applying actuarial assumptions to adjust the accumulated plan benefits and vested plan benefits to reflect the time value of money (through discounts for interest) and the probability of payment (by means of decrements such as for death, disability, withdrawal, or retirement) between June 30, 1983 and the expected date of payment. The significant actuarial assumptions used in the valuations as of June 30, 1983 were (a) life expectancy of participants (the Modified Group for men and women set back two years), (b) retirement age assumptions (the assumed average retirement age was 60), and (c) investment return. The valuations included assumed average investment returns of 7.0%. The actuarial assumptions are based on the presumption the Plan will continue. Were the Plan to terminate, different actuarial assumptions and other factors might be applicable in determining the actuarial present value of accumulated plan benefits and vested plan benefits.

Professional School Board employees participate in the Virginia Supplemental Retirement System. The employees' contribution is based on 5% of creditable compensation, which is paid by the City for the employee. These payments totaled $1,099,982 for the year ended June 30, 1984. All other funding for the professional School Board employees is the responsibility of the Commonwealth of Virginia. Data concerning the actuarial present value of accumulated plan benefits and vested plan benefits and net assets available for benefits which are relevant to the City are not available since such determinations are made on a system-wide basis and not for individual local governments.

**XI** Segment Information for Enterprise Funds

The City maintains five Enterprise Funds which provide transit, water, sewage, airport, and civic center services. Key financial data for the year ended June 30, 1984 for those services are as follows:

|  | Transit company | Water | Sewage treatment | Airport | Civic center | Total |
|---|---|---|---|---|---|---|
| Operating revenues | $ 807,707 | $ 3,531,855 | $ 6,397,330 | $ 1,660,008 | $ 802,983 | $13,199,883 |
| Operating expenses: | | | | | | |
| Depreciation | 247,289 | 563,977 | 763,668 | 581,396 | 310,823 | 2,467,153 |
| Other | 2,079,607 | 3,135,358 | 4,359,312 | 1,375,205 | 1,256,527 | 12,206,009 |
| | 2,326,896 | 3,699,335 | 5,122,980 | 1,956,601 | 1,567,350 | 14,673,162 |
| Operating income (loss) | $(1,519,189) | $ (167,480) | $ 1,274,350 | $ (296,593) | $ (764,367) | $ (1,473,279) |
| Operating grants | $ 1,001,989 | $ — | $ — | $ — | $ — | $ 1,001,989 |
| Operating transfers | $ 261,793 | $ 918 | $ 2,808 | $ 432 | $ 626,872 | $ 892,823 |
| Non operating income (expense) | $ 19,921 | $ 219,616 | $ (37,251) | $ 175,385 | $ 30,677 | $ 408,348 |
| Net income (loss) | $( 235,486) | $ 53,054 | $ 1,239,907 | $ (120,776) | $ (106,818) | $ 829,881 |
| Current capital contributions | $ 1,544,667 | $ 11,428 | $ 29,054 | $ 2,646,136 | $ — | $ 4,231,285 |
| Bonds payable | $ | $ 1,400,000 | $ 3,345,000 | $ 564,510 | $ — | $ 5,309,510 |
| Net working capital | $ 236,600 | $ 2,330,390 | $ 3,010,001 | $ 2,936,910 | $ 572,397 | $ 9,086,298 |
| Acquisition of fixed assets | $ 1,434,583 | $ 523,994 | $ 186,784 | $ 2,765,046 | $ 50,376 | $ 4,960,783 |
| Total assets | $ 4,521,491 | $15,393,392 | $40,271,003 | $20,644,738 | $11,567,433 | $92,398,057 |
| Total liabilities | $ 188,586 | $ 1,854,547 | $ 3,692,810 | $ 837,460 | $ 129,885 | $ 6,703,288 |
| Total equity | $ 4,332,905 | $13,538,845 | $36,578,193 | $19,807,278 | $11,437,548 | $85,694,769 |

**XII** Joint Venture

The City of Roanoke, Town of Vinton, and Roanoke County jointly own a regional sanitary landfill operated by the Roanoke Valley Regional Solid Waste Management Board. The Board is composed of six members, three of whom are appointed by Roanoke City Council. The remaining three members are appointed by the other joint owners. The City of Roanoke has control over budget and financing of the venture only to the extent of representation by the three board members appointed.

|  | June 30, 1984 |
|---|---|
| Operating revenues | $1,259,740 |
| Operating expenses | 988,912 |
| Operating income | 270,828 |
| Non-operating income | 59,295 |
| Net income | $ 330,123 |
| | |
| Total fund balance July 1, 1983 | $3,091,667 |
| Net income | 330,123 |
| Contributed capital | 168,145 |
| Total fund balance June 30, 1984 | $3,589,935 |
| | |
| Total assets | $3,959,717 |
| Total liabilities | $ 369,782 |
| Total equity | $3,589,935 |
| City of Roanoke equity June 30, 1983 | $1,694,887 |
| Increase in equity | 107,593 |
| City of Roanoke equity June 30, 1984 | $1,802,480 |

**XIII** Contingent Liabilities

The Transit Company is in the process of developing an Intermodal Transportation Center in downtown Roanoke. Approximately eighty percent of the cost of the project will be financed by the Urban Mass Transportation Administration. On July 26, 1984, a portion of the structure collapsed. Management feels that additional costs to complete the structure and any potential claims arising from the incident will not have a significant impact on the Company's financial condition.

The City is named as a defendant in litigation involving claims for personal injury or property damages for which the City Attorney estimates any ultimate liability will be immaterial.

Special Purpose Grants are subject to audit to determine compliance with their requirements. City officials believe that if any refunds are required, they will be immaterial.

# APPENDIX 13-3: Statistical Data[36]

### TABLE 1
### City of Roanoke, Virginia
### General Fund Revenues by Sources
### Last Ten Fiscal Years

|  | 1983–84 | 1982–83 | 1981–82 | 1980–81 |
|---|---|---|---|---|
| Revenues |  |  |  |  |
| Local taxes | $ 54,850,470 | $50,678,835 | $47,745,724 | $44,945,851 |
| Permits, fees, and licenses | 359,348 | 337,510 | 260,915 | 268,585 |
| Fines and forfeitures | 475,635 | 425,737 | 422,377 | 428,144 |
| Rents and interest | 991,940 | 838,563 | 958,274 | 897,201 |
| Intergovernmental | 40,706,223 | 37,143,944 | 35,944,327 | 35,192,662 |
| Charges for services | 4,891,791 | 6,571,280 | 6,866,930 | 6,369,041 |
| Miscellaneous | 895,284 | 984,056 | 1,618,522 | 1,135,199 |
| Total revenue | $103,170,691 | $96,979,925 | $93,817,069 | $89,236,683 |

### TABLE 2
### City of Roanoke, Virginia
### General Fund Expenditures and Other Uses by Function
### Last Ten Fiscal Years

|  | 1983–84 | 1982–83 | 1981–82 | 1980–81 |
|---|---|---|---|---|
| Expenditures |  |  |  |  |
| General government | $ 4,567,405 | $ 4,384,589 | $ 4,077,914 | $ 3,778,261 |
| Judicial | 1,503,621 | 1,399,792 | 1,551,089 | 1,547,481 |
| Public safety | 14,035,745 | 12,452,196 | 11,718,443 | 10,970,204 |
| Public works | 11,595,662 | 13,041,841 | 12,894,708 | 12,586,725 |
| Health and welfare | 8,173,448 | 7,670,434 | 8,451,191 | 7,693,208 |
| Education | 41,477,043 | 37,926,364 | 36,418,517 | 34,608,259 |
| Parks, recreation and cultural | 1,940,994 | 1,891,030 | 2,016,666 | 1,599,743 |
| Community development | 481,309 | 389,917 | 891,053 | 1,005,436 |
| Nondepartmental | 7,418,667 | 7,677,411 | 7,556,206 | 5,423,889 |
| Transfers to other funds: |  |  |  |  |
| Debt service | 7,331,935 | 7,130,134 | 7,045,561 | 8,387,479 |
| Capital projects | 2,463,968 | 570,548 | 291,457 | 1,070,503 |
| Proprietary | 949,194 | 865,602 | 639,424 | 737,516 |
| Total expenditures and transfers to other funds | $101,938,991 | $95,399,858 | $93,552,229 | $89,408,704 |

**TABLE 1**
*(continued)*

| 1979–80 | 1978–79 | 1977–78 | 1976–77 | 1975–76 | 1974–75 |
|---|---|---|---|---|---|
| $44,894,938 | $44,301,702 | $43,362,437 | $39,299,417 | $31,904,184 | $27,204,424 |
| 224,949 | 206,721 | 234,530 | 235,312 | 116,317 | 110,046 |
| 339,816 | 435,495 | 359,452 | 325,327 | 333,262 | 286,497 |
| 860,051 | 1,625,951 | 1,333,626 | 1,530,368 | 654,299 | 685,126 |
| 30,836,176 | 27,881,833 | 25,710,145 | 23,696,419 | 24,734,385 | 21,783,093 |
| 5,805,948 | 5,937,017 | 6,167,643 | 5,353,651 | 4,612,938 | 4,525,755 |
| 1,704,914 | 1,024,504 | 858,064 | 1,113,881 | 1,334,888 | 893,682 |
| $84,666,792 | $81,413,223 | $78,025,897 | $71,554,375 | $63,690,273 | $55,488,623 |

**TABLE 2**
*(continued)*

| 1979–80 | 1978–79 | 1977–78 | 1976–77 | 1975–76 | 1974–75 |
|---|---|---|---|---|---|
| $ 3,524,999 | $ 3,005,509 | $ 2,533,875 | $ 2,157,781 | $ 2,174,027 | $ 1,914,309 |
| 1,953,224 | 1,753,826 | 1,754,973 | 1,372,951 | 1,286,550 | 1,188,015 |
| 9,709,420 | 7,804,665 | 7,356,773 | 6,400,399 | 6,675,160 | 5,743,678 |
| 13,187,911 | 12,106,763 | 11,084,502 | 9,579,606 | 9,186,229 | 8,851,567 |
| 8,574,927 | 7,305,727 | 6,611,389 | 9,015,248 | 9,650,248 | 8,864,005 |
| 31,129,300 | 27,815,856 | 26,823,221 | 24,340,382 | 23,559,450 | 21,269,612 |
| 1,489,684 | 1,388,290 | 1,222,154 | 1,085,920 | 1,097,091 | 1,151,959 |
| 714,630 | 1,151,108 | 1,029,816 | 1,015,645 | 1,450,968 | 728,923 |
| 6,753,268 | 4,847,581 | 4,300,191 | 5,885,300 | 4,133,822 | 3,211,790 |
| 8,265,232 | 8,612,172 | 8,583,543 | 7,052,269 | 4,079,246 | 3,038,491 |
| 1,431,177 | 5,977,470 | 1,529,118 | 1,097,092 | (25,473) | 826,578 |
| 924,762 | 789,983 | 340,000 | 505,000 | 585,000 | 565,700 |
| $87,658,534 | $82,558,950 | $73,169,555 | $69,507,593 | $63,852,318 | $57,354,627 |

## TABLE 3
### City of Roanoke, Virginia
### Local Tax Revenues by Source
### Last Ten Fiscal Years

|  | 1983–84 | 1982–83 | 1981–82 | 1980–81 |
|---|---|---|---|---|
| General property taxes | $31,930,382 | $29,550,130 | $27,699,966 | $24,875,487 |
| Sales tax | 8,378,391 | 7,287,463 | 6,907,344 | 6,852,472 |
| Business and occupational licenses | 5,458,028 | 5,330,945 | 5,256,760 | 5,209,339 |
| Utility consumer tax | 6,430,235 | 5,888,956 | 5,602,388 | 5,909,334 |
| Motor vehicle licenses | 1,102,049 | 1,055,914 | 1,047,227 | 1,051,024 |
| Franchise tax | 515,373 | 641,928 | 433,223 | 461,268 |
| Cigarette tax | 285,963 | 265,325 | 299,643 | 272,926 |
| Admissions tax | 110,506 | 82,712 | 75,926 | 81,376 |
| Other taxes | 639,543 | 575,462 | 423,247 | 232,625 |
| Total local taxes | $54,850,470 | $50,678,835 | $47,745,724 | $44,945,851 |

## TABLE 4
### City of Roanoke, Virginia
### General Property Tax Levies and Collections
### Last Ten Years

|  | 1983–84 | 1982–83 | 1981–82 | 1981[2] |
|---|---|---|---|---|
| Total tax levies | $31,519,015 | $29,696,698 | $27,720,599 | $16,175,209 |
| Current tax collections | $30,570,519 | $28,583,100 | $26,713,823 | $15,597,335 |
| Delinquent tax collections | 1,359,863 | 967,030 | 986,143 | 599,941 |
| Total tax collections | $31,930,382 | $29,550,130 | $27,699,966 | $16,197,276 |
| Current tax collections as percent of levies | 96.99% | 96.25% | 96.37% | 96.43% |
| Total tax collection as percent of levies | 101.31% | 99.51% | 99.93% | 100.14% |

[1] Calendar-year levies compared to calendar-year collections.
[2] Short tax year, effective January 1, 1981 to June 30, 1981, adopted for real estate and public service corporation taxes. All future real estate and public service corporation taxes will be levied on a fiscal-year basis (July 1 through June 30) in lieu of a calendar year (January 1 through December 31).

## TABLE 3
(*continued*)

| 1979–80 | 1978–79 | 1977–78 | 1976–77 | 1975–76 | 1974–75 |
|---|---|---|---|---|---|
| $24,855,280 | $24,674,260 | $24,238,783 | $20,926,065 | $15,730,686 | $12,959,483 |
| 6,697,527 | 6,466,365 | 5,840,342 | 5,132,972 | 4,198,742 | 3,932,175 |
| 5,233,731 | 4,884,286 | 4,985,167 | 4,929,483 | 4,567,287 | 3,857,556 |
| 6,108,892 | 6,332,552 | 6,549,060 | 6,540,758 | 5,788,379 | 5,094,726 |
| 956,177 | 951,614 | 956,875 | 937,513 | 878,510 | 715,456 |
| 452,141 | 440,742 | 225,143 | 206,322 | 209,162 | 188,517 |
| 279,262 | 269,531 | 285,868 | 287,599 | 239,775 | 212,775 |
| 71,237 | 69,116 | 79,557 | 145,849 | 132,672 | 131,087 |
| 240,691 | 213,236 | 201,642 | 192,856 | 158,971 | 112,649 |
| $44,894,938 | $44,301,702 | $43,362,437 | $39,299,417 | $31,904,184 | $27,204,424 |

## TABLE 4
(*continued*)

| 1980[1] | 1979[1] | 1978[1] | 1977[1] | 1976[1] | 1975[1] |
|---|---|---|---|---|---|
| $24,842,952 | $24,428,315 | $25,051,696 | $23,504,507 | $17,784,629 | $13,363,611 |
| $24,371,760 | $23,844,873 | $23,898,323 | $22,637,957 | $17,102,986 | $12,822,781 |
| 675,620 | 693,487 | 519,688 | 503,931 | 500,296 | 388,583 |
| $25,047,380 | $24,538,360 | $24,418,011 | $23,141,888 | $17,603,282 | $13,211,364 |
| 98.10% | 97.61% | 95.40% | 96.31% | 96.17% | 95.95% |
| 100.83% | 100.45% | 97.47% | 98.46% | 98.98% | 98.86% |

## TABLE 5
## City of Roanoke, Virginia
## Assessed and Estimated Actual Value of Taxable Property
## Last Ten Years

| | Real property | | | Personal property | | |
|---|---|---|---|---|---|---|
| Year | Assessed value | Estimated actual value | Assessment ratio | Assessed value | Estimated actual value | Assessment ratio |
| 1975 | $ 266,460,313 | $ 666,150,783 | .40 | $ 76,461,069 | $127,435,115 | .60 |
| 1976[1] | 370,260,800 | 925,652,000 | .40 | 94,527,797 | 157,546,328 | .60 |
| 1977[2] | 1,042,800,437 | 1,042,800,437 | 1.00 | 99,516,031 | 165,860,052 | .60 |
| 1978 | 1,173,765,091 | 1,173,765,091 | 1.00 | 108,962,808 | 181,604,680 | .60 |
| 1979 | 1,180,785,998 | 1,180,785,998 | 1.00 | 121,410,523 | 202,350,872 | .60 |
| 1980 | 1,220,029,310 | 1,220,029,310 | 1.00 | 128,396,201 | 213,993,668 | .60 |
| 1981[3] | 1,242,865,377 | 1,242,865,377 | 1.00 | 137,691,401 | 229,485,668 | .60 |
| 1982 | 1,406,766,757 | 1,406,766,757 | 1.00 | 155,627,970 | 259,379,950 | .60 |
| 1983 | 1,545,023,968 | 1,545,023,968 | 1.00 | 173,969,410 | 289,949,017 | .60 |
| 1984 | 1,599,177,720 | 1,599,177,720 | 1.00 | 203,756,120 | 339,593,533 | .60 |

## TABLE 6
## City of Roanoke, Virginia
## Property Tax Rates and Tax Levies
## Last Ten Years

| | Real property | | Personal property | | Public service corporations | | |
|---|---|---|---|---|---|---|---|
| Year | Tax rate per $100 | Levy | Tax rate per $100 | Levy | Tax rate per $100 | Levy | Total tax levies |
| 1975 | $3.45 | $ 9,191,282 | $3.45 | $2,657,300 | $3.45 | $1,515,029 | $13,363,611 |
| 1976[1] | 3.45 | 12,773,246 | 3.45 | 3,283,971 | 3.45 | 1,727,412 | 17,784,629 |
| 1977[2] | 1.64 | 17,041,969 | 4.10 | 4,100,414 | 1.64 | 2,362,124 | 23,504,507 |
| 1978 | 1.60 | 18,245,113 | 4.10 | 4,480,467 | 1.60 | 2,326,116 | 25,051,696 |
| 1979 | 1.50 | 17,346,425 | 4.10 | 4,986,071 | 1.50 | 2,095,819 | 24,428,315 |
| 1980 | 1.46 | 17,822,730 | 3.75 | 4,787,789 | 1.46 | 2,232,433 | 24,842,952 |
| 1981[3] | .73 | 9,072,917 | 3.75 | 5,163,428 | .73 | 1,938,864 | 16,175,209 |
| 1982 | 1.38 | 19,392,276 | 3.75 | 5,830,632 | 1.38 | 2,497,691 | 27,720,599 |
| 1983 | 1.35 | 20,857,610 | 3.75 | 6,512,416 | 1.35 | 2,326,672 | 29,696,698 |
| 1984 | 1.33 | 21,625,513 | 3.70 | 7,522,453 | 1.33 | 2,371,049 | 31,519,015 |

[1]Includes increased assessed value from annexation effective January 1, 1976.
[2]Effective January 1, 1977 all real estate assessed at 100 percent of fair market value; prior to January 1, 1977 real estate assessed at 40 percent of fair market value.
[3]Short tax year, effective January 1, 1981 to June 30, 1981, adopted for real estate and public service corporation taxes. All future real estate and public service corporation taxes will be levied on a fiscal-year basis (July 1 through June 30) in lieu of a calendar year (January 1 through December 31).

## TABLE 5
(*continued*)

| Public service corporations ||| Total assessed value |
|---|---|---|---|
| Assessed value | Estimated actual value | Assessment ratio | Total assessed value |
| $ 43,913,895 | $139,853,169 | .314 | $ 386,835,277 |
| 50,069,907 | 154,536,750 | .324 | 514,858,504 |
| 124,873,643 | 134,562,115 | .928 | 1,267,190,111 |
| 130,757,967 | 142,904,882 | .915 | 1,413,485,866 |
| 126,613,127 | 143,715,241 | .881 | 1,428,809,648 |
| 147,446,807 | 162,207,708 | .909 | 1,495,872,318 |
| 147,263,111 | 153,239,450 | .961 | 1,527,819,889 |
| 167,643,344 | 184,223,455 | .910 | 1,730,038,071 |
| 166,099,146 | 191,800,400 | .866 | 1,885,092,524 |
| 174,921,919 | 188,900,560 | .926 | 1,977,855,759 |

## TABLE 7
### City of Roanoke, Virginia
### Ratio of Net General Bonded Debt to Total Assessed Value and Net Bonded Debt per Capita
### Last Ten Fiscal Years

| Fiscal year | Population | Total assessed value | Net bonded debt | Ratio of net bonded debt to assessed value | Net bonded debt per capita |
|---|---|---|---|---|---|
| 1974–75 | 89,200[a] | $ 386,835,277 | $33,578,000 | 8.68 | $376.44 |
| 1975–76[1] | 101,500[a] | 514,858,504 | 31,156,000 | 6.05 | 306.96 |
| 1976–77 | 97,000[a] | 1,267,190,111[2] | 51,049,000 | 4.03 | 526.28 |
| 1977–78 | 98,200[a] | 1,413,485,866 | 47,557,000 | 3.36 | 484.29 |
| 1978–79 | 96,600[a] | 1,428,809,648 | 44,065,000 | 3.08 | 456.16 |
| 1979–80 | 100,220[c] | 1,495,872,318 | 53,110,000 | 3.55 | 529.93 |
| 1980–81 | 100,200[a] | 1,527,819,889 | 49,745,000 | 3.26 | 496.46 |
| 1981–82 | 100,200[a] | 1,730,038,071 | 45,880,000 | 2.65 | 457.88 |
| 1982–83 | 100,200[b] | 1,885,092,524 | 53,190,000 | 2.82 | 530.84 |
| 1983–84 | 100,200[b] | 1,977,855,759 | 49,450,000 | 2.50 | 493.51 |

Source: [a]Tayloe Murphy Institute
[b]City of Roanoke Department of Finance
[c]U.S. Census Bureau
[1]Includes increased population and assessed value from annexation effective January 1, 1976.
[2]Effective January 1, 1977 all real estate asessed at 100 percent of fair market value; prior to January 1, 1977 real estate assessed at 40 percent of fair market value.

## TABLE 8
### City of Roanoke, Virginia
### Computation of Legal Debt Margin*
### June 30, 1984

| | | |
|---|---:|---:|
| Assessed value of real estate, 1984 | | $1,599,177,720 |
| Legal debt limit, 10% of $1,599,177,720 | | $ 159,917,772 |
| Total bonded debt | $54,195,000 | |
| Other long-term debt | 5,067,911 | |
| Less: available in debt service fund | (5,803,854) | |
| Less: water and sewage revenue bonds | (4,745,000) | 48,714,057 |
| Legal debt margin | | $ 111,203,715 |

*The charter of the city of Roanoke limits the legal debt margin to 10 percent of the assessed valuation of real estate within the city limits.

## TABLE 9
### City of Roanoke, Virginia
### Ratio of Net Debt Service Expenditures for
### General Long-Term Debt to Total General Fund Expenditures
### Last Ten Fiscal Years

| Fiscal year | Principal | Interest | Total debt service | Total general expenditures | Percent of debt service to general expenditures |
|---|---:|---:|---:|---:|---:|
| 1974–75 | $1,901,577 | $1,136,914 | $3,038,491 | $ 57,354,627 | 5.30% |
| 1975–76 | 2,375,827 | 1,703,419 | 4,079,246 | 63,852,318 | 6.39 |
| 1976–77 | 4,722,853 | 2,329,416 | 7,052,269 | 69,507,593 | 10.15 |
| 1977–78 | 5,792,958 | 2,790,585 | 8,583,543 | 73,169,555 | 11.73 |
| 1978–79 | 6,035,742 | 2,576,430 | 8,612,172 | 82,558,950 | 10.43 |
| 1979–80 | 5,738,054 | 2,527,178 | 8,265,232 | 87,658,534 | 9.43 |
| 1980–81 | 5,617,646 | 2,769,833 | 8,387,479 | 89,408,704 | 9.38 |
| 1981–82 | 4,306,879 | 2,738,682 | 7,045,561 | 93,552,229 | 7.53 |
| 1982–83 | 4,017,889 | 3,112,245 | 7,130,134 | 95,399,858 | 7.47 |
| 1983–84 | 4,181,036 | 3,150,899 | 7,331,935 | 101,938,991 | 7.19 |

## TABLE 10
### City of Roanoke, Virginia
### Revenue Bond Coverage
### Water and Sewage Treatment Bonds
### Last Ten Fiscal Years

| Fiscal year | Gross revenue | Expenses, net of depreciation and interest | Net revenue available for debt service | Debt service requirements | | | Coverage |
| | | | | Principal | Interest | Total | |
|---|---:|---:|---:|---:|---:|---:|---:|
| 1974–75 | $ 4,478,756 | $3,025,160 | $1,453,596 | $1,004,000 | $486,908 | $1,490,908 | .97 |
| 1975–76 | 5,269,513 | 3,425,014 | 1,844,499 | 738,000 | 586,134 | 1,324,134 | 1.39 |
| 1976–77 | 5,385,027 | 3,851,445 | 1,533,582 | 756,000 | 506,580 | 1,262,580 | 1.21 |
| 1977–78 | 5,638,029 | 4,174,018 | 1,464,011 | 812,000 | 450,249 | 1,262,249 | 1.16 |
| 1978–79 | 6,399,804 | 5,006,254 | 1,393,550 | 756,000 | 421,335 | 1,177,335 | 1.18 |
| 1979–80 | 7,501,573 | 5,422,255 | 2,079,318 | 785,000 | 432,430 | 1,217,430 | 1.71 |
| 1980–81 | 8,005,759 | 6,048,176 | 1,957,583 | 659,000 | 352,680 | 1,011,680 | 1.93 |
| 1981–82 | 9,260,253 | 7,334,029 | 1,926,494 | 647,000 | 320,390 | 967,390 | 1.99 |
| 1982–83 | 9,806,773 | 7,495,024 | 2,311,749 | 535,000 | 291,314 | 826,314 | 2.80 |
| 1983–84 | 10,373,790 | 7,494,670 | 2,879,120 | 546,000 | 262,240 | 808,240 | 3.56 |

## TABLE 11
### City of Roanoke, Virginia
### Summary of Bonded Debt Principal Requirements to Maturity
### June 30, 1984

| Fiscal year | General obligation serial bonds[1] | | General obligation revenue serial bonds | | Total | |
|---|---|---|---|---|---|---|
| | Principal | Interest | Principal | Interest | Principal | Interest |
| 1984–85 | $ 3,965,000 | $ 2,909,066 | $ 535,000 | $ 240,825 | $ 4,500,000 | $ 3,149,891 |
| 1985–86 | 4,415,000 | 2,669,657 | 535,000 | 211,430 | 4,950,000 | 2,881,087 |
| 1986–87 | 4,265,000 | 2,423,578 | 535,000 | 184,035 | 4,800,000 | 2,607,613 |
| 1987–88 | 4,315,000 | 2,167,374 | 535,000 | 156,390 | 4,850,000 | 2,323,764 |
| 1988–89 | 4,365,000 | 1,905,460 | 535,000 | 128,495 | 4,900,000 | 2,033,955 |
| 1989–90 | 4,435,000 | 1,635,978 | 535,000 | 100,350 | 4,970,000 | 1,736,328 |
| 1990–91 | 4,510,000 | 1,363,170 | 535,000 | 76,800 | 5,045,000 | 1,439,970 |
| 1991–92 | 4,440,000 | 1,080,369 | 250,000 | 53,250 | 4,690,000 | 1,133,619 |
| 1992–93 | 4,165,000 | 796,331 | 250,000 | 38,000 | 4,415,000 | 834,331 |
| 1993–94 | 4,240,000 | 507,600 | 250,000 | 22,500 | 4,490,000 | 530,100 |
| 1994–95 | 2,815,000 | 280,725 | 250,000 | 11,250 | 3,065,000 | 291,975 |
| 1995–96 | 2,390,000 | 118,013 | — | — | 2,390,000 | 118,013 |
| 1996–97 | 1,130,000 | 25,425 | — | — | 1,130,000 | 25,425 |
| | $49,450,000 | $17,882,746 | $4,745,000 | $1,223,325 | $54,195,000 | $19,106,071 |

[1]Debt service on $564,510 outstanding general obligation serial bonds is included but is being repaid by revenues of the airport fund.

## TABLE 12
### City of Roanoke, Virginia
### Demographic Statistics
### Last Ten Fiscal Years

| Fiscal year | Population[1] | Per capita income[2] | School enrollment[3] | Unemployment rate[4] |
|---|---|---|---|---|
| 1974–75 | 89,200 | $ 5,925 | 16,461 | 7.3% |
| 1975–76 | 101,500 | 6,376 | 16,255 | 7.0 |
| 1976–77 | 97,000 | 6,791 | 15,973 | 6.0 |
| 1977–78 | 98,200 | 7,582 | 17,988 | 6.3 |
| 1978–79 | 96,600 | 8,438 | 17,289 | 4.9 |
| 1979–80 (U.S. Census) | 100,220 | 8,885 | 16,546 | 5.3 |
| 1980–81 | 100,200 | 9,734 | 15,821 | 7.2 |
| 1981–82 | 100,200 | 10,275 | 15,421 | 8.7 |
| 1982–83 | 100,200[5] | 10,846(est.) | 15,237 | 7.0 |
| 1983–84 | 100,200[5] | 11,449(est.) | 14,800 | 4.7[6] |

[1]Source: University of Virginia, Tayloe Murphy Institute
[2]Source: University of Virginia, Tayloe Murphy Institute
[3]Source: Roanoke City School Board
[4]Source: Virginia Employment Commission
[5]Source: City of Roanoke, Department of Finance
[6]Rate as of June 30, 1984

## TABLE 13
### City of Roanoke, Virginia
### Construction and Bank Deposits
### Last Ten Fiscal Years

| Fiscal year | Commercial construction[1] | | Residential construction[1] | | Bank deposits[2] |
|---|---|---|---|---|---|
| | Number of permits | Value | Number of permits | Value | |
| 1974–75 | 368 | $10,119,620 | 1,178 | $ 4,375,212 | $ 559,769,000 |
| 1975–76 | 482 | 20,915,608 | 1,136 | 4,160,634 | 577,643,000 |
| 1976–77 | 451 | 20,477,906 | 1,186 | 6,168,961 | 597,994,000 |
| 1977–78 | 483 | 25,342,438 | 1,070 | 6,437,859 | 716,404,000 |
| 1978–79 | 492 | 16,833,188 | 1,032 | 7,523,251 | 726,316,000 |
| 1979–80 | 505 | 28,880,018 | 1,009 | 7,843,422 | 991,632,000[3] |
| 1980–81 | 458 | 34,330,883 | 915 | 13,525,907 | 1,043,530,000 |
| 1981–82 | 421 | 19,498,189 | 737 | 5,826,143 | 1,097,236,000 |
| 1982–83 | 480 | 36,731,520 | 948 | 7,903,644 | 1,224,213,000 |
| 1983–84 | 497 | 32,243,884 | 924 | 16,772,850 | 1,365,854,444(est.) |

[1]*Source:* City of Roanoke, Department of Engineering, Planning, and Building Inspection
[2]*Source:* Federal Deposit Insurance Corporation
[3]Effective 1980 deposits for savings and loan associations are included in bank deposits.

## TABLE 14
### City of Roanoke, Virginia
### Principal Property Taxpayers
### June 30, 1984

| Taxpayer | Description | 1984 assessed valuation | Percentage of total assessed valuation |
|---|---|---|---|
| C&P Telephone Co. | Communications | $ 61,119,883 | 3.09% |
| Norfolk Southern Corp. | Transportation | 40,233,522 | 2.03 |
| Appalachian Power Co. | Public utility | 38,183,832 | 1.93 |
| American Telephone and Telegraph Communications of Virginia | Communications | 16,185,987 | .82 |
| General Services Administration | Federal office building | 13,000,000 | .66 |
| Roanoke Electric Steel | Primary metal industry | 11,860,587 | .60 |
| American Motor Inns | Hotel lodging | 11,635,823 | .59 |
| Blue Cross and Blue Shield of Southwest Virginia | Health insurance | 10,883,586 | .55 |
| American Telephone & Telegraph Co. | Communications | 9,565,406 | .48 |
| Prudential Insurance Co. (shopping center) | Insurance | 9,459,281 | .48 |
| | | $222,127,907 | 11.23% |

## APPENDIX NOTES

**34** City of Roanoke, Virginia, *Comprehensive Annual Financial Report, City of Roanoke, Virginia, Year Ended June 30, 1984* (Roanoke, Virginia: City of Roanoke, Virginia, 1984), pp. 3–4.
**35** Ibid., pp. 26–35.
**36** Ibid., pp. 70–80.

# PART TWO

# ACCOUNTING AND FINANCIAL REPORTING FOR OTHER NONBUSINESS ORGANIZATIONS

Conceptually, the principles and practices of fund accounting for any nonbusiness organization should be comparable. Operationally, however, fund accounting for churches, private foundations, universities and colleges, labor unions, health and welfare organizations, hospitals, and other nonbusiness organizations can be quite different from governmental fund accounting.

Part I listed some of the basic assumptions, principles, and standards that could be used to distinguish nonbusiness accounting and financial reporting from that of business. These assumptions, principles, and standards were used in Part I to explain the distinctions between accounting and financial reporting for governmental and business entities. They also were used to make a distinction between the different entities in government.

These basic assumptions, standards, and principles will continue to be used in Part II. However, instead of using them to distinguish the differences in accounting and financial reporting for these other nonbusiness organizations from *only* business organizations, they will also be used to distinguish the accounting and financial reporting for these other nonbusiness organizations from each other as well as from those of government.

Chapter 14 will explain and illustrate the accounting and financial reporting for health and welfare organizations and certain other nonprofit organizations; Chapter 15, for colleges and universities; and Chapter 16, for hospitals. After studying and learning the principles and practices associated with accounting and financial reporting for the majority of nonbusiness organizations, you should be ready for Parts III and IV concerning management accounting and management control for all nonbusiness organizations.

# CHAPTER 14

# VOLUNTARY HEALTH AND WELFARE AND CERTAIN NONPROFIT ORGANIZATIONS

Only within the past two decades has the accounting profession made a serious attempt to provide appropriate guidance concerning accounting principles and reporting practices for nonprofit organizations other than governments, hospitals, and colleges and universities. This guidance is necessary if there is to be any consistency in the application of accounting principles in the preparation of financial statements for external reporting purposes for these organizations. Thus, when an auditor expresses an opinion on the fairness of presentation of the financial statements of a labor union or a health and welfare organization, there can be some assurance to third parties that the statements are fairly presented in accordance with generally accepted accounting principles consistently applied.

Current guidance on principles of accounting for voluntary health and welfare organizations is given by the American Institute of Certified Public Accountants in their *Industry Audit Guide. Audits of Voluntary Health and Welfare Organizations*.[1] For certain nonprofit organizations, the AICPA has prepared *Statement of Position (SOP) 78-10*, concerning *Accounting Principles and Reporting Practices for Certain Nonprofit Organizations*.[2] *SOP 78-10* was released on December 31, 1978, after quite some controversy among accountants concerning principles of accounting for these other nonprofit organizations. Proponents of *SOP 78-10* are concerned with acceptable accounting principles for certain nonbusiness organizations for which no acceptable principles had been stated. The subcommittee on nonprofit organizations of the AICPA also prepared an audit and accounting guide for audits of certain nonprofit organizations. *SOP 78-10* is included in this guide as an appendix. While no effective date has been set for adoption of the accounting principles set forth in *SOP 78-10*, this statement and the *Audit and Accounting Guide* are the best statements of principles available.

The discussion in this chapter will be concerned with accounting and financial reporting for voluntary health and welfare organizations and these other certain nonbusiness organizations.

## VOLUNTARY HEALTH AND WELFARE ORGANIZATIONS

Voluntary health and welfare organizations provide services for particular segments of our society not generally provided by the government. As the AICPA in their *Health and Welfare Audit Guide* says: "They are tax exempt (organized for the benefit of the public), supported by the public, and operated on a 'not-for-profit' basis."[3] Most of the revenue for these types of organizations comes from voluntary contributions that are expended for improved conditions pertaining to health, welfare, and community services.

While some progress had been made before 1960 in developing accounting principles for health and welfare organizations, the first formal industrywide guide for voluntary health and welfare organizations was promulgated by the National Health Council in 1964. In 1966, the AICPA published its first guide on auditing voluntary health and welfare organizations and revised this guide in 1974. The 1974 guide is the most current one available.

The discussion on voluntary health and welfare accounting will be approached in the following order:

1 Fund accounting
2 Basis of accounting
3 Special accounting considerations
4 Illustrative transactions
5 Financial reporting

## FUND ACCOUNTING

As discussed in the governmental accounting section, fund accounting is concerned with separate entity accounting. As a general rule, voluntary health and welfare organizations can have as many as six separate accounting entities (funds):

1 Current unrestricted fund
2 Current restricted fund
3 Land, building, and equipment fund (plant fund)
4 Custodian funds
5 Loan and annuity funds
6 Endowment funds

### Current Unrestricted Fund

The current unrestricted fund of voluntary health and welfare organizations is somewhat comparable to the general fund in government. It is employed to account for all revenues and expenditures of the organization for which the governing board has placed no restrictions regarding the appropriate use of the resources. The exception is actions concerning unrestricted resources invested in fixed assets; these latter actions are accounted for in the land, buildings, and equipment fund. Resources that are normally unrestricted as to their use come from such sources as contributions, sales of goods and services, investment income, service fees, and legacies and bequests. When the governing board—and not an outside source—places certain restrictions on the resources, then these resources are a part of the unrestricted funds. These resources, in turn, are accounted for much as a reservation of retained earnings of the fund balances in business or enterprise funds in governmental accounting. In other words, they are a reservation of the fund balance of the current unrestricted fund.

### Current Restricted Fund

Somewhat as special revenue funds in government, the current restricted fund is employed to account for activities for which the donor or grantor specifically restricts the use of the resources. Such resources come from gifts, grants, and income from endowments that the donor has required to be used for specific purposes.

### Land, Building, and Equipment Fund

The land, building, and equipment fund of voluntary health and welfare organizations is employed to accumulate resources for the investment in fixed assets as well as to account for the net investment in those assets. Net investment means that the liabilities, such as mortgages payable, are also included in the fund. Generally accepted accounting principles require that the fixed assets be depreciated, so the depreciation on the fixed assets is also accounted for in this fund.

### Custodian Funds

Because the assets and the income from the assets of custodian funds are disbursed only on instruction from the person or organizations from which they were received, custodian funds seldom are accounted for as a part of the resources of voluntary health and welfare organizations. They are somewhat comparable to agency funds of government.

### Loan and Annuity Funds

These funds are shown separately only when they are material and usually can be accounted for in one of the other funds.

### Endowment Funds

Endowment funds of voluntary health and welfare organizations are used to account for the principal of gifts or bequests for which the donor indicates the use of the funds. Usually, the principal remains intact while the income is used, either for restricted or unrestricted current fund purposes. The principal in the fund remains in the endowment funds only as long as restrictions on the funds apply. They are then transferred to either the restricted or unrestricted current funds or the plant fund.

## BASIS OF ACCOUNTING

The "accrual basis" is used in accounting and financial reporting for voluntary health and welfare organizations. The "modified accrual basis" of expenditure accounting, as used in government, is replaced by the term "expense" accounting. This is because of the full accrued expenditure basis used in the current funds and the application of depreciation accounting—expense accounting—in the land, building, and equipment fund. They are all brought together as accrual-based reporting in the combined financial statements.

Except for proprietary funds and nonexpendable trust funds in government, this is the first time in our discussions concerning nonbusiness accounting that accounting and financial reporting for depreciation is a required accounting principle. "Depreciation expense, therefore," according to the *Audit Guide* for these voluntary health and welfare organizations, "should be recognized as a cost of rendering current services and should be included as an element of expense in the statement of support, revenue, and expenses of the fund in which the assets are recorded and in the statement of financial expenditures."[4]

Under the accrual basis of accounting, pledges are considered as revenue when received, with an allowance deducted for possible uncollectible pledges. Contributions of investments that are restricted as to use normally are included in the endowment fund. Those investments that are unrestricted as to use are considered contributions in the current unrestricted fund. In some states, gains on investments in endowment funds can be considered available for unrestricted use.

Grants to others are usually recorded as an expense, and are thus accrued, when the recipient is entitled to the grant.

## SPECIAL ACCOUNTING CONSIDERATIONS

Budgets are not required in voluntary health and welfare organizations but can be used for control purposes. When used, it is not necessary to compare the budget with actual information in the financial statements. Fixed assets are capitalized and depreciated in the land, building, and equipment fund. The expense is also shown in the statement of functional expenses.

Much as in governmental accounting, transfers between funds are recorded as transfers and not expenditures or expenses. Donated materials or services can be recorded as revenue or expenses when the goods or services are normally received in cash. Alternatively, these donations can be converted to cash or are comparable to those normally paid for as an expenditure. Investments can be carried either at cost or market value.

## FINANCIAL REPORTING

The required financial statements are: (1) the balance sheet and (2) a statement of activity, with expenses shown on a functional or program basis. Supporting services also are shown separately from the program's functional services. In these statements, fund-raising expenses are shown separately from operating expenses. It is also desirable to have combined statements showing the total of each category in all of the funds. The principal types of restricted fund balances must also be disclosed.

CHAPTER 14: VOLUNTARY HEALTH AND WELFARE AND CERTAIN NONPROFIT ORGANIZATIONS   **419**

Functional classifications relate to the programs being provided by the health and welfare organization as contrasted to the normal object-of-expenditure classification. Yet, programs for supporting services must be distinguished from program services. Examples of program services include welfare research, welfare training, professional training, and community services; examples of supporting services include fund raising and general management.

## ILLUSTRATIVE TRANSACTIONS—VOLUNTARY HEALTH AND WELFARE ORGANIZATIONS

The following illustration depicts a fictitious, fairly large, independent public welfare organization. The stated purpose is to try to develop means to help those in need of welfare assistance so that such individuals need not rely on government or other welfare agencies. Their basic programs, in addition to some community services, include welfare research, training and education of welfare recipients, and training of welfare professionals. The organization is also involved in running a well-organized fund-raising effort. The support services are: (1) management and general and (2) fund raising.

Since principles of accounting suggest that program services must be separated from functional services, it is necessary to keep subsidiary records for the program and support costs, in addition to the normal object-of-expenditure record keeping.

The Community Welfare Organization has three funds:

1. Current unrestricted fund
2. Current restricted fund
3. Land, buildings, and equipment fund

The trial balance of each of these three funds on January 1, 19X1 is shown in Exhibit 14-1.

### Current Unrestricted Fund

The transactions and journal entries for the current year for the current unrestricted fund are as follows:

**1** Received pledges of $1,230,000, with expected bad debt losses of $30,000. The journal entry is:

|  | Dr. | Cr. |
|---|---|---|
| Pledges receivable | $1,230,000 |  |
|    Allowance for estimated |  |  |
|       uncollectible pledges |  | $ 30,000 |
|    Contributions |  | 1,200,000 |

**2** Collected cash from last year's pledges, $80,000; wrote off $20,000; collected $1,110,000 on this year's pledges. The journal entry is:

|  |  |  |
|---|---|---|
| Cash | $1,190,000 |  |
| Allowance for estimated |  |  |
|    uncollectible pledges | 20,000 |  |
|       Pledges receivable |  | $1,210,000 |

## EXHIBIT 14-1
### Community Welfare Organization
### Trial Balances
### January 1, 19X1
(In Thousands of Dollars)

| Accounts | Current fund unrestricted | | Current fund restricted | | Land, buildings, and equipment fund | |
|---|---|---|---|---|---|---|
| | Dr. | Cr. | Dr. | Cr. | Dr. | Cr. |
| Cash | $1,020 | | $3 | | $ 10 | |
| Short-term investments | 500 | | | | | |
| Long-term investments | 1,000 | | | | | |
| Pledges receivable | 100 | | | | | |
| Allowance for estimated uncollectible pledges | | $ 20 | | | | |
| Investments | 50 | | | | | |
| Prepaid expense | 10 | | | | | |
| Investment income receivable | 20 | | | | | |
| Land | | | | | 5 | |
| Building | | | | | 100 | |
| Allowance for depreciation | | | | | | $ 30 |
| Equipment | | | | | 30 | |
| Allowance for depreciation | | | | | | 15 |
| Accounts payable | | 50 | | | | |
| Grants payable | | 100 | | | | |
| Deferred revenue | | 100 | | | | |
| Mortgages payable | | | | | | 30 |
| Fund balance: | | | | | | |
| Unrestricted | | 1,330 | | | | |
| Restricted | | 1,100 | | 3 | | |
| Unexpended—restricted | | | | | | 10 |
| Expended | | | | | | 60 |
| Totals | $2,700 | $2,700 | $3 | $3 | $145 | $145 |

3 Reversed end of the year's investment income receivable to current year's investment income, $20,000. The journal entry is:

| | | |
|---|---|---|
| Investment income | $20,000 | |
|     Investment income receivable | | $20,000 |

4 Collected cash from:

| | |
|---|---|
| Legacies and bequests | $ 80,000 |
| United fund | 100,000 |
| Membership dues | 20,000 |
| Investment income | 160,000 |
| Total | $360,000 |

The journal entry is:

| | | |
|---|---|---|
| Cash | $360,000 | |
|     Legacies and bequests | | $ 80,000 |
|     United fund | | 100,000 |
|     Membership dues | | 20,000 |
|     Investment income | | 160,000 |

**5** Expenses payable were as follows:

| | |
|---|---|
| Salaries | $310,000 |
| Employee benefits | 38,000 |
| Contracts and professional fees | 34,000 |
| Supplies | 59,000 |
| Telephone and telegraph | 49,000 |
| Postage | 27,000 |
| Space rental | 90,000 |
| Equipment rental | 68,000 |
| Transportation | 108,000 |
| Conferences | 69,000 |
| Printing and publications | 48,000 |
| Miscellaneous | 10,000 |
|     Total | $910,000 |

The journal entry is:

| | | |
|---|---|---|
| Salaries | $310,000 | |
| Employee benefits | 38,000 | |
| Contracts and professional fees | 34,000 | |
| Supplies | 59,000 | |
| Telephone and telegraph | 49,000 | |
| Postage | 27,000 | |
| Space rental | 90,000 | |
| Equipment rental | 68,000 | |
| Transportation | 108,000 | |
| Conferences | 69,000 | |
| Printing and publication | 48,000 | |
| Miscellaneous | 10,000 | |
|     Accounts payable | | $910,000 |

**6** Grants of $300,000 were awarded. The journal entry is:

| | | |
|---|---|---|
| Awards and grants | $300,000 | |
|     Awards and grants payable | | $300,000 |

**7** Accounts paid, $890,000; awards and grants paid, $280,000. The journal entry is:

| | | |
|---|---|---|
| Accounts payable | $890,000 | |
| Awards and grants payable | 280,000 | |
|     Cash | | $1,170,000 |

### EXHIBIT 14-2
### Community Welfare Organization
### Current Unrestricted Fund
### Distribution of Expenses to Program and Supporting Services
### For Year 19X1

| Expenses | Total | Total program services | Program services — Welfare research | Program services — Welfare training | Program services — Professional training | Program services — Community services |
|---|---|---|---|---|---|---|
| Salaries | 310 | 200 | 80 | 60 | 31 | 29 |
| Employee benefits | 38 | 25 | 9 | 7 | 4 | 5 |
| Contracts and professional fees | 34 | 30 | 10 | 5 | 10 | 5 |
| Supplies | 49 | 40 | 10 | 5 | 5 | 20 |
| Telephone and telegraph | 49 | 40 | 10 | 10 | 10 | 10 |
| Postage | 27 | 20 | 5 | 5 | 5 | 5 |
| Space rental | 90 | 90 | 30 | 30 | 15 | 15 |
| Equipment rental | 68 | 50 | 25 | 10 | 10 | 5 |
| Transportation | 108 | 100 | 40 | 30 | 15 | 15 |
| Conferences | 69 | 60 | 25 | 15 | 10 | 10 |
| Printing and publication | 48 | 40 | 15 | 10 | 10 | 5 |
| Awards and grants | 300 | 300 | 200 | 40 | 30 | 30 |
| Miscellaneous | 10 | 5 | 1 | 3 | — | 1 |
| Total | 1,200 | 1,000 | 460 | 230 | 155 | 155 |

**8** Purchased short-term investments, $100,000; long-term investments, $200,000. The journal entry is:

| | | |
|---|---|---|
| Short-term investments | $100,000 | |
| Long-term investments | 200,000 | |
|     Cash | | $300,000 |

The adjustments needed at the end of the year were as follows:

**A1** Inventories for community services increased by $10,000. The journal entry is:

| | Dr. | Cr. |
|---|---|---|
| Inventories | $10,000 | |
|     Supplies—community service | | $10,000 |

**A2** Investment income receivable was determined, $10,000. The journal entry is:

| | | |
|---|---|---|
| Investment income receivable | $10,000 | |
|     Investment income | | $10,000 |

No adjustments are needed for prepaid expenses and deferred revenue; the amounts are the same for each of the two years for each account. Exhibit 14-2 distributes expenses to program and supporting services.

The closing entries needed were as follows:

**EXHIBIT 14-2**
(*continued*)

| | Supporting services | | |
|---|---|---|---|
| Total supporting services | | Management and general | Fund raising |
| 110 | | 50 | 60 |
| 13 | | 6 | 7 |
| 4 | | — | 4 |
| 9 | | 5 | 4 |
| 9 | | 5 | 4 |
| 7 | | 3 | 4 |
| — | | — | — |
| 18 | | 15 | 3 |
| 8 | | 4 | 4 |
| 9 | | 3 | 6 |
| 8 | | 4 | 4 |
| — | | — | — |
| 5 | | 5 | — |
| 200 | | 100 | 100 |

**1** To close support, revenue, and expense accounts to restricted and unrestricted fund balances, the journal entry is:

| | | Dr. | Cr. |
|---|---|---|---|
| C1 | Contributions | $1,200,000 | |
| | Legacies and bequests | 80,000 | |
| | United fund | 100,000 | |
| | Membership dues | 20,000 | |
| | Investment income | 150,000 | |
| | Salaries | | $310,000 |
| | Employee benefits | | 38,000 |
| | Contracts and professional services | | 34,000 |
| | Supplies | | 49,000 |
| | Telephone and telegraph | | 49,000 |
| | Postage | | 27,000 |
| | Space rental | | 90,000 |
| | Equipment rental | | 68,000 |
| | Transportation | | 108,000 |
| | Conferences | | 69,000 |
| | Printing and publications | | 48,000 |
| | Miscellaneous | | 10,000 |
| | Awards and grants | | 300,000 |
| | Fund balances: | | |
| |   Restricted for investments | | 150,000 |
| |   Unrestricted | | 200,000 |

**EXHIBIT 14-3**
**Community Welfare Organization**
**Transactions and Journal Entries**
**Current Unrestricted Fund**
**For Fiscal Year 19X1**
(In Thousands)

| No. | Transaction | | Journal entry | Dr. | Cr. |
|---|---|---|---|---|---|
| 1 | Received pledges of $1,230, with expected bad debt losses of $30 | | Pledges receivable<br>  Allowance for estimated<br>    uncollectible pledges<br>  Contributions | $1,230 | $ 30<br>1,200 |
| 2 | Collected cash from last year's pledges, $80; wrote off $20; collected $1,110 on this year's pledges | | Cash<br>Allowance for estimated<br>  uncollectible pledges<br>    Pledges receivable | 1,190<br><br>20 | <br><br>1,210 |
| 3 | Reversed investment income receivable to investment income, $20 | | Investment income<br>  Investment income receivable | 20 | 20 |
| 4 | Collected cash from:<br>  Legacies and bequests<br>  United fund<br>  Membership dues<br>  Investment income | $ 80<br>100<br>20<br>160<br>$360 | Cash<br>  Legacies and bequests<br>  United fund<br>  Membership dues<br>  Investment income | 360 | 80<br>100<br>20<br>160 |
| 5 | Expenses payable were as follows:<br>  Salaries<br>  Employee benefits<br>  Contracts and professional fees<br>  Supplies<br>  Telephone and telegraph<br>  Postage<br>  Space rental<br>  Equipment rental<br>  Transportation<br>  Conferences<br>  Printing and publication<br>  Miscellaneous | 310<br>38<br><br>34<br>59<br>49<br>27<br>90<br>68<br>108<br>69<br>48<br>10<br>$910 | Salaries<br>Employee benefits<br>Contracts and professional fees<br>Supplies<br>Telephone and telegraph<br>Postage<br>Space rental<br>Equipment rental<br>Transportation<br>Conferences<br>Printing and publication<br>Miscellaneous<br>  Accounts payable | 310<br>38<br>34<br>59<br>49<br>27<br>90<br>68<br>108<br>69<br>48<br>10 | 910 |
| 6 | Grants of $300 were awarded | | Awards and grants<br>  Awards and grants payable | 300 | 300 |
| 7 | Accounts were paid, $890; awards and grants were paid, $280 | | Accounts payable<br>Awards and grants payable<br>  Cash | 890<br>280 | 1,170 |
| 8 | Purchased short-term investments, $100; long-term investments, $200 | | Short-term investments<br>Long-term investments<br>  Cash | 100<br>200 | 300 |
| A1 | Inventories for community service increased by $10 | | Inventories<br>  Supplies—community<br>    service | 10 | 10 |

## EXHIBIT 14-3
*(continued)*

| No. | Transaction | Journal entry | Dr. | Cr. |
|---|---|---|---|---|
| A2 | Investment income receivable was determined, $10 | Investment income receivable<br>    Investment income | 10 | 10 |
|  | No adjustments are needed for prepaid expenses and deferred revenue. The amounts are the same for the two years for each account. | | | |
| C1 | To close support, revenue, and expense accounts to restricted and unrestricted fund balances<br><br>(See Exhibit 14-2 for distribution of expenses to program and supporting services) | Contributions<br>Legacies and bequests<br>United fund<br>Membership dues<br>Investment income<br>    Salaries<br>    Employee benefits<br>    Contracts and professional services<br>    Supplies<br>    Telephone and telegraph<br>    Postage<br>    Space rental<br>    Equipment rental<br>    Transportation<br>    Conferences<br>    Printing and publications<br>    Miscellaneous<br>    Awards and grants<br>    Fund balance—restricted for investments<br>    Fund balance—unrestricted | 1,200<br>80<br>100<br>20<br>150 | <br><br><br><br><br>310<br>38<br><br>34<br>49<br>49<br>27<br>90<br>68<br>108<br>69<br>48<br>10<br>300<br><br>150<br><br>200 |

Exhibit 14-3 summarizes all of the previous transactions and journal entries. Exhibit 14-2 organizes the objects of expenditure into functional classifications. This information normally would be kept in a subsidiary ledger. From the transactions and journal entries, a worksheet for the unrestricted current fund is prepared (see Exhibit 14-4), from which the balance sheet (see Exhibit 14-9), the statement of support, revenue, expenses, and changes in fund balances (see Exhibit 14-10), and the statement of functional expenses (see Exhibit 14-11) can be prepared. The financial statements combine all funds in order to have a statement reflecting the activities of the total organization.

## Current Restricted Fund

The transactions and journal entries for the current restricted fund of the Community Welfare Organization for the year 19X1 are as follows:

**EXHIBIT 14-4**
**Community Welfare Organization**
**Unrestricted Current Fund**
**Worksheet for Year 19X1**
(In Thousands)

| Accounts | Beginning balance | | Transaction | | | | Ending trial balance | | Statement of support, revenues, expenses, & changes in fund balance | | Balance sheet | |
|---|---|---|---|---|---|---|---|---|---|---|---|---|
| | Dr. | Cr. | No. | Dr. | No. | Cr. | Dr. | Cr. | Dr. | Cr. | Dr. | Cr. |
| Cash | 1,020 | | 2 | 1,190 | 7 | 1,170 | 1,100 | | | | 1,100 | |
| | | | 4 | 360 | 8 | 300 | | | | | | |
| Short-term investments | 500 | | 8 | 100 | | | 600 | | | | 600 | |
| Long-term investments | 1,000 | | 8 | 200 | | | 1,200 | | | | 1,200 | |
| Pledges receivable | 100 | | 1 | 1,230 | 2 | 1,210 | 120 | | | | 120 | |
| Allowance for estimated uncollectible pledges | | 20 | 2 | 20 | 1 | 30 | | 30 | | | | 30 |
| Inventories | 50 | | A1 | 10 | | | 60 | | | | 60 | |
| Prepaid expenses | 10 | | | | | | 10 | | | | 10 | |
| Investment income receivable | 20 | | A2 | 10 | 3 | 20 | 10 | | | | 10 | |
| Accounts payable | | 50 | 7 | 890 | 5 | 910 | | 70 | | | | 70 |
| Awards and grants payable | | 100 | 7 | 280 | 6 | 300 | | 120 | | | | 120 |
| Deferred revenue | | 100 | | | | | | 100 | | | | 100 |
| Fund balances: | | | | | | | | | | | | |
| Restricted for investments | | 1,100 | | | | | | 1,100 | | | | 1,100 |
| Unrestricted | | 1,330 | | | | | | 1,330 | | | | 1,330 |

|  |  |  |  |  |  |  |  |  |
|---|---|---|---|---|---|---|---|---|
| Contributions |  |  |  | 1 | 1,200 |  | 1,200 | 1,200 |
| Legacies and bequests |  |  |  | 4 | 80 |  | 80 | 80 |
| United fund |  |  |  | 4 | 100 |  | 100 | 100 |
| Membership dues |  |  |  | 4 | 20 |  | 20 | 20 |
| Investment income |  | 3 | 20 | 4 | 160 |  | 150 | 150 |
|  |  |  |  | A2 | 10 |  |  |  |
| Salaries |  | 5 | 310 |  |  | 310 | | 310 |
| Employee benefits |  | 5 | 38 |  |  | 38 | | 38 |
| Contracts and professional |  |  |  |  |  |  |  |  |
| services |  | 5 | 34 |  |  | 34 | | 34 |
| Supplies |  | 5 | 59 | A1 | 10 | 49 | | 49 |
| Telephone and telegraph |  | 5 | 49 |  |  | 49 | | 49 |
| Postage |  | 5 | 27 |  |  | 27 | | 27 |
| Space rental |  | 5 | 90 |  |  | 90 | | 90 |
| Equipment rental |  | 5 | 68 |  |  | 68 | | 68 |
| Transportation |  | 5 | 108 |  |  | 108 | | 108 |
| Conferences |  | 5 | 69 |  |  | 69 | | 69 |
| Printing and publication |  | 5 | 48 |  |  | 48 | | 48 |
| Miscellaneous |  | 5 | 10 |  |  | 10 | | 10 |
| Awards and grants |  | 6 | 300 |  |  | 300 | | 300 |
|  | 2,700 |  | 5,520 |  | 5,520 | 4,300 | 1,550 | 1,200 |
|  | 2,700 |  |  |  |  | 4,300 |  | 1,200 |
| To |  |  |  |  |  |  |  |  |
| Restricted fund balance— |  |  |  |  |  |  |  |  |
| investment |  |  |  |  |  | 150 | | 150 |
| Unrestricted fund balance |  |  |  |  |  | 200 | | 200 |
|  |  |  |  |  |  | 1,550 | 3,100 | 1,550 |
|  |  |  |  |  |  |  | 3,100 | 3,100 |
|  |  |  |  |  |  |  | 2,750 | |
|  |  |  |  |  |  |  | 150 | |
|  |  |  |  |  |  |  | 200 | |
|  |  |  |  |  |  |  | 3,100 | |

**1** Cash received for research, $12,000. The journal entry is:

|  | Dr. | Cr. |
|---|---|---|
| Cash | $12,000 | |
|     Contributions—research | | $12,000 |

**2** Research expenditures for salaries, $10,000. The journal entry is:

| Salaries—research | $10,000 | |
|---|---|---|
|     Cash | | $10,000 |

**3** The closing journal entry is:

| Contributions—research | $12,000 | |
|---|---|---|
|     Salaries—research | | $10,000 |
|     Fund balance—restricted | | 2,000 |

These transactions and journal entries are summarized for the current restricted fund in Exhibit 14-5. From these transactions and journal entries, a worksheet for the current restricted fund is prepared (see Exhibit 14-6), from which the balance sheets (see Exhibit 14-9), the statement of support, revenue, expenses, and changes in fund balances (see Exhibit 14-10), and the statement of functional expenses (see Exhibit 14-11) can be prepared.

## Land, Buildings, and Equipment Fund

The transactions and journal entries for the land, buildings, and equipment fund for the Community Welfare Organization for the year 19X1 are as follows:

**1** Contribution in cash to the building fund was $10,000. The journal entry is:

|  | Dr. | Cr. |
|---|---|---|
| Cash | $10,000 | |
|     Contribution to building fund | | $10,000 |

**EXHIBIT 14-5**
**Community Welfare Organization**
**Transaction and Journal Entries**
**Current Restricted Fund**
**Fiscal Year 19X1**
(In Thousands)

| No. | Transactions | Journal entry | Dr. | Cr. |
|---|---|---|---|---|
| 1 | Cash received for research | Cash | 12 | |
| | |     Contributions—research | | 12 |
| 2 | Research expenditures for salaries | Salaries—research | 10 | |
| | |     Cash | | 10 |
| 3 | Closing entry | Contributions—research | 12 | |
| | |     Salaries—research | | 10 |
| | |     Fund balance—restricted | | 2 |

**EXHIBIT 14-6**
**Community Welfare Organization**
**Current Restricted Fund**
**Worksheet**
**For Year 19X1**
(In Thousands)

| Accounts | Trial balance | | Transactions | | | | Support, revenue, expenses, and changes in fund balance | | Balance sheet | |
|---|---|---|---|---|---|---|---|---|---|---|
| | Dr. | Cr. | No. | Dr. | No. | Cr. | Dr. | Cr. | Dr. | Cr. |
| Cash | 3 | | 1 | 12 | 2 | 10 | | | 5 | |
| Fund balance—restricted | | 3 | | | | | | | | 3 |
| Contribution—research | | | | | 1 | 12 | | 12 | | |
| Salaries—research | | | 2 | 10 | | | 10 | | | |
| | 3 | 3 | | 22 | | 22 | 10 | 12 | 5 | 3 |
| To fund balance | | | | | | | 2 | | | 2 |
| | | | | | | | 12 | 12 | 5 | 5 |

**2** Paid $2,000 interest on mortgage and $5,000 on the mortgage. The journal entry is:

| | | |
|---|---|---|
| Interest—management and general | $2,000 | |
| Mortgages payable | 5,000 | |
| Cash | | $7,000 |

**3** Depreciated the buildings at $5,000 and the equipment at $5,000 for the following programs and services: welfare research, $1,000; welfare training, $2,000; professional training, $2,000; community service, $2,000; management and general, $2,000; and fund raising, $1,000. The journal entry is:

| | | |
|---|---|---|
| Depreciation | $10,000 | |
| Allowance for depreciation: | | |
| Building | | $5,000 |
| Equipment | | 5,000 |

**C1** Since the mortgage and interest were paid from the money received from the contributions, the unexpended—restricted fund balance would increase by $3,000 (contribution, $10,000, less amount paid for mortgage, $5,000, less amount paid for interest, $2,000, equals $3,000). The expended fund balance would decrease by $5,000 (depreciation, $10,000, less reduction in mortgage, $5,000, equals $5,000). The closing entry is:

| | | |
|---|---|---|
| Contribution to building fund | $10,000 | |
| Fund balance—expended | 5,000 | |
| Interest | | $ 2,000 |
| Depreciation | | 10,000 |
| Fund balance—unexpended— restricted | | 3,000 |

These transactions and journal entries are summarized in Exhibit 14-7. From these transactions and journal entries, a worksheet (see Exhibit 14-8) is prepared, from which the balance sheets (see Exhibit 14-9), the statement of support, revenue, expenses, and changes in fund balances (see Exhibit 14-10), and the statement of functional expenses (see Exhibit 14-11) can be prepared.

## Financial Statements

Exhibits 14-9, 14-10, and 14-11 illustrate the required statements for a voluntary health and welfare organization. Notice the segregation of revenues and support in the statement of support, revenue, expenses, and changes in fund balance as well as the classification in that statement of expenses by program category (see Exhibit 14-10). The statement of functional expenses (see Exhibit 14-11) brings together the objects of

**EXHIBIT 14-7**
**Community Welfare Organization**
**Transaction and Journal Entries**
**Land, Buildings, and Equipment Fund**
**Fiscal Year 19X1**
(In Thousands)

| No. | Transactions | Journal entry | Dr. | Cr. |
|---|---|---|---|---|
| 1 | Contribution in cash to building fund, $10 | Cash<br>    Contribution to building fund | 10 | 10 |
| 2 | Paid interest on mortgage, $2 and mortgage $5 | Interest—management and<br>    general<br>Mortgages payable<br>    Cash | 2<br><br>5 | <br><br>7 |
| 3 | Depreciated buildings at $5 and equipment at $5 for the following programs and services: welfare research $1; welfare training $2; professional training $2; community service, $2; management and general, $2; and fund raising, $1. | Depreciation<br>    Allowance for depreciation—<br>      building<br>    Allowance for depreciation—<br>      equipment | 10 | <br><br>5<br><br>5 |
| C1 | Closing entry—to fund balances as follows: expended $5, dr.; unexpended—restricted $3, cr. | Contribution to building fund<br>Fund balance—expended<br>    Interest<br>    Depreciation<br>    Fund balance—unexpended—<br>      restricted | 10<br>5 | <br><br>2<br>10<br><br>3 |

expenditures along with the functional or program category. Note also that the title of the fund balance is both expended and unexpended.

## CERTAIN NONPROFIT ORGANIZATIONS

Numerous nonprofit organizations exist for which no particular accounting principles had been developed prior to the issuance in December 1978 of the AICPA's *Statement of Position 78-10 (SOP 78-10)*. SOP 78-10 provides guidance on accounting principles for certain nonbusiness organizations not covered by GAAP guidelines issued by other sources. The following listing illustrates the included organizations:

| | |
|---|---|
| Cemetery organizations | Private and community foundations |
| Civic organizations | Private elementary and secondary schools |
| Fraternal organizations | Professional associations |
| Labor unions | Public broadcasting stations |
| Libraries | Religious organizations |
| Museums | Research and scientific organizations |
| Other cultural institutions | Social and country clubs |
| Performing arts organizations | Trade associations |
| Political parties | Zoological and botanical societies |

**EXHIBIT 14-8**
**Community Welfare Organization**
**Land, Buildings, and Equipment Fund**
**Worksheet for Year 19X1**
(In Thousands)

| Accounts | Trial balance Dr. | Trial balance Cr. | Transactions No. | Transactions Dr. | Transactions No. | Transactions Cr. | Support, revenue, expenses, and changes in fund balance Dr. | Support, revenue, expenses, and changes in fund balance Cr. | Balance sheet Dr. | Balance sheet Cr. |
|---|---|---|---|---|---|---|---|---|---|---|
| Cash | 10 | | 1 | 10 | 2 | 7 | | | 13 | |
| Land | 5 | | | | | | | | 5 | |
| Building | 100 | | | | | | | | 100 | |
| Allowance for depreciation—building | | 30 | | | 3 | 5 | | | | 35 |
| Equipment | 30 | | | | | | | | 30 | |
| Allowance for depreciation—equipment | | 15 | | | 3 | 5 | | | | 20 |
| Mortgages payable | | 30 | 2 | 5 | | | | | | 25 |
| Fund balances: | | | | | | | | | | |
| Unexpended—restricted | | 10 | | | | | | | | 10 |
| Expended | | 60 | | | | | | | | 60 |
| Contribution to building fund | | | | | 1 | 10 | | 10 | | |
| Interest | | | 2 | 2 | | | 2 | | | |
| Depreciation | | | 3 | 10 | | | 10 | | | |
| Totals | 145 | 145 | | 27 | | 27 | 12 | 10 | 148 | 150 |
| To fund balance— | | | | | | | | | | |
| Unexpended—restricted | | | | | | | 3 | | | 3 |
| Expended | | | | | | | | 5 | 5 | |
| | | | | | | | 15 | 15 | 153 | 153 |

## EXHIBIT 14-9
### Community Welfare Services
### Balance Sheets
### December 31, 19X1
(In Thousands)

| Assets | 19X1 | 19X0 | Liabilities and fund balances | 19X1 | 19X0 |
|---|---|---|---|---|---|
| Current funds—unrestricted | | | Current funds—unrestricted | | |
| Cash | 1,100 | 1,020 | Accounts payable | 70 | 50 |
| Short-term investments | 600 | 500 | Awards and grants payable | 120 | 100 |
| Long-term investments | 1,200 | 1,000 | Deferred revenue | 100 | 100 |
| Pledges receivable, less allowance for uncollectibles, $30, and $20 | 90 | 80 | Fund balance Designated for long-term investment | 1,250 | 1,100 |
| Inventories | 60 | 50 | Undesignated | 1,530 | 1,330 |
| Prepaid expenses | 10 | 10 | | | |
| Interest receivable | 10 | 20 | | | |
| | 3,070 | 2,680 | | 3,070 | 2,680 |
| Current funds—restricted | | | Current funds—restricted | | |
| Cash | 5 | 3 | Fund balance—research | 5 | 3 |
| Land, building, and equipment fund | | | Land, building, and equipment fund | | |
| Cash | 13 | 10 | Mortgages payable | 25 | 30 |
| | | | Fund balances: | | |
| Land, buildings, and equipment, less depreciation of $55 and $45 | 80 | 90 | Unexpended—restricted | 13 | 10 |
| | | | Expended | 55 | 60 |
| | 93 | 100 | | 93 | 100 |

Organizations for which audit guides have been issued by the AICPA, including one for health and welfare organizations, are not included in the *Statement of Position 78-10* for certain nonprofit organizations.

## Summary of Accounting Principles and Reporting Practices

The following statement, taken from a monograph prepared by the certified public accounting firm 'Price Waterhouse & Co.' adequately discusses and summarizes the more important provisions of the *AICPA Statement of Position, 78-10* on "Accounting Principles and Reporting Practices for Certain Nonprofit Organizations."

*Accrual basis reporting:* Probably the most far-reaching of all of the accounting principles in the Statement is the requirement that nonprofit organizations report on the accrual basis of accounting. While most profit-oriented organizations use accrual accounting, a large number of small and medium-sized nonprofit organizations continue to follow cash basis accounting for reporting purposes.

The requirement is for accrual basis financial statements which does not necessarily mean accrual basis bookkeeping. Many nonprofit organizations find it practical to keep their records on a cash basis and then, at the end of a period, prepare accrual basis financial statements through worksheet adjustments or formal journal entries.

*Emphasis on fund accounting reduced:* The Statement indicates that the use of fund accounting for reporting purposes continues to be appropriate where necessary to disclose prop-

## EXHIBIT 14-10
## Community Welfare Services
## Statement of Support, Revenue, Expenses, and Changes in Fund Balances
(In Thousands)

|  | Current fund — Unrestricted | Current fund — Restricted | Land, buildings, and equipment fund | Total |
|---|---|---|---|---|
| **Public support and revenue** | | | | |
| Public support: | | | | |
| Contribution | 1,200 | 12 | 10 | 1,222 |
| Legacies and bequests | 80 | | | 80 |
| United fund | 100 | | | 100 |
| Revenue: | | | | |
| Membership dues | 20 | | | 20 |
| Investment income | 150 | | | 150 |
|  | 1,550 | 12 | 10 | 1,572 |
| **Expenses** | | | | |
| Program services: | | | | |
| Welfare research | 460 | 10 | 1 | 471 |
| Welfare education and training | 230 | | 2 | 232 |
| Professional training | 155 | | 2 | 157 |
| Community service | 155 | | 2 | 157 |
| Total program services | 1,000 | 10 | 7 | 1,017 |
| Supporting services: | | | | |
| Management and general | 100 | | 4 | 104 |
| Fund raising | 100 | | 1 | 101 |
| Total supporting services | 200 | | 5 | 205 |
| Total expenses | 1,200 | 10 | 12 | 1,222 |
| Excess (deficiencies) of public support and revenue over expenses | 350 | 2 | (2) | 350 |
| Fund balances—beginning of year | 2,430 | 3 | 70 | 2,503 |
| Fund balances—end of year | 2,780 | 5 | 68 | 2,853 |

erly the nature and amount of significant resources which have been restricted by persons outside the organization. The emphasis, however, is on the clarity and usefulness of the information to be disclosed rather than on the use of fund accounting per se.

This is a subtle but important distinction. In the past, many have assumed that fund accounting was mandatory for nonprofit organizations and that the use of fund accounting for recordkeeping dictated, in turn, the use of detailed multi-fund reporting formats. Unfortunately, such financial statements are often complicated and confusing to many readers.

Thus, the Statement of Position has redirected emphasis from the form of disclosure to the appropriateness and quality of disclosure. While it reaffirms that traditional, by-fund financial statements may in some instances still be the most appropriate way to communicate certain information, it has not mandated the use of such disclosure.

*Required financial statements:* The Statement of Position does not prescribe the form of the financial statements to be used. Rather, it emphasizes the information appropriate for fair disclosure and leaves each organization to choose the specific format most appropriate for its

## EXHIBIT 14-11
## Community Welfare Services
## Statement of Functional Expenses
## For Year 19X1
(In Thousands)

|  | Program services |  |  |  | Supporting services |  |  | Total expenses |
|---|---|---|---|---|---|---|---|---|
|  | Welfare research | Welfare education and training | Professional education and training | Community services | Total | Managerial and general | Fund raising | Total |  |
| Salaries | 90 | 60 | 31 | 29 | 210 | 50 | 60 | 110 | 320 |
| Employee benefits | 9 | 7 | 4 | 5 | 25 | 6 | 7 | 13 | 38 |
| Contracts and professional fees | 10 | 5 | 10 | 5 | 30 | — | 4 | 4 | 34 |
| Supplies | 10 | 5 | 5 | 20 | 40 | 5 | 4 | 9 | 49 |
| Telephone and telegraph | 10 | 10 | 10 | 10 | 40 | 5 | 4 | 9 | 49 |
| Postage | 5 | 5 | 5 | 5 | 20 | 3 | 4 | 7 | 27 |
| Space rental | 30 | 30 | 15 | 15 | 90 | — | — | — | 90 |
| Equipment rental | 25 | 10 | 10 | 5 | 50 | 15 | 3 | 18 | 68 |
| Transportation | 40 | 30 | 15 | 15 | 100 | 4 | 4 | 8 | 108 |
| Conferences | 25 | 15 | 10 | 10 | 60 | 3 | 6 | 9 | 69 |
| Printing and publication | 15 | 10 | 10 | 5 | 40 | 4 | 4 | 8 | 48 |
| Awards and grants | 200 | 40 | 30 | 30 | 300 | — | — | — | 300 |
| Miscellaneous | 1 | 3 | — | 1 | 5 | 7 | — | 7 | 12 |
| Total expenses before depreciation | 470 | 230 | 155 | 155 | 1,010 | 102 | 100 | 202 | 1,212 |
| Depreciation of building and equipment | 1 | 2 | 2 | 2 | 7 | 2 | 1 | 3 | 10 |
| Total expenses | 471 | 232 | 157 | 157 | 1,017 | 104 | 101 | 205 | 1,222 |

435

use. The Statement does specify, however, three basic financial statements as normally being "required":

**1** A Balance Sheet, showing the assets, liabilities and fund balances of the organization. The Balance Sheet, or notes thereto, should also disclose the nature of significant restrictions on resources.

Moreover, the Statement provides that nonprofit organizations having only unrestricted funds must prepare a classified Balance Sheet. (A classified Balance Sheet is one in which assets and liabilities are separated into categories, i.e., "current" and "long-term.") Organizations having both unrestricted and restricted funds should also prepare a classified Balance Sheet, unless the fund classifications themselves adequately disclose the current and long-term nature of the assets and liabilities.)

**2** A Statement of Activity, which shows all of the activity of the organization from the beginning to the end of the year. This Statement of Activity could be titled with any one of a number of different names, including Statement of Revenue, Expenses and Changes in Fund Balances; Statement of Changes in Fund Balances; Statement of Revenue, Expenses, Capital Additions and Changes in Fund Balances; or Statement of Income and Expense.

**3** A Statement of Changes in Financial Position, which summarizes all changes in the assets, liabilities and deferred accounts for the period. This statement is not required by the AICPA's previously-issued nonprofit industry audit guides, but it is required for most profit-oriented entities. The reader is directed to APB Opinion 19 for further explanation and discussion of this statement.

*Financially interrelated organizations:* The Statement of Position requires that combined financial statements be presented if any one of the following circumstances exists:

**1** Separate entities solicit funds in the name of the reporting organization, and substantially all of the funds solicited are to be transferred to the reporting organization or used at its discretion, or

**2** An organization transfers some of its resources to another entity (such as a foundation or investment trust) whose resources are held for the benefit of the reporting organization, or

**3** An organization assigns functions to a controlled entity whose funding is primarily derived from sources other than public contributions.

Combined financial statements may be, but are not required to be, prepared in circumstances other than the above.

Religious organizations will not be required to present combined statements, although they are still encouraged to do so when combination would be meaningful.

*Required disclosure:* While format has not been specifically set forth, it should be noted that some of the required disclosures in effect dictate format. However, most details of format are left to each reporting organization.

The following are some of the Statement's specific disclosure requirements:

**1** The fund balance section of the Balance Sheet should clearly disclose:
   **a** the total amount of unrestricted fund balances,
   **b** the total amounts of the major types of restricted fund balances, and
   **c** the total amount of fund balance invested in fixed assets

This disclosure could be handled through the use of either a multiple column presentation or by careful use of line item descriptions.

**2** The Statement of Activity should show operating income and expenses segregated from legally restricted, non-expendable or capital-type gifts and income.

**3** The Statement of Activity should clearly label the excess of operating income over expenses before, and after, the addition of legally restricted, nonexpendable or capital-type gifts and income.

**4** The Statement of Activity should show the total of all unrestricted revenue and support.

**5** The Statement of Activity should show the principal sources of restricted revenue.

*Combining fund groupings:* In many instances it may be entirely appropriate to combine various fund groupings into only "unrestricted" and "restricted" columns. This is the type of format illustrated in the Price Waterhouse Position Paper on College and University Reporting, issued in 1975. Still other organizations may prefer the classifications "expendable" and "nonexpendable." Expendable funds would include those amounts which are available for current activities, both restricted and unrestricted. Likewise, nonexpendable funds would include those amounts which are not available for current activities, either because of donor-imposed restrictions or because of their nature (such as fixed assets).

*Nonexpendable or capital-type gifts:* Legally restricted, nonexpendable or capital-type gifts and income have a different character from expendable gifts, and for this reason should be reported separately from amounts which can be currently spent. The two most common types of nonexpendable transactions are gifts for endowment and gifts for purchases of fixed assets.

In addition, capital gains and investment income which are specifically restricted by the donor, or by law, for nonexpendable purposes should also be reflected separately. It must be noted, however, that amounts which the Board internally designates as endowment do not meet this definition and should not be included as nonexpendable.

*Pledges recorded but income deferred:* Pledges that an organization could legally enforce should be recorded as a receivable on the Balance Sheet, net of an allowance for the estimated portion that may not be collected. While few organizations attempt to enforce legal collection, most can estimate fairly accurately the amount which will ultimately be collected, and this net amount should be recorded. This treatment provides appropriate recognition that pledges represent assets and should be reflected on the Balance Sheet.

The timing of the recognition of pledges as income in the Statement of Activity will depend on the donors' intentions. Where a donor has not specified the period he intends his pledge to be used, the pledge should be included as income in the year that he had indicated his pledge will be paid. Until that time, the pledge would be reflected as deferred income on the Balance Sheet.

*Current restricted gifts deferred:* Current restricted gifts are those amounts which are restricted for a specific "current" or operating purpose. The Statement requires that restricted gifts, including those made or fixed asset additions, be recorded as deferred income on the Balance Sheet until the organization has expended funds which meet the restrictions imposed by the donor. Once expenditures have been made that meet the terms of the restrictions, such gifts would be reflected as income in the Statement of Activity.

Such amounts are deferred, however, only so long as the organization has not expended funds, from whatever source, which meet the terms of the restrictions. There is no requirement that a specific restricted gift be spent—only that the legal restriction be met. For example, assume a donor gives $5,000 for a specific research project, and, subsequent to the receipt of the gift, the organization uses $25,000 of its unrestricted funds to perform this same research project. The restriction has thus been met, and the $5,000 restricted gift must be reflected as income in the period.

*Current restricted fund effectively eliminated:* Under the treatment discussed in the previous paragraphs, there will no longer be a "fund balance" for current restricted funds in the Balance Sheet. Unspent amounts will be reflected as deferred income outside the fund balance section. For this reason it may be expected that the use of a separate column for current restricted funds will disappear from many financial statements. This will require careful captioning to disclose specific current restricted assets in the Balance Sheet, as well as sources of current restricted revenue in the Statement of Activity.

*Grant income deferred:* There has been confusion in the past over the timing of recognition of grant income. Under the treatment outlined in the Statement, grants are to be handled in the same manner as current restricted gifts. Accordingly, grants received before expenditures were made would be deferred on the Balance Sheet. Income recognition would take place at the time funds were expended which meet the terms of the grant, again without regard to the specific funds actually used.

*Grants recorded by grantors at the time of award:* Some nonprofit organizations, such as foundations, make grants to other organizations. Grantor organizations should record as a liability, and as an expense, the total amount of a grant awarded at the time the grantee is "entitled" to the grant. Normally, this either is at the time that the Board of Trustees has approved the specific grant or at the time the grantee is notified that he has been awarded the grant.

Some grants provide for payment over a several-year period. Where the grantee will routinely receive such payments without the necessity of a subsequent review and formal decision by the grantor, the Statement dictates that the full amount of the grant, including the amounts payable in future years, be recorded at the time awarded. If, instead, the grantor indicates that the future payments are subject to an extensive review by the grantor prior to making payment, such subsequent payments would not be recorded as a liability and expense until after this subsequent review. In these circumstances, each subsequent payment effectively would be treated as a new grant.

*Donated and contributed services:* The Statement of Position establishes strict criteria for an organization's recording the monetary value of services contributed by volunteers. Before an organization records the value of such services as contributions or support, and an equivalent amount as expense, all of the following must exist:

"**1** The services performed are significant and they form an integral part of the efforts of the organization.... (They would be performed by salaried personnel if donated or contributed services were not available....)

"**2** The organization controls the employment and duties of the donors of the services...in a way comparable to the control it would exercise over employees with similar responsibilities....

"**3** The organization has a clearly measurable basis for the amount to be recorded.

"**4** The program services of the reporting organization are not principally intended for the benefit of the organization's members...."

*Expenses reported on a functional basis:* For those organizations receiving support in the form of contributions from the general public, expenses should be reported on a functional or programmatic basis that discloses the purposes for which expenses have been incurred. This is in contrast to reporting on a natural expense basis, where amounts spent for salaries, rent, office supplies, etc. are shown. Supporting services should be reported separately from program services and would normally include management and general expenses, as well as fund raising expenses.

Functional reporting is appropriate since nonprofit organizations exist to carry out programs, not just to pay salaries or incur expenses. Reporting on a functional basis forces the organization to identify specific programs, and equally important, to identify the costs of such programs. Those organizations not receiving significant support from the general public are encouraged, although not required, to report on a functional basis.

*Management and general expenses:* Management and general expenses are narrowly defined in the Statement as "... those which are not identifiable with any single program or fund-raising activity but are indispensable to the conduct of all these activities and to an organization's existence. They include expenses for the overall direction of the organization's general board activities, business management, general record-keeping, budgeting, and related purposes."

The above definition suggests that only expenses which are not identifiable with another function should be considered management and general. Thus, it is important that an organization record carefully the administration of its projects so that appropriate allocations of staff time, and the costs associated therewith, can be made. This includes the chief officer of the organization and his staff, the activities of whom should also be prorated among the various program and supporting categories where their time is spent.

*Fund raising expenses:* Fund raising expenses are defined as the costs involved in inducing others to contribute money, materials, time or facilities without receiving any economic benefit in return. Fund raising costs should include a fair allocation of overhead as well as direct expenses.

The Statement also discusses the question of deferring fund raising expenses which may benefit future periods, but concludes that such costs should not be deferred. The rationale is simply that it is too difficult to establish that future benefits will in fact result from such costs, with the resulting risk of significant abuse if deferral were permitted. Further, with the adverse publicity surrounding fund raising costs, it seems essential to adopt a conservative approach that would appear reasonable to both legislators and regulators.

In addition, the Statement discusses the appropriateness of allocating certain costs between the program and fund raising functions and concludes that this should be done where the facts warrant. An example would be an allocation of costs for literature which is to be distributed to the public and which has both educational and fund raising objectives.

*Valuation of investments:* The proper carrying value for investments was a major concern for the AICPA during development of its nonprofit standards. It was finally determined in the Statement of Position that a nonprofit organization's marketable securities portfolio may be carried in its financial statements at either market value or the lower of cost or market. For bonds expected to be held to maturity, amortized cost is also an appropriate method. Other kinds of investments, such as real estate and oil and gas interests, may also be carried at either the lower of cost or fair value or at fair value. Unrealized appreciation or depreciation of current investments carried at the lower of cost or market and all investments carried at market will be recorded as current revenue or expense; unrealized appreciation or depreciation of long-term investments carried at the lower of cost or market will be recorded as a direct addition or deduction to the fund balance.

*Fixed assets capitalized:* The Statement provides that fixed assets must be capitalized. This will be one of the more controversial recommendations because many nonprofit organizations presently do not capitalize these assets.

The Statement discusses the reasons for this conclusion, and the readers who are concerned with this proposal are urged to refer to it. The essence of that discussion is that, for many organizations, fixed assets are a major asset for which the Board is accountable, and failure to reflect these assets on the Balance Sheet is misleading.

For many, the most difficult aspect will be the requirement for retroactive recording of fixed assets—the reconstruction of the historical cost of those assets purchased in prior years that are still in service. In those instances, however, where the organization does not have historical cost information, the Statement provides that other reasonable bases may be used for the purpose of this initial recording, including cost-based appraisals, insurance appraisals, replacement costs, or property tax appraisals adjusted for market. (This pragmatic approach applies only to the initial recording of assets at the effective date and only where historical cost records are not available; all subsequent additions must be recorded at cost, or at fair value if donated.)

*Depreciation:* A requirement related to the capitalization of fixed assets is that depreciation accounting must also be followed, except for those structures which are used primarily as houses of worship (but these must still be capitalized). Also excluded from this depreciation requirement are "inexhaustible" assets, such as landmarks, monuments, cathedrals or historical treasures.

Depreciation accounting is a method of spreading the cost of an asset over its useful life; it is not intended to be either a valuation process or a method to provide replacement funds. While many nonprofit organizations do not follow depreciation accounting, the Statement of Position provides that the Statement of Activity should reflect the cost of operations for the period so that the reader can better judge financial results. Buildings and equipment wear out, and if one is trying to measure cost, this cost "expiration" or depreciation must be considered.[5]

## Illustrative Reports

There are so many types of organizations for which *Statement of Position, 78-10* states the accounting principles and reporting practices that trying to show a representative sampling of the accounting transactions for these numerous types of organizations would be prohibitive. It is better, for learning purposes, to show the financial statements for a few representative organizations.

As stated in the Price Waterhouse & Co. summary of principles, "The emphasis (on fund accounting), however, is on the clarity and usefulness of the information to be disclosed rather than on the use of fund accounting per se."[6] The first set of illustrative reports concerns a country club (see Exhibit 14-12, balance sheet; Exhibit 14-13, statement of revenue, expenses, and changes of cumulative excess of revenue over expenses; and Exhibit 14-14, statement of changes in financial position) and shows only one fund. The second set of illustrative reports concerns a religious organization (see Exhibit 14-15, balance sheet; Exhibit 14-16, statement of support and revenue, expenses, capital additions, and changes in fund balance; and Exhibit 14-17, statement of changes in financial position) and classifies the funds as expendable and nonexpendable funds, along with a plant fund. The expendable and nonexpendable funds are further classified into other funds. The third set of illustrative reports concerns a union (see Exhibit 14-18, balance sheet; Exhibit 14-19, statement of revenue, expenses, and changes in fund balance; and Exhibit 14-20, statement of changes in financial position) and uses the terms "designated" and "undesignated" to show the restrictions placed upon the funds.

These statements, from the AICPA's *Statement of Position, 78-10,* reflect current reporting standards. Note that the titles of each of the statements may be a little different from organization to organization, and that depreciation is recorded in each of the types of organizations. Some of the statements have references to notes to the financial statements. These notes are not shown.

**EXHIBIT 14-12**
**Sample Country Club[7]**
**Balance Sheet**
**March 31, 19X1 and 19X0**

|  | 19X1 | 19X0 |
|---|---|---|
| **Assets** | | |
| Current assets | | |
| Cash | $ 44,413 | $ 37,812 |
| Investments (Note 2) | 289,554 | 388,007 |
| Accounts receivable, less allowances of $5,000 in 19X1 and $6,000 in 19X0 | 71,831 | 45,898 |
| Inventories at lower of cost (FIFO) or market | 27,930 | 28,137 |
| Prepaid expenses | 19,154 | 13,948 |
| Total current assets | 452,882 | 513,802 |
| Property and equipment, at cost (Note 3) | | |
| Land and land improvements | 1,085,319 | 1,098,828 |
| Buildings | 1,331,590 | 1,200,585 |
| Furniture, fixtures, and equipment | 274,761 | 254,540 |
|  | 2,691,670 | 2,553,953 |
| Less accumulated depreciation | 864,564 | 824,088 |
|  | 1,827,106 | 1,729,865 |
| Other assets | | |
| Deferred charges | 15,077 | 16,524 |
| Beverage license | 10,500 | 10,500 |
|  | 25,577 | 27,024 |
|  | $2,305,565 | $2,270,691 |
| **Liabilities and Membership Equity** | | |
| Current liabilities | | |
| Accounts payable and accrued expenses | $ 61,426 | $ 63,600 |
| Deferred revenues—initiation fees (Note 1) | 15,677 | 7,755 |
| Due to resigned members | 16,400 | 12,900 |
| Taxes | 20,330 | 23,668 |
| Total current liabilities | 113,833 | 107,923 |
| Membership equity | | |
| Proprietary certificates, 500 at $1,500 each—no change during the years | 750,000 | 750,000 |
| Cumulative excess of revenue over expenses | 1,441,732 | 1,412,768 |
|  | 2,191,732 | 2,162,768 |
|  | $2,305,565 | $2,270,691 |

**EXHIBIT 14-13**
**Sample Country Club**
**Statement of Revenue, Expenses, and Changes in Cumulative Excess of Revenue Over Expenses**
**Years Ended March 31, 19X1 and 19X0**

|  | 19X1 | 19X0 |
|---|---:|---:|
| **Revenue** | | |
| Dues | $ 590,000 | $ 600,000 |
| Restaurant and bar charges | 270,412 | 265,042 |
| Greens fees | 171,509 | 163,200 |
| Tennis and swimming fees | 83,829 | 67,675 |
| Initiation fees | 61,475 | 95,220 |
| Locker and room rentals | 49,759 | 49,954 |
| Interest and discounts | 28,860 | 28,831 |
| Golf cart rentals | 26,584 | 24,999 |
| Other—net | 4,011 | 3,893 |
| Total revenue | 1,286,439 | 1,298,814 |
| **Expenses** | | |
| Greens | 241,867 | 244,823 |
| House | 212,880 | 210,952 |
| Restaurant and bar | 153,035 | 136,707 |
| Tennis and swimming | 67,402 | 48,726 |
| General and administrative | 533,838 | 690,551 |
| Net (gains) losses on investments | 98,453 | (98,813) |
| Total expenses | 1,307,475 | 1,232,946 |
| Excess (deficiency) of revenue over expenses before capital additions | (21,036) | 65,868 |
| **Capital additions** | | |
| Assessments for capital improvements | 50,000 | — |
| Excess (deficiency) of revenue over expenses after capital additions | 28,964 | 65,868 |
| Cumulative excess of revenue over expenses—beginning of year | 1,412,768 | 1,346,900 |
| Cumulative excess of revenue over expenses—end of year | $1,441,732 | $1,412,768 |

## SUMMARY

Chapter 14 brings together financial accounting and reporting for two basic types of nonbusiness organizations: (1) health and welfare organizations and (2) certain nonprofit organizations.

Those involved in accounting and auditing of health and welfare organizations have had fairly good guidance in principles and practices for over twenty-five years. How-

**EXHIBIT 14-14**
**Sample Country Club**
**Statement of Changes in Financial Position**
**Years Ended March 31, 19X1 and 19X0**

|  | 19X1 | 19X0 |
|---|---|---|
| **Sources of funds** | | |
| Excess (deficiency) of revenue over expenses before capital additions | $(21,036) | $65,868 |
| Capital additions | 50,000 | — |
| Excess (deficiency) of revenue over expenses after capital additions | 28,964 | 65,868 |
| Add-back provision for depreciation, which does not affect working capital | 40,476 | 61,618 |
| Total from operations | 69,440 | 127,486 |
| Decrease in deferred charges—net | 1,447 | — |
| Total sources | 70,887 | 127,486 |
| **Application of funds** | | |
| Purchases of property and equipment | 137,717 | 84,377 |
| Increase in deferred charges—net | — | 8,909 |
| Total applications | 137,717 | 93,286 |
| Increase (decrease) in working capital | $(66,830) | $34,200 |
| **Changes in the components of working capital are summarized as follows:** | | |
| Increase (decrease) in current assets | | |
| Cash | $ 6,601 | $(70,928) |
| Investments | (98,453) | 98,813 |
| Accounts receivable | 25,933 | 5,000 |
| Inventories | (207) | 8,112 |
| Prepaid expenses | 5,206 | 2,056 |
|  | (60,920) | 43,053 |
| (Increase) decrease in current liabilities | | |
| Accounts payable and accrued expenses | 2,174 | (5,597) |
| Deferred revenues—initiation fees | (7,922) | (3,517) |
| Due to resigned members | (3,500) | (2,700) |
| Taxes | 3,338 | 2,961 |
|  | (5,910) | (8,853) |
| Increase (decrease) in working capital | $(66,830) | $ 34,200 |

## EXHIBIT 14-15
### Sample Religious Organization[8]
### Balance Sheet
### December 31, 19X1

| | Expendable funds | | | | Nonexpendable funds | | Total all funds |
|---|---|---|---|---|---|---|---|
| | Operating | Deposit and loan | Total | Plant fund | Endowment | Annuity and life income | |
| **Assets** | | | | | | | |
| Cash | $1,750,000 | $ 10,000 | $ 1,760,000 | $ 408,000 | $ 20,000 | $ 2,000 | $ 2,190,000 |
| Accounts receivable, less allowance for doubtful receivables of $12,000 | 520,000 | — | 520,000 | — | — | — | 520,000 |
| Pledges receivable, less allowance for doubtful pledges of $25,000 | 500,000 | — | 500,000 | 80,000 | — | — | 580,000 |
| Investments (Note 2) | 3,800,000 | 300,000 | 4,100,000 | 260,000 | 1,300,000 | 178,000 | 5,838,000 |
| Loans receivable, less allowance for doubtful loans of $350,000 | — | 2,600,000 | 2,600,000 | — | — | — | 2,600,000 |
| Advances to plant funds | — | 3,500,000 | 3,500,000 | — | — | — | —* |
| Land, buildings, and equipment at cost, less accumulated depreciation of $23,500,000 (Note 3) | — | — | — | 44,800,000 | — | — | 44,800,000 |
| Other assets | 150,000 | — | 150,000 | — | — | — | 150,000 |
| Total assets | $6,720,000 | $6,410,000 | $13,130,000 | $45,548,000 | $1,320,000 | $180,000 | $56,678,000 |

| Liabilities and fund balances | | | | | | | |
|---|---|---|---|---|---|---|---|
| Accounts payable and accrued expenses | $ 600,000 | — | $ 600,000 | $ 20,000 | — | $120,000 | $ 740,000 |
| Deferred amounts (Note 6) | | | | | | | |
|   Unrestricted | 160,000 | — | 160,000 | — | — | — | 160,000 |
|   Restricted | 870,000 | — | 870,000 | 328,000 | — | 60,000 | 1,258,000 |
| Advances from expendable funds | — | — | — | 3,500,000 | — | — | —* |
| Deposits payable | — | $7,310,000 | 7,310,000 | — | — | — | 7,310,000 |
| Long-term debt (Note 4) | — | — | — | 2,800,000 | — | — | 2,800,000 |
|   Total liabilities | 1,630,000 | 7,310,000 | 8,940,000 | 6,648,000 | — | 180,000 | 12,268,000 |
| Fund balances (deficit) | | | | | | | |
| Unrestricted | | | | | | | |
|   Designated for long-term investment | 3,800,000 | — | 3,800,000 | — | — | — | 3,800,000 |
|   Undesignated | 1,290,000 | (900,000) | 390,000 | — | — | — | 390,000 |
| | 5,090,000 | (900,000) | 4,190,000 | — | — | — | 4,190,000 |
| Restricted | — | — | — | — | $1,320,000 | — | 1,320,000 |
| Net investment in plant | — | — | — | 38,900,000 | — | — | 38,900,000 |
|   Total fund balances (deficit) | 5,090,000 | (900,000) | 4,190,000 | 38,900,000 | 1,320,000 | — | 44,410,000 |
| Total liabilities and fund balances | $6,720,000 | $(900,000) | $13,130,000 | $45,548,000 | $1,320,000 | $180,000 | $56,678,000 |

*Interfund borrowings eliminated in combination.

**EXHIBIT 14-16**
Sample Religious Organization
Statement of Support and Revenue, Expenses,
Capital Additions, and Changes in Fund Balances
Year Ended December 31, 19X1

| | Expendable funds | | | | Plant fund | Nonexpendable endowment funds | Total all funds |
|---|---|---|---|---|---|---|---|
| | Operating | | Deposit and loan | Total | | | |
| | Unrestricted | Restricted | | | | | |
| Support and revenue | | | | | | | |
| Contributions and bequests | $ 6,800,000 | $180,000 | — | $ 6,980,000 | — | — | $ 6,980,000 |
| Fees for services | 4,000,000 | — | — | 4,000,000 | — | — | 4,000,000 |
| Endowment and other investment income | 200,000 | 40,000 | — | 240,000 | — | — | 240,000 |
| Net gain on investment transactions | 250,000 | — | — | 250,000 | — | — | 250,000 |
| Contributed services | 950,000 | — | — | 950,000 | — | — | 950,000 |
| Auxiliary activities | 205,000 | — | $ 535,000 | 740,000 | — | — | 740,000 |
| Total support and revenue | 12,405,000 | 220,000 | 535,000 | 13,160,000 | — | — | 13,160,000 |
| Expenses | | | | | | | |
| Program services | | | | | | | |
| Pastoral | 3,300,000 | 45,000 | — | 3,345,000 | $ 300,000 | — | 3,645,000 |
| Education | 4,000,000 | 80,000 | — | 4,080,000 | 460,000 | — | 4,540,000 |
| Health care | 2,800,000 | 25,000 | — | 2,825,000 | 250,000 | — | 3,075,000 |
| Social services | 900,000 | 50,000 | — | 950,000 | 85,000 | — | 1,035,000 |
| Cemeteries | 220,000 | 20,000 | — | 240,000 | 20,000 | — | 260,000 |
| Religious personnel development | 600,000 | — | — | 600,000 | 55,000 | — | 655,000 |
| Auxiliary activities | 160,000 | — | 685,000 | 845,000 | 5,000 | — | 850,000 |
| Total program services | 11,980,000 | 220,000 | 685,000 | 12,885,000 | 1,175,000 | — | 14,060,000 |

| | | | | | | | |
|---|---|---|---|---|---|---|---|
| Supporting services | | | | | | | |
| General administration | 180,000 | — | — | 180,000 | 15,000 | — | 195,000 |
| Fund raising | 120,000 | — | — | 120,000 | 10,000 | — | 130,000 |
| Total supporting services | 300,000 | — | — | 300,000 | 25,000 | — | 325,000 |
| Total expenses | 12,280,000 | 220,000 | 685,000 | 13,185,000 | 1,200,000 | — | 14,385,000 |
| Excess (deficiency) of support and revenue over expenses before capital additions | 125,000 | — | (150,000) | (25,000) | (1,200,000) | — | (1,225,000) |
| Capital additions | | | | | | | |
| Contributions and bequests | — | — | — | — | 310,000 | 200,000 | 510,000 |
| Investment income | — | — | — | — | 15,000 | — | 15,000 |
| Net gain on investment transactions | — | — | — | — | — | 80,000 | 80,000 |
| Total capital additions | — | — | — | — | 325,000 | 280,000 | 605,000 |
| Excess (deficiency) of support and revenue over expenses after capital additions | 125,000 | — | (150,000) | (25,000) | (875,000) | 280,000 | (620,000) |
| Fund balances (deficit) at beginning of year | 5,315,000 | — | (750,000) | 4,565,000 | 39,425,000 | 1,040,000 | 45,030,000 |
| Transfers to plant funds for plant acquisitions and principal debt service payments financed from operating funds | (350,000) | — | — | (350,000) | 350,000 | — | — |
| Fund balances (deficit) at end of year | $ 5,090,000 | — | $(900,000) | $ 4,190,000 | $38,900,000 | $1,320,000 | $44,410,000 |

## EXHIBIT 14-17
### Sample Religious Organization
### Statement of Changes in Financial Position
### Year Ended December 31, 19X1

|  | Expendable funds | | | | Nonexpendable funds | | Total all funds |
|---|---|---|---|---|---|---|---|
|  | Operating | Deposit and loan | Total | Plant fund | Endowment | Annuity and life income |  |
| **Resources provided** | | | | | | | |
| Excess (deficiency) of support and revenue over expenses before capital additions | $ 125,000 | $(150,000) | $ (25,000) | $(1,200,000) | — | — | $(1,225,000) |
| Capital additions | | | | | | | |
| Contributions and bequests | — | — | — | 310,000 | $200,000 | — | 510,000 |
| Investment income | — | — | — | 15,000 | — | — | 15,000 |
| Net gain on investment transactions | — | — | — | — | 80,000 | — | 80,000 |
| Excess (deficiency) of support and revenue over expenses after capital additions | 125,000 | (150,000) | (25,000) | (875,000) | 280,000 | — | (620,000) |
| Items that do not use (provide) resources | | | | | | | |
| Provision for depreciation | — | — | — | 1,200,000 | — | — | 1,200,000 |

| | | | | | | |
|---|---:|---:|---:|---:|---:|---:|
| Net gain on investment transactions | (250,000) | (15,000) | (265,000) | — | (80,000) | $(12,000) | (357,000) |
| Issuance of long-term debt | — | — | — | 400,000 | — | — | 400,000 |
| Increase in deferred amounts | 650,000 | — | 650,000 | 3,000 | — | 2,000 | 655,000 |
| Proceeds from sale of investments | 1,800,000 | 210,000 | 2,010,000 | 332,000 | 590,000 | 49,000 | 2,981,000 |
| Total resources provided | 2,325,000 | 45,000 | 2,370,000 | 1,060,000 | 790,000 | 39,000 | 4,259,000 |
| Resources used | | | | | | | |
| Purchases of building and equipment | — | — | — | 755,000 | — | — | 755,000 |
| Reduction of long-term debt | — | — | — | 320,000 | — | — | 320,000 |
| Purchases of investments | 1,830,000 | 70,000 | 1,900,000 | — | 784,000 | 36,000 | 2,720,000 |
| Increase in accounts and pledges receivable | 400,000 | — | 400,000 | 5,000 | — | — | 405,000 |
| Increase in loans receivable | — | 45,000 | 45,000 | — | — | — | 45,000 |
| Decrease in accounts payable and accrued expenses | 70,000 | — | 70,000 | 10,000 | — | 2,000 | 82,000 |
| Decrease in deposits payable | — | 10,000 | 10,000 | — | — | — | 10,000 |
| Total resources used | 2,300,000 | 125,000 | 2,425,000 | 1,090,000 | 784,000 | 38,000 | 4,337,000 |
| Transfers to plant funds for plant acquisitions and principal debt service payments financed from operating funds | (350,000) | — | (350,000) | 350,000 | — | — | — |
| Increase (decrease) in cash | $ (325,000) | $ (80,000) | $ (405,000) | $ 320,000 | $ 6,000 | $ 1,000 | $ (78,000) |

**EXHIBIT 14-18**
Sample Union[9]
Balance Sheet
December 31, 19X1
(With Comparative Totals for 19X0)

|  | General fund (undesignated) | Strike insurance fund (designated) | December 31, 19X1 total | December 31, 19X0 total |
|---|---:|---:|---:|---:|
| **Assets** | | | | |
| Current assets | | | | |
| Cash (including savings accounts of $2,100,000 and $1,050,000) (Note 3) | $ 650,800 | $ 1,710,000 | $ 2,360,800 | $ 1,238,100 |
| Investments at market | 491,800 | 9,054,200 | 9,546,000 | 9,640,400 |
| Per capita dues receivable | 51,800 | 133,200 | 185,000 | 189,500 |
| Accrued interest receivable | 1,800 | 210,700 | 212,500 | 214,600 |
| Loans to affiliated organizations (Note 4) | 21,400 | — | 21,400 | 27,300 |
| Accounts receivable (less allowance for doubtful accounts of $2,300 and $2,500) | 67,900 | — | 67,900 | 68,900 |
| Prepaid expenses | 74,900 | — | 74,900 | 71,500 |
| Total current assets | 1,360,400 | 11,108,100 | 12,468,500 | 11,450,300 |
| Property, furniture, and equipment at cost (Note 1) | | | | |
| Land | 678,400 | — | 678,400 | 678,400 |
| Buildings (net of accumulated depreciation of $743,500 and $675,600) | 1,973,400 | — | 1,973,400 | 1,515,500 |
| Furniture and equipment (net of accumulated depreciation of $314,800 and $278,200) | 50,800 | — | 50,800 | 87,400 |
| Total property, furniture, and equipment | 2,702,600 | — | 2,702,600 | 2,281,300 |
| Total assets | $4,063,000 | $11,108,100 | $15,171,100 | $13,731,600 |
| **Liabilities and Fund Balances** | | | | |
| Current liabilities | | | | |
| Accounts payable | $ 337,600 | — | $ 337,600 | $ 423,100 |
| Notes payable | 13,100 | — | 13,100 | 19,600 |
| Affiliation dues payable | 48,800 | — | 48,800 | 49,600 |
| Accrued salaries | 31,500 | — | 31,500 | 33,000 |
| Payroll taxes and employee deductions payable | 89,300 | — | 89,300 | 90,400 |
| Total current liabilities | 520,300 | — | 520,300 | 615,700 |
| Fund balances | 3,542,700 | $11,108,100 | 14,650,800 | 13,115,900 |
| Total liabilities and fund balances | $4,063,000 | $11,108,100 | $15,171,100 | $13,731,600 |

## EXHIBIT 14-19
### Sample Union
### Statement of Revenue, Expense, and Changes in Fund Balances
### Year Ended December 31, 19X1
### (With Comparative Totals for 19X0)

|  | General fund (undesignated) | Strike insurance fund (designated) | December 31, 19X1 total | December 31, 19X0 total |
|---|---|---|---|---|
| **Revenue** | | | | |
| Per capita dues (Note 2) | $9,385,500 | $ 3,532,300 | $12,917,800 | $13,219,800 |
| Initiation fees | 24,100 | — | 24,100 | 22,800 |
| Sales of organizational supplies | 26,700 | — | 26,700 | 17,900 |
| Rental income | 216,300 | — | 216,300 | 216,100 |
| Administrative fees—apprentice training | 11,800 | — | 11,800 | 12,100 |
| Interest income | 28,100 | 609,000 | 637,100 | 644,100 |
| Total revenue | 9,692,500 | 4,141,300 | 13,833,800 | 14,132,800 |
| **Expense (Note 6)** | | | | |
| Program services | | | | |
| Strike assistance to local unions | 877,900 | 2,630,500 | 3,508,400 | 3,345,600 |
| Constitutional convention | 154,600 | — | 154,600 | 132,800 |
| Field office services | | | | |
| Organization | 2,054,000 | — | 2,054,000 | 2,106,500 |
| Negotiation | 2,156,700 | — | 2,156,700 | 2,212,000 |
| Grievance | 924,300 | — | 924,300 | 947,900 |
| Total program services | 6,167,500 | 2,630,500 | 8,798,000 | 8,744,800 |
| Administrative and general | 3,537,700 | 57,600 | 3,595,300 | 1,425,200 |
| Net (gains) losses on investments | (94,400) | — | (94,400) | 2,062,800 |
| Total expense | 9,610,800 | 2,688,100 | 12,298,900 | 12,232,800 |
| Excess of revenue over expense | 81,700 | 1,453,200 | 1,534,900 | 1,900,000 |
| Fund balances, beginning of year | 3,461,000 | 9,654,900 | 13,115,900 | 11,215,900 |
| Fund balances, end of year | $3,542,700 | $11,108,100 | $14,650,800 | $13,115,900 |

ever, those involved in accounting or auditing of certain nonprofit organizations, such as labor unions, churches, trade associations, performing arts organizations, professional organizations, and so forth, have not been as fortunate. They have had little guidance in accounting principles and auditing standards for these organizations until 1978 when *SOP 78-10* was issued by the AICPA.

Fund accounting for all nonprofit organizations is still appropriate for most situations. However, the emphasis on fund accounting was not stressed to any great extent in accounting for these certain other nonprofit organizations. Both types of organizations use full accrual accounting, including depreciation accounting. Financial reporting in both types of organizations covered in this chapter stress combined statements instead of single fund statements.

## EXHIBIT 14-20
### Sample Union
### Statement of Changes in Financial Position
### Year Ended December 31, 19X1
### (With Comparative Totals for 19X0)

|  | General fund (undesignated) | Strike insurance fund (designated) | December 31, 19X1 total | December 31, 19X0 total |
|---|---|---|---|---|
| **Sources of working capital** |  |  |  |  |
| Excess of revenue over expense | $ 81,700 | $1,453,200 | $1,534,900 | $1,900,000 |
| Add charges not affecting working capital |  |  |  |  |
| Depreciation | 104,500 | — | 104,500 | 100,300 |
| Working capital provided | 186,200 | 1,453,200 | 1,639,400 | 2,000,300 |
| **Use of working capital** |  |  |  |  |
| Purchase of property, furniture, and equipment | 525,800 | — | 525,800 | 352,000 |
| Increase (decrease) in working capital | $(339,600) | $1,453,200 | $1,113,600 | $1,648,300 |
| **Changes in working capital** |  |  |  |  |
| Increase (decrease) in current assets |  |  |  |  |
| Cash | $(413,900) | $1,536,600 | $1,122,700 | $ 186,300 |
| Investments | (15,900) | (78,500) | (94,400) | 1,425,200 |
| Per capita dues receivable | (1,300) | (3,200) | (4,500) | (2,300) |
| Accrued interest receivable | (400) | (1,700) | (2,100) | (1,200) |
| Loans to affiliated organizations | (5,900) | — | (5,900) | (2,600) |
| Accounts receivable | (1,000) | — | (1,000) | (100) |
| Prepaid expenses | 3,400 | — | 3,400 | 2,900 |
|  | (435,000) | 1,453,200 | 1,018,200 | 1,608,200 |
| Increase (decrease) in current liabilities |  |  |  |  |
| Accounts payable | (85,500) | — | (85,500) | (32,200) |
| Notes payable | (6,500) | — | (6,500) | (6,500) |
| Affiliation dues payable | (800) | — | (800) | (200) |
| Accrued salaries | (1,500) | — | (1,500) | (800) |
| Payroll taxes and employee deductions payable | (1,100) | — | (1,100) | (400) |
|  | (95,400) | — | (95,400) | (40,100) |
| Increase (decrease) in working capital | $(339,600) | $1,453,200 | $1,113,600 | $1,648,300 |

## QUESTIONS

1 List some of the organizations that would follow the accounting principles discussed in the American Institute of Certified Public Accountants' *Statement of Position 78-10* concerning certain nonprofit organizations.

2 Are the principles of accounting discussed in the AICPA's *Statement of Position 78-10* required

for voluntary health and welfare organizations? If not, where can the principles of accounting for financial reporting for voluntary health and welfare organizations be found?

**3** Are there any significant differences between the principles of accounting for voluntary health and welfare organizations and those for certain nonprofit organizations?

**4** Because the nonprofit organization is required to present its statements on the accrual basis, does it likewise mean that the organization must keep its books and records on the accrual basis? Explain how the books and records can be kept on one basis and the statements prepared on another.

**5** How are pledges recorded in the books of a nonprofit organization and then presented in the statements?

**6** Explain the differences between funds in government and funds in voluntary health and welfare organizations.

**7** Explain the differences between the basis of accounting in voluntary health and welfare organizations and in governmental funds in government.

**8** Do certain nonprofit organizations use accrual or modified accrual accounting?

**9** Explain the distinctions between accrual accounting and modified accrual accounting.

**10** How can depreciation expense be shown in the functional financial statements of a voluntary health and welfare organization if depreciation is recorded in the land, building, and equipment fund?

## PROBLEMS

**14-1** Choose the best answer for each of the following questions.

**1** Voluntary health and welfare organizations, unlike some not-for-profit organizations, record and recognize depreciation of fixed assets because:
  **a** Fixed assets are more likely to be material in amount in a voluntary health and welfare organization than in other not-for-profit organizations.
  **b** Voluntary health and welfare organizations purchase their fixed assets and, therefore, have a historical cost basis from which to determine amounts to be depreciated.
  **c** A fixed asset used by a voluntary health and welfare organization has alternative uses in private industry, and this opportunity cost should be reflected in the organization's financial statements.
  **d** Contributors look for the most efficient use of funds, and since depreciation represents a cost of employing fixed assets, it is appropriate that a voluntary health and welfare organization reflect it as a cost of providing services.

**2** Which of the following funds of a voluntary health and welfare organization does not have a counterpart fund in governmental accounting?
  **a** Current unrestricted
  **b** Land, building, and equipment
  **c** Custodian
  **d** Endowment

**3** Which of the following are considered certain nonprofit organizations?
  **a** Museums, professional associations, social and country clubs
  **b** Religious organizations, private foundations, and colleges and universities
  **c** Labor unions, fraternal organizations, and voluntary health and welfare organizations
  **d** Cemetery associations, civic organizations, and hospitals

**4** The AICPA's *SOP 78-10* recognizes as the appropriate basis of accounting for certain nonprofit organizations:
  **a** The cash basis
  **b** The accrual basis

   **c** The modified accrual basis
   **d** None of the above
  **5** In accounting for certain nonprofit organizations:
   **a** Fund accounting is required for both accounting and reporting
   **b** Fund accounting is appropriate for reporting purposes where necessary
   **c** Fund accounting should not be used
   **d** A single fund is appropriate for both accounting and reporting
  **6** For certain nonprofit organizations:
   **a** The form of the financial statement is prescribed
   **b** The form of the financial statement is not prescribed, but the emphasis is on disclosure
   **c** The only statement required is a statement of activity
   **d** The only statement required is a balance sheet
  **7** Combined statements are required for certain nonprofit organizations if:
   **a** Separate entities solicit funds in the name of the reporting organization and if the funds are transferred to the reporting organization
   **b** The organization is a religious organization
   **c** Combined statements are never required
   **d** The organization assigns functions to a controlled entity through which funding is derived from sources other than public contributions

**14-2** Choose the most appropriate answer for the following:
  **1** The current unrestricted fund of a voluntary health and welfare organization is somewhat comparable to which fund of government?
   **a** General fund
   **b** Special revenue fund
   **c** Capital projects fund
   **d** Debt service fund
  **2** The current restricted fund of a voluntary health and welfare organization is somewhat comparable to which fund of government?
   **a** General fund
   **b** Special revenue fund
   **c** Enterprise fund
   **d** Debt service fund
  **3** Custodian funds of a voluntary health and welfare organization are somewhat comparable to which fund of government?
   **a** General fund
   **b** Special revenue fund
   **c** Agency fund
   **d** Enterprise fund
  **4** Endowment funds of a voluntary health and welfare organization are somewhat comparable to which fund or account group of government?
   **a** Trust fund
   **b** Agency fund
   **c** General fund
   **d** Fixed assets account group
  **5** The basis of accounting for voluntary health and welfare organizations is:
   **a** Full accrual basis
   **b** Modified accrual basis
   **c** Cash basis
   **d** None of the above

**6** In voluntary health and welfare organizations, donated services are recorded as:
  **a** Revenue or expenses
  **b** Only revenue
  **c** Only expenses
  **d** None of the above

**7** Financial statements for voluntary health and welfare organizations are normally prepared on:
  **a** A functional basis
  **b** An object-of-expenditure classification basis
  **c** An organizational basis
  **d** A departmental basis

**14-3** The characteristics of voluntary health and welfare organizations differ in certain respects from the characteristics of state or local governmental units. As an example, voluntary health and welfare organizations derive their revenues primarily from voluntary contributions from the general public, while governmental units derive their revenues from taxes and services provided to their jurisdictions.

**Required**:
**1** Describe fund accounting and discuss whether its use is consistent with the concept that an accounting entity is an economic unit that has control over resources, accepts responsibilities for making and carrying out commitments, and conducts economic activity.
**2** Distinguish between accrual accounting and modified accrual accounting and indicate which method should be used for a voluntary health and welfare organization.
**3** Discuss how methods used to account for fixed assets differ between voluntary health and welfare organizations and governmental units.[10]

**14-4** Local Union 123 of the National Association of _____ is an independently organized union. While the national union often helps during a local strike, the local union decided to provide for any strike contingency by setting up a strike contingency fund. Local members contribute an amount for this fund in addition to the regular due for the general fund.

The trial balances for the two funds of the local union as of January 1, 19X5, appear on page 456.

The following transactions took place during the year:

| | |
|---|---:|
| Billed members for dues: | |
|   General fund | $100,000 |
|   Strike assistance fund | 80,000 |
| Collected dues: | |
|   General fund | 106,500 |
|   Strike assistance fund | 95,000 |
| Accrued national dues | 12,000 |
| Paid national dues | 14,000 |
| Invested surplus cash in treasury notes: | |
|   General fund | $100,000 |
|   Strike assistance fund | 250,000 |
| Interest receivable on investments: | |
|   General fund | 10,000 |
|   Strike assistance fund | 25,000 |
| Interest receivable paid: | |
|   General fund | 11,000 |
|   Strike assistance fund | 30,000 |
| Paid convention expenses | 3,000 |

Paid strike assistance:
  General fund                                         50,000
  Strike assistance fund                              125,000
Expenses payable during year:
  Organization expenses           $5,000
  Negotiation expenses             6,000
  Grievance expenses               4,000               15,000
Expenses paid                                          16,000
Salaries payable during year                           30,000
Taxes payable during year                               5,000
Salaries paid during year                              37,000
Taxes paid during year                                  3,000
Depreciation:
  Building 10 percent
  Furniture and equipment 20 percent

## Trial Balances
### Local Union 123
### National Association of _____
### January 1, 19X5

|  | General fund | | Strike assistance fund | |
| --- | --- | --- | --- | --- |
| Accounts | Dr. | Cr. | Dr. | Cr. |
| Cash | $ 375,000 |  | $ 750,000 |  |
| Investments | 275,000 |  | 1,000,000 |  |
| Dues receivable | 11,500 |  | 25,000 |  |
| Interest receivable | 2,000 |  | 4,000 |  |
| Land | 40,000 |  |  |  |
| Building | 360,000 |  |  |  |
| Allowance for depreciation |  | $ 100,000 |  |  |
| Furniture and equipment | 100,000 |  |  |  |
| Allowance for depreciation |  | 40,000 |  |  |
| Accounts payable |  | 3,000 |  |  |
| National dues payable |  | 5,000 |  |  |
| Accrued salaries payable |  | 12,000 |  |  |
| Payroll taxes payable |  | 2,000 |  |  |
| Fund balances |  | 1,001,500 |  | $1,779,000 |
| Total | $1,163,500 | $1,163,500 | $1,779,000 | $1,779,000 |

**Required**:

Prepare journal entries, record the above transactions for the year on a worksheet, and prepare the following:

1 Balance sheet for 19X5 and compare with previous year.
2 Statement of revenue, expenses, and changes in fund balance with comparative statements.
3 Statement of changes in financial position.

14-5 John Smith, president of the Barlow Furniture Manufacturing Company, has just recently been appointed to act as chairman of the board of the Local United Fund Program during the coming year. In his business activities, he works very closely with his local CPA and uses her advice in statement interpretation and the general uses of accounting in his business, both for management purposes and for financial reporting.

So, upon becoming chairman of the board of the local voluntary health and welfare organization, he reviewed the financial statements and found they were quite different from those he was normally used to in his business. Assume he has asked you to help him understand the distinction between business accounting and statement preparation and the nonprofit voluntary health and welfare organization accounting and statement preparation. You are to respond to his request.

**14-6** In 1950 a group of civic-minded merchants in Albury City organized the "Committee of 100" for the purpose of establishing the Community Sports Club, a nonprofit sports organization for local youth. Each of the committee's 100 members contributed $1,000 toward the club's capital, and each received a participation certificate. In addition, each participant agreed to pay dues of $200 a year for the club's operations. All dues have been collected in full by the end of each fiscal year ending March 31. Members who have discontinued their participation have been replaced by an equal number of new members through transfer of the participation certificates from the former members to the new ones. Following is the club's trial balance at April 1, 19X2:

|  | Dr. | Cr. |
|---|---|---|
| Cash | $ 9,000 | |
| Investments (at market, equal to cost) | 58,000 | |
| Inventories | 5,000 | |
| Land | 10,000 | |
| Building | 164,000 | |
| Accumulated depreciation—building | | $130,000 |
| Furniture and equipment | 54,000 | |
| Accumulated depreciation—furniture and equipment | | 46,000 |
| Accounts payable | | 12,000 |
| Participation certificates (100 at $1,000 each) | | 100,000 |
| Cumulative excess of revenue over expenses | | 12,000 |
| | $300,000 | $300,000 |

Transactions for the year ended March 31, 19X3 were as follows:

| | |
|---|---|
| Collections from participants for dues | $20,000 |
| Snack bar and soda fountain sales | 28,000 |
| Interest and dividends received | 6,000 |
| Additions to accounts payable: | |
|   House expenses | 17,000 |
|   Snack bar and soda fountain | 26,000 |
|   General and administrative | 11,000 |
| Accounts paid | 55,000 |
| Assessments for capital improvements not yet incurred (assessed on March 20, 19X3; none collected by March 31, 19X3; deemed 100 percent collectible during year ending March 31, 19X4) | 10,000 |
| Unrestricted bequest received | 5,000 |

The following adjustments were made:

**1** Investments are valued at market, which amounted to $65,000 at March 31, 19X3. There were no investment transactions during the year.

**2** Depreciation for the year:

| | |
|---|---|
| Building | $4,000 |
| Furniture and equipment | 8,000 |

**3** Allocation of depreciation:

| | |
|---|---|
| House expenses | 9,000 |
| Snack bar and soda fountain | 2,000 |
| General and administrative | 1,000 |

**4** Actual physical inventory at March 31, 19X3 was $1,000, and it pertains to the snack bar and soda fountain.

**Required**:

On a functional basis:

**1** Record the transactions and adjustments in journal entry form for the year ended March 31, 19X3. Omit explanations.

**2** Prepare the appropriate all-inclusive activity statement for the year ended March 31, 19X3.[11]

**14-7** At the end of the fiscal year 19X2, the trial balance for the three funds of the Apple Valley Church was as shown in Exhibit 14-21.

**EXHIBIT 14-21**
**Apple Valley Church**
**Trial Balances**
**Beginning of Fiscal Year—19X2**

| Accounts | Operating fund Dr. | Operating fund Cr. | Missionary fund Dr. | Missionary fund Cr. | Plant fund Dr. | Plant fund Cr. |
|---|---|---|---|---|---|---|
| Cash | $ 175,000 | | $ 25,000 | | $ 100,000 | |
| Pledges receivable | 225,000 | | 80,000 | | | |
| Allowance for uncollectible pledges | | $ 25,000 | | $ 5,000 | | |
| Investments | 800,000 | | | | 500,000 | |
| Interest receivable | 10,000 | | | | 5,000 | |
| Advance to plant fund | 20,000 | | | | | |
| Other assets | 10,000 | | | | | |
| Land | | | | | 150,000 | |
| Buildings | | | | | 1,500,000 | |
| Allowance for depreciation | | | | | | $ 400,000 |
| Equipment | | | | | 500,000 | |
| Allowance for depreciation | | | | | | 100,000 |
| Accounts payable | | 50,000 | | | | |
| Accrued expenses | | 5,000 | | | | |
| Advance from operating fund | | | | | | 20,000 |
| Fund balance—unrestricted | | 1,160,000 | | 100,000 | | |
| Net investment in plant | | | | | | 2,235,000 |
| | $1,240,000 | $1,240,000 | $105,000 | $105,000 | $2,755,000 | $2,755,000 |

During the year the following transactions took place in the operating fund.

**1** Pledges received during the year totalled $425,000, $25,000 of which was not expected to be collected.

**2** Cash received on current and last year's pledges was $525,000.

**3** Of the pledges receivable, $25,000 worth were considered uncollectible and were written off.

**4** Cash contributions were $100,000.

**5** Fees for services were $75,000.

**6** Cash received from investment income was $80,000. Interest receivable at year end was $5,000.

**7** Services contributed for general administrative purposes were valued at $10,000.

**8** Other assets (prepaid insurance) in the amount of $5,000 were used during the year (administrative expenses).

**9** Payments in cash for personal services were as follows:

| | |
|---|---:|
| Pastoral | $100,000 |
| Educational | 40,000 |
| Health care | 50,000 |
| Social services | 40,000 |
| Fund raising | 25,000 |
| Auxiliary activities | 75,000 |
| General administration | 50,000 |
| Total | $380,000 |

Personal services accrued at year end were $5,000. The beginning and ending balances were posted to pastoral services.

**10** Purchases for other objects of expenditures were allocated to the following functions:

| | |
|---|---:|
| Pastoral | $25,000 |
| Educational | 10,000 |
| Health care | 10,000 |
| Social services | 5,000 |
| Auxiliary activities | 5,000 |
| General administration | 20,000 |
| Fund raising | 5,000 |
| Total | $80,000 |

Payments on account were $100,000.

**11** An amount of $100,000 was transferred to the plant fund.

**12** An amount of $100,000 was transferred to the missionary fund.

**13** Additional investments of $100,000 were purchased.

The following transactions took place during the year in the missionary fund.

**1** Pledges amounted to $110,000. It was expected that $10,000 would not be collected.

**2** Cash collected on pledges was $150,000, and $5,000 of uncollectible pledges were written off.

**3** The operating fund transferred $100,000 to the missionary fund.

**4** Missionary support during the year amounted to $200,000.

The following transactions took place during the year in the plant fund.

**1** Transfer of cash from the operating fund was $100,000.

**2** Interest received in cash on investments was $50,000. Interest receivable at the end of the year was $10,000.

**3** An addition to the building costing $100,000 was completed during the year.

**4** The buildings were expected to last forty years with appropriate upkeep. The addition to the building was completed in time to use it for six months.

**5** The equipment was expected to last ten years.

**Required**:

1 Post the yearly transactions to a worksheet for each of the funds. Head the columns on the worksheets as follows:

| (1) | (2) | | (3) | | (4) | | (5) | | (6) | |
|---|---|---|---|---|---|---|---|---|---|---|
| | Beginning balances | | Transactions | | Trial balance | | Statement of activity | | Balance sheet | |
| Accounts | Dr. | Cr. | Dr. | Cr. | Dr. | Cr. | Dr. | Cr. | Dr. | Cr. |

2 Prepare comparative financial statements needed for the Apple Valley Church.

# NOTES

1 See American Institute of Certified Public Accountants, *Industry Audit Guide. Audits of Voluntary Health and Welfare Organizations* (New York: American Institute of Certified Public Accountants, Inc., 1978).

2 See American Institute of Certified Public Accountants, *Audit and Accounting Guide. Audits of Certain Nonprofit Organizations* (New York: American Institute of Certified Public Accountants, 1981).

3 AICPA, *Industry Audit Guide: Health and Welfare Organizations*, p. v.

4 Ibid., p. 12.

5 Price Waterhouse & Company, *Accounting Principles and Reporting Practices for Certain Nonprofit Organizations. A Discussion of the More Important Provisions of the AICPA Statement of Position* (Washington, D.C.: Price Waterhouse & Company, 1979), pp. 3–9.

6 Ibid., p. 3.

7 AICPA *Audit and Accounting Guide. Audits of Certain Nonprofit Organizations*, pp. 114–117.

8 Ibid., pp. 146–152.

9 Ibid., pp. 160–166.

10 Adapted from American Institute of Certified Public Accountants. *Uniform CPA Examination Questions and Unofficial Answers* (New York: American Institute of Certified Public Accountants, May 1977).

11 Ibid., May 1983.

# CHAPTER 15

# COLLEGES AND UNIVERSITIES

Since the end of World War II, enrollment in colleges and universities has increased considerably. Universities formerly having only 3,000 to 5,000 students now have 20,000 to 30,000 students. In addition, much of the funded research done in the United States takes place in colleges and universities. Funded research from the federal government, state governments, and private foundations requires strict accountability for those monies. Grants often must be accounted for in funds that are restricted for these special research purposes—separate and distinct from the money used for educational purposes. Therefore, fund accounting is used in colleges and universities, much as it is in governmental units.

The concepts of fund accounting are comparable, whether the funds are in government or in colleges and universities. Yet there are sufficient differences in the practice of fund accounting in the two types of organizations to warrant discussion and illustrations of each type. For example, accounting for state and local governments generally requires the use of the modified accrual basis of accounting. College and university accounting, on the other hand, frequently uses the accrual (expenditure) basis of accounting. In addition, the titles of the various funds are somewhat different in the two types of organizations. For example, in local government, the title used for the general operations of the entity is the "general fund." In college and university accounting, the title of the operating fund is the "current fund." Moreover, instead of having special revenue funds, the current fund is divided into unrestricted current funds and restricted current funds, the latter being comparable to special revenue funds. Another major distinction is the requirement in government for a statement comparison, when budgets are used, between the budget and the actual revenue and expenditures. Budgets often are not required to be used in college and university accounting, but they are in the general fund of government.

The purpose of this chapter, therefore, is to describe and illustrate the particular characteristics of college and university accounting. The major differences between college and university accounting and governmental accounting will often be used to point out those particular characteristics.

## PARTICULAR CHARACTERISTICS OF COLLEGE AND UNIVERSITY ACCOUNTING

The discussion of the similarities and differences between the two types of organizations will center upon the following topics:

1 Accounting principles for colleges and universities
2 Budgetary accounting
3 Funds used in college and university accounting

The principles and practices illustrated and explained in this chapter will be for the purpose of external financial reporting. Parts III and IV will go into the basic approaches to accounting for internal decision making.

### Accounting Principles for Colleges and Universities

The National Association of College and University Business Officers (NACUBO) has provided the most authoritative statement of accounting principles for colleges and universities, while the Governmental Accounting Standards Board (GASB) does the same for state and local governmental units. The American Institute of Certified Public Accountants (AICPA) recognizes the principles provided by these two bodies as those principles that CPAs should use when making audits of these two types of organizations.

The statement of the principles of accounting by NACUBO requires that the accrual basis of revenue and expenditure accounting be used for all funds in college and university accounting, unless the amount is immaterial. Thus, prepaid expenses and interest are recognized in college and university accounting. Depreciation is not required in any fund except in endowment or similar funds on depreciable assets held for investment. Thus, *revenues are recorded when earned and expenditures are recorded when materials are received or services are used*. Expenditures would include those for capital assets as well as for current expenditures. Depreciation, however, can be recorded in plant funds in order to determine expired capital costs for evaluating management performance or for managerial decision making, much as is done in governmental accounting in the general fixed assets account group. In general, all purchases, including investments, are reported at cost, and gifts are reported at fair market value. Transfers between funds, except temporary loans, should be recorded as transfers rather than as revenue.

As in any profit-type entity, profit-type activities in colleges and universities use the full accrual method. Thus, current expenses are accrued in the current period, and future period expenses are deferred to the future period. Auxiliary enterprises (departments) of colleges and universities, such as rooms and meals, are a part of the current fund operations and are not considered profit-type activities. The only profit-type activities in college and university operations would be those not considered a part of the normal operations of the university or college and basically set up for revenue and expense purposes; such an example would be a research organization that provides services to the government and businesses and additional income to the faculty.

## Budgetary Accounting

Accounting practices may vary among the different kinds of colleges and universities; for example, some colleges and universities use budgetary accounting and some do not. Many colleges and universities are public institutions funded by state or local government. Their primary revenues come from the governmental body, which is controlled by a budget. So revenue and expenditure recognition for this group of universities and colleges closely follows governmental accounting principles as they pertain to budgetary practices.

This approach to accounting, however, is not essential to private or church-related colleges and universities. These colleges and universities, more often than not, must rely on tuition and fees as the primary source of their revenue. So, revenue and cost recognition of a private institution is more closely related to practices in profit-type activities than to those costs supported by revenue from state or local government appropriations. GAAP for colleges and universities, therefore, do not require budget and budget comparisons, even though many of the institutions follow the practices for budgetary control found in governmental units. When colleges and universities are state or municipality supported, they still follow GAAP for colleges and universities, even though they may follow many governmental practices. If the state or municipality requires certain governmental principles to be followed, they also must be incorporated into the accounting system.

## Similarities and Differences Between College and University and Governmental Principles of Accounting

The following is a comparison of the preceding principles of accounting with those previously discussed for governmental accounting.

*Accrual accounting:* Current funds use the full accrual revenue and expenditure basis. Thus, fixed assets are not capitalized in current funds; prepaid expenditures and deferred revenues are shown; allowances for doubtful accounts are shown. Purchases are shown at cost, and gifts are shown at fair-market value. Long-term liabilities and long-term assets are recorded in the plant funds and not in the current funds.

*Budgetary control:* Budgetary control is optional and not required. If used, it is comparable to budgetary control in government.

*Interfund transfers:* Mandatory transfers, such as interest, must be segregated from nonmandatory transfers in the statements. Transfers between funds must be shown as transfers and not revenues. A permanent advance between funds should be recorded as a permanent advance to the fund balance of the recipient fund. Interfund short-term borrowing should be shown as a current receivable of the fund making the loan and a current payable of the fund receiving the loan.

## Funds Used in College and University Accounting

The funds most commonly found in college and university accounting are:

1 Current funds—unrestricted and restricted
2 Loan funds
3 Endowment and similar funds
4 Annuity and life income funds
5 Plant funds
6 Agency funds

**Current Funds—Unrestricted** These funds are those resources that can be spent, without restriction, to accomplish the primary missions of the college or university—teaching, research, and public service. Unrestricted current funds may also include auxiliary services, such as dormitories and dining facilities, that are necessary to accomplish the primary missions of the college or university.

**Current Funds—Restricted** These funds are those resources that can be spent only for specified purposes, such as a grant for a specific research project. While the restricted current funds are a part of the total current funds, the accounting for the resources in those funds is similar to that for any other specific separate entity. The results of the restricted funds transactions are shown together with the unrestricted funds only in the statements. Transactions in the restricted funds are kept separate from the transactions in the unrestricted current funds. Thus, interfund transactions between restricted current funds and unrestricted current funds—both the debits and the credits—would have to take place in both of the funds.

When resources are moved from one fund to another, other than temporary loans, the amounts should be recorded as transfers. This includes amounts that are required to be transferred—mandatory transfers—such as required amounts transferred to the plant funds for payment of interest and principal on indebtedness. It also includes nonmandatory transfers—voluntary transfers—which should be treated separately from mandatory transfers in the statements. The statement of current fund revenues, expenditures, and other changes, therefore, includes both mandatory and nonmandatory transfers.

When budgets are used and proposed expenditures are encumbered, comparable to current principles of local government accounting, these encumbrances are not shown as current-year expenditures in the financial statements. Thus, it can be seen that current funds in college and university accounting are comparable to general and special revenue funds in governmental accounting.

Since restricted current funds are restricted by the donor to specific purposes, revenue is generally recognized only when expenditures are made for the restricted purpose. Prior to revenue recognition, the balance available for expenditure is carried in a fund balance account that is restricted for the donor's purpose.

**Loan Funds** The purpose of loan funds is to account for loans to students, faculty, and staff. Since the fund is an interest-earning fund, the accounting for the resources of these funds is on the accrual basis as they relate to income and expenses, including such items as estimated losses on bad debts. No such type of fund ordinarily exists in governmental accounting.

**Endowment and Similar Funds**  Endowment funds are nonexpendable funds established by gifts from outside donors, usually authorizing the income to be used for operations of the institution or for other purposes. This type of endowment fund is called a *pure endowment fund*. *Term endowment funds* are those whose principal, all or part, may be used by the institution after a certain period of time. *Quasi-endowment funds* are those whose resources come from the governing body of the university rather than from outside donors.

In the past, income stabilization reserves were used as a means of keeping the income from the endowment resources comparable from year to year. These reserves are no longer allowed under current accounting principles. Current principles of accounting also allow the institution to value investments at current market as well as at cost. These funds can be related to fiduciary funds of government.

**Annuity and Life Income Funds**  Some donors give investments to colleges and universities with the stipulation they will receive a certain amount from the investments each year until they die or some other occasion occurs. Then, the corpus will go to the college or university. *Annuity funds* provide for the payment of a specific amount periodically to the donor or to specified individuals until the expiration of an agreed-upon time. **Life income funds** agree to pay to the donor or specified individuals the income from the assets donated for the lifetime of the income beneficiaries. After the designated time, usually the life of the beneficiaries, the principal of the fund then becomes the property of the institution, usually as an endowment to the university. Such funds as annuity and life income funds seldom are used in governmental accounting.

**Plant Funds**  Plant funds in a college or university include not only the typical fixed assets and long-term debt found in the account groups of a local governmental unit, but also include resources that can be used to acquire additional fixed assets or to retire indebtedness. Since fixed assets and long-term debt are not recorded in the current funds of the institution, plant funds are used to keep the record of these assets and long-term debt. In addition, these funds are used to accumulate resources for the replacement or renewal of the fixed assets. Likewise, these funds also accumulate sums for the retirement of indebtedness, usually by transfers from the current funds. Thus, plant funds operate much as governmental debt service funds, capital projects funds, general long-term debt account groups, and general fixed assets account groups.

**Agency Funds**  These funds hold resources that belong to others. The college or university holds monies on deposit from students or others that never become a part of the assets of the institution. Agency funds in colleges and universities are similar to agency funds in government.

## Similarities and Differences Between Funds in Colleges and Universities and Funds in Government

The following listing provides a comparison of funds in college and university accounting and funds in governmental accounting.

*Current funds:* Unrestricted current funds and restricted current funds are separate accounting entities for operating purposes but are combined for reporting purposes. They include only current assets to be used for current operating purposes. Current restricted resources, however, must be used in accordance with restrictions provided by the grantor. These funds are comparable to the general fund and special revenue funds of government.

*Loan funds:* These funds account for resources used to provide loans to students, faculty, and staff. There is no comparable fund in government.

*Endowment funds:* These funds include three types: (1) pure endowment funds account for resources in which the principal lasts in perpetuity and the income is used in accordance with stipulations of outside agency or persons; (2) term endowment funds account for resources for which after a period, all or part of the principal can be expended; and (3) quasi-endowment funds account for funds stipulated by the institution to be retained to be invested. These funds are comparable to trust funds of government.

*Plant funds:* These funds include four subgroups: (1) unexpended funds for acquisition of fixed assets, (2) unexpended funds for renewal or replacement, (3) unexpended funds to be used for retirement of long-term debt, and (4) capitalized fixed assets and fixed liabilities. The plant funds include much of what would be in the general fixed assets and general long-term debt account groups, the capital projects funds, and the debt service funds in government.

*Annuity and life income funds:* These entities are used to account for resources that provide annuities or life income to others upon the death of the beneficiary. The balance of the fund goes to the university. They are not used in government.

*Agency funds:* These funds are used to account for resources kept by the college or university as a custodian for others. They are comparable to agency funds in government.

## Financial Reporting

For current funds, the statements should include: (1) a balance sheet, (2) a statement of changes in fund balance, and (3) a statement of current funds revenues, expenditures, and other changes. For all other funds, only a balance sheet and a statement of changes in fund balance are needed.

Reporting should be by function. No separate report needs to be made between program and supporting services.

Depreciation accounting can be shown in plant funds, but not in current funds. Unfunded grants are not accrued, but can be shown in the footnotes to the statements.

If budgetary accounting is used, comparable to governmental accounting, encumbrances are not shown as expenditures and the reserve for encumbrances is a part of the fund balance and not shown as a liability.

## ILLUSTRATIVE TRANSACTIONS

The preceding discussion on college and university accounting has brought out the distinctions and characteristics of this type of accounting practice. Two basic fund categories will be used to illustrate the accounting for colleges and universities—the current unrestricted part of current funds and all of the subgroups of plant funds. With these illustrations, the reader should be able to grasp the concepts and practices for the other funds from the prior illustrations of governmental accounting.

Since one of our purposes is to show the similarities and differences between college and university accounting and governmental accounting, three particular distinctions should be noted in the illustrations: (1) the differences between the modified accrual basis and the accrual basis of revenue and expenditure accounting; (2) the equivalent of more than one fund or account group specifically illustrated in the plant funds; and (3) the difference between statement presentation for the college and university funds and governmental financial reports.

## Unrestricted Current Funds

Much as is found in general and special revenue funds of government, restricted current funds of colleges and universities follow the same basic accounting practices as are found in the unrestricted funds, except for revenue recognition as discussed previously. However, restricted current funds are concerned with the revenues, expenditures, assets, liabilities, and fund balances as they pertain to the restricted requirements for the fund.

The balances at the beginning of the year in the unrestricted current fund of Loriann State University are as follows:

**Loriann State University**
**Unrestricted Current Fund**
**Trial Balance**
**July 1, 19X1**
(In Thousands)

| Accounts | Dr. | Cr. |
|---|---|---|
| Cash | $ 200 | |
| Investments | 600 | |
| Accounts receivable | 350 | |
| Allowance for bad debts | | $ 40 |
| Inventory | 140 | |
| Prepaid expenses | 40 | |
| Accounts payable | | 180 |
| Student deposits | | 50 |
| Due to other funds | | 260 |
| Deferred credits | | 40 |
| Fund balance | | 760 |
| | $1,330 | $1,330 |

Exhibit 15-1, a list of all transactions and journal entries, brings together all of the transactions in summary form for the financial activities during the year in the unrestricted current fund. The adjusting entries of the prior year for student deposits and deferred credits are reversed at the beginning of the year in order to place the deferrals into the proper revenue accounts for this year. The journal entries, also shown in this exhibit, are posted to the worksheet (see Exhibit 15-2) from which these statements are developed: Exhibit 15-3, the balance sheet; Exhibit 15-4, statement of changes in fund balances; and Exhibit 15-5, statement of current funds revenues, expenditures, and other changes.

## EXHIBIT 15-1
## Loriann State University
## Unrestricted Current Fund
## Transactions and Journal Entries for Year 19X1
(In Thousands)

| No. | Transactions | | | Journal entries | Dr. | Cr. |
|---|---|---|---|---|---|---|
| 1 | Reversed student fees for prepaid deposits—$50 | | | Student deposits<br>Student fees | 50 | 50 |
| 2 | Reversed amount for deferred sales—auxiliary departments—$40 | | | Deferred credits<br>Sales and services—auxiliary departments | 40 | 40 |
| 3 | Accrued amount due from state appropriation—$5,000 | | | Due from state<br>State appropriation | 5,000 | 5,000 |
| 4 | Collected appropriation—$5,000 | | | Cash<br>Due from state | 5,000 | 5,000 |
| 5 | Student fees billed—$5,350 | | | Accounts receivable<br>Student fees | 5,350 | 5,350 |
| 6 | Collection on student fees—$5,280 | | | Cash<br>Accounts receivable | 5,280 | 5,280 |
| 7 | Sold goods and services—education department, $100; auxiliary departments, $300 | | | Cash<br>Sales and services—educational departments<br>Sales and services—auxiliary departments | 400 | 100<br><br>300 |
| 8 | Purchased short-term investments—$50 | | | Investments<br>Cash | 50 | 50 |
| 9 | Billed students for auxiliary services—$2,000; cash collected on sales of auxiliary services—$1,000 | | | Accounts receivable<br>Cash<br>Sales and services—auxiliary departments | 2,000<br>1,000 | <br><br>3,000 |
| 10 | Received cash from accounts receivable—$2,000 | | | Cash<br>Accounts receivable | 2,000 | 2,000 |
| 11 | Due to other funds for mandatory and nonmandatory transfers—$2,880<br>Debt service—educational<br>Debt service—auxiliary departments<br>Renewals and replacements<br>Loan fund—matching grant<br>Nonmandatory—transfers | | 200<br>500<br>800<br>200<br>1,180 | Mandatory transfers—<br>Debt service—educational<br>Debt service—auxiliary departments<br>Renewals and replacement<br>Loan fund—matching grant<br>Nonmandatory transfers<br>Due to other funds | <br>200<br>500<br>800<br>200<br>1,180 | <br><br><br><br><br>2,880 |
| 12 | Paid $2,900 to other funds | | 2,880 | Due to other funds<br>Cash | 2,900 | 2,900 |
| 13 | Set up accounts payable for expenditures:<br>Instruction<br>Research<br>Public service<br>Academic support<br>Student service<br>Institutional service<br>Operation and maintenance of plant | | 5,000<br>580<br>500<br>300<br>200<br>600<br><br>1,020 | Expenditures:<br>Instruction<br>Research<br>Public service<br>Academic support<br>Student service<br>Institutional service<br>Operation and maintenance of plant<br>Scholarships and fellowships | 5,000<br>580<br>500<br>300<br>200<br>600<br><br>1,020<br>300 | |

**EXHIBIT 15-1**
(*continued*)

| No. | Transactions | Journal entries | Dr. | Cr. |
|---|---|---|---|---|
| | Scholarships and fellowships 300 | Accounts payable | | 8,500 |
| 14 | Paid accounts—$8,440 | Accounts payable<br>Cash | 8,440 | 8,440 |
| 15 | Set up accounts payable for expenditure for auxiliary departments—$2,500 | Expenditures—auxiliary departments<br>Accounts payable | 2,500 | 2,500 |
| 16 | Paid accounts—$2,500 | Accounts payable<br>Cash | 2,500 | 2,500 |
| 17 | Wrote off $20 of bad debts | Allowance for bad debts<br>Accounts receivable | 20 | 20 |
| 18 | Cash collected from miscellaneous sources of revenue | Cash<br>Other revenue sources | 200 | 200 |
| 19 | Students deposited $60 for payment of future fees | Cash<br>Student deposits | 60 | 60 |
| A1 | Adjustments to bad debts: estimated to need $40 in account—add $20 more—related to research | Expenditures—research<br>Allowance for bad debts | 20 | 20 |
| A2 | Inventory showed a decrease of $40 related to operation and maintenance of plant | Inventory<br>Expenditures—operation and maintenance of plant | 20 | 20 |
| A3 | Revenue of $40 from auxiliary departments deferred to new period | Sales and services—auxiliary departments<br>Deferred credits | 40 | 40 |

## Plant Funds

Plant funds have been described previously in this chapter. As has been seen, the equivalents of four funds and account groups of government are included in the single classification, "plant funds," of colleges and universities. They are unexpended plant fund, renewals and replacements fund, retirement of indebtedness fund, and investment in plant fund. The beginning balances for each of these categories are shown on page 472.

Exhibit 15-6, the transactions and journal entries for each of these categories of plant funds, shows the type of activities that are encountered in these funds. While the plant fund is considered as one fund for college and university accounting and reporting purposes, the accounting transactions take place in the equivalent of four funds. Note that the investment in plant fund is not considered an account group but a part of the plant funds. Exhibit 15-6 brings together all of the activities for the year in terms of transactions and journal entries for the plant funds. Exhibit 15-7 records each of these journal entries in a worksheet, from which the following statements can be prepared: Exhibit 15-8, the balance sheet, and Exhibit 15-9, the statement of changes in fund balances.

## EXHIBIT 15-2
## Unrestricted Current Fund
## Loriann State University
## Worksheet for Year 19X1
(In Thousands)

| Accounts | Beginning balances Dr. | Beginning balances Cr. | Transactions for the year No. | Transactions for the year Dr. | Transactions for the year No. | Transactions for the year Cr. |
|---|---|---|---|---|---|---|
| **Assets:** | | | | | | |
| Cash | 200 | | 4 | 5,000 | 8 | 50 |
| | | | 6 | 5,280 | 14 | 8,440 |
| | | | 7 | 400 | 12 | 2,900 |
| | | | 9 | 1,000 | 16 | 2,500 |
| | | | 10 | 2,000 | | |
| | | | 18 | 200 | | |
| | | | 19 | 60 | | |
| Investments | 600 | | 8 | 50 | | |
| Accounts receivable | 350 | | 5 | 5,350 | 6 | 5,280 |
| | | | 9 | 2,000 | 10 | 2,000 |
| | | | | | 17 | 20 |
| Allowance for bad debts | | 40 | 17 | 20 | | |
| Due from state | | | 3 | 5,000 | 4 | 5,000 |
| Inventory | 140 | | | | | |
| Prepaid expenses | 40 | | | | | |
| **Liabilities:** | | | | | | |
| Accounts payable | | 180 | 14 | 8,440 | 13 | 8,500 |
| | | | 16 | 2,500 | 15 | 2,500 |
| Student deposits | | 50 | 1 | 50 | 19 | 60 |
| Due to other funds | | 260 | 12 | 2,900 | 11 | 2,880 |
| Deferred credits | | 40 | 2 | 40 | | |
| Fund balance | | 760 | | | | |
| **Revenues:** | | | | | | |
| Student fees | | | | | 1 | 50 |
| | | | | | 5 | 5,350 |
| State appropriation | | | | | 3 | 5,000 |
| Sales and services—education departments | | | | | 7 | 100 |
| Sales and services—auxiliary departments | | | | | 2 | 40 |
| | | | | | 7 | 300 |
| | | | | | 9 | 3,000 |
| Other revenue sources | | | | | 18 | 200 |
| **Expenditures:** | | | | | | |
| Instruction | | | 13 | 5,000 | | |
| Research | | | 13 | 580 | | |
| Public service | | | 13 | 500 | | |
| Academic support | | | 13 | 300 | | |
| Student services | | | 13 | 200 | | |
| Institutional services | | | 13 | 600 | | |
| Operation and maintenance of plant | | | 13 | 1,020 | | |
| Scholarships and fellowships | | | 13 | 300 | | |
| Auxiliary departments | | | 15 | 2,500 | | |

## EXHIBIT 15-2
*(continued)*

| Trial balance | | Adjustments | | | | Statement of changes in fund balances | | Balance sheet | |
|---|---|---|---|---|---|---|---|---|---|
| Dr. | Cr. | No. | Dr. | No. | Cr. | Dr. | Cr. | Dr. | Cr. |
| 250 | | | | | | | | 250 | |
| | | | | | | | | | |
| 650 | | | | | | | | 650 | |
| 400 | | | | | | | | 400 | |
| | 20 | | | A1 | 20 | | | | 40 |
| 140 | | A2 | 20 | | | | | 160 | |
| 40 | | | | | | | | 40 | |
| | 240 | | | | | | | | 240 |
| | 60 | | | | | | | | 60 |
| | 240 | | | | | | | | 240 |
| | | | | A3 | 40 | | | | 40 |
| | 760 | | | | | | | | 760 |
| | 5,400 | | | | | | 5,400 | | |
| | 5,000 | | | | | | 5,000 | | |
| | 100 | | | | | | 100 | | |
| | 3,340 | A3 | 40 | | | | 3,300 | | |
| | 200 | | | | | | 200 | | |
| 5,000 | | | | | | 5,000 | | | |
| 580 | | A1 | 20 | | | 600 | | | |
| 500 | | | | | | 500 | | | |
| 300 | | | | | | 300 | | | |
| 200 | | | | | | 200 | | | |
| 600 | | | | | | 600 | | | |
| 1,020 | | | | A2 | 20 | 1,000 | | | |
| 300 | | | | | | 300 | | | |
| 2,500 | | | | | | 2,500 | | | |

**EXHIBIT 15-2**
*(continued)*

| Account | Beginning balances Dr. | Beginning balances Cr. | Transactions for the year No. | Transactions for the year Dr. | Transactions for the year No. | Transactions for the year Cr. |
|---|---|---|---|---|---|---|
| Mandatory transfers: | | | | | | |
|   Debt service—educational | | | 11 | 200 | | |
| Renewals and replace-<br>  ments | | | 11 | 800 | | |
| Loan fund matching<br>  grant | | | 11 | 200 | | |
| Debt service—auxiliary<br>  departments | | | 11 | 500 | | |
| Nonmandatory transfers | | | 11 | 1,180 | | |
| | $1,330 | $1,330 | | $54,370 | | $54,370 |
| To fund balance | | | | | | |

**Loriann State University**
**Plant Funds**
**Trial Balances**
**July 1, 19X0**
*(In Thousands)*

| | Unexpended | Renewals and replacements | Retirement of indebtedness | Investment in plant |
|---|---|---|---|---|
| Assets: | | | | |
|   Cash | $ 800 | $ 10 | $100 | |
|   Investments | 3,000 | 500 | | |
|   Due from unrestricted<br>    current funds | 240 | 5 | | |
|   Deposits with trustees | | | 500 | |
|   Land | | | | $ 1,000 |
|   Land improvements | | | | 2,000 |
|   Buildings | | | | 48,000 |
|   Equipment | | | | 28,000 |
|   Library books | | | | 150 |
| Total assets | $4,040 | $515 | $600 | $79,150 |
| Liabilities and fund balances: | | | | |
|   Accounts payable | $ 10 | | | |
|   Notes payable | 100 | | | $ 1,600 |
|   Bonds payable | | | | 5,000 |
|   Mortgages payable | | | | 500 |
|   Net investment in plant | | | | 72,050 |
|   Fund balances | | | | |
|     Restricted | 2,500 | $150 | $250 | |
|     Unrestricted | 1,430 | 365 | 350 | |
| Total liabilities and fund<br>  balances | $4,040 | $515 | $600 | $79,150 |

**EXHIBIT 15-2**
(*continued*)

| Trial balance | | Adjustments | | | | Statement of changes in fund balances | | Balance sheet | |
|---|---|---|---|---|---|---|---|---|---|
| Dr. | Cr. | No. | Dr. | No. | Cr. | Dr. | Cr. | Dr. | Cr. |
| 200 | | | | | | | 200 | | |
| 800 | | | | | | | 800 | | |
| 200 | | | | | | | 200 | | |
| 500 | | | | | | | 500 | | |
| 1,180 | | | | | | | 1,180 | | |
| $15,360 | $15,360 | | $80 | | $80 | $13,880 | $14,000 | $1,500 | $1,380 |
| | | | | | | 120 | | | 120 |
| | | | | | | $14,000 | $14,000 | $1,500 | $1,500 |

The unexpended plant fund has built or purchased part of the property through the issuance of bonds. While it is not shown in the illustration, the expenditures for the construction in progress can be immediately reflected in the investment in plant fund as work in progress (along with the bonds payable) or shown upon completion of the project. Assuming the projects were completed during the year, the following transactions would be made (turn to page 480):

**EXHIBIT 15-3**
**Loriann State University**
**Balance Sheet—Unrestricted Current Fund**
**June 30, 19X1**
(In Thousands)

| | Current year | Prior year |
|---|---|---|
| Assets: | | |
| Cash | $ 250 | $ 200 |
| Investments | 650 | 600 |
| Accounts receivable | 400 | 350 |
| Less allowance for bad debts | (40) | (40) |
| Inventories | 160 | 140 |
| Prepaid expenses | 40 | 40 |
| Total assets | $1,460 | $1,290 |
| Liabilities and fund balances: | | |
| Accounts payable | 240 | 180 |
| Student deposits | 60 | 50 |
| Due to other funds | 240 | 260 |
| Deferred credits | 40 | 40 |
| Fund balance | 880 | 760 |
| Total liabilities and fund balance | $1,460 | $1,290 |

## EXHIBIT 15-4
## Loriann State University
## Statement of Changes in Fund Balances—
## Unrestricted Current Fund
## Year Ended June 30, 19X1
### (In Thousands)

| | | |
|---|---:|---:|
| Revenues and other additions: | | |
|   Unrestricted current fund revenues | | $14,000 |
| Expenditures and other deductions: | | |
|   Educational and general expenditures | | 8,500 |
|   Auxiliary departments expenditures | | 2,500 |
| Transfers among funds: | | |
|   Mandatory: | | |
|     Principal and interest | $700 | |
|     Renewals and replacements | 800 | |
|     Loan fund matching grant | 200 | 1,700 |
|   Nonmandatory | | 1,180 |
| Total expenditures and other deductions | | 13,880 |
| Net increase in fund balance | | 120 |
| Fund balance—beginning of year | | 760 |
| Fund balance—end of year | | $ 880 |

## EXHIBIT 15-5
## Loriann State University
## Statement of Current Funds Revenues, Expenditures,
## and Other Changes
## Unrestricted Current Fund
## For Year Ended June 30, 19X1
### (In Thousands)

| | |
|---|---:|
| Revenues: | |
|   Tuition and fees | $ 5,400 |
|   State appropriations | 5,000 |
|   Sales and services—education departments | 100 |
|   Sales and services—auxiliary departments | 3,300 |
|   Other revenue sources | 200 |
| Total revenues | 14,000 |
| Expenditures and mandatory transfers: | |
|   Educational and general | |
|     Instruction | 5,000 |
|     Research | 500 |
|     Public service | 500 |
|     Academic support | 300 |
|     Student services | 200 |
|     Institutional services | 600 |
|     Operation and maintenance of plant | 1,000 |
|     Scholarships and fellowships | 300 |
|   Educational and general expenditures | 8,500 |
|   Mandatory transfers | |
|     Principal and interest | 200 |
|     Renewals and replacements | 800 |
|     Loan fund matching grants | 200 |
| Total educational and general | 9,700 |

## EXHIBIT 15-5
*(continued)*

| | | |
|---|---:|---:|
| Auxiliary departments | | |
|   Expenditures | | 2,500 |
|   Mandatory transfers for principal and interest | | 500 |
|   Total auxiliary departments | | 3,000 |
| Total expenditures and mandatory transfers | | 12,700 |
| Nonmandatory transfers to other funds | | 1,180 |
| Total expenditures and transfers | | 13,880 |
| Net increase in fund balance | | $ 120 |

## EXHIBIT 15-6
### Loriann State University
### Plant Funds
### Transactions and Journal Entries
### For Year 19X1
*(In Thousands)*

| No. | Transactions | Journal entries | Dr. | Cr. |
|---|---|---|---:|---:|
| | | **Unexpended Plant Fund** | | |
| 1 | State appropriated $100, which was accrued | Due from state<br>  State appropriation—restricted | $ 100 | $ 100 |
| 2 | Cash was collected for investment income, $10 | Cash<br>  Investment income—restricted | 10 | 10 |
| 3 | Amount due from current fund unrestricted, $200, was accrued | Due from unrestricted current fund<br>  Transfers—unrestricted | 200 | 200 |
| 4 | Cash was collected from expired term endowment, $100 | Cash<br>  Expired term endowment—restricted | 100 | 100 |
| 5 | Another note payable for $100 was issued | Cash<br>  Notes payable | 100 | 100 |
| 6 | Cash was received from the issuance of $800 of bonds | Cash<br>  Bonds payable | 800 | 800 |
| 7 | Cash of $250 was received from a private gift | Cash<br>  Private gifts, grants, and contracts | 250 | 250 |
| 8 | Cash of $232 was received from the current fund, unrestricted | Cash<br>  Due from unrestricted current funds | 232 | 232 |
| 9 | Cash of $100 was collected from the state | Cash<br>  Due from state | 100 | 100 |
| 10 | Accounts payable for expenditures for plant facilities were set up, $1,302 | Expenditures—plant facilities<br>  Accounts payable | 1,302 | 1,302 |
| 11 | Paid $1,292 on the accounts payable | Accounts payable<br>  Cash | 1,292 | 1,292 |
| 12 | Purchased $500 of additional investments | Investments<br>  Cash | 500 | 500 |
| 13 | Bonds payable transferred to investment in plant fund along with the assets built or purchased | Bonds payable<br>  Fund balance—restricted | 800 | 800 |

## EXHIBIT 15-6
*(continued)*

| No. | Transactions | Journal entries | Dr. | Cr. |
|---|---|---|---|---|
| | | **Renewals and Replacements Fund** | | |
| 1 | Cash received from private grant, $20 | Cash<br>  Private gifts, grants, and contracts—restricted | 20 | 20 |
| 2 | Mandatory amount from current fund, unrestricted, was accrued, $800 | Due from unrestricted current fund<br>  Transfer from current funds—mandatory renewals and replacements | 800 | 800 |
| 3 | Cash of $795 was received from current funds, unrestricted | Cash<br>  Due from unrestricted current funds | 795 | 795 |
| 4 | Received $100 from sale of investment | Cash<br>  Investments | 100 | 100 |
| 5 | Accrued expenditures of $913 for renewals and replacements of plant facilities | Expenditures—plant facilities<br>  Accounts payable | 913 | 913 |
| 6 | Paid accounts | Accounts payable<br>  Cash | 913 | 913 |
| | | **Retirement of Indebtedness Fund** | | |
| 1 | Cash was received from unrestricted current funds for payment of principal and interest, $700; from unexpended plant funds for accrued interest on sale of bonds, $6; from investment income, $10; and from private gifts, $150; for a total of $866 | Cash<br>  Mandatory transfers—current fund, unrestricted—principal and interest<br>  Accrued interest on sale of bonds<br>  Private gifts, grants, and contracts, restricted<br>  Investment income, restricted | 866 | 700<br><br>6<br><br>150<br>10 |
| 2 | Retired debt, $500; paid interest on indebtedness, $345; had administrative costs of $1 | Retirement of indebtedness<br>Interest on indebtedness<br>Administrative costs<br>  Cash | 500<br>345<br>1 | 846 |
| | | **Investment in Plant Fund** | | |
| 1 | Debt was retired as follows: notes payable, $200; bonds payable, $200; and mortgages payable, $100 | Notes payable<br>Bonds payable<br>Mortgages payable<br>  Retirement of indebtedness | 200<br>200<br>100 | 500 |
| 2 | Renewal and replacement investments in buildings, $500; equipment, $300; land improvements, $75; library books, $25; disposed of plant facilties, $300, which consisted of building ($100) and equipment ($200) | Buildings<br>Equipment<br>Land improvements<br>Library books<br>Disposal of plant facilities<br>  Expenditures for:<br>    Plant facilities<br>    Buildings<br>    Equipment | 500<br>300<br>75<br>25<br>300 | <br><br><br><br><br><br>900<br>100<br>200 |
| 3 | Expenditures for new facilities from unexpended plant funds: land, $50; buildings, $1,252. Issued bonds payable $800, with net investments of $502 | Land<br>Buildings<br>  Bonds payable<br>  Net investment | 50<br>1,252 | <br><br>800<br>502 |

## EXHIBIT 15-7
### Loriann State University
### Worksheet—Plant Funds
### Year Ended June 30, 19X1
(In Thousands)

| Accounts | Beginning balances | | Transactions | | | | Ending balances | | Statement of changes in fund balance | | Balance sheet | |
|---|---|---|---|---|---|---|---|---|---|---|---|---|
| | Dr. | Cr. | No. | Dr. | No. | Cr. | Dr. | Cr. | Dr. | Cr. | Dr. | Cr. |
| Unexpended plant fund: | | | | | | | | | | | | |
| Cash | 800 | | 9 | 100 | 11 | 1,292 | 600 | | | | 600 | |
| | | | 6 | 800 | 12 | 500 | | | | | | |
| | | | 5 | 100 | | | | | | | | |
| | | | 2 | 10 | | | | | | | | |
| | | | 4 | 100 | | | | | | | | |
| | | | 7 | 250 | | | | | | | | |
| | | | 8 | 232 | | | | | | | | |
| Investments | 3,000 | | 12 | 500 | | | 3,500 | | | | 3,500 | |
| Due from unrestricted current funds | 240 | | 3 | 200 | 8 | 232 | 208 | | | | 208 | |
| Due from state | | | 1 | 100 | 9 | 100 | | | | | | |
| Accounts payable | | 10 | 11 | 1,292 | 10 | 1,302 | | 20 | | | | 20 |
| Notes payable | | 100 | | | 5 | 100 | | 200 | | | | 200 |
| Bonds payable | — | | 13 | 800 | 6 | 800 | | | | | | |
| Fund balances: | | | | | | | | | | | | |
| Restricted | | 2,500 | | | 13 | 800 | | 3,300 | | | | 3,300 |
| Unrestricted | | 1,430 | | | | | | 1,430 | | | | 1,430 |
| Expired term endowment (restricted) | | | | | 4 | 100 | | 100 | | 100 | | |
| State appropriations (restricted) | | | | | 1 | 100 | | 100 | | 100 | | |
| Private gifts, grants, and contracts (restricted) | | | | | 7 | 250 | | 250 | | 250 | | |
| Investment income—restricted | | | | | 2 | 10 | | 10 | | 10 | | |
| Expenditures—plant facilities | | | 10 | 1,302 | | | 1,302 | | 1,302 | | | |
| Transfers (unrestricted) | | | | | 3 | 200 | | 200 | | 200 | | |
| Totals | 4,040 | 4,040 | | 5,786 | | 5,786 | 5,610 | 5,610 | 1,302 | 660 | 4,308 | 4,950 |
| To fund balance— | | | | | | | | | | | | |
| restricted | | | | | | | | | | 612 | | 612 |
| unrestricted | | | | | | | | | | 30 | | 30 |
| | | | | | | | | | 1,302 | 1,302 | 4,950 | 4,950 |

**EXHIBIT 15-7**
*(continued)*

| Accounts | Beginning balances | | Transactions | | | | Ending balances | | Statement of changes in fund balance | | Balance sheet | |
|---|---|---|---|---|---|---|---|---|---|---|---|---|
| | Dr. | Cr. | No. | Dr. | No. | Cr. | Dr. | Cr. | Dr. | Cr. | Dr. | Cr. |
| Renewals and replacements fund: | | | | | | | | | | | | |
| Cash | 10 | | 3 | 795 | 6 | 913 | 12 | | | | 12 | |
| | | | 4 | 100 | | | | | | | | |
| | | | 1 | 20 | | | | | | | | |
| Investments | 500 | | | | 4 | 100 | 400 | | | | 400 | |
| Due from unrestricted current funds | 5 | | 2 | 800 | 3 | 795 | 10 | | | | 10 | |
| Accounts payable | | | 6 | 913 | | 913 | | | | | | |
| Fund balances: | | | | | | | | | | | | |
| Restricted | | 150 | | | | | | 150 | | | | 150 |
| Unrestricted | | 365 | | | | | | 365 | | | | 365 |
| Private gifts, grants, and contracts, restricted | | | | | 1 | 20 | | 20 | | 20 | | |
| Mandatory transfers Renewals and replacement | | | | | 2 | 800 | | 800 | | 800 | | |
| Expenditures—plant facilities | | | 5 | 913 | | | 913 | | 913 | | | |
| Totals | 515 | 515 | | 3,541 | | 3,541 | 1,335 | 1,335 | 913 | 820 | 422 | 515 |
| To fund balance: | | | | | | | | | | | | |
| Restricted | | | | | | | | | | 20 | 20 | |
| Unrestricted | | | | | | | | | | 73 | 73 | |
| | | | | | | | | | 913 | 913 | 515 | 515 |

| Account | Dr | Cr | Ref | Dr | Cr | Dr | Cr | Dr | Cr |
|---|---|---|---|---|---|---|---|---|---|
| **Retirement of indebtedness fund:** | | | | | | | | | |
| Cash | 100 | | 1 | 866 | 120 | | 846 | | 120 |
| Deposits with trustees | 500 | | | | 500 | | | | 500 |
| **Fund balances:** | | | | | | | | | |
| Restricted | | 250 | | | | 250 | | | 250 |
| Unrestricted | | 350 | | | | 350 | | | 350 |
| Private gifts, grants, and contracts, restricted | | | | | 150 | 150 | | 150 | |
| Investment income, restricted | | | | | 10 | 10 | | 10 | |
| Accrued interest on sale of bonds | | | | | 6 | 6 | | 6 | |
| Administrative costs | | | 2 | 1 | | | 1 | | |
| Retirement of indebtedness | | | 2 | 500 | | | 500 | 500 | |
| Interest on indebtedness | | | 2 | 345 | | | 345 | 345 | |
| Mandatory transfer—principal and interest | | | | | 700 | 700 | | 700 | |
| Totals | 600 | 600 | | 1,712 | 1,466 | 1,466 | 1,712 | 1,705 | 1,220 |
| To fund balance—unrestricted | | | | | | | | 20 | |
| | | | | | | 846 | 866 | 866 | 866 |
| | | | | | | 866 | 866 | | |
| **Investment in plant fund:** | | | | | | | | | |
| Land | 1,000 | | 3 | 50 | | 1,050 | | 1,050 | |
| Land improvements | 2,000 | | 2 | 75 | | 2,075 | | 2,075 | |
| Buildings | 48,000 | | 2 | 500 | | 49,652 | | 49,652 | |
| | | | 3 | 1,252 | 100 | | | | |
| Equipment | 28,000 | | 2 | 300 | 200 | 28,100 | | 28,100 | |
| Library books | 150 | | 2 | 25 | | 175 | | 175 | |
| Notes payable | | 1,600 | 1 | 200 | | | 1,400 | | 1,400 |
| Bonds payable | | 5,000 | 1 | 200 | 800 | | 5,600 | | 5,600 |
| Mortgages payable | | 500 | 1 | 100 | | | 400 | | 400 |
| Net investment | | 72,050 | 3 | | 502 | | 72,552 | | 72,252 |
| Expended for plant facilities | | | 2 | | 900 | 900 | | 900 | |
| Retirement of indebtedness | | | 1 | | 500 | 500 | | 500 | |
| Disposal of plant facilities | | | 2 | 300 | | | 300 | 300 | |
| Totals | 79,150 | 79,150 | | 3,002 | 3,002 | 81,352 | 81,352 | 1,400 | 1,400 |
| Increase in net investment in plant | | | | | | | | 1,100 | |
| | | | | | | | | 1,400 | 1,400 |

479

**1** Unexpended plant fund:

|  | Dr. | Cr. |
|---|---|---|
| Bonds payable | $ 800,000 | |
|     Fund balance, restricted | | $800,000 |

**2** Investment in plant fund:

| | | |
|---|---|---|
| Land | 50,000 | |
| Buildings | 1,252,000 | |
|     Bonds payable | | 800,000 |
|     Net investment in plant | | 502,000 |

The bonds payable could have been recorded in the investment in plant fund upon issuance of the bonds, with a debit to the net investment in plant and a credit to bonds payable. In the unexpended plant fund, a credit would have gone to fund balance, restricted, instead of to bonds payable.

## Financial Reporting

Exhibits 15-8 and 15-9 are illustrative and representative of the financial statements necessary for college and university plant funds reporting.

## SUMMARY

Fund accounting is employed in college and university accounting much as it is in governmental accounting. However, instead of the general and special revenue funds found in government, current funds—restricted and unrestricted—are found in college and university accounting. While both of the funds (restricted and unrestricted) are considered current funds, they must be accounted for and reported on separately.

Plant funds, however, include four separate categories: unexpended, renewals and replacements, retirement of indebtedness, and investment in plant. The accounting for these four categories is kept separately. However, all categories are shown in the balance sheet and the statement of changes in fund balances.

Loan funds are used to account for loans to students, faculty, and staff. Endowment funds are nonexpendable funds and are used to account for gifts from outside donors. Annuity and life income funds are used to account for gifts from others that provide an amount to beneficiaries until an agreed-upon time, then the corpus goes to the university. Agency funds in college and university accounting are comparable to agency funds in governmental accounting: they account for monies held for others.

Colleges and universities are not required to use budgets. But, when owned by state or local governments, they often are required to follow governmental accounting practice regarding budgets. Colleges and universities use an accrued expenditure accounting basis—thus, they account for all expenditures on the accrual basis. They do not account for expenses.

**EXHIBIT 15-8**
**Loriann State University**
**Plant Funds**
**Balance Sheet**
**June 30, 19X1**
(In Thousands)

| Assets | Current year | Prior year | Liabilities and fund balance | Current year | Prior year |
|---|---|---|---|---|---|
| Unexpended: | | | | | |
| Cash | 600 | 800 | Accounts payable | 20 | 10 |
| Investments | 3,500 | 3,000 | Notes payable | 200 | 100 |
| Due from unrestricted current fund | 208 | 240 | Bonds payable | | |
| | | | Fund balance: | | |
| | | | Restricted | 2,688 | 2,500 |
| | | | Unrestricted | 1,400 | 1,430 |
| Total unexpended | 4,308 | 4,040 | | 4,308 | 4,040 |
| Renewals and replacements: | | | | | |
| Cash | 12 | 10 | Fund balances: | | |
| Investments | 400 | 500 | Restricted | 130 | 150 |
| Due from unrestricted current fund | 10 | 5 | Unrestricted | 292 | 365 |
| Total renewals and replacements | 422 | 515 | | 422 | 515 |
| Retirement of indebtedness: | | | | | |
| Cash | 120 | 100 | Fund balances: | | |
| Deposit with trustees | 500 | 500 | Restricted | 250 | 250 |
| | | | Unrestricted | 370 | 350 |
| Total retirement of indebtedness | 620 | 600 | | 620 | 600 |
| Investment in plant: | | | | | |
| Land | 1,050 | 1,000 | Notes payable | 1,400 | 1,600 |
| Land improvements | 2,075 | 2,000 | Bonds payable | 5,600 | 5,000 |
| Buildings | 49,652 | 48,000 | Mortgages payable | 400 | 500 |
| Equipment | 28,100 | 28,000 | Net investment in plant | 73,652 | 72,050 |
| Library books | 175 | 150 | | | |
| Total investment in plant | 81,052 | 79,150 | | 81,052 | 79,150 |

## EXHIBIT 15-9
### Loriann State University
### Plant Funds
### Statement of Changes in Fund Balances
(In Thousands)

|  | Unexpended | Renewals and replacements | Retirement of indebtedness | Investment in plant |
|---|---|---|---|---|
| **Revenues and other additions:** | | | | |
| Expired term endowments (restricted) | 100 | | | |
| State appropriation (restricted) | 100 | | | |
| Private gifts, grants, and contracts (restricted) | 250 | 20 | 150 | |
| Investment income (restricted) | 10 | | 10 | |
| Expended for plant facilities | | | | 900 |
| Retirement of indebtedness | | | 6 | 500 |
| Total revenue and other additions | 460 | 20 | 166 | 1,400 |
| **Expenditures and other deductions:** | | | | |
| Administration and collection costs | | | 1 | |
| Expended for plant facilities | 1,302 | 913 | | |
| Retirement of indebtedness | | | 500 | |
| Interest on indebtedness | | | 345 | |
| Disposal of plant facilities | | | | 300 |
| Total expenditures and other deductions | 1,302 | 913 | 846 | 300 |
| **Transfers among funds:** | | | | |
| Mandatory | | | | |
| Principal and interest | | | 700 | |
| Renewals and replacements | | 800 | | |
| Unrestricted gifts | 200 | | | |
| Total transfers | 200 | 800 | 700 | |
| Net increase or decrease for year | (642) | (93) | 20 | 1,100 |
| Fund balance at beginning of year | 3,930 | 515 | 600 | 72,050 |
| Fund increase from bonds payable | 800 | | | |
| Fund balance at end of year | 4,088 | 422 | 620 | 73,450 |

## QUESTIONS

1. Discuss the relationships and distinctions between fund accounting for governmental units and for colleges and universities and other nonprofit organizations.
2. At the present time, which organization has the primary responsibility for setting accounting principles for colleges and universities and for other nonprofit organizations?

3 Is budgetary accounting required for college and university accounting and financial reporting? Discuss.
4 What are the principal funds found in college and university accounting? Explain the purpose of each of the funds.
5 Make a distinction between plant funds in college and university accounting and the general fixed assets account group in governmental accounting.
6 Accrual accounting is required in college and university accounting. Make a distinction between accrual accounting found in college and university accounting and the modified accrual basis found in local and municipal governmental accounting.
7 Are the financial statements found in college and university accounting and financial reporting the same as those found in governmental accounting? Discuss each of the required statements.
8 Make a distinction between mandatory and nonmandatory transfers between funds in college and university accounting.
9 Are there any major differences between agency funds in college and university accounting and state and local governmental accounting?
10 Refer to Exhibit 15-1, transaction number 1. Explain this type of transaction.
11 Refer to Exhibit 15-1, transaction number 11, and Exhibit 15-4. Explain the placement of mandatory and nonmandatory transfers on the statement of changes in fund balances.

## PROBLEMS

15-1 Select the best answer for each of the following questions.[1]
  1 What is the recommended method of accounting to be used by colleges and universities?
   a Cash
   b Modified cash
   c Restricted accrual
   d Accrual
  2 In the loan fund of a college or university, each of the following types of loans would be found except:
   a Student
   b Staff
   c Building
   d Faculty
  3 Which of the following receipts is properly recorded as restricted current funds on the books of a university?
   a Tuition
   b Student laboratory fees
   c Housing fees
   d Research grants
  4 Tuition waivers for which there is no intention of collection from the student should be classified by a not-for-profit university as

| | Revenue | Expenditures |
|---|---|---|
| a | No | No |
| b | No | Yes |
| c | Yes | Yes |
| d | Yes | No |

**5** For the fall semester of 19X1, Cranbrook College assessed its students $2,300,000 for tuition and fees. The net amount realized was only $2,100,000 because of the following revenue reductions:

| | |
|---|---|
| Refunds occasioned by class cancellations and student withdrawals | $ 50,000 |
| Tuition remissions granted to faculty members' families | 10,000 |
| Scholarships and fellowships | 140,000 |

How much should Cranbrook report for the period for unrestricted current funds revenues from tuition and fees?
a  $2,100,000
b  $2,150,000
c  $2,250,000
d  $2,300,000

**6** Which of the following is utilized for current expenditures by a not-for-profit university?

| | Unrestricted current funds | Restricted current funds |
|---|---|---|
| a | No | No |
| b | No | Yes |
| c | Yes | No |
| d | Yes | Yes |

**15-2** During the years ended June 30, 19X0 and 19X1, Sonata University conducted a cancer research project financed by a $2,000,000 gift from an alumnus. This entire amount was pledged by the donor on July 10, 19W9, although he paid only $500,000 at that date. The gift was restricted to the financing of this particular research project. During the two-year research period, Sonata's related gift receipts and research expenditures at year's end (June 30) were as follows:

| | 19X0 | 19X1 |
|---|---|---|
| Gift receipts | $1,200,000 | $ 800,000 |
| Cancer research expenditures | 900,000 | 1,100,000 |

How much gift revenue should Sonata report in the restricted column of its statement of current funds, revenues, expenditures, and other changes for the year ended June 30, 19X1? Explain your answer.[2]

**15-3** Presented on page 485 is the current funds balance sheet of Burnsville University as of the end of its fiscal year ended June 30, 19X7.[3]

The following transactions occurred during the fiscal year ended June 30, 19X8:

**1** On July 7, 19X7, a gift of $100,000 was received from an alumnus. The alumnus requested that one-half of the gift be used for the purchase of books for the university library and the remainder be used for the establishment of a scholarship fund. The alumnus further requested that the income generated by the scholarship fund be used annually to award a scholarship to a qualified disadvantaged student. On July 20, 19X7, the board of trustees resolved that the funds of the newly established scholarship fund would be invested in savings certificates. On July 21, 19X7, the savings certificates were purchased.

**2** Revenue from student tuition and fees applicable to the year ended June 30, 19X8 amounted to $1,900,000. Of this amount, $66,000 was collected in the prior year and $1,686,000 was collected during the year ended June 30, 19X8. In addition, at June 30,

## Burnsville University
## Current Funds Balance Sheet
## June 30, 19X7

| Assets | | | Liabilities and fund balances | | |
|---|---|---|---|---|---|
| Current funds: | | | Current funds: | | |
| Unrestricted: | | | Unrestricted: | | |
| Cash | $210,000 | | Accounts payable | $ 45,000 | |
| Accounts receivable student tuition and fees, less allowance for doubtful accounts of $9,000 | 341,000 | | Deferred revenues | 66,000 | |
| | | | Fund balances | 515,000 | $626,000 |
| State appropriations receivable | 75,000 | $626,000 | | | |
| Restricted: | | | Restricted: | | |
| Cash | 7,000 | | Fund balances | | 67,000 |
| Investments | 60,000 | 67,000 | | | |
| Total current funds | | $693,000 | Total current funds | | $693,000 |

19X8, the university had received cash of $158,000 representing fees for the session beginning July 1, 19X8.

**3** During the year ended June 30, 19X8, the university had collected $349,000 of the outstanding accounts receivable at the beginning of the year. The balance was determined to be uncollectible and was written off against the allowance account. At June 30, 19X8, the allowance account was increased by $3,000.

**4** During the year, interest charges of $6,000 were earned and collected on late student fee payments.

**5** During the year, the state appropriation was received. An additional unrestricted appropriation of $50,000 was made by the state but had not been paid to the university as of June 30, 19X8.

**6** An unrestricted gift of $25,000 cash was received from alumni of the university.

**7** During the year, investments of $21,000 were sold for $26,000. Investment income amounting to $1,900 was received.

**8** During the year, unrestricted operating expenses of $1,777,000 were recorded. At June 30, 19X8, $59,000 worth of these expenses remained unpaid.

**9** Restricted current funds of $13,000 were spent for authorized purposes during the year.

**10** The accounts payable at June 30, 19X7 were paid during the year.

**11** During the year, $7,000 in interest was earned and received on the savings certificates purchased in accordance with the board of trustees resolution, as discussed in item 1.

**Required**:

**1** Prepare journal entries to record in summary the preceding transactions for the year ended June 30, 19X8. Each journal entry should be numbered to correspond with the transaction described above. Your answer sheet should be organized as follows:

| | Current funds | | | | Endowment fund | |
|---|---|---|---|---|---|---|
| | Unrestricted | | Restricted | | | |
| Accounts | Dr. | Cr. | Dr. | Cr. | Dr. | Cr. |

**2** Prepare a statement of changes in fund balances for the year ended June 30, 19X8.

**15-4** The following accounts were taken from a state university's chart of accounts. Determine in which fund they may be found, and make a check mark in the column in which each account is found.

| Account | Current fund Unrestricted | Current fund Restricted | Loan fund | Endowment fund | Plant fund | Agency fund |
|---|---|---|---|---|---|---|
| Cash | | | | | | |
| Investments | | | | | | |
| Inventory | | | | | | |
| Accounts receivable | | | | | | |
| Notes receivable | | | | | | |
| Interest and dividends receivable | | | | | | |
| Allowance for doubtful accounts | | | | | | |
| Appropriations receivable | | | | | | |
| Capital appropriations receivable | | | | | | |
| Investment in plant | | | | | | |
| Advance from treasury | | | | | | |
| Accounts payable | | | | | | |
| Deferred revenue | | | | | | |
| Accrued expenditures | | | | | | |
| Fund balance | | | | | | |
| Accrued administrative expenses | | | | | | |
| Endowment—unrestricted | | | | | | |
| Quasi-endowment—restricted | | | | | | |
| Bonds payable | | | | | | |
| Mortgages payable | | | | | | |
| Funds held in custody for others | | | | | | |
| Revenues—unrestricted | | | | | | |
| Revenues—restricted | | | | | | |
| Grants and contracts | | | | | | |
| Appropriations | | | | | | |
| Private gifts | | | | | | |
| Investment income | | | | | | |
| Retirement of indebtedness | | | | | | |
| Expended for plant facilities | | | | | | |
| Proceeds from disposal of plant facilities | | | | | | |
| Educational and general expenditures | | | | | | |
| Auxiliary enterprise expenditures | | | | | | |
| Mandatory transfers | | | | | | |
| Nonmandatory transfers | | | | | | |
| Land | | | | | | |
| Buildings | | | | | | |

**15-5** All of the following transactions are independent of each other. They occurred in a rather small, independently owned university during the year 19XX.

**1** During the year, $15,000 of restricted current funds were spent.

**2** A private donor made a $50,000 contribution. The funds could be spent in any manner desired by the university.

**3** Investments purchased during the year amounted to $100,000. During the year, interest and dividends received amounted to $6,000. Interest accrued at the end of the year was $500, and the fair market value of the investments at the end of the year was $105,000.

**4** Cash collected on tuition and fees during the year was $750,000. Of this amount, $50,000 pertained to receivables from the prior year. Students, on their receivables for tuition and fees, still owed $75,000 at the end of the year.

**5** One of the university's alumni died during the year, leaving $250,000 to the university. Of this amount, $40,000 was specifically provided for the accounting department to be used in any way they desired. Of the balance, $100,000 could be used by the university in its current operations, while $110,000 should remain in trust, with the income being used for general operations.

**6** A building was constructed during the year, costing $300,000.

**7** A mortgage of $500,000 was obtained from the X Bank. The money received from the mortgage was for a small dormitory. The rent received from students for the rooms in the dormitory was to be used to pay off the mortgage.

**Required**:

**1** State the fund or funds in which the preceding transactions will be recorded.

**2** Make the journal entries to record the transactions.

**15-6** A partial balance sheet of Rapapo State University as of the end of its fiscal year July 31, 19X2 is presented below.[4]

**Rapapo State University**
**Current Funds Balance Sheet**
**July 31, 19X2**

| Assets | | Liabilities and fund balances | |
|---|---|---|---|
| Unrestricted: | | Unrestricted: | |
| Cash | $200,000 | Accounts payable | $100,000 |
| Accounts receivable— | | Due to other funds | 40,000 |
| tuition and fees, less al- | | Deferred revenue—tuition | |
| lowance for doubtful ac- | | and fees | 25,000 |
| counts of $15,000 | 360,000 | Fund balance | 435,000 |
| Prepaid expenses | 40,000 | | |
| Total unrestricted | 600,000 | Total unrestricted | 600,000 |
| Restricted: | | Restricted: | |
| Cash | 10,000 | Accounts payable | 5,000 |
| Investments | 210,000 | Fund balance | 215,000 |
| Total restricted | 220,000 | Total restricted | 220,000 |
| Total current funds | $820,000 | Total current funds | $820,000 |

The following information pertains to the year ended July 31, 19X3:

**1** Cash collected from students' tuition totaled $3,000,000. Of this $3,000,000, $362,000 represented accounts receivable outstanding at July 31, 19X2; $2,500,000 was for current-year tuition; and $138,000 was for tuition applicable to the semester beginning in August 19X3.

**2** Deferred revenue at July 31, 19X2 was earned during the year ended July 31, 19X3.

**3** Accounts receivable at July 31, 19X2, which were not collected during the year ended July 31, 19X3, were determined to be uncollectible and were written off against the allowance account. At July 31, 19X3, the allowance account was estimated at $10,000.

**4** During the year, an unrestricted appropriation of $60,000 was made by the state. This state appropriation was to be paid to Rapapo sometime in August 19X3.

**5** During the year, unrestricted cash gifts of $80,000 were received from alumni. Rapapo's board of trustees allocated $30,000 of these gifts to the student loan fund.

**6** During the year, investments costing $25,000 were sold for $31,000. Restricted fund investments were purchased at a cost of $40,000. Investment income of $18,000 was earned and collected during the year.

**7** Unrestricted general expenses of $2,500,000 were recorded in the voucher system. At July 31, 19X3, the unrestricted accounts payable balance was $75,000.

**8** The restricted accounts payable balance at July 31, 19X2 was paid.

**9** The $40,000 due to other funds at July 31, 19X2 was paid to the plant fund as required.

**10** One quarter of the prepaid expenses at July 31, 19X2 expired during the current year and pertained to general education expense. There was no addition to prepaid expenses during the year.

**Required**:

**1** Prepare journal entries in summary form to record the foregoing transactions for the year ended July 31, 19X3. Number each entry to correspond with the number indicated in the description of its respective transaction. Your answer sheet should be organized as follows:

|  |  | Current funds | | | |
| --- | --- | --- | --- | --- | --- |
|  |  | Unrestricted | | Restricted | |
| **Entry no.** | **Accounts** | Dr. | Cr. | Dr. | Cr. |

**2** Prepare a statement of changes in fund balances for the year ended July 31, 19X3.

## NOTES

**1** Adapted from American Institute of Certified Public Accountants, *Uniform CPA Examination Questions and Unofficial Answers* (New York: American Institute of Certified Public Accountants, various dates).
**2** Ibid., May 1982.
**3** Ibid., Nov. 1978.
**4** Ibid., Nov. 1983.

# CHAPTER 16

# HOSPITALS

Within the last generation, medical care, including hospitalization, of those who are ill or need surgery, has grown by leaps and bounds. Partially or fully financed by employers, individual and family hospital and physician insurance has provided needed medical care in hospitals that previously was taken care of in the home, in the doctor's office, or not taken care of at all. For the senior citizen, Medicare and Medicaid, partially financed through governmental resources, provide hospital facilities and physicians' services that often were not available to those older persons.

In addition, medical knowledge for the diagnosis and treatment of illness, disease, and needed surgery has advanced rapidly in recent years. Only fifty years ago, who would have thought that the chest could be opened and the heart provided with new arteries or new valves so an individual could continue living? Who would have thought that the function of the kidneys could be transplanted from one person to another? And, think of the numerous drugs, such as penicillin, that have provided the means for controlling dangerous infections.

It is fairly obvious that most of the functions now provided in a modern hospital could not have been provided in previous generations through the means of the physician's little black bag or even in the physician's office. Costs to finance modern facilities and equipment needed by the physician and surgeon are way beyond the financial capacity of most single physicians, or even a small group of physicians and surgeons. The modern hospital, however, does provide the facilities and equipment for the doctors, physicians, and nurses to provide medical care for the ill.

The cost of hospital and medical care, however, has increased so rapidly in recent years that the federal and state governments and insurance companies have adopted cost containment programs to overcome some of this rapid rise. For example, the methods of payments to hospitals and doctors for treatment rendered under Medicare and Medicaid have been changed in order to reduce the total payment. Charges for outpatient treatment for certain types of surgery and medical care have become allowable types of payment by insurance companies. While the methods of determining allowable charges may change, the basic ideas of hospital accounting remain fairly consistent.

The purpose of this chapter, therefore, is to explain and illustrate the financial accounting and reporting principles and practices that are needed to provide financial information to third parties concerning the financing and operation of a hospital. Management accounting, including cost accounting, is also very important for hospital administrators in order for them to have information with which to efficiently, economically, and effectively manage the hospital. The subjects of cost and management accounting, however, will not be discussed and illustrated to any extent in this chapter, but they will be provided in Parts III and IV of this book.

## THE OPERATIONS OF A MODERN HOSPITAL

Hospitals are not owned or operated by any one organizational type. Some hospitals are government owned and operated; the Veteran Administration's hospitals and the military hospitals are examples of federally operated institutions. Most states also own and operate various types of hospitals—mental care hospitals, for example. And, most localities—counties, cities, and even hospital districts—own and operate full-service hospitals. Some of these hospitals receive fees from patients for services from the hospitals. Others, such as military hospitals and state mental hospitals, are fully supported through appropriations from the government.

The majority of hospitals, however, are owned and operated by not-for-profit organizations—religious groups; educational institutions; federal, state, and local governments; and community organizations. "Not-for-profit" in this case means that the hospital has to receive financial help. This help comes not only from fee-paying patients but also from outside sources through donations, grants, gifts, and other such resources. Thus these organizations often solicit funds for their capital construction and operations, use governmental and private grants for both capital construction and operations, and try not to use more of their financial resources each year than they take in. In the past few years, because of the ability of hospitals to be assured of sufficient revenue to operate profitably through Medicare, Medicaid, and hospital insurance payments, some hospitals have become investor owned—the purpose being to make a profit for the investors. These hospitals now, because of the cost-containment practices of Medicare, Medicaid, and insurance companies, are having to adopt modern financial management practices in order to continue profitable operations. Parts III and IV discuss these modern practices in more depth.

Contrary to what was done in the past, in recent years, governmental and philanthropic institutions have not been contributing sufficient resources to the hospitals to provide for the necessary capital construction and medical equipment. Many hospitals, therefore, have gone to long-term borrowing and long-term leasing for the procurement of capital assets. Private solicitation of contributions is also a method used to obtain the resources needed for the normal operations of the hospital, as well as for capital construction.

Thus one can easily see that because of the diverse types of ownership and debt financing used to construct, maintain, and operate a modern hospital, third parties require a great deal of financial information concerning the hospital's operations. Accountants who audit these organizations and provide opinions to third parties regarding the financial statements need to know that generally accepted accounting principles have been used and consistently applied by hospital management in the preparation of the financial statements.

To cover the diverse needs of third parties for financial reports, our discussion of hospital accounting and financial reporting will be as follows:

1 GAAP for hospitals
2 Fund accounting in hospitals
3 Application of hospital accounting principles
   a To various assets and liabilities
   b To revenues and expenses
   c To the fund balance
4 Financial statements for hospitals
5 Variations and special needs

By now, most students of fund accounting are capable of preparing the normal journal entry for a transaction, posting that entry to ledger accounts, and preparing a trial balance, from which statements can be prepared. Therefore, instead of showing all hospital transactions through an illustrative case, only transactions that differ from those previously learned will be illustrated in this chapter. However, illustrative financial statements, the results of all of the hospital's financial transactions, will be shown.

## GENERALLY ACCEPTED ACCOUNTING PRINCIPLES FOR HOSPITALS

In their *Hospital Audit Guide*, the AICPA says: "the Committee on Health Care Institutions unanimously concludes that they (financial statements of hospitals) should be prepared in accordance with generally accepted accounting principles."[1] Thus the statements of principles of accounting issued by the Financial Accounting Standards Board, and preceding organizations, are applicable to hospitals and are the principles that must be used and consistently applied when CPAs express an opinion on the financial statements of a hospital.

This means that accrual expense accounting—not expenditure accounting—along with full accrual revenue accounting, must be employed to produce financial statements for third parties. Unlike governments and universities, capital assets of hospitals (i.e., property, plant, and equipment) are accounted for as a part of the unrestricted fund—the current operating fund—since segregation in a separate fund would imply the existence of restrictions on asset use.[2]

In addition to GAAP stated by the Financial Accounting Standards Board, the principle of fund accounting is stated in the AICPA's *Hospital Audit Guide*.[3] In addition, the American Hospital Association and the Hospital Financial Management Association provide guidance on accounting principles and practices to its members.[4] The AICPA's *Hospital Audit Guide* says that the "recommendations in the revised American Hospital Association's *Chart of Accounts for Hospitals* are generally compatible with accepted accounting principles and this Guide."[5]

## FUNDS IN HOSPITAL ACCOUNTING

Fund accounting for business is usually not considered a generally accepted accounting principle by the FASB. Fund accounting for hospitals, however, is recognized in the *Audit Guide* as an appropriate principle of accounting for hospitals. Comparable to funds in university accounting, several groups and funds are recognized in each of two classes of funds used in hospital accounting. They are:

1 Unrestricted funds
   a  Current
   b  Board-designated
   c  Plant (property, plant, and equipment)
2 Restricted funds
   a  Specific purpose funds
   b  Plant replacement and expansion funds
   c  Endowment funds
   d  Other restricted funds

### Unrestricted Funds

All resources of the hospital on which an outside donor has not placed a restriction on their use, and the debt and capital equity pertaining to those resources, fall in the unrestricted fund. This includes:

1 Current operating resources
2 Board-designated resources, such as those restricted to the purchase of a special piece of equipment
3 Property, plant, and equipment
4 Current liabilities and deferred revenue pertaining to the operating resources
5 Long-term debt related to the acquisition of the property, plant, and equipment
6 The capital equity—fund balance—related to the acquisition of the property, plant, and equipment and the operations of the fund

The term "fund balance" is the name of the account that reflects fund equity, the difference between the assets and the liabilities.

While a separate classification of resources is made within the unrestricted fund for financial reporting purposes—current, board-designated, and plant—this classification has no effect on the accounting operations of the fund. All of the assets, liabilities, fund equity, revenue, and expenses are within the framework of a single entity. However, transactions occur among accounts within these three classifications, but the accounts are all a part of the unrestricted fund; these include cash coming from accounts receivable, the board designating cash to purchase investments for expanding a wing on the hospital, and the fixed assets being depreciated in order to provide the current operating expense for determining the appropriate amount for revenues over the expenses for the period. All of these types of transactions are within the single entity—the unrestricted fund.

Transactions do occur, however, between the unrestricted and restricted funds that are interentity transactions. Thus a single transaction will affect both entities, the unrestricted and the restricted funds.

To illustrate, restricted funds can be transferred to the unrestricted fund for such purposes as acquiring long-term assets or general operations. When transferred in accordance with the donor's restrictions, these funds then become a part of the assets and fund balance of the unrestricted fund. For example, suppose that the income from a certain endowment fund is to be used for operating purposes. The income from this specific endowment fund (X endowment fund) during the year was $50,000. It is then due to the unrestricted fund, and the journal entry in the unrestricted fund would be:

|  | Dr. | Cr. |
|---|---|---|
| Due from X endowment fund | $50,000 | |
|     Income from endowment fund | | $50,000 |

To record amount due from X endowment fund for the income earned during the year.

When the X endowment fund pays the amount to the unrestricted fund, the entry would be:

| Cash | $50,000 | |
|---|---|---|
|     Due from X endowment fund | | $50,000 |

To record cash received from X endowment fund for income earned during the year.

The transactions in the X endowment fund—income fund would be:

| Income | $50,000 | |
|---|---|---|
|     Due to unrestricted fund | | $50,000 |

To record income for the year to be transferred to unrestricted fund.

When paid, the entry would be:

| Due to unrestricted fund | $50,000 | |
|---|---|---|
|     Cash | | $50,000 |

To record payment made to unrestricted fund.

Interfund transactions of this type can also originate in the specific purpose funds and in the plant replacement and expansion funds, as well as the endowment funds. For example, suppose the unrestricted fund had spent $100,000 for equipment during the year and, according to the donor's restrictions, is to be reimbursed by the plant replacement and expansion fund for this expenditure. The entries in the unrestricted fund for the purchase of equipment would be:

| Equipment | $100,000 | |
|---|---|---|
|     Cash | | $100,000 |

To record purchase of equipment.

For reimbursement from the plant replacement and expansion fund, the entry is:

| Cash | $100,000 | |
|---|---|---|
|     Fund balance | | $100,000 |

To record reimbursement of cost of equipment from the replacement and expansion fund.

In the plant replacement and expansion fund, the entry would be as follows:

| | | |
|---|---|---|
| Fund balance | $100,000 | |
|     Cash | | $100,000 |

To record reimbursement of cost of equipment in the unrestricted fund.

## Restricted Funds

All resources on which an outside donor has placed a restriction on their use fall within the classification of restricted funds. Unlike the unrestricted fund, which is a single entity, each of the restricted funds is a single entity. Thus, within the classification of specific purpose funds, there may be many entities, each being a fund by itself. For financial reporting, these many individual funds are combined into three specific reporting entities:

1. Specific purpose funds
2. Plant replacement and expansion funds
3. Endowment funds

In addition to these three combined funds for reporting purposes, a hospital may have other restricted resources, such as student loan, annuity, and life income funds.

**Specific Purpose Funds** These types of funds could be called specific operating purpose funds because the resources are restricted to specific operating purposes, such as for charity services. These funds can also be shown as deferred revenue in the unrestricted funds and deducted from the expense or shown as revenue when the appropriate time occurs, such as when a charity case is paid from these funds.

**Plant Replacement and Expansion Funds** When a donor restricts his giving to be used only for plant replacement or expansion, the amount is shown as a specific fund in the plant replacement and expansion funds. If the amount of the giving is restricted only in general and not specifically related to the individual gift, then only one plant replacement and expansion fund is necessary. When transferred to the unrestricted fund, amounts from the plant replacement and expansion funds are shown as increases in the assets acquired and in the fund balance. This type of transaction was previously illustrated in the discussion on unrestricted funds.

**Endowment Funds** Much as in governmental accounting's fiduciary funds and university accounting's endowment funds, hospital accounting may have many or only a few endowment funds. Each of these funds is a separate fund, and thus a separate entity. For accounting purposes, endowment funds may be separated into principal and income funds as was illustrated in Chapter 10. When transferred to the unrestricted funds in accordance with the provision of the endowment, the revenue is shown as nonoperating revenue in the unrestricted fund.

As was discussed in Chapter 10 concerning trust funds in government and in Chapter 15 on university endowment funds, there are two major types of endowment funds:

(1) those in which the principal lasts in perpetuity, the income being used as the donor stipulates; and (2) those in which the principal—either all or a portion of it—and the income can be used after a period of time. When a fund of the second type becomes available for general operations but is restricted to specific purposes, it should be transferred to a specific purpose fund instead of to the unrestricted fund.

It is fairly obvious that restrictions on endowment funds have been placed by the donors on the income and the principal. Accounting for these endowment funds, then, should be in accordance with the provisions of the donor.

## APPLICATION OF HOSPITAL ACCOUNTING PRINCIPLES— UNRESTRICTED FUND

When applied, accounting principles for the unrestricted fund of a hospital affect not only revenues and expenses, but also the assets, liabilities, and fund balance. In this section, we will illustrate the application of unrestricted fund accounting principles as follows:

1. Assets
2. Liabilities
3. Revenues
4. Expenses
5. Fund balances

### Assets

Each asset that is shown on the balance sheet of a hospital may have some characteristics that differ from those of other types of organizations. These distinctions will be discussed by type of asset, where there might be a difference from normal accounting transactions.

**Cash** While cash in hospital funds can be recorded in one bank account and not segregated from other cash uses, some donors require that the cash in one particular fund (e.g., an endowment fund) be separated from other operating funds. In this case, it is usually better to have separate bank accounts. Otherwise, one bank account, with separate accounts for each particular purpose shown in the records, can be used. However, some organizations prefer that cash for each separate purpose be separated by having different bank accounts for each purpose.

**Accounts Receivable** The accounts receivable from charges to patients for services rendered are recorded at the full accrual rate. Yet, seldom is the full accrual rate the amount that the hospital receives for the patient's charges. Courtesy discounts, charity allowances, and contractual adjustments with third-party payors are reasons for not receiving the full amount of the charges. Courtesy discounts are amounts allowed to privileged patients, such as doctors, nurses, employees, clergymen, and employee dependents. Charity allowances are the difference between the established rates and the amounts the hospital will collect from indigent patients or organizations established to help indigent patients. Contractual adjustments are the difference between the established rates and the contract rates to third-party payors, such as insurance companies and the government. Sometimes, the full charges are reduced to the correct amount owed, by a charge to an account that will be deducted from the full rate revenue, when third-party payors are billed for the amount of the services. At other times, the reduced rate is not shown until the amount to be received is actually received.

Under the accrual accounting method, however, before the financial statements can be prepared, an allowance for discounts, bad debts, adjustments, or otherwise uncollectible amounts must be determined in order to reflect the amounts that are expected to be collected from the accounts receivable at the balance sheet date.

One of the major accounting considerations in nonprofit accounting is the numerous subsidiary ledgers that must be maintained. This has been discussed and illustrated in Chapters 5 and 6 for governmental accounting. Yet, subsidiary ledgers become extremely important in accounting for receivables in hospitals. Patient receivables may be classified in more than a dozen different subsidiary ledgers. For example, the *Audit Guide* recommends that accounts receivable controls should be maintained under four primary headings:

1 Inpatients not discharged
2 Inpatients discharged
3 Outpatients
4 Other accounts receivable

The patient receivables accounts are then broken down into the types of payors of the accounts:

1 Blue Cross
2 Medicare
3 Medicaid
4 Compensation and liability cases
5 Other

Accounts receivables from sources other than patients come from:

1 Government appropriations
2 Community Chests/United Fund
3 Tuitions and fees
4 Pledges
5 Sundry other sources[6]

To illustrate transactions concerning receivables and the revenue earned from patient services, suppose that patient charges at established rates during the year were $5,000,000. Of this amount, contractual adjustments of $600,000 and charity services of $150,000 would account for $750,000 that would need to be written off before the total amount is collected.

The entry to record the receivables for patient services while the patients were in the hospital is:

|  | Dr. | Cr. |
|---|---|---|
| Accounts and notes receivable—inpatients not discharged | $5,000,000 | |
| Patient service revenue | | $5,000,000 |

To record gross billings for inpatient services.

When the patients are discharged the entry would be:

| | | |
|---|---|---|
| Accounts and notes receivable—inpatients discharged | $5,000,000 | |
| Accounts and notes receivable—inpatients not discharged | | $5,000,000 |

To record transfer of accounts from patients in the hospital to patients discharged.

Assuming that the amounts written off for charity services and contractual adjustments are made when the receivables from third-party payors are established, the following entries are made:

| | | |
|---|---|---|
| Cash | $ 50,000 | |
| Accounts receivable—Blue Cross | 2,200,000 | |
| Accounts receivable—Medicare | 1,800,000 | |
| Charity services | 150,000 | |
| Contractual adjustments | 600,000 | |
| Accounts and notes receivable—inpatients discharged | | $4,800,000 |

To record amount received in cash from patients, $50,000; amounts due from Blue Cross, $2,200,000, and Medicare, $1,800,000; and amounts written off to charity services, $150,000, and contractual adjustments, $600,000.

Of the $200,000 left in the accounts and notes receivable account at the end of the year, it was estimated that $100,000 would be collected, $85,000 would have to be written off as bad debts, and there would be an additional charity services adjustment of $15,000.

The entry for this year-end adjustment is as follows:

| | | |
|---|---|---|
| Provision for bad debts | $85,000 | |
| Charity services | 15,000 | |
| Estimated uncollectibles and allowances | | $85,000 |
| Accounts and notes receivable—inpatients discharged | | 15,000 |

To record the year-end adjustments for possible bad debts and write off of amounts for charitable services.

The revenue from patient services is then shown as a gross amount in the statement of revenue and expenses along with a deduction for all of the allowances and deductions illustrated here in order to show the net patient service revenue.

Often hospitals receive gifts or grants from donors who restrict the amounts to payments for charity cases. These amounts would be recorded in a specific purpose fund and transferred to the unrestricted fund when the amount of charitable deductions is known. In the financial statements of the unrestricted fund, these donations are shown as deductions from charity service, which are then shown as net charity services to be deducted from gross revenue.

To illustrate these principles, assume that donors have given $25,000 to support charity cases in the hospital. This would be recorded in the specific purpose fund as follows:

|  | Dr. | Cr. |
|---|---|---|
| Cash | $25,000 | |
|     Fund balance | | $25,000 |

To record gifts and grants restricted to payment for charity cases.

If $50,000 was shown as a deduction from revenue for charity cases, the full $25,000 would be paid from the specific purpose fund to the unrestricted fund as follows:

| Fund balance | $25,000 | |
|---|---|---|
|     Cash | | $25,000 |

To record payment to the unrestricted fund for charity cases.

In the unrestricted fund, the cash received from the specific purpose fund for these charity cases would be:

| Cash | $25,000 | |
|---|---|---|
|     Charity services | | $25,000 |

To record cash received from the specific purpose fund for charity cases.

To illustrate the financial statement presentations of accounts receivable, revenues, and the allowances made, let us use the amounts from the previous illustrations. Patient services revenue is $5,000,000 at standard rates. Deductions and allowances during the year include: charity services of $150,000, less $25,000 from specific purpose fund for payment of charitable services, leaving $125,000; and contractual adjustments of $600,000. The accounts receivable balance at end of year was $200,000. The estimated provision for bad debts was $85,000, and the estimated charity service was $15,000.

The balance sheet presentation in the unrestricted fund for these accounts receivable would be:

| Receivables | | $200,000 |
|---|---|---|
|     Less estimated uncollectibles | | |
|         and allowances | | 100,000 |
| Net receivables | | $100,000 |

In the statement of revenues and expenses for the unrestricted fund, the presentation of patient services revenues and the related deductions would be as follows:

| | |
|---|---|
| Patient service revenue | $5,000,000 |
| Less allowances and uncollectible accounts (after deduction of related gifts and grants, $25,000) | 825,000 |
| Net patient revenue | $4,175,000 |

The amount $825,000 for allowances and uncollectible accounts consists of the following:

| | | |
|---|---|---|
| Charity services | $150,000 | |
| Year-end charity services | 15,000 | |
| | 165,000 | |
| Less gifts for charity services | 25,000 | $140,000 |
| Contractual adjustments | | 600,000 |
| Estimated bad debts | | 85,000 |
| | | $825,000 |

**Investments** Concerning investments, the AICPA's *Hospital Audit Guide* says:

Some noteworthy features of accounting for hospital investments are: (1) accounting by specific fund, (2) differentiating between principal and income transactions, and (3) pooling of investments.

In order to obtain investment flexibility, hospitals frequently pool resources of various funds for investment purposes. Because net results of operating the pool do not usually show up as such in financial statements, it is important that the net profit be allocated equitably to, and reported in, statements of participating funds. In order to accomplish an equitable allocation, investment pools should be operated on the market-value method. Under the market-value method, each participating fund is assigned a number of units based on the percentage it owns of the total pool.

Market value is used to determine the number of units to be allocated to new funds entering the pool, or to calculate equity of funds withdrawing from the pool. Net profit of pool operations should be allocated to participating funds based on the funds' equity or share of the pool.[7]

In their recommendation to the FASB, the AICPA's Subcommittee on Health Care Matters, in their *Statement of Position, 78-1*, suggested that all marketable securities be valued at either cost or market. In the unrestricted fund, changes in the valuation of current marketable securities would be shown in the statement of revenues and expenses as a nonoperating revenue or loss, while in the noncurrent assets, such as investments in board-designated funds, the reevaluation allowance would be shown in the statement of changes in fund balance. In the restricted funds, both current and noncurrent asset valuation allowances would be shown in the statement of changes in fund balance. Income from investments in board-designated funds also would be a nonoperating revenue in the unrestricted fund's statement of revenues and expenses.

*Statement of Position, 78-1* also suggests that marketable equity securities of investor-owned hospitals should follow the requirements stated in FASB *Statement No. 12*, which specifies the accounting and disclosure requirements for these types of organizations. *SOP, 78-1* also suggests that marketable equity securities for not-for-profit hospitals should be grouped into separate portfolios as follows:

**1** Marketable equity securities included in unrestricted funds should be grouped into separate portfolios according to the current or noncurrent classification of the securities.

**2** Marketable equity securities included in different types of restricted funds should be grouped into separate portfolios according to types of funds (for example, portfolios of marketable equity securities included in various specific purpose funds should be grouped together but not with those in endowment funds).

**3** The current portfolios of unrestricted funds of entities that are combined in financial statements should be treated as a single combined portfolio; the noncurrent unrestricted portfolios of those entities should also be treated as a single combined portfolio; similar restricted fund portfolios of entities that are combined in financial statements should be treated as single portfolios (for example, portfolios of marketable equity securities included in the various specific purpose funds of a not-for-profit hospital should be combined with the portfolios of marketable equity securities held in the various specific purpose funds of an entity whose financial statements are combined with those of the not-for-profit hospital).[8]

**Property, Plant, and Equipment** In contrast to the accounting for fixed assets used for current operations in governmental funds, which are recorded in the general fixed assets account group, fixed assets used for current operations of hospitals are recorded in the unrestricted fund. Depreciable property in this fund is then depreciated each accounting period, and the depreciations expense is shown in the statement of revenues and expenses as a separate line-item operating expense. The accumulated depreciation is shown in the balance sheet as a deduction from the fixed assets. Technological improvements may lessen the useful life of hospital plant and equipment. So, in determining useful life as a basis for ascertaining periodic depreciation on hospital plant and equipment, obsolescence should be taken into consideration as one of the factors used to determine the depreciation rate.

Fixed assets held for investment or for other nonoperating purposes should be shown separately in the balance sheet from those fixed assets used for operations.

Long-term leases for the use of property, plant, and equipment would have to follow Accounting Principles Board *Opinion No. 5, Reporting of Leases in Financial Statements of Lessee*, and FASB *Statement 13, Accounting for Leases*. This subject has been discussed and illustrated in Chapter 11.

To illustrate the statement presentation for fixed assets and the related depreciation, in the unrestricted fund, let us assume that the property, plant, and equipment for a hospital at year end amounted to $8,000,000. Prior years' accumulated depreciation amounted to $3,000,000, and this year's depreciation amounted to $250,000. The balance sheet presentation would be as follows:

| | |
|---|---|
| Property, plant, and equipment | $8,000,000 |
| Less accumulated depreciation | 3,250,000 |
| Net property, plant, and equipment | $4,750,000 |

As a special line item under operating expenses in the statement of revenues and expenses, in the unrestricted fund, depreciation expenses would be shown as follows:

Operating expenses:
   Nursing services, etc.     —
   Provision for depreciation     $250,000
      Total operating expenses     —

## Liabilities

Liabilities in hospital accounting include all of the liabilities found in a normal business organization, such as current and long-term debt, deferred revenue, and accrued expenses. Instead of carrying long-term debt in a general long-term debt account group, as is done in government, hospitals carry them as long-term debt, pay interest on the debt, and retire the debt in the unrestricted fund. Long-term debt is not isolated from the other operating activities, as is done in some other fund organizations.

## Revenues

Operating revenues in a hospital not only come from patient services but also from research and other grants, educational programs, nonpatient meals, sales of scrap and waste, and miscellaneous other sources. Nonoperating revenues include unrestricted gifts, income from endowment funds, donated services, rental income, and gains from investments.

Deductions from patient services revenue include: those previously discussed under accounts and notes receivable and charity allowances; policy discounts to employees, doctors, and others; and contractual adjustments to third-party payors.

**Donated Services** Some of the revenue received from hospital operations is that of donated services. The donated services are recorded at fair value as an other operating revenue and also as an operating expense if an employer-employee relationship exists and the value of the service can be determined objectively. For example, if certain nurses donated their services to the hospital, objectively valued at $10,000, the entry for that donation would be:

|  | Dr. | Cr. |
|---|---|---|
| Nursing services expense | $10,000 |  |
|    Donated services revenue |  | $10,000 |

To record nursing services donated to the operations of the hospital.

**Other Revenue Sources** Fees for physicians and surgeons who carry out their functions in a hospital usually are not considered as hospital revenue. Hospital revenue from patient services includes such items as nursing services and room and board. Daily patient services may also be classified by type of service as: medical, surgical, pediatrics, intensive care, psychiatric, obstetric, newborn nurseries, premature nurseries, and other. Revenue also may be classified in terms of the place at which the nursing services were performed, such as operating room, recovery room, emergency service, and so forth. In addition, other professional services include laboratories, blood bank, radiology, anesthesiology, physical therapy, and electrocardiology. These types of revenue are sometimes classified as (1) revenue from daily patient services (routine services), (2) revenue from other nursing services, or (3) revenue from other professional services (ancillary services).[9]

## Expenses

Expenses may be classified either functionally or by object of expenditures. The normal functional classification is: (1) nursing services, (2) other professional services, (3) general services, and (4) fiscal and administrative services including depreciation. Object-of-expenditure classifications include: (1) salaries and wages, (2) employee benefits, (3) fees to individuals and organizations, (4) supplies, (5) purchased services, and (6) other expenses, including depreciation. Exhibit 16-1 shows a schedule listing the detailed accounts under these expense categories used in the accounting system.[10]

Expenses of fund raising may be deducted from the related revenue, or they may be disclosed separately in the financial statements.

Revenue and expenses of the restricted funds would be similar to those discussed in the governmental section on fiduciary funds in Chapter 10, in the restricted funds discussion in Chapter 15 on university accounting, and in Chapter 14 regarding other nonbusiness accounting. Interfund transactions from the restricted funds to the unrestricted fund have already been illustrated.

## Fund Balance

Capital equity of the various funds of a hospital does not usually include more than one type of capital equity account—the fund balance account. An account such as retained earnings is not necessary, since all capital equity transactions (e.g., transfers of property, plant, and equipment funds from the restricted account, that is, the plant replacement and expansion fund) would go directly to fund balance. This type of transaction has been illustrated in the section on funds.

Likewise, donations to both the unrestricted funds of property and equipment, at fair market value, go directly to the fund balance account.

## APPLICATION OF ACCOUNTING PRINCIPLES—RESTRICTED FUNDS

The basic idea concerning applying accounting principles in restricted funds is that there would be no restricted fund unless a restriction was placed on the use of certain resources by an outside donor. So, the wishes of the donor must be met before the funds can be released from their restrictions and transferred to unrestricted funds.

As previously noted, restricted funds can be classified as: (1) funds for specific operating purposes, (2) funds for additions to property, plant, and equipment, and (3) endowment funds.

**EXHIBIT 16-1**
**Sample Hospital**
**Schedule of Operating Expenses**[11]
**Year Ended December 31, 19__**
**With Comparative Figures for 19__**

|  | Current year | | Prior year | |
|---|---|---|---|---|
|  | Personal services | Supplies and other expense | Personal services | Supplies and other expense |
| Nursing services: | $ | | | |
|   Administrative office | | | | |
|   Medical and surgical | | | | |
|   Pediatrics | | | | |
|   Intensive care | | | | |
|   Psychiatric | | | | |
|   Obstetric | | | | |
|   Newborn nurseries | | | | |
|   Premature nurseries | | | | |
|   Other units | | | | |
|   Operating rooms | | | | |
|   Recovery rooms | | | | |
|   Delivery and labor rooms | | | | |
|   Central services and supply | | | | |
|   Intravenous therapy | | | | |
|   Emergency service | | | | |
|   Education | | | | |
|   Other | | | | |
|  | $ | | | |
| Other professional services: | $ | | | |
|   Administrative office | | | | |
|   Laboratories | | | | |
|   Blood bank | | | | |
|   Electrocardiology | | | | |
|   Electroencephalography | | | | |
|   Radiology | | | | |
|   Clinics | | | | |
|   Inhalation therapy | | | | |
|   Medical records | | | | |
|   Pharmacy | | | | |
|   Anesthesiology | | | | |
|   Physical therapy | | | | |
|   Social service | | | | |
|   Education | | | | |
|   Research | | | | |
|   Other | | | | |
|  | $ | | | |

**EXHIBIT 16-1**
(*continued*)

|  | Current year | | Prior year | |
|---|---|---|---|---|
|  | Personal services | Supplies and other expense | Personal services | Supplies and other expense |
| General services: | $ | | | |
|   Administrative office | | | | |
|   Dietary | | | | |
|   Plant engineering | | | | |
|   Power plant | | | | |
|   Electricity and refrigeration | | | | |
|   Maintenance shops | | | | |
|   Automotive service | | | | |
|   Elevator operators | | | | |
|   Security | | | | |
|   Housekeeping | | | | |
|   Laundry and linen | | | | |
|   Personnel quarters | | | | |
|   Printing and duplicating | | | | |
|   Physicians' offices | | | | |
|   Auxiliary units | | | | |
|  | $ | | | |
| Fiscal services: | $ | | | |
|   Administrative office | | | | |
|   Accounting | | | | |
|   Admitting | | | | |
|   Credits and collections | | | | |
|   Data processing | | | | |
|   Receiving | | | | |
|   Cashier | | | | |
|   Communications | | | | |
|   Storerooms | | | | |
|   Other | | | | |
|  | $ | | | |
| Administrative services: | $ | | | |
|   Executive office | | | | |
|   Personnel | | | | |
|   Purchasing | | | | |
|   Public relations | | | | |
|   Governing board | | | | |
|   Medical staff | | | | |
|   Employee benefits | | | | |
|   Insurance | | | | |
|   Auxiliaries | | | | |
|   Interest | | | | |
|   Other | | | | |
|  | $ | | | |

## Specific Purpose Funds

Specific purpose funds are restricted by the donor to operating purposes. When transferred to the unrestricted fund, they will be a part of the operations of the hospital and will be shown in the revenue and expense statement, usually as operating revenue.

## Plant Replacement and Expansion Funds

Contributions by donors specifically for property, plant, and equipment replacement or additions, when transferred to the unrestricted fund for expenditures made, become a part of the capital equity of the unrestricted fund. They do not become a part of the operations until the plant and equipment are depreciated.

However, when contributions are made by outside donors and restricted to reimbursing the unrestricted fund for depreciation expense in order to replace or add new assets, the contribution would be included as revenue in the unrestricted fund. But an amount would not be taken from the unrestricted fund's fund balance and transferred to a restricted fund until actual expenditures are made. When the actual expenditures for additions or replacement are made, the restricted fund would transfer sufficient resources to the unrestricted fund to cover the costs of the new assets. The transfer would go directly to the fund balance account and not be shown as a revenue account.

## Endowment Funds

Endowment funds consist primarily of two types:

**1** Those whose principal remains in perpetuity and the income can be expended (pure endowment fund)
**2** Those whose principal (and/or interest) can be expended after a certain period of time or after a particular event (such as a death) takes place (term endowment fund)

When endowment fund income is restricted as to its use (or term endowment fund principal when released), the funds should be transferred to a restricted fund (either plant fund or specific purpose fund) and then transferred to the unrestricted fund when the restrictions have been met. Otherwise, the purpose of the endowment fund would determine whether the income (or term endowment fund principal when released) would be operating revenue, nonoperating revenue, or an increase in fund balance.

## FINANCIAL STATEMENTS

Hospital accounting requires the preparation of the following financial statements for the unrestricted fund:

**1** Balance sheet
**2** Statement of revenues and expenses
**3** Statement of changes in fund balance
**4** Statement of changes in financial position

For the restricted funds, the following statements must be prepared:

1 Balance sheet
2 Statement of changes in fund balance

### Illustrative Balance Sheet

**Unrestricted Fund** Exhibit 16-2, taken from the AICPA's *Hospital Audit Guide*, shows the normal presentation of a hospital balance sheet. Note the following in this statement:

1 The assets are classified as current and other. The "other" classification includes both board-designated funds (including cash and investments) and property, plant, and equipment, less depreciation.
2 Receivables are shown less estimated uncollectibles and allowances, as previously illustrated.
3 Liabilities are classified as current, deferred revenue—third-party payors, long-term debt, and fund balance.
4 The balance sheets are shown for two years.

**Restricted Funds** The restricted funds balance sheets are shown as a continuation of Exhibit 16-2. (The notes referred to in the body of Exhibit 16-2 and the other exhibits that follow are not included here.) Note the following in these statements:

1 Restricted funds are classified as follows:
   a Specific purpose funds
   b Plant replacement and expansion funds
   c Endowment funds

Each of these classifications may have several funds in them; they are, however, combined into one fund for statement purposes.

2 The plant replacement and expansion fund has pledges receivable, net of estimated uncollectibles.

### Illustrative Statement of Revenues and Expenses—Unrestricted Fund

A revenues and expenses statement is needed only in the unrestricted fund. Exhibit 16-3 provides an illustration of this statement. Note the following in the statement:

1 Allowances and uncollectible amounts are deducted from patient services revenue.
2 Revenue is classified as operating revenue and other operating revenue.
3 Expenses are classified as operating expenses and nonoperating expenses.
4 Operating expenses are classified in this statement by functions as follows:
   a Nursing services
   b Other professional services
   c General services

**d** Fiscal services
   **e** Administrative services (including interest)
   **f** Provision for depreciation

   **5** Nonoperating revenue includes unrestricted gifts and bequests, unrestricted income from endowment funds, and gains and income from board-designated investments.

## Illustrative Statement of Changes in Fund Balances

A statement of changes in fund balance must be prepared for both unrestricted funds and restricted funds.

**Unrestricted Funds** Exhibit 16-4 shows a sample statement of changes in fund balances for a hospital's unrestricted fund. Note that in addition to the net excess of revenue over expenses, changes include amounts transferred from the plant replacement and expansion fund (a restricted fund) for expenditures for replacements or additions to property, plant, and equipment in the unrestricted fund. Likewise, donations for replacement of property, plant, and equipment that were given to the unrestricted fund and not expended are transferred to the restricted fund.

**Restricted Funds** The restricted funds changes in fund balance statement is classified by: (1) specific purpose funds, (2) plant replacement and expansion funds, and (3) endowment funds.

By observing the classification of items in the changes in fund balance for the specific purpose funds, one can determine the types of items received in these funds: restricted gifts and bequests, grants, income from investments, and gain on sale of investments. Payments made are those pertaining to operations in the unrestricted fund: other operating revenue and deductions from allowances and uncollectible accounts, such as charity cases.

The plant replacement and expansion fund increases in fund balance can come from restricted gifts and bequests, income from investments, and transfers from other funds. Decreases in the fund balance usually pertain to the amounts transferred to the unrestricted fund for plant replacement and expansion, property, and equipment.

**Endowment Funds** Endowment funds often go for several years with only increases in the fund balance. This illustration shows only amounts received and income earned, not amounts transferred to other funds.

## Illustrative Statement of Changes in Financial Position—Unrestricted Fund

Exhibit 16-5 is an illustrative statement of changes in financial position. Note those items that are a little different from the normal statement of changes in financial position pertaining to funds provided.

## EXHIBIT 16-2
### Sample Hospital
### Balance Sheet[12]
### December 31, 19___
### With Comparative Figures for 19___

### Unrestricted funds

| Assets | Current year | Prior year | Liabilities and fund balances | Current year | Prior year |
|---|---|---|---|---|---|
| Current: | | | Current: | | |
| Cash | $ 133,000 | $ 33,000 | Notes payable to banks | $ 227,000 | $ 300,000 |
| Receivables (Note 3) | 1,382,000 | 1,269,000 | Current installments of long-term debt (Note 5) | 90,000 | 90,000 |
| Less estimated uncollectibles and allowances | (160,000) | (105,000) | Accounts payable | 450,000 | 463,000 |
| | 1,222,000 | 1,164,000 | Accrued expenses | 150,000 | 147,000 |
| Due from restricted funds | 215,000 | — | Advances from third-party payors | 300,000 | 200,000 |
| Inventories (if material, state basis) | 176,000 | 183,000 | Deferred revenue | 10,000 | 10,000 |
| Prepaid expenses | 68,000 | 73,000 | Total current liabilities | 1,227,000 | 1,210,000 |
| Total current assets | 1,814,000 | 1,453,000 | Deferred revenue—third-party reimbursement (Note 4) | 200,000 | 90,000 |
| Other: | | | Long-term debt (Note 5): | | |
| Cash (Note 2) | 143,000 | 40,000 | Housing bonds | 500,000 | 520,000 |
| Investments (Notes 1 and 2) | 1,427,000 | 1,740,000 | Mortgage notes | 1,200,000 | 1,270,000 |
| Property, plant, and equipment (Notes 4 and 5) | 11,028,000 | 10,375,000 | Total long-term debt | 1,700,000 | 1,790,000 |
| Less accumulated depreciation | (3,885,000) | (3,000,000) | Fund balance* | 7,400,000 | 6,918,000 |
| Net property, plant, and equipment | 7,143,000 | 6,775,000 | | | |
| Total (Note 2) | $10,527,000 | $10,008,000 | Total | $10,527,000 | $10,008,000 |

## Restricted Funds

| | | | | |
|---|---:|---|---:|---:|
| **Specific purpose funds:** | | **Specific purpose funds:** | | |
| Cash | $ 1,260 | Due to unrestricted funds | $ 215,000 | $ — |
| Investments (Note 1) | 200,000 | Fund balances: | | |
| Grants receivable | 90,000 | Research grants | 15,000 | 30,000 |
| | | Other | 61,260 | 41,000 |
| | | | 76,260 | 71,000 |
| Total specific purpose funds | $ 291,260 | Total specific purpose funds | $ 291,260 | $ 71,000 |
| **Plant replacement and expansion funds:** | | **Plant replacement and expansion funds:** | | |
| Cash | $ 10,000 | Fund balances: | | |
| Investments (Note 1) | 800,000 | Restricted by third-party payors | $ 380,000 | $ 150,000 |
| Pledges receivable, net of estimated uncollectible | 20,000 | Other | 450,000 | 950,000 |
| Total plant replacement and expansion funds | $ 830,000 | Total plant replacement and expansion funds | $ 830,000 | $ 1,100,000 |
| **Endowment funds:** | | **Endowment funds:** | | |
| Cash | $ 50,000 | Fund balances: | | |
| Investments (Note 1) | 6,100,000 | Permanent endowment | $ 4,850,000 | $ 2,675,000 |
| | | Term endowment | 1,300,000 | 1,300,000 |
| Total endowment funds | $ 6,150,000 | Total endowment funds | $ 6,150,000 | $ 3,975,000 |
| | $ 3,975,000 | | | |

*Composition of the fund balance may be shown here, on the statement of changes in fund balances (such as illustrated in Exhibit 16-4), or in a footnote.

## EXHIBIT 16-3
### Sample Hospital
### Statement of Revenues and Expenses[13]
### Year Ended December 31, 19___
### With Comparative Figures for 19___

|  | Current year | Prior year |
|---|---:|---:|
| Patient service revenue | $8,500,000 | $8,000,000 |
| Allowances and uncollectible accounts (after deduction of related gifts, grants, subsidies, and other income— $55,000 and $40,000) (Notes 3 and 4) | (1,777,000) | (1,700,000) |
| Net patient service revenue | 6,723,000 | 6,300,000 |
| Other operating revenue (including $100,000 and $80,000 from specific purpose funds) | 184,000 | 173,000 |
| Total operating revenue | 6,907,000 | 6,473,000 |
| Operating expenses: | | |
| Nursing services | 2,200,000 | 2,000,000 |
| Other professional services | 1,900,000 | 1,700,000 |
| General services | 2,100,000 | 2,000,000 |
| Fiscal services | 375,000 | 360,000 |
| Administrative services (including interest expense of $50,000 and $40,000) | 400,000 | 375,000 |
| Provision for depreciation | 300,000 | 250,000 |
| Total operating expenses | 7,275,000 | 6,685,000 |
| Loss from operations | (368,000) | (212,000) |
| Nonoperating revenue: | | |
| Unrestricted gifts and bequests | 228,000 | 205,000 |
| Unrestricted income from endowment funds | 170,000 | 80,000 |
| Income and gains from board-designated funds | 54,000 | 41,000 |
| Total nonoperating revenue | 452,000 | 326,000 |
| Excess of revenues over expenses | $ 84,000 | $ 114,000 |

1 Increase in deferred third-party reimbursements

2 Revenue restricted to property, plant, and equipment replacement transferred to plant replacement and expansion fund

3 Decrease in board-designated funds, and property, plant, and equipment expenditures financed by plant replacement and expansion funds

As to funds applied, the only major difference from the normal statement of changes in financial position is that pertaining to increase in board-designated funds.

## VARIATIONS IN ACCOUNTING AND SPECIALIZED NEEDS

Several areas of accounting not discussed in the preceding sections of the chapter need to be considered whenever discussing hospital accounting. They are.

1 Budgetary accounting
2 Cost accounting

EXHIBIT 16-4
Sample Hospital
Statement of Changes in Fund Balances[14]
Year Ended December 31, 19__
With Comparative Figures for 19__

|  | Current year | Prior year |
|---|---|---|
| **Unrestricted Funds** | | |
| Balance at beginning of year | $6,918,000 | $6,242,000 |
| Excess of revenues over expenses | 84,000 | 114,000 |
| Transferred from plant replacement and expansion funds to finance property, plant, and equipment expenditures | 628,000 | 762,000 |
| Transferred to plant replacement and expansion funds to reflect third-party payor revenue restricted to property, plant, and equipment replacement | (230,000) | (200,000) |
| Balance at end of year | $7,400,000 * | $6,918,000 |
| **Restricted Funds** | | |
| Specific purpose funds: | | |
| Balance at beginning of year | $ 71,000 | $ 50,000 |
| Restricted gifts and bequests | 35,000 | 20,000 |
| Research grants | 35,000 | 45,000 |
| Income from investments | 35,260 | 39,000 |
| Gain on sale of investments | 8,000 | — |
| Transferred to: | | |
| Other operating revenue | (100,000) | (80,000) |
| Allowances and uncollectible accounts | (8,000) | (3,000) |
| Balance at end of year | $ 76,260 | $ 71,000 |
| Plant replacement and expansion funds: | | |
| Balance at beginning of year | $1,100,000 | $1,494,000 |
| Restricted gifts and bequests | 113,000 | 150,000 |
| Income from investments | 15,000 | 18,000 |
| Transferred to unrestricted funds (described above) | (628,000) | (762,000) |
| Transferred from unrestricted funds (described above) | 230,000 | 200,000 |
| Balance at end of year | $ 830,000 | $1,100,000 |
| Endowment funds: | | |
| Balance at beginning of year | $3,975,000 | $2,875,000 |
| Restricted gifts and bequests | 2,000,000 | 1,000,000 |
| Net gain on sale of investments | 175,000 | 100,000 |
| Balance at end of year | $6,150,000 | $3,975,000 |

*Composition of the balance may be shown here, on the balance sheet, or in a footnote.

**EXHIBIT 16-5**
**Sample Hospital**
**Statement of Changes in Financial Position of**
**Unrestricted Fund[15]**
**With Comparative Figures for 19__**
**Year Ended December 31, 19__**

|  | Current year | Prior year |
|---|---:|---:|
| Funds provided: |  |  |
| Loss from operations | $ (368,000) | $ (212,000) |
| Deduct (add) items included in operations not requiring (providing) funds: |  |  |
| Provision for depreciation | 300,000 | 250,000 |
| Increase in deferred third-party reimbursement | 110,000 | 90,000 |
| Revenue restricted to property, plant, and equipment replacement transferred to plant replacement and expansion fund | (230,000) | (200,000) |
| Funds required for operations | (188,000) | (72,000) |
| Nonoperating revenue | 452,000 | 326,000 |
| Funds derived from operations and nonoperating revenues | 264,000 | 254,000 |
| Decrease in board-designated funds | 210,000 | — |
| Property, plant, and equipment expenditures financed by plant replacement and expansion funds | 628,000 | 762,000 |
| Decrease in working capital | — | 46,000 |
|  | $1,102,000 | $1,062,000 |
| Funds applied: |  |  |
| Additions to property, plant, and equipment | $ 668,000 | $ 762,000 |
| Reduction of long-term debt | 90,000 | 90,000 |
| Increase in board-designated funds | — | 210,000 |
| Increase in working capital | 344,000 | — |
|  | $1,102,000 | $1,062,000 |
| Changes in working capital: |  |  |
| Increase (decrease) in current assets: |  |  |
| Cash | $ 100,000 | $ (50,000) |
| Receivables | 58,000 | 75,000 |
| Due from restricted funds | 215,000 | (100,000) |
| Inventories | (7,000) | 16,000 |
| Prepaid expenses | (5,000) | 1,000 |
|  | 361,000 | (58,000) |
| Increase (decrease) in current liabilities: |  |  |
| Note payable to banks | (73,000) | 50,000 |
| Accounts payable | (13,000) | 10,000 |
| Accrued expenses | 3,000 | 2,000 |
| Advances from third-party payors | 100,000 | 40,000 |
| Deferred revenue | — | 2,000 |
|  | 17,000 | 104,000 |
| Increase (decrease) in working capital | $ 344,000 | $ (46,000) |

3 Hospitals as a part of other organizations
4 Board-designated funds
5 Hospitals operated by governmental units
6 Malpractice loss contingencies

## Budgetary Accounting

Enterprise or profit-type funds generally do not use the fixed budget found in governmental fund accounting. Thus, when budgeting is used in hospital accounting, unless the hospital is a governmental hospital, the type of budget found is the flexible budget, in order to accommodate the level of operations that may occur. Since this type of budgeting is for management control, it is discussed in Part III, Chapter 19.

## Cost Accounting

Because of the contractual arrangements with third-party payors, costs of particular functions become very important in hospital accounting. Without cost accounting, it is very difficult to determine the actual costs of operation, from which many third-party payors base their determination of reimbursement rates.

Cost accounting is not discussed in this chapter, but is thoroughly discussed and illustrated in Chapters 17, 18, and 19.

## Hospitals as a Part of Other Organizations

The *Hospital Audit Guide* as amended by the AICPA's *Statement of Position, 81-2* says concerning reporting practices of hospital-related organizations:

9 Not-for-profit hospitals may be related to one or more separate not-for-profit organizations. For purposes of this statement of position, a separate organization is considered to be related to a hospital if
 a The hospital controls the separate organization through contracts or other legal documents that provide the hospital with the authority to direct the separate organization's activities, management, and policies;
 b The hospital is for all practical purposes the sole beneficiary of the organization. The hospital should be considered the organization's sole beneficiary if any one of the three following circumstances exist:
  (1) The organization has solicited funds in the name of the hospital, and with the expressed or implied approval of the hospital, and substantially all the funds solicited by the organization were intended by the contributor, or were otherwise required, to be transferred to the hospital or used at its discretion or direction.
  (2) The hospital has transferred some of its resources to the organization, and substantially all of the organization's resources are held for the benefit of the hospital.
  (3) The hospital has assigned certain of its functions (such as the operation of a dormitory) to the organization, which is operating primarily for the benefit of the hospital.[16]

When the above conditions apply, the financial statements should be consolidated, combined, or references made in the notes to the financial statements. Accounting Research Bulletin No. 51, *Consolidated Financial Statements*, provides guidance as to whether the financial statements should be consolidated, combined, or the information shown in the notes to the statements.

The following summary, taken from *SOP, 81-2*, shows the conditions under which the statements are consolidated, combined, or notes to the financial statements made.

SUMMARY OF REQUIREMENTS OF THE HOSPITAL[17]

| Circumstances | Requirements |
| --- | --- |
| The hospital is related to a separate organization and meets the criteria stated in ARB no. 51. | Consolidate or combine in accordance with ARB no. 51. |
| The hospital does not meet the criteria stated in ARB no. 51 but controls and is the sole beneficiary of the related organization's activities. | In a note to the financial statements, disclose summarized financial data of the related organization, such as total assets, total liabilities, changes in fund balances, total revenue, total expenses, and amount of distributions to the hospital; and disclose the nature of the relationship between the hospital and the related organization. |
| Neither of the above is present, but the related organization holds significant amounts of funds designated for the hospital. | Disclose the existence and nature of the relationship. |
| There have been material transactions between the hospital and the related organization. (This could be present in any of the above circumstances.) | In the notes to the financial statements, (a) disclose the existence and nature of the relationship and (b) describe and quantify the transactions. |

## Board-Designated Funds

The governing board of a hospital may designate certain unrestricted funds for restricted purposes. For example, each year the board may appropriate $100,000 of the unrestricted funds for the construction of a wing on the hospital. This designation of board-designated funds does not change the classification of the funds from unrestricted to restricted, but the resources are shown as board-designated funds in the unrestricted portion of the records and the financial statements.

## Hospitals Operated by Governmental Units

As stated in the opening section of the chapter, governmental units may own and operate hospitals as do private investors and other non-profit organizations, such as churches and universities. In the past, governmental organizations often operated the hospital either as a special revenue fund or as an enterprise fund. *Statement of Position, 78-7* provides a suggested guide for auditors who audit government-owned and government-operated hospitals. It says:

Hospitals that are operated by governmental units should follow the requirements of the AICPA's *Hospital Audit Guide*. Since the accounting recommended in that guide can best be accommodated in the enterprise funds, such funds should be used in accounting for governmental hospitals.[18]

## Malpractice Loss Contingencies

The accounting profession has consistently maintained that if a loss contingency has occurred that can result in a probable loss, then that contingency should be reflected in the financial statements as an accrued expenditure. *FASB Statement No. 5, Accounting for Contingencies*, FASB *Interpretation No. 14, Reasonable Estimation of the Amount of a Loss*, and the AICPA's *Statement on Auditing Standards No. 12, Inquiry of a Client's Lawyer Concerning Litigation, Claims, and Assessments* are examples of the accountant's interest in this subject.

In recent years, malpractice suits against professionals and certain organizations, such as hospitals, have become increasingly common, and many times the individual bringing the suit is awarded very large sums of money. Therefore, some professionals and organizations have been dropping their malpractice insurance because of the cost. This automatically brings about a possibility of a large malpractice loss contingency.

In a *1978 Statement of Position* concerning malpractice loss contingencies, the AICPA's Subcommittee on Health Care Matters says that: ''The estimated loss contingency resulting from malpractice risks should be accrued for and disclosed in conformity with the provisions of FASB *Statement No. 5* and FASB *Interpretation No. 14*.''[19]

## SUMMARY

Since a majority of hospitals are of the nonprofit type, hospital accounting is considered to fall within the scope of accounting for nonbusiness organizations, even though the accounting principles are basically the same as for most business organizations. Hospitals must follow accounting principles normally considered generally accepted accounting principles. A major variation from normal GAAP is that hospital accounting is accomplished through two funds: unrestricted and restricted.

Within the unrestricted fund are three groups: current, board-designated, and plant. These groups operate as if they were only one fund; the separation into groups is primarily for financial statement presentation. Within the restricted funds are also three distinctive funds: specific purpose; additions to property, plant, and equipment; and endowment. These groups operate as individual funds, each with its own separate set of records. However, the individual funds within each separate group are shown separately when presented in financial statements.

The titles of the accounts found in hospital accounting may differ from those found in normal enterprise accounting. Presently, the major portion of current revenue of a hospital is predominantly financed through third-party payors, such as Blue Cross/Blue Shield, Medicare, and Medicaid. Contractual arrangements by the hospital with third-party payors usually provide for discounts on the regular billed price. The original billings are at the normal billed price, and the adjustments for contractual agreements, charity cases, and policy discounts are then provided when the bill is presented to third-party payors or when the bill is actually paid by them. Yet, GAAP accrual accounting for hospitals requires that the provisions for contractual adjustments and bad debts be provided in the financial statements. This is usually done through year-end adjustments.

Financial statements for the unrestricted fund are: balance sheet, statement of revenues and expenses, statement of changes in fund balance, and a statement of changes in financial position. Financial statements for the restricted fund are the balance sheet and statement of changes in fund balance; thus the net changes in fund balance normally shown in the statement of revenues and expenses are shown in the statement of changes in fund balance in the restricted funds.

Often, hospitals are related to other types of organizations, such as fund-gathering organizations, a cafeteria, or nurses' dormitories. Under most related organizations, their financial statements must be consolidated, combined, or explained in the notes to the financial statements.

Board-designated funds, much as in other nonbusiness organizations, are a part of the current operating fund and are not a restricted fund. Government-owned and government-operated hospitals must follow the same accounting principles found in all other types of hospitals.

## QUESTIONS

1 Describe the importance of good accounting for hospitals as it relates to third-party users.
2 Where are the generally accepted accounting principles for hospitals obtained?
3 What basis of accounting is used for hospital accounting?
4 What funds are used in hospital accounting? Describe the components of each fund.
5 The governing board of the Riverside Community Hospital sets aside $25,000 each year in order to purchase newer operating equipment. Their argument has been that these funds are restricted for general operations and, therefore, should be placed in the restricted fund, especially in the additions to property, plant, and equipment fund. Are they applying appropriate accounting principles when they record this transaction in this manner?
6 A city has a special revenue fund that is used to pay for a part of the operations of the Johnston City Community Hospital. Should the hospital operate as a special revenue fund of the city or as an enterprise fund?
7 Explain the reasoning behind billing patients of a hospital at the standard rate rather than at the payment rate, with the allowances for policy discounts and charitable services, along with contractual adjustments being shown separately and deducted from the gross billing rate in the statement.
8 This is the last chapter in the book on fund accounting and financial reporting for nonbusiness entities. Distinguish among the various types of fund accounting as related to hospital accounting.
9 Prepare the journal entries for both the unrestricted fund and the restricted funds when the additions to property, plant, and equipment fund reimburses the unrestricted fund for all purchases of new equipment. The unrestricted fund purchases $45,000 worth of new equipment during the accounting period.

10 Explain the difference between accounting for fixed assets, including depreciation, in hospital accounting and in college and university accounting; in hospital accounting and governmental fund accounting; and in certain nonprofit organization accounting and hospital accounting.
11 Pooling of investment resources in hospital accounting is a common occurrence. Explain how the pool allocates earnings and investments.
12 Are securities recorded in the accounting records of a hospital carried at cost, at market, or at cost or market, whichever is lower? Which is the procedure suggested by GAAP? By the American Hospital Association?
13 Do hospitals carry long-term debts and fixed assets in account groups? If not, explain how these two items are accounted for.
14 Explain how donated services are accounted for in hospital accounting.
15 Which financial statements are prepared for the funds in hospital accounting?
16 Do hospitals use fixed budgets? Explain which types of budgets are commonly used.
17 Is cost accounting a common type of accounting for hospitals?
18 Hospitals and other organizations quite commonly work together as related organizations. Explain how separate organizations may be considered related to the hospital.
19 Contingent liabilities arising from malpractice suits may be an important consideration in hospital accounting. Explain how malpractice loss contingencies are handled in the financial statements.

## PROBLEMS

16-1 Choose the best answer for each of the following questions.
1 From an accounting and financial reporting standpoint, hospitals are preponderantly of the:
   a Nonprofit type
   b Governmental type
   c Privately owned
   d None of the above
2 Hospital accounting basically follows:
   a GAAP for profit-type organizations
   b GAAP for governmental-fund-type organizations
   c GAAP for universities
   d GAAP for certain nonprofit organizations
3 Uncollectible debts in hospital accounting are:
   a Shown as expenses in the operating statement
   b Deducted from revenue before placing in the accounts
   c Deducted from revenue in the revenue and expense statement
   d Shown as a nonoperating expense in the revenue and expense statement
4 The basic types of funds in hospital accounting are:
   a Profit and nonprofit funds
   b Operating fund, plant fund, and unrestricted fund
   c General, special revenue, endowment, and plant funds
   d Restricted and unrestricted funds
5 In hospital accounting, subsidiary ledgers are
   a Seldom used

    **b** Used, but not to any great extent
    **c** Commonly used
    **d** Extensively used
**6** The standard rate for a private room in Providence Hospital is $215 per day. Mr. John Smith, a Medicare patient, occupies the room for six days. Medicare pays the hospital only $180 per day for the room. The journal entry (entries) to record this transaction is (are):

    **a**  Accounts receivable—Medicare     $1,080
          Patient services revenue                   $1,080
    **b**  Accounts receivable—inpatients not discharged     $1,080
          Patient services revenue                   $1,080
       Accounts receivable—Medicare     $1,080
          Accounts receivable—inpatients not discharged         $1,080
    **c**  Accounts receivable—Medicare     $1,080
       Allowance for bad debts     210
          Patient services revenue                   $1,290
    **d**  Accounts receivable—inpatients not discharged     $1,290
          Patient services revenue                   $1,290
       Accounts receivable—inpatients discharged     $1,290
          Accounts receivable—inpatients not discharged         $1,290
       Accounts receivable—Medicare     $1,080
       Contractual adjustments     210
          Accounts receivable—inpatients discharged         $1,290

**7** The financial statements needed for the unrestricted fund of a hospital are:
    **a** The balance sheet and income statement
    **b** The balance sheet, the statement of revenues and expenses, and the statement of changes in financial position
    **c** the balance sheet and the statement of revenues, expenses, and changes in fund balance
    **d** The balance sheet, the statement of revenues and expenses, the statement of changes in financial position, and the statement of changes in fund balance

**8** The financial statements needed for the restricted funds of a hospital are:
    **a** The balance sheet and the statement of changes in fund balance
    **b** The balance sheet and the income statement
    **c** The balance sheet, the income statement, the statement of changes in financial position, and the statement of changes in fund balance
    **d** The balance sheet, the statement of revenues and expenses, the statement of changes in financial position, and the statement of changes in fund balance

**16-2** Choose the best answer from each of the following questions.[20]
    **1** Which of the following would normally be included in other operating revenues of a voluntary not-for-profit hospital?
        **a** Unrestricted interest income from an endowment fund

b An unrestricted gift
c Donated services
d Tuition received from an educational program

2 Donated medicines that normally would be purchased by a hospital should be recorded at fair market value and should be credited directly to
a Other operating revenue
b Other nonoperating revenue
c Fund balance
d Deferred revenue

3 A gift to a voluntary not-for-profit hospital that is not restricted by the donor should be credited directly to
a Fund balance
b Deferred revenue
c Operating revenue
d Nonoperating revenue

4 Depreciation should be recognized in the financial statements of
a Proprietary (for-profit) hospitals only
b Both proprietary (for-profit) and not-for-profit hospitals
c Both proprietary (for-profit) and not-for-profit hospitals, only when they are affiliated with a college or university
d All hospitals, as a memorandum entry not affecting the statements of revenues and expenses

5 An unrestricted pledge from an annual contributor to a voluntary not-for-profit hospital made in December 19X1 and paid in cash in March 19X2 would generally be credited to
a Nonoperating revenue in 19X1
b Nonoperating revenue in 19X2
c Operating revenue in 19X1
d Operating revenue in 19X2

6 On July 1, 19X1, Lilydale Hospital's Board of Trustees designated $200,000 for expansion of outpatient facilities. The $200,000 is expected to be expended in the fiscal year ending June 30, 19X4. In Lilydale's balance sheet at June 30, 19X2, this cash should be classified as a $200,000
a Restricted current asset
b Restricted noncurrent asset
c Unrestricted current asset
d Unrestricted noncurrent asset

7 Glenmore Hospital's property, plant, and equipment (net of depreciation) consists of the following:

| | |
|---|---|
| Land | $ 500,000 |
| Buildings | 10,000,000 |
| Movable equipment | 2,000,000 |

What amount should be included in the restricted fund grouping?
a $0
b $2,000,000
c $10,500,000
d $12,500,000

**16-3** The following selected information was taken from the books and records of Glendora Hospital (a voluntary hospital) as of and for the year ended June 30, 19X2.[21]

1 Patient service revenue totaled $16,000,000, with allowances and uncollectible accounts amounting to $3,400,000. Other operating revenue aggregated $346,000 and included $160,000 from specific purpose funds. Revenue of $6,000,000 recognized under cost-reimbursement agreements is subject to audit and retroactive adjustment by third-party payors. Estimated retroactive adjustments under these agreements have been included in allowances.

2 Unrestricted gifts and bequests of $410,000 were received.

3 Unrestricted income from endowment funds totaled $160,000.

4 Income from board-designated funds aggregated $82,000.

5 Operating expenses totaled $13,370,000 and included $500,000 for depreciation computed on the straight-line basis. However, accelerated depreciation is used to determine reimbursable costs under certain third-party reimbursement agreements. Net cost reimbursement revenue amounting to $220,000, resulting from the difference in depreciation methods, was deferred to future years.

6 Also included in operating expenses are pension costs of $100,000, in connection with a noncontributory pension plan covering substantially all of Glendora's employees. Accrued pension costs are funded currently. Prior service cost is being amortized over a period of twenty years. The actuarially computed value of vested and nonvested benefits at year's end amounted to $3,000,000 and $350,000, respectively. The assumed rate of return used in determining the actuarial present value of accumulated plan benefits was 8 percent. The plan's net assets available for benefits at year's end was $3,050,000.

7 Gifts and bequests are recorded at fair market values when received.

8 Patient service revenue is accounted for at established rates on the accrual basis.

**Required**:

1 Prepare a formal statement of revenues and expenses for Glendora Hospital for the year ended June 30, 19X2.

2 Draft the appropriate disclosures in separate notes accompanying the statement of revenues and expenses, referencing each note to its respective item in the statement.

**16-4** The Board of Directors of the Edgemont Hospital determined that they needed to add a new wing onto the hospital to take care of the overload they currently had.

They determined that $1,800,000 would be needed. Of this amount, $800,000 could be obtained from government grants, if $1,000,000 could be raised from local contributions. A campaign to raise the $1,000,000 was started by obtaining pledges. The campaign chairman determined that of the total pledges received, about 90 percent would be paid. So, the goal was to receive pledges of $1,200,000, which goal campaign workers achieved. Cash of $1,080,000 was paid on the pledges, and the grant was obtained.

The wing on the hospital was built for the amount estimated, $1,800,000. The money left over from the campaign was left in the additions to property, plant, and equipment fund for any further additions needed to property, plant, and equipment. It was invested in interest-paying securities.

**Required**:

1 Prepare journal entries to record the above transactions in the appropriate fund or funds.

2 Prepare the balance sheet and the statement of changes in fund balance for the restricted fund.

**16-5** At the beginning of 19X5, the Mountain View Hospital's trial balances were as follows:

## Mountain View Hospital
### Trial Balances
### January 1, 19X5

#### Unrestricted Fund

| | | |
|---|---:|---:|
| Cash | $ 20,000 | |
| Accounts receivable | 50,000 | |
| Estimated uncollectibles and allowances | | $ 5,000 |
| Inventory of supplies | 18,000 | |
| Prepaid insurance | 12,000 | |
| Property, plant, and equipment | 7,500,000 | |
| Accumulated depreciation | | 1,500,000 |
| Accounts payable | | 22,000 |
| Accrued salaries payable | | 3,000 |
| Bonds payable | | 4,000,000 |
| Fund balance | | 2,070,000 |
| Totals | $7,600,000 | $7,600,000 |

#### Restricted Funds

| | | |
|---|---:|---:|
| Specific purpose fund: | | |
| Cash | $ 25,000 | |
| Fund balance | | $ 25,000 |
| Totals | $ 25,000 | $ 25,000 |
| Endowment fund: | | |
| Investments | $2,618,856 | |
| Fund balance | | $2,618,856 |
| Totals | $2,618,856 | $2,618,856 |

The following is information concerning the operations of the year.

**1** Cash collected on the prior year's accounts receivable was $45,000, and $5,000 was written off.

**2** During the year, inpatients were charged, at the standard rate, $2,500,000 for services rendered. Of this amount, charges for services to patients who were still in the hospital were $50,000. All of the others had been discharged, and $2,300,000 had been billed to third-party insurance payors. Contractual adjustments of $125,000 were made at the time of billing the insurance companies. Charitable cases at the standard rate amounted to $25,000. Outpatients were charged, at the standard rate, $100,000 for services rendered during the year. Of this amount, $80,000 was billed to insurance carriers, $10,000 was written off to contractual adjustments, and $10,000 was related to charity cases.

**3** Of the balance of $100,000 of accounts receivable left on the books at the end of the year, it was estimated that $5,000 would be written off as uncollectible accounts and a contractual adjustment would be made for $10,000 for accounts billed to insurance companies.

**4** Cash collected on the current year's accounts receivable was $2,330,000.

**5** Gifts and grants were received that were restricted to payment of charity cases that amounted to $75,000. The charity cases written off, however, were only $35,000. The balance remained in the specific purpose fund. The balance was also invested.

**6** During the year, $2,197,000 was paid on the $2,200,000 of accounts payable incurred for operating expenses as follows:

**a** Salaries, wages, and employee benefits, $2,000,000
  **b** Fees to individuals and organizations, $100,000
  **c** Supplies, $100,000
**7** Accrued salaries and wages at the end of the year were $10,000.
**8** Insurance used during the year was $4,000.
**9** Supplies inventory at the end of the year was $20,000.
**10** The property, plant, and equipment was purchased from donations received and a serial bond issue of $5,000,000 worth of 8 percent bonds. The bonds were to be retired at an annual basis of $200,000. Several wealthy donors had agreed to an endowment of $1,000,000 per year for ten years for the payment of principal and interest. The provision was made in the endowment that any amount, after sufficient resources had been received for payment of the total principal and interest, was to be transferred to the plant replacement and expansion fund, a restricted fund. This amount, with any earnings (assume earnings to be 10 percent a year) was to be used to reimburse the unrestricted fund for any additions to property, plant or equipment until the fund was exhausted.
**11** The average life of the plant and equipment was estimated to be twenty-five years.

**Required**:
Prepare journal entries for the transactions for the year, post the entries to a work sheet, and from the work sheet prepare the statements for the year.

**16-6** The following portfolios of the Hillside Community Hospital were pooled to obtain the maximum revenue from investments:

|  | Cost | Market |
|---|---|---|
| Unrestricted fund | $ 145,000 | $ 150,000 |
| Restricted funds: |  |  |
| Endowment fund A | 60,000 | 50,000 |
| Endowment fund B | 190,000 | 200,000 |
| Endowment fund C | 1,100,000 | 1,000,000 |
| Plant fund | 500,000 | 500,000 |

The pooled funds were expected to earn 10 percent on the investments.

**Required**:
Determine the amounts that should be allocated to each of the portfolios for the earnings on the investments in the pool.

**16-7** The unrestricted fund of the Oceanside Hospital purchased some modern equipment for the operating room at a cost of $250,000. The restricted fund "additions to property, plant, and equipment fund" had solicited sufficient resources to reimburse the unrestricted fund for this transaction.

**Required**:
Prepare general journal entries, with explanations, to record the above transactions in the proper fund or funds.

# NOTES

**1** Subcommittee on Health Care Matters, American Institute of Certified Public Accountants, *Industry Audit Guide. Hospital Audit Guide*, Fourth Edition (New York: American Institute of Certified Public Accountants, 1982), p. 3.
**2** Ibid., p. 4.

3 Ibid., pp. 4–10.
4 See American Hospital Association, *Chart of Accounts for Hospitals* (Chicago: American Hospital Association, 1978); also see *Hospitals*, the journal of American Hospital Association; and *Hospital Financial Management*, the journal of the Hospital Financial Association.
5 *Hospital Audit Guide*, p. 4.
6 Ibid., p. 19.
7 Ibid., pp. 17–18.
8 Ibid., p. 76.
9 Ibid., pp. 29–30.
10 Ibid., pp. 35–36.
11 Ibid., pp. 51–52.
12 Ibid., pp. 40–41.
13 Ibid., p. 42.
14 Ibid., p. 43.
15 Ibid., pp. 44–45.
16 Ibid., pp. 90–91.
17 Ibid., p. 96.
18 Ibid., p. 86.
19 Ibid., p. 67.
20 American Institute of Certified Public Accountants, *Uniform CPA Examination Questions and Unofficial Answers* (New York: American Institute of Certified Public Accountants, various dates).
21 Ibid., Nov. 1982.

# PART THREE

# ACCOUNTING FOR MANAGEMENT PLANNING AND CONTROL

The focus in earlier chapters has been on the development of accounting systems capable of producing financial reports for fiscal control, for compliance purposes, and for the benefit of external decision makers. Most management decisions, however, are based on inputs provided by other types of information. In the past fifteen years, management accounting techniques have been developed in a profit-oriented environment to provide a basis for the broader informational needs of management. Although to date their applications have been relatively limited, the existing techniques of management accounting can be successfully adapted to management control and planning systems in governmental and other not-for-profit settings. These techniques will be examined in further detail in Part III.

*Management accounting* is concerned with providing information to assist in management decisions. These decisions typically focus on the efficient and effective use of resources in the achievement of organizational objectives. *Cost accounting* involves methods of accumulating and assigning costs to products, projects, or services produced. Both cost accounting and management accounting are concerned with cost behavior and cost-measurement methods. Questions of efficiency often are defined and answered in least-cost terms. Effectiveness must be measured in terms of the results achieved and by the people served, that is, in terms of performance. Efficiency and effectiveness are not mutually exclusive concepts, however, which is why in recent years efforts have been made to combine management and cost accounting principles to form the basis for achieving both these aims—doing things right and doing the right things.

Doing the right things involves the development of an overall perspective in which the goals and objectives of the organization or community can be defined. This is provided in the introduction to Chapter 17. The balance of Chapter 17 acquaints the reader with the role of *management accounting* within the management control structure. In addition, basic cost concepts and cost-estimation techniques are introduced—techniques that support future-oriented management decisions. *Cost accounting systems* applicable to the management control procedures generally found in governmental and not-for-profit settings are discussed in Chapter 18, and management accounting techniques are outlined in Chapter 19.

CHAPTER 17

# MANAGEMENT ACCOUNTING IN THE MANAGEMENT PROCESS

In previous chapters, our primary purpose has been to introduce the reader to accounting principles and techniques for governmental and other nonbusiness organizations. These principles and techniques, for the most part, have been related to financial accounting and reporting. One of the primary responsibilities of management in any organization is to provide external users with timely and accurate accounting information that is in accordance with generally accepted accounting principles. Management, however, has other important information needs. These include the need to know: (1) that the organization is effectively accomplishing its goals and objectives, (2) that the resources of the organization are being used efficiently, and (3) the basis for timely corrective actions, if needed, when conditions (1) and/or (2) are not being met. These needs are usually supplied through what is called a *management control system*.

## Management Control Defined

Some form of management control has been applied for as long as formal organizations have existed. More recently, however, increased emphasis on *accountability*, in both the public and private sectors, has made the adoption of more effective techniques of management control all the more imperative. Accounting departments traditionally have served as the primary locus of the management control function in most organizations. Financial controls (as described in Parts I and II in relation to financial accounting and reporting) are essential to organizational survival. Information provided by an accounting system that is designed to serve the needs of internal decision making as well as external financial reporting is an integral component of a contemporary management control system.

Early definitions of control emphasized the importance of initiating corrective action when problems were discovered. In current definitions, greater emphasis is placed on the more positive aspects of control (rather than merely after-the-fact corrective actions). Management control is now looked upon as a continuous monitoring process. Robert J. Mockler suggests that management control is:

> a systematic effort to set performance standards consistent with planning objectives, to design information feedback systems, to compare actual performance with these predetermined standards, to determine whether there are any deviations and to measure their significance, and to take any action required to assure that all corporate resources are being used in the most effective and efficient way possible in achieving corporate objectives.[1]

From the standpoint of this book, management control is concerned primarily with ensuring that resources are obtained and used in an effective and efficient manner. In this context, accounting systems should be designed to facilitate the comparison of actual performance with the planned performance of the organization.

Management control involves several interrelated activities, as shown schematically in Exhibit 17-1. Budgets must first be established against which planned activities can be evaluated as they are carried out. Monitoring devices *measure* the performance of individuals, activities, and/or programs within the organization. The measurements obtained are then *compared* with the standards to determine whether the current state of affairs approximates the planned state. Finally, action devices must be applied to *correct* any significant deviations. Corrective action may involve bringing performance in line with plans or modifying plans to more closely reflect performance.

**EXHIBIT 17-1** A corrective model for management control.

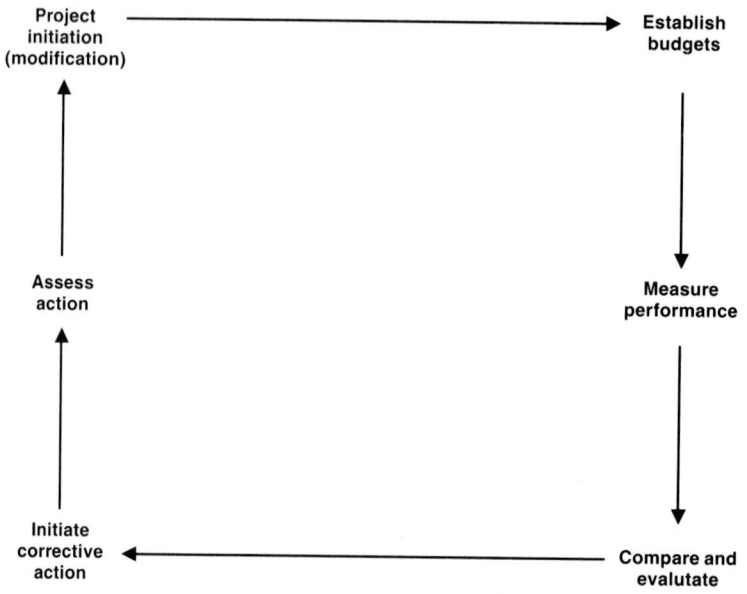

Project initiation (modification) → Establish budgets → Measure performance → Compare and evaluate → Initiate corrective action → Assess action → Project initiation (modification)

Taken in this context, controls can provide the tools for determining whether an organization is proceeding toward established objectives and can alert decision makers when actual performance deviates from planned performance. These procedures also can help to identify the magnitude of the deviation and appropriate corrective actions to bring the activities back on course.

## Establishing a Basis for Comparison

Standards may be based on input measures (costs) or may be expressed in terms of performance criteria and measures of output and effectiveness, such as profit expected or return on investment in an enterprise fund of government. Performance criteria in the not-for-profit sectors include productivity ratios, work load measures, and other indices that provide some bench marks against which to evaluate the actual activities of the organization in terms of economy and efficiency.

Identification of appropriate standards to be used in the budget begins with the design of program schedules and the development of estimates of resource needs. A program schedule details the specific tasks to be undertaken in terms of their sequence, time duration, and interdependence. A *work breakdown schedule* (WBS) might be prepared to show the various program tasks, milestones, technical performance goals, or other indicators. WBS techniques are widely used in business and industry and are beginning to find application in government and other not-for-profit organizations.

Resource estimates are then determined for each task; these estimates usually are expressed in dollar terms (i.e., as budgets) but also may include personnel requirements, special equipment and facility needs, and so forth. The starting and completion times for each task must be established and interdependences or linkages among tasks must be determined. Finally, the responsibility for carrying out each task should be assigned.

## Measuring Performance

A control system should include the means for measuring program achievements, that is, performance measures and measures of effectiveness. Such measurement may entail automated reporting procedures (monthly accounting summaries, for example, can provide a good basis for such measurement). Sometimes, the measurement may be undertaken by those groups or individuals whose performance is to be controlled. Self-measurement may result in a loss of meaningful control, however. Data that might reduce access to rewards (or serve as a basis for sanctions) may be concealed or distorted.

To counter this inherent tendency, special organizational units often are established to serve as sensors in the evaluation of certain activities of other organizational units. *Internal auditors,* for instance, are being assigned these responsibilities with increasing frequency in state government, larger universities, and municipal governments of major cities.

Work load and cost measures were adopted in the early 1900s to provide greater accountability in the delivery of public services. Work load measures represent *output measures* in that, in the aggregate, they indicate the volume of goods and/or services delivered by a program or activity. Cost measures, on the other hand, represent one important category of *input measures,* that is, data that indicate the resources employed to operate a program or project. When work load or output measures are related to costs or input measures, the resulting index often is called a *performance measure.*

*Work load measures* relate to the volume of work performed during some time period. In a welfare department, for example, it may be possible to determine the number of cases in various categories that can be handled by a case worker daily, weekly, or annually. With this information and an estimate of the total number of cases to be processed, the department head could calculate the amount of employee work hours required during any fiscal period. Other common work load measures include: tons of trash collected; number of arrests made; number of vaccinations given; number of inspections made; number of library books circulated; number of emergency calls responded to; number of full-time equivalent university students; number of hospital patients served daily; number of X-rays processed; and so forth. Work load measures serve as basic budget-building information and, often retrospectively, can provide an indication of the adequacy of previous resource allocation decisions.

Such measures often are used as indicators of operating efficiency: for example, the cost per patient-day of hospital service; the number of cases successfully prosecuted per law enforcement officer; or the response time involved in providing some public service. As may be seen from these examples, not all performance measures are expressed in cost terms. Performance measures provide basic management information on program economics, that is, such measures reveal the relationship between initial resource allocations (inputs) and the delivery of services (outputs).

**Comparison and Evaluation**

The comparison step indicates if deviations from the original plans are occurring in actual activities and results and, if so, the magnitude of these deviations. Suppose that the program involves the conversion of all work stations in the accounting office to a computerized data and word processing network. The objective is to accomplish this conversion over a period of six months at a cost not to exceed $1,500 per work station (including the computer terminals, training of personnel, etc.). This objective provides the standard in terms of performance criteria. At the end of three months, an assessment is made, and it is determined that only one-third of the stations have actually been converted at an average cost of $1,800 per station. It should be evident that the standards—time duration to accomplish the program and unit cost—have not been met to this point.

This comparison of actual versus planned performance is extremely important. Although basic information is provided, not all deviations from the plan are of equal significance. Therefore, judgments must be made to determine whether the deviations from the plan warrant corrective action.

Evaluation involves a diagnosis of the types, amounts, and possible causes of reported deviations. The control system detects and reports exceptions, but it must also identify those deviations that, taken together, hold the greatest threat to the successful achievement of program objectives. The program manager must be able to evaluate those deviations in actual performance that significantly impact the consumption of scarce resources or affect the timely completion of schedule activities. Returning to the previous example, upon further evaluation it might be determined that the delays in work-station conversion and the additional costs incurred per station can be traced to problems with the available computer software to accommodate the needs of the accounting department.

**Corrective Action**

When standards are not met, the control process provides a signal that an investigation may be needed. The problem should be investigated whenever a significant deviation is identified. Sometimes, the cause of a deviation is an unrealistic plan, and a revision in initial goals and objectives for the program or project may be required.

The program to automate the accounting office, for example, may have been too optimistic from the outset in terms of the time required to make the work-station conversion. Therefore, the expectations may have to be revised in light of the actual accomplishments through the first three months of the program.

Sometimes, the gap between actual performance and the plan reflects a lack of effort. Sometimes, the gap in performance is the consequence of a simple misunderstanding or a failure to communicate expectations (goals and objectives). Before setting in motion corrective actions directed at the apparent source of the problem, managers should ask themselves: "Have I clearly identified and communicated what I expected will be achieved in terms of this program or activity?" At times, it must be recognized that a reduction in productivity may be the result of events outside the immediate control of management.

In terms of the office automation program outlined previously, the problem of inadequate computer software may be outside the immediate control of management. However, if the evaluation revealed that the problem is tied to the attitudes of the staff toward the conversion to computerized data and word-processing capabilities, then the solution may well lay in a more effective program of education and communication with the affected personnel (e.g., that automation is not going to eliminate jobs, result in increased workloads, or create an undesirable work environment).

Finally, management must make a systematic assessment of the effects of corrective actions. Did the corrective action actually close the gap between planned and actual performance? If the answer is yes, then the various tasks can continue to be implemented and monitored. However, if the answer is no, then it is necessary to reevaluate the possible causes of the deviation and to examine more closely the alternative courses of remedial action. Management accounting represents a significant portion of the financial base providing information within the management decision-making framework. In fulfilling this role, it is necessary that various techniques beyond those provided for financial reporting purposes be used by the accountant to develop information for decision makers at the various levels in the management structure.

## COMPONENTS OF ACCOUNTING

The major components of accounting might be viewed in the following manner.

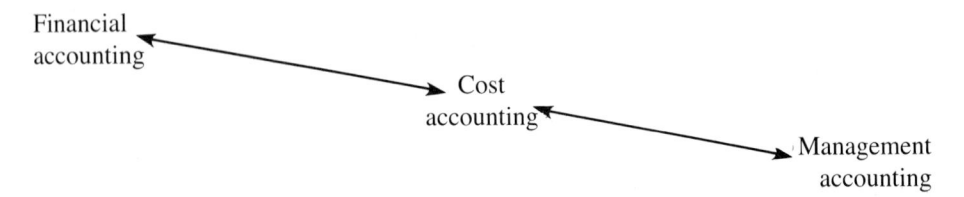

Financial accounting ↔ Cost accounting ↔ Management accounting

The schematic diagram suggests that cost accounting acts as a link between financial accounting and management accounting. Although this may be an oversimplification of the relationships involved, it does suggest that cost accounting encompasses a body of concepts and techniques used in both financial and management accounting.

### Financial Accounting

A major purpose of financial accounting is to provide information on: (1) the results of financial operations and (2) the entity's financial position. Financial statements are expected to conform to consistently applied generally accepted accounting principles established by the accounting profession. Information contained in the statements is in large part directed to external parties for investment or compliance purposes.

### Cost Accounting

Costs are a major component in determining the income and financial position of an organization. Cost allocation is a factor of considerable importance in overall cost determination and financial statement preparation. Specifically, cost accounting is concerned with cost estimation, cost-allocation methods, and cost determination.

### Management Accounting

The principle purpose of management accounting is to provide information for management planning and control. Basically, management accounting deals with the following areas:

**1** *Cost estimation*  In management accounting, the emphasis on cost estimation is for planning or control purposes rather than on financial reporting, as is the case with cost accounting.

**2** *Planning*  A planning decision might involve decisions on adding a project, service, or facility. Management accounting input is generally required for such decisions.

**3** *Cost control*  It is essential that costs be monitored in some effective fashion so that one can determine if costs are reasonable for the activities performed.

**4** *Performance measurement*  Management accounting information is used to evaluate managerial performance. Information is supplied to help answer questions such as, was management effective in running the city government, or did management comply with regulations in carrying out a project?

**5** *Management motivation*  An important aspect of management control is concern for goal congruence. Standards, budgets, and performance-measurement methods should be developed with proper motivation in mind.

While differences between cost and management accounting may exist, as indicated, the terms are often used interchangeably. In an attempt to minimize cumbersome terminology, the term ''management accounting'' will be used to mean both cost and management accounting.

Exhibit 17-2 outlines some of the more frequently used management accounting techniques, suggesting how and where they might be used within the management decision-making framework.

Although some accounting techniques may be used at the strategic-planning level (the goal-setting or goal-revision level), such use is extremely limited because of the nature of decision making at that level. Most accounting techniques are first used at the management control level. After their initial use for management control purposes, many of the same techniques are then used in the operating control area. Having reviewed in a general way where accounting fits within the management structure, management accounting can be examined more specifically.

## MANAGEMENT ACCOUNTING AND MANAGEMENT CONTROL

It is important to recognize that the management control structure should be dictated by the overall environment and organizational complexities. The application of specific kinds of accounting techniques employed should then be determined by particular needs of the management control system. In the governmental accounting environment, some budgeting, responsibility accounting, and performance-measurement

**EXHIBIT 17-2**  RELATION OF ACCOUNTING TECHNIQUES TO MANAGEMENT NEEDS

|  | Strategic planning | Management control | Operating control | Financial reporting |
|---|---|---|---|---|
| Cost-estimation methods | X | X | X |  |
| Master budgets |  | X |  | X |
| Cost-allocation methods |  |  |  | X |
| Product-cost-determination systems |  |  |  | X |
| Cost-volume-profit analysis | X | X | X |  |
| Capital budgeting, cost-benefit analysis | X | X |  |  |
| Responsibility accounting |  | X | X |  |
| Performance-evaluation methods |  | X | X |  |
| Special decision analysis | X | X |  |  |

techniques might be expected to be used. Others, such as cost accounting systems, breakeven analysis, and capital budgeting, would also be used.

**The Management Accounting Framework**

The environment of management accounting may be thought of as a diverse set of organizations that have some goal or series of goals and that operate under conditions of uncertainty. Under such conditions, decision making becomes the essence of management. The minimization of uncertainty surrounding the decision becomes the challenge of the management accountant.

Various concepts relevant to the area will become more significant as you begin to understand management accounting and to make use of the different techniques. For instance, in this chapter, the terms "measurement," "communications," "information," and "cost" have already been used, along with various other concepts in discussing management accounting. These concepts provide part of the structure needed for an understanding of management accounting. The following definitions are provided for reference.

**1** *Measurement* This concept is defined as a "special language which represents real world phenomena by means of numbers and relations of numbers that are predetermined within the number system." In an accounting sense, it refers to the assignment of numbers to an entity's economic phenomena based on observations and according to rules.[2]

**2** *Communication* This concept identifies "...the procedure by means of which one mechanism affects another mechanism" or in effect "...the procedures by which one mind may affect another."[3]

**3** *Systems* A system represents a number of objects with an identifiable relationship between the objects and the properties. Only when it is understood that management accounting is contained within a structure of systems, subsystems, and smaller elements is one in a position to relate the subject matter to the other components and to recognize their interrelationship. Management accounting systems are part of the overall information and management systems of an entity.

**4** *Planning* Planning, because of its diverse elements, is difficult to define in an operational manner. However, it may be generally thought of as the development of goals and the establishment of operational guidelines within restrictions imposed by technology and the environment.

**5** *Control* Control represents the monitored state of a system. Ideally, its components consist of criteria derived from planning, a mechanism for feedback, and some systematic output.

**6** *Cost* Cost refers to "some type of measured sacrifice evolving from an operational sequence of events and centering upon a particular activity or product."[4] More simply stated, it might represent a release of value in order to generate some benefit.

A possible outline for the management accounting structure in the governmental and nonprofit environment might be as shown in Exhibit 17-3. The current state of the

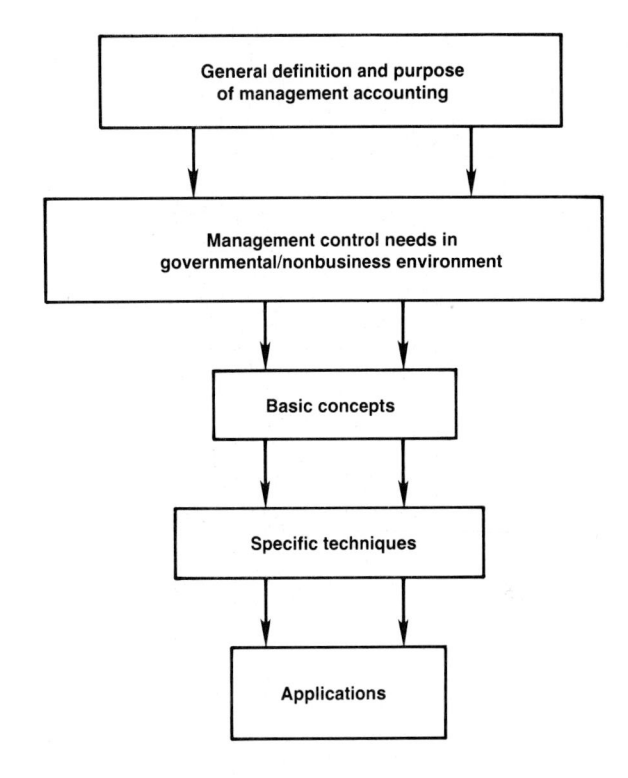

```
                    ┌─────────────────────────────┐
                    │ General definition and purpose │
                    │   of management accounting    │
                    └──────────────┬──────────────┘
                                   ▼
                    ┌─────────────────────────────┐
                    │  Management control needs in │
                    │ governmental/nonbusiness     │
                    │        environment           │
                    └──────────────┬──────────────┘
                                   ▼
                    ┌─────────────────────────────┐
                    │       Basic concepts         │
                    └──────────────┬──────────────┘
                                   ▼
                    ┌─────────────────────────────┐
                    │     Specific techniques      │
                    └──────────────┬──────────────┘
                                   ▼
                    ┌─────────────────────────────┐
                    │        Applications          │
                    └─────────────────────────────┘
```

**EXHIBIT 17-3**  Possible structure for management accounting.

structure, down through the underlying concepts, has been discussed in the preceding material. Chapter 17 will be devoted to development of specific techniques for use by management in financial reporting and problem-solving applications.

## THE ROLE OF THE MANAGEMENT ACCOUNTANT

As might be expected, some accountants have moved beyond basic accounting responsibilities to become managers in the nonbusiness and governmental sectors. However, at this point, of primary concern are the titles and responsibilities held by accountants in accounting positions.

Management uses the organizational chart to set forth key positions and to help in the definition of authority and responsibility. Exhibit 17-4 shows a partial organizational chart for the town of Buzzard's Bay. From the chart, one can only guess where problem-solving information is developed. It probably comes from a combination of the budget and finance manager, analysis manager, and the town manager. Exhibit 17-5 provides us with a partial outline of the organizational arrangement in a university setting. The university chart shows the accounting function under the responsibility of the financial vice-president. Accounting work, whether of a financial-reporting or problem-solving nature, would likely be coordinated through the financial vice-president.

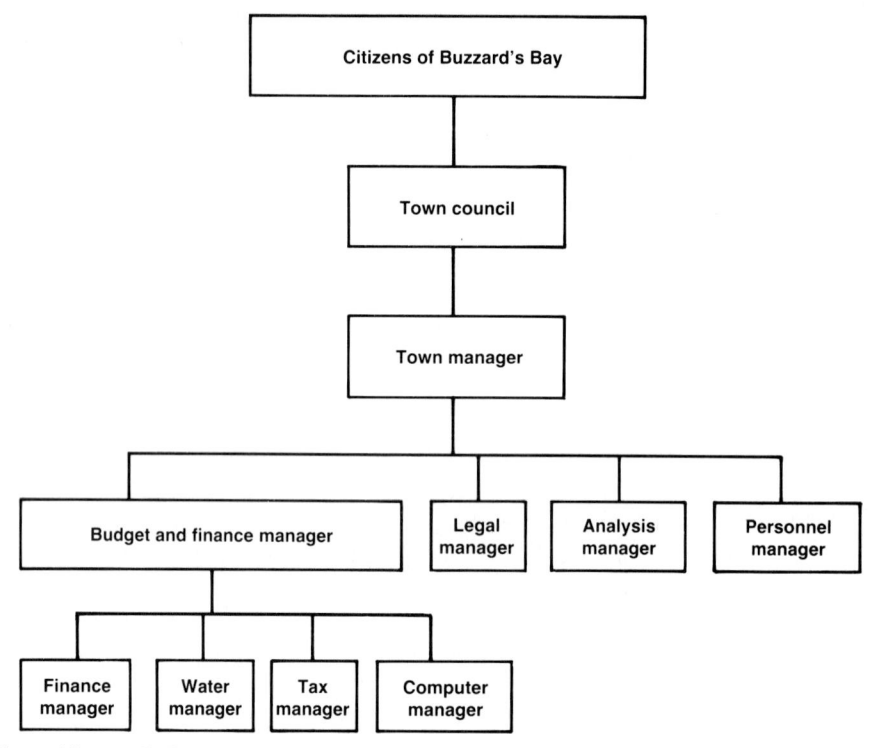

**EXHIBIT 17-4** Town of Buzzard's Bay organizational chart.

## The Duties of the Controller

The controller, or someone in a similar capacity, should have the primary responsibility for developing and communicating financial information. As can be seen from Exhibits 17-4 and 17-5, the controller or budget and finance manager typically has staff responsibility for financial and management accounting. It is also typical to include within the controllership function those areas responsible for systems and procedures and budgeting. Even the internal audit function is often included within the controllership function. However, it is preferable that the internal auditors report directly to some higher level because, on occasion, they should review the actions of top management, including the controller and financial vice-president.

## COST CONCEPTS AND TERMINOLOGY

Even though "cost" is one of the more frequently used terms in management accounting, it is extremely difficult to define. A committee of the American Accounting Association wrote: "Cost is foregoing value, measured in monetary terms, incurred or potentially to be incurred, to achieve a specific objective."[5] As indicated in earlier dis-

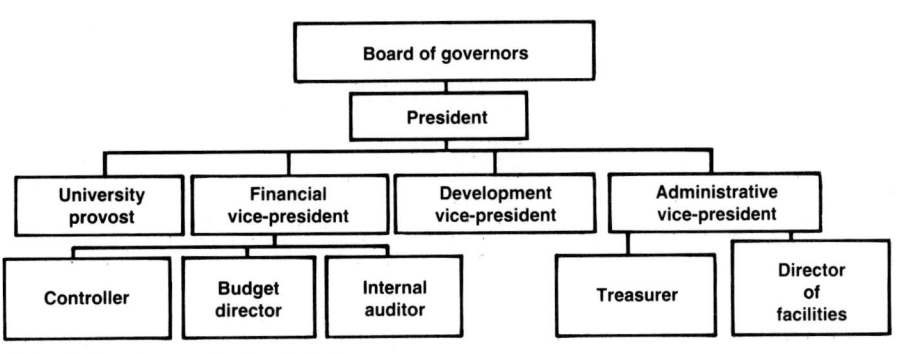

```
                        Board of governors
                              |
                          President
     _____|_____
     |              |                   |                  |
 University     Financial          Development      Administrative
  provost      vice-president     vice-president    vice-president
                  |                                        |
         _____|_____                     _____|_____
         |       |        |                      |                   |
                                                              Director
     Controller Budget  Internal               Treasurer        of
                director auditor                              facilities
```

**EXHIBIT 17-5**   Union University organizational chart.

cussion, "cost" might generally be defined as a release of value required in order to accomplish some goal or purpose. From such a definition, it may be concluded that costs are incurred for purposes of deriving some benefit. For instance, a public utility incurs costs for generating revenues in excess of cost consumed (expenses). Costs are incurred by the city to provide services required such as police or fire protection.

Obviously, "cost" standing alone is a difficult concept to understand, but it can be made somewhat more understandable by providing a modifier such as "variable," "fixed," "direct," "controllable," or some other term. For an example of the many variations of "cost," refer to Exhibit 17-6. Although not all of the terms will be covered, the purpose of the next few paragraphs is to provide an introduction to some basic cost terminology used in management accounting.

## Full Costs and Partial Costs

The question of cost was discussed at the outset of the section. For many different reasons, there is a need to determine proper costs. Tax levels, utility rates, and patient billings, for instance, are all tied to the question: "What is the proper cost?" In full costing, the accountant is attempting to identify all costs properly associated with some activity. For instance, in the hospital environment, patient-care costs involve hospital room costs, meals, laundry, drugs, surgery, therapy, and other items that are more or less directly attributable to the patient. What about admission/discharge costs, nursery care, heat, light, and power and other similar costs?

Under full costing, an attempt is made to include all costs—costs generated specifically by the patient as well as costs of providing the overall resources. In the governmental and nonprofit areas, full costs are often called *program costs*.

In many cases, it may be desirable to attempt to identify those costs that result specifically from treating the patient. Such costs would not be expected to be incurred if the patient did not exist. Such *partial costs* (e.g., direct costs) are often used to gauge contributions made to overall costs when the patient is billed on some type of recovery basis.

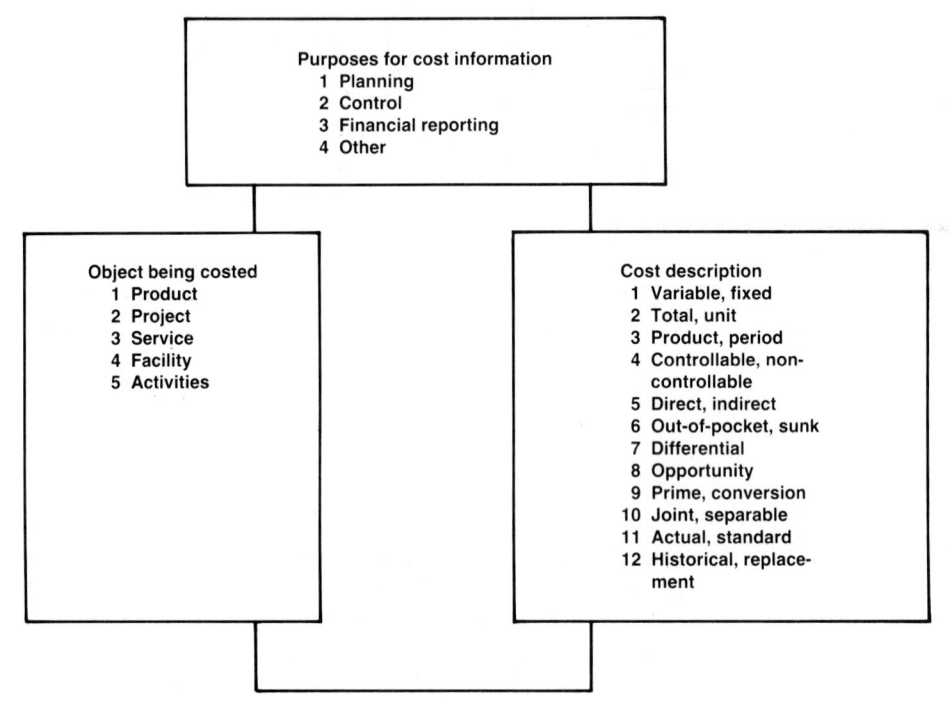

```
                    ┌─────────────────────────────────┐
                    │  Purposes for cost information  │
                    │    1 Planning                   │
                    │    2 Control                    │
                    │    3 Financial reporting        │
                    │    4 Other                      │
                    └─────────────────────────────────┘
```

| Object being costed | Cost description |
|---|---|
| 1 Product | 1 Variable, fixed |
| 2 Project | 2 Total, unit |
| 3 Service | 3 Product, period |
| 4 Facility | 4 Controllable, non-controllable |
| 5 Activities | 5 Direct, indirect |
|  | 6 Out-of-pocket, sunk |
|  | 7 Differential |
|  | 8 Opportunity |
|  | 9 Prime, conversion |
|  | 10 Joint, separable |
|  | 11 Actual, standard |
|  | 12 Historical, replacement |

**EXHIBIT 17-6** Framework for cost terminology. (*Source:* Adapted from Wilber C. Haseman, "An Interpretive Framework For Cost," *The Accounting Review*, October 1968, p. 251.)

## Direct and Indirect Costs

A *direct cost* represents a cost incurred for a specific purpose and uniquely associated with that purpose. Cost of the town manager is a direct cost of the town. The salary of the manager of a day-care center would be considered a direct cost of the center. However, if the center were broken down into departments by different age groups, with a part of the manager's salary being allocated to each department, the salary would be an *indirect* cost of each of the individual departments. In this case, the cost assigned to each of the departments would have to be allocated on some more or less arbitrary basis. Indirect costs are often called *overhead costs*. In many situations, service departments exist to provide some type of support or service to primary activities. A motor pool is considered a service-type activity in a local government or university. For reporting purposes, costs of service activities may often be allocated to the main activities.

An *indirect cost* might then be defined as a cost that is associated with more than one activity or program but that cannot be traced to any one of the activities individually.

## Controllable or Noncontrollable Costs

All costs are controllable by someone in the organization given a long-enough time period. As a result, costs assigned to the manager of a department at a lower level in the organization may contain both controllable and noncontrollable elements. *Controllable costs* are defined as those costs that can be significantly influenced by the manager of the department. For instance, the supervisor of a town's maintenance department might exercise significant control over cost of supplies, maintenance, and staff of the department, but would have little or no control over insurance costs allocated to the department.

## Differential Costs

These costs may be defined as the difference in total costs between alternatives or as the difference between costs (*incremental*) at two different activity levels. Since decisions are generally based on differentials between competing alternatives, we should expect differential costs to be future oriented and, therefore, very useful for planning purposes.

## Opportunity Costs

Opportunity costs measure the maximum return that might have been expected had a resource been committed to an alternative. We are simply looking at the effect of having given up one opportunity in order to select another alternative. If you were offered a job paying a salary but selected some other earning possibility, the salary would represent the opportunity foregone (opportunity cost) because of the decision made.

## Variable and Fixed Costs

Whether providing information for product costing or management decision-making purposes, one of the most important jobs of the management accountant is to analyze cost behavior. This kind of classification indicates how costs react or respond to changes in levels of business activity within a relevant range. The relevant range is the range of activity in which the cost (dependent variable) and activity relationships (independent variable) are considered valid. As activity levels change, some costs change; others remain constant.

In attempting to relate costs to activity, four basic cost and activity relationships are often considered: fixed costs, semifixed costs, semivariable costs, and variable costs. These relationships, as presented in Exhibit 17-7, provide a classification of cost behavior that is useful for a variety of purposes, including planning and control.

*Fixed costs,* as outlined in Exhibit 17-7(A), indicate there is no change in costs with changes in activity. Fixed-cost levels are usually tied to time periods and capacity levels rather than to activity levels. For instance, salaries are typically fixed for a reasonable period of time. Rent expense is likely to be related to time periods.

If a cost changes directly in response to changes in the activity measure being used, it is called a *variable* cost. At zero activity, there would be no variable costs. Then, as units of activity are increased, the related costs are expected to increase at some constant rate. This variable relationship is shown in Exhibit 17-7(D). Supplies, labor, and energy costs are often identified as variable costs. To illustrate, assume that it requires

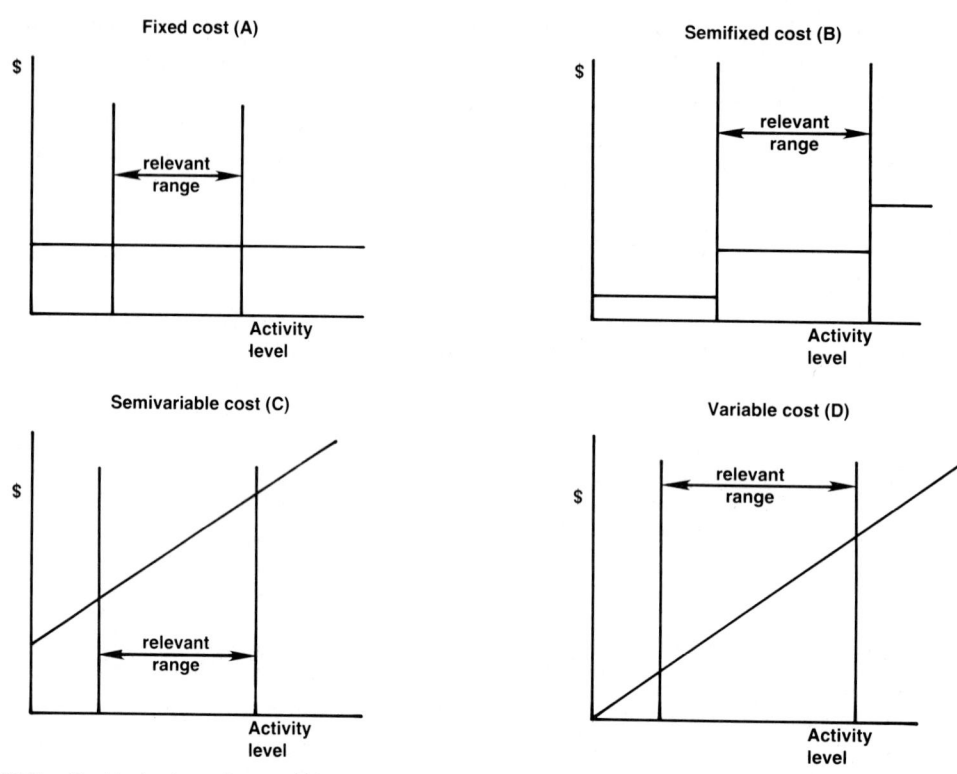

**EXHIBIT 17-7** Cost behavior patterns within a relevant range.

approximately $5,000 to clean streets each time it snows in Newport, Rhode Island. As snow days increase, cost of snow removal should increase in direct proportion to the number of snow days.

A *semifixed* (step-fixed) *cost* can be described by means of a step function as shown in Exhibit 17-7(B). Supervisory salaries might be considered a semifixed cost, since at some level of increased activity another supervisor will be required. If, within the prescribed relevant range, only one supervisor is required, then the cost is considered fixed. But, if additional supervisors are called for as activity continues to increase within the relevant range of activity being analyzed, the cost is considered semifixed.

A *semivariable* (mixed) *cost* includes both fixed and variable components as shown in Exhibit 17-7(C). For example, an electric utility might use a flat rate plus a rate per unit used. There is some minimum cost at zero activity, but costs increase as activity increases. Knowledge of these cost-behavior patterns is required if managers are to be successful in product costing and predicting results of various alternatives.

## COST-ESTIMATION METHODS

How much will it cost to carry out a new program, provide a service, or produce a product? What price should we bid in order to get a job? These are just a few of the problem situations in which it is necessary to identify costs by the different behavior patterns. Costs for direct material and direct labor are often based on engineering studies. Indirect cost behavior is likely determined by some type of cost-estimation study.

In cost estimation, an attempt is made to find predictable relationships between an activity component (independent variable) and the cost (dependent variable) so that costs can be estimated based on projections of the behavior of the independent variable. Activity components typically used include units of product, hours worked, machine hours, miles driven, patients treated, or other evidence of activity. Although one cannot determine indirect (overhead) costs at different levels with precision, a function, $y = a + bx$, can usually be developed that will provide an acceptable representation of cost behavior for the purpose sought.

When using cost-estimation techniques, we assume that linear functions can be used to approximate nonlinear situations and that all costs can be categorized as either fixed or variable within a relevant range. If these assumptions are found to be realistic, then reasonable approximations of costs can often be developed by various methods, including (1) a direct analysis of each cost component, (2) the high-low method, (3) the scattergraph approach, and (4) regression analysis.

### Initial Approach to Developing Cost Estimates

One way of obtaining initial cost estimates is by direct analysis of each component of cost. Indirect costs sometimes are estimated by one or more people who simply rely on their knowledge of existing cost behavior. For example, in one company, management brought together the employees they considered to be most knowledgeable in the cost area and requested that they identify each item as fixed or variable. Having made the separation of costs, personnel then had to relate the variable costs (dependent variable) with some activity component (independent variable) for the purpose of estimating costs at different levels of activity. Although the estimates were unreliable for decision-making purposes, results enabled management to make a rough allocation of indirect costs.

### The High-Low Method

The high-low method calls for identifying total costs at two different activity levels, usually at the low point and high point within the relevant range. The specific approach can be described as follows, with an application of the approach shown in Exhibit 17-8.

1 Select the highest observed value of the independent variable and the corresponding value of the dependent variable.
2 Select the lowest observed value of the independent variable and the corresponding value of the dependent variable.
3 Determine the difference between the dependent variables selected.
4 Determine the difference between the independent variables selected.
5 Divide the difference between the dependent variables by the difference of the independent variables. The result is the estimated slope ($b$) of the line.

## EXHIBIT 17-8
### Use of High-Low Method for Estimating Costs

| Month | Patient days | Indirect labor cost |
|---|---|---|
| January | 550 | $4,800 |
| February | 575 | 4,900 |
| March | 425 | 4,100 |
| April | 400 | 4,050 |
| May | 350 | 3,750 |
| June | 200 | 2,800 |
| July | 400 | 3,900 |
| August | 450 | 4,250 |

Steps:
1. Highest value: independent 575, dependent $4,900
2. Lowest value: independent 200, dependent $2,800
3. $4,900 − $2,800 = $2,100
4. 575 − 200 = 375
5. $2,100 ÷ 375 = $5.60
6. $4,900 − (575 × $5.60) = $1,680

Indirect labor cost equation:
  y = 1,680 + 5.60x

---

**6** Multiply the high or low independent variable by the slope of the line and subtract from the corresponding value of the dependent variable. The remainder represents the y-intercept of the line ($a$).

## The Scattergraph Method

A more accurate way of determining the estimated variability rate of an indirect cost than the high-low method is to plot all points of observed cost data on a graph. A line is then visually fitted to the plotted points, taking into consideration all points. Typically, the line is fitted so that approximately an equal number of points fall above and below the line. Using the example from Exhibit 17-8, the points of observed cost data are plotted on a graph shown in Exhibit 17-9.

The graph is called a scattergraph, and the fitted line is the cost line. The variability rate can then be calculated by determining the total cost for some point on the line and subtracting the y-intercept value to arrive at total variable costs. The variable cost is then divided by the activity level to arrive at the variable cost per unit of activity. In the example, the variable cost rate is $5.57.

In this method, rather than simply fitting a line to high and low points, all points are considered, providing a regression line based on averages. This eliminates the problem inherent in using extremes to determine the regression line.

## Regression Analysis

Regression analysis (least-squares method) is a more sophisticated approach than the scattergraph method. It assures that we will have the best fit of a straight line drawn be-

```
                              y
                          5,000
                                                                        x    x
                          4,000
                                                              x    x
                                                         x  x
                          3,000
                                            x
                          2,000

                          1,000

                               └────────┬─────┬─────┬─────┬─────┬─────┬────
                                       100   200   300   400   500   600   x

                    Total cost for 350 days:    $3,750
                    y intercept value            1,800
                          Total variable costs  $1,950

                    $1,950 ÷ 350 days = $5.57 variable cost per day

                    Indirect labor cost equation
                          y = 1,800 + 5.57x
```

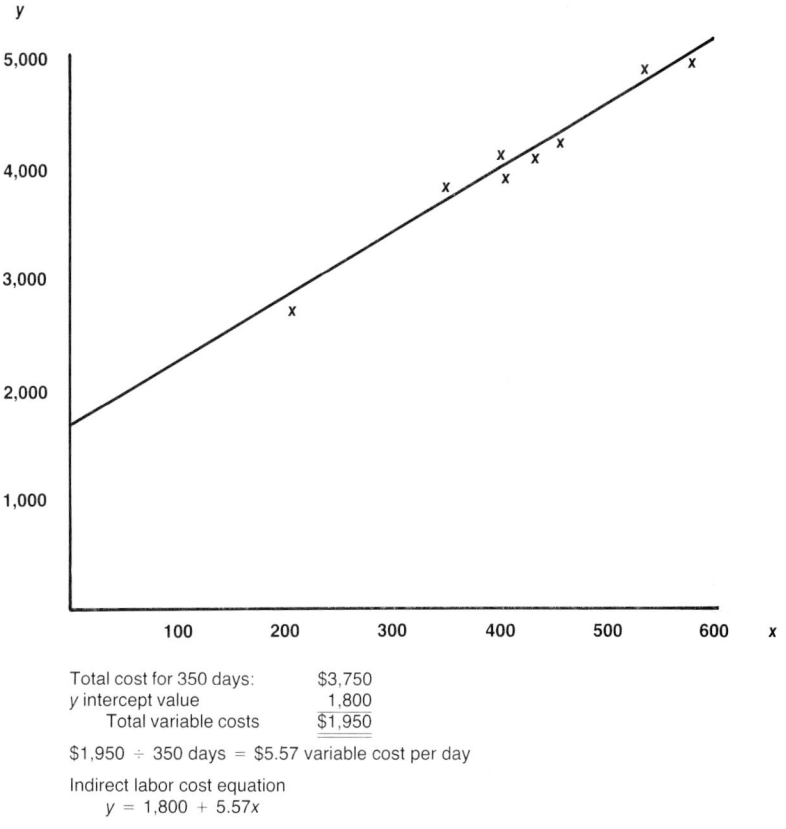

**EXHIBIT 17-9** Use of scattergraph method for estimating costs.

tween the plots on a scattergraph. Indeed, the term "regression analysis" simply identifies a process by which the average amount of change in a variable that is associated with changes in one or more other variables is measured. Although coverage of the subject is too extensive to be dealt with here, it is useful to look at the basic example provided in Exhibit 17-10, which uses data from Exhibit 17-9. Solving simultaneously the normal equations of simple regression, the values of $a$ and $b$ are determined.

Regardless of the estimation method employed, it is important in management accounting to have reliable predictions of indirect costs as well as other costs. If it is determined that the equations developed (see Exhibits 17-8 and 17-10) are reliable, then they can be employed in providing cost information for reporting or decision-making purposes.

## SUMMARY

This chapter provides insight into the field of management control and the language of management accounting. More specifically, the reader should now be familiar with a wide variety of cost terms. Many of these terms will be used throughout the remainder of this book, particularly variable cost and fixed cost. Methods are available for

## EXHIBIT 17-10
## Use of Regression Analysis
## For Estimating Costs

| n | Patient days (x) | Indirect labor cost (y) | $x^2$ | xy |
|---|---|---|---|---|
| 1 | 550 | $ 4,800 | 302,500 | 2,640,000 |
| 2 | 575 | 4,900 | 330,625 | 2,817,500 |
| 3 | 425 | 4,100 | 180,625 | 1,742,500 |
| 4 | 400 | 4,050 | 160,000 | 1,620,000 |
| 5 | 350 | 3,750 | 122,500 | 1,312,500 |
| 6 | 200 | 2,800 | 400,000 | 560,000 |
| 7 | 400 | 3,900 | 160,000 | 1,560,000 |
| 8 | 450 | 4,250 | 202,500 | 1,912,500 |
|   | 3,350 | $32,550 | 1,498,750 | 14,165,000 |

Regression equations:
1. $\Sigma y = na + b\Sigma x$
2. $\Sigma xy = a\Sigma x + b\Sigma x^2$

Solving simultaneously:
1. $32,550 = 8a + 3,350b$
2. $14,165,000 = 3,350a + 1,498,750b$

3. $13,630,313 = 3,350a + 1,402,813b$
4. $14,165,000 = 3,350a + 1,498,750b$

$534,687 = 0 + 95,937b$
$b = 5.57$
$a = 1,735$

Indirect labor cost equation
$y = 1,735 + 5.57x$

Steps in solving simultaneously
1. Multiply (1) by 418.75 to equalize values of a
2. Subtract (3) from (2)

separating indirect costs into fixed and variable components. Four methods were outlined in this chapter, namely, (1) committee, or direct analysis method; (2) high-low method; (3) scattergraph technique; and (4) regression analysis.

Unfortunately, however, all costs cannot be conveniently classified as one or the other; certain assumptions must be made to make this two-way classification all-inclusive. When these assumptions are valid, they can be utilized to help management in the decision-making function.

## QUESTIONS

1 Identify and define the components of the management system.
2 In what phase of the management system does accounting play the most important role? Why?
3 Within the management system a number of subcomponents are required. Identify these subcomponents.
4 Identify the basic concepts essential for an understanding of management accounting.
5 Why can we describe cost accounting as a link between financial accounting and management accounting? Discuss fully.
6 Define cost accounting.

7 Define management accounting.
8 Describe, in your own words, the role of the management accountant.
9 Why is the term "cost" difficult to define?
10 Discuss the relevant range of activity. Why is this assumption made?
11 Why is it often difficult to classify costs as either variable or fixed? How are semivariable and semifixed costs handled?
12 What are direct costs? What are indirect costs?
13 When are costs controllable?
14 Are all direct costs also variable? Explain.
15 Are all controllable costs also direct costs? Explain.
16 Identify the different methods for estimating cost behavior.
17 Is regression analysis a better method for estimating costs than the high-low method? Discuss.
18 Should the scattergraph be used in conjunction with the high-low method and regression analysis? Discuss.

## PROBLEMS

17-1 Classify the following costs as either fixed, semifixed, semivariable, or variable.
1 Payments in lieu of taxes
2 Supervisory personnel
3 Indirect labor
4 Direct labor
5 Royalty payments
6 Machinery depreciation
7 Insurance on inventory
8 Electric power
9 Insurance on hospital building
10 Indirect materials
11 Town manager's salary

17-2 Determine which costs are controllable and which costs are noncontrollable by the manager of the Williams Nursing Home.
1 Heat
2 Depreciation of the building
3 Supervision
4 Repairs on nursing equipment
5 Light
6 Supplies
7 Labor wage rates
8 Overtime wages
9 Maintenance
10 Insurance on the building

17-3 Repair and maintenance expenses of Radford Water Authority are to be analyzed for purposes of constructing a budget. Examination of past records reveals the following costs and related activity:

|  | High | Low |
|---|---|---|
| Cost per month | $39,200 | $32,000 |
| Machine hours | 24,000 | 15,000 |

**Required:**
Using the high-low method, develop values for $a$ and $b$ in $y = a + bx$.

**17-4** The highway department wants to calculate the fixed portion of its fuel expense, as measured against truck mileage, for the first three months of 19X7. Information for the first three months of 19X7 is as follows:

| Month | Truck mileage | Fuel expense |
|---|---|---|
| January | 34,000 | 610 |
| February | 31,000 | 585 |
| March | 34,000 | 610 |

**Required:**
Calculate the fixed portion of the highway department's fuel expense, rounded to the nearest dollars.

**17-5** Total project costs for Richmond Deepwater Terminal are budgeted at $460,000 for 100,000 units of budgeted output and at $560,000 for 120,000 units of budgeted output. Because of the need for additional facilities, budgeted fixed costs for 120,000 units are 25 percent more than budgeted fixed costs for 100,000 units.

**Required:**
Calculate the terminal's budgeted variable cost per unit of output.

**17-6** Ron Jones, controller of City Hospital, has been requested by management to separate overhead costs of the delivery room into variable-cost and fixed-cost components. The following information is available.

| Month | Activity component units produced | Costs incurred |
|---|---|---|
| January | 1,000 | $25,000 |
| February | 1,200 | 28,000 |
| March | 1,400 | 34,000 |
| April | 1,600 | 37,000 |
| May | 1,800 | 40,000 |

**Required:**
1 Identify and discuss methods available for separating the cost components.
2 Using the high-low method, calculate the value for $a$ and $b$ in $y = a + bx$.

**17-7** The city's fire department needs an estimate of the variable portion of its water expense, as measured against fires responded to for the first six months of 19X8. Information for the first six months of 19X8 is as follows:

| Month | Fires | Water expense |
|---|---|---|
| January | 34 | $6,100 |
| February | 31 | 5,850 |
| March | 34 | 6,200 |
| April | 36 | 6,400 |
| May | 30 | 5,500 |
| June | 28 | 5,400 |

**Required:**
1 Determine the variable rate using the high-low method.
2 Estimate the variable rates using the scattergraph rate.
3 Using regression analysis, calculate the variable rate.

**17-8** Hish Bartley, manager of the city of Nashville's inventory department, has been asked by the town manager to separate expenses of the inventory department into variable-cost and fixed-cost components. The following information has been provided:

| Month | Units shipped | Expenses |
|---|---|---|
| January | 5,000 | $10,000 |
| February | 6,000 | 11,600 |
| March | 8,000 | 17,100 |
| April | 12,000 | 26,000 |
| May | 11,000 | 19,000 |
| June | 14,000 | 29,000 |
| July | 10,000 | 24,000 |

**Required:**
Using regression analysis, calculate the value for $a$ and $b$ in $y = a + bx$.

# NOTES

1. Robert J. Mockler, *The Management Control Process* (New York: Appleton-Century-Crofts, 1972), p. 2.
2. Yuji Ijiri, *The Foundations of Accounting Measurement* (Englewood Cliffs, N.J.: Prentice-Hall, Inc., 1967), p. 19.
3. Claude E. Shannon and Warren Weaver, *The Mathematical Theory of Communication* (Urbana, Ill.: The University of Illinois Press, 1949), p. 95.
4. Wilber E. Haseman, "An Interpretive Framework for Cost," *The Accounting Review,* October 1968, pp. 742–43.
5. "Report of the Committee on Cost Concepts and Standards," *The Accounting Review,* Supplement to vol. 27 (Sarasota, Fla.: American Accounting Association, 1952), vol. 27, p. 176.

# CHAPTER 18

# COST ACCOUNTING TECHNIQUES

Early cost accounting systems were developed to provide information for product cost determination and pricing purposes. As cost accounting systems in the private sector evolved, management found more and more uses for data available from the basic cost system. As a result, break-even analysis, standard costing, responsibility accounting, and other management accounting techniques were developed. Today, these and other techniques are widely used in business and industry.

As a rule, governmental and other nonbusiness efforts have not focused attention on product cost determination or pricing, until recently. Consequently, decision making and control techniques in the governmental and other nonbusiness sectors have lagged seriously behind developments in the business sector. Management accounting techniques introduced in this chapter should prove to be useful in a wide variety of situations in the governmental and not-for-profit areas.

## AREAS IN NEED OF MANAGEMENT ACCOUNTING

Numerous organizations in the overall nonbusiness area have special needs for management accounting information. Several types of organizations—especially the utility, health care, and educational areas—have attributes similar to profit-oriented organizations. In such cases, it becomes fairly easy to see how management accounting tools can be used to satisfy management's information needs. However, in the area of state and local government, revenues are often not related to services provided. Goals and objectives become clouded, and the political influence makes it difficult to address such important questions as: "What is the cost of a proper level of police protection?" or "What benefits can be derived from providing snow removal service?" Nevertheless, there is need for sound management accounting information if state and local governments are to make use of management control systems.

While relevant models for each of the nonbusiness areas cannot be identified at this point, a start can be made by highlighting some of the more generalized techniques and by providing examples. This chapter will concentrate for the most part on cost accounting techniques. Chapter 19 will then cover planning and control techniques.

## COST MEASUREMENT AND ASSIGNMENT

Cost measurement and assignment are important because cost-related information should play a key role in any management control system. In Chapter 17, we indicated that cost information was needed for financial reporting, planning, and control. Services have to be priced (e.g., patient billings, water service, and recreational facilities), budgets have to be established, decisions must be made, and financial reports must be prepared.

Different notions of cost must be related to purpose and object being costed. In cost measurement and assignment, full (program) costs, differential costs, controllable costs, and direct costs are used. Some type of cost system is usually needed for data accumulation and proper measurement and assignment purposes.

## COST ACCOUNTING SYSTEMS

A cost accounting system involves using particular processes for accumulating costs and assigning them to a program, project, or service (see Exhibit 18-1). The nature of the cost-accumulation process in governmental and other non-profit-oriented situations should indicate whether a *process* or *job order cost* would be more appropriate for accumulating costs. Before outlining specific costing procedures, however, the significance of cost allocation and the procedures needed for accumulating cost components (identified in Exhibit 18-1) should be discussed.

### Cost Allocation

Cost allocation is necessary whenever an attempt is made to determine the full cost of a service or product. This need often arises in dealing with government grants and con-

**EXHIBIT 18-1** The cost accounting process.

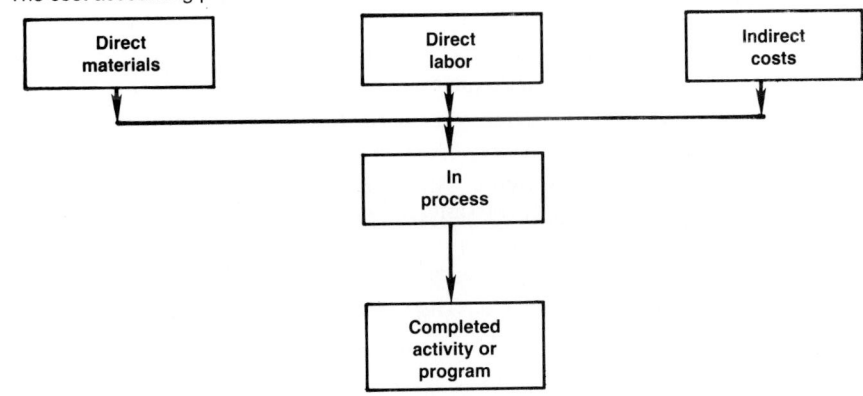

tracts. A similar need exists when public utilities attempt to set equitable rates or when a hospital establishes billing rates at levels expected to recover all costs associated with the provision of patient care. A comparable situation might be encountered in which an organization operates a cafeteria for its employees on a break-even (recovery of costs) basis. In attempting to develop a unit cost for meals, an effort would be made to consider not only the direct cost of food and wages of cafeteria personnel, but also utility costs, equipment costs, and other indirect costs.

The other problem relates to direct but fixed costs of a specific department. In a cafeteria, for instance, there are numerous costs that might be specifically identified with that department (direct costs) but that, for costing purposes, cannot be traced directly to meals (indirect costs). Costs such as these are often allocated by assuming some level of operation (number of meals, loads of garbage, or supplies planned for the year) and dividing the total annual cost by estimated activity for the year, so as to arrive at a unit rate.

As a consequence, where it is considered essential to reflect full costs, two different kinds of allocation problems are likely to arise in developing unit costs for a service or program. One problem involves costs identified as direct to the total agency or program—for instance, salaries of the hospital administrator and director of nurses. Although salaries for these staff personnel are direct costs of the hospital as a whole, where full unit costs were being developed for intensive care, nursery, surgery, cafeteria, and other components of the hospital, they would be allocated to the separate departments (and become indirect costs). The basis for the allocation, although arbitrary, would have to be reasonable and based on services provided.

The other problem relates to direct but fixed costs of a specific department. In a cafeteria, for instance, there are numerous costs that might be specifically identified with that department (direct costs) but that, for costing purposes, cannot be traced directly to meals (indirect costs). Costs such as these are often allocated by assuming some level of operation (number of meals, loads of garbage, or supplies planned for the year) and dividing the total annual cost by estimated activity for the year, so as to arrive at a unit rate.

A city hospital might be considered a governmental endeavor. Exhibit 18-2 provides a hypothetical example of a city's hospital costs, along with some indication of the nature of the allocation problem. The hospital has three revenue or mission centers (primary activity) and two general service (supporting) departments. Assume that the hospital is attempting to determine the full costs of providing the services of the primary activities. This objective requires that three different kinds of costs be charged to the centers. Direct expenses can be traced to the individual centers. Administrative expenses (e.g., salaries of hospital administrators) represent direct expenses of the hospital as a whole but indirect costs with respect to the individual centers. If full costs of those centers are to be estimated, the expenses of the service centers must be allocated to the primary mission centers. The allocations in Exhibit 18-2 are based on floor space for expenses and units processed for laundry expenses.

A number of methods exist for allocating service center costs to primary activities or mission centers. The method selected should be the best method for reflecting the utilization of the costs. Two of the most widely used methods for allocation are the

## EXHIBIT 18-2
## MN Hospital Costs

|  | Mission centers | | | Service centers | | |
|---|---|---|---|---|---|---|
|  | General care | Intensive care | Emergency care | Maintenance | Laundry | Total |
| Direct expenses | $ 600,000 | $ 500,000 | $300,000 | $ 350,000 | $ 250,000 | $2,000,000 |
| Administrative expenses | $ 300,000 | $ 200,000 | $200,000 | $ 440,000 | $ 370,000 | $1,510,000 |
| Total | $ 900,000 | $ 700,000 | $500,000 | $ 790,000 | $ 620,000 | $3,510,000 |
| Allocation of service center costs: | | | | | | |
| Maintenance (a) | $ 474,000 | $ 237,000 | $ 79,000 | $(790,000) | | |
| Laundry (b) | $ 310,000 | $ 232,500 | $ 77,500 | | $(620,000) | |
|  | $1,684,000 | $1,169,500 | $656,500 | 0 | 0 | $3,510,000 |

(a) Allocation of maintenance based on floor space:

|  | Sq. feet | | |
|---|---|---|---|
| General care | 60,000 × $7.90 | $474,000 |
| Intensive care | 30,000 × $7.90 | $237,000 |
| Emergency care | 10,000 × $7.90 | $ 79,000 |
|  | 100,000 × $7.90 | $790,000 |

(b) Allocation of laundry based on units laundered:

|  | Units | | |
|---|---|---|---|
| General care | 100,000 × $3.10 | $310,000 |
| Intensive care | 75,000 × $3.10 | $232,500 |
| Emergency care | 25,000 × $3.10 | $ 77,500 |
|  | 200,000 × $3.10 | $620,000 |

*method of neglect* and the *step (step-down) method*. The method of neglect disregards service provided by one or more service departments to other service departments. In the hospital example, for instance, it is possible, even likely, that the two service departments made use of each other's service. If so, they were ignored in the calculations in Exhibit 18-2.

The step method gives partial recognition to services rendered by other service departments. Assume, in Exhibit 18-2, that reciprocal services were provided by the service centers. In the step method, a decision would have to be made regarding the order of allocation. If the maintenance center is to be allocated first, part of its services would be allocated to laundry, and then laundry's revised costs would be allocated to the mission centers (review the calculations in Exhibit 18-3). By using algebra or matrix algebra the full reciprocal relationship of the departments could be considered. For information on the matrix algebra you should refer to a cost accounting textbook.

## Cost Accounting Record-keeping Procedures

To ensure that the cost flows and the transformation process are properly recorded, various accounting procedures must be established. Basic procedures for recording inventory, labor, and indirect costs are outlined below.

**EXHIBIT 18-3**
**Step-down Allocation Procedure**

(a) Allocation of maintenance based on floor space:

|  | Sq. feet |  |  |  |
|---|---|---|---|---|
| General care | 60,000 | × $6.93 | = | $415,800 |
| Intensive care | 30,000 | × 6.93 | = | $207,900 |
| Emergency care | 10,000 | × 6.93 | = | $ 69,300 |
| Laundry | 14,000 | × 6.93 | = | $ 97,000* |
|  | 114,000 |  |  | $790,000 |

(b) Allocation of laundry based on units laundered:

|  | Units |  |  |  |
|---|---|---|---|---|
| General care | 100,000 | × $3.5850 | = | $358,500 |
| Intensive care | 75,000 | × 3.5850 | = | 268,875 |
| Emergency care | 25,000 | × 3.5850 | = | 89,625 |
|  | 200,000 |  |  | $717,000 |

*Rounded down from $97,020.

**Direct Material** Overall, materials, especially direct materials, are not a significant factor in governmental and other nonprofit cost accounting systems. Nevertheless, inventories are maintained for supplies in many situations, and direct materials might be a significant factor in a number of programs and projects.

Minimal procedures and records are needed in a periodic system in which physical inventory counts are used to update inventory balances. Accounts are charged directly from approved invoices. Balances in the inventory accounts are adjusted periodically through a physical inventory count to reflect actual usage of inventories. This process is reflected in Exhibit 18-4.

Smaller organizations usually account for inventory of materials and supplies through periodic physical inventories. At this minimum level of record keeping, materials and supplies purchased would initially be charged to expenditures as invoices are approved for payment. At the year's end, a physical count would be made of items on hand, and the inventory would be recorded with an offsetting credit to expenditures.

It is necessary to establish a subsidiary stores ledger to provide an up-to-date record of the items on hand where perpetual inventory records are desired. The individual stores records would be debited for amounts received in addition to debiting the general ledger control account for purchases. The entry into the stores ledger is usually made from a copy of the receiving report. To provide an up-to-date record, items removed from stores would also have to be posted both to the general ledger and the stores ledger, by posting from copies of the store's requisitions.

In larger organizations, inventory of supplies and materials should be accounted for by means of a perpetual inventory system of the type described above.

**Direct Labor** Direct labor is not purchased in advance of its use. As labor is used for various projects (e.g., to build a road or to provide library services), procedures may be needed to identify the amount and kind of labor expended for that particular

## CHAPTER 18: COST ACCOUNTING TECHNIQUES   553

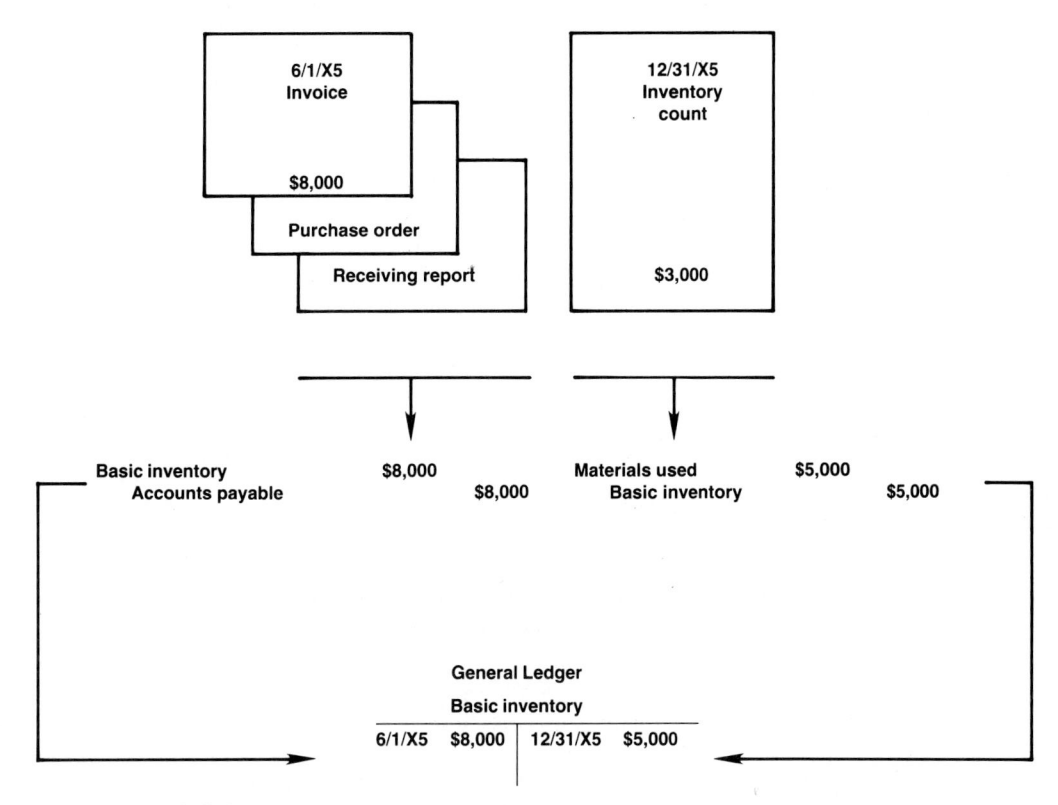

**EXHIBIT 18-4**  Periodic inventory system.

activity. For hourly employees, time cards are often used to accumulate the total labor. Hours may be recorded through the use of a computer system, mechanically by a time clock as the worker punches in and out daily, or they may be recorded manually. The hours are summarized at the end of each pay period, and gross and net pay are calculated for each worker, based on pay and withholding authorizations.

During the pay period, each worker may have worked on a number of different jobs or projects or in several different departments. Those work assignments should be supported by job tickets, field labor reports, or other evidence for each job. At the end of each pay period, job tickets or other evidence must be summarized to form the basis for the *labor distribution*—the charges to projects or departments by means of a work and cost ledger or job cost sheet.

Information from the time cards is then used to prepare the payroll register, checks, and journal entries. The journal entries serve as the basis for entries into control accounts and subsidiary records. This overall process is outlined in Exhibit 18-5.

The number of hours on the job tickets should be less than or equal to hours on the time cards. The nonchargeable hours might indicate indirect labor, idle time, or something else, depending on the organization and system used.

```
                            Employee X
                                │
        ┌───────────────────────┴───────────────────────┐
        │                                               │
┌───────────────┐                               ┌───────────────┐
│   Time        │                               │   Job         │
│   card        │                               │   tickets     │
│               │                               │               │
│  M       8    │                               │  Job 30    6  │
│  T       8    │                               │               │
│  W       8    │                               │  Job 31    7  │
│  Th      8    │                               │               │
│  F       8    │                               │  Job 32    8  │
│         ──    │                               │               │
│         40    │                               │  Job 32    6  │
│               │                               │               │
│               │                               │  Job 33    8  │
│               │                               │               │
│               │                               │  Misc.     5  │
└───────┬───────┘                               └───────┬───────┘
        │                                               │
        └───────────────────────┬───────────────────────┘
                                │
┌───────────────┐       ┌───────────────┐       ┌───────────────┐
│   Rate        │       │   Payroll     │       │   Employee    │
│  authorizations│       │   register    │       │   check       │
│               │       │               │       │               │
│  Withholding  │       │               │       │               │
│  authorizations│       │               │       │               │
└───────────────┘       └───────┬───────┘       └───────────────┘
                                │
                          Journal entry
```

| | | |
|---|---|---|
| Work and cost ledger, direct labor | xx | |
| Indirect labor | xx | |
| Wages payable | | xx |

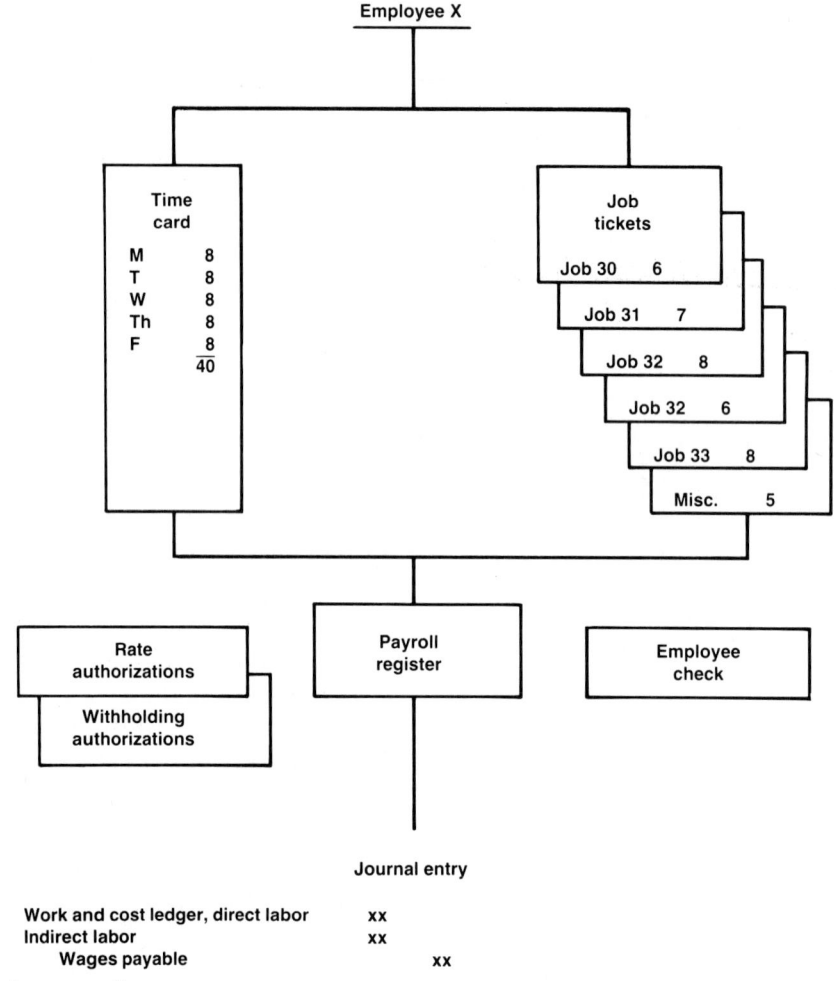

**EXHIBIT 18-5** Labor accounting.

**Indirect Costs** Given a basic cost-accumulation system, the cost of direct materials and direct labor can be measured reasonably well. Procedures used to measure many indirect costs are usually less satisfactory because of the indirect nature of costs; nevertheless, such procedures are necessary to cost accounting. (For a review, refer back to the section on cost allocation.)

For example, a hospital provides some number of radiologic service units for a given period of time. It might be expected that the costs of film, drugs, and power directly associated with the units have been reasonably well identified and assigned directly to the units. Can the same thing be said for the salary of the radiologist, technician costs, depreciation, maintenance costs of equipment, and other similar costs? The answer is obviously no. These costs cannot be traced directly to the service provided, even though they may have been a necessary part of the service. Indeed, some of the costs are directly identifiable with the basic service but not with a specific radiologic unit, because of their fixed nature.

With respect to cost systems, indirect costs are divided into two categories: (1) actual indirect costs incurred and (2) indirect costs applied to the revenue-producing function or projects in process. Actual indirect costs incurred are typically recorded by means of a control account and some type of subsidiary record, such as departmental expense analysis or overhead cost sheets. Examples of entries to record indirect cost are as follows:

|  | Dr. | Cr. |
|---|---|---|
| Repairs | $1,000 | |
|     Accounts payable | | $1,000 |

Distribution: Department M, $500; Department N, $500.

|  | Dr. | Cr. |
|---|---|---|
| Electricity | $1,000 | |
|     Accounts payable | | $1,000 |

Distribution: Department M, $300; Department N, $500; Department O, $200.

|  | Dr. | Cr. |
|---|---|---|
| Depreciation—equipment | $2,000 | |
|     Accumulated depreciation | | $2,000 |

Distribution: Department M, $800; Department N, $400; Department O, $800.

These entries might be recorded in the accounts as shown in Exhibit 18-6.

### EXHIBIT 18-6
### Indirect Cost Accounts

**Overhead control**

| Repairs | $1,000 |
| Electricity | 1,000 |
| Depreciation | 2,000 |

**Overhead cost sheet—department M**

| Repairs | Electricity | Depreciation | Total |
|---|---|---|---|
| $500 | $300 | $800 | $1,600 |

**Overhead cost sheet—department N**

| Repairs | Electricity | Depreciation | Total |
|---|---|---|---|
| $500 | $500 | $400 | $1,400 |

**Overhead cost sheet—department O**

| Repairs | Electricity | Depreciation | Total |
|---|---|---|---|
| | $200 | $800 | $1,000 |

Some of the overhead items can be identified directly with the departments (i.e., they were direct costs of the departments). Others may have been arbitrarily allocated to the departments because they represented costs of the departments but cannot be traced directly to the individual departments.

The amount of indirect costs to be applied to each department is developed by estimating both indirect costs and activity for the year, which gives a predetermined rate. Consider the following example:

A hospital uses a predetermined indirect cost rate based on radiological units in connection with the cost accounting system. Data relating to March and the entire year were as follows:

|  | Actual for March | Budgeted for the year |
|---|---|---|
| Radiological units | 10,000 | 120,000 |
| Radiological overhead | $100,000 | $960,000* |

*Based on regression analysis.

Calculate this predetermined overhead rate, overhead charged to service, and the amount of overapplied or underapplied overhead for the month.

Solution:

Predetermined rate: $960,000/120,000 = $8 per unit

| Department overhead for the month | $100,000 |
|---|---|
| Overhead applied ($8 × 10,000) | 80,000 |
| Underapplied overhead | $ 20,000 |

Where predetermined rates are used, it is expected that underapplied or overapplied overhead will develop and that significant differences might arise from month to month. Nevertheless, differences accumulated should become insignificant by the year's end if cost-estimation methods used have produced reliable estimates. In some cases, the activity for the period is divided into actual overhead for the period (by department or overall), and this rate is used to allocate total overhead. This method is likely to create significant variations in costs where activity is not constant from period to period and fixed costs are a significant part of total overhead costs.

## Process Costing

When very similar units are processed on a continuous basis, *process-costing systems* are typically used. *Unit costs* derived from costs accumulated by department and time period reflect averages developed for the department on a period basis. The cost for individual services provided, except as an average, cannot be determined from a process cost accounting system. For example, in the case of water and electric utilities, the cost of providing water or electricity service would likely be accounted for on a process-costing basis. A large component of the total cost would likely be direct labor and indirect costs. The product (service) would be the same from month to month. Costs of producing the product (service) would be quite similar also. There is really no way to distinguish cost of services provided to customer *A* versus customer *B* except in terms of the amount of the service. A type of process costing might also be used in a per diem reimbursement method in which total costs of patient care are divided by patient days. For example, assume that a government-sponsored program provides patient counseling. Unit costs need to be developed for purposes of comparison with other programs and for reimbursement purposes. Program costs for one month are $26,000, with 5,000 patients being counseled. The cost per patient was $5.20. This example is fairly typical of the level of process costing experienced in governmental and other nonbusiness areas.

## Job-Order Cost Accounting Systems

A job-order costing system is needed when it is important to identify costs by individual services or projects. Some type of job-order cost is usually utilized in activities of non-business-oriented entities such as highway departments and the output of printing and maintenance shops or the accumulation of project or program costs.

As reasonable accuracy becomes important in determining costs of programs, projects, and services, specific cost procedures must be established to determine, assign, and transfer the relevant costs from one stage to another until the assignment has been completed. As indicated earlier, a job-order costing system will typically be used where the item to be produced is to conform to certain specifications or the duration of the project is so long that several time periods may elapse before the primary output is completed.

**Basic Components** The process begins with instructions being issued to provide some project or provide some service. Inventory items are issued, labor is expended, and indirect costs are incurred. Since the first two costs, inventory items and direct labor, can be identified directly with the job, the system should be designed so that their costs can easily be charged to the proper job. Some type of job cost sheet is usually set up to accumulate these costs with the actual entries being made from material requisitions and labor time tickets, or other evidence of the costs incurred.

Since most overhead cannot be directly identified with specific jobs, it is largely allocated on some arbitrary but logical basis. Sometimes, as indicated in an earlier section, overhead is estimated for a normal level of activity, and this balance is then divided by the estimated activity base (labor hours, number of patients, units, or some other activity base) to arrive at a predetermined overhead rate. Overhead is then allocated to the job based on actual activity for the period times the rate. Such an approach to overhead allocation should eliminate the unusual fluctuations sometimes encountered when actual overhead incurred is periodically allocated to jobs. The basic documents and data flows are shown in Exhibit 18-7.

Exhibit 18-7 shows a job cost sheet being set up by client and/or job number. Materials used in producing the item called for in the job are recorded from basic material requisitions. Labor used on the job is recorded from labor tickets, and overhead is allocated on some predetermined basis from an overhead distribution schedule. Cost flows are also outlined for the balance of the accounting system. In a job-order costing system, work in process is represented by uncompleted job cost sheets, and finished goods are represented by completed job sheets that have been transferred from work in process.

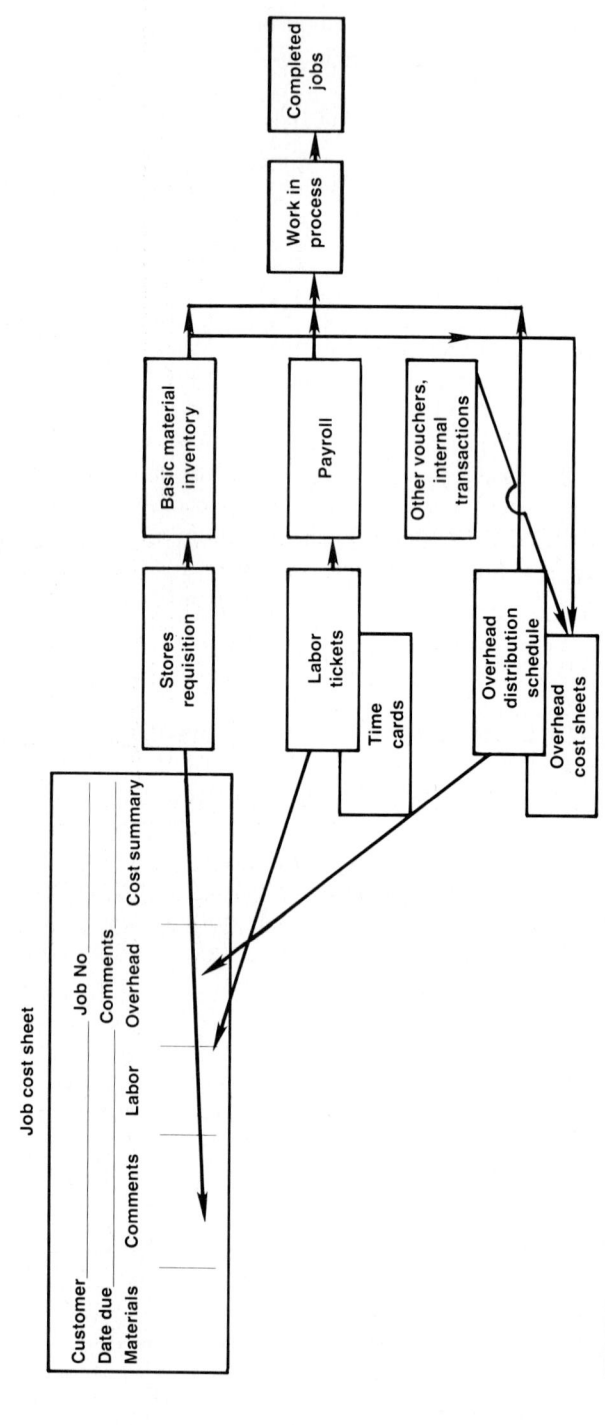

**EXHIBIT 18-7** Job order costing system.

**Job Costing in Project Control** In project control, such as the construction of major capital facilities, three different components of the project must be monitored: cost of the project, quality of the work, and time involved. Job-order costing can be used to provide an auditable record of costs incurred, and the system can be established so that actual costs can be compared with budgeted costs for control purposes.

A job cost sheet would be established for each major facilities project, with an assigned number indicating the individual projects. As materials are received and labor expended, costs would be charged to the applicable jobs based on the assigned numbers. Overhead costs would be allocated in one of the ways previously discussed. Periodically, actual costs to date should be combined with estimated costs to complete and the results compared with original budgeted costs as a means of monitoring possible cost overruns and underruns.

**Job Costing in Public Programs** Several classes of cost accounts may be relevant in measuring the cost of public programs. Unless an accrual accounting system has been installed, however, this approach may encounter several problems. Misleading figures may result from the common method of determining unit costs by simply dividing the performance unit (e.g., number of street lights maintained) into the current expenditures for the activity. Even if the costs are limited to expenditures, current unit costs may be overstated if new capital equipment is included in the expenditure, or if there is a large increase in inventories. On the other hand, unit costs may be understated in many municipal accounting systems because of a failure to account for the drawing down of inventories or for depreciation—the user costs of equipment.

As indicated earlier, indirect cost or overhead includes the cost of items that cannot be conveniently charged directly to the jobs or operations benefited, including general administrative expense. It can be argued, for example, that the public works department should be assigned part of the costs of the personnel department, the accounting department, and other service or auxiliary agencies. These indirect costs are often distributed to operating departments on a formula basis, as determined by labor hours, labor costs, or total direct cost of each job or operation.

The procedural steps for summarizing and posting to the cost accounts are diagramed in Exhibit 18-8. Field reports provide the primary record of work performed and expenses incurred in the basic information for cost accounting. The particular design and maintenance of these reports depend on local conditions. For example, a job order system might be installed to record and monitor costs of highway maintenance. A crew foreman or project supervisor may prepare these reports, or it may be desirable to have each individual employee prepare a daily or weekly time sheet or time and effort report, indicating work assignments and the time spent on each operation. Supervisory personnel will have to provide a separate bill of materials used and a statement of the equipment service rendered for each job and operation. Field reports need to be summarized before posting to job cost sheets or work and cost ledgers.

The field report may consist of several separate forms, but, in some situations, it may be possible to combine the requisite information in one report. Field labor reports are used to determine the costs of labor entering into each operation or job; these data can also provide a basis for payroll preparation (a general accounting function). Daily

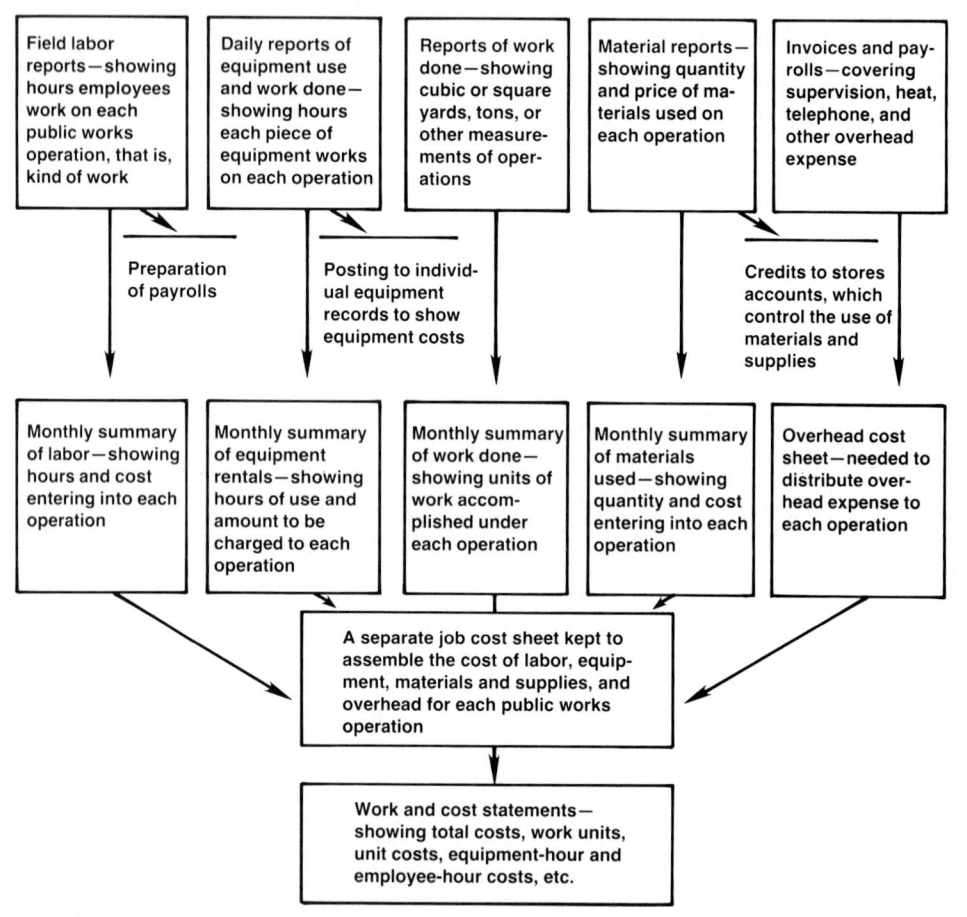

```
┌─────────────┐ ┌─────────────┐ ┌─────────────┐ ┌─────────────┐ ┌─────────────┐
│ Field labor │ │ Daily       │ │ Reports of  │ │ Material    │ │ Invoices    │
│ reports—    │ │ reports of  │ │ work done—  │ │ reports—    │ │ and pay-    │
│ showing     │ │ equipment   │ │ showing     │ │ showing     │ │ rolls—      │
│ hours       │ │ use and     │ │ cubic or    │ │ quantity    │ │ covering    │
│ employees   │ │ work done—  │ │ square      │ │ and price   │ │ supervision,│
│ work on     │ │ showing     │ │ yards, tons,│ │ of ma-      │ │ heat,       │
│ each public │ │ hours each  │ │ or other    │ │ terials used│ │ telephone,  │
│ works       │ │ piece of    │ │ measure-    │ │ on each     │ │ and other   │
│ operation,  │ │ equipment   │ │ ments of    │ │ operation   │ │ overhead    │
│ that is,    │ │ works on    │ │ operations  │ │             │ │ expense     │
│ kind of work│ │ each        │ │             │ │             │ │             │
│             │ │ operation   │ │             │ │             │ │             │
└─────────────┘ └─────────────┘ └─────────────┘ └─────────────┘ └─────────────┘
```

**EXHIBIT 18-8**   Field reports used in cost accounting.

(Diagram, continued: Preparation of payrolls; Posting to individual equipment records to show equipment costs; Credits to stores accounts, which control the use of materials and supplies. These feed into: Monthly summary of labor; Monthly summary of equipment rentals; Monthly summary of work done; Monthly summary of materials used; Overhead cost sheet. All feed into: A separate job cost sheet kept to assemble the cost of labor, equipment, materials and supplies, and overhead for each public works operation. Final box: Work and cost statements—showing total costs, work units, unit costs, equipment-hour and employee-hour costs, etc.)

reports of equipment operators provide summaries of the equipment rental charges to be distributed to the jobs on the cost ledger. These reports can also be used to post individual equipment records (showing for each piece of equipment the expense for labor, gasoline, oil and other supplies, repair costs, overhead, and depreciation). Materials and supplies reports indicate withdrawal of stores from stockrooms, providing credit to stores accounts as well as charges to operating costs accounts.

Many indirect costs are reported in substantially the same manner as direct costs, from time reports, store records, and so forth. Certain indirect costs may also be determined from invoices on such items as travel expenses, utility services, and general office expenses. These indirect costs are posted initially to an overhead cost sheet and then allocated to jobs and activities on a predetermined proportionate basis.

The job cost sheet is the final assemblage of the information with respect to all work performed and all costs incurred. Accounts in the work and cost ledger are generally posted monthly and closed upon completion of a specific job or are closed at the end of the regular accounting period when unit costs on an activity/program are recorded.

The administrator will find cost accounting useful as a basis for decision and action only to the extent that significant information is properly presented. Job cost sheets may be the essential link between costs records and the administrator's use of the information. Monthly summary statements of work completed, expenses, unit costs, and employee-hour production are desirable. Such statements may be readily compiled from the information that appears on the job cost sheets. Other statements may be prepared periodically, according to management needs, on such subjects as total labor costs, employee productivity, equipment rental resources, analysis of noneffective time and idle equipment, and losses of supplies due to waste or spoilage.

## STANDARD COSTING AND VARIANCE ANALYSIS

In a business setting, standard costing has been widely used to simplify the record keeping involved in traditional product and project cost determination systems while providing a means for control by means of variance analysis. However, its use in the governmental and nonbusiness area has been extremely rare, although standard costing and variance analysis may have potential application in a number of such environments.

In setting up standards, a unit cost and some measure of time, weight, or other unit are established for a job or activity. Total variances are derived by comparing actual results with planned performance. This variance can be developed for differences between planned performance and actual performance. Once the total variance is developed, it may be possible to further break the variance down into price and volume components and possibly mix differences.

**Volume Variance** If a city bus service planned on offering service to 500,000 customers at a fare of $.50, and only 400,000 customers used the service, the bus company's volume variance would be $50,000 ([500,000 − 400,000] × $.50).

**Price Variance** In the volume variance example, if the actual fare charged had been $.60 instead of $.50 the bus company's total variance would have been only $10,000 ([500,000 × $.50] − [400,000 × $.60]). Yet, the volume variance is still $50,000. In this case, there is a favorable price variance of $40,000 ([400,000 × $.60] − [400,000 × $.50]).

**Mix Variance** In the above examples, a mix variance does not exist. However, if different routes called for different fares, and the actual mix of routes used was different from those budgeted, a mix variance would result.

## SUMMARY

This chapter provided an introduction and discussion of cost accounting techniques most likely to be used by governmental and other nonprofit entities. The various cost accounting systems such as process and job order costing were briefly discussed. Standard costing and variance analysis were outlined.

The importance of cost allocation was stressed and the various methods for allocating service development costs were explained. Finally, some suggestions were made regarding record keeping for cost accounting purposes.

## QUESTIONS

1 What is job-order costing?
2 Describe the difference between job-order costing and process costing.
3 Why isn't process costing likely to be used widely in the governmental and nonprofit areas?
4 Discuss the significance of cost allocation.
5 Describe the differences between periodic and perpetual inventory record keeping.
6 How are labor costs generally accumulated?
7 Describe some of the problems involved in indirect cost accounting.
8 Describe the two methods discussed in this chapter for allocating service department costs.
9 What is standard costing?
10 What is variance analysis?
11 Describe the difference between a volume variance and a price variance.

## PROBLEMS

**18-1** The town of Salem is constructing sidewalks for one of its newest subdivisions. The following information has been obtained on costs during construction:

1 Direct materials, primarily concrete and forms, were purchased at $200,000. At the end of construction 10 percent of the material remained in inventory.
2 Direct labor on the project amounted to $150,000.
3 Indirect costs related to the job were allocated based on 50 percent of direct labor.

**Required**:
Determine costs of constructing the sidewalks.

**18-2** The city of Radford's highway department has responsibility for maintenance and repair of city streets. At the beginning of the fiscal year, only one repair project was in process. All major jobs are accounted for by a job-order costing system. Costs applicable to the job in process are as follows:

|  | Job 1050 |
|---|---|
| Direct material | $4,000 |
| Direct labor | 2,000 |
| Overhead | 2,500 |
|  | $8,500 |

During the first month of the new year, the following transactions took place:

1 Materials totaling $60,000 were purchased on account.
2 Direct material requisitions for the following jobs were prepared and used:

| Job 1050 | $ 1,000 |
|---|---|
| 1051 | 4,000 |
| 1052 | 2,000 |
| 1053 | 2,500 |
| 1054 | 2,000 |
|  | $11,500 |

3 Wages paid to employees were related to current-month activities and totaled $10,000. Labor tickets indicated direct labor should be charged to the following jobs:

| Job 1050 | $  500 |
|---|---|
| 1051 | 2,500 |
| 1052 | 2,000 |
| 1053 | 2,600 |
| 1054 | 1,000 |
| | $8,600 |

    **4** Depreciation applicable to the highway department for the month was $6,000.
    **5** Indirect material charged to overhead was $2,000.
    **6** Miscellaneous overhead totaled $920 for the month.
    **7** Jobs 1050 and 1051 were completed. Overhead is applied to the jobs on an actual basis using direct labor cost as the activity component.

**Required**:
Prepare summary cost sheets for each job.

**18-3** Assume you are using a process-costing system and the goal is to establish a cost per patient using dialysis units in the hospital. The hospital has several of the units, and the process is similar for each patient using the equipment. The following represents a summary of costs involved in providing the dialysis service:

| Direct medical supplies: | |
|---|---|
|   Blood tubing | $ 20,000 |
|   Saline solution | 16,000 |
|   Needles and syringes | 26,000 |
|   Dializers | 12,000 |
|   Other | 30,000 |
| | $104,000 |
| Direct wages: | |
|   Nursing | $120,000 |
|   Technicians | 100,000 |
| | $220,000 |
| Allocated costs: | $150,000 |

During the period, 6,000 patients were treated.

**Required**:
Determine the cost per patient.

**18-4** The city hospital's maintenance department costs are to be allocated to the hospital's primary mission centers on the following basis: Allocation of maintenance costs of $450,000 based on floor space. Floor space estimates at the hospital are:

| | Sq. feet |
|---|---|
| General care | 50,000 |
| Intensive care | 25,000 |
| Emergency care | 25,000 |
| Administration | 10,000 |
| Maintenance | 5,000 |
| Cafeteria | 10,000 |
| Laundry | 10,000 |

**Required**:
**1** Identify the primary mission departments.
**2** Allocate the maintenance department costs.

**18-5** The city of Oakville operates its own motor pool for transportation services and power plant to provide heat to the town hall, police building, and fire station. The following expenses were incurred by the two service functions:

| | |
|---|---|
| Motor pool | $160,000 |
| Power plant | 200,000 |
| Total | $360,000 |

Use made of the services was as follows:

| | Power (KWH) | Transportation (miles) |
|---|---|---|
| Town hall | 20,000 | 10,000 |
| Police department | 30,000 | 100,000 |
| Fire department | 60,000 | 20,000 |
| Power plant | 10,000 | 2,000 |
| Motor pool | 5,000 | 4,000 |

**Required**:
1. Allocate the service department costs to the mission centers using the method of neglect.
2. Allocate the costs using the step method.

**18-6** In Problem 18-5 the power plant made use of the motor pool's services, and energy generated by the power plant was used to heat the motor pool facilities. Explain how the reciprocal relationship between these two service departments might be given full recognition in allocating costs.

**18-7** The Montgomery County Hospital budgeted 5,000 patient days per month at $400 per day. For the year, the hospital had 4,500 patient days at $400.

**Required**:
Calculate the total variance and volume variance.

**18-8** The city of Radford installed a bus system in 19X6. In planning for the bus service, the city's fixed offices projected 100,000 customers for the year at a per customer fare of $.60. During 19X6, 100,000 customers made use of the bus service. After 50,000 customers had used the service, the fare was raised by 60 percent.

**Required**:
Calculate the total variance and price variance.

**18-9** Assume a university budgets 20,000 students for the fall semester, at a tuition rate of $1,800 per student. Shortly before the start of the semester, the university's trustees approve a tuition increase, and the academic-year tuition is set at $4,000 effective immediately. After registration for the fall term, enrollment was determined to be 18,900 students.

**Required**:
1. Determine the total difference between expected and actual tuition fees.
2. Break the total difference down into applicable variances.

**18-10** The printing department of the town of Blacksburg uses a standard-costing system with a standard overhead rate of $6 per unit. In developing this rate, a normal capacity of 10,000 units was used. At this level, the flexible budget included $20,000 of fixed costs and $40,000 of variable costs. In the current period, 8,000 units were completed and shipped to other departments in the town. Actual overhead costs for the period were $54,000.

**Required**:
Calculate the relevant overhead variances.

CHAPTER 19

# MANAGEMENT ACCOUNTING TECHNIQUES

In Chapter 18, various cost accounting techniques used for financial reporting purposes were introduced. Standard costing and variance analysis, which are used for management control purposes, were also introduced. In this chapter, a number of techniques that have been successfully used in the business sector for planning and control purposes are discussed and illustrated.

As with the case of cost accounting systems, managers in government and other nonbusiness activities have not, until recently, attempted to adopt available planning and control techniques from the business sector for their use in decision making, although most of them can be readily adapted to both the for-profit and the not-for-profit segments of nonbusiness organizations. This chapter introduces a number of management accounting techniques that are readily adaptable to all situations in nonbusiness organizations in which: (1) revenues or benefits have a direct relationship to costs, (2) cost containment is an important issue, and (3) management performance should be measured. These techniques should prove to be quite useful to nonbusiness accounting managers in providing information for planning and control purposes.

## BREAK-EVEN ANALYSIS

Sound planning and budgeting procedures dictate that significant attention be given to the relationship between differential costs and volume of operations. The primary purpose of break-even analysis (cost-volume-profit analysis) is to estimate the level of activity at which total revenues are equal to total costs. The analysis requires that a separation between variable and fixed costs be made so that the effect of changes in volume on revenues and costs can be estimated. For instance, costs of $80,000 for a facility operating at 80 percent capacity would fall to $60,000 when the facility was operated at 60 percent capacity, if all costs related to the operation were variable. However, if all costs were fixed, a change in volume would have no effect on costs.

Break-even analysis assumes that costs related to a particular operation can be broken down into fixed and variable components. This enables us to express the cost function by using the cost-estimating equation:

$$y = a + bx$$

where $x$ = output
$a$ = fixed costs
$b$ = unit of variability
(variable cost per unit)

The revenue function can be expressed as:

$$y = cx$$

where $c$ = unit of variability
(unit sale price)

Graphically, the break-even point is found where the cost and revenue functions intersect, as indicated in Exhibit 19-1. That figure also shows how the break-even equation can be derived. In the resulting equation, $x$ equals units needed to break even, $b$ represents fixed costs, and $(c - b)$ represents the contribution margin per unit of the product or service.

**EXHIBIT 19-1** Break-even analysis.

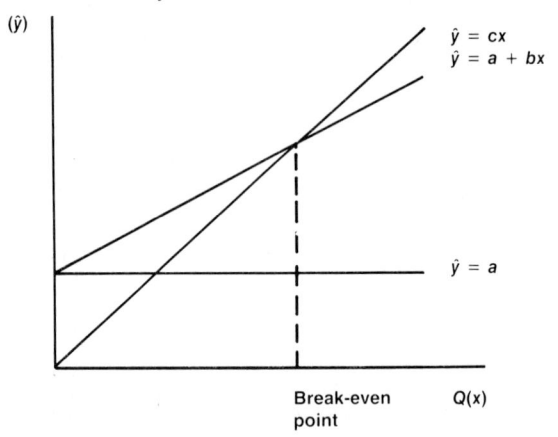

$$\begin{aligned}
\text{Sales} &= \text{variable expenses} + \text{fixed expenses} \\
cx &= bx + a \\
\hline
cx - bx &= a \\
x(c - b) &= a \\
x &= \frac{a}{(c - b)}
\end{aligned}$$

From this base, units needed to break even can be calculated by dividing fixed costs by contribution margin per unit ($c - b$). Dollar revenue can be derived by dividing fixed costs by the profit-volume ratio (contribution margin divided by sales). Minimum sales (units or dollars) needed for a certain profit level can be developed by adding profit desired to fixed costs and dividing by contribution margin (unit or ratio). Consider the following example:

The city of X, which operates a cafeteria for the benefit of employees, is attempting to identify the amount of revenue needed to cover costs of the cafeteria operation. Last year's results, broken down by fixed and variable components, are as follows:

|  | Fixed | Variable | Total |
|---|---|---|---|
| Salaries | $ 80,000 |  | $ 80,000 |
| Wages | 20,000 | $100,000 | 120,000 |
| Food |  | 200,000 | 200,000 |
| Supplies | 5,000 | 20,000 | 25,000 |
| Rent | 4,000 |  | 4,000 |
| Other | 1,000 |  | 1,000 |
|  | $110,000 | $320,000 | $430,000 |

The number of meals served last year was 320,000. This year, cafeteria personnel project that approximately 440,000 meals will be served. What price should be set in order to break even?

The solution would be as follows. The variable cost for a meal the previous year was

$$\$320,000 \div 320,000 = \$1 \text{ variable cost per meal}$$

Expected costs for the coming year are:

$$\$1 \times 440,000 = \$440,000 \text{ variable costs}$$
$$\phantom{\$1 \times 440,000 = \ }110,000 \text{ fixed costs}$$
$$\phantom{\$1 \times 440,000 = \ }\$550,000 \text{ total costs}$$

Projected price per meal is:

$$\$550,000 \div \$440,000 = \$1.25 \text{ price per meal}$$

Break-even or cost-volume-profit analysis requires several assumptions.

1 Fixed and variable components can be separated.
2 Some common activity base, such as number of meals, can be found for developing the necessary relationship.
3 The analysis is assumed to contain a common unit.
4 Relationships can be expressed by means of linear equations.
5 Analysis is limited to some relevant range in which even though the functions may not be linear, the relationships can be approximated by linear functions.

In this example, assume that last year's costs were within the same range as the coming year's costs, the separation of fixed and variable components was reasonable, use of the assumption of a basic meal as the activity unit was valid, and the meal projection was reasonable.

## FLEXIBLE BUDGETS

If costs are related to some identifiable activity, and if the costs can be broken down into variable-cost and fixed-cost components, budgets can be constructed to reflect different levels of activity. In the planning stage, budgets developed at different levels of activity might provide valuable insights to those responsible for making decisions based on certain levels of funding and activity expectations. Even where costs to be incurred are constrained by legal appropriations, the knowledge gained by observing impact of cost behavior on objectives sought is invaluable.

Flexible budgeting should prove to be quite valuable in nonconstrained activities, such as proprietary and capital project funds as well as responsibility accounting situations. Activities represented by proprietary funds, and possibly activities represented by capital project funds, cannot operate efficiently and effectively unless budgeted amounts for costs are varied in relationship to the principal activities planned and experienced. Indeed, a basic assumption of responsibility accounting systems is that managers will be held responsible for controllable costs at the level of activity achieved.

Even where budget constraints of one type or another prohibit costs above a certain amount, flexible budgets can be used by managers to point out why costs allowed are inadequate to achieve certain stated objectives. For instance, if $200,000 has been provided for removal of tree leaves based on last year's costs for 100,000 houses, and 20,000 additional houses have been added through annexation, it is likely that some changes will be required in order to live within the budget constraint.

## COST-BENEFIT ANALYSIS

In Chapter 17, it was suggested that *costs* can be defined as "a release of value required to accomplish some goal or purpose." From this definition, it may be concluded that costs are incurred for the purposes of deriving some *benefits*. Cost data derived from a cost-management accounting system can provide significant inputs to the analysis of costs and benefits.

### Elements of Cost-Benefit Analysis

The purpose of cost-benefit analysis is to provide information so that the best alternative for achieving an objective can be determined. As such, cost-benefit analysis seeks: (1) to determine whether or not a particular program or project is justified, (2) to rank various alternatives appropriate to a given set of objectives, and (3) to ascertain the optimal course of action to attain these objectives. In contrast to more traditional forms of evaluation that tend to be short-range and narrow in scope, cost-benefit analysis operates within an extended time horizon. The analysis focuses attentions on those aspects of a decision that can be quantified. This means, in the case of some public projects and programs, alternative costs are highlighted.

Cost-benefit analysis assists in the resource allocation problem through an identification of (1) an objective function, (2) constraints, (3) externalities, (4) time dimensions, and (5) risk and uncertainty. Selecting an *objective function* involves the identification (in dollar terms, to the extent possible) of the costs and benefits associated with each alternative. In this way, various alternatives can be compared with one another in terms of the cost of attaining the desired benefits. *Constraints* specify the rules of the game, that is, the limitations within which a solution must be sought. Frequently, optimal solutions must be discarded because they do not conform to these imposed rules. Constraints are incorporated into mathematical models as parameters or boundary conditions. *Externalities* are those factors—inputs (costs), outputs (benefits), and constraints—that initially are excluded from the problem statement in order to make it more manageable. Ultimately, the long-range effects of these phenomena must be considered, however. This further evaluation usually is undertaken after the objective function and model have been tested and the range of feasible alternatives has been tested.

In examining the *time dimensions* of various alternatives, it is necessary to delineate long-term costs and benefits. The timing of costs and benefits cannot be ignored. It is not sufficient merely to add the total benefits and subtract the total costs estimated for a given alternative. Rather, it is necessary to consider a measure that reflects the impacts of deferred benefits and future costs. And in so doing, the analyst encounters the problems of *risk and uncertainty*.

Time is a valuable resource in any organization. And yet, the value of time often is overlooked, particularly when dollars spent this year are compared with those of last year or next year. In developing a cost-benefit analysis, however, it is important to recognize that dollar values are not equal over time. Benefits that accrue in the present are worth more to their recipients than benefits that occur at some time in the more distant future. Similarly, funds that must be invested today cost more than funds that must be invested in the future, since presumably one alternative use of such funds would be to invest them at some rate of return that would increase their value.

Therefore, the *present value* of both costs and benefits (to the extent possible) should be determined by multiplying each stream by an appropriate *discount factor*. This factor gets smaller as the costs or benefits occur farther in the future. If the alternative is to invest available funds at some interest rate ($i$), then an appropriate discount factor can be expressed as:

$$\frac{1}{(1 + i)^n}$$

where $i$ is the relevant interest rate per period and $n$ is the number of periods into the future that the benefits and costs will accrue. Since $i$ is positive, the farther an event is in the future, the smaller is its present value. A high discount rate means that the present is valued considerably over the future; that is, there is a significant time preference, a higher regard for present benefits than for equal future benefits, and/or incentives for investment.

Choice of an appropriate discount rate continues to be a significant problem in the governmental and other nonbusiness areas. It is not uncommon for governmental decision makers to ignore the problem and not use a discount rate or for them to use the interest rate on bonds issued. In the federal government, average rates for private sector investments as well as rates prescribed by various agencies have been used.

**EXHIBIT 19-2**
**Discounting $10,000 Annually over Ten Years**

| Year | Discount factor at 8 percent | Value | Discount factor at 10 percent | Value |
|---|---|---|---|---|
| 1 | 0.925926 | $ 9,259.26 | 0.909090 | $ 9,090.90 |
| 2 | 0.857339 | 8,573.39 | 0.826446 | 8,264.46 |
| 3 | 0.793832 | 7,938.32 | 0.751315 | 7,513.15 |
| 4 | 0.735030 | 7,350.30 | 0.683013 | 6,830.13 |
| 5 | 0.680583 | 6,805.83 | 0.620920 | 6,209.20 |
| 6 | 0.630170 | 6,301.70 | 0.564472 | 5,644.72 |
| 7 | 0.583490 | 5,834.90 | 0.513156 | 5,131.56 |
| 8 | 0.540269 | 5,402.69 | 0.466505 | 4,665.05 |
| 9 | 0.500249 | 5,002.49 | 0.424095 | 4,240.95 |
| 10 | 0.463193 | 4,631.93 | 0.385541 | 3,855.41 |
| Total | | $67,100.81 | | $61,445.53 |

Although the choice of the particular discount rate may be difficult to justify, the procedures for discounting are quite simple. Once an appropriate rate is chosen, a table of discount factors can be consulted to determine the appropriate figure to apply to each year in the stream of costs and benefits. However, as the data in Exhibit 19-2 illustrate, the selection of the discount rate can significantly affect the final decision.

## Discounting Methods Used

Cost-benefit analysis was introduced in the public sector as part of the Flood Control Act of 1936, which required that water resources development projects not be initiated unless an evaluation showed that a project's expected "benefits to whomsoever they may accrue (are) in excess of estimated costs." The *internal rate of return* is widely used in business and reflects a legacy of prominent economists such as John Maynard Keynes and Kenneth Boulding.

Since the costs associated with any investment decision usually accrue first, the undiscounted sum of benefits must be considerably larger in order to yield a favorable project. This characteristic of long-term investments is implicit in the analytical technique of internal rate of return ($r$), which is defined by the following equation:

$$r: \sum_{n=0}^{N} \frac{B_n}{(1+r)^n} = \sum_{n=0}^{N} \frac{C_n}{(1+r)^n}$$

Note that the internal rate of return is not set equal to anything—the right-hand side of the equation is the present value of costs, and the left-hand side is the present value of benefits. The internal rate of return is that interest rate $r$ that brings the two sides of the equation into equilibrium, that is, when the return on investment (discounted benefits) equals the cost of capital.

To illustrate the application of this criterion, assume that a city-owned utility is confronted with the decision of whether or not to initiate a new plant that will require a

**EXHIBIT 19-3**
**Internal Rate of Return Calculations**

| | | | | Present value | |
|---|---|---|---|---|---|
| Year | Benefits | Costs | Discount rate at 11.6% | Benefits | Costs |
| 1 | 0 | $100,000 | 0.89606 | 0 | $ 89,606 |
| 2 | $100,000 | 40,000 | 0.80292 | $ 80,292 | 32,117 |
| 3 | 100,000 | 40,000 | 0.71946 | 71,946 | 28,778 |
| 4 | 100,000 | 40,000 | 0.64468 | 64,468 | 25,787 |
| 5 | 0 | 70,000 | 0.57767 | | 40,437 |
| Total | $300,000 | $290,000 | | $216,706 | $216,725 |

first-year investment in start-up costs of $100,000 with estimated annual operating costs of $40,000. In the fifth year of operations, it is anticipated that major modifications in the project line will be required and the current line will be shut down at a cost of $70,000. It is estimated that the firm will have three years of operations in this plant during which net return will average $100,000 annually. In short, for an investment of $290,000 over five years, the firm will obtain a return of $300,000. The costs and benefits of this project are illustrated in Exhibit 19-3.

As illustrated by the calculations on the right-hand side of Exhibit 19-3, an internal rate of return of approximately 11.6 percent provides *one* solution to the equation. If capital "costs" less than 11.6 percent (in terms of the interest rate in the current market), the proposed project would be desirable. In practice, of course, the utility would likely examine several alternative investments and select the alternative that exhibits the greatest margin of return.

The internal rate of return provides a reasonably good measure of investment potential when all alternatives are of the same magnitude. When the alternatives are of different scales, it is of lesser practical value, since very little is revealed about the absolute size of the net benefits in the application of this technique.

A more recently developed indicator is *net present value*, in which the present value of benefits is subtracted from the present value of costs. Net present value is the criterion recommended, if not used, more frequently in contemporary cost-benefit analysis. The formula for calculating the present value of net benefits is:

$$N = -C_0 + \frac{(B_1 - C_1)}{(1 + i)} + \frac{(B_2 - C_2)}{(1 + i)^2} + \cdots + \frac{(B_n - C_n)}{(1 + i)^n}$$

Two projects with equal net benefits might be regarded indifferently, however. Assume that two projects each offered net benefits of $10,000. However, one involves a present value of benefits of $2 million and a present value of costs of $1.99 million, while the other project has a present value of benefits of $100,000 and a present value of costs of $90,000. Suppose that something goes wrong, so that the calculations of costs and benefits are off by 10 percent. The first project might have a negative benefit of as much as $200,000, whereas the second would do no worse than break even.

## Value of Cost-Benefit Analysis

It is virtually impossible to eliminate the need for subjective judgments in the process of making decisions for any organization. Nonetheless, a more "systematic" approach to cost and benefit comparison, as provided by cost-benefit analysis, and the consideration of time-preference of capital investment, can contribute significantly to a more rational basis for such decisions. This is particularly true when compared with the uncoordinated, haphazard, and intuitive approaches that characterize many more traditional methods. Examining expenditures in terms of programs and objectives instead of merely by spending entities and considering total benefits of expenditures for alternative programs alongside total costs of the inputs are important contributions of cost-benefit techniques.

## RESPONSIBILITY ACCOUNTING AND PERFORMANCE MEASUREMENT

As you have already learned, financial reporting provides aggregated facts relevant to a fund, group of funds, or some other activity. From a management control point of view, it is necessary to have periodic reporting on performance by individual managers, departments, and programs so that those responsible for the activities can be evaluated and timely corrective action taken when necessary.

In fact, budgets and standards tied in with a responsibility accounting system provide the bases for control and performance measurement within an entity.

### Responsibility Accounting

The basic notion of responsibility accounting involves provision of information to managers directly responsible for an activity as well as to the next higher level of responsibility. Responsibility accounting attempts to report results so that significant differences can be identified, responsibility determined, explanations obtained, and corrective action taken. In this system, departments, functions, and programs are referred to as *responsibility centers*. In a municipal government, for instance, the costs of the operations of police and fire protection would be accumulated separately so that the police and fire commissioners could be held accountable for their respective areas of responsibility.

For responsibility centers to be operational, costs charged to them should be separated into direct and indirect costs as well as controllable and uncontrollable costs. Since not all direct costs are controllable at the responsibility center level, the direct expenses should be broken down into controllable and uncontrollable components. Indirect costs will often be allocated to the responsibility center in an attempt to estimate the full cost of operations or programs at that level. In Exhibit 18-2, the schedule failed to provide for responsibility reporting. For instance, within intensive care, the costs would have been broken down as shown in Exhibit 19-4, to reflect controllable costs needed in a responsibility reporting system.

### Performance Measurement

In a profit-oriented environment, most performance measurement models are tied to profits: profits, profit percentage (profits/sales), return on investment (profit/invest-

**EXHIBIT 19-4**
**Costs of Intensive Care**

| Direct expenses | Actual | Budget | Difference |
|---|---|---|---|
| Controllable: | | | |
| Nurses' salaries | $160,000 | $150,000 | ($10,000) |
| Wages of attendants | 65,000 | 60,000 | (5,000) |
| Supplies | 39,000 | 40,000 | 1,000 |
| Energy costs | 40,000 | 40,000 | — |
| Total | $304,000 | $290,000 | ($14,000) |
| Uncontrollable: | | | |
| Residents' and interns' salaries | $160,000 | $160,000 | — |
| Supervisor's salary | 40,000 | 40,000 | — |
| Depreciation | 100,000 | 100,000 | — |
| Other | 10,000 | 10,000 | — |
| | $310,000 | $310,000 | — |
| Total expenses | $614,000 | $600,000 | ($14,000) |

ment), and residual income (profit minus a deduction for capital costs). In other cases, performance measurement is provided by comparing actual costs against budget by responsibility center.

Since profits are not typically a factor in the governmental and other nonbusiness areas, a comparison of actual with budgeted costs is often the best and perhaps the only means of performance measurement available to management. Although a number of attempts have been made to develop productivity measures, they have generally been inadequate because management has not been able to identify valid output representations. Consequently, managers in the nonbusiness area have been left with few means for controlling and measuring costs.

## PROBLEMS IN CONTROLLING NONBUSINESS COSTS

If the purpose of the nonbusiness unit is to control cost as well as to control the expenditures against the appropriation, then the accounting system must provide total costs as well as expenditures.

### Costs Versus Expenditures

The requirements for *full costing* in terms of accrual accounting may be more than many smaller units are prepared to undertake. A shift to full accrual accounting may initially be difficult and costly, involving a level of sophistication in accounting methods sometimes not found in small governmental organizations. Most organizations will not undertake this conversion unless it is obvious that better management results will be attained. However, where detailed procedures have been employed in conjunction with cash-obligation accounting systems, it often has been found that a shift to the accrual basis does not increase costs of accounting; instead it results in measurable savings in some cases. Many of the exceptions from the full accrual basis can be accommodated in the accounting system through adjusting entries in worksheets rather than in the general ledger records. Changing from an expenditure basis to an accrual cost basis involves adjustments for inventories, depreciation of fixed assets, and other accounts. These adjustments are helpful in answering such questions as the following: How much does the program cost? Is there good cost control in departments and agencies? How much should be charged for services? What contributions can the municipality make toward a matching grant program?

Matching the actual costs of various programs and activities against the budget (in terms of direct benefits and/or program effectiveness in achieving identified objectives) is a key component in program budgeting. Costs can then be accumulated at a departmental, agency, or program level and compared with budgets, costs of other departments, or with costs of earlier periods. This can serve as an important means of monitoring and controlling repetitive operating costs. Although cost recovery is a standard fixture of commercial-type funds, the problem also exists to a lesser extent in some governmental operating funds. For example, the public works department of a city may work on a cost reimbursement basis to repair a street torn up in installing lines for a private utility company. The charge for this service should include a fair share of equipment costs, which are often overlooked without an accrual accounting system. Likewise, costs of long-term municipal resources can often be applied as part of a city's contribution to a state or federal grant program.

## Accounting for Department, Fund, or Program Responsibility Centers

Expenditures, as related to a budget, under the modified accrual basis of accounting for local governments were discussed for line-item expenditures in Part I and are illustrated graphically in Exhibit 19-5, along with a comparison to amounts appropriated. While these illustrations apply to a governmental unit, they will apply equally to other nonbusiness organizations.

Current standards also suggest that expenditures can be classified into function or programs, objects of expenditures, departments, and character. These are illustrated in Exhibits 19-6 and 19-7 for departmental responsibility centers M, N, O, P, and Q and program centers V, W, X, Y, and Z. A comparison is also made in Exhibit 19-8 between line items and responsibility centers for budget and expenditures and in Exhibit 19-9 for line items and program expenditures.

**EXHIBIT 19-5**
**Line-Item Budget and Actual Expenditures**
(In Thousands)

| Line items | Budget | Actual | Difference |
|---|---|---|---|
| Personal services | $ 700 | $ 680 | $20 |
| Materials and supplies | 450 | 440 | 10 |
| Travel | 250 | 240 | 10 |
| Contractual services | 100 | 100 | — |
| Capital outlay | 200 | 200 | — |
| Debt service | 150 | 140 | 10 |
| Totals | $1,850 | $1,800 | $50 |

### EXHIBIT 19-6
### Departmental Responsibility Center—Budget and Actual
(Expenditure Basis, in Thousands)

| Responsibility center | Budget | Actual | Difference |
|---|---|---|---|
| M | $ 640 | $ 610 | $30 |
| N | 290 | 285 | 5 |
| O | 290 | 285 | 5 |
| P | 340 | 335 | 5 |
| Q | 290 | 285 | 5 |
| Total | $1,850 | $1,800 | $50 |

For comparison with other operating units on a periodic basis or for other analytical reasons, expenditures are a poor means of keeping records. Costs should be determined as well as expenditures. For example, if the city illustrated in Exhibit 19-5 is interested in departmental costs (or cost-center costs) or program costs, it must convert the modified accrual expenditures into costs. Using the figures in Exhibit 19-5, assume the following:

```
Personal services:
   Annual and sick leave accrued                          +$ 50,000
Supplies:
   Beginning inventory              +$ 20,000
   Ending inventory                 −  10,000        +    10,000
Travel:
   Accrued                                            +     5,000
Capital outlay:
   Expenditures                     −  200,000
   Depreciation                     +  450,000       +   250,000
Contractual services:
   Prepaid expenses, beginning                        +    10,000
Debt service:
   Total expenditures               +  140,000
   Less debt payment                −   40,000       +   100,000
```

### EXHIBIT 19-7
### Program Budget and Actual
(Expenditure Basis, in Thousands)

| Program | Budget | Actual | Difference |
|---|---|---|---|
| V | $ 420 | $ 405 | $15 |
| W | 335 | 330 | 5 |
| X | 310 | 310 | — |
| Y | 305 | 300 | 5 |
| Z | 480 | 455 | 25 |
| Total | $1,850 | $1,800 | $50 |

## EXHIBIT 19-8
### Line-Item Expenditures by Responsibility Center
### Budget and Actual
(In Thousands)

| | Responsibility centers | | | | | |
|---|---|---|---|---|---|---|
| Line items | M | N | O | P | Q | Totals |
| Personal services | [245]<br>237 | [120]<br>117 | [ 95]<br>92 | [120]<br>117 | [120]<br>117 | [ 700]<br>680 |
| Supplies | [105]<br>95 | [ 55]<br>55 | [105]<br>105 | [105]<br>105 | [ 80]<br>80 | [ 450]<br>440 |
| Travel | [ 60]<br>58 | [ 35]<br>33 | [ 60]<br>58 | [ 60]<br>58 | [ 35]<br>33 | [ 250]<br>240 |
| Contractual services | [ 25]<br>25 | [ 25]<br>25 | [ 0] | [ 25]<br>25 | [ 25]<br>25 | [ 100]<br>100 |
| Capital outlay | [ 55]<br>55 | [ 55]<br>55 | [ 30]<br>30 | [ 30]<br>30 | [ 30]<br>30 | [ 200]<br>200 |
| Debt service | [150]<br>140 | | | | | [ 150]<br>140 |
| Totals | [640]<br>610 | [290]<br>285 | [290]<br>285 | [340]<br>335 | [290]<br>285 | [1,850]<br>1,800 |

[Budget]
Actual

## EXHIBIT 19-9
### Line-Item Expenditures by Programs
### Budget and Actual
(In Thousands)

| | Programs | | | | | |
|---|---|---|---|---|---|---|
| Line items | V | W | X | Y | Z | Totals |
| Personal services | [100]<br>95 | [200]<br>195 | [150]<br>150 | [150]<br>145 | [100]<br>95 | [ 700]<br>680 |
| Supplies | [100]<br>95 | [ 50]<br>50 | [100]<br>100 | [100]<br>100 | [100]<br>95 | [ 450]<br>440 |
| Travel | [ 50]<br>45 | [ 50]<br>50 | [ 25]<br>25 | [ 25]<br>25 | [100]<br>95 | [ 250]<br>240 |
| Contractual services | [ 20]<br>20 | [ 20]<br>20 | [ 20]<br>20 | [ 20]<br>20 | [ 20]<br>20 | [ 100]<br>100 |
| Capital outlay | [150]<br>150 | [ 15]<br>15 | [ 15]<br>15 | [ 10]<br>10 | [ 10]<br>10 | [ 200]<br>200 |
| Debt service | | | | | [150]<br>140 | [ 150]<br>140 |
| Totals | [420]<br>405 | [335]<br>330 | [310]<br>310 | [305]<br>300 | [480]<br>455 | [1,850]<br>1,800 |

[Budget]
Actual

**EXHIBIT 19-10**
**Actual Expenditures Compared to Costs**
(In Thousands)

| Line item expenditure | Total expenditures | Additions | Subtractions | Total costs |
|---|---|---|---|---|
| Personal services | $ 680 | $ 50 | | $ 730 |
| Supplies | 440 | 20 | $ 10 | 450 |
| Travel | 240 | 5 | | 245 |
| Contractual services | 100 | 20 | 10 | 110 |
| Capital outlay | 200 | 450 | 200 | 450 |
| Debt service | 140 | | 40 | 100 |
| Total | $1,800 | $545 | $260 | $2,085 |

The changes between expenditures and costs can be shown in a table, reflected in accounts, or shown as items on a worksheet. Exhibits 19-10 and 19-11 show the changes in worksheet form.

The costs can then be shown by type and by department. With these adjustments, the departments become potential responsibility centers and, more specifically, cost centers. Cost centers other than departments may be used to determine costs for a particular activity, such as a certain type of police service rather than for the total department. Exhibit 19-12 shows the differences between costs and expenditures by department and object, both budget and actual. Another useful distribution of costs would be to programs rather to cost centers.

The budget and expenditure data are displayed in Exhibit 19-13 on a *program* basis. These programs are labeled V, W, X, Y, and Z in the exhibit. However, they could have been designated as any type of program that a jurisdiction or nonprofit organization

**EXHIBIT 19-11**
**Comparison of Budgeted Line Items by Expenditures and Costs**
(In Thousands)

| | Total | Personal services | Supplies | Travel | Contract services | Capital assets | Debt service |
|---|---|---|---|---|---|---|---|
| Expenditures and costs: | | | | | | | |
| Expenditures | $1,800 | $680 | $440 | $240 | $100 | $200 | $140 |
| Costs | 2,085 | 730 | 450 | 245 | 110 | 450 | 100 |
| Difference | $ 285 | $ 50 | $ 10 | $ 5 | $ 10 | $250 | $-40 |
| Budget and actual expenditures: | | | | | | | |
| Budget | $1,850 | $700 | $450 | $250 | $100 | $200 | $150 |
| Actual | 1,800 | 680 | 440 | 240 | 100 | 200 | 140 |
| Difference | $ 50 | $ 20 | $ 10 | $ 10 | — | — | $ 10 |
| Budget expenditures— budgeted costs: | | | | | | | |
| Budget expenditures | $1,850 | $700 | $450 | $250 | $100 | $200 | $150 |
| Budgeted costs | 2,135 | 750 | 460 | 255 | 110 | 450 | 110 |
| Difference | $ 285 | $ 50 | $ 10 | $ 5 | $ 10 | $250 | $-40 |

**EXHIBIT 19-12**
**Line-Item Costs by Cost Centers**
(In Thousands)

|  | Cost centers | | | | | |
| --- | --- | --- | --- | --- | --- | --- |
| Line items | M | N | O | P | Q | Totals |
| Personal services | 253 | 128 | 98 | 128 | 123 | 730 |
| Supplies | 100 | 55 | 110 | 105 | 80 | 450 |
| Travel | 63 | 33 | 58 | 58 | 33 | 245 |
| Contractual services | 30 | 30 |  | 25 | 25 | 110 |
| Capital outlay | 135 | 135 | 60 | 60 | 60 | 450 |
| Debt service | 100 |  |  |  |  | 100 |
| Totals | 681 | 381 | 326 | 376 | 321 | 2,085 |

may have established; for example, health, public safety, transportation, housing, recreation, and so forth. While programs often are coterminous with cost centers, they may cut across organizational units, as is the case in this example. Therefore, in order to determine where the costs come from, it is necessary to know the amount of costs from each departmental cost center that goes into each program. This cost allocation is illustrated in Exhibit 19-14.

The budget must be based on costs rather than expenditures in order to make analytical comparisons. These budgets are illustrated in Exhibits 19-15 and 19-16.

**EXHIBIT 19-13**
**Line-Item Costs by Programs**
(In Thousands)

|  | Programs | | | | | |
| --- | --- | --- | --- | --- | --- | --- |
| Line items | V | W | X | Y | Z | Totals |
| Personal services | 110 | 200 | 160 | 150 | 110 | 730 |
| Supplies | 100 | 50 | 100 | 100 | 100 | 450 |
| Travel | 45 | 50 | 25 | 25 | 100 | 245 |
| Contractual services | 20 | 25 | 25 | 20 | 20 | 110 |
| Capital outlay | 100 | 100 | 100 | 100 | 50 | 450 |
| Debt service |  |  |  |  | 100 | 100 |
| Totals | 375 | 425 | 410 | 395 | 480 | 2,085 |

**EXHIBIT 19-14**
**Cost-Center Costs by Programs**
(In Thousands)

|  | Programs | | | | | |
|---|---|---|---|---|---|---|
| Cost centers | V | W | X | Y | Z | Totals |
| M | 51 | 125 | 60 | 195 | 250 | 681 |
| N | 56 | 50 | 150 | 75 | 50 | 381 |
| O | 51 | 150 | 25 | 50 | 50 | 326 |
| P | 176 | 25 | 75 | 50 | 50 | 376 |
| Q | 41 | 75 | 100 | 25 | 80 | 321 |
| Totals | 375 | 425 | 410 | 395 | 480 | 2,085 |

## SUMMARY

This chapter has provided an orientation to various accounting techniques that might be applicable to the nonbusiness area for management planning and control purposes. Various techniques for planning purposes such as break-even analysis, flexible budgeting, and cost-benefit analysis were introduced. Methods for control, specifically through standards and responsibility accounting, were also discussed. Finally, certain problems in controlling governmental costs were outlined.

**EXHIBIT 19-15**
**Line-Item Costs by Cost Centers**
**Budget and Actual**
(In Thousands)

|  | Cost centers | | | | | |
|---|---|---|---|---|---|---|
| Line items | M | N | O | P | Q | Totals |
| Personal services | [260] | [130] | [100] | [135] | [125] | [ 750] |
|  | 253 | 128 | 98 | 128 | 123 | 730 |
| Supplies | [100] | [ 60] | [110] | [110] | [ 80] | [ 460] |
|  | 100 | 55 | 110 | 105 | 80 | 450 |
| Travel | [ 65] | [ 35] | [ 60] | [ 60] | [ 35] | [ 255] |
|  | 63 | 33 | 58 | 58 | 33 | 245 |
| Contractual services | [ 30] | [ 30] | [ 0] | [ 25] | [ 25] | [ 110] |
|  | 30 | 30 |  | 25 | 25 | 110 |
| Capital outlay | [135] | [135] | [ 60] | [ 60] | [ 60] | [ 450] |
|  | 135 | 135 | 60 | 60 | 60 | 450 |
| Debt service | [110] |  |  |  |  | [ 110] |
|  | 100 |  |  |  |  | 100 |
| Totals | [700] | [390] | [330] | [390] | [325] | [2,135] |
|  | 681 | 381 | 326 | 376 | 321 | 2,085 |

[Budget]
Actual

## EXHIBIT 19-16
### Line-Item Costs by Programs
### Budget and Actual
(In Thousands)

| Line items | Programs V | W | X | Y | Z | Totals |
|---|---|---|---|---|---|---|
| Personal services | [115] 110 | [205] 200 | [165] 160 | [155] 150 | [110] 110 | [ 750] 730 |
| Supplies | [105] 100 | [ 50] 50 | [105] 100 | [100] 100 | [100] 100 | [ 460] 450 |
| Travel | [ 50] 45 | [ 50] 50 | [ 25] 25 | [ 20] 25 | [105] 100 | [ 255] 245 |
| Contractual services | [ 20] 20 | [ 25] 25 | [ 25] 25 | [ 20] 20 | [ 20] 20 | [ 110] 110 |
| Capital outlay | [100] 100 | [100] 100 | [100] 100 | [100] 100 | [ 50] 50 | [ 450] 450 |
| Debt service | | | | | [110] 100 | [ 110] 100 |
| Totals | [390] 375 | [430] 425 | [420] 410 | [400] 395 | [495] 480 | [2,135] 2,085 |

[Budget]
Actual

## QUESTIONS

1. Define and discuss responsibility accounting.
2. What is meant by performance measurement and evaluation?
3. Discuss the significance of break-even analysis.
4. Discuss the problems of cost versus expenditure as it relates to governmental units.
5. What is a flexible budget? Discuss when flexible budgets should be used.
6. Discuss the importance of cost-benefit analysis.
7. Discuss the problem of performance measurement in the nonbusiness area.
8. What is control?
9. Why is a good understanding of costs essential to the proper functioning of a responsibility accounting system?
10. What are the major uses of a flexible budget?
11. Discuss the problems in attempting to develop a suitable discount rate for cost-benefit analysis.

## PROBLEMS

**19-1** The Broadhurst Nursing Home has fixed costs of $20,000, variable costs per patient day of $36, and bills its patients at a rate of $80 per patient day. What is its break-even volume in number of patient days?

**19-2** The town of Water Valley's electric utility is currently attempting to justify the rate per KWH before the public utility commission. The utility has fixed costs of $100,000, variable expenses of $5 per KWH, and is currently charging customers $10 per KWH. The utility expects to sell about 40,000 KWH next year with the same price structure.

**Required:**
1. What will the utility's expected break-even point be?
2. Calculate total expected revenues and expenses for the utility.

**19-3** Montgomery County Hospital's cost-center report for its radiological unit is shown below:

| Expense | 19X6 |
|---|---|
| Supplies (all variable) | $42,000 |
| Outside lab services (all variable) | 4,000 |
| Salaries and wages (fixed) | 60,000 |
| Electric expense (variable) | 2,600 |
| Other expenses (fixed) | 4,000 |

In 19X6, the unit handled 100 patients per week. Next year, patients are expected to decrease by about 20 percent. As a result, one part-time technician, at a salary of $4,800 will be terminated. In addition to the costs shown above, the cost center is allocated $40,000 of administrative costs.

**Required:**
What charge per patient should be assessed in order for the cost center to break even, assuming they must recover full cost of their department?

**19-4** The Board of Trustees of the United Methodist Church is meeting to prepare a budget for the next year. The treasurer of the church has given each member of the board the statement of receipts and disbursements.

**Statement of Cash Receipts and Disbursements**
**For the Year Ended June 30, 19XX**

| | | |
|---|---:|---:|
| Cash receipts | | $250,000 |
| Cash disbursements: | | |
|   Salaries and wages | $68,000 | |
|   Mortgage payments | 42,000 | |
|   Transportation | 7,500 | |
|   Foreign missions | 86,000 | |
|   Operating expenses | 18,000 | |
|   Various | 6,000 | 227,500 |
|   Excess of receipts over disbursements | | $ 22,500 |

A newly appointed member of the board complains that the information provided is too highly aggregated to be of much use in preparing a new budget. Another long-standing member indicates that the board has always been able to work with the submitted report.

**Required:**
Discuss additional information you might like to have made available before working on the budget.

**19-5** In 19X5, the city of Bedford's snow-removal costs were $200,000, three-fourths of which was variable based on inches of snow. Last year the city had twenty-five inches of snow. Overall costs of snow removal are expected to increase in 19X6 by 10 percent due to inflation.

**Required:**
Set up a flexible budget for snow removal for 19X6 based on 20, 25, 30, and 40 inches of possible snow.

**19-6** Melford Hospital operates a general hospital but rents space and beds to separately owned entities rendering specialized services such as pediatrics and psychiatry. Melford charges each separate entity for common services such as patients' meals and laundry and for administrative services such as billings and collections. Space and bed rentals are fixed charges for the year, based on bed capacity rented to each entity.[1]

Melford charged the following costs to pediatrics for the year ended June 30, 19X2:

|  | Patient days (variable) | Bed capacity (fixed) |
|---|---|---|
| Dietary | $ 600,000 | — |
| Janitorial | — | $ 70,000 |
| Laundry | 300,000 | — |
| Laboratory | 450,000 | — |
| Pharmacy | 350,000 | — |
| Repairs and maintenance | — | 30,000 |
| General and administrative | — | 1,300,000 |
| Rent | — | 1,500,000 |
| Billings and collections | 300,000 | — |
| Totals | $2,000,000 | $2,900,000 |

During the year ended June 30, 19X2, pediatrics charged each patient an average of $300 per day, had a capacity of 60 beds, and had revenue of $6,000,000 for 365 days. In addition, pediatrics directly employed the following personnel:

|  | Annual salaries |
|---|---|
| Supervising nurses | $25,000 |
| Nurses | 20,000 |
| Aides | 9,000 |

Melford has the following minimum departmental personnel requirements based on total annual patient days:

| Annual patient days | Aides | Nurses | Supervising nurses |
|---|---|---|---|
| Up to 21,900 | 20 | 10 | 4 |
| 21,901 to 26,000 | 26 | 13 | 4 |
| 26,001 to 29,200 | 30 | 15 | 4 |

These staffing levels represent full-time equivalents. Pediatrics always employs only the minimum number of required full-time equivalent personnel. Salaries of supervising nurses, nurses, and aides are therefore fixed within ranges of annual patient days.

Pediatrics operated at 100 percent capacity on 90 days during the year ended June 30, 19X2. It is estimated that during these 90 days the demand exceeded 20 patients more than capacity. Melford has an additional 20 beds available for rent for the year ending June 30, 19X3. Such additional rental would increase pediatrics' fixed charges based on bed capacity.

**Required:**
**1** Calculate the minimum number of patient days required for pediatrics to break even for the year ending June 30, 19X3, if the additional 20 beds are not rented. Patient demand

is unknown, but assume that revenue per patient day, cost per patient day, cost per bed, and salary rates will remain the same as for the year ended June 30, 19X2.

2 Assume that patient demand, revenue per patient day, cost per patient day, cost per bed, and salary rates for the year ending June 30, 19X3, remain the same as for the year ended June 30, 19X2. Prepare a schedule of increase in revenue and increase in costs for the year ending June 30, 19X3 in order to determine the net increase or decrease in earnings from the additional 20 beds if pediatrics rents this extra capacity from Melford.

19-7 DeMars College has asked your assistance in developing its budget for the coming 19X1–X2 academic year. You are supplied with the following data.[2]

1 For the current year:

|  | Lower division (freshman-sophomore) | Upper division (junior-senior) |
| --- | --- | --- |
| Average number of students per class | 25 | 20 |
| Average salary of faculty member | $10,000 | $10,000 |
| Average number of credit hours carried each year per student | 33 | 30 |
| Enrollment including scholarship students | 2,500 | 1,700 |
| Average faculty teaching load in credit hours per year (10 classes of 3 credit hours) | 30 | 30 |

For 19X1–X2, lower-division enrollment is expected to increase by 10 percent, while the upper-division enrollment is expected to remain stable. Faculty salaries will be increased by a standard 5 percent, and additional merit increases to be awarded to individual faculty members will be $90,750 for the lower division and $85,000 for the upper division.

2 The current budget is $210,000 for operation and maintenance of plant and equipment; this includes $90,000 for salaries and wages. Experience of the past three months suggests that the current budget is realistic but that expected increases for 19X1–X2 are 5 percent in salaries and wages and $9,000 in other expenditures for operation and maintenance of plant and equipment.

3 The budget for the remaining expenditures for 19X1–X2 is as follows:

| | |
| --- | --- |
| Administrative and general | $240,000 |
| Library | 160,000 |
| Health and recreation | 75,000 |
| Athletics | 120,000 |
| Insurance and retirement | 265,000 |
| Interest | 48,000 |
| Capital outlay | 300,000 |

4 The college expects to award twenty-five tuition-free scholarships to lower-division students and fifteen to upper-division students. Tuition is $22 per credit hour, and no other fees are charged.

5 Budgeted revenues for 19X1–X2 are as follows:

| | |
| --- | --- |
| Endowments | $114,000 |
| Net income from auxiliary services | 235,000 |
| Athletics | 180,000 |

The college's remaining source of revenue is an annual support campaign held during the spring.

**Required:**
1. Prepare a schedule computing by division for 19X1–X2 (a) the expected enrollment, (b) the total credit hours to be carried, and (c) the number of faculty members needed.
2. Prepare a schedule computing the budget for faculty salaries by division for 19X1–X2.
3. Prepare a schedule computing the tuition revenue budget by division for 19X1–X2.
4. Assuming that the faculty salaries budget computed in number 2 was $2,400,000 and that the tuition revenue budget computed in number 3 was $3,000,000, prepare a schedule computing the amount that must be raised during the annual support campaign in order to cover the 19X1–X2 expenditures budget.

**19-8** Prince George County is planning to acquire some new snow-removal equipment at a total cost of $306,000. The estimated life of the machinery is expected to be about six years with an estimated residual value of $6,000. County officials expect cash savings from using the new equipment to be $80,000 per year. The county has determined that it has a discount rate of 10 percent. The present value of $1 at 10 percent for six years is .564. The present value of an annuity of $1 in arrears at 10 percent for six years is 4.355.

**Required:**
Calculate the net present value for the project.

**19-9** The town manager of Blacksburg has decided not to accept the council's proposal to build a parking garage unless the town can get a 14 percent return. The project is expected to cost $1,400,000, with expected income of $200,000 a year for 10 years.

**Required:**
Calculate the internal rate of return for the project.

**19-10** An important concept in management accounting is that of responsibility accounting.[3]

**Required:**
1. Define the term responsibility accounting.
2. What are the conditions that must exist for there to be effective responsibility accounting?
3. What benefits are said to result from responsibility accounting?
4. Listed below are two charges found on the monthly report of a department that provides surgical care. Performance is evaluated by the use of comparison of costs with budget. State which, if any, of the following charges are consistent with the responsibility accounting concept. Support each answer with a brief explanation.
    a. A charge for general hospital administration at 10 percent of department billings.
    b. A charge for the use of the hospital computer facility. The charge is determined by taking actual annual computer department costs and allocating an amount to each user on the ratio of its use to total hospital use.

**NOTES**

1. Adapted from American Institute of Certified Public Accountants, *Uniform CPA Examination Questions and Unofficial Answers* (New York: American Institute of Certified Public Accountants, 1973).
2. Ibid., 1970.
3. Ibid., 1976.

# PART FOUR

## ADVANCED TOPICS

Building on the foundations established in the first three parts of this book, Part IV extends these topics to a more advanced level—especially as they apply to contemporary techniques for strategic management, budgeting, and auditing in complex organizations. The objective is to place the principles and practices of accounting into a broader context of modern management.

A structure for understanding and applying these advanced topics in the context of the planning and control systems of governmental and other nonbusiness organizations is detailed in Chapter 20. Various systemic procedures for a more effective achievement of organizational goals are discussed and illustrated in terms of management responsibilities for maintaining a planning-control continuum. Planning and control procedures at the strategic, management, and operational levels are outlined, and the role of a management information system is delineated. The chapter concludes with an examination of the techniques of strategic planning and program budgeting and their linkages to, and dependency upon, accounting data organized on a program basis.

Techniques for monitoring and evaluating the efficiency of operations of a governmental or other nonbusiness unit provide the focus of Chapter 21. The budget of an organization is presented as a work program, in the tradition of performance budgeting. Performance measures discussed in Part III are further extended to serve a dual purpose of management planning and control. The procedures of service level analysis are discussed to illustrate how broader participation in performance accountability can be achieved.

These two chapters do not discuss double-entry bookkeeping systems as they relate to the newer types of budgetary planning. It is assumed that the student should be capable by now of making debit and credit entries; posting those entries to accounts, whether the accounts are general or subsidiary ledger accounts; relating budgetary accounts to actual accounts; and preparing reports for management from those records and accounts.

The processes of performance auditing are described and illustrated in Chapter 22. These processes are applied to determine the efficiency of operations and the effectiveness of goal accomplishment of the organizational unit. Knowing the processes for determining whether management has appropriately carried out its responsibilities should be the final cap on the student's understanding of the accounting and control responsibilities in governmental and other nonbusiness sectors.

As noted at the outset, these final chapters go beyond the standard approach to accounting for public and nonbusiness entities. In so doing, however, the objective is to prepare the student for a more active role in the overall financial management of these organizations—for a level of participation that is responsive to contemporary needs and that capitalizes upon the significant contributions that professionals in the field of accounting can make to these organizations.

# CHAPTER 20

# A STRATEGIC MANAGEMENT FRAMEWORK

For the most part, the principles and techniques presented in Parts I and II were related to financial accounting and reporting. The management of any organization has a responsibility to provide external users with timely and accurate accounting information, in accordance with generally accepted accounting principles. In Part III, the principles and techniques of management accounting were described in an effort to show how accounting information can also be used for the purposes of management control.

As noted in Chapter 17, management has other important information needs, however. These include the need to know: (1) that organizational resources are being used as efficiently and economically as possible, (2) that the organization is effective in the accomplishment of its goals and objectives, and (3) that corrective actions will be taken on a timely basis when conditions (1) and/or (2) are not met. Fortunately, generally accepted accounting principles suggest that, in providing the basis for budgetary control, accounts can be classified by programs as well as by functions, objects of expenditures, or other classifications. With a program-based accounting classification, a basis can be established for determining the effectiveness of organizational programs. Program *effectiveness* can be determined, for example, by measuring actual program results against program objectives or the desired results stated in the budget of a program. When anticipated costs are stated in the program's budget, the basis for determining the *efficiency* of an operation can be established by measuring actual costs against budgetary costs.

## MANAGEMENT: THE ART OF GETTING THINGS DONE

The concept of management evokes many images. Making a profit in a business, constructing a public works facility, winning a military battle, passing a college examination, or preparing a municipal budget all require management skills. Management can be generalized to cover these five diverse activities and all other similar tasks that might be identified.

Management is frequently referred to as "the art of getting things done." It is a dynamic art, involving the direction, coordination, and control of human and physical resources in an effort to bring into focus and give consistency to those activities designed to achieve some purpose, goal, or objective efficiently and effectively. In this context, the *purpose* of an organization is its reason for existence, often stated in rather broad, immeasurable, and abstract terms. Measurable statements of desired results or outputs must be drawn from the broad purpose (or mission statement) of the organization. These more immediate statements represent the *goals* of the organization. Goals, in turn, must be translated into more specific *program objectives* to give guidance to management and operational personnel at all levels within the organization. Objectives may also be detailed to the level of individual participants within an organization, as often is the case when the techniques of "management by objectives" are employed. For the purposes of this discussion, however, objectives will be limited to program activities and will be assumed to represent subsets of an organization's goals.

The term *effectiveness* relates to the accomplishment of an organization's goals and objectives. An organization is effective when its goals are accomplished; it is ineffective when they are not. The concept of *efficiency* is linked to the use of organizational resources. When fewer resources are used to accomplish the same results or when additional results are attained using the same resources, then a program or set of activities is said to be more efficient. In this context, efficiency can be equated with *doing things right,* whereas effectiveness involves *doing the right things.*

In recent years, an approach that combines the basic management objectives of efficiency and effectiveness has come to be labeled *strategic management.* Strategic management can be defined in terms of the procedural tasks with which it must be concerned:

  **1** Establishing overall strategic goals and selecting objectives of a particular program or enterprise.
  **2** Determining resource requirements (personnel, equipment, materials, time, and money) and allocating these resources in accordance with agreed-upon program objectives.
  **3** Controlling the entire process from the point of decision or commitment to completion by reacting in a timely manner to deviations between the planned and actual progress toward the achievement of goals and objectives.[1]

Strategic management is concerned with deciding in advance what an organization should do (planning), determining who will do it and how it will be done (resource management), and monitoring and enhancing ongoing activities and operations (control and evaluation). The functions of strategic management are best performed as a balance between objective method and subjective ability. The effectiveness of such management is measured by the results (performance or output) achieved and, particularly, by the response time required to make necessary adjustments when things go wrong.

## THE PLANNING-CONTROL CONTINUUM

While various terminology has been used to describe the functions of management, most authors agree that management must be carried out within a basic planning and control framework. As Martin J. Gannon has observed: "planning and control are intimately related and, in fact, represent opposite sides of the same coin. Without planning, there can be no control."[2] Managers make use of goals, objectives, plans, programs, budgets, and various types of organizational, operational, and financial controls to carry out their responsibilities. Thus planning and control mechanisms form a continuum, as illustrated in Exhibit 20-1. While the relative mix of planning and control may be determined by management styles and the complexity of organizational structure, a basic discussion of this planning-control continuum can provide a better understanding of the role of accounting in contemporary management systems.

### Strategic, Management, and Operational Planning

*Strategic planning* involves the formulation of organizational purposes (goals) and the determination of objectives and strategies (the means) for the acquisition and application of the resources necessary to attain those purposes. Decisions must be made at fairly high levels within any organization (business, governmental unit, or other not-for-profit entity) as to the kind of products or services to be provided and who the beneficiaries will be. Such decisions are strategic to the long-term success of the organization, and typically, only key decision makers are involved at this level. Often, such strategic planning may not be considered continuous or formally structured.

**EXHIBIT 20-1**   The planning-control continuum.

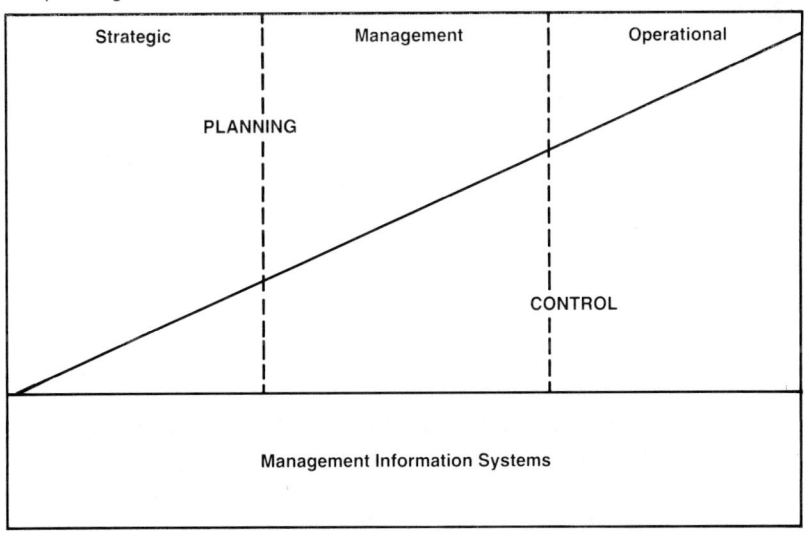

Although at times given different labels or merged with other processes, some form of strategic planning is essential in all organizational activities. It is a more far-sighted, long-range approach than the incremental, disjointed, and cumulative pattern that characterizes many organizational decisions.

To illustrate strategic planning in the context of local government, assume that members of a city council are aware of the problems of declining business in the downtown area due to congestion, lack of adequate parking, and the problems of access among various segments of the community (e.g., the elderly, low-income families, handicapped, etc.). Various alternatives are considered, and a decision is reached to inaugurate a public transit system in an effort to increase access and relieve some of the congestion. A decision of this nature involves strategic planning—first, the problem is defined, then relevant alternatives are considered, and finally, certain overall objectives and guidelines are established for the new transit system.

As can be seen from this example, accounting data seldom have been a significant factor in the strategic planning process. However, information derived from a management accounting system sometimes can provide important inputs to strategic planning.

*Management planning* involves: (1) programming approved goals into specific projects, programs, and activities; (2) designing and staffing organizational units to carry out approved programs; and (3) budgeting and procuring the necessary resources to implement these programs over some time period. A basic responsibility of management planning is to identify and budget the wherewithal of financial resources and personnel and to provide a framework within which the use of these resources can be evaluated.

Using the public transit system to illustrate this process, management planning might include an assessment of various modes of public transit in terms of costs and benefits, analyses of various route configurations, the development and evaluation of budget priorities, and so forth. The management plan would likely culminate in the development and presentation of specific funding approaches and budget requests.

*Operational planning* focuses on the tactics of performance and the setting of standards for the use of specific resources to achieve overall goals and objectives that are integral parts of the strategic and management plans. Operational planning is concerned primarily with scheduling of detailed program activities. Scheduling involves a determination of the times and amounts for resource utilization. It must take into account the availability of resources, the sequence of activities or jobs, and the resource requirements and possible starting times for each activity. In the public transit example, operational planning would involve the determination of equipment-acquisition schedules, training programs for operators, the actual route designations, and the development of related public improvement projects.

Effective and efficient operational planning can mean the difference between "on time" and "late" in the achievement of a specific project. Successful management planning can mean the difference between effective resource utilization and waste. Effective and comprehensive strategic planning may mean the difference between success and failure in the delivery of vital services.

## Strategic, Management, and Operational Control

*Strategic controls* are used to evaluate the overall performance of an organization or a significant part thereof. In the private sector, standards such as profitability, ratio of assets to liabilities, and sales growth provide a broad basis on which to assess the overall performance of an organization. Standards applicable to public sector activities have been detailed in recent years in terms of *measures of effectiveness*. A city council, for example, may outline certain expectations regarding the overall ridership of the public transit system, the desirable ratio of costs to benefits to be attained, and so forth. These broad criteria provide the bench marks against which the transit system ultimately should be evaluated.

When an organization fails to meet such broad standards, the remedies may be equally broad. They may include the recasting of goals and objectives, a reformulation of plans and programs, changes in organizational structure, improved internal and external communications and so forth. Strategic controls are needed to assist decision makers in determining appropriate corrective actions when unpredictable changes occur in the broader environment of the organization. A strategic control system provides a basis by which both the desired goals and objectives and the methods of control can be modified. Since large amounts of data may be required to achieve effective strategic control in complex organizations, continuous monitoring of activities through the application of management controls may be more appropriate to ensure that corrective action is taken on a timely basis.

*Management control* involves the measurement and evaluation of program activities to determine if policies and objectives are being accomplished as efficiently and effectively as possible. It is in the area of management control that accounting information and procedures have made the most significant contributions. Consequently, management control provided the primary focus for the discussion in Part III.

Management control provides the basic structure for coordinating the day-to-day activities of an organization, encompassing all those activities involved in ensuring that the organization's resources are appropriately used in the pursuit of goals and objectives. Output from the accounting system provides managers with important performance-measurement information as decisions are made and actions taken that are expected to lead to desired results.

Continuing with the example of the transit system, studies would have to be made of the most effective means of implementation (city operated versus privately operated system), the routes to be served, number of personnel and facilities needed to operate the route, and so forth. Service facilities would have to be acquired. Projections would be needed on expected revenue and costs. Most of the controls would be based on guidelines established in the strategic and management planning processes. Operating budgets must be established for the various routes, and these budgets, in turn, serve as a basis to measure performance at various levels in the transit system.

Management controls are often designed to anticipate and identify problems before they happen. An obvious approach is to try to anticipate possible deviations from some established standards or criteria of performance. This is the primary objective of statistical quality control. This approach also can be applied as a budgetary control. If, for example, a major expenditure is proposed, the possibility that it might exceed the budget should be ascertained ahead of time rather than after the fact. Such controls may involve various forecasting and projection techniques.

*Operational controls* seek to assure that specific tasks or programs are carried out efficiently and in compliance with established policies. These processes involve a determination of requirements for program resources and their necessary order of commitment to achieve specific program objectives. It often is difficult to distinguish between management control and operational control. Techniques used initially for management control may become more specific in application when converted to operational control purposes.

Operational control techniques focus on specific responsibilities for carrying out those tasks identified at the strategic and management control levels. These techniques must provide management with the ability to: (1) consider the costs of several alternatives in dollars and time; (2) establish criteria for resource allocation and scheduling; (3) provide a basis for evaluating the accuracy of estimates and the effects of change; and (4) assimilate and communicate data regarding program activities and revise or update the operations plan.

Operational controls are very specific and situation-oriented. They measure day-to-day performance by providing comparisons with various criteria to determine areas that require more immediate corrective actions. Productivity ratios, work-load measures, and unit costs are examples of such performance measures. Such measures most frequently focus on issues of efficiency and economy.

In the transit system example, budgets and standards are established as part of the processes of management control. Levels of inventory supplies and parts will likely be established for operation of the bus system. Subsequent control of daily operations by individual routes will be the responsibility of route supervisors or comparable personnel. Thus, while the budget originates as part of the management planning and control process, subsequent implementation of many phases of the budget becomes an operational control function.

## Management Information Systems

Every management information system should incorporate these basic planning-control perspectives. Operationally, they often are indivisible. Note, however, the subtle, yet important shift in emphasis among these components—from broad issues of effectiveness to specific problems of efficiency. Thus the "mix" among these processes may vary considerably. Moreover, these planning and control processes often require quite different skills and have different informational requirements. Information needs vary in terms of time spans, levels of aggregation, linkages with operating units, and focus on input-output relationships.

A solution is to design a *management information system* (MIS) that can serve the multiple needs of this planning-control continuum. As a concept, MIS often is vaguely described and broadly misunderstood. Some people confuse management information systems with electronic data-processing procedures. Many management information systems do make effective use of modern data-processing and word-processing equipment. However, an MIS is much more than an electronic "black box" to direct and control complex organizations. First and foremost, an MIS is a *process* by which information is organized and communicated in a timely fashion to resolve management problems.

Information is different from data, and this distinction is very important. Data are facts and figures that currently are not being used in a decision process. Files, records, and reports not under immediate consideration are examples of data. By contrast, information consists of classified and interpreted data that are being used for decision making. In addition to storing raw data, the memory of a management information system is a repository for information by which decisions can be tested for acceptability.

Contemporary financial management activities are both *information demanding* and *information producing*. The information input and output requirements of the accounting techniques described in Chapters 17, 18, and 19 can provide important feedback to management—soundings, scanning, and evaluations of changing financial conditions that result from previous program decisions and actions.

Management involves the development, adaptation, and implementation of strategic, tactical, and technical decisions to enhance the capacity of the organization to meet the demands and expectations that impinge on it. An MIS facilitates the development of decisions in planning, organizing, implementing, and controlling the programs and activities of the organization. This is what gives purpose to an MIS. The specific objective of an MIS is to communicate information for decision making in a synergistic fashion—where the whole becomes greater than the sum of the individual parts.

## ACCOUNTING AND PROGRAM EFFECTIVENESS

To be truly effective and responsive to public needs, governmental accounting procedures should reflect a longer-range perspective, that is, a planning perspective. The same can be said for not-for-profit organizations—a planning perspective is essential to formulate appropriate responses to client needs. Most plans—or decisions with future consequences—have financial implications, and, therefore, a strong relationship must exist between the objectives of planning and those of accounting. An accounting system that is responsive to the contemporary needs of management must be able to serve the purposes of both *control* and *planning*. In this longer-range perspective, the accounting system is part of a more comprehensive management information system that supports the data requirements of strategic planning, program analysis, and evaluation. The balance of this chapter will be devoted to these three basic activities of management and their implications for more effective programs in government and not-for-profit organizations.

### Strategic Planning Defined

The term *strategic* has been applied to planning activities to denote linkages with the goal-setting process, the formulation of more immediate objectives, and the specific actions required in the deployment of organizational resources to achieve these goals and objectives. The concept of strategic planning first found application in business and industry in the late 1950s and early 1960s. According to William R. King and David I. Cleland, strategic planning in the private sector "deals primarily with the contrivance of organizational efforts directed to the development of organizational purpose, direction, and future generation of products and services, and the design of implementation policies by which the goals and objectives of the organization can be accomplished."[3]

Efforts to apply strategic planning in the public sector began to surface in the late 1960s and early 1970s, in part as a response to criticisms of comprehensive planning—a process advocated (but seldom achieved) in government for over four decades. As applied in government, it has been suggested that strategic planning "is the process of identifying public goals and objectives, determining needed changes in those objectives, and deciding on the resources to be used to attain them. It entails the evaluation of alternative courses of action and the formulation of policies that govern the acquisition, use, and disposition of public resources."[4]

Both of these definitions have several elements in common:

1 Formulation of goals, objectives, and implementation strategies
2 Analysis of program alternatives
3 Measurement of program results and accomplishments

Traditional planning efforts have tended to be one-shot optimizations, often initiated under conditions of stress. Once "the best plans" were laid, little attempt was made to test their continued efficacy against the realities of emerging conditions. It has been said that few plans survive contact with the enemy. Indeed, rarely are policies and programs executed exactly as originally conceived. Random events, environmental disturbances, competitive tactics, and unforeseen circumstances may all conspire to thwart the smooth implementation of plans, policies, and programs. In short, fixed targets, static plans, and repetitive programs are of relatively little value in a dynamic society.

Strategic planning provides a framework within which decisions can be subjected to continuous testing, correction, and refinement. Through such an approach, alternative courses of action can be identified and analyzed, and estimates can be made of the likely consequences resulting from their implementation (see Exhibit 20-2). Within this framework, the actual impact of resource commitments can be evaluated in terms of program performance. And this evaluation is then fed back to recycle the process.

## Programs in Strategic Planning

Programs are the fundamental building blocks for strategic planning. A program can be defined as a group of interdependent, closely related activities or services that possess or contribute to a common goal or set of allied objectives. A program is a distinct organization of resources directed toward a specific goal of either:

1 Eliminating, containing, or preventing a problem
2 Creating, improving, or maintaining a condition affecting the organization and/or its clientele
3 Supporting or controlling other identifiable programs

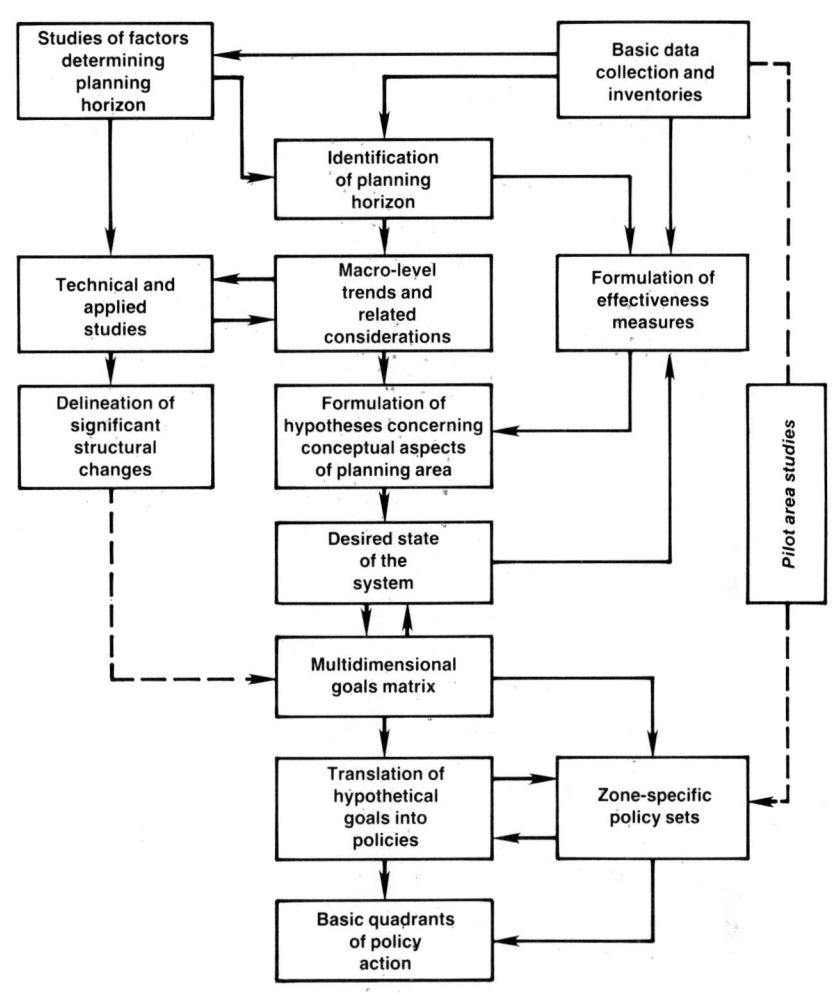

**EXHIBIT 20-2** The strategic planning process.

A set of activities that cuts across several public agencies while focusing on the problems of juvenile delinquency can constitute a program. The establishment of a trauma unit in a hospital emergency room is an example of a program. The internal auditing unit within the controller's office may be defined as a program. A university research center concentrating on composite materials may be treated as a program or may have a number of programs associated with its research mission.

## Goal Statements

Under traditional management processes, decision making in government and not-for-profit organizations frequently becomes *input oriented*. That is to say, analyses of alternative methods of achieving goals and objectives are based on expenditure-related issues rather than policy-based issues. Seldom is an assessment made of the *effectiveness* of these inputs in terms of meeting identified client needs or the performance of public services. As a consequence, there is no guarantee that decisions will be coherently responsive to comprehensive goals and objectives.

Goals are developed at the strategic planning level as measurable standards that reflect the desired results to be achieved by a program. Each goal should lend itself to at least partial quantification and should bring together all costs associated with the execution of the program. Since a program is concerned with a time span of expenditures, goals extend beyond the current fiscal period, often into an uncertain future.

Precision in the identification of organizational goals is a vital prerequisite to sound analysis of financial commitments. The formulation of precise, qualitative statements of an organization's purpose is not an easy task, however. A common tendency is to describe *what* the organization does, instead of addressing the question of *why* these activities are appropriate within its mandate.

## Program Objectives

In identifying program objectives, an effort should be made to specify the key results to be accomplished within a specific time period. Program or agency objectives should be quantifiable. While they should be realistic and attainable, they also should present a challenge to improve conditions consistent with existing policies, practices, and procedures and directly related to program purposes. Program objectives must also be consistent with the resources available (or anticipated) and should assign singular responsibility and accountability, even in joint efforts.

Program objectives should specify the *what* and the *when* of anticipated agency activities. There is a tendency, however, to focus on the *how*. Thus an appropriate program objective of a municipal fire department might be: "To reduce current response time of all fire and emergency vehicles by 25 percent during the next two years." A statement: "To build, equip, and man a third fire station during the next two years" tells how the program might be accomplished and should be reserved for the delineation of specific program actions.

Resources provided to achieve program objectives often are interchangeable for the maximum achievement of a program goal. That is to say, given a budget target at the program level, an organization must determine how to distribute the financial and personnel resources available among the program components to achieve an optimal output. It is at this level that the detailed object codes of traditional financial accounts often are used to identify resource inputs.

## How Statements: Identification of Implementation Strategies

Agencies should also be required to describe specific actions or strategies—*how* and *where* specific resources (personnel, equipment, materials, capital expenditures, etc.) will be used. Such justifications often are designed as *strategy statements*—specifying means for achieving a single key result based on the resources (fiscal and personnel) available or anticipated.

These statements, in turn, should be related to *performance measures*. These measures can be used in the accounting system to identify the products, service units, and/or clients associated with the activities of the agency, providing the mechanisms to determine the success (or lack thereof) of a program in achieving agreed-upon goals. These measures may be equated to costs or inputs. Efforts must be made, however, to go beyond the more common work-load measures that tend to assess only efficiency. Measures such as number of employee-days spent, number of requests received, or number of cases per worker may be appropriate in measuring agency/program efficiency. They do not provide a measurable base for assessing the effectiveness of programs, however. *Effectiveness measures* examine the relationship of the outputs to objectives—the standards for the outputs.

While these procedural steps may be initiated sequentially, more often they are performed through a series of iterations (see Exhibit 20-3). Identifying objectives, for example, may further clarify the appropriate programs and subprograms of an agency. This clarification, in turn, may assist in determining which activities should be placed within each subprogram. It may not be possible, however, to formulate precise statements of objectives until activity schedules have been examined in some detail. The establishment of such schedules, in turn, may require careful examination of alternative strategies and associated measures of efficiency and effectiveness. Thus the process must be viewed from the top down in terms of objectives and from the bottom up in terms of organizational activities designed to carry out these objectives.

## Analysis of Program Alternatives

The systematic analysis of program alternatives is a cornerstone of more effective financial management. The same dollars spent on different program goals (or on alterna-

**EXHIBIT 20-3**  Iterative process for setting goals and objectives.

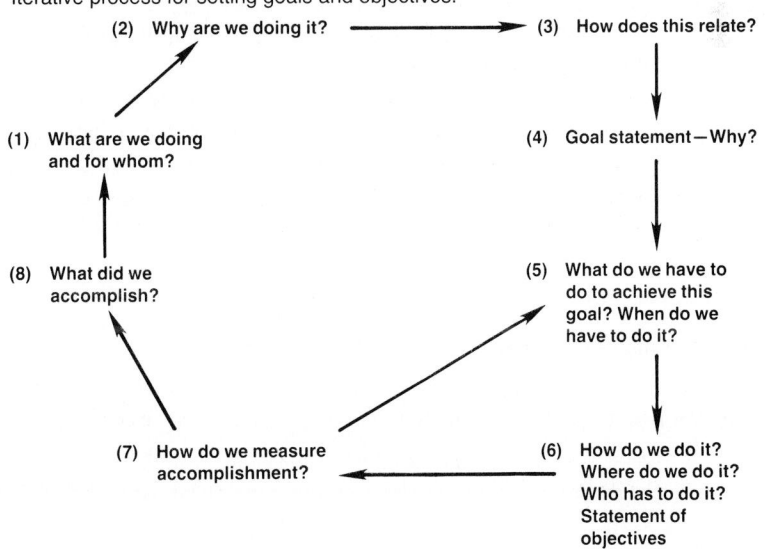

(1) What are we doing and for whom?
(2) Why are we doing it?
(3) How does this relate?
(4) Goal statement—Why?
(5) What do we have to do to achieve this goal? When do we have to do it?
(6) How do we do it? Where do we do it? Who has to do it? Statement of objectives
(7) How do we measure accomplishment?
(8) What did we accomplish?

tive approaches to the same program goal) may yield greatly varied results. Resources should be spent where they can produce the greatest net benefits. Programs should be selected through a systematic analysis of associated costs and benefits. Such analyses draw heavily upon information found within a management accounting and control system.

To undertake such analyses, explicit measures of program outputs must be identified and quantified. This task frequently is a difficult one, particularly for organizations more accustomed to measuring activity levels in terms of inputs rather than the outputs produced.

In general, there are two basic approaches to program analysis: (1) the *fixed cost* approach, in which the goal is to maximize benefits for an established level of costs or predetermined budget allocation; and (2) the *fixed benefits* approach, in which the goal is to ascertain the minimum level of expenditure necessary to achieve some agreed-upon level of benefits. The first approach often characterizes cost-benefit analysis. The second is frequently followed in cost-effectiveness analysis. While the fixed level of budget or benefits may be predetermined outside the analysis, often a major part of the analysis will center on a determination of this constraint.

Program analysis seeks to:

1 Determine whether or not a particular program or proposal is justified
2 Rank various program alternatives appropriate to a given goal or set of objectives
3 Ascertain the optimal course(s) of action to attain such goals

In program analysis, it is important to be aware of the feedback from the accounting system and subsequent revisions in the programs that have been formulated to meet agreed-upon objectives. Thus programming must be an iterative process, involving continuous refinement and modification as dictated by changing circumstances in program delivery. The probability that program revisions will be required increases significantly as the time span of decisions increases. These processes seek ever-increasing precision in an accounting system in the identification of relationships between inputs (resources) and outputs (accomplishments).

Program costs are obtained from the accounting system and are projected to match revenue projections. It is possible through such procedures to determine the adequacy of revenue sources to support proposed programs. It also is possible to identify future cost commitments generated by current programs. Once the budget is framed in program terms, total costs can be disaggregated by type of inputs (e.g., salaries and wages, materials and supplies, equipment, etc.). Multiyear program and financial plans serve as the critical link between goals (outputs), on the one hand, and resource inputs on the other. When these budget costs and outputs are included as a part of the accounting records, "real-time" comparisons can be made between budgeted costs and outputs and actual costs and outputs.

## Program Measurement

Once programs are implemented, measurement techniques should be applied to help in the determination of needed improvements and modifications. While program analysis tends to be prospective, program measurement focuses on the actual performance of ongoing or recently completed activities. The purpose of measurement often is to suggest changes in resource allocations, to improve current operations, or to plan future activities. Program measurement seeks to evaluate the overall success of the chosen course of action and to identify where improvements might be made to more fully realize the projected program benefits. In short, program analysis and program measurement represent an *iterative cycle*—a cycle in which analysis precedes program commitments and measurement evaluates the impacts and effectiveness of these decisions and commitments.

Accounting measurements must be built primarily upon program data. Activities of local government frequently involve programs that are amenable to financial measurements. Such measurements, in turn, can be readily adapted to accounting systems. Thus the effectiveness and efficiency of many program activities of local (and state) governments and not-for-profit organizations are appropriately measured and evaluated within a management accounting format.

The "output" of many nonbusiness or public activities, however, may be difficult to define and measure in direct terms. As a consequence, secondary measures of effectiveness—*surrogates*—often must be used to test alternative approaches and to evaluate costs. For example, the total direct benefits to be realized from a program that reduces the incidence of high school dropouts may be difficult to measure. However, a surrogate measure would be the increase in earning capacity that individuals who complete a high school education can anticipate over those who drop out. Such figures are available in terms of national averages and can be applied as a rough measure of benefits to be derived.

Problems with such measurements frequently emerge from the data-gathering and record-keeping procedures of public agencies and not-for-profit organizations. And, of course, management accounting and control data are a significant part of these record systems and procedures.

## Strategic Planning and Program Budgeting

The budget process offers an opportunity for periodic reevaluation of broad purposes and objectives. It also affords the opportunity to compare programs and their costs in light of these longer-range purposes. A budget document can provide a common terminology for describing the plans and programs that relate to diverse organizational operations. This planning potential within the budgetary process, however, has been largely overshadowed by the fiscal control focus of traditional accounting and budgeting procedures.

The Planning-Programming-Budgeting System (PPBS) was introduced at the federal level in the mid-sixties to provide a broader basis for policy analysis and decision making within the context of a central review by the chief executive and governing body. As shown in Exhibit 20-4, PPBS represented a "top-down" budget format, with decisions and directives flowing from the policy levels to the operating levels of the organization. As Allen Schick has observed:

PPB reverses the information and decisional flow. Before the call for estimates is issued, top policy has to be made, and this policy constrains the estimates prepared below. For each lower level, the relevant policy instructions are issued by the superior level prior to the preparation of estimates. Accordingly, the critical decisional process—that of deciding on purpose and plans—has a downward and disaggregative flow.[5]

PPBS was received with enthusiasm by the proponents of a more rational and comprehensive approach to planning and control. It was greeted with great skepticism, however, by many who had survived earlier experiments with performance and program budgeting.

Unfortunately, PPBS was never fully integrated with the "bottom-up" informational flow that characterizes more traditional accounting and budget formats. Consequently, operating agencies often were left on the periphery of the process. These agencies were required to provide new responses to important policy directives (e.g., measures of effectiveness). However, they had little understanding or appreciation of how these responses would impact their resource allocations.

Operating in a realm of uncertainty, agency personnel tended to be suspicious of the consequences of PPBS. These suspicions were reinforced by an emphasis in PPBS on "across-the-board" program structures that carried the threat of agency reorganization. The pendulum had swung to the opposite extreme from the focus of traditional financial management practices. And many agencies were totally unprepared for (and unwilling to participate in) the transition.

By the early seventies, even the proponents of PPBS were eulogizing its demise. PPBS had attempted to go too far too fast in reforming the budget process. The emphasis on strategic planning to the near exclusion of the management planning and control functions proved disorienting to both operating agencies and policy makers. The latter group often was unable to fully absorb the implications of the more abstract information about broad public programs.

**EXHIBIT 20-4** BASIC DIFFERENCES AMONG BUDGET ORIENTATIONS

| Characteristic | Objects of expenditure | Performance budget | PPBS/Program budget |
|---|---|---|---|
| Control responsibility | Central | Operating | Operating |
| Management responsibility | Dispersed | Central | Supervisory |
| Planning responsibility | Dispersed | Dispersed | Central |
| Role of budget agency | Fiduciary | Efficiency | Policy |
| Decision/information flow | Bottom-up aggregative | Bottom-up aggregative | Top-down disaggregative |
| Information focus | Objects | Activities | Programs |
| Decision basis | Incremental | Incremental | Programmatic |
| Key budget stage | Execution | Preparation | Analysis |
| Basic personnel skills | Accounting | Administration | Economics |
| Appropriation-organization linkages | Direct | Activity-based | Across-the-board |

Adapted from Allen Schick, "The Road to PPB: The Stages of Budget Reform," in *Planning Programming Budgeting: A Systems Approach to Management,* ed. Fremont J. Lyden and Ernest G. Miller (Chicago: Markham Publishers, 1968), p. 50.

Many localities and organizations that experimented with PPBS in the sixties and early seventies more recently have adopted (and adapted) the techniques of *program budgeting* as a more realistic compromise to achieve a more systematic and comprehensive approach to budget making. Program budgeting offers considerably more flexibility through which the underlying planning framework can be combined with the basic functions of management and control. Therefore, program budgeting holds the potential of a more appropriate interface between long-range planning and decision making and the day-to-day operations of not-for-profit organizations. It provides a foundation for an accounting system that is more fully attuned to the basic goals of greater accountability, efficiency, and effectiveness. This multipurpose approach will be discussed in the final section of this chapter.

## ACCOUNT DATA CROSSWALKS

As discussed in Chapter 4, the more detailed object-of-expenditure classification offers two distinct advantages not possessed by other classification systems: (1) *accountability*—a pattern of accounts is established that can be controlled and audited, and (2) *personnel management information*—the control of personnel requirements can be used to control the entire budget. These two characteristics have sustained the object-of-expenditure format for over sixty-five years. Recent efforts to develop financial information systems that are more responsive to the needs of management have found these features somewhat intransigent to other objectives, however.

An accounting system that is more responsive to the needs of management can be built upon these two basic characteristics of an object-of-expenditure classification. To illustrate the first stage in such a system, a comparison can be made at the line-item level between the amounts budgeted and actual expenditures. Such data are shown in Exhibit 20-5. These data build on the materials presented previously in Chapter 19, with minor modifications to illustrate a program-based approach.

These budget and expenditure data can then be crosswalked to provide an accounting summary on a *program* basis. The term "crosswalk" refers to any data conversion that involves a change in classification systems (for example, from objects of expenditure to programs or vice versa). The programs in Exhibit 20-6 are labeled V, W, X, Y,

**EXHIBIT 20-5**
**Line-Item Budget and Actual Expenditures**
(In Thousands)

| Line items | Budget | Actual | Difference |
|---|---|---|---|
| Personal services | $ 700 | $ 730 | −$30 |
| Materials and supplies | 450 | 440 | 10 |
| Travel | 250 | 240 | 10 |
| Contractual services | 100 | 100 | — |
| Capital outlay | 200 | 200 | — |
| Debt service | 150 | 100 | 50 |
| Totals | $1,850 | $1,810 | $40 |

### EXHIBIT 20-6
### Line-Item Expenditures by Programs Budget and Actual
### (In Thousands)

| Line items | Programs | | | | | Totals |
|---|---|---|---|---|---|---|
| | V | W | X | Y | Z | |
| Personal | [100] | [200] | [150] | [150] | [100] | [ 700] |
| services | 105 | 210 | 155 | 155 | 105 | 730 |
| Materials and | [100] | [ 50] | [100] | [100] | [100] | [ 450] |
| supplies | 95 | 50 | 100 | 100 | 95 | 440 |
| Travel | [ 50] | [ 50] | [ 25] | [ 25] | [100] | [ 250] |
| | 45 | 50 | 25 | 25 | 95 | 240 |
| Contractual | [ 20] | [ 20] | [ 20] | [ 20] | [ 20] | [ 100] |
| services | 20 | 20 | 20 | 20 | 20 | 100 |
| Capital | [150] | [ 15] | [ 15] | [ 10] | [ 10] | [ 200] |
| outlay | 150 | 15 | 15 | 10 | 10 | 200 |
| Debt | | | | | [150] | [ 150] |
| service | | | | | 100 | 100 |
| Totals | [420] | [335] | [310] | [305] | [480] | [1,850] |
| | 415 | 345 | 315 | 310 | 425 | 1,810 |

[Budget]
Actual

and Z. However, they could have been designated as any type of program that a jurisdiction or nonprofit organization may have established—for example, health, public safety, transportation, housing, recreation, and so forth.

Programs often cut across organizational units—such is the case in this example. Managers often are interested in knowing how much each program costs in terms of the resources allocated to their organizational unit. The first step in determining these

### EXHIBIT 20-7
### Line-Item Costs by Departments
### (In Thousands)

| Line items | Departments | | | | | Totals |
|---|---|---|---|---|---|---|
| | M | N | O | P | Q | |
| Personal services | 238 | 134 | 115 | 132 | 111 | 730 |
| Materials and supplies | 147 | 82 | 70 | 81 | 70 | 450 |
| Travel | 80 | 45 | 38 | 44 | 38 | 245 |
| Contractual services | 36 | 20 | 17 | 20 | 17 | 110 |
| Capital outlay | 147 | 82 | 70 | 81 | 70 | 450 |
| Debt service | 33 | 18 | 16 | 18 | 15 | 100 |
| Totals | 681 | 381 | 326 | 376 | 321 | 2,085 |

costs is to identify departmental costs by line item. These cost allocations are illustrated in Exhibit 20-7. In Chapter 19, these entities were discussed in terms of *cost centers* and *responsibility centers*. At this point, however, these costs can be attributed to more familiar organizational units, that is, departments or agencies.

It is important to note that costs exceed recorded expenditures by $275,000. From the discussion of the basis of accounting (Chapter 1), it may be recalled that expenditures represent costs measured by the amount of actual cash paid out during a given fiscal period. Under an accrued cost basis, however, adjustments must be made for inventories, the depreciation of fixed assets, and other accounts. Such adjustments are critical in answering the question: How much does a program cost?

The distribution of accrued costs by programs is shown in Exhibit 20-8. The major adjustment occurs in capital outlay ($250,000). Other adjustments are evident in supplies ($10,000), travel ($5,000), and contractual services ($10,000).

From an accounting standpoint, perhaps the most valuable type of program crosswalk is that which brings together the types of costs by department or cost center for each program. In order to compare program costs with the overall effectiveness of program activities, it is essential that a program budget be based on costs rather than expenditures. Such a comparison can readily be developed from the accounting data in Exhibits 20-7 and 20-8. Departmental costs by programs are summarized in Exhibit 20-9, completing the program crosswalk.

## SUMMARY

The approaches to planning, budgeting, and accounting discussed in this chapter are designed to offer expanded information formats to program managers and decision

**EXHIBIT 20-8**
**Line-Item Costs by Programs**
(In Thousands)

| Line items | V | W | X | Y | Z | Totals |
|---|---|---|---|---|---|---|
| Personal services | 110 | 200 | 160 | 150 | 110 | 730 |
| Materials and supplies | 100 | 50 | 100 | 100 | 100 | 450 |
| Travel | 45 | 50 | 25 | 25 | 100 | 245 |
| Contractual services | 20 | 25 | 25 | 20 | 20 | 110 |
| Capital outlay | 100 | 100 | 100 | 100 | 50 | 450 |
| Debt service | | | | | 100 | 100 |
| Totals | 375 | 425 | 410 | 395 | 480 | 2,085 |

**EXHIBIT 20-9**
**Department Costs by Programs**
(In Thousands)

|  | Programs | | | | | |
|---|---|---|---|---|---|---|
| Departments | V | W | X | Y | Z | Totals |
| M | 51 | 125 | 60 | 195 | 250 | 681 |
| N | 56 | 50 | 150 | 75 | 50 | 381 |
| O | 51 | 150 | 25 | 50 | 50 | 326 |
| P | 176 | 25 | 75 | 50 | 50 | 376 |
| Q | 41 | 75 | 100 | 25 | 80 | 321 |
| Totals | 375 | 425 | 410 | 395 | 480 | 2,085 |

makers. The traditional object-of-expenditure budget and financial accounting techniques serve well the purposes of administrative analysis and operations control.

The basic premise of Part IV of this book, however, is that program budgeting and management accounting are intended primarily for the purposes of planning, program analysis, and management control.

Strategic planning and program analysis precede budget commitments, whereas administrative analysis and operational control must be applied during the execution of the budget. Additional control mechanisms can be maintained throughout these processes by adopting management accounting and cost accounting techniques, as described in Part III. These functions tend to overlap, such that no clear-cut distinctions can be made. However, the informational needs of management can be greatly facilitated by the multipurpose approach to accounting introduced in this chapter and further developed throughout the balance of Part IV.

## QUESTIONS

1. Identify information that is important to the management of any organization.
2. Distinguish between the purpose, goals, and program objectives of an organization.
3. What procedural areas are of particular concern under the concept of strategic management?
4. What are the principal distinctions among strategic planning, management planning, and operational planning?
5. What are the principal distinctions among strategic control, management control, and operational control?
6. What is a basic difference between data and information?
7. What are the three basic components of strategic planning, whether applied in the private sector or in government?
8. In strategic planning terms, what is a program?
9. What are the basic distinctions among goals, program objectives, and implementation strategies?
10. Distinguish between performance measures and effectiveness measures.
11. What is the basic purpose of program analysis?
12. Describe the characteristics of PPBS that earned this budget format the label of a "top-down" approach.
13. What is the basic function of a multipurpose accounting and budgetary system?

## CASE 20-1 PROGRAM CROSSWALK

Problem 4-1, presented at the conclusion of Chapter 4, focused on the development of an agency budget under traditional procedures. A line-item budget for the financial management department of the city of Rurbania served to illustrate this process. Expenditures for the previous fiscal year and the current departmental budget are shown in Exhibit 20-10.

As noted in the discussion of this line-item budget, five agencies comprise the financial management department: the city treasurer's office, the budget division, the division of accounts, the data-processing section, and the purchasing office. The city treasurer's office is responsible for (1) cash disbursements, (2) maintenance of the city's cash position, (3) administration of tax collections, and (4) management of investments. The budget division supervises the formulation and administration of the city's operating and capital budgets. The

**EXHIBIT 20-10** CURRENT LINE-ITEM BUDGET COMMITMENTS

| FUND | DEPARTMENT | FUNCTION |
|---|---|---|
| General | Financial management | General government |

**BUDGET COMMENTS**

The current budget for the financial management department is 7.14 percent (or $30,339) higher than the level of expenditure for the previous fiscal year. The projected budget request for the next fiscal year represents a 25.2 percent increase over the current budget. The major increases anticipated are in personal services (31.24 percent), employee benefits (30.86 percent), and contractual services (20.49 percent). Staff increases (nine new positions are requested) are required to accommodate the additional workload brought about by proposed changes in budget format and accounting procedures. These additional positions account for $61,440 (69.4 percent) of the $88,480 increase in salaries. The remaining increase is the result of scheduled salary adjustments. The major increase under contractual services is for data processing (25 percent). A decrease in data-processing equipment costs is anticipated, however.

| Object classifications | Last fiscal year | Current budget |
|---|---:|---:|
| Personal services | | |
| 1100 Salaries | $278,020 | $363,760 |
| 1120 Wages | 0 | 0 |
| 1130 Special payments | 0 | 0 |
| 1140 Overtime payments | 5,250 | 7,990 |
| Subtotal: Personal services | $283,270 | $371,750 |
| Contractual services | | |
| 1210 General repairs | $    700 | $    755 |
| 1220 Utility services | 3,600 | 3,900 |
| 1230 Motor vehicle repairs | 500 | 540 |
| 1240 Travel | 2,100 | 2,270 |
| 1250 Professional services | 5,725 | 6,185 |
| 1260 Communications | 6,780 | 7,320 |
| 1270 Printing | 1,000 | 1,080 |
| 1280 Computing services | 64,725 | 80,900 |
| 1290 Other contract services | 3,000 | 3,240 |
| Subtotal: Contractual services | $ 88,130 | $106,190 |

**EXHIBIT 20-10** (continued)

| Object classifications | Last fiscal year | Current budget |
|---|---:|---:|
| Supplies and materials | | |
| 1310 Office supplies | $ 29,440 | $ 32,200 |
| 1320 Fuel supplies | 0 | 0 |
| 1330 Operating supplies | 1,000 | 1,060 |
| 1340 Maintenance supplies | 900 | 955 |
| 1350 Drugs and chemicals | 0 | 0 |
| 1360 Food supplies | 0 | 0 |
| 1370 Clothing and linens | 0 | 0 |
| 1380 Education and recreation supplies | 0 | 0 |
| 1390 Other supplies | 1,500 | 1,590 |
| Subtotal: Supplies and materials | $ 32,840 | $ 34,805 |
| Equipment | | |
| 1410 Office equipment | $ 700 | $ 845 |
| 1420 Electrical equipment | 250 | 270 |
| 1430 Motor Vehicles | 0 | 0 |
| 1440 Highway equipment | 0 | 0 |
| 1450 Medical and lab equipment | 0 | 0 |
| 1480 Data-processing equipment | 15,000 | 12,000 |
| 1490 Other equipment | 0 | 0 |
| Subtotal: Equipment | $ 16,020 | $ 13,115 |
| Current obligations | | |
| 1510 Payments to sinking funds | 0 | 0 |
| 1520 Interest on temporary loans | 0 | 0 |
| 1530 Rental charges | 0 | 0 |
| 1540 Insurance | 300 | 350 |
| 1550 Dues and subscriptions | 5,000 | 5,300 |
| 1560 Electrostatic reproduction | 1,640 | 1,740 |
| 1590 Other obligations | 0 | 0 |
| Subtotal: Current obligations | $ 6,940 | $ 7,390 |
| Employee benefits | | |
| 1610 Retirement and pension benefits | $ 8,780 | $ 11,495 |
| 1620 Social security contribution | 8,229 | 10,768 |
| 1630 Federal old-age insurance | 1,168 | 1,529 |
| 1640 Group insurance | 724 | 945 |
| 1650 Medical/hospitalization insurance | 8,899 | 11,643 |
| Subtotal: Employee benefits | $ 27,800 | $ 36,380 |
| Totals | $455,000 | $569,630 |

division of accounts directs the general accounting and payroll activities and coordinates the debt administration programs of the city. The data-processing section provides management information to assist officials in their management and decision-making responsibilities. The purchasing office acts as the central procurement agency for the city.

As part of the city of Rurbania's efforts to develop improved financial management and accounting procedures, a program budget has been adopted on an experimental basis. Four major programs have been identified for the financial management department (see Exhibit 20-12). To some extent, these programs cut across the organizational lines of the five agencies. The city manager has asked Bud G. Etary to identify the anticipated cost of each of these programs in terms of the commitments required of the five organizational units.

The first step is to distribute the line-item budget by agency. In all likelihood, this distribution was accomplished in the budget-building phase and/or is reflected in the administration of the current budget in terms of allocations and allotments (see Chapter 4). Exhibit 20-11 summarizes these line-item budget allocations across the five agencies of the financial management department. The staff assignments for each of these agencies are as follows:

**Treasurer's office**

| | |
|---|---|
| City treasurer | $18,105 |
| Administrative analyst | 11,500 |
| Administrative assistant | 9,720 |
| Secretary | 7,343 |
| Clerk-typist | 5,945 |
| Total salaries | $52,613 |

**Division of accounts**

| | |
|---|---|
| Accountant III | $14,060 |
| Accountant II (2) | 21,100 |
| Cashier | 7,130 |
| Account clerks (2) | 12,480 |
| Bookkeeping machine operator | 6,480 |
| Clerk-typists (3) | 14,945 |
| Total salaries | $76,195 |

**Purchasing office**

| | |
|---|---|
| Purchasing Manager | $15,975 |
| Buyer | 12,460 |
| Secretary | 7,344 |
| Clerk-Typists (2) | 11,880 |
| Total salaries | $47,659 |

**Budget division**

| | |
|---|---|
| Budget director | $17,890 |
| Systems analyst | 14,700 |
| Budget analyst II (3) | 33,205 |
| Budget analyst I | 9,000 |
| Secretary | 7,343 |
| Clerk-typist | 5,945 |
| Total salaries | $88,083 |

**Data processing section**

| | |
|---|---|
| Data processing director | $17,570 |
| Systems analyst | 14,700 |
| Senior programmer | 12,780 |
| Programmers (2) | 19,825 |
| Computer operator (2) | 16,270 |
| Key punch operator | 12,120 |
| Clerk-typist | 5,945 |
| Total salaries | $99,210 |

Note that the funds budgeted for overtime payments were allocated by Etary on the basis of total salaries assigned to each agency (at approximately 2.2 percent of salary commitments). Employee benefits also are driven salary commitments (i.e., at approximately 10 percent of salary costs). The budget allocation for office equipment ($1,115) was assigned to the division of accounts, whereas the allocation for data-processing equipment was assigned to the data-processing section. The $350 for insurance under object code 1540 was assigned to the treasurer's office.

The next step is to prepare a parallel distribution of the line-item budget by the four programs that have been identified for the department's operations during the current fiscal year. This distribution is likely to be somewhat less definite than the budget allocations to the five agencies, but nevertheless some preliminary estimates can be made, as shown in Exhibit 20-12.

In some instances, staff effort has been reassigned to accommodate the objectives of these programs. For example, the administrative analyst will divide his or her time equally between

## EXHIBIT 20-11
### Line-Item Allocations by Agencies

| Line items | Agencies | | | | | Totals |
|---|---|---|---|---|---|---|
| | CT | BUD | ACC | DP | PUR | |
| Personal services | 52,613 | 88,083 | 76,195 | 99,210 | 47,659 | 363,760 |
| Overtime | 1,155 | 1,935 | 1,674 | 2,179 | 1,047 | 7,990 |
| Benefits | 5,262 | 8,810 | 7,620 | 9,922 | 4,766 | 36,380 |
| Contractual services | 3,655 | 6,120 | 5,300 | 87,800 | 3,315 | 106,190 |
| Supplies and materials | 5,035 | 8,425 | 7,295 | 9,490 | 4,560 | 34,805 |
| Equipment | — | — | 1,115 | 12,000 | — | 13,115 |
| Current obligations | 1,370 | 1,705 | 1,475 | 1,920 | 920 | 7,390 |
| Totals | 69,090 | 115,078 | 100,674 | 222,521 | 62,267 | 569,630 |

CT = City treasurer's office
BUD = Budget division
ACC = Division of accounts
DP = Data-processing section
PUR = Purchasing office

the cash and debt management program and the procurement and inventory maintenance program. The cashier is reassigned to the treasurer's office. The systems analyst in the data-processing section will divide his or her effort equally between the development of a program budget and the management accounting program. The budget director will devote 10 percent of his or her effort to each of the Programs A, C, and D and the remaining 70 percent of his or her effort will be devoted to Program B.

The major adjustments in staff assignments occur with the data-processing section, which will provide support to all four programs. This distribution of these efforts, as well as the other reassignments, are summarized below:

### Program A

| | | |
|---|---|---|
| Cashier | | $ 7,130 |
| Data-processing director | (25%) | 4,395 |
| Senior programmer | (33%) | 4,260 |
| Programmer | | 9,600 |
| Other DP staff | | 8,600 |
| Budget director | (10%) | 1,790 |
| Less: | | |
| Administrative analyst II | (50%) | (5,750) |
| Net adjustment | | $30,025 |

### Program B

| | | |
|---|---|---|
| Data processing director | (25%) | $ 4,395 |
| Senior programmer | (33%) | 4,260 |
| Programmer | | 10,225 |
| Systems analyst | (50%) | 7,350 |
| Other DP staff | | 8,600 |
| Less: | | |
| Budget director | (30%) | (5,370) |
| Net adjustment | | $29,460 |

### Program C

| | | |
|---|---|---|
| Systems analyst | (50%) | $ 7,350 |
| Senior programmer | (33%) | 4,260 |
| Data processing director | (25%) | 4,390 |
| Other DP staff | | 8,600 |
| Budget director | (10%) | 1,790 |
| Less: | | |
| Cashier | | (7,130) |
| Net adjustment | | $19,260 |

### Program D

| | | |
|---|---|---|
| Administrative analyst | (50%) | $ 5,750 |
| Data processing director | (25%) | 4,390 |
| Other DP staff | | 8,535 |
| Budget director | (10%) | 1,790 |
| Net adjustment | | $20,465 |

## EXHIBIT 20-12
### Line-Item Allocations by Programs

| Line items | Programs | | | | Totals |
|---|---|---|---|---|---|
| | A | B | C | D | |
| Personal services | 82,638 | 117,543 | 95,455 | 68,124 | 363,760 |
| Overtime | 1,815 | 2,582 | 2,097 | 1,496 | 7,990 |
| Benefits | 8,265 | 11,755 | 9,545 | 6,815 | 36,380 |
| Contractual services | 34,480 | 29,885 | 27,070 | 14,755 | 106,190 |
| Supplies and materials | 7,195 | 11,490 | 9,785 | 6,335 | 34,805 |
| Equipment | 3,250 | 4,210 | 4,090 | 1,565 | 13,115 |
| Current obligations | 1,890 | 2,380 | 1,950 | 1,170 | 7,390 |
| Totals | 139,533 | 179,845 | 149,992 | 100,260 | 569,630 |

A = Cash and debt management program
B = Program budgeting and service level analysis
C = Financial and management accounting
D = Procurement and inventory maintenance

It should be noted that the sum of the net adjustments equals the initial salary allocation to the data-processing section.

The budget allocations for overtime payments and employee benefits are again distributed on the basis of salary commitments. Operating funds for contractual services, supplies and materials, and current obligations have been left with the agency having primary responsibility for each of the programs. Operating funds assigned to the data-processing section have been distributed to the four programs on the basis of the salary commitments for data-processing personnel assigned to each of these programs. The $12,000 for data-processing equipment acquisition has also been reallocated on this same basis.

**Required:**
Using the information provided in support of the line-item allocations in Exhibits 20-11 and 20-12, complete the program crosswalk by distributing the estimated program costs by agencies in Exhibit 20-13. The agency and program totals are provided in the exhibit.

## EXHIBIT 20-13
### Agency Costs by Programs

| Agencies | Programs | | | | Totals |
|---|---|---|---|---|---|
| | A | B | C | D | |
| CT | | | | | 69,090 |
| BUD | | | | | 115,078 |
| ACC | | | | | 100,674 |
| DP | | | | | 222,521 |
| PUR | | | | | 62,267 |
| Totals | 132,881 | 187,175 | 149,858 | 99,716 | 569,630 |

**NOTES**

1 Alan Walter Steiss, *Strategic Management and Organizational Decision Making* (Lexington, Mass.: Lexington Books, 1985), p. 21.
2 Martin J. Gannon, *Management: An Organizational Perspective* (Boston: Little, Brown, 1977), p. 140.
3 William R. King and David I. Cleland, *Strategic Planning and Policy* (New York: Van Nostrand Reinhold, 1978), p. 6.
4 Alan Walter Steiss, *Public Budgeting and Management* (Lexington, Mass.: Lexington Books, 1972), p. 148.
5 Allen Schick, "The Road to PPB: The Stages of Budget Reform," in *Planning Programming Budgeting: A Systems Approach to Management,* ed. Fremont J. Lyden and Ernest G. Miller (Chicago: Markham Publishers, 1968), p. 42.

# CHAPTER 21

# MANAGEMENT EMPHASIS ON PERFORMANCE AND ACCOUNTABILITY

As discussed in Chapter 4, the traditional purpose of a budget in government has been to provide a legal basis from which to control public spending. Accounting, in turn, provides a data base and a set of procedures with which to assess fiscal accountability, financial integrity, and legal compliance with legislative and administrative mandates, as set forth in laws, ordinances, and regulations. As a management tool, the budget can be used to determine where operating economies and performance efficiencies can be attained. In this connection, accounting systems can provide information to assist in making appropriate decisions regarding the most efficient allocation of fiscal resources. On the basis of such information, public agencies can be held more accountable for the implementation of these decisions.

## THE BUDGET AS A WORK PROGRAM

Recognition that budgeting and accounting could serve important management purposes began to emerge in the public sector in the mid-thirties, culminating in the concept of *performance budgeting*. Performance budgeting had its heyday in the late forties and early fifties. It seldom is discussed in any detail in contemporary textbooks, being relegated for the most part to a historical footnote. Nevertheless, many of the attributes of performance budgeting—and the accounting techniques that were developed to support this budget format—have survived to become important, integral parts of contemporary financial management systems.

### Performance Classification Systems

The management objective of efficiency derives much of its conceptual and technical basis from cost accounting. The budget is envisioned as a *work program*, the principal focus being at and below the departmental level where the efficiency of operating units can be assessed. Work-cost data are reduced into discrete, measurable units to facilitate the more efficient performance of prescribed activities.

The relationship among various classification systems is further illustrated in Exhibit 21-1, based on typical municipal functions of "provision of streets and roads." As the data in this exhibit demonstrate, in relatively uncomplicated activity areas, it is possible to move with comparative ease from a functional classification—which may cut across organizational lines—to programs and to performance units. It also is possible to use the objects-of-expenditure classification to supplement performance schedules.

Two key components that distinguish performance budgeting from other budgetary approaches are the identification of *performance units* within work programs and the

**EXHIBIT 21-1** PERFORMANCE CLASSIFICATION SYSTEM

| Category | Department or bureau | Number of units | Unit cost |
|---|---|---|---|
| **Function** | | | |
| 1.0 Provision of streets and roads | Public works department | | |
| **Programs** | | | |
| 1.1 Street construction | Bureau of streets | | |
| 1.2 Street maintenance | Bureau of streets | | |
| 1.3 Traffic control | Traffic department Police department | | |
| 1.4 Street lighting | Street lighting division | | |
| **Performance** | | | |
| 1.41 Replacement of lamps | | | |
|     Incandescent | | 13,800 | $ 3.50 |
|     Mercury vapor | | 1,100 | $ 15.25 |
| 1.42 Washing luminaries | | 12,000 | $ 1.85 |
| 1.43 Painting standards | | 3,500 | $ 21.14 |
| 1.44 Maintenance of standards | | 1,440 | $ 16.26 |
| 1.45 Cable repairs | | 400 | $ 90.00 |
| 1.46 Damage repairs | | 350 | $305.00 |
| 1.47 Miscellaneous maintenance | | 200 | $ 11.80 |
| **Objects of expenditure** | | | |
| 1.47 Miscellaneous maintenance | | | |
|     (a) Personal services | $1,100 | | |
|     (b) Materials and supplies | 504 | | |
|     (c) Equipment | 756 | | |
|     (d) Overhead | 385 | | |
|     Subtotal | $2,745 | | |

efforts to provide full measurement of *performance costs*. A performance unit might be described in terms of a team of workers assigned the responsibility to carry out a specific task or series of tasks, whereas performance costs would be those costs directly associated with carrying out these activities. While these two components represent the particular strengths of performance budgeting, in another sense, they also reflect the basic shortcomings of this approach in terms of its implementation.

Program gaps and potential conflicts and inconsistencies in data were major limitations to the application of performance budgeting as an aid to management decision making. Work programs can be related to particular processes or functions carried out by governmental agencies or units within a not-for-profit organization. However, very few functions are conducted by only one agency or department. While functions may cut across organizational lines, in application, work programs usually were identified within the established structure of the organization.

An inability to achieve a uniform and consistent basis for identifying performance units and a reluctance to adopt accrual accounting procedures to assist in measuring performance costs added significantly to the problems of implementation in many local governments. As a consequence, many applications of performance budgeting focused only on selected components, such as activity classification systems and performance measures. These components, however, remain as major contributions to financial management procedures emerging from this period.

## Activity Classification

As discussed in Chapter 4, the principal purpose of an *object classification* system is the control of expenditures at the agency or unit level. Agencies tend to buy the same things; therefore, it is possible to establish a chart of accounts that is uniform through the whole of government. Thus the accounting system is linked directly with budgetary accounts. Object classifications show in great detail *what* is purchased, but not *why*, that is, the nature of organizational programs and accomplishments under those programs.

To overcome this shortcoming, purchases can be organized and aggregated according to the activities they serve, not as things in themselves. *Activity classifications* seek to relate activities to the functions and work responsibilities of distinct operating units. All the expenditure data required by an administrator are gathered under a single rubric. Activity classifications can provide a great deal of information about what the organization is doing and thereby, help make managers more cost conscious in the evaluation of their units in terms of the efficient use of resources.

The term ''activity'' can be broadly applied under various circumstances to mean process, project, or purpose. A *process* approach, for example, would list as activities the various steps in carrying out an agency's work program. A *project* approach might list the individual projects (often involving fixed assets and capital facilities) that make up the total activities of an agency. A *purpose* classification might group activities according to broad functions or by clientele groups. Considerable confusion can arise, however, from mixing these approaches in a single agency or not-for-profit organization.

The use of activity classifications requires an accounting crosswalk to track expenditures from the more traditional categories to the chosen activity units. Exhibit 21-2 illustrates this crosswalk, building on the activities of department M under program Y (as previously identified in Exhibit 20-9). In the earlier days of performance budgeting, these sorts had to be carried out largely by hand. Today, modern electronic data-processing software facilitates the sorting of accounting data according to a number of categories and subcategories.

## Performance Measures

Performance measures often are adopted to provide a basis for greater accountability in the delivery of public services. A performance measure combines some indicator of *output*, such as the volume of goods or services delivered, with some measure of *input*, that is, data that indicate the resources employed to operate a program or project.

Performance measures often are used as indicators of operating efficiency—for example, the cost per patient-day of hospital service; the number of cases successfully prosecuted per law enforcement officer; or the response time involved in providing some public service. As may be seen from these examples, not all performance measures are expressed in cost terms. Performance measures provide basic management information on program economics, that is, such measures reveal the relationship between initial resource allocations (inputs) and the delivery of services (outputs).

The most common measures of output are *work-load measures*, which relate to the volume of work performed during some time period. In a public health clinic, for

**EXHIBIT 21-2**
**Activity Costs by Departmental Unit**
**Budget and Actual**

| Departmental units | Activities | | | | |
|---|---|---|---|---|---|
| | Y1 | Y2 | Y3 | Y4 | Totals |
| M1 | [ 6,000] | [10,000] | [ 6,000] | [ 8,000] | [30,000] |
| | 5,830 | 9,550 | 5,880 | 8,500 | 29,760 |
| M2 | [11,000] | [10,000] | [10,000] | [ 9,000] | [40,000] |
| | 10,500 | 10,200 | 9,800 | 9,500 | 40,000 |
| M3 | [11,500] | [10,500] | [12,500] | [10,500] | [45,000] |
| | 12,030 | 10,400 | 12,440 | 10,550 | 45,420 |
| M4 | [15,000] | [15,000] | [10,000] | [10,000] | [50,000] |
| | 14,550 | 14,200 | 9,800 | 9,900 | 48,450 |
| M5 | [ 8,000] | [ 9,000] | [10,000] | [ 8,000] | [35,000] |
| | 7,150 | 8,000 | 9,020 | 7,200 | 31,370 |
| Totals | [51,500] | [54,500] | [48,500] | [45,500] | [200,000] |
| | 50,060 | 52,350 | 46,940 | 45,650 | 195,000 |

[Budget]
Actual

example, it may be possible to determine the number of cases in various categories that can be handled by a public health nurse on a daily, weekly, or annual basis. With this information and an estimate of the total number of cases to be processed, the clinic director could calculate the nursing staff required during any fiscal period. Common work-load measures include: tons of trash collected; number of arrests made; number of vaccinations given; number of inspections made; number of library books circulated; number of emergency calls responded to; number of full-time equivalent university students; number of hospital patients served daily; number of X-rays processed; and so forth. Work-load measures provide basic information for the development of an agency's budget. And often, on a retrospective basis, these measures can provide an indication of the appropriateness of previous resource allocation decisions.

As indicated in Chapter 17, *unit cost measures* refer to the expenses incurred per component unit to carry out some regular, recurring operation or activity. Unit cost measures aggregate all of the relevant costs associated with the delivery of a particular service. These costs are then divided by the total units of service provided. Case 21-1 at the end of this chapter provides a more comprehensive example of how unit costs are determined.

In some situations, it may be important to build unit costs on a full cost basis. In Exhibit 21-1, for example, the "total cost" figure for miscellaneous maintenance, built on unit cost data, differs from the total cost using the object-of-expenditure approach. This difference, of course, stems from the inclusion of overhead in the object-of-expenditure figure. This illustrates one of the technical problems in the use of unit cost data for budget-building purposes. To ensure that a full cost figure is presented, some mechanism must be developed to prorate indirect or overhead costs to the individual activities or end products that represent the performance units.

An overemphasis on performance measures can result in pseudoefficiency. Performance measures can be understated, that is, the objectives can be set relatively low to ensure achievement. Or organizations may resort to "creaming"—doing the easy assignments first and deferring or neglecting the more difficult ones—in order to meet such measures of efficiency. For example, a forensic laboratory might be evaluated in terms of the number of tests performed. As a result, priority might be given to the relatively simple tests, leaving the more involved ones until the "volume" tests have been completed. Such problems suggest the need for careful review of performance data by disinterested third parties.

Although seldom practiced today in its pure form, many characteristics of performance budgeting have survived. Performance measures—work-load measures and unit cost measures—and the concept of performance levels or *levels of service* have been incorporated into many contemporary financial management applications that seek greater efficiency and economy in the allocation of limited resources. The focus on cost efficiency, which was a hallmark of performance budgeting, has its parallel emphasis in current budget and accounting formats. Cost accounting systems also are beginning to receive wider application in local and state governments and not-for-profit organizations, particularly in support of the techniques of cost-benefit and cost-effectiveness analysis.[1]

## SERVICE DELIVERY ACCOUNTABILITY

For over sixty years, the incremental aspects of public financial management have been criticized as arbitrary and irrational. Critics have pointed to the lack of coordination and the neglect of important values in traditional budget-building procedures. They have suggested that budgets built on an incremental basis produce only small changes in the status quo. Supporting accounting systems also have been designed to provide decision makers with incremental information by comparing expenditures from the prior fiscal period with those in the current fiscal period. In incremental budgeting, the results from previous fund allocations are accepted as the primary decision criteria. Therefore, existing programs are continued into the future without being subjected to intensive reexamination.

Incremental budgeting and accounting are suspect in their ability to allocate scarce resources in the most efficient, economical, and effective manner. Therefore, new procedures have been proposed to promote greater rationality, comprehensiveness, and accountability. Under these procedures, every program—new and old—must compete equally for available resources. Rather than reviewing only the incremental adjustments over previous levels of funding and expenditures, the budget is analyzed in its entirety. In this way, inefficient and obsolete programs can be revised or eliminated, thereby freeing more resources for new or higher-priority programs. This more comprehensive budget format sometimes is referred to as a *zero-base* approach because no incrementally established budget base is accepted as permanent.

### Service Level Analysis

Service is the primary mission of local government and of many not-for-profit organizations. Therefore, the activities of such organizations can be readily identified and often can be measured and analyzed in service delivery terms. In an era of increasing public demand for accountability in the delivery of services, the shortcomings of more traditional practices of budgeting and accounting are becoming more widely recognized by the management of these organizations. Among these shortcomings are:

1 *Insufficient Information*—Conventional accounting and budgeting practices provide relatively little useful information about (a) the type and level of services provided, (b) the objectives and beneficiaries of the service, or (c) the special resources required in the provision of specific levels of service.

2 *Lack of Choice Mechanisms*—With increasing frequency, local governments and not-for-profit organizations have insufficient financial resources to fund all services at the requested levels. Conventional practices provide no workable mechanisms, however, to help make choices or to identify the trade-offs among different services in anything even approaching a cost-benefit basis.

3 *Impact of Change Unclear*—No meaningful processes exist to: (a) predict how significant changes in funding will affect service delivery, (b) determine the benefits in services afforded by increases in funding, or (c) identify the absolute minimum level of service that a nonbusiness organization can provide.

Service level analysis attempts to overcome these shortcomings by drawing attention to the elements of the budget base along with recommended changes in the level of services to be delivered.

### Actionable Programs versus Fixed Expenditures

Service level analysis can be applied to all actionable programs or activities. An *actionable program* is one in which there is some discretion as to the courses of action pursued. All activities that compete for general fund revenues (or equivalent funds in not-for-profit organizations) should be included in the service level analysis. In addition, intergovernmental grants and formula-funded programs, often excluded from conventional budget analysis, should be identified to determine the importance of such special funds to organizational activities.

Service level analysis can have only limited application to programs where the levels of expenditures are imposed by laws or statutes, intergovernmental commitments, or other legal or fiscal constraints. It can assist, however, in identifying the public costs of such constraints.

Actionable or discretionary programs (i.e., those for which expenditure levels are not fixed) may make up only a portion of the total budget (less than 25 percent, according to some estimates).[2] However, they often represent activities that are more difficult to analyze and plan. Thus more effective management control of these budget components through service level analysis can greatly affect the entire budget.

Unfortunately, some confusion exists between fixed expenditures and *essential levels of service*. Labeling a service as "essential" is not the same thing as defining its supporting expenditures as "fixed." Local governments, for example, may have relatively little choice about the funding of essential service levels, and such service levels may comprise a major portion of the annual budget. One of the basic objectives of service level analysis, however, is to identify these essential service levels so that an organization can maintain and deliver—and be held accountable for—such programs in a more efficient and effective manner. Essential services can be provided more efficiently (at less cost) or more effectively (with greater benefits). With experience, the categories of expenditures excluded from service level analysis can be reduced significantly in relation to the total budget.

### Components of Service Level Analysis

While the terminology may vary from application to application, the three basic components to a service level analysis are as follows:

**1** *Identification of Budget Units*—the designation of the basic building blocks within the organizational structure responsible for decision making and an examination of goals and objectives, current purposes and methods of operation, ways of measuring performance and effectiveness, and relations with other budget units.[3]

**2** *Decision Package Analysis*—the identification of alternative ways of providing essential services and the justification of various levels of service at which each budget unit might operate.

**3** *Priority Ranking and Evaluation*—the arrangement of all levels of service in descending order of importance and the determination of a funding cut-off point.

The linkages between these analytical components, as applied in local government, is shown in Exhibit 21-3.

It is important that *budget units* be of such a size that their data needs can be served adequately by the available accounting system. In most municipalities, for example, budget units will correspond with established divisions within the departments or agencies of city government. Large multifunctional divisions may be further subdivided to reflect more specific functions.

Initially, the identification of appropriate budget units may be a fairly time-consuming effort, requiring considerable thought and organizational analysis. It is unlikely,

**EXHIBIT 21-3** Flow chart for service level analysis.

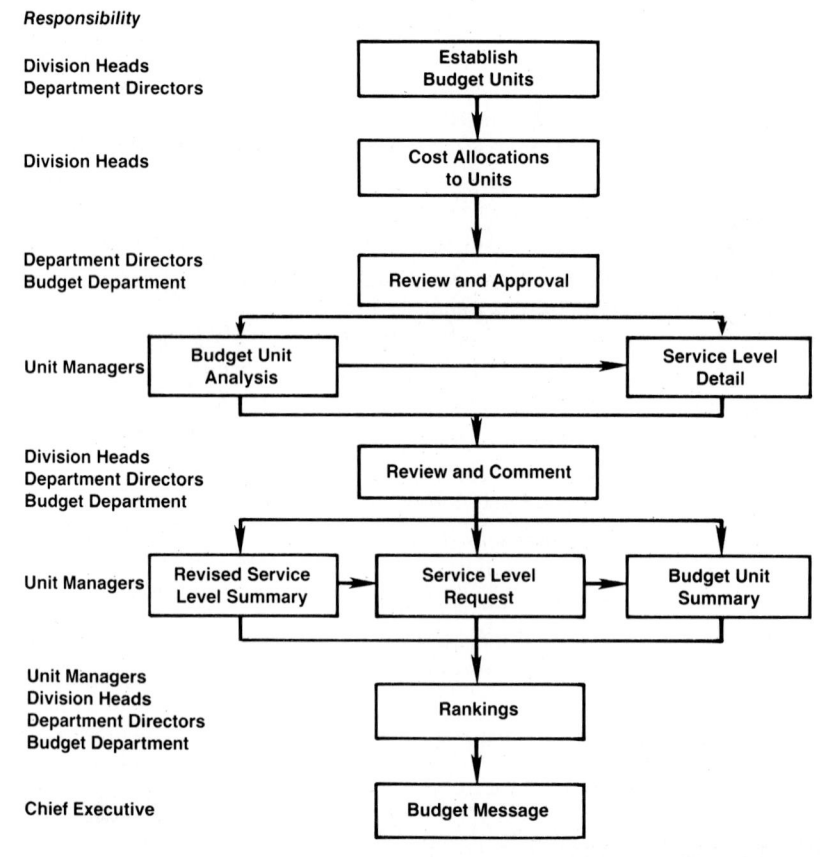

*Responsibility*

| Responsibility | Process |
|---|---|
| Division Heads / Department Directors | Establish Budget Units |
| Division Heads | Cost Allocations to Units |
| Department Directors / Budget Department | Review and Approval |
| Unit Managers | Budget Unit Analysis → Service Level Detail |
| Division Heads / Department Directors / Budget Department | Review and Comment |
| Unit Managers | Revised Service Level Summary ↔ Service Level Request ↔ Budget Unit Summary |
| Unit Managers / Division Heads / Department Directors / Budget Department | Rankings |
| Chief Executive | Budget Message |

however, that budget units will change dramatically from one year to the next. Consequently, the identification of budget units generally is a one-time task, requiring only minor adjustments in subsequent years as new program responsibilities are assumed or major program revisions are initiated.

A *decision package* represents a discrete set of services, activities, and resources that are applied to the performance of a given operation or the accomplishment of a program objective. A decision package should describe the set of activities in such a way that management can: (1) evaluate it and rank it against other activities competing for limited resources and (2) decide whether to approve or disapprove it.[4] Decision packages may involve alternative methods for delivering a service (for example, contracting out part of the activities involved versus carrying out these functions in-house). Or they may be alternative approaches which make use of more or less of the same basic resource inputs (for example, full-time salaried personnel versus part-time wage personnel hired on an as-needed basis).

Exhibit 21-4 illustrates a summary sheet for the service level analysis of the rescue squad/ambulance service in the city of Rurbania, which forms the basis for Case 21-3 at the conclusion of this chapter. Three decision packages are identified: (1) the current approach, involving free, around-the-clock ambulance service provided as part of the operations of the fire department; (2) a contractual option frequently used in the past in smaller communities, involving the local mortuary; and (3) a contractual option relying on the ambulance service of the city-county hospital.

For some essential services, only one decision package may be readily evident—the level of investment from prior budget years may be such that a continuation of the current approach may be the only feasible decision. However, such prior program investments—whether in dollar terms or in terms of other administrative (or psychological) commitments—should not preclude searching for alternative decision packages. Maintaining an existing program simply because it represents the way business has always been done is one of the underlying sources of waste and inefficiency in organizational operations.

### Minimum Service Levels

After a decision package is chosen, a minimum level of service should be identified for each package. By definition, the maintenance of an existing program or the initiation of a new program would not be feasible below this minimum level. Minimum service levels include only the most essential elements or activities within chosen decision packages. These elements provide the highest priority services or meet the most critical needs of the government or organization. The minimum service level also defines the minimum level of funding for each package. The minimum service level shown in Exhibit 21-4 would involve the operation of the rescue squad/ambulance service strictly on a volunteer basis.

It often is difficult to get agency personnel to think in such terms, that is, to identify a level of service/funding below the present level of support. In such cases, a percentage of the current level may be arbitrarily set as the minimum level—65 to 80 percent

### EXHIBIT 21-4 SERVICE LEVEL IMPACT SUMMARY

| FUND | DEPT./PROGRAM | DIVISION/ELEMENT |
|---|---|---|
| General | Fire Safety | Operations |

*Current Operations and Resources*
Free ambulance service provided to all people in the city. Calls for emergency transportation are dispatched over the fire emergency communications network. Vehicle responds to the scene of need. One vehicle, four drivers, and two paramedics provide around-the-clock service 365 days per year.

*Alternative Methods of Operation*
Contract with Digger O'Dell's Mortuary—save about $10,000 per year but run the risk of not having dedicated vehicle.

Contract with city-county hospital—hospital ambulance sometimes dispatched to remote parts of the county or to other medical facilities outside the county.

#### Service Level Summary

| | Service level | | Cumulative | | Cumulative percent | |
|---|---|---|---|---|---|---|
| Service level title | Total | Positions | Total | Positions | Total | Positions |
| 1 Volunteer service | $ 7,660 | 0 | $ 7,660 | 0 | 8.6% | 0% |
| 2 Assigned drivers | $41,025 | 3 | $48,685 | 3 | 54.7% | 50% |
| 3 Add paramedic team | $40,360 | 3 | $89,045 | 6 | 100.0% | 100% |
| 4 Add second paramedic team | $24,220 | 2 | $113,265 | 8 | 127.2% | 133% |
| 5 Add second ambulance unit | $57,345 | 4 | $170,610 | 12 | 191.6% | 200% |

#### Program Objectives

1 Ten-minute response time; no medical or first-aid assistance.
2 Seven-minute response time; no medical or first-aid assistance.
3 Add medical assistance and reduce complications due to no first-aid assistance.
4 Paramedic services provided around-the-clock.
5 Response time less than ten minutes to all parts of city.

---

of the current appropriation frequently is used. The budget unit manager then is asked to identify the level of service that could be provided at this reduced funding level (and what current activities would have to be sacrificed to accommodate this funding level).

Additional levels of service should then be identified. Each succeeding level should expand the services available, step by step, until the level of service is back to and even above current service standards. Each level of service must be analyzed in terms of the specific quantities and qualities of work to be performed (and services to be provided). Appropriate costs should be assigned to each level. Potential service impacts should be described. And the importance of each level should be justified (in terms of program goals). Several levels of service may be identified between the minimum or survival level and the current level—two or three in smaller units, perhaps four or more for larger units.

Level 3 in Exhibit 21-4 represents the current level of service, involving four drivers and a two-person paramedic team (identified by the 100 percent of service designation). Thus two service levels are shown below the current level, and two levels are indicated above the current level. The addition of a second paramedic team is the level identified above current services, while a second ambulance unit (requiring four additional drivers) is the next projected level.

A summary for each budget unit should reflect all the resources required to deliver each level of service, including detailed costs from all funding sources and a summary of personnel, equipment, and other major resource requirements. At this point, the mechanisms of the object-of-expenditure format can be reintroduced (see Exhibit 21-5). In effect, once the detailed cost data have been established for the minimum level of service, these costs are then built upon in a cumulative fashion for each successive level. It is not necessary to prepare a separate object-of-expenditure budget for each service level. The budget for service level 3 is simply the sum of all entries under each object code in the first three columns of Exhibit 21-5. In exceptional cases, where decision packages present distinctive service delivery alternatives (as, for example, a labor-intensive versus a capital-intensive approach), separate budget summaries may be necessary.

**EXHIBIT 21-5**
**Objects of Expenditure for Five Service Levels**

| Object codes | Service levels | | | | |
|---|---|---|---|---|---|
| | 1 | 2 | 3 | 4 | 5 |
| 1110 Salaries and wages | 0 | $36,775 | $26,405 | $18,765 | $39,155 |
| 1140 Overtime | 0 | 0 | 3,160 | 1,895 | 3,915 |
| Subtotal: personal services | 0 | $36,775 | $29,565 | $20,660 | $43,070 |
| 1330 Operating supplies | $1,085 | 0 | 145 | 500 | 400 |
| 1340 Maintenance supplies | 0 | 0 | 400 | 0 | 200 |
| 1350 Drugs and medical supplies | 0 | 0 | 760 | 0 | 400 |
| Subtotal: supplies and materials | $1,085 | 0 | $ 1,305 | $   500 | $ 1,000 |
| 1430 Motor vehicles | $6,575 | 0 | $ 2,425 | 0 | $ 6,000 |
| 1450 Medical and lab equipment | 0 | 0 | 1,000 | 0 | 600 |
| Subtotal: equipment | $6,575 | 0 | $ 3,425 | 0 | $ 6,600 |
| 1610 Retirement and pension benefits | 0 | $   692 | $   988 | $   498 | $ 1,086 |
| 1620 Social security contributions | 0 | 1,914 | 2,731 | $ 1,378 | $ 3,006 |
| 1640 Group insurance | 0 | 82 | 118 | 60 | 131 |
| 1650 Medical hospital insurance | 0 | 1,562 | 2,228 | 1,124 | 2,452 |
| Subtotal: employee benefits | 0 | $ 4,250 | $ 6,065 | $ 3,060 | $ 6,675 |
| Budget unit total | $7,660 | $41,025 | $40,360 | $24,220 | $57,345 |

## Ranking Service Levels

The difference between formulating levels of service and ranking them is similar to the distinction between efficiency and effectiveness. Peter Drucker has defined efficiency as "doing things right" and effectiveness as "doing the right things."[5] The formulation of levels of service, in essence, involves a determination of how to do things right. Deciding to do the right things is the objective of the ranking process.

Before ranking can begin, a set of criteria must be established on which to base these decisions. Criteria should address such questions as: Is the program or service legally required? Does the organization possess the necessary technical skills to implement the activities? Does the proposed approach have a previous record of success? Will lower-level management accept and execute the program? Will the service delivery be cost effective? Can the organization (or municipality) afford not to implement the proposed program?

In each successive review, ranking establishes an order of priority for each service level. Highest-priority (most important) service levels are ranked until all levels have been included. This process of ranking or prioritizing should be quite familiar to those organizations with established procedures for capital improvements programming (CIP). It is merely the CIP priority system applied to an analysis of the operating budget.

It is likely that more service levels will be presented than can be funded from available revenues. Therefore, three alternatives can be employed, either singularly or in concert, to bring projected revenue and proposed expenditures in balance:

1. Funds can be withheld from the lowest priority service levels.
2. Efforts can be made to reduce the cost of providing one or more levels of service.
3. Revenues can be increased (e.g., by raising taxes, liquidating assets, etc.).

The final priority list can be used to fund service levels in order of priority until anticipated revenues are exhausted. At this point, a funding cut-off line is drawn, and those service levels below this line are not funded. Unfunded service levels should be reexamined, and, if deemed necessary to the well-being of the municipality (or nonprofit organization), the other two alternatives should be explored.

## Driving Accountability Deeper into the Organization

An examination of the consequences of various funding levels is important in any organization, especially when funding requests must be balanced within relatively fixed fiscal resources. The ranking techniques used in service level analysis assures that high-priority activities will be funded.

Without a ranking process, budgeting is little more than a juggling act—trying to find the proper pieces in a hit-and-miss fashion that will add up to an acceptable whole. Unable to discern which programs or activities are of lower priority and, therefore, which can be deferred or eliminated, decision makers often are forced to make across-the-board cuts. Service level analysis minimizes this need by creating an explicit priority listing.

Service level analysis also can be helpful in driving accountability for budgeting and budget execution deeper into the organization. From the outset, these analytical techniques require the involvement of program managers, thus tapping a larger reservoir of program knowledge and analytical skills. Direct involvement of program managers in budget making, in turn, often increases their concern for the proper implementation of organizational policies and programs. Thus service level analysis helps to facilitate the transformation of policies into plans and plans into action.

First and foremost, service level analysis, like zero-base budgeting in which it is frequently applied, is an attack on incremental approaches to budgeting and accounting. Service level analysis goes beyond an examination of new programs and incremental changes to existing programs. It involves a close scrutiny of all activities, old and new. In this sense, service level analysis serves as a mechanism of management control, seeking to eliminate unnecessary spending that may be the consequence of obsolete, inefficient programs or duplications of effort. Funds are thus channeled to more important demands, thereby increasing overall efficiency.

## SUMMARY

This chapter has examined some of the basic objectives of management control, and in particular, the concepts of performance efficiency, operating economy, and service delivery accountability. Management control involves a "systematic effort to compare current performance to a predetermined plan or objectives, presumably to take any immediate action required."[6] The actions precipitated by the management controls, in general, are directed at (1) increasing the efficiency of performance, (2) achieving further economies in operations, or (3) increasing the accountability in the use of limited resources for the delivery of critical services. The use of performance measures and the techniques of service level analysis, as outlined in this chapter, are designed to support these management control objectives in governmental agencies and not-for-profit organizations.

## QUESTIONS

1. What two components distinguish performance budgeting from other budgetary approaches?
2. What is the basic distinction between an object classification and an activity classification?
3. Define the following measures of performance: (a) unit cost measure, (b) work load measure, (c) effectiveness measure.
4. What are the basic objectives of service level analysis?
5. What is an actionable program, and how does it relate to (differ from) a fixed expenditure?
6. Identify the three basic components of service level analysis.
7. Define the concept of decision packages as applied in service level analysis.
8. What are the essential criteria for the selection of a minimum level of service?
9. What is the basic objective of the ranking process?
10. How can service level analysis influence accountability in government and not-for-profit organizations?

## CASE 21-1  UNIT COST ANALYSIS

Citizen groups have recently petitioned the city council of Rurbania for an upgrading of the street lighting systems in their neighborhoods. They have requested that conventional incandescent lights be replaced with mercury vapor lamps similar to those currently in operation in some commercial districts of the city.

The city of Rurbania is eligible to participate in a federal program under the Safe Streets Act through which all incandescent street lights in the city could be replaced, with only 25 percent of the conversion costs to be borne by the city. The city engineer and the public works director have estimated that the total cost of this conversion program would be $1 million. To justify participation in this program, the city council has asked some assurances be given that such a program would result in an appropriate cost savings over the first four to five years of operation to warrant the initial investment of $250,000 in city funds.

To provide such assurances, the city manager asked Joe Furd, an analyst in the financial management department, to: (1) develop cost data on the current operations of the street lighting system in Rurbania and (2) formulate a cost comparison of these current figures with the projected operating costs for the new mercury vapor lighting system. In the process of developing these data, Furd decided that it would be useful to prepare an overall cost analysis of the total operations of the city's annual street lighting maintenance program. The following information and questions will help the reader to duplicate the analysis that Furd undertook.

1 In discussing the problem with the director of public works, Furd learned that mercury vapor lamps, while initially more expensive, require replacement only once every three years under normal maintenance procedures. Incandescent lamps, on the other hand, are routinely replaced with the following frequencies:
   a Lamps that burn all night are replaced every four months.
   b Lamps that burn from dusk to midnight are replaced every eight months.
   c Multiple lamps (two or more lamps per pole) are replaced every two months.
   If, at present, there are 2,600 all-night-burning incandescent lamps in Rurbania, 1,200 midnight-burning lamps, and 400 multiple lamps in the street lighting system, how many work units (lamp replacements) must be carried out on an annual basis?

2 If, at present, there are 3,000 mercury vapor lamps in the street lighting system, how many work units (lamp replacements) must be carried out on an annual basis under the normal maintenance program? How many work units would be required if the total system (7,200 lamps) were converted to mercury vapor lamps?

3 The public works director also pointed out to Furd that the maintenance records show 15 percent of the incandescent lamps and 10 percent of the mercury vapor lamps must be replaced before the normal maintenance periods due to early burnouts. These lamps are replaced between normal maintenance periods even though they are replaced again according to the established preventive maintenance schedule. How many additional work units result from early burnouts among incandescent lamps? From the mercury vapor lamps? How many additional work units would be required if the total system used mercury vapor lamps?

4 Furd's next task was to develop unit costs for each of the operations associated with the maintenance of the street lighting system. In discussing the problem with crew leaders, Furd determined that, on the average, a crew member can replace five incandescent lamps per hour or two mercury vapor lamps per hour. In checking with the payroll department, Furd determined that members of the maintenance crew responsible for replacing lamps receive $5.00 per hour. What is the unit labor cost of replacing each incandescent lamp? What is the unit labor cost of replacing each mercury vapor lamp?

5 Furd next determined the unit cost data for materials and supplies used in the various lamping operations of the street lighting maintenance crews. From the records of the purchasing office, he found that incandescent lamps cost $3.25 each and that mercury vapor lamps cost $18.50 each. Equipment costs for incandescent lamping run $3.75 per hour, while equipment costs for maintaining the mercury vapor lamps run $3.00 per hour. Given these data, what is the

total unit cost (unit labor cost, materials cost, and equipment cost) for replacing an incandescent lamp? For replacing a mercury vapor lamp?

6 Each time an incandescent lamp is replaced through the preventive maintenance program, the maintenance crew also washes the luminaries (reflectors). Mercury lamps are self-contained, that is, they do not have separate reflectors. On the average, two employees can wash ten luminaries in an hour. Materials used to wash luminaries (soap, cloths, etc.) cost, on the average, $25 per day for each two-member crew, while the equipment cost involved in this phase of the operation is $5.00 per hour. If luminaries are washed only during normal maintenance and not when a lamp is replaced due to early burnout, what is the total unit cost and total annual cost for this phase of the street lighting maintenance program?

7 With these unit cost data, it is possible to make a comparison between the present system of incandescent and mercury vapor lamps and the proposed system of all mercury vapor lamps. By multiplying work units times unit costs for each phase of the operation, an annual cost for each system can be determined. Will there be a sufficient annual cost savings from the total mercury vapor lamp system to cover Rurbania's share of the cost of conversion (i.e., $250,000) over a four-year to five-year period?

## CASE 21-2  ANNUAL BUDGET BUILT ON UNIT COSTS

Furd decided to continue his analysis of the street lighting maintenance program to determine a total annual budget built on unit costs. He learned that the light standards must be repainted every other year, and as the public works director pointed out, these standards must be repaired from time to time. The circuits within the cable system also must receive periodic repairs, wind damage to the standards occurs with some frequency, and other types of maintenance must be made as required.

In checking the records of the various maintenance crews, Furd determined that over the past several years, 10 percent of all light standards over eighteen feet high have required some form of annual maintenance, while 30 percent of the light standards under eighteen feet required some form of repair each year. Of the 500 circuits in the cable system, 80 percent required some form of maintenance each year. Wind damage results in replacement of 5 percent of all light standards annually. And some 200 employee-hours are required each year for miscellaneous maintenance of the street lighting system.

With this background information, Furd was able to develop unit cost estimates for each of these operations, as shown in Exhibit 21-6. With these unit cost estimates, he was able to prepare an annual routine maintenance budget for the current street lighting system.

**Required:**
By completing the last column in Exhibit 21-7, determine the total cost of this annual maintenance budget.

## CASE 21-3  SERVICE LEVEL ANALYSIS

Members of the Rurbania City Council have expressed various concerns in the wake of state and local initiatives to limit government spending and increases in property taxes. They are particularly troubled by the type of information on which they must make decisions regarding the allocation of fiscal resources among competing public programs. Some council members argue that appropriate information does not now exist to determine: (1) the minimum levels of service that the city should provide, (2) how the delivery of services will be affected by changes in funding, or (3) the actual benefits afforded by increases in program funding.

EXHIBIT 21-6   UNIT COSTS FOR STREET LIGHT MAINTENANCE REPORT

| Operation | Unit employee-hours | Rate per employee hour | Unit-labor costs | Unit materials | Unit equipment | Total unit costs |
|---|---|---|---|---|---|---|
| Replacement of lamps | | | | | | |
|   Incandescent | 0.20 | $5.00 | $ 1.00 | $ 3.25 | $ 0.75 | $ 5.00 |
|   Mercury vapor | 0.50 | $5.00 | $ 2.50 | $ 18.50 | $ 1.50 | $ 22.50 |
| Washing luminaries | 0.20 | $5.00 | $ 1.00 | $ 0.30 | $ 0.50 | $ 1.80 |
| Painting of standards | | | | | | |
|   Over 18 feet | 4.50 | $6.00 | $ 27.00 | $ 1.25 | $ 3.25 | $ 31.50 |
|   Under 18 feet | 3.00 | $6.00 | $ 18.00 | $ 1.00 | $ 2.50 | $ 21.50 |
| Maintenance of standards | | | | | | |
|   Over 18 feet | 2.00 | $5.60 | $ 11.20 | $ 12.80 | $ 5.00 | $ 29.00 |
|   Under 18 feet | 1.50 | $5.60 | $ 8.40 | $ 9.75 | $ 3.00 | $ 21.15 |
| Damage repairs | 30.00 | $6.90 | $207.00 | $170.00 | $47.00 | $424.00 |
| Cable repairs | 10.00 | $6.80 | $ 68.00 | $ 40.00 | $16.00 | $124.00 |
| Maintenance not otherwise classified | | $6.80 | $ 6.80 | $ 4.00 | $ 4.50 | $ 15.30 |

EXHIBIT 21-7   ANNUAL ROUTINE MAINTENANCE BUDGET FOR STREET LIGHTING

| Operation | Inventory | Annual frequency | Work Units | Unit costs | Annual costs |
|---|---|---|---|---|---|
| Replacement of lamps | | | | | |
|   All-night burning | 2,600 | 3.00 | 7,800 | $ 5.00 | |
|   Midnight burning | 1,200 | 1.50 | 1,800 | $ 5.00 | |
|   Multiple lamps | 400 | 6.00 | 2,400 | $ 5.00 | |
|   Early burnouts | 12,000 | 0.15 | 1,800 | $ 5.00 | |
|   Mercury vapor | 3,000 | 0.33 | 1,000 | $ 22.50 | |
|     Early burnouts | 1,000 | 0.10 | 100 | $ 22.50 | |
| Washing luminaries | 12,000 | 1.00 | 12,000 | $ 1.80 | |
| Painting of standards | | | | | |
|   Over 18 feet | 3,300 | 0.50 | 1,650 | $ 31.50 | |
|   Under 18 feet | 3,700 | 0.50 | 1,850 | $ 21.50 | |
| Maintenance of standards | | | | | |
|   Over 18 feet | 3,300 | 0.10 | 330 | $ 29.00 | |
|   Under 18 feet | 3,700 | 0.30 | 1,110 | $ 21.15 | |
| Damage repairs | 7,000 | 0.05 | 350 | $424.00 | |
| Cable repairs | 500 | 0.80 | 400 | $124.00 | |
| Maintenance not otherwise classified | | 200 employee-hours | | $ 15.30 | |
| Annual total costs | | | | | |

These council members are interested in specific mechanisms for a continuous evaluation of ongoing programs. Through such an evaluation, they hope to identify unnecessary spending resulting from the redundant or obsolete program activities. If this can be achieved, they argue, funds can be channeled to more important public service demands, thereby increasing the overall efficiency of government spending.

In an effort to develop such an approach, the city council has authorized the city manager to hire Mr. Eric Snerdley of Zackery, Bottomwell, and Brinkerdorf, a certified public accounting firm specializing in municipal finance and budgeting. Mr. Snerdley has selected the fire department for a demonstration project, and Sparky Le Feu, an analyst with the department of financial management, has been assigned to work with him. The following information and questions will help the reader duplicate the analysis that Snerdley and Le Feu have undertaken.

1 The first step in the development of this process involved the identification of appropriate budget units within the fire department and the allocation of current resources to these units based on the existing budget. Budget units should be selected so as to correspond to the responsibility structure for budget decision making. Given a typical municipal fire department, what are some of the appropriate budget units that could serve in this analytical capacity?

2 Each authorized position and its cost should be assigned to one of the budget units. All nonpersonal costs should be examined to determine the appropriate share to be distributed to each unit. The primary purpose of this cost assignment is to provide a data baseline from which subsequent comparisons can be made. Exhibit 21-8 illustrates the cost allocation that Snerdley and Le Feu made to the rescue squad budget unit under the fire safety program. Given this traditional budget format, what sort of analytical statements can be made about the activities of the rescue squad?

3 An important step in service level analysis involves the formulation of goals and objectives. In this context, a goal is the long-term outcome (end product) desired from the delivery of some particular public service. An objective is a more precisely defined target for ac-

### EXHIBIT 21-8
### Cost Allocation to the Rescue Squad Budget Unit

| Object/subobject codes | Allocations |
|---|---|
| 1110 Salaries and wages | $63,180 |
| 1140 Overtime payments | 3,160 |
| Subtotal: personal services | $66,340 |
| 1330 Operating supplies | $ 1,230 |
| 1340 Maintenance supplies | 400 |
| 1350 Drugs and medical supplies | 760 |
| Subtotal: supplies and materials | $ 2,390 |
| 1430 Motor vehicles | $ 9,000 |
| 1450 Medical and lab equipment | 1,000 |
| Subtotal: equipment | $10,000 |
| 1610 Retirement and pension benefits | $ 1,680 |
| 1620 Social security contributions | 4,645 |
| 1640 Group insurance | 200 |
| 1650 Medical/hospital insurance | 3,790 |
| Subtotal: employee benefits | $10,315 |
| Budget unit total | $89,045 |

**EXHIBIT 21-9  SERVICE LEVEL IMPACT SUMMARY**

| FUND | DEPT./PROGRAM | DIVISION/ELEMENT |
|---|---|---|
| General | Fire Safety | Operations |

*Goals and Objectives*
Reduce and eliminate complications due to injury or other medical need because individuals cannot be transported rapidly and adequately to medical facilities. Provide free ambulance service to those who cannot pay for medical transportation.

*Current Operations and Resources*
Free ambulance service provided to all people in the city. Calls for emergency transportation are dispatched over the fire emergency communications network. Vehicle responds to the scene of need. One vehicle, four drivers, and two paramedics provide around-the-clock service 365 days per year.

*Alternative Methods of Operation*
Contract with Digger O'Dell's Mortuary—save about $10,000 per year but run the risk of not having dedicated vehicle.

Contract with city-county hospital—hospital ambulance sometimes dispatched to remote parts of the county or to other medical facilities outside the county.

*Critical Linkages*
Fire emergency communications—receive dispatch services
City garage—routine maintenance and repairs

### Service Level Summary

| Service level title | Service level Total | Service level Positions | Cumulative Total | Cumulative Positions | Cumulative percent Total | Cumulative percent Positions |
|---|---|---|---|---|---|---|
| 1 Volunteer service | $ 7,660 | 0 | $ 7,660 | 0 | 8.6% | 0% |
| 2 Assigned drivers | $41,025 | 3 | $ 48,685 | 3 | 54.7% | 50% |
| 3 Add paramedic team | $40,360 | 3 | $ 89,045 | 6 | 100.0% | 100% |
| 4 Add second paramedic team | $24,220 | 2 | $113,265 | 8 | 127.2% | 133% |
| 5 Add second ambulance unit | $57,345 | 4 | $170,610 | 12 | 191.6% | 200% |

### Program Objectives

1 Ten-minute response time; no medical or first-aid assistance.
2 Seven-minute response time; no medical or first-aid assistance.
3 Add medical assistance and reduce complications due to no first-aid assistance.
4 Paramedic services provided around-the-clock.
5 Response time less than ten minutes to all parts of city.

### Cumulative Program Measures

| Level | Average number of calls/year | Average response time | Average turn-around time | Responses > 10 minutes |
|---|---|---|---|---|
| 1 | 125 | 10 min. | 25 min. | 25 |
| 2 | 125 | 7 min. | 19 min. | 15 |
| 3 | 125 | 5 min. | 15 min. | 10 |
| 4 | 125 | 5 min. | 15 min. | 7 |
| 5 | 250 | 3 min. | 10 min. | 0 |

complishment within a specific time period. Objectives should be measurable to the extent possible. Several goals and objectives are identified in Exhibit 21-9. What additional goals and objectives might be suggested for the Rurbania rescue squad?

4  The next step taken by Snerdley and Le Feu was to describe current methods of operations for each budget unit, including the resources required. Such a description should briefly describe the flow of work and the expected outcome from that work. Alternative methods of operation also should be identified and consideration might be given to: (a) cost reductions through new equipment or modernization of facilities, (b) reorganization of processes and/or people, (c) shifts in contractual service arrangements, (d) changes in ordinances to permit more economic operations, and so forth. A capsule summary of these analyses for the rescue squad is provided in Exhibit 21-9. Given the stated goals and objectives for the budget unit, what other alternative methods of operation might be considered?

5  Snerdley and Le Feu next identified the critical linkages between various budget units. A budget unit may provide services to clients referred from another unit and, in turn, may provide information on these clients/services to a third unit. To ensure maximum coordination, critically linked budget units should exchange their respective service level analyses. In some cases, it may be desirable to plan service levels on a joint basis. What additional critical linkages might Snerdley and Le Feu have identified beyond those shown in Exhibit 21-9?

6  Program measures are descriptors of those aspects of an activity or program that can be quantified. Such measures cannot characterize every important aspect of a program, but they can help to clarify and add meaning to words such as "more," "better," "increased," and so forth. Program measures give some idea of what a municipality can expect to obtain at different levels of funding within a program or activity. Measures identified by Snerdley and Le Feu for the rescue squad/ambulance service are shown in Exhibit 21-9. How do these program measures relate to the critical allocation decisions that must be made in the budget process?

7  Snerdley and Le Feu identified five service levels for the rescue squad/ambulance service, as summarized in the second part of Exhibit 21-9. The minimum level involves the provision of one ambulance/rescue vehicle, operated on a volunteer basis or by fire operations personnel. This service level results in a relatively high average response time (ten minutes) for the estimated number of calls per year (125), with 20 percent of the calls requiring a response time of greater than ten minutes. No medical attendant or first-aid service can be provided under this initial level of service. The cost of this minimum service level is estimated at $7,660.

The second level of service involves the assignment of drivers from among the fire operations personnel to operate the ambulance/rescue vehicle. Since the drivers will be in the station when the calls come in, the response time will be reduced by 30 percent (to seven minutes), while the average turnaround time will be reduced by six minutes. An increase of funding of $41,025 would be required to carry out this second service level, which approximates the current level of service provided in Rurbania.

The service level analysis and request forms for these first two service levels, as completed by Snerdley and Le Feu, are shown as Exhibits 21-10 and 21-11. Blank forms are provided as Exhibits 21-12, 21-13, and 21-14 and should be filled out based on the following information.

8  The third service level involves the addition of a paramedic team to the rescue squad, as well as the assignment of fire operations personnel on an around-the-clock basis to drive the vehicle (adding one ambulance driver to the three assigned in the previous level). The around-the-clock assignment would further reduce the average response time and the average turnaround time by two and four minutes respectively. More importantly, this service level would reduce the risk of medical complications by providing early first-aid assistance and would re-

## EXHIBIT 21-10  SERVICE LEVEL ANALYSIS AND REQUEST

| SERVICE LEVEL<br>Fire operations/<br>volunteer service | BUDGET UNIT<br>Resuce squad/<br>ambulance service | RANK<br>1 of 5 |
|---|---|---|

*Operations and Services Provided/Resources Used*
Provide ambulance/rescue vehicle at Firehouse #1. Operated on a volunteer basis or by fire operations personnel. Police required to respond to assist drivers with emergency medical cases.

*Difference Between Service Level and Current Level*
Eliminates regular fire operations personnel assigned to a vehicle on around-the-clock basis, 365 days per year. Will increase response time. No medical attendant or first-aid service provided.

*Increment Justification/Consequence for City Services*
This level is needed to provide free emergency medical transportation to those who cannot pay. Most emergencies will be responded to within ten minutes. No capacity for disaster situations. At a lower level of service, no around-the-clock service is available.

| Resources | Service level | Cumulative | Position titles |
|---|---|---|---|
| Personal services | 0 | 0 | No assigned |
| Contractual services | 0 | 0 | positions |
| Supplies and materials | $1,085 | $1,085 | |
| Equipment | $6,575 | $6,575 | |
| Employee benefits | 0 | 0 | • |
| Total budget | $7,660 | $7,660 | |

**Program Measures**

| | Average number<br>of calls/year | Average<br>response time | Average turn-<br>around time | Responses<br>> 10 minutes |
|---|---|---|---|---|
| Service level | 125 | 10 min. | 25 min. | 25 |
| Cumulative | 125 | 10 min. | 25 min. | 25 |
| Budget | 125 | 5 min. | 15 min. | 10 |

duce the danger of injury in transport (since the paramedic team would ride with the accident victim). This service level would add $48,060 to the cost of the budget unit. Complete the service level analysis and request form for this third level using Exhibit 21-12.

9  The fourth service level would add a second paramedic team (at a cost of $24,220), thus providing medical attendants and first-aid service around-the-clock. While this additional service capacity would have no immediate impact on the average response time or average turnaround time, it is estimated that the number of calls for which the response time was greater than ten minutes could be reduced to seven (out of 125). It is recommended that this additional service capacity be adopted in the next two years. Complete the service level analysis and request form for this fourth level of service using Exhibit 21-13.

10  The final service level calls for the addition of a second ambulance unit located at Firehouse #2 to provide around-the-clock ambulance and paramedic services from two locations to better serve the growth and shifts in the population of Rurbania. It is estimated that this additional unit would reduce the response time to an average of three minutes, reduce turnaround

**EXHIBIT 21-11** SERVICE LEVEL ANALYSIS AND REQUEST

| SERVICE LEVEL<br>Fire operations/<br>volunteer service | BUDGET UNIT<br>Resuce squad/<br>ambulance service | RANK<br>2 of 5 |
|---|---|---|

*Operations and Services Provided/Resources Used*
Provide ambulance/rescue vehicle at Firehouse #1. Operated by fire operations personnel, supplemented by volunteers. Police required to respond to assist drivers with emergency medical cases.

*Difference Between Service Level and Current Level*
Current level

*Increment Justification/Consequence for City Services*
This will reduce response time by 30 percent. No medical attendant or first-aid service provided. No capacity for disaster situations.

| Resources | Service level | Cumulative | Position titles |
|---|---|---|---|
| Personal services | $36,775 | $36,775 | Ambulance |
| Contractual services | 0 | 0 | drivers |
| Supplies and materials | 0 | $ 1,085 | |
| Equipment | 0 | $ 6,575 | |
| Employee benefits | $ 4,250 | $ 4,250 | |
| Total budget | $41,025 | $48,685 | |

**Program Measures**

| | Average number of calls/year | Average response time | Average turn-around time | Responses > 10 minutes |
|---|---|---|---|---|
| Service level | 0 | −3 min. | −6 min. | −10 |
| Cumulative | 125 | 7 min. | 19 min. | 15 |
| Budget | 125 | 5 min. | 15 min. | 10 |

**EXHIBIT 21-12** SERVICE LEVEL ANALYSIS AND REQUEST

| SERVICE LEVEL<br>Fire operations/<br>volunteer service | BUDGET UNIT<br>Resuce squad/<br>ambulance service | RANK<br>3 of 5 |
|---|---|---|

*Operations and Services Provided/Resources Used*
Provide ambulance/rescue vehicle at Firehouse #1 with two-member paramedic team. Drivers provided from fire operations personnel on around-the-clock basis, 365 days per year.

*Difference Between Service Level and Current Level*
Adds medical attendant and first-aid services. Assigns fire operations personnel on an around-the-clock basis. No volunteers required.

*Increment Justification/Consequence for City Services*
Reduce risk of medical complications by providing early first-aid to those in need of help. Reduce danger of injury in transport. Further reduction in response time possible.

**EXHIBIT 21-12** (continued)

| Resources | Service level | Cumulative | Position titles |
|---|---|---|---|
| Personal services | | | Ambulance |
| Contractual services | | | drivers |
| Supplies and materials | | | Paramedics |
| Equipment | | | |
| Employee benefits | | | |
| Total budget | | | |

| | Program Measures | | | |
|---|---|---|---|---|
| | Average number of calls/year | Average response time | Average turn- around time | Responses > 10 minutes |
| Service level | | | | |
| Cumulative | | | | |
| Budget | 125 | 5 min. | 15 min. | 10 |

**EXHIBIT 21-13** SERVICE LEVEL ANALYSIS AND REQUEST

| SERVICE LEVEL Fire operations/ volunteer service | BUDGET UNIT Resuce squad/ ambulance service | RANK 4 of 5 |
|---|---|---|

Operations and Services Provided/Resources Used

Difference Between Service Level and Current Level

Increment Justification/Consequence for City Services

| Resources | Service level | Cumulative | Position titles |
|---|---|---|---|
| Personal services | | | |
| Contractual services | | | |
| Supplies and materials | | | |
| Equipment | | | |
| Employee benefits | | | |
| Total budget | | | |

| | Program Measures | | | |
|---|---|---|---|---|
| | Average number of calls/year | Average response time | Average turn- around time | Responses > 10 minutes |
| Service level | | | | |
| Cumulative | | | | |
| Budget | 125 | 5 min. | 15 min. | 10 |

## CHAPTER 21: MANAGEMENT EMPHASIS ON PERFORMANCE AND ACCOUNTABILITY

**EXHIBIT 21-14**  SERVICE LEVEL ANALYSIS AND REQUEST

| SERVICE LEVEL<br>Fire operations/<br>volunteer service | BUDGET UNIT<br>Resuce squad/<br>ambulance service | RANK<br>5 of 5 |
|---|---|---|

*Operations and Services Provided/Resources Used*

*Difference Between Service Level and Current Level*

*Increment Justification/Consequence for City Services*

| Resources | Service level | Cumulative | Position titles |
|---|---|---|---|
| Personal services<br>Contractual services<br>Supplies and materials<br>Equipment<br>Employee benefits<br>Total budget | | | |

| | Program Measures | | | |
|---|---|---|---|---|
| | Average number of calls/year | Average response time | Average turn-around time | Responses > 10 minutes |
| Service level<br>Cumulative<br>Budget | 125 | 5 min. | 15 min. | 10 |

time to ten minutes, and eliminate any response delays of more than ten minutes. This service level is recommended for implementation within the next three to four years and would add $57,345 to the cost of operations, bringing the cumulative total to $170,610 (in present-dollar terms). Complete the service level analysis and request form for this final level using Exhibit 21-14. In general, what improvements do you perceive in the information provided under a service level analysis to program managers and decision makers as contrasted to more traditional budget and accounting formats?

## NOTES

1 Ernest Enke, "The Accounting Precondition of PPB," *Management Accounting*, vol. 53, January 1972, pp. 33-37.
2 Allen Schick, "Putting It All Together," *Sunset, Zero-Base Budgeting and Program Evaluation*, Proceedings of a Conference on Legislative Oversight (Richmond, Va.: Joint Legislative Audit and Review Commission, 1977), p. 17.

3 Logan M. Cheek, *Zero-Base Budgeting Comes of Age* (New York: AMACOM, 1977), p. 22. Cheek, Graeme Taylor, and others refer to these basic building blocks as "decision units," whereas other writers have used the term "budget units," as adopted here, to avoid possible confusion with the concept of "decision packages."
4 Peter A. Pyhrr, *Zero-Base Budgeting* (New York: John Wiley & Sons, 1973), p. 6.
5 Peter F. Drucker, "The Effective Decision," *Harvard Business Review*, 45, January-February 1967, p. 95.
6 William Travers Jerome III, *Executive Control—The Catalyst* (New York: John Wiley & Sons, 1961), p. 24.

CHAPTER 22

# CONTROL THROUGH PERFORMANCE AUDITING

Management control through budgeting, accounting, and financial reporting for organizations that use fund accounting has been discussed in previous chapters. Several additional methods may be employed, however, both for internal management control and for external reporting to achieve control for appropriate management performance.

Budgetary accounting and financial reporting are most appropriate management control tools when the expected results of individuals and organizations can be stated in financial terms. Thus business-type funds in nonbusiness organizations, in which profit or return on investment is the type of results measured, can best use financial reports that measure results against a profit budget to achieve management control. When actual operations are evaluated against budgetary expectations, such as in nonbusiness-type funds, budgetary accounting and reporting is the financial type of management control most appropriate for certain nonbusiness entities.

Appropriate supervisory and management techniques and performance auditing, in addition, can be used. Their use is to control the organization's efficient and economical operations, effective goal achievement, compliance with laws and regulations, and operations in which fraud or intent to deceive are prevalent.

## APPROPRIATE SUPERVISORY AND MANAGERIAL TECHNIQUES

Numerous books and articles are currently available on appropriate supervisory and managerial techniques that any business or nonbusiness unit can employ to achieve better operating capability, so there is no need to discuss those techniques in detail in this chapter. However, performance auditing, as applicable to both business and nonbusiness entities and as the subject of this chapter, is directly related to evaluating the appropriate use of some of those managerial techniques. Those techniques that apply to operating more efficiently, economically, and effectively, especially as they apply to nonbusiness entities, will be considered here. They include:

**1** *Planning*—developing appropriate standards or plans for efficient and economical operation or effective goal accomplishment that should be followed.

**2** *Executing*—carrying out the appropriate plans, often called "operations" or "doing."

**3** *Controlling*—measuring the results of the operations (executing) against the appropriate standards (planning) to assure others that the appropriate plans are being or have been carried out, and when they are not, communicating to others what caused this discrepancy. Other terms are "reviewing" and "auditing."

The planning process can be subdivided into three major stages: (1) strategic planning, (2) organizational planning, and (3) operational planning. As discussed in Chapter 20, generally speaking, during the strategic planning stage, the goals of the organization are developed and stated or reexamined and restated. Also at this stage, long-term plans requisite to the accomplishment of the goals are articulated.

To accomplish the goals of the organization, personnel and other resources must be appropriately organized. Appropriate organizational plans for use of human and other resources are developed at the organizational planning stage.

Once the goals have been stated and the human and other resources needed to accomplish the goals have been organized, the specific operational standards needed to achieve the goals must be developed and stated before being carried out. For example, operations that need to be planned include such activities as production, marketing, research, personnel, accounting, and so forth.

At each stage of planning, action must be taken in order to achieve the planned result. The results of action at the strategic planning stage are the goals and long-term plans. The results of action at the organizational planning stage are organizational charts, statements of organizational responsibility, and other guidelines concerning the use of resources. The results of carrying out the operational standards are the work results desired. Depending upon the various operational organizations used, these results could be products or services that achieve the goal of the organization as a whole. Intermediate operations that help achieve the final results include: marketing operations, warehousing, storing, advertising, selling, research operations to provide possible newer products or services, and so forth.

Controls are developed at each stage of planning to assure that the action at the executing stage accomplishes the results contemplated from the agreed-upon plans. Operational controls are needed to measure the accomplishment of the plans at the operational stage. Management controls are needed to measure the accomplishment of the various plans developed at the organizational stage. And, effectiveness controls are needed to assure the development of appropriate goals for the organization and the appropriate timing for the accomplishment of those goals.

## Management's Accountability Function

In summary, the management of an organization is accountable for setting appropriate goals, for developing standards needed to accomplish those goals, for effectively carrying out those standards, and for developing organizational and operational standards for economical and efficient operations. Management is responsible for checking to see whether the standards are appropriate, and when appropriate, that they have been carried out properly.

### Auditor's Responsibility

Independent auditors often are employed to assure third parties, including higher levels within the organization, that the particular level of management has carried out its accountability function. As independent reviewers of the overall or a particular level of management's accountability, auditors can determine whether management has effectively accomplished the stated goals; whether the resources are economically organized and efficiently carried out; whether laws, regulations, and policies have been complied with; and whether any fraud or intended deceit has been employed by management or employees of the organization. The review of management's operations for efficient, economical, and effective performance is often called a performance audit.

## PERFORMANCE AUDITING

The term "performance auditing" goes by many other descriptive titles—operational auditing, internal auditing, management auditing, program auditing, program results auditing, program evaluations, being only a few. Compliance auditing and fraud auditing, in addition, are sometimes placed within the definition of performance auditing, but usually are considered as parts of a financial statement audit, especially for governmental and nonbusiness organizations.

### Types of Performance Audits

Reporting on the accountability of management for all levels of management activities, as well as for all types of programs, can be considered under the title of performance auditing. Yet, because performance auditing does have two different purposes, it often is broken down into two different types: efficiency and economy auditing and effectiveness auditing.

*Efficiency and economy auditing* is considered to be the reviewing and reporting on organizational and operational activities of management. This includes organizational and operational planning, production, organizing, selling, personnel, accounting, marketing, and other functions for the purpose of determining how efficiently and economically those activities are conducted. *Effectiveness auditing* is considered to be the review of all of the activities necessary to effectively accomplish the goals of a particular organizational unit, program area of responsibility, or other entity. For example, effectiveness auditing would be the review of all activities of a particular program, contract, or entity to determine whether the goals have been accomplished and reporting the results of the review to a third party. Effectiveness auditing, then, could consider the programs of education, employment, health, welfare, environment, and highways in government; education, research, and public service in colleges and universities; research, training, and welfare in health and welfare organizations; and member services, conferences and meetings, technical services, and general administration in a trade association.

In efficiency and economy auditing, the auditor evaluates the activities of management and the personnel under them to see whether they have carried out those activities efficiently and economically, which means that the activities have been carried out for the least cost or with the least use of resources or that the outputs increase at a faster rate than costs. Efficiency and economy, therefore, pertains to the relationship of inputs (costs of labor, material, and overhead) to outputs (revenue, benefits, or other final results).

In effectiveness auditing, the auditor evaluates the activities of the management and the personnel under them to determine the effectiveness of the achievement of the goal of the entity or program for which management is responsible. Effectiveness is the relationship of outputs to the goals of the program. If the goals are appropriate and they have been accomplished, then the program is judged to be effective.

To illustrate the results of an efficiency and economy audit, let us consider the following audit situation. A city manager is looking for ways to save money. At present, garbage is collected from the rear of dwellings. Consider the following audit conclusion:

> Instead of collecting garbage from the rear of dwellings, the city's garbage collection department could save $50,000 each year by requiring the city's residents to place garbage at the street and then making streetside collections.

Note that this conclusion pertains to operations only and does not consider the political or social purposes of garbage collecting. Also, note that there are three elements to this efficiency and economy audit conclusion:

**1** The actions of the garbage collection department (management and the personnel under them)—the collecting of garbage from the rear of buildings.

**2** The standards that the garbage collection department should have followed in order to accomplish the trash collection in the most efficient and economical manner—to require residents to place garbage at the street and then to make streetside collections.

**3** The results if the appropriate standard is followed—an additional savings of $50,000 each year, the difference between collecting garbage from the rear of the building and making streetside collections.

Or consider the following audit conclusion on a state program that has the goal of providing safe highways through proper snow and ice removal.

> Article 12 of the State's Constitution authorizes the commissioner of the Department of Transportation to contract with counties to remove ice and snow from the state's roads. Under this "first preference" clause of the constitution, counties are allowed to select sections of the State's roads to plow or sand. Counties have elected to service one section of state highways but not adjoining sections, then resume service at another point on the road. Or, they may spread salt on one section that later has to be serviced by the State. By allowing the counties to follow this skip-patchwork pattern, instead of suggesting a change in the constitution that would require counties to follow a logical and well-defined pattern of snow and ice removal that is coordinated with the State's pattern, so that sufficient ice and snow is removed to make

the roads safely passable, the State is not effectively providing safe highways because of improper snow and ice removal.[1]

Note that this conclusion has the same three elements as those for an efficiency and economy audit—an appropriate standard, the action of management and their personnel as to whether they have carried out those standards, and the results, that is, the measurement of the actions against the appropriate standards. The difference, however, is that instead of measuring the dollar value of costs for the same output, the result is that when the goal of the program is measured against the output (unsafe roads) it can be determined that the goal is not being carried out effectively.

1 The actions: Counties (county management and personnel) were removing ice and snow in a skip-patchwork pattern, leaving many sections of the highway improperly cleared, and the State Department of Transportation (State Department of Transportation management and their personnel) was unable to prevent this because of the "first preference" clause of the constitution.

2 The appropriate standard that should have been followed is: The counties should "follow a logical and well-defined pattern of snow and ice removal, that is coordinated with the State's pattern, so that sufficient ice and snow is removed to make the roads safely passable."

3 The results of not following the proper standard: The goal of the program—to make the roads and highways safely passable through proper snow and ice removal—is not being effectively accomplished.

## Audit Evidence and Audit Objectives

*Audit evidence* has been defined as "facts and information used to come to a conclusion on an audit objective." The previous two conclusions came about because the auditor gathered information on an audit objective. An *audit objective* is the question to which the conclusion provides the answer. So, the audit objective for the efficiency and economy audit might have been stated as follows:

> Can the city save $50,000 each year (results) by the garbage collection service not collecting garbage at the rear of buildings and by requiring residents (actions) to place garbage at streetside so that it can be picked up at that point (standard)?

Likewise, the audit objective for the effectiveness audit might have been stated as follows:

> Can the state's roads and highways be made safer, that is, can a more effective snow and ice removal method be found (results) by the state Department of Transportation, instead of allowing the counties to remove ice and snow in a skip-patchwork pattern that leaves many sections of the highway improperly cleared, requiring them (actions) to follow a well-defined and logical pattern of snow and ice removal that is coordinated with the state's pattern so that sufficient ice and snow is removed to make the roads safely passable (standard)?

It can be seen that the audit objective has the same three elements as were found in the conclusion. Auditors often call these three elements: *criteria* for the appropriate standard; *causes* for the action of management and their personnel that caused the results; and *effects* for the results.[2]

The elements in the audit objective, obviously, would not be exactly the same as those found in the conclusion. The major difference would be that the amount of the effects in the audit objective would have to be of sufficient merit to warrant further examination. The amount of the effects in the conclusion normally would be much more significant than that in the objective. Also, the audit objective does not just happen. The auditor has a well-defined pattern that allows (1) the development of a tentative audit objective, (2) the development of a firm audit objective, from the tentative audit objective, (3) the gathering of evidence on the firm audit objective in order to come to a conclusion on that objective, and (4) the reporting of that conclusion to third parties. These are the phases of the audit process and are often called: (1) the preliminary survey, (2) the review and testing of management control, (3) the detailed audit, and (4) the report development.

Effectiveness audits use as the appropriate standards for the audit objective (criteria) proper goals that were developed or that should have been developed at the strategic planning stage. Efficiency and economy audits use as the appropriate standards (criteria) for the audit objective proper standards developed or that should have been developed at the organizational and work planning stages. Thus it can be seen that efficiency and economy audits can be made without considering an effectiveness audit, or an effectiveness audit can be made without considering efficiency and economy audits. Quite often, to be effective, it requires the use of more resources rather than less resources.

To clearly show the distinction between effectiveness audits and efficiency and economy audits, our illustrative case of these types of audits will be of only one contract—approached both as an effectiveness audit and as an efficiency and economy audit. This example, which concerns contracting for computer software programs, can be found in all types of organizations—business as well as nonbusiness, governmental as well as nongovernmental. Our illustrative case will be from a large state university.

The efficiency and economy audit goes through the audit processes of determining the audit objective, using as the criteria of the audit objective appropriate organizational and operational standards; developing evidence on all three elements of that audit objective; coming to a conclusion; and then reporting the conclusion to a third party. The effectiveness audit is concerned with the effectiveness of the accomplishment of the goals of the contract, using as the criteria of the audit objective the goals developed at the strategic planning stage. Stated in a different way, the effectiveness audit is concerned with measuring the outputs, the developed software, against the goals of the contract for developing computer software. The efficiency audit is concerned with the measurement of the output stated in dollar values against the standards for input stated in terms of costs.

## THE PHASES OF A PERFORMANCE AUDIT

Some auditors are often told exactly what the client (third party) wants in the way of an audit; the audit objective is often well stated so the auditor can gather evidence on that objective in order to come to a conclusion. Other auditors, however, must go through the various phases in order to develop a tentative audit objective into a firm one before gathering evidence on the objective in order to come to a conclusion that can be reported to a third party.

## Reasons for Conducting a Performance Audit

An auditor's approach to identifying specific managerial weaknesses in an activity or the effectiveness of goal accomplishment for the program, organization, or contract follows a logical, not a haphazard, approach. There are sound reasons for examining a particular organization or area and a logical process for identifying specific managerial weaknesses in the various activities of the overall area.

Among others, the following are the usual reasons why an auditor is asked to examine a broad area of management for which specific managerial weaknesses can be identified in one of the activities or management's effectiveness can be determined.

1 Large amounts of money are spent in that area.

2 Executives, legislators, or other parties have a particular interest in one particular area.

3 The auditor, because of particular knowledge of the area, suspects possible weaknesses in specific activities in an area.

4 The area has a history of poor management control.

5 Specific allegations are received from others, including the press, who have a reason to suspect poor management practices in the area.

In an efficiency and economy audit, an auditor usually searches for managerial weaknesses in an activity, and in an effectiveness audit, the auditor usually searches for ineffectiveness of the organization, program, or other entity. However, to be fair and impartial, the auditor should use a balanced approach in auditing and reporting. When reporting on a management weakness, the auditor should also identify specific activities that follow good managerial practices. The reason for auditing management's performance in the first place is to improve that performance. Balanced reporting—citing instances of good management practices as well as deficient practices—should lead to a desire by management for improved performance.

One often hears that an auditor has no business examining specialized activities of others, since he or she is not an expert in that specialized field. Yet, if one considers that the audit team should be experts in gathering evidence on an audit objective, they should be able to gather evidence on any type of activity whether specialized or not. If the auditor is not an expert in developing an audit objective, gathering evidence on that objective, coming to a conclusion on the objective, and reporting that conclusion to others, government audit standards suggest that someone else should make the audit. If the audit team collectively possesses this expertise, they should be able to gather evidence on: (1) whether the standards for action were appropriate, and if not, what standards should have been used for the activity (criteria); (2) the various actions followed by management, employees, or others—these actions are usually those that followed improper standards (causes); and (3) measuring the results of the actions of management, management's employees, or others involved in carrying out the inappropriate standard by using the appropriate standard as the measuring stick (effects).

For an efficiency and economy audit, the auditor usually goes through four separate and distinct phases: the preliminary survey, the review and testing of management control, the detailed audit, and the report development. The purpose of the preliminary survey phase is to gather background and general information from which the auditor can become acquainted with the activity and from which a tentative audit objective can be determined. The purpose of the review and testing of management control phase is to test the management control system sufficiently to gather evidence on each element of the tentative audit objective in order to ascertain whether the objective is firm enough for a detailed audit. The purpose of the detailed audit phase is for the auditor to gather sufficient, relevant material, and competent evidence on the firm audit objective so that the conclusion drawn on the audit objective is the proper conclusion. And, the purpose of the report development phase is to report the conclusion, with evidence to support it, to third parties.

Each of these phases will be illustrated in the following efficiency and economy audit. This audit concerns the use of a contractor to supply the design and the software for an automatic data-processing system for accounting and administrative purposes for a large university. Note that in this audit we are not looking for the effectiveness of the achievement of the goals of this contract, but rather how much can be saved if the contract is carried out properly. This is one easy way to make a distinction between an effectiveness audit and an efficiency and economy audit.

## ILLUSTRATIVE PHASES OF AN EFFICIENCY AND ECONOMY AUDIT— A CONTRACT BY UNIVERSITY *A* FOR A COMPUTERIZED ACCOUNTING AND ADMINISTRATIVE RECORDS SYSTEM[3]

In an efficiency and economy audit, the auditor usually goes through four clearly defined stages: the preliminary survey, the review and testing of management control, the detailed audit, and the report development.

### Preliminary Survey

**Background Information**  Computer programs are what make the computers run and are referred to as "software." Rather than have a staff of system analysts and programmers design the system and write the programs, these functions often are contracted out. However, before anyone can design a system and program for its operations, the agency must determine what the system is to be used for and draft adequate design specifications.

Computer software development has historically been a problem and is further complicated by contracting for it. Literature on the subject contains many discussions of software development projects that were late, cost too much, or failed completely. Causes for these problems have included the difficulty of defining the work to be done, changes to the scope of the work during the project, and the lack of communication between automatic data processing (ADP) users and specialists.

Many universities contract for software development because of the lack of staff or skill to develop programs in-house.

The university's internal auditor was asked by the president of the university to review the contract for the acquisition of the computer system to determine whether the university had received the full value for the money spent for this contract. The auditor found information comparable to that given in the previous section and in addition, came up with the following information.

University A is one of the larger users of ADP resources in the country. It is estimated that the costs of ADP resources in the university alone were over $10,000,000 each year, and the costs are continuing to escalate. These computer resources are used for a variety of reasons concerning education, but one of the uses will be that of accounting and administrative applications.

In August 19X0, University A let a contract to a computer firm for an estimated cost of $131,000 for the development, implementation, and conversion of an accounting and administrative records system to a computerized system. Work exceeding the scope of the contract was to be quoted on the basis of time and materials used, based on rates listed in the contract. The contract called for work to be done in three stages but did not stipulate that each stage should be completed and approved before work could begin on the next stage. The milestone chart (work schedule), moreover, indicated that work might be done concurrently on all stages.

The agreement required the contractor to draft an acceptance test plan for each stage of development and stipulated that the university could withhold payment for each calendar day's delay. The contractor also was liable for damages sustained because of negligence or failure to perform, unless caused by the university.

The contract also required written authorization from the university before the contractor could make modifications. The programming language was specified in the contract, and the documentation desired was described. Quality standards levied on the contractor, however, were stated in general terms, such as "the highest quality standards reasonably attainable in the data-processing industry," and "the system will edit data to ensure validity," without any measures of either quality or validity. The university used systems specifications prepared under a previous contract to solicit bids for the development of the system.

## A Tentative Audit Objective

From this background and general information, the auditor could assert, without knowing for sure, an audit objective such as:

> Will University A, by contracting with a computer firm for the development, implementation, and conversion of the accounting and administrative records system to a computerized system (causes), without having complete design and systems specifications (criteria), not be provided with a workable system after spending the total cost of the contract of $131,000 (effects)?

It is obvious that some additional evidence needs to be obtained on the various elements of the audit objective before attempting a full-scale, detailed audit. The auditor gathers this additional information and evidence by carrying out the review and testing of management control phase.

### Review and Testing of Management Control

This phase is undertaken for the purpose of firming up the audit objective before spending a great deal of time examining countless documents, interviewing numerous people, and observing the operation of the ADP equipment. Each element of the audit objective will be considered separately to show that the criteria are acceptable, the causes can be identified, and effects are significant.

**Criteria** The criteria as stated, that is, have complete design and system specifications before letting a contract, undoubtedly are appropriate and acceptable. However, additional criteria may be found that will increase the significance of the effects. Thus the criteria can be used as a basis for the audit if the effects are significant and the causes can be identified.

**Causes** To identify the causes in order to make corrections in the operations and to determine the significance of the effects, the auditor needs to know a little more about the university's letting of the contract, the contractor's administration of the contract, the university's review of the contract, and the results from the contract.

A review of specifications used as a basis for soliciting bids showed that these specifications were only 50 percent to 80 percent complete. Information concerning the contract showed that it was let in August 19X0. In November 19X0, the university approved stage I of the system's development. The approval letters stated that stage I appeared to be reasonably sound. It also stated that many portions of stage II programming were already well underway. Stage III was completed in May 19X1.

The university's methods and procedures committee reviewed and approved the acceptance test plan for each stage. Despite the testing and approval of each stage, the manager of the ADP operations stated that numerous problems were encountered immediately after the system was placed in operation and throughout 19X1. The manager also stated that the number of problems suggested that the quality of review of the work in progress was poor (additional information on criteria). University management later stated that the reports generated by the system were grossly inaccurate.

**Effects** Because of the poor results from the contract, in March 19X2, the university made an offer to pay 70 percent of the unpaid billings of $400,000, an escalation of the contract cost of over 250 percent. Statements from university personnel indicated that a great deal more time would be needed to modify the program before it could be operated successfully. They also said that a large sum would also need to be spent to arbitrate the price of the contract.

### A Firm Audit Objective

From this information, a firm audit objective could be developed and used as a basis for making the detailed audit. Note in the following objective, that when information is available to determine the approximate amount of the effects, the amount can be stated in the objective. Otherwise, some amount that is significant to the auditor and to third parties may be stated, such as "a very large amount." The correct amount will be shown in the conclusion to the objective.

Also note that the criteria of the objective have been expanded from the tentative objective to include "that of a proper review at each of the stages." The objective would be stated somewhat as follows:

> Has University A, by their using a computer contractor to develop their computerized accounting and administrative records system and before granting the contract not providing (causes) complete design and systems specifications and during the carrying out of the contract nor the proper review of the work at each stage of development of the system before approving starting the next stage of development (criteria), (1) lost control over the university's financial functions, even though being billed for as much as $250,000 more than the original contract cost of $131,000; (2) spent a very large amount for outside system analysts and arbitration support (as much as $100,000), and (3) have to spend an additional large sum of money (as much as $50,000) to bring the system up to an acceptable level of performance (effects)?

## The Detailed Audit

As has been stated, the purpose of the detailed audit is to gather sufficient, relevant, material, and competent evidence on each element of the audit objective so that the auditor can come to a reportable conclusion on that objective. The following evidence, in summary form, was used to come to a conclusion on the firm audit objective.

**Evidence on Criteria**  No additional evidence is needed on the criteria.

**Evidence on Causes**  University officials told the internal auditor that the problems became so severe that eventually they were unable to prepare financial statements on the results of their operations. The university comptroller attributed this lack of ability to prepare the financial statements to multiple financial and statistical problems caused by the failure of the computer contractor to meet his contractual obligations. The university hired a CPA firm to review the problems experienced with the contract. The firm reported that the computer system did not meet the criteria established by the university for accountability of program operations and cited about seventy-five deficiencies, covering twenty-two major system requirements.

In their review of the system, the CPA firm concluded that, if an audit could be performed at all, it would be so extensive that the cost would make it prohibitive. They stated that the accounting system was unable to prepare financial statements or to properly identify the function's operating cost.

The CPA firm also concluded that the first step necessary to bring the system up to par was to complete the specifications "because the system was never really designed." At best, they stated, the specifications were only 80 percent complete. Also, the specifications implied too many things rather than being specific about any of them. The incomplete system specifications indicated that the university's system development posture was not as advanced as it was perceived to be.

The CPA firm also said that the poor quality of the university's review of the contractor's work was first reflected in the acceptance of incomplete specifications from the previous contract. Then, in the present contract, a system that was approved by the university at the completion of each developed stage showed serious problems immediately after installation.

University personnel and the CPA firm listed the following deficiencies in the system:

**1** Numerous controls outside the system have had to be established to assure the integrity of the data processed.
**2** The system does not provide the needed statistical data.
**3** Very little documentation (i.e., systems manuals, procedures, etc.) was obtained from the contractor.
**4** The existing system lacks the standardization normally associated with integrated systems (e.g., inconsistency in program terminology).
**5** The system is not designed to facilitate modifications to meet changing requirements.

Officials of the university stated that the system did not perform some of its planned functions and performed others incorrectly or inadequately.

The contractor, in his defense, pointed to instances in which university management took excessive amounts of time to render decisions necessary to resolve matters and thus delayed efficient construction and operation of the system. He also claimed that the data provided by the university as system input contained errors.

University officials concluded that adequate requirements had not been included in the initial system design and that the specifications approved later proved to be inadequate. Also, they concluded that they had not provided the technical expertise needed to adequately monitor the contractor's development of the system.

The auditors' review of the contracting system shows that the university did not have an environment conducive to successful contracting and that university management failed to recognize and deal with the following factors concerning contract management:

**1** All conditions were not addressed in the contract and/or in specifications.
**2** Delays occurred because of untimely management decisions.
**3** Provisions were not made to ensure the quality of input data.

**Evidence on Effects** In March 19X2, the university made an offer to the contractor to pay about 70 percent of its unpaid billings that had been withheld to settle the contract. The contractor demanded formal arbitration. On November 1, 19X2, the arbitration proceedings were terminated by mutual consent of the parties. The termination agreement was formally executed containing a settlement of $350,000 on the contractor's claim of $400,000. Meanwhile, the university had paid the CPA firm over $100,000 in fees to review the system, provide support for arbitration, test, and conduct system planning. The university assumed control of the system once the contract was terminated.

According to an analysis of the system by the university's auditor and the CPA firm, an estimated 700 additional staff-days, at an estimated cost of $50,000, would be needed to bring the system up to an acceptable level, as a result of the system deficiencies. The university's ADP manager stated that the system design had never been completed and that the contractor had deviated from the fragments of design that did exist.

**Conclusion** The conclusion on the audit objective that the auditor—or others who would examine the evidence—would reach would be somewhat as follows:

University A, by their using a computer contractor to develop a computerized accounting and administrative records system for the university and before granting the contract and during the carrying out of the contract by their not providing (causes) complete design and systems specifications and a proper review of the work at each stage of development of the system before approving starting the next stage of development (criteria), lost control over the University's financial and administrative functions even though spending more than $220,000 beyond the original cost of $131,000 for the contract; spent over $100,000 for systems analysts and arbitration support for outside consultants, and found that there would be an additional cost of over $50,000 to bring the system up to an acceptable level of performance (effects).

## The Report Development

The purpose of the report development phase is to take the conclusion and evidence developed in the detailed audit phase and place it in a form that can be reported to third parties. The report would contain the same conclusion developed in the detailed audit, along with sufficient evidence to convince others that the conclusion is the correct one. While the conclusion and evidence may be stated in different rhetorical forms, the basic information and conclusion from the audit would be the same as for the report.

In addition, the auditor would recommend to the university president that the university should write, manage, and monitor software development contracts if they planned to use them in the future; that they should have proper review and approval procedures to monitor each phase of development of the contract; and that they should have clauses in the contract to ensure the university's ability to deny payment for the contract when the contractor does not perform properly.

## ILLUSTRATIVE PHASES OF AN EFFECTIVENESS AUDIT— UNIVERSITY A'S CONTRACT FOR A COMPUTERIZED ACCOUNTING AND ADMINISTRATIVE RECORDS SYSTEM

The same four phases take place in effectiveness auditing as occur in efficiency and economy auditing: the preliminary survey, the review and testing of management control, the detailed audit, and the report development. Since an effectiveness audit usually deals with only one organization, one contract, or one program rather than many individual activities, a significant difference between the two types of performance audit is that the auditor, in an effectiveness audit, usually combines the two early phases—the preliminary survey and the review and testing of management control. And, ordinarily, the auditor uses the same reasons for identifying a program, a contract, or other entity to audit as those listed on page 641 for identifying areas in which to look for activities to audit for more efficient and economical management performance.

Since the purpose of an effectiveness audit is to determine whether the manager is effectively accomplishing the goals of the organization, contract, or program, the goals must be specifically identified early in the stages of the audit. The development of a goal in a rather new area, when one has not previously been stated, often demands skills other than those concerned with evidence gathering. Therefore, auditors often use consultants or other experts with quantitative or other types of skills on the audit team. This expertise often provides the auditor with evidence needed to support the goals and standards required as the basis for the audit. The consultants can also define and supply the evidence needed to support the criteria used to measure the accomplishment of the goals.

This illustration is a continuation of the previous example concerning efficiency and economy audits. This audit, however, is concerned with effectiveness, rather than efficiency and economy. To be effective, the auditor may have to recommend more resources to do the job rather than fewer resources. The preliminary stages in an effectiveness audit are more often than not combined into one stage rather than two.

**Preliminary Survey and Review and Testing of Management Control**

In addition to the background information provided in the previous section, alternative information or new information is as follows. The university president requested the internal auditor to review the contract concerning the acquisition of programs for the computer system to automate accounting and administrative operation. The president told the university auditor that the controller had said that the clerical tasks of accounting and administrative applications had become too large for her to handle with the present staff. The controller also said that if the university converted to an automated system these tasks could be accomplished not only more effectively but also more efficiently. She further stated that she would like to have a contractor promptly provide her with computer programs (1) that would automate necessary accounting and administrative tasks for the university, (2) that are usable as delivered, (3) that have reasonable operating and maintenance costs, and (4) that are written so that they can easily be modified later to meet changing requirements. The president said that he told the controller to go ahead if she was sure the contractor could effectively do, at a reasonable cost, what the controller said she wanted done. The president said that he would have another audit made to determine the reasonableness of the cost of the contract, but right now he was interested in determining whether the conditions stated by the controller were being fulfilled by the contractor.

To make this type of effectiveness audit, the goals of the program would have to be stated specifically. The evidence to support the goals would come from the statement by the president and would be: promptly deliver computer programs that (1) automate necessary tasks for the university, (2) are usable as delivered, (3) have reasonable operating and maintenance costs, and (4) are written so they can be easily modified later to meet changing requirements. Reasonable operating and maintenance costs require that the programs be skillfully written (to minimize their costs), thoroughly tested for correctness, and well documented for ease of operation and interpretation. If later modification is to be made with ease, the programs must be well documented for the maintenance programmers who will modify them. The goals of the program also should have been stated in the contract, so the contractor would know what was expected of him.

In August 19X0, University A let a contract to a computer firm for an estimated cost of $131,000 for the development, implementation, and conversion of an accounting and administrative records system to a computerized system. Work exceeding the scope of the contract was to be quoted on the basis of time and materials used, based on rates listed in the contract. The contract called for work to be done in three stages, but did not stipulate that each stage should be completed and approved before work could begin on the next stage. The milestone chart (work schedule), moreover, indicated that work might be done concurrently on all stages.

The agreement required the contractor to draft an acceptance test plan for each stage of development and stipulated that the agency could withhold payment for each calendar day's delay. The contractor also was liable for damages sustained because of negligence or failure to perform, unless caused by the agency.

The contract also required written authorization from the agency before the contractor could make modifications. The programming language was specified in the contract, and the documentation desired was described. Quality standards levied on the contractor, however, were stated in general terms, such as "the highest quality standards reasonably attainable in the data-processing industry," and "the system will edit data to ensure validity," without any measures of either quality or validity. The university used systems specifications prepared under a previous contract to solicit bids for the development of the system. There was nothing in the contract that specifically said that the computer programs should be usable as delivered or that they could be easily modified later to meet changing conditions.

A review of specifications used as a basis for soliciting bids showed that these specifications were only 50 percent to 80 percent complete. Information concerning the contract showed that it was let in August 19X0. In November 19X0, the university approved stage I of the system's development. The approval letters stated that stage I appeared to be reasonably sound. It also stated that many portions of stage II programming were already well underway. Stage III was completed in May 19X1.

The university's methods and procedures committee reviewed and approved the acceptance test plan for each stage. Despite the testing and approval of each stage, the manager of the ADP operations stated that numerous problems were encountered immediately after the system was placed in operation and throughout 19X1. The manager also stated that the number of problems suggested that the quality of review of the work in progress was poor. Agency management later stated that the reports generated by the system were grossly inaccurate.

Because of the poor results from the contract, in March 19X2, the university made an offer to pay 70 percent of the unpaid billings of $400,000, an escalation of the contract cost of over 250 percent. Statements from agency personnel indicated that a great deal more time would be needed to modify the program before they could operate it successfully. They also said that a large sum would also need to be spent to arbitrate the price of the contract.

**A Firm Audit Objective**

As has been stated earlier, the audit objective will consist of criteria, causes, and effects. The criteria for an effectiveness audit are the goals of the program, contract, or organization. Goals that are fairly firm for this contract should be to have promptly delivered computer programs that: (1) automate necessary tasks for the university's accounting and administrative operations, (2) are usable as delivered, (3) have reasonable operating and maintenance costs, and (4) are written so that they can easily be modified later to meet changing requirements.

Causes will be either the university's or the contractor's actions concerning what was done in letting the contract and in developing the programs and using them to automate the tasks needed to achieve the goals suggested. The effects will be that the university or the contractor either did or did not effectively achieve the goals desired.

To audit this contract, the following audit objective could be used:

> Has University A in its contracting for and the contractor in its development of programs for development, implementation, and conversion of the accounting and administrative records system to a computerized system (causes) been ineffective in accomplishing the goals (effects) of promptly delivering computer programs that (1) automate necessary tasks for the university, (2) are usable as delivered, (3) have reasonable operating and maintenance costs, and (4) are written so that they can easily be modified later to meet changing requirements (criteria)?

## The Detailed Audit

In the detailed audit, the auditor gathers, analyzes, and summarizes sufficient, relevant, material, and competent evidence in order to come to a conclusion on the audit objective. Quite a lot of evidence on the three elements has already been obtained. But the auditor needs evidence on the criteria, on the causes, and on the effects that is sufficient and reliable so that he can come to a conclusion on each of the elements and on the audit objective as a whole.

**Evidence on Criteria** The criteria must be in such a form that they can be used as the basis of measuring whether the actions of both the university and the contractor will achieve the goals of the program. The contract has an acceptance test plan and a statement regarding each day's delay. So, the term "promptly" can be measured. The terms "usable," "reasonable," and "easily modified," unless defined in the contract, would have to be the normal and reasonable meanings. The definition of reasonableness is measurable to a certain extent: "Reasonable operating and maintenance costs require that the programs be skillfully written (to minimize their costs), thoroughly tested for correctness, and well documented for ease of operation and interpretation." Also, "easily modified" can be defined as: "If later modification is to be made with ease, the programs must be well documented for the maintenance programmers, who will modify them."

**Causes** The university controller told the auditor that the inability of the system to prepare financial statements was caused by the failure of the computer contractor to meet his contractual obligations.

The contractor, in his defense, pointed to instances where university management took excessive amounts of time to render decisions necessary to resolve matters and thus delayed efficient construction and operation of the system. He also claimed that the data provided by the university as system input contained errors.

University officials concluded that adequate requirements had not been included in the initial system design and that the specifications approved later proved to be inadequate. Also, they concluded that they had not provided the technical expertise needed to adequately monitor the contractor's development of the system.

The auditors' review of the contracting system shows that the university did not have an environment conducive to successful contracting and that university management failed to recognize and deal with the following factors concerning contract management:

1 All conditions were not addressed in the contract and/or in specifications.
2 Delays occurred because of untimely management decisions.
3 Provisions were not made to ensure the quality of input data.

The university hired a CPA firm to review the problems experienced with the contract. The firm reported that the computer system did not meet the criteria established by the university for accountability of program operations and cited about seventy-five deficiencies, covering twenty-two major system requirements.

In March 19X2, the university made an offer to the contractor to pay about 70 percent of its unpaid billings that had been withheld to settle the contract. The contractor demanded formal arbitration. On November 1, 19X2, the arbitration proceedings were terminated by mutual consent of the parties. The termination agreement was formally executed containing a settlement of $350,000 on the contractor's claim of $400,000. Meanwhile, the university had paid a CPA firm over $100,000 in fees to review the system, provide support for arbitration, test, and conduct system planning. The university assumed control of the system once the contract was terminated.

The CPA firm also concluded that the first step necessary to bring the system up to par was to complete the specifications "because the system was never really designed." At best, they stated, the specifications were only 80 percent complete. Also, the specifications implied too many things rather than being specific about any of them. The incomplete system specifications indicated that the university's system development posture was not as advanced as it was perceived to be.

The CPA firm also said that the poor quality of the university's review of the contractor's work was first reflected in the acceptance of incomplete specifications from the previous contract. Then, in the present contract, a system that was approved by the university at the completion of each developed stage showed serious problems immediately after installation.

**Effects** University officials told the auditor that the problems became so severe that eventually they were unable to prepare financial statements on the results of their operation. In their review of the system, the CPA firm concluded that, if an audit could be performed at all, it would have to be so extensive that the cost would make it prohibitive. They stated that the accounting system was unable to prepare financial statements or to properly identify the function's operating cost.

University personnel and the CPA firm listed the following deficiencies in the system.

1 Numerous controls outside the system have had to be established to assure the integrity of the data processed.

2 The system does not provide the needed statistical data.

3 Very little documentation (i.e., systems manuals, procedures, etc.) was obtained from the contractor.

4 The existing system lacks the standardization normally associated with integrated systems (e.g., inconsistency in program terminology).

5 The system is not designed to facilitate modifications to meet changing requirements.

Officials of the university stated that the system did not perform some of its planned functions and performed others incorrectly or inadequately.

In summary, the effects were that the system was very ineffective.

**Conclusion** The conclusion the auditor would reach on the audit objective from this evidence would be somewhat as follows:

> University A, in its contracting, and the contractor, in carrying out the contract for development, implementation, and conversion of the accounting and administrative records system to a computerized system (causes), were ineffective (effects) in achieving the goal of promptly delivering computer programs that (1) automate necessary accounting and administrative tasks for the university, (2) are usable as delivered, (3) have reasonable operating and maintenance costs, and (4) are written so that they can easily be modified later to meet changing requirements (criteria).

## The Report Development

Although containing the same information, the conclusion in the audit report may be written in a somewhat different style from that in the summary of the working papers, as follows:

> The goal of promptly delivering computer programs that (1) automate necessary accounting and administrative tasks for the university, (2) are usable as delivered, (3) have reasonable operating and maintenance costs, and (4) are written so that they easily can be modified later to meet changing requirements was endorsed by both the university's controller and president. This goal was to be achieved by contracting for these programs through an independent contractor. A contract was signed in August 19X0, but in March 19X2, the university was unable to prepare financial statements, identify the function's operating costs, or provide the needed statistical data. The cause of this inability of the computer system to operate properly through the programs provided by the contractor appears to be the university's lack of system design and the poor quality of the university's review of the contractor's work. The contractor's programs also did not meet the criteria established by the university for accountability of program operations.

The purpose of the report development phase is to take the conclusion and the evidence developed in the detailed audit phase and place it in a form that can be reported to third parties. A great deal of the evidence shown in summary form in the working papers for the audit would also be presented in the report. Several recommendations could also be made to the president of the university—the basic one being that the university should not have contracted for the design of a computer system until they knew exactly what they wanted. Most of the problems in this case were due to the lack of system design procedures.

## ACCOUNTING SYSTEMS AND PERFORMANCE AUDITING

After studying Chapter 20 on program budgeting and Chapters 18 and 19 on cost accounting, one can easily see that by developing the accounting system to include the appropriate standards (usually standard costs) into the accounting system, measurement of efficiency and economy can be done as a matter of the accounting processes. Then, the accounting system's developer must determine the program, contract, or organization accounting entity's goals. By including the goals (the measurable standards from the strategic planning stage of the entity) into the accounting system as the benefits desired, one can measure the effectiveness of the system through the accounting system.

Little has been done toward the measurement of either efficiency and economy or effectiveness in nonbusiness entities through the accounting system. Yet, the measurements of both of these types of entities or activities through the accounting system is done daily in the business sector of our economy.

## SUMMARY

This chapter provides a basis for the student to understand (1) the distinction between efficiency of operations and effectiveness of goal accomplishment and (2) the methods of determining through an audit whether the operations have been efficient or whether the goals have been accomplished.

Through one case concerning development of an administrative accounting system for a university, both of the concepts—auditing for efficient operations and for effective goal accomplishment—are explained and illustrated. An appropriate accounting system with built-in goal standards and efficiency cost measures can provide management with a basis for determining whether it has accomplished its goals or whether it has attained the standards for efficient operations. Until these measures and measurements are provided through an appropriate accounting system, efficiency and effectiveness audits are the only bases for providing management with that information.

## QUESTIONS

1. As related to auditing the performance of management, what are the three elements or techniques discussed in the chapter?
2. Discuss the three major stages of planning.
3. What is management's accountability function?
4. What is the auditor's responsibility when it comes to assessing the accountability of management for its functions?
5. Define performance auditing. What are the two most prominent types of performance auditing?
6. What is the purpose of an efficiency and economy audit?
7. What is the purpose of an effectiveness audit?

8 What are the three elements always found in any conclusion to a performance audit?
9 Define "evidence" as it pertains to a performance audit.
10 What is the conclusion to an audit objective? Define audit objective.
11 Why does an auditor usually start into any management area?
12 What are the phases of a performance audit? Define and describe the purposes of each of the phases.
13 From the illustrative cases in the chapter, can you easily delineate the phases of the audit function?
14 What is the difference between the conclusion in the detailed examination and the conclusion in the audit report?
15 What level of management planning determines the standards to be used for an efficiency and economy audit? For an effectiveness audit?

## CASE 22-1  USER CHARGES IN THE STATE

The following is a preliminary report prepared by a legislative auditor for the State of Z.[4]

### Preliminary Report to the Legislature—User Charges

User charges promote economy and efficiency in government operations. They address two current public problems—taxes and regulation. User charges can help reduce general state collections by partially substituting for taxes and by reducing the demand for goods and services whose production is currently financed by general tax receipts. They can also reduce the cost to business and society of complying with certain types of state regulations.

This report describes principles and pricing practices which, from the standpoint of economical and efficient operations, would be beneficial if adopted by the legislature in formulating user charge guidelines. This is not to imply that these principles could always be adhered to. In addition, other social policy objectives might sometimes justify departing from the objective of maximum economical and efficient operations. Nevertheless, adopting these principles would permit a more informed comparison between a policy based on economic efficiency and that actually being pursued. The consequences of deviating from equitable and economically efficient pricing principles could be more accurately assessed. It is in this sense that we believe this document to be of use to the state legislature.

A note of caution is called for regarding these pricing principles. Sometimes there might be legal impediments to the full implementation of pricing practices that would be beneficial on economic grounds. Thus the legality of implementing any pricing practice must always be determined before any action can be taken.

### Past and Present User Charge Policy

User charges have been employed by the state since its inception. The importance of charges in the state budget has varied. Presently, they account for about 3 percent of total receipts.

Many studies on particular user charges have revealed problems.

1 Pricing practices are inconsistent both within and across agencies.
2 The total costs of providing special benefits are not always being collected.
3 The state may be earning less than fair market value on the leases on some of its properties.

The existence of these problems indicates a need for a comprehensive review of state user charge policy. As a result, existing charges might be changed or charges might be imposed where none now exist.

### The Equity and Efficiency of User Charges

User charges that collect the total cost of goods produced and services provided at public expense place these costs on those who benefit, rather than on other taxpayers who do not. User charges that collect total costs may also act as a market test, assuring that the benefits derived are at least as great as their production cost. Also, charging for goods and services allocates them to those who value them most highly (and perhaps to those best able to afford them).

### Principles of Pricing for Economic Efficiency of Produced Goods

These principles apply to goods and services, the supply of which is not fixed, but they could be adjusted by the state's making additional expenditures on some production process.

1  When identifiable individuals are the recipients of goods produced and services provided at state expense, charges should be levied that will cover the production costs incurred on behalf of the recipient.

2  Incremental production costs should be reflected in price when possible, consistent with the objective of recovering full production cost.

### Nonproduced Goods

These principles apply to goods, the supply of which is fixed either by natural limits or as a matter of policy.

1  When nonproduced goods are controlled (through ownership or regulation) by the state but are used for the benefit of identifiable individuals, charges should be levied that will equate the amount of the goods desired at those charges with the supply.

2  If consistent with law, the charge that will "clear" the market may either be determined in advance, such as through appraisal techniques for determining fair market value, or be established through a mechanism for auctioning the supply.

### Exceptions to Pricing for Economic Efficiency

These principles are aimed at maximizing economic efficiency, but other social policy goals might, in particular situations, warrant deviation from these principles. For example, it might be appropriate, because of potential benefits to society, to encourage the consumption of some goods (e.g., food, shelter, and education) by charging less than their full cost or fair market value. Similarly, it might be appropriate to assure low-income individuals the opportunity to benefit from certain state-provided goods and services by reducing charges. It would also be appropriate to adjust the charges when individuals not directly involved in the activity are affected (favorably or adversely) by a recipient's consumption of a publicly provided good or use of a public service. Finally, legal and administrative factors must be considered. Charges may be levied only as permitted by law. And, in general, charges should not be imposed when the administrative costs of doing so would exceed the revenues collected.

### Matters for Legislative Consideration

There is a lack of information on user charges, and there is evidence that some present charges do not conform with the pricing guidelines discussed in this report. The legislature could:

1 Require agencies to determine the correspondence between current user charges, whether mandated by statute or set by the agencies, and these principles.

2 Require agencies to present this information to it through the office of the governor and then decide what changes, if any, were necessary.

3 Amend existing legislation or instruct agencies to implement these changes, monitored and assisted by the office of the governor.

**Required**:

1 Would you consider this report one based on a detailed audit? If so, see if you can state the audit conclusion. Also, show the elements of the conclusion—criteria, causes, and effects. If not based on the detailed examination, at what phase of the examination would you consider this report to be?

2 Can you come up with an audit objective for this case? Does this case have sufficient evidence in it for you to specifically identify each of the elements of the audit objective? If not, what would you have to do to specifically identify each of those elements?

3 Would you consider it necessary in all cases to make a detailed audit before rendering a report?

4 What type of audit would you believe could come from this preliminary report—an efficiency and economy audit or an effectiveness audit?

### CASE 22-2  THE EFFECTIVENESS OF GRANT AUDITING

The following is a digest of a report by the United States General Accounting Office on grant auditing.[5]

### Digest

Federal grant-making agencies are responsible for seeing that grant funds are spent for authorized purposes. Audits of grantees' records are one of the principal methods of carrying out this responsibility. Many such audits are made by federal auditors, but an increasing number are made by state and local auditors and independent public accountants.

Federal agencies that rely on audits by state and local auditors and independent accountants are responsible for seeing that the audits are performed in accordance with (1) applicable standards and (2) audit guidelines provided by the agency. It is important that the agencies examine the audit work because the audits are one of the principal bases the agencies have to see that grantees have properly handled their federal funds. Moreover, they need such audits to see that the government is getting what it pays for.

GAO has reviewed the procedures followed by three federal agencies in making such examinations and has found them ineffective in identifying low quality work. For instance, GAO reviewed twelve audits that had been through the agencies' review process and found that eight lacked one or more attributes necessary for a quality job. For instance:

One agency did not detect that the auditors had not properly evaluated grantee controls over cash; GAO found that the controls were weak and fraud or embezzlement would have been easy.

In another case, the agency reviewed the independent accountant's workpapers and a supplemental statement of work performed and then concluded that the accountant's performance had been satisfactory. GAO found, however, that while the accountant had said the compliance review had been performed, the grantee was violating fire and safety requirements.

Other items the agencies failed to learn about were an error in the cash account, a lack of documentation to support over $40,000 of reported nonfederal contributions, and a $120,000 embezzlement.

All the audits GAO examined had been made by independent accountants. GAO cautions that while the group it tested is believed to indicate weakness in agency review procedures, the number reviewed is too small to warrant any overall conclusions about the adequacy of work by independent public accountants in general.

The three agencies—the Departments of Commerce and of Health, Education, and Welfare and the Community Services Administration—followed different procedures in making such examinations but all relied principally on a desk review (a reading of the auditor's report) to detect weaknesses in audit work or other problems. In some cases, the agencies also examined the auditor's workpapers. GAO's review of the workpapers disclosed many of the deficiencies, including some overlooked by the agencies. Also, none of the three agencies normally reviewed grantee's records to check the accuracy of some of the audit work by the independent accountants. GAO did and found errors.

## Recommendations

GAO believes the agencies' procedures for examining the work of such accountants are too superficial and is recommending that the director, Office of Management and Budget, require federal grant-making agencies to develop and implement complete and balanced quality testing processes for identifying substandard audit work. GAO is making this recommendation because it believes that with improvements in the review process, the government's ability to detect and recoup federal funds used for unauthorized purposes would be increased. More significantly, better audits should result in quicker and better identification of weaknesses in grantee internal controls, placing the government in a better position to bring about needed corrections. GAO feels this problem warrants prompt corrective measures.

The agencies involved told GAO that they had too few in-house auditors to do this work more extensively. GAO is recommending that the agencies reassess the priorities for their auditors to see if more time can be devoted to this work. GAO is also recommending a procedure to follow in making the reviews.

## Agency Comments

The Office of Management and Budget agrees that federal agencies should apply effective quality testing processes to audits made by nonfederal auditors. The agencies included in our review generally agreed with our recommendations; however, Commerce and the Community Services Administration responded that a shortage of audit staff contributes to the problems addressed in our report.

**Required**:
1 What type of audit would you consider that this report represents? Can you identify the conclusion to this audit? Specifically state the elements of the conclusion.
2 The characteristics that distinguish an effectiveness audit from an efficiency and economy audit are often cleverly disguised. Can you, by stating an audit objective for an efficiency and economy audit for this case and then an audit objective for an effectiveness audit, delineate those characteristics?

## NOTES

1 Comptroller General of the United States, *Examples of Findings from Governmental Audits* (Washington, D.C.: U.S. General Accounting Office, 1973), pp. 24–25.
2 See Leo Herbert, *Auditing the Performance of Management* (Belmont, Calif.: Lifetime Learning Publications, 1979), p. 21.
3 Adapted from a U.S. General Accounting Office Report, *Contracting for Computer Software Development—A Serious Problem Requiring Management Attention*, FGMSD-80-4 (Washington, D.C.: U.S. General Accounting Office, November 9, 1979).
4 Adapted from a U.S. General Accounting Office Report, *The Congress Should Consider Exploring Opportunities to Expand and Improve the Application of User Charges by Federal Agencies*, PAD-80-25 (Washington, D.C.: U.S. General Accounting Office, March 25, 1980).
5 Report to the Congress by the Comptroller General of the United States, *Quality Testing of Audits of Grantees Records—How It Is Done by Selected Federal Agencies and What Improvements Are Needed*, FGMSD 79-38 (Washington, D.C.: U.S. General Accounting Office, July 19, 1979).

# INDEX

Account classifications, 35, 90–91
Account groups, 11, 12, 16–17, 280-284, 342, 345
Account titles, 38
Accountability, 1, 2, 5, 6, 22, 85, 343, 461, 527, 585, 596, 601, 611, 616, 623–624
   of management, 636–637
Accounting, basis of, 13, 18–20, 21, 38, 391–392, 418
   for certain nonprofit entities, 433
   for colleges and universities, 463
   for fiduciary funds, 255–256
   for governmental funds, 117–118, 191, 212–213, 236
   for hospitals, 491
   for proprietary funds, 38, 40
   for voluntary health and welfare organizations, 416, 418
Accounting, meaning of, 2, 7–9
Accounting control, 2, 22–23, 189, 281, 282
Accounting entity, 9, 10–11, 12, 13, 309
Accounting equation, 7, 17–18, 38, 99–100
Accounting for certain nonprofit organizations, 430, 441–443, 450–451, 453
Accounting for colleges and universities, 464, 465, 467, 473
Accounting for governmental entities
   account groups, 280–281, 284–292, 293–302
   fiduciary funds, 254–274
   governmental funds, 110–139, 146–173, 185–205, 211–228, 234–247

   proprietary funds, 37–63, 71–78
Accounting for hospitals, 492, 493, 494–496
Accounting for voluntary health and welfare organizations, 416–430
Accounting principles, 343, 415, 433–434, 436–440
Accounting Principles Board, 500
Accounting Research Bulletin, 514
Accounts payable, 19
Accounts receivable, 19, 130, 495–496, 498
Accrual accounting, 463, 491, 496, 516, 559, 573
Accrual basis, 18, 19, 156, 255–256, 418, 433, 461, 462, 467, 573, 574
Accrued expense accounting, 491
Accrued interest, 191–192
Actionable or discretionary programs, 617
Activity classifications, 613–614
Adjusting entries, 53, 151–152, 265
Ad valorem taxes, 118–121
Agency funds, 4, 15, 16, 123, 124, 147, 254–255, 256, 272–273, 391, 464, 465, 466
Allocation and allotment systems, 28, 95–96, 115–117
American Accounting Association, 536–537
American Hospital Association, 491
American Institute of Certified Public Accountants (AICPA), 6, 21, 168, 321–322, 345, 362, 415, 430–431, 440, 451, 462, 491, 499, 506, 513, 515
Annuity and life income funds, 465, 466
Annuity tables, 217, 218

## 660　INDEX

Appropriation ordinance, 94
Appropriations, 12, 21, 23, 94, 97, 114, 115, 246, 282, 490, 568, 573
Assessor, 26
Asset control, 125
Assets, 16, 17, 19, 22, 98, 256, 272, 280, 342, 492, 495–501
Audit conclusions, 639, 640, 641, 647, 652
Audit evidence, 639, 640, 641, 643, 645–646, 650–652
Audit objectives, 639, 640, 641, 643, 644–645, 649
Audit reports, 362, 363, 647, 652–653
Audit standards, 321, 322, 362, 638, 641
Auditing, 2, 22, 24, 28, 29, 88, 98, 309, 377, 585, 636–653
Auditor's accountability, 637
Auditor's opinion, ex. 377
Auxiliary enterprises, 462–463
Availability fee, 237

Bad debt, 496
Balance sheet, 59, 77, 202, 204, 215, 224, 244, 245, 259, 260, 267, 290, 297, 299, 344, 345, 418, 435, 440, 441, 444–446, 450, 495, 498, 506, 508–509
Basic accounting equation, 7, 17–18, 38, 99–100
Basis of accounting (see Accounting, basis of)
Board-designated funds, 492, 514, 516
Bond and interest register, 282
Bond discounts and premiums, 191, 192, 216, 217, 220, 223, 263
Bond indentures, 212
Bond interest, 212, 236, 238
Bond principal, 212, 236, 238, 281
Bonded debt ledger, 282
Bonds, 185, 186, 188, 189, 191, 211, 214–215, 216, 217, 218, 224, 225, 238, 281, 284, 287, 293, 294, 295–299
Bonds payable account, 214, 239, 298, 299
Borrowing, 188, 299, 490
Breakeven analysis, 548, 565–567
Breakeven operations, 38, 550
Budget adjustments, 97–98, 103–104
Budget adoption transactions, 101, 126, 127
Budget calendar, 26, 90
Budget classifications, 90–93
Budget comparison schedule, 165
Budget cycle, 88–89
Budget document, 93–94
Budget execution, 94–98
Budget guidance memorandum, 90
Budget manual, 88
Budget officer, 26, 27, 90

Budget ordinance, 46, 88, 94
Budget procedures, 23, 887–88, 585
Budget units, 617, 618, 620, 621
Budgetary accounting, 3, 18, 49, 96, 100, 115, 126, 146, 156, 188–189, 213, 236, 245, 392, 418, 462, 463, 635
Budgetary controls, 2, 22, 69, 146, 213, 463, 587, 591
Budgets, 23, 85, 86–87, 115, 146, 168, 234, 461, 464, 528, 529, 533, 568, 572, 589

Capital acquisitions, 186, 235
Capital assets, 186, 235, 236
Capital budget, 87, 186, 187, 236
Capital equipment, 281
Capital equity, 43, 492, 502
Capital facilities planning, 28, 88, 186, 187
Capital grants, 43, 44
Capital improvements program (CIP), 87–88, 186, 234, 622
Capital lease accounting, 300–301
Capital outlay, 149–150, 157–158, 187
Capital project funds, 3, 12, 15, 16, 185, 188, 211, 216, 234, 236, 237, 280, 286–289, 314–315, 346, 363, 364, 390, 568
 basis of accounting for, 191
 budgetary accounting in, 188–191
 capital budget and, 157–158
 financing of, 186
 issuance of bonds, 193
 premiums, discounts, and accrued interest in, 191–192
 special uses of, 185–186
Capitalization of fixed assets, 162
Cash basis, 18, 151, 170
Cash in hospital funds, 495
Cash-obligation accounting systems, 573
Causes for audits, 639, 641, 644, 645, 650
Charitable deductions, 497
Charity allowances, 495, 497
Charity services, 497, 498
Chart of accounts, 613
Claims, judgments, and compensated leave liability, 301–302
Closing entries, 55, 76, 104, 162–163, 195, 198, 199, 240, 243, 245–246, 258, 266–267, 428
Colleges and universities (see Accounting for colleges and universities)
Combined balance sheet, 147, 344, 365–366
Combined fund groupings, 437
Combined statements, 10, 13, 147, 343, 399, 418, 436–437
 balance sheets in, 147, 345, ex. 346–349, 365–366

INDEX    **661**

statement of changes in financial position. 349
statement of revenues, expenditures, and changes in fund balance, 345, ex. 350
statement of revenues, expenditures, and changes in fund balance for funds with annual budgets, 351, ex. 355–359, ex. 358–361
statement of revenues, expenses, and changes in retained earnings/fund balance, ex. 352
Combining statements, 10, 13, 114, 204, 226, 344, 346–348, ex. 365–373
Communications, in auditing procedures, 534, 591
Compliance auditing, 637
Comprehensive annual financial report, 343–364, 373–374
Comptroller General, 6
Computer software development, 642
Conclusions (see Audit conclusions)
Consolidated financial statements, 10, 11, 342, 345
Constraints, in cost-benefit analysis, 569, 598
Consumption method of inventory accounting, 147
Contingency liabilities, 403
Contractual adjustments, 496, 497
Contractual services, 149, 156–157
Contributed capital, 44, 45
Controllable costs, 538–539, 572
Controller, 26, 27, 536, 648, 650
Controlling, in auditing, 636, 637
Corpus, 253
Corrective action, 528, 531–532
Cost accounting, 26, 71, 86, 283, 490, 513, 525, 532, 548–562, 565, 611, 615
Cost allocation, 532, 550, 578
Cost behavior, 525, 534, 568
Cost-benefit and cost-effectiveness analysis, 9, 187, 565, 568–572, 598, 615
Cost centers, 9, 575, 577, 578, 603
Cost containment programs, 489, 490, 565
Cost control, 532, 579
Cost estimation, 532, 540–543, 556
Cost ledger, 560
Cost measurement, 525, 530, 549
Cost reimbursement, 574
Cost-volume-profit analysis, 565, 567
Courtesy discounts, 495
Criteria for audits, 639, 640, 641, 644, 645, 649
Crosswalks, 93, 601–603, 605–609
Current restricted and unrestricted funds, 417–418, 419–428, 437–438, 461, 464, 465–466, 492–495, 499
Custodian funds, 417

Debits and credits, 12, 17, 98, 100, 464
Debt financing, 45, 491
Debt service funds, 3, 12, 15, 16, 118, 211, 212, 213, 216, 235, 237, 239, 296, 297, 309, 312–313, 315–316, 346, 361, 362, 390
  accounting for serial bonds in, 214–215, 224
  accounting for term bonds in, 215–223
  basis of accounting for, 212
  budgetary accounting in, 213
  finances for repayment of debt, 212
  special use of, 211
Debt servicing, 150, 158, 223, 236
Decision packages, in service level analysis, 618, 619, 621
Deferred revenues, 41, 223, 492
Delinquent assessments, 241
Depreciation, 14, 15, 20, 55, 75, 283, 290, 418, 440, 462, 492, 502, 559, 574
Detailed audit, 645–646, 650–652
Deviations from planned performance, 529, 530
Differential costs, 539
Direct costs, 537, 538, 550, 572
Discount factor or rate, 569–570
Discount on bond investment, 220
Discount on sale of bonds, 191, 192, 220, 223
Discount on taxes paid, 124, 496
Donated and contributed services, 438, 501
Donor's restrictions, 493
Double-entry accounting, 5, 99, 101, 114, 283, 302

Earnings investments, 191, 192, 263
Effectiveness audits, 637, 638, 640, 642, 647
Effectiveness measures, 9, 529, 591, 596, 597, 617
Effects, in audits, 639, 641, 644, 646, 651
Efficiency and economy, 587, 592, 614, 635, 636, 637, 653
Efficiency and economy audits, 637, 638, 642, 647
Efficiency and effectiveness, 85, 93, 525, 585, 587, 588, 599, 622, 636, 637, 638
Encumbrances, 23, 96, 97, 98, 99, 101–102, 236, 393, 464
Encumbrances accounting, 101–104, 146, 149, 151, 160, 170, 213, 236
Endowment funds, 417, 418, 465, 466, 493, 494–495, 501, 505, 507

Enterprise funds, 14, 15, 39, 72, 280, 365–369, 390–391, 401–402, 513
  basis of accounting for, 40
  capital equity in, 43
  capital grants and, 44–45
  debt financing of, 45–46
  expenses and other uses of financial resources in, 42–43
  interfund transactions and, 47
  profit versus break-even operations of, 39
  revenue and other sources of financing of, 40–42
  residual equity transfers in, 43–44
  retained earnings and, 45
Entitlement, 271–272
Entity, 3, 9–11, 37
Essential service levels, 617
Estimated loss on receivables, 117, 118, 119, 120
Estimated revenues, 99–100, 103, 189
Evaluation, 530–531
Evidence, audit (see Audit evidence)
Executing, in auditing procedures, 636
Executive budget, 90, 93
Expendable funds, 11, 254, 257–260, 345
Expenditure accounting, 146
Expenditure controls, 96–97
Expenditures, 12, 18, 19, 23, 25, 90, 92, 93, 98, 99, 100, 105, 106, 114, 117, 146, 191, 246, 345, 462, 574, 575, 577, 616
Expense accounting, 418
Expenses, 17, 18, 98, 99, 117, 492, 502
Extended time horizon, 568
External financial reporting, 342–343, 527, 635
Externalities, in cost-benefit analysis, 569

Fair market value of gifts, 191
Field reports, 559–560
Financial Auditing Standards Board (FASB), 183, 269, 491, 499, 515
Fiduciary funds, 3, 12, 14, 16, 18, 20, 114, 147, 254–279, 284, 345, 373, 494, 502
  Agency funds as, 272–273
  Basis of accounting for, 255–257
  Characteristics of, 255
  Expendable trust funds as, 257–260
  Nonexpendable trust funds as, 256–257
  Pension trust funds as, 260–270
  Revenue sharing funds as, 270
Finance department, 26, 28
Financial accounting, 8, 21, 86, 376, 527, 531, 587, 604
Financial management, 8, 25, 86
Financial reporting, 2, 6, 8, 10, 18, 23, 25, 90, 114, 299, 343, 345, 376, 413, 416, 466, 480, 527, 531, 533, 535, 565, 572, 587
Financial reporting pyramid, 344
Financial statement audit, 637
Financial statements, 3, 9, 10, 11, 17, 20, 21, 90, 104, 165, 199, 204, 215, 267, 272, 323, 343, 345, 362, 430, 434, 436, 491, 505–510, 516
  for certain nonprofit organizations, 430
  for colleges and universities, 474
  for governmental entities, 59–61, 76–77, 165, 199–202, 204, 215, 223, 240–241, 244, 258–259, 267–269
  for hospitals, 505–512
  for voluntary health and welfare organizations, 433–434
Financially interrelated organizations, 436
Financing capital acquisitions, 186, 188
Fiscal controls, 11, 12, 85, 146, 527
Fiscal entity, 13
Fixed assets, 4, 11, 12, 15, 16, 17, 48, 87, 98, 125, 126, 149, 185, 188, 191, 238, 280, 281, 309, 316–317, 393, 417, 436, 439–440, 463, 465, 492, 500, 574
Fixed assets control, 281–282
Fixed assets held for investments, 500
Fixed costs, 539–540, 550, 565, 567
Fixed expenditures, 617
Flexible budgets, 513
Flood Control Act of 1936, 570
Fraud auditing, 637
Full costing, 537, 573
Full faith, credit, and taxing power, 46, 186, 234
Functional classifications, 419, 438
Fund accounting, 11, 12, 13, 29, 310, 413, 416–417, 433–434, 440, 461, 463, 464–466, 492, 635
Fund balance, 18, 98, 99, 103, 104, 151, 237, 240, 241, 246, 258, 260, 280, 342, 345, 492, 499, 502
Fund equity balances, 396–397, 492
Fund-raising expenses, 418, 439, 502
Funds, 10, 91, 342, 572

General Accounting Office (GAO), 6, 21
General fixed assets account group, 4, 11, 12, 16, 17, 185, 186, 188, 195, 198, 235, 281, 282, 283, 289–290, 302, 400, 462, 465
General fixed assets schedule, 291
General fund, 12, 15, 16, 106, 114, 234, 237, 254, 260, 265, 280, 285–286, 309, 310, 346, 354, 355–357, 358–361, 390, 461, 466

adjusting entries in, 151
basis of accounting for, 117–118
budgets and budgetary accounting in, 115–117, 126–127
closing entries in, 162–164
expenditure accounting in, 146–147, 149–150, 153–154, 155–157
financial statements for, 165
prior year's reserve for encumbrances in, 151, 160–161
revenue accounting in, 118–121, 123, 128–133
residual equity transfers in, 150, 158
subsidiary revenue ledgers in, 133, 160
General ledger, 23, 105, 573
General long-term debt account group, 4, 11, 12, 16, 17, 85, 87, 89, 129, 185, 188, 191, 195, 236, 281, 284, 465
General obligation bonds, 186, 234, 282
Generally accepted accounting principles (GAAP), 2, 6, 20, 23, 24, 28, 117, 151, 165, 223, 272, 345, 362–363, 375, 431, 463, 491, 515, 587
Gifts, 45, 257, 437, 501
Goal achievement, in auditing procedures, 635, 637, 647
Goals and objectives, 10, 85, 92, 187, 525, 527, 534, 548, 568, 572, 585, 587, 588, 589, 590, 591, 594, 595–596, 617, 638, 648, 649, 653
Government Finance Officers Association, 106
Governmental Accounting Standards Board (GASB), 20, 117, 345, 462
Governmental Auditing Standards, 641
Governmental funds, 10, 12, 14, 15, 20, 37, 44, 49, 51, 99, 100, 106, 254, 345
Governmental fund accounting, 3, 196
Grant accounting, 129, 438
Grant expense, 161
Grant income deferred, 438
Grant revenue, 118, 186, 271
Gross national product (GNP), 1, 5, 29

Health and welfare organizations (see Accounting for voluntary health and welfare organizations)
High low method of cost estimation, 541–542
Hospital accounting (see Accounting for hospitals)
Hospital Financial Management Association, 491
Hospital insurance, 489, 491
Hospitals, 550, 554
 as a part of other organizations, 513–514

Income, 19, 117
Income, deferred, 437
Income taxes, 118
Income trust fund, 256, 258–260
Incremental budgeting, 616
Indirect costs, 538, 550, 555, 557, 572, 615
Input measures, 529, 530, 569, 597, 598, 638, 640
Interentity transactions, 46, 310, 312–321
Interest, 462
Interest-earning fund, 464
Interest payable ledger, 282
Interfund eliminations, 344–345
Interfund receivables and payables, 399
Interfund transactions, 4, 46, 309, 310, 312–321, 463, 464, 493
Intergovernmental services, 118
Internal accounting controls, 22, 23
Internal auditing, 98, 529, 536, 637, 643
Internal improvement laws, 186
Internal management controls, 37, 635
Internal rate of return, 570–571
Internal service funds, 14, 15, 37, 39, 71, 72, 78, 280, 311–312, 370–372, 391, 395
International City Management Association (ICMA), 25
Inventory, 1, 147, 281, 393, 552, 557, 559, 574
Investment in plant, 476
Investments, 191, 192, 261, 263, 393, 418, 439, 499

Job-order costs, 557–561
Job tickets, 553
Joint ventures, 402
Journal entries, 73, 115, 193, 266, 297, 310, 419, 553

Labor distribution, 553, 557
Land, building, and equipment fund, 417, 428
Legal requirements, special report for, 376
Liabilities, 16, 17, 19, 24, 98, 99, 256, 272, 280, 342, 492, 501
Line items, 23, 97, 106, 574
Linear functions, 567
Loan and annuity funds, 417, 464, 466
Long-term assets and liabilities, 12, 14, 16, 98, 281, 463, 493
Long-term debt, 4, 10, 17, 186, 188, 211, 280, 282, 284, 302, 309, 397–399, 465, 492
Long-term debt control, 281–282
Long-term investments, 570, 572
Long-term leasing, 186, 188, 490
Long-term notes, 186, 281
Long-term planning, 601, 636

Malpractice loss contingencies, 515
Management accounting, 2, 8, 10, 37, 86, 490, 525, 531, 534, 587, 590, 599
Management and general expense, 439
Management auditing, 637
Management by objectives, 588
Management control, 2, 3, 9, 21, 24, 28, 86, 513, 527, 528, 532–535, 565, 591, 599, 623, 635, 636, 641, 643, 647, 648–649
Management decision-making, 531
Management information systems, 592–593
Management motivation, 533
Management performance, 462, 565, 635
Management planning, 590
Management techniques, 635
Managerial weaknesses, as a reason for a performance audit, 641
Mandatory transfers, 463, 464
Marketable equity securities, 500
Materials and supplies, 147–149, 155–156, 552
Measurement, 534
Measurement focus, 25
Medical care insurance, 489
Memorandum only totals, 345
Milestone chart, 643
Minimum service levels, 619–621
Model City Charter, 25
Modified accrual basis, 18, 19, 20, 117, 151, 165, 170, 191, 214, 236, 255–256, 345, 418, 461, 467
Multiple periods, 195
Municipal bonds, 88, 99, 234
Municipal Finance Officers Association, 106, 117, 151, 213

National Association of Colleges and Universities Business Officers (NACUBO), 21, 462
National Council on Governmental Accounting (NCGA), 1, 2, 6, 13, 14, 18, 20, 97, 117, 147, 165, 212, 223, 240, 254, 267, 268–269, 271–272, 280, 283, 343, 345, 346, 363, 391
National Municipal League, 25
Net benefits, 571
Net present value, 571
Noncontrollable costs, 538–539
Noncurrent assets, 499
Nonexpendable funds, 20, 39, 254, 255, 256–257
Nonexpendable gifts, 437
Nonmandatory transfers, 413
Nonoperating revenues, 41, 501
Nonprofit organizations, 430–440
Not-for-profit entities, 37, 490, 525, 529
Not-for-profit funds, 11, 14, 15, 37, 99, 254
Notes receivable account, 497
Notes to financial statements, 349, 354

Object codes, 11, 23, 91–92, 106, 613
Objective function, 568–569
Objects of expenditure, 12, 22, 86, 91, 93, 106, 146, 419, 502, 615, 621
Obligations, 23
Office of Management and Budget, 321, 322
Operating and maintenance costs, 648, 650
Operating budget, 87–88
Operating control, 533, 574
Operating efficiency, 530
Operating expenses, 42, 43
Operating grants, 41
Operating revenues, 40, 47, 501
Operating transactions, 73
Operating transfers, 42, 43, 48, 150, 191, 212, 215, 217
Operational auditing, 637
Operational control, 592
Operational planning, 590, 636, 637
Operational standards, 636
Opportunity costs, 539
Organizational planning, 636, 637
Output measures, 529–530, 569, 588, 597, 598, 638, 640
Overhead, 557, 559
Oversight responsibility, 343
Owner's equity, 17, 98–99

Partial costs, 537
Pay-as-you-go, 186, 188
Payroll register, 553
Pension plans, 393, 400–401
Pension trust funds, 255, 260–270, 312–313
Performance audits, 24, 586, 635, 637–642
  accounting system development for, 653
  phases of, 640
  reasons for conducting, 641
  types of, 637, 640
Performance budgeting, 585, 611–615
Performance classification systems, 611–613
Performance costs, 613
Performance effectiveness, 9, 25, 525
Performance evaluation, 88
Performance measures, 9, 528, 529–530, 532–533, 572–573, 585, 588, 591, 597, 614, 615, 617, 623
Performance standards, 528, 529
Performance units, 612–613, 615
Perpetual inventory records, 552
Personal services, 87, 147, 153–154

Planned performance, 528, 529, 530
Planning, 2, 85, 86, 187, 281, 528, 532, 534, 565, 589, 636
Planning-control continuum, 585, 589–592
Planning-Programming-Budgeting Systems (PPBS), 85–86, 599–600
Plant funds, 463, 465, 469–480
Plant replacement and expansion funds, 493, 494, 502, 505
Pledge accounting, 418, 437
Policies, 594, 623, 637
Pre- and postaudits, 28, 98
Preliminary survey, 642, 647
Premium on bond sales, 191, 192, 220, 223
Premium on investments, 220, 223
Prepaid expenses, 462
Present value, 569
Price, Waterhouse & Co., 433, 440
Principal and interest funds, 494
Principal trust fund, 256, 258, 417
Principles of accounting, 40, 72, 235, 255, 256, 279, 283, 284
Priority rankings, 618
Private solicitation of funds, 490
Proceeds from sale of bonds, 191
Process costs, 549, 556–557
Product cost determination, 548
Productivity ratios, 529, 592
Profit funds, 3, 11
Profit-type entities, 48, 462
Profit-volume ratio, 567
Program analysis, 594, 597, 599, 604
Program auditing, 637
Program budgeting, 9, 25, 85–86, 91, 574, 599, 601
Program costs, 537
Program effectiveness, 25, 593
Program evaluations, 598–599, 637
Program objectives, 531
Program schedules, 529
Program services, 419
Programming, 97, 188, 598
Programs, 10, 85, 419, 577, 587, 589, 594–595, 616
Property, plant, and equipment funds, 491, 492, 500
Property taxes, 234–235
Proprietary funds, 3, 14, 15, 18, 19, 37–38, 71, 185, 211, 254, 280, 284, 309, 310–311, 345, 347, 353, 568
 basis of accounting for, 38, 40
 enterprise funds as, 37–63
 internal service funds as, 71–78
Public employee retirement systems (PERS), 267–268

Public hearings, 94
Purchase method of inventory accounting, 148
Purchasing agent, 27
Pure endowment funds, 465, 466, 505
Pyramidal chart, ex., 344

Quasi-endowment funds, 465
Quasi-external transactions, 41, 310

Real property, 119
Regression analysis, 542–543
Renewals and replacements fund, 476, 478
Rental income, 501
Report development, 647, 652–653
Reporting entity, 343
Reserve for encumbrances, 99, 100, 101, 103, 151, 159, 160, 162, 163, 189, 194, 240
Residual equity transfers, 43, 44, 48, 49, 150, 158, 191, 311
Resource allocations, 592, 614
Responsibility accounting, 533, 548, 568, 572–573
Responsibility centers, 9, 572, 574, 577, 603
Restricted funds, 175, 176, 180, 181, 464, 493, 494–495, 499, 502–505, 506, 515
 endowment funds as, 492, 494–495, 505
 other types of, 492
 plant replacement and expansion funds as, 494, 503
 specific purpose funds as, 492, 494, 503
Retained earnings, 43, 45, 55, 62, 76
Retirement of indebtedness fund, 476, 479
Revenue, 17–18, 23, 25, 40, 87, 90, 91, 93, 98, 99, 100, 105, 106, 114, 118, 128, 129, 130, 131, 132, 146, 246, 345, 462, 492, 501
Revenue accounting, 123
Revenue bonds, 186, 212, 237, 300
Revenue sharing, 114, 118, 123, 270–272
Revenue transactions, 51, 73–74, 128, 132
Review and testing of management control, 644, 648
Reviewing, in auditing procedures, 636
Revolving funds, 71
Risk and uncertainty, 569
Roanoke, Virginia, financial reports of, 330–341, 342, 345, 377, 387–412

Sales taxes, 118
Scattergraph method of cost estimation, 542
Scheduling, 590, 592
Self-assessment taxes, 118, 121, 122
Serial bonds, 214, 224, 236, 242, 281, 284, 293–294
Serial debt, 211, 212, 214, 215, 281, 293, 294
Service charges, 47

Service level analysis, 585, 615, 616–623, 625–633
Single audit, 4, 309, 321–323, 324, 330
Sinking fund, 45, 46, 216–217, 237
Special assessment bonds, 234, 237
Special assessment funds, 3, 15, 16, 20, 185, 186, 211, 234–238, 239, 280, 284, 289, 316
Special assessments deferred, 236–237, 241
Special reports, 376
Special revenue funds, 3, 12, 15, 16, 114, 185, 214, 237, 272, 280, 461, 466
Specific purpose funds, 494, 505
Standard costing, 548, 561, 565
Standards, 529, 531, 533, 572, 590, 591, 636, 638, 640, 643
Statement of activity, 418, 436
Statement of changes in financial position, 59, 76, 118, 181, 267, 347, 353, 368, 369, 436, 448–449, 452, 507, 512
Statement of changes in fund balance, 204, 258, 446–447, 474, 507, 511
Statement of current fund revenues, expenditures, and other changes, 464, 474
Statement of revenue and expenses, 442, 451, 497, 498–499, 510
Statement of revenues, expenditures, and changes in fund balance, 165, 202, 204, 345, 348, 350, 351
Statement of revenues, expenses, and changes in retained earnings, 59–60, 77, 347, 352, 367
Statement of revenues, expenses, and changes in reserve accounts and fund balances, 267, 347
Step-down method, 551
Strategic control, 591
Strategic management, 585, 588
Strategic planning, 533, 585, 588, 589, 593–601, 604, 636, 640
Strategy statements, 596–597
Subsidiary accounts, 26, 105–106
Subsidiary ledger controls, 22, 23, 24, 104–106, 132, 146, 158, 160, 165, 281–282, 496
Subsidiary revenue ledger, 132
Sunset legislation, 25
Supervisory techniques, 636
Surrogates, 599
Suspense accounts, 121, 122

T accounts, 52, 53–54, 56–57, 75
Tax anticipation notes, 123, 124
Taxes paid in advance, 123
Taxes receivables, 117, 119, 120, 121, 130

Term bonds, 215, 224–225, 236, 281, 284, 295–299
Term debt, 212
Term endowment funds, 465, 466, 505
Time cards, 553
Time preference of capital investments, 572
Transactions, 22, 309–321, 492
Transfers between funds, 42, 48, 49, 72, 150, 158, 191, 212, 214, 309, 310, 311, 312–321, 462, 463
Treasurer, 27
Trust funds, 4, 15, 16, 20, 185, 186, 256–270, 271, 374, 375
Trust principal, 254
Tuition and fees, 463

Uncertainty, 87, 569
Uncollectable pledges, 418
Uncontrollable costs, 572
Unit costs, 550, 556, 559, 566, 592, 612, 615, 623–625
Unit of variability, 566
Unrestricted funds, 416–417, 419, 464, 467–469, 491, 492–494, 497, 499, 500, 506–507, 514, 515
User charges, 71, 234, 559

Valuation of investments, 439
Variable costs, 539–540, 550, 565
Variance analysis, 561, 565
Vested interest in pensions, 255, 262
Volume of work, 530
Voluntary health and welfare organizations (see Accounting for voluntary health and welfare organizations)
Voluntary transfers, 464

Withholding taxes, accounting for, 122
Work and cost ledger, 560
Work breakdown schedule (WBS), 529
Work-load measures, 529–530, 592, 612, 614–615
Work programs, 611, 612, 613
Working capital, 19
Worksheets of transactions, 60–61, 74–75, 136–137, 165–169, 264
  for account groups, 291, 296–297
  for capital project funds, 200–201
  for debt service funds, 220–221
  for fiduciary funds, 259, 267
  for general funds, 165–169
  for special assessment funds, 244

Year-end encumbrances, 102–103
Year-end reversions, 97

Zero-base budgeting, 9, 86, 616, 623